AFTER GENOCIDE

PHIL CLARK AND ZACHARY D. KAUFMAN

editors

After Genocide

*Transitional Justice, Post-Conflict Reconstruction
and Reconciliation in Rwanda and Beyond*

HURST & COMPANY, LONDON

First published in the United Kingdom by
HURST Publishers Ltd,
41 Great Russell Street, London, WC1B 3PL
© Phil Clark and Zachary D. Kaufman, 2008
All rights reserved.
Printed in India

The right of Phil Clark and Zachary D. Kaufman
and the Contributors to be identified as the authors
of this volume has been asserted by them in accordance
with the Copyright, Designs and Patents Act, 1988.

A catalogue data record for this volume is available
from the British Library.

ISBNs
978-1-85065-918-1 *casebound*
978-1-85065-919-8 *paperback*

www.hurstpub.co.uk

CONTENTS

ACKNOWLEDGEMENTS

The compilation and editing of this anthology involved more people than we could possibly thank here.

We are immensely grateful for the work of Nastasya Tay, our Editorial Assistant. Lara Warren also assisted with the production of the final manuscript. For their comments on key aspects of the draft manuscript, we would like to thank Ligia Abreu, Fahim Ahmed, Adrienne Bernhard, Mauro De Lorenzo, Len Epp, Howard Kaufman, Sarah Martin, Vipin Narang, Kirk Simpson, Katherine Southwick and Jennifer M. Welsh.

We are grateful for the support of various institutions during our work on this anthology. We both thank the University of Oxford, particularly the Department of Politics and International Relations, Magdalen College, St. Antony's College, and Rhodes House. Phil additionally thanks Balliol College, St. Cross College, the Rhodes Trust, the Centre for Socio-Legal Studies (University of Oxford), and the Transitional Justice Institute (University of Ulster). Zachary also thanks Stanford University's Center on Democracy, Development, and the Rule of Law; Yale Law School; and the Marshall Aid Commemoration Commission.

We also would like to express our appreciation to Michael Dwyer, Managing Director, Hurst Publishers Ltd, for his encouragement throughout the production of this anthology.

Finally, we are immensely grateful for the love and support of our family and friends throughout our work on this volume.

Phil Clark and *Zachary D. Kaufman*

NOTE

Wanting to make our own concrete contribution to development in post-genocide Rwanda, the editors will donate profits from this book to the construction of the Kigali Public Library, Rwanda's first public library. For more information about the Kigali Public Library, and to make your own contribution, please visit: www.kigalilibrary.org.

Phil Clark and *Zachary D. Kaufman*

ABBREVIATIONS

AE	African Enterprise
AFDL	Alliance des Forces Démocratiques pour la Libération du Congo-Zaire
AI	Amnesty International
ASF	Avocats Sans Frontières
AU	African Union
AVEGA	Association des Veuves du Génocide
CAVR	Comissão de Acolhimento, Verdade e Reconciliacão
CELA	Centre for the Learning of African Languages
CSDG	Conflict, Security and Development Group
DPA	Department of Political Affairs (United Nations)
DPKO	Department of Peacekeeping Operations (United Nations)
DRC	Democratic Republic of Congo
ECOWAS	Economic Community of West African States
EDS	Electronic Disclosure System
FAR	Forces Armées Rwandaises
FCO	Foreign and Commonwealth Office (UK Government)
FIDH	Fédération Internationale des Droits de l'Homme
GELOD	Global Evidence for Legal Officers Database
GIS	Geographic Information Systems
GoR	Government of Rwanda
GoS	Government of Sudan
GTZ	Gesellschaft für Technische Zusammenarbeit
HCIC	Humanitarian Community Information Centre
HRW	Human Rights Watch
ICC	International Criminal Court
ICISS	International Commission on Intervention and State Sovereignty
ICRC	International Committee of the Red Cross
ICTR	International Criminal Tribunal for Rwanda (United Nations)
ICTY	International Criminal Tribunal for the Former Yugoslavia (United Nations)

IDPs	Internally Displaced Persons
IMF	International Monetary Fund
INCORE	International Conflict Research (University of Ulster)
IPEP	International Panel of Eminent Personalities
KFOR	Kosovo Force (United Nations)
KJPC	Kosovo Judicial and Prosecutorial Council
KLA	Kosovo Liberation Army (also known as Ushtria Çlirimtare e Kosovës (UÇK) in Albanian)
KWECC	Kosovo War and Ethnic Crimes Court
LAS	Legal Advisory Section
LDGL	Ligue des Droits de la personne dans la région des Grands Lacs
LIPRODHOR	Ligue Rwandaise pour la Promotion et la Défense des Droits de l'Homme
MRND	Mouvement Républican National la Démocratie et le Développement
NAM	Non-Aligned Movement
NIF	Neutral International Force
NURC	National Unity and Reconciliation Commission
OAU	Organisation of African Unity
OCHA	Office for the Coordination of Humanitarian Affairs (United Nations)
ODA	Official Development Assistance
ONUMOZ	UN Operation in Mozambique
OSCE	Organisation for Security and Co-operation in Europe
OTP	Office of the Prosecutor
PDD	Presidential Decision Directive
PDK	Party of Democratic Kampuchea
PRI	Penal Reform International
PSD	Parti Social-Démocratique
R2P	Responsibility to Protect
RDR	Rassemblement Républicain pour la Démocratie au Rwanda
RGF	Rwandan Government Forces
RPF	Rwandan Patriotic Front
RTLM	Radio Télévision Libre des Mille Collines
SRSG	Special Representative of the Secretary General (United Nations)
TRC	Truth and Reconciliation Commission
UN	United Nations
UNAMIR	United Nations Assistance Mission in Rwanda

ABBREVIATIONS

UNAVEM II	United Nations Angola Verification Mission II
UNDP	United Nations Development Programme
UNHCR	United Nations High Commissioner for Refugees
UNMIK	United Nations Mission for Kosovo
UNMO	United National Military Observers
UNOMUR	United Nations Observer Mission Uganda-Rwanda
UNOSOM I	United Nations Operation in Somalia I
UNOSOM II	United Nations Operation in Somalia II
UN/PR	United Nations Permanent Representative
UNPROFOR	United Nations Protection Force
UNSC	United Nations Security Council
UNTAC	United Nations Transitional Authority in Cambodia
US/DoS	United States Department of State
USG	United States Government
WFP	World Food Programme

GLOSSARY

abakuzi (Kinyarwanda)	"the workers"
abunzi (Kinyarwanda)	mediators or reconcilers (especially in disputes within communities)
amahoro (Kinyarwanda)	peace
amasasu (Kinyarwanda)	machetes
auto-défense-civile (French)	civilian self-defence
Banyarwanda (Kinyarwanda)	people of Rwanda
bourgmestre (French)	local mayor
cellule (French)	the smallest unit of Rwandan administration
commune (French)	a unit of Rwandan public administration, larger than a *secteur*
gacaca (Kinyarwanda)	grass; name given to system of community-based courts for prosecuting genocide suspects
gacaca nkiristu (Kinyarwanda)	Christian *gacaca*, practised in some parishes, mainly in rural Rwanda
ibuka (Kinyarwanda)	to remember
Impuzamugambi (Kinyarwanda)	"those who have the same goal"; term given to a genocidal militia
ingando (Kinyarwanda)	to reflect; solidarity camps or civic education centres
Inkotanyi (Kinyarwanda)	a tireless warrior; self-referential term for the RPA
Interahamwe (Kinyarwanda)	"those who work together"; name given to genocidal militias
inyangamugayo (Kinyarwanda)	honourable elders or people of integrity; name given to *gacaca* judges
inyenzi (Kinyarwanda)	cockroach; derogatory term for Tutsi rebels, or Tutsi generally, during the genocide
kubabara (Kinyarwanda)	to suffer (in a physical or moral sense)
kubabarira (Kinyarwanda)	to forgive

kwiha amahoro (Kinyarwanda)	to calm a situation before it escalates
kwishyira mu Mutuzo (Kinyarwanda)	synonym for kwiha amahoro
négationisme (French)	denial (e.g. of the genocide)
préfet (French)	prefect
préfecture (French)	prefecture
ratione loci (Latin)	territorial jurisdiction
ratione materiae (Latin)	subject-matter jurisdiction
ratione personae	personal jurisdiction
ratione tempore (Latin)	temporal jurisdiction
Reseau Zéro (French)	Zero Network
Sbchutztruppe (German)	armed forces of the German colonial administration
secteur (French)	a unit of public administration, smaller than a commune
ukuri kurakiza (Kinyarwanda)	"the truth heals"
umubyeyi (Kinyarwanda)	parent
umudugudu (Kinyarwanda)	village
urubanza (Kinyarwanda)	*secteur*-level mediators of non-genocide-related disputes, similar to *gacaca* jurisdictions; in a judicial setting, signifies "a trial"

THE CONTRIBUTORS

Editors

Phil Clark is a Research Fellow in Courts and Public Policy at the Centre for Socio-Legal Studies, University of Oxford, and co-convenor of Oxford Transitional Justice Research. He has a DPhil in Politics from Balliol College, University of Oxford, where he studied as a Rhodes Scholar. His doctoral research, based on extensive fieldwork, explored issues of post-genocide justice and reconciliation in Rwanda, focusing on the *gacaca* community courts. Following his doctoral work, he was the researcher and author of a forthcoming book project for the Open Society Justice Initiative, exploring issues of the complementarity of the International Criminal Court (ICC) and national and community-level institutions in the Democratic Republic of Congo (DRC) and Uganda. The project was based on seven months' fieldwork in the DRC and Uganda in 2006-2008. Clark was also technical advisor and co-author of a 2007 UN Office of the High Commissioner for Human Rights project surveying popular perceptions of transitional justice and peace-building in northern Uganda. He has advised the Danish, Sudanese, Ugandan and UK governments, the ICC, the UN International Criminal Tribunal for Rwanda, Human Rights Watch and Crisis Group on conflict issues in Africa.

Zachary D. Kaufman is a JD candidate at Yale Law School, where he is the Editor-in-Chief of the *Yale Law & Policy Review* and was named an Olin Fellow of the John M. Olin Center for Law, Economics, and Public Policy. At Yale Law School, Kaufman has also served as Managing Editor of the *Yale Human Rights & Development Law Journal*, Articles Editor of the *Yale Journal of International Law*, and Policy Editor of the *Yale Law and Policy Review*. At the same time, Kaufman is completing his DPhil degree in International Relations at the University of Oxford, where he is a Marshall Scholar and writing a dissertation on the role of the United States in the establishment of war crimes tribunals. Kaufman has worked at Google and the international law firm of O'Melveny & Myers. He has served at the US Departments of State and Justice and the UN International Criminal Tribunals for Rwanda (ICTR) and for the Former Yugoslavia (ICTY). He also was the first American to serve at the ICC, where he was policy clerk to Chief Prosecutor Luis Moreno Ocampo. Kaufman is the founder, president, and chairman of the Board of Directors of the American Friends of the Kigali Public Library; co-founder and Executive Director of Marshall Scholars for the Kigali Public Library; and an Honorary Member of the Rotary Club of Kigali-Virunga, Rwanda. He is a Board Member and Senior Fellow of Humanity in Action and he serves as a consultant on other non-profit and social entrepreneurial ventures. A 2005-06 Fellow of Stanford University's Center on Democracy, Development, and the Rule of Law, Kaufman received his BA degree in Political Science from Yale University, where he was the student body president.

Contributors

Morten Bergsmo is Senior Researcher at the International Peace Research Institute, Oslo. He was formerly (2002-5) Senior Legal Advisor and Chief of the Legal Advisory Section, Office of the Prosecutor, ICC, and previously (1994-2002) Legal Adviser, ICTY. He was also Legal Advisor to the UN Commissionof Experts for the Former Yugoslavia, which was established pursuant to Security Council resolution 780 (1992) in 1993-94, and represented the ICTY to the UN negotiation process to establish the ICC, 1996-2002.

Susanne Buckley-Zistel is the director of the research project, "The Politics of Building Peace," about strategies of dealing with the past after violent conflicts, at the Free University Berlin. She previously worked as a research fellow at the Peace Research Institute Frankfurt; the Conflict, Security, and Development Group at King's College, London; as well as for a number of UK-based, conflict-related NGOs. Buckley-Zistel holds a PhD from the London School of Economics and has published widely on post-conflict transformation. She is the author of the book, *Conflict Transformation and Social Change in Uganda: Remembering After Violence* (Palgrave/Macmillan) and is currently finalising a book on post-conflict justice and reconciliation in Rwanda.

Alison J. Cole is an Associate Legal Officer for the joint Appeals Chamber of the ICTR and the ICTY. She previously worked as an independent consultant at the Office of the Prosecutor of the ICTR, working with rape witnesses and the expert witness on the sexual violence committed as a mode of the genocide. She has conducted several human rights investigations, including on death row in Jamaica, in refugee camps in Northern Uganda, in the tribal regions of Gujarat, and in the Palestinian Territories.

Solomon Nsabiyera Gasana is a Congolese-born consultant on conflict and post-conflict issues in the Great Lakes region and founder of Abundant Life Institute, a peace-building, justice, and development organisation. As a Fulbright scholar, he completed a Master's degree at Eastern Mennonite University, Virginia. He was previously Director of the Healing, Peace, and Reconciliation Program, World Vision Rwanda.

Helen Hintjens teaches on two new Masters programmes at the Institute of Social Studies in The Hague: Human Rights, Development and Social Justice and Violent Conflict, Reconstruction and Human Security. She previously worked for many years at the Centre for Development Studies at Swansea University in Wales. Her main publications on Rwanda include: "Explaining the 1994 Genocide in Rwanda," *Journal of Modern African Studies,* 37 (2) (1999); "When Identity becomes a Knife: Reflecting on the Genocide in Rwanda," *Ethnicities,* 1 (1) (2001). With David Kiwuwa, she has authored a chapter entitled, "Not Ethnicity but Race: Unity and Conflict in Rwanda since the Genocide" in S. Saha (ed.) *Perspectives on Contemporary Ethic Conflict,* (Lanham, MD: Lexington Books, 2006). Hintjens also publishes on asylum and refugee issues, social movements, and on the politics of Caribbean non-sovereign territories.

Hassan Bubacar Jallow is Prosecutor of the ICTR. He studied law at the University of Dar es Salaam, Tanzania (1973), the Nigerian Law School (1976), and University College, London (1978). He then worked as State Attorney in the Attorney-General's Chambers in The Gambia from 1976 until 1982, when he was appointed Solicitor General. Justice Jallow served as The Gambia's Attorney-General and Minister of Justice from 1984 to 1994, and subsequently as a Judge of The Gambia's Supreme Court from 1998 to 2002. In 1998, he was appointed by the UN Secretary-General to serve as an international legal expert and carry out a judicial evaluation of the ICTR and the ICTY. He also has served as a legal expert for the Organisation of African Unity and worked on the drafting and conclusion of the African Charter on Human and Peoples' Rights, which was adopted in 1981. He has also served the Commonwealth in various ways, including chairing the Governmental Working Group of Experts in Human Rights. Until his commencement as Prosecutor of the ICTR, Justice Jallow was a Judge of the Appeals Chamber of the Special Court for Sierra Leone on the appointment of the UN Secretary-General in 2002, as well as a member of the Commonwealth Secretariat Arbitral Tribunal. Justice Jallow was awarded the honour of Commander of the National Order of the Republic of The Gambia.

Paul Kagame is President of the Republic of Rwanda. From 1990 to 1994, he was military commander of the Rwandan Patriotic Front (RPF), the insurgent armed force that halted the genocide in Rwanda in 1994. He was appointed Vice-President and Minister for Defence in the Government of National Unity in July 1994, and in 1998 was elected Chairman of the RPF, a partner in the Government of National Unity. On 17 April 2000, Paul Kagame was elected President of the Republic of Rwanda by the Transitional National Assembly;

after winning the 2003 elections he was sworn in as President, ending the transition period. He was elected First Vice President of the African Union during the Second Ordinary Session of the Assembly of Heads of State and Government of the African Union in July 2003. He is currently Chairman of the Common Market for Eastern and Southern Africa.

Jean Baptiste Kayigamba was born and educated in Rwanda, graduating from the National University of Rwanda in 1992 with an MA in English and Linguistics. He also has an MA in Publishing from Oxford Brookes University. When the genocide started in Rwanda, he was working for Inter Press Service (IPS) and the Third World News Agency, and after the genocide he worked in the Office of the President of Rwanda, initially as Press Attaché, then as Director of Media and Public Relations. He later left public administration to work as a correspondent for numerous international news organisations, most notably Reuters. Since 2001, Kayigamba has lived in the UK with his wife and three children.

René Lemarchand is Emeritus Professor of Political Science at the University of Florida. He has written extensively on the Great Lakes region of Africa and was the recipient of the Herskovits Award in 1971 for *Rwanda and Burundi* (1970). He is also the author of a companion volume, *Burundi: Ethnic Violence and Genocide* (1994), and more recently of *The Dynamics of Violence in Central Africa* (University of Pennsylvania Press, 2008). He served as Regional Advisor on governance and democracy with the United States Agency for International Development in Abidjan from 1992 to 1996 and in Accra from 1996 to 1998, and has been a visiting lecturer at the Universities of Berkeley, Bordeaux, Copenhagen, Helsinki and Antwerp.

Linda Melvern is the author of six works of non-fiction, including a fifty-year history of the United Nations. Her two books about the Rwandan genocide are: *A People Betrayed: The Role of the West in Rwanda's Genocide*, published in September 2000 by Zed Books, London, and St. Martin's Palgrave, New York; and *Conspiracy to Murder: The Rwandan Genocide*, Verso, 2004. A fully updated paperback edition of *Conspiracy to Murder* was published in April 2006.

Martin Ngoga is Prosecutor-General of the Republic of Rwanda and formerly the Rwandan government's special envoy to the ICTR in Arusha.

Tom Ndahiro is a Rwandan journalist and human rights activist. Until May 1999, he was the Editor-in-Chief of a weekly Rwandan newspaper, after which he was elected by the parliament to be one of the first seven members of the Rwandan Commission for Human Rights. In this institution, he served as a Commissioner in charge of Civil and Political Rights. Ndahiro extensively lectures and publishes nationally and internationally on the subject of genocide. Since he left the Commission in March 2006, he has been researching and writing a book on "genocide ideology".

Kalypso Nicolaïdis is a University Lecturer in International Relations and a Fellow of St. Antony's College, University of Oxford. She is also the director of the European Studies Centre and chair of Southeastern European Studies. In 2005-06 Nicolaïdis held the professorial chair on Visions of Europe at the College of Europe in Bruges; previously she was Vincent Wright Chair at the Sciences-Po in Paris and Associate Professor at Harvard University's Kennedy School of Government, and taught at the Ecole Nationale d'Administration in Paris. Nicolaïdis holds a PhD in Political Economy and Government from Harvard University, a Master's degree in Public Administration from the Kennedy School of Government, a Master's degree in International Economics and a Diploma from the Institut d'Etudes Politiques in Paris. She has published widely on the EU, as well as preventive diplomacy, dispute resolution, and other issues in international affairs, in numerous journals including *Foreign Affairs, Foreign Policy*, the *Journal of Common Market Studies*, the *Journal of European Public Policy*, and *International Organization*. Her latest publications include: *Whose Europe? National Models and the Constitution of the European Union* (Oxford University Press, 2003) and *The Federal Vision: Legitimacy and Levels of Governance in the US and the EU* (Oxford University Press, 2001).

Luis Moreno Ocampo is the first Chief Prosecutor of the ICC, unanimously elected in April 2003. Between 1984 and 1992, as a prosecutor in Argentina, Moreno Ocampo was involved in precedent-setting trials of top military commanders for mass killings and other large-scale human rights abuses. In 1992, he resigned as Chief Prosecutor of the Federal Criminal Court of Buenos Aires and established a private law firm, Moreno Ocampo & Wortman Jofre, which specialises in corruption control programmes for large firms and organisations and criminal and human rights law. Until his election as Chief Prosecutor of the ICC, Moreno Ocampo worked as a lawyer and as Private Inspector General for large companies. He also took on a number of *pro bono* activities, including as legal representative for the victims in the extradition of the former Nazi officer Erich Priebke to Italy, the trial of the chief of the Chilean secret police for the murder of General Carlos Prats, and several cases concerning political bribery, journalists' protection, and freedom of expression. Moreno Ocampo has also worked with various local, regional and international NGOs. He was the president of Transparency International for Latin America and the Caribbean, as well as serving on its global Advisory Board. The founder and president of Poder Ciudadano, Moreno Ocampo has served as a member of the Advisory Board of the "Project on Justice in Times of Transition" and "New Tactics on

Human Rights." Moreno Ocampo has also been a visiting professor at both Stanford University and Harvard University.

William A. Schabas is the Director of the Irish Centre for Human Rights at the National University of Ireland, Galway, where he also holds the professorship in human rights law. From 2000 to 2004, Schabas served as one of three international commissioners in the Sierra Leone Truth and Reconciliation Commission. He is the author of numerous monographs and articles, including *Genocide in International Law*, *Introduction to the International Criminal Court*, *The Abolition of the Death Penalty in International Law*, and *The UN International Criminal Tribunals*. He is an Officer of the Order of Canada.

John Steward gained his PhD from Adelaide University in 1972, after completing his undergraduate degree in agriculture, and then completed an Honours degree in Divinity from the Melbourne College of Divinity. In Indonesia from 1974 to 1983, he was a lecturer in theology, agriculture, and community development before joining World Vision in Jakarta to initiate a leadership training programme for village development motivators. Steward went on to facilitate adult learning processes for indigenous community workers from over 50 countries. In 1997-98 he was involved in post-genocide reconstruction with World Vision in Rwanda. He returns to Rwanda every six months to discuss progress with Rwandan peace workers.

Maria Warren served as Chief of Information and Evidence in the Office of the Prosecutor of the ICTR from 2000 to 2006. She was previously Director of Knowledge Management in one of Australia's largest corporate law firms. In both positions, Warren was able to integrate sound principles of legal practice and information management to mobilise key information, technical, human and legal resources to develop and implement innovative and effective trial strategies. She is now combining her private and public experience to assist in the institution-building efforts at the ICC as Chef de Cabinet in the Office of the Prosecutor.

Philippa Webb is currently Special Assistant to the President of the International Court of Justice, President Rosalyn Higgins. She was formerly Associate Legal Advisor to the Prosecutor of the ICC, before which she worked at the United Nations Secretariat in New York and an international law firm in Sydney and Tokyo. Webb holds Arts and Law degrees from the University of New South Wales and a Master of Laws from Yale Law School. She is a doctoral candidate at Yale Law School, writing on the development of international humanitarian law by international courts and tribunals.

Jennifer M. Welsh holds a BA in Political Science from the University of Saskatchewan (where she won the Governor General's Medal) and Master's and

Doctorate degrees in International Relations from the University of Oxford (where she studied as a Rhodes Scholar). She is a former Jean Monnet Fellow of the European University Institute in Florence and was a Cadieux Research Fellow in the Policy Planning Staff of the Canadian Department of Foreign Affairs. Welsh has taught international relations at the University of Toronto, McGill University, and the Central European University (Prague). She is currently University Lecturer in International Relations at the University of Oxford, where she is a Fellow of Somerville College. Welsh is the author and co-author of five books and a series of articles on international relations. Her most recent publications include *Humanitarian Intervention and International Relations* (Oxford University Press, 2004) and *At Home in the World: Canada's Global Vision for the 21st Century* (HarperCollins Canada, 2004). The latter was a Globe 100 Best Book of the Year (2004) and was also nominated for the Shaughnessy Cohen Prize for Political Writing. Her current research projects include the evolution of the notion of the "responsibility to protect" in international society, the ethics of post-conflict reconstruction, and changing directions in Canadian foreign aid policy. In 2008, Oxford University Press published a book she co-edited with Vaughan Lowe, Adam Roberts, and Dominik Zaum entitled, *The United Nations Security Council and War: The Evolution of Thought and Practice since 1945*.

Paul D. Williams is an Associate Professor in the Elliott School of International Affairs at the George Washington University, USA. He is author of *British Foreign Policy under New Labour 1997-2005* (Palgrave-Macmillan, 2005), co-author of *Understanding Peacekeeping* (Polity, 2004), co-editor of *Africa in International Politics* (Routledge, 2004) and editor of *Security Studies: An Introduction* (Routledge, 2008). His main research interests are UK foreign policy and contemporary peace operations.

Dominik Zaum is Lecturer in International Relations at the University of Reading. He is the author of *The Sovereignty Paradox: The Norms and Politics of International Statebuilding* (Oxford University Press, 2007), and editor, together with Vaughan Lowe, Sir Adam Roberts, and Jennifer Welsh, of *The United Nations Security Council and War* (Oxford University Press, 2008). He has written in particular on post-conflict state-building and international administrations, and has previously worked for the Office of the High Representative in Bosnia and the Lessons Learned and Analysis Unit of the UNMIK/ EU Pillar in Kosovo.

PREFACE

President Paul Kagame

The years since the Rwandan genocide, during which an estimated one million people were murdered in an attempt to eradicate all Tutsi from the face of the earth, have involved much soul-searching and rebuilding. Rwanda and the whole world have had to ask what went so terribly wrong in 1994: why and how were so many innocent civilians allowed to be butchered while the world watched, yet refused to intervene? Why was so little done to attempt to save them? Who is responsible for these crimes and how should we deal with them? How do we now go about rebuilding a Rwandan society that was so decimated—physically, emotionally, psychologically and spiritually—by the genocide? How can we ensure that such destruction is not wrought again in Rwanda or anywhere else in the future?

The events of 1994 reverberate through the daily lives of all Rwandans and all inhabitants of the Great Lakes region, just as they should reverberate through the memories and consciences of all of humanity. The genocide touched the lives of all Rwandans; no individual or community was spared. Every Rwandan is either a genocide survivor or a perpetrator, or the friend or relative of a survivor or perpetrator. The entire Great Lakes region also became volatile because of the genocide, particularly because so many of its orchestrators and perpetrators fled into neighbouring countries, principally the Democratic Republic of Congo (DRC), taking with them their ideology of ethnic hatred and a desire to spread it throughout the region.

The terrible impact of the genocide is felt not just in Rwanda; it has afflicted the whole region, and it should serve as a lesson to the world that turned its back on Rwanda in its hour of greatest need.

The UN and the international community as a whole abandoned Rwanda in 1994. Before the beginning of the slaughter on 7 April 1994, the leadership of the Rwandan Patriotic Front (RPF) as well as many other voices, including the UN's own personnel on the ground and in New York, repeatedly warned the UN of our fears that Rwanda's government of the day was plotting widespread killings of Tutsi. The UN ignored these messages and acted even more cowardly and reprehensibly after the genocide began, by decreasing and subsequently withdrawing the bulk of its contingent of peacekeepers on the ground, which was supposed to oversee the implementation of the Arusha Peace Accord. The UN's failure to intervene in Rwanda in 1994 shook my faith, and that of most Rwandans, in the UN system and the international community generally. We in Rwanda have drawn lasting lessons from the 1994 calamity: never to allow such a thing to happen in our country or elsewhere. This explains our total commitment to peacemaking in our region and in Africa as a whole. It is this moral obligation that led us to contribute directly to the African Union's and United Nations' peacekeeping efforts in Darfur.

The failings of the international community are not only those of abandoning Rwanda during the genocide; some countries directly aided the slaughter. I hold the French government, in particular, responsible for helping to arm and train the militias that dispersed throughout the country to wipe out the Tutsi population. This has been confirmed in a recent report by an independent Commission that investigated the role of France in the genocide. The report concludes that France gave political, military, diplomatic and logistical support before and during the genocide to the government that committed the crime. There were other Rwandans who were killed during the genocide, especially those perceived as opposing the agenda of the genocidal government—but, make no mistake, the agenda of the perpetrators was to exterminate the entire Tutsi population. I hope that those responsible for abetting the most heinous of crimes will be brought to justice.

As though aiding such atrocities were not enough, France and other Western countries have provided safe havens for many of the planners and key perpetrators of the genocide. Just as the hunt for Holocaust criminals continues unabated more than half a century after the Second World War, the global pursuit of perpetrators of the Rwandan genocide, particularly the masterminds of the most serious crimes, must go on until every culprit has been brought to account. It is a scandal that, even today, supposedly respectable members of the international community of nations should harbour those who committed genocide and crimes against humanity.

A new phenomenon has emerged in the form of individuals and groups who seek to revise history for their own gain, including many who deny outright that genocide took place in Rwanda in 1994. These revisionists, including Rwandan and non-Rwandan ideologues, academics, journalists and political leaders, now claim that the genocide was a myth; that what occurred in 1994 was simply a civil war between two equal sides or the spontaneous flaring of ancient tribal hatred. Those who have divergent interpretations of how and why genocide occurred are revisionists and/or proponents of the theory of double genocide. This, as we know, is another phase of genocide. It must be noted that the 1994 genocide of the Tutsi was the only genocide to be recognised both at the political and judicial levels. At the political level, it was recognised when the UN passed resolution 955, which created the International Criminal Tribunal for Rwanda (ICTR) in Arusha, Tanzania, to try genocide perpetrators. At the judicial level, it was recognised in the case of *The Prosecutor vs. Edward Karemera*, in which the ICTR's Appeals Chamber ruled that all defendants before the Tribunal could argue against their involvement in the genocide but could not question whether genocide had taken place in Rwanda.

Even worse than denial of the genocide, some sources accuse the RPF, the force that halted the genocide, of seeking to exterminate the Hutu population. This is an absolute falsehood, sheer nonsense. While some rogue RPF elements committed crimes against civilians during the civil war after 1990, and during the anti-genocidal campaign, individuals were punished severely according to the RPF's internal procedures of the day. To try to construct a case of moral equivalency between genocide crimes and isolated crimes committed by rogue RPF members is morally bankrupt and an insult to all Rwandans, especially survivors of the genocide. Objective history illustrates the degeneracy of this emerging revisionism. The fact that there was no mass revenge in the post-genocide period—which could have easily occurred—is evidence of the clarity of purpose of the Rwandan leadership that actively mobilised the Rwandan population for higher moral purposes than some commentators contend. That the Government of National Unity formed after the genocide involved all political parties except the party that spearheaded the genocide is further proof of the RPF's moral leadership.

There are many flawed interpretations of that leadership, as illustrated in this book, in chapter 4 by René Lemarchand, cleverly hidden under the question of contesting ethnicity. The premise on which Lemarchand's chapter is based is mistaken. It is not reference to Hutu/Tutsi terminologies that forms the basis of the problem of ethnicity in Rwanda. Rather, it is distortions and prejudices that for decades were associated with these terms for political ends. These distortions and prejudices were introduced by colonialists, sustained by the post-colonial regimes, and used to foment the 1994 genocide. This is the philosophy and associated stereotypes that we have to criminalise. A discussion limited to niceties of terminologies is simplistic. Lemarchand should note that for decades the Rwandan people, for survival reasons, were inclined to identify with the favoured "ethnic" group and made entries in their identity cards accordingly. Lemarchand's attempt to see everything Rwandan through the ethnic prism will not help bring Rwandans together. It is also wrong for Lemarchand to assume that there has been global criminalisation of the Hutu community. Genocide happened in broad daylight, and the population knows who is guilty and who is innocent of genocide crimes.

Similarly, Lemarchand is wrong to suggest that the memory of the Hutu victims of genocide has been thwarted or that there has been a clash of ethnic memories in Rwanda. In fact, the key issue has never been crimes committed by the Rwandan Patriotic Army (RPA) nor that victims of these crimes should not be allowed to remember their loved ones. The issue has been, and will always be, that Hutu and Tutsi were not "victims of a calamity for which responsibility is shared by elements of both communities." The point I have always made is that in 1994 there was, on one side, a government-sponsored genocide with perpetrators using the state machinery at their disposal, and on the other side, the RPA fighting to stop the genocide. In the process, and as mentioned above, some of the RPA soldiers committed crimes for which they have been punished and are still being punished. Lemarchand attempts to put the blame for genocide squarely on the liberation war launched by the RPF but deliberately ignores the central cause of that liberation war: the fact that Rwandan refugees had remained stateless for over thirty years, their plight ignored by the world.

It is an established fact that the victims of genocide were the Tutsi and, in that respect, when we commemorate the genocide, we remember them primarily as the group that was targeted for extermination. That does not mean that we do not recognise the heroism of the Hutu who refused to identify themselves with the killers and were opposed to their agenda. When the world remembers the Holocaust, it has in mind the Jews who were singled out for extermination. And yet there were Germans and others who died because they refused to identify with the Nazis.

Attempts to hide the systematic orchestration of the genocide by those in power before and during the genocide serve the purposes of many revisionists and deniers who themselves are guilty of genocide crimes. Many foreign countries continue to harbour these self-serving manipulators of history, just as they provide succour to *génocidaires* in their midst. The revisionists must receive justice for their crimes against historical truth and the affront of their fraudulent narratives to Rwandan people and every survivor of the genocide, just as the *génocidaires* must be found and brought to account for their crimes.

The genocide deniers must be countered at every turn. A volume such as this—edited by two young scholars, Phil Clark and Zachary D. Kaufman, originally of the University of Oxford, and including the work of a unique array of academics and practitioners, Rwandans (including genocide survivors, whose voices are all too rarely heard internationally) and non-Rwandans—is a vital riposte to the cynical re-writers of history. This volume is a commemoration of the genocide that demands active responses in the form of appropriate mechanisms of justice and reconciliation in Rwanda; not simply a remembrance of the cataclysm of 1994, but a call to seek the most culturally-relevant and long-lasting means to rebuild Rwandan lives, individually and collectively. I congratulate the editors on assembling such a comprehensive work on the challenges, and possible means, of reconstructing Rwanda after the genocide.

Rebuilding Rwandan society requires responses to conflict that draw upon our own culture. Efforts to achieve justice, peace, healing and reconciliation must derive from concepts and practices that the Rwandan population recognises and can own. This is the spirit behind the *gacaca* jurisdictions, our revived and reformed traditional conflict resolution system that involves the population intimately in the prosecution of genocide suspects. All Rwandans own *gacaca*, a system which allows those accused of lesser crimes to face their accusers, and permits in turn their communities to participate in deciding whether to acquit or punish those charged with genocide crimes. Rwandans have practiced *gacaca* for centuries and believe in its capacity to punish and to reconcile, to ultimately reintegrate perpetrators, and in the process, to assist in rebuilding the fabric of society torn by criminality and conflict. I hope that *gacaca* will become an inspiration for other post-conflict societies across Africa and elsewhere, as a home-grown, innovative means of justice and reconciliation. It shows how countries emerging from conflict can draw on their own principles and practices to overcome animosity, and build more vibrant, sustainable societies.

Sadly, sections of the international community have ignored the need for locally relevant responses to the genocide, and have tried instead to impose on the Rwandan population institutions and processes that fail to address the particular needs of our society. The ICTR, established by the UN against the wishes of the Rwandan government, as demonstrated by its vote in 1994 as a non-permanent member of the UN Security Council, encapsulates the wider problem of international responses to the genocide. The ICTR has spent more than $1bn. on the prosecution of only a handful of cases. Its physical detachment from Rwanda has prevented it from meaningfully engaging with the Rwandan people.

The immense resources being spent on the ICTR could be better used to support local Rwandan institutions, such as the Rwandan national court system and *gacaca*, which contribute significantly and quantifiably to justice, peace, healing and reconciliation. The ICTR's own donors initially ordered it to complete its work by the end of 2008, long before it would have processed its caseload. I have demanded for many years that cases of the orchestrators and most serious perpetrators of the genocide be transferred to Rwanda's national courts. Fortunately, the early closure of the ICTR seems likely to pave the way for these suspects to be tried in the country that suffered greatest at their hands, and where survivors will have the chance to see with their own eyes justice being done. Only justice delivered in Rwanda, mainly by Rwandans, according to Rwandan and universal principles, can genuinely contribute to peace, healing and reconciliation. Those critical of Rwanda's ways of dispensing justice should join hands in improving the existing judicial system, instead of positioning themselves as adversaries. As the International Criminal Court has selected the conflicts in the DRC, northern Uganda, Darfur and the Central African Republic for its first-ever investigations, it must learn from the mistakes of the ICTR, particularly regarding the dangers of doing international justice in ways detached from the societies it claims to help rebuild after mass conflict.

The 1994 genocide in Rwanda is a blight on all of humanity. The world's failure to intervene to halt the genocide has scarred the world's conscience and begs serious questions about the role of the UN and other international actors in resolving conflict. We must not forget what Rwandans experienced in 1994, what the perpetrators did, and what the international community failed to do. Meaningful commemoration of the genocide means confronting those who would deny or rewrite the suffering of the Rwandan people. As Clark's and Kaufman's book recognises, ultimately, looking back means looking forward: commemorating the genocide means seeking the most appropriate, sustainable ways of doing justice, achieving reconciliation, and rebuilding a strong, vibrant society for all Rwandans.

FOREWORD

ENDING THE CULTURE OF IMPUNITY TO PREVENT CRIMES

Luis Moreno Ocampo

The 1994 Rwandan genocide was an event that shamed the world. The outrage felt by the international community helped focus efforts to establish new methods to address atrocities. As a consequence of the Rwandan genocide and its aftermath, the UN Security Council established the UN International Criminal Tribunal for Rwanda (ICTR) to punish those most responsible for the massive crimes that took place in 1994. In 1998, 120 states signed the Rome Statute, agreeing to create a permanent International Criminal Court (ICC).

The ratification of the Rome Statute by more than 100 states stands testament to growing agreement on the principles of international justice and the means of their enforcement. The Rome Statute served to galvanise a network of national and international actors dedicated to holding perpetrators of atrocities accountable. In the Rome system, the ICC is complementary to domestic systems and intervenes only when a state fails to genuinely act. It is therefore states that remain primarily responsible for investigating and prosecuting crimes committed within their jurisdiction. When the ICC does initiate a case, its Statute requires states parties to cooperate. Working together, this system is confronting centuries-old methods of behaviour, those of conflict and war, the abuse of civilians, women and children, to reshape the norms of human conduct. Nonetheless, the idea of a permanent international criminal justice system is young and fraught with challenges.

The ICC represents a piece of the prevention equation, not a complete formula. Yet, it is a piece that did not exist in April 1994. Ultimately, a comprehensive international justice network that effectively prevents genocide would be the most fitting memorial to the massive destruction and degradation of human life that took place in Rwanda.

The tragic history of the Rwandan genocide is replete with lessons on prevention for the ICC and the rest of the emerging transitional justice network. The identification and articulation of these lessons in this book are an important contribution to the collective task and responsibility of preventing further genocides. This unique and valuable anthology is co-edited by Phil Clark and Zachary D. Kaufman, young scholars from the University of Oxford and experts in transitional justice. The contributors are not only important thinkers and commentators on the Rwandan genocide and transitional justice, but they have also researched and worked in the field, whether in Rwanda, other atrocity sites or in transitional justice institutions, such as the ICC, the ICTR and the UN International Criminal Tribunal for the former Yugoslavia. The work of this anthology is all the more crucial because transitional justice, especially when carried out during ongoing conflict, is a new and rapidly evolving field that academics and practitioners are in the daily process of defining and developing.

I congratulate the editors of this book and the other contributors for unearthing and addressing the lessons of Rwanda. Learning from them is part of our commitment to ending the culture of impunity for atrocious crimes.

PART I
INTRODUCTION AND BACKGROUND

AFTER GENOCIDE

Phil Clark and Zachary D. Kaufman

Introduction

The impact of the 1994 Rwandan genocide continues to echo throughout Rwanda, the Great Lakes region of Africa and the world. Its reverberations are felt acutely in the lives of all Rwandans, for whom the genocide is still a daily reality. The effects of the genocide extend far beyond Rwanda, in refugee flows and the spillover of ethnic antagonisms into neighbouring countries, and in evolving international principles and policies of humanitarian intervention, conflict resolution and transitional justice. It is not only the sheer magnitude and speed of the genocide—an estimated 800,000 Tutsi and their perceived Hutu and Twa sympathisers murdered in only three months, many by their own neighbours, friends and family—that continue to hold our attention today, but also the complexity of its causes and effects.

The purpose of this book is to assess the impact of the genocide in Rwanda, Africa and beyond, and at the same time to analyse the nuances of the national and international, academic and political debates that have consequently developed. What is currently lacking in the growing literature on Rwanda and the genocide are holistic, multi-disciplinary analyses. Holistic approaches explore responses to the physical, psychological and psycho-social needs of individuals and groups during and after conflict, reflecting the intricacies of the situations they seek to address. Often standing in the way of holistic analyses, the legal paradigm has become dominant in the study of conflict and post-conflict societies, proffering procedural, academic and institutional "remedies" that too often fail to recognise other important perspectives. Legal processes have their place as responses to mass violence, but they reflect only one among many means of addressing atrocities. They may not constitute the initial response, may need to be delivered locally rather than internationally, and may eventually need to play a supporting role to more fundamental political and social processes.

1

This volume grew out of three conferences that we organised at the University of Oxford between May 2004 and May 2005. Through these events, we believed that a fitting way to commemorate the hundreds of thousands of innocent lives lost in 1994 was to explore with a broad range of engaged individuals the most appropriate ways to help rebuild Rwanda today. That is the ethos of this anthology, which comprises chapters delivered in draft form at the conferences and others especially commissioned for this collection. The wounds of 1994 are still fresh, but sufficient time has passed to analyse with some clarity the genocide and its aftermath.

In choosing contributors to the conferences and this volume, we gathered scholars and practitioners, Rwandans and non-Rwandans, from a variety of fields. We asked contributors to speak about conflict and post-conflict issues across four dimensions: individual, community, national and international. In addition to offering expert analysis of the genocide and its consequences, this volume provides a space for genocide survivors to tell their stories, which are too seldom heard in such gatherings. We also engage practitioners, to garner their reflections from work in the field. The immensity of the genocide and its aftermath requires this multi-faceted examination.

What became clear through the Oxford conferences is that important voices on Rwanda are rarely heard in the same forum, to the detriment of mutual understanding and effective collaboration. Scholars and practitioners seldom have the chance to exchange ideas and debate with one another directly. Relations between the Rwandan government, the United Nations International Criminal Tribunal for Rwanda (ICTR) and human rights NGOs, for example, have often been fraught, undermining the possibility of productive engagement among them. We have sought to bring many of these parties together in order to generate discussions and debates about the genocide and its consequences. We assemble these contributors not because we necessarily endorse all of their views, but because drawing them into the same space, and hearing them alongside one another, sparks debates in a constructive manner that otherwise might not occur.

This volume seeks to highlight key points of contention, not to find easy resolutions or syntheses (because these probably could not be reached without severe distortions of the views considered), but to provide the basis for the complex discussions the genocide demands. Although we cast our net wide, many of the invited academics and practitioners working on Rwanda-related issues, including some who presented papers at the Oxford events, were for various reasons unable to contribute to this book. Nevertheless, we believe this volume represents a comprehensive exploration of issues related to the Rwandan genocide and its aftermath.

Key concepts

As the title of this book suggests, three topics dominate discussions here: transitional justice, post-conflict reconstruction and reconciliation. Ruti Teitel offers a useful definition of transitional justice as "the conception of justice associated with periods of political change, characterized by legal responses to confront the wrongdoings of repressive predecessor regimes."[1] We contend, however, that transitional justice should not be limited, and should not necessarily afford primacy, to judicial responses. John Hamre and Gordon Sullivan employ the World Bank's definition of "post-conflict reconstruction", which incorporates "the rebuilding of the socioeconomic framework of society" and the "reconstruction of the enabling conditions for a functioning peacetime society [to include] the framework of governance and rule of law."[2] They add that "post-conflict reconstruction" should include "providing and enhancing not only social and economic well-being and governance and the rule of law but also other elements of justice and reconciliation and, very centrally, security."[3] Finally, we broadly interpret "reconciliation" as rebuilding fractured individual and communal relationships after conflict, with a view to encouraging cooperation among former antagonists. As John Paul Lederach argues, "to enter reconciliation processes is to enter the domain of the internal world, the inner understandings, fears and hopes, perceptions and interpretations of the relationship itself."[4]

While transitional justice, post-conflict reconstruction and reconciliation are united by notions of rebuilding, there is much debate among the contributors over how best to define these terms and how they should apply to post-genocide Rwanda and other societies that have suffered similar tragedies. For example, while "transitional justice" has become the dominant phrase used to describe theoretical and operational responses to mass conflict—again, undoubtedly because of the dominance of legal perspectives in this realm—it is not clear why justice should be accorded primacy over other objectives, such as truth, peace, healing and reconciliation, nor whether the pursuit of justice will in fact facilitate meaningful society-wide transition from violence to order and stability.

The final chapter of this volume, by Clark, Kaufman and Kalypso Nicolaïdis, investigates the appropriateness of the terms "transitional justice" and

---

1   R. Teitel, "Transitional Justice Genealogy," *Harvard Human Rights Journal*, 16 (Spring 2003), 69.

2   World Bank, *Post-Conflict Reconstruction: The Role of the World Bank* (Washington: World Bank, 1998), 14.

3   J. Hamre and G. Sullivan, "Toward Postconflict Reconstruction", *The Washington Quarterly*, 25, 4 (Autumn 2002), 89.

4   J. Lederach, "Five Qualities of Practice in Support of Reconciliation Processes" in R. Helmick and R. Petersen (eds), *Forgiveness and Reconciliation: Religion, Public Policy, and Conflict Transformation* (Philadelphia: Templeton Foundation Press, 2001), 185.

3

"post-conflict reconstruction" to describe responses to conflict and post-conflict situations. The growth in academic discussions of transitional justice and post-conflict reconstruction is relatively recent, and the terms of reference are still fluid, as commentators mould contested concepts to suit specific circumstances. Recent anniversaries of the Rwandan genocide have provided critical opportunities to debate the direction of studies of transition and reconstruction. To this end, this book explores six key terms outlined in detail by Clark in Chapter 10—reconciliation, peace, justice, healing, forgiveness and truth. Many debates over these issues relate to contentious definitions of these concepts. For example, as the wide-ranging discussions in this volume show, debates over "justice"—what it is, what it should achieve, who should administer it—are often heated and not always resolved or resolvable. This volume is intended to help clarify the theory and practice of transitional justice, post-conflict reconstruction and reconciliation.

Key themes

The six terms just outlined are critical to exploring three major themes in this volume: the history and memory of the Rwandan genocide; post-genocide justice, reconstruction and reconciliation; and the relevance of the genocide beyond Rwanda. The intersections and entanglements of these themes are crucial to grasping key debates in present-day Rwanda and to formulating effective responses to the genocide and atrocities elsewhere: how history is constructed and the past is remembered inevitably shapes questions about who is culpable for crimes, how they should be punished, who warrants redress and how society as a whole should be reconstructed.

The politics of genocide history and memory

One motivation for this volume was our dissatisfaction with the content and tone of many commemorations of the tenth and subsequent anniversaries of the genocide. Two worrying trends were discernible: a neglect of basic truths about the genocide, and the proliferation of genocide denial and other forms of damaging revisionism. The benefit of recent films such as *Hotel Rwanda*, *Sometimes in April* and *Shooting Dogs*,[5] which brought the genocide to a gen-

---

5   It should be noted that, while helping to widen popular understanding of the genocide, these films have also proven highly controversial. For example, some commentators have claimed that Paul Rusesabagina, the manager of the *Hotel des Mille Collines* in Kigali during the genocide and the "hero" of *Hotel Rwanda*, did not act as valiantly as portrayed in the movie, alleging—among other claims—that he charged Tutsi exorbitant sums for the rooms in which they hid from the *génocidaires*. See, for example, E. Musoni, "Rusesabagina Dodges Radio Talk Show", *The New Times* (6 February 2006), http://www.newtimes.co.rw/index.php?option=com_content&task=view&id=3375&Itemid=61.

eral audience, has been undermined by inaccurate depictions of the genocide elsewhere. Many journalistic reports and academic commentaries on the tenth anniversary of the genocide focused disproportionately on secondary historical issues, such as who was responsible for shooting down President Juvénal Habyarimana's plane on 6 April 1994, the event that "triggered" the genocide. The long-term planning of the genocide which preceded the plane crash and the plight of Rwandan genocide survivors were often forgotten in the rush to report the controversy that erupted when, in March 2004, *Le Monde* printed excerpts of a report by the French investigating judge Jean-Louis Bruguière, alleging that the Rwandan Patriotic Front (RPF) had deliberately shot down the plane and allowed the subsequent murder of hundreds of thousands of Tutsi to justify the RPF's insurgency against the Hutu government. Bruguière's allegations received even greater media attention when, two days after *Le Monde*'s story broke, UN headquarters in New York discovered what it believed (erroneously, as it turned out) was the flight recorder from Habyarimana's plane, which investigators had considered lost.

Bruguière's allegations are serious and warrant further investigation. However, in concentrating on the plane crash and the discovery of the flight recorder, many discussions of the tenth anniversary of the genocide missed the fundamental point: that the crash, while important in itself, not least because it involved the assassination of two heads of state, is more important because it precipitated a deliberate catastrophe with much more significant causes. One aim of this volume is to return the events of the genocide, its causes and aftermath, and especially the plight of victims and survivors, to the centre of the genocide narrative and analysis.

The murder spree against the Tutsi was no spontaneous flaring of ancient ethnic antagonisms. As Linda Melvern outlines in her chapter in this volume and in other works,[6] and as one of our conference participants, Alison Des Forges, has documented extensively,[7] the genocide was systematically orchestrated by the Hutu-led government. High-level meetings in the early 1990s

---

Other commentators, including the director of *Hotel Rwanda*, Terry George, have argued that the Rwandan government has initiated a "smear campaign" against Rusesabagina because of his criticism of the Kagame administration during speaking tours of the US and Europe. See T. George, "Smearing a Hero", *Washington Post* (10 May 2006) http://www.washingtonpost.com/wp-dyn/content/article/ 2006/05/09/ AR2006050901242.html.

6   See L. Melvern, *A People Betrayed: The Role of the West in Rwanda's Genocide* (New York: Zed Books, 2000); L. Melvern, *Conspiracy to Murder: The Rwanda Genocide and the International Community* (London, Verso Books, 2004). A fully revised and updated paperback edition of *Conspiracy to Murder* was published by Verso Books in April 2006.

7   A. Des Forges, *Leave None to Tell the Story: Genocide in Rwanda* (New York: Human Rights Watch, 1999).

called for the training of youth militias, the stockpiling of weapons and "rehearsal" pogroms of Tutsi as preparation for the genocide.

There is a serious problem of causality in recent analyses of the alleged role of the RPF in the genocide. Even if it were proven that Kagame and the RPF were responsible for shooting down Habyarimana's plane—and there is currently far from compelling evidence of this—the genocide would likely have happened anyway, such was the government's degree of planning. Roméo Dallaire, head of the failed UN peacekeeping mission in Rwanda during the genocide, questions in his 2003 autobiography whether the RPF deliberately plotted the genocide to justify a counter-offensive that would allow it to take over the country: "I found myself thinking such dire thoughts as whether . . . the genocide had been orchestrated to clear the way for Rwanda's return to the pre-1959 status quo in which Tutsi had called all the shots," Dallaire says. "Had the Hutu extremists been bigger dupes than I? Ten years later, I still can't put these troubling questions to rest."[8] Dallaire's claim contradicts his own evidence, described painstakingly in his book, that the Hutu extremists had been plotting the genocide for years and had begun to prepare the Hutu population for the killing spree far in advance.

Second, equally troubling is the growing revisionism regarding the genocide. A range of voices, from Hutu ideologues to Western academics, has grown louder in recent years, claiming either that there was no genocide of Tutsi in 1994 or that there is little substantive difference between crimes against Tutsi and those perpetrated against Hutu by the RPF and Tutsi civilians. Genocide revisionism is not new, as displayed by the host of deniers of the Holocaust, which has prompted the passing of anti-denial legislation in many countries. In the Rwandan case, genocide deniers have a variety of motivations: scholars pursuing the latest academic fads that revel in "alternative narratives", no matter how spurious or morally questionable; génocidaires seeking to deflect attention from their crimes; and critics of the current RPF government who try to connect alleged RPF atrocities in 1994 to unrelated concerns with its current policies.

Certainly crimes committed by the RPF and Tutsi civilians in 1994 should be investigated; as Lemarchand, Hintjens and Buckley-Zistel rightly argue in this volume, Hutu survivors of the 1994 violence are also entitled to redress for the crimes they have suffered. However, such crimes, while requiring robust legal and political responses, are not morally equivalent to genocide, what the ICTR has called the "crime of crimes."[9] It is unjustified to argue, for example,

8   R. Dallaire, *Shake Hands with the Devil: The Failure of Humanity in Rwanda* (Toronto: Random House Canada, 2003), 476.

9   *Prosecutor v. Kambanda* (Case No. ICTR-97-23-S), Judgement and Sentence (4 September 1998) Paragraph 16; *Prosecutor v. Serashugo* (Case Number ICTR-98-39-S), Sentence

as Rory Carroll did in *The Guardian* in January 2005, that the Hutu population's supposed "sense of grievance is likely to be compounded by a Hollywood film, *Hotel Rwanda*, depicting horrors perpetrated by Hutu militias."[10]
Although Hutu were also victims of crimes in 1994, why must a film like *Hotel
Rwanda*, designed to portray the immense horror of the genocide, show both
"sides"? While it is true that both "sides" committed crimes in 1994, it is being increasingly forgotten that only one "side" committed genocide.

Several authors in this volume respond explicitly to the problem of revisionism relating to the events of 1994. Tom Ndahiro, a genocide survivor, tackles
what he claims is the most virulent and systematic programme of revisionism, that of the *Rassemblement Républicain pour la Démocratie au Rwanda*
(RDR). Ndahiro argues that the RDR engages in "genocide-laundering" by
denying that the genocide occurred and thus continues the oppression of Tutsi
by seeking to purge the violent campaign against them from global memory.
René Lemarchand argues that revisionism and denial by some Hutu ideologues
have been greatly boosted by revisionist tendencies among certain Western
academics.

Several contributors confront revisionism implicitly by focusing on the degree to which the genocide was planned by the Habyarimana government.
Linda Melvern and Paul Williams explore the planning of the genocide and the
international community's neglect, while Jean Baptiste Kayigamba, a Rwandan genocide survivor and journalist, in an extraordinary first-hand account,
describes his harrowing experiences of living in Kigali in the months before
and during the genocide. These chapters highlight just how bereft much of
the recent commentary has been in ignoring the Hutu government's careful
orchestration of the genocide.

These analyses constitute a starting-point for further exploration. What is
also needed are increasingly detailed accounts of what happened in 1994 (in
the vein of Des Forges' *Leave None to Tell the Story: Genocide in Rwanda,*[11]
African Rights' *Rwanda: Death, Despair and Defiance*[12] and Scott Straus's
The Order of Genocide: Race, Power, and War in Rwanda[13]), linking specific
dates, times, names and places (especially those in rural areas in Rwanda that
are often overlooked), and vigorous debates over their significance. It is also

---

(2 February 1999) Paragraph 15.

10   R. Carroll, "Genocide Tribunal 'Ignoring Tutsi Crimes'", *The Guardian* (13 January
      2005) http://www.guardian.co.uk/rwanda/story/0,14451,1389194,00.html.

11   Des Forges, *Leave None to Tell the Story,* op. cit.

12   African Rights, *Rwanda: Death, Despair and Defiance* (New Expanded Edition, London:
      African Rights, August 1995).

13   S. Straus, *The Order of Genocide: Race, Power, and War in Rwanda* (Ithaca: Cornell
      University Press, 2006).

necessary to situate the genocide in the broader history of colonial and national political manipulation of Hutu-Tutsi antagonisms throughout the 20th century. The general narrative of the genocide is currently clear in the existing literature. It is now time to discuss details reaching down to the lives of individual and everyday Rwandans. Perhaps what is most insidious about much of the recent commentary is that it obscures—without convincing justification—the broad brushstrokes of the genocide, thus rendering the personal experiences, particularly those of the victims and survivors, near-invisible.

History and memory: outline of chapters. Chapters 1 to 9 of this volume cover the history and memory of the genocide. Melvern, arguing that "the past is prologue", not only explores the nature of the Habyarimana government's genocidal conspiracy and the ways in which previous pogroms of Tutsi paved the way for the violence of 1994 (a theme also explored in Kayigamba's first-hand account of violence in the build-up to, and during, the genocide), but she also provides a useful way to frame issues of history and memory of the genocide: by understanding that the genocide is critical to Rwanda's future. How we interpret atrocities shapes how we respond to them. Unifying all the chapters is the contention that history is invariably politicised and that Rwanda's future hinges on the ability to navigate divergent interpretations of the past.

Kayigamba expresses anger at the *génocidaires* who killed members of his family and a sense of betrayal by the international community that refused to intervene to save innocent lives. He cautions against expecting the rapid renewal of Rwandan society. The past must be dealt with slowly, methodically, he argues, if Rwanda is to have a secure future. Kayigamba expresses scepticism over calls for forgiveness and reconciliation after the genocide and argues that, because decades of impunity in Rwanda convinced the *génocidaires* that they could commit atrocities without fear of being held accountable, those convicted of genocide must be punished to protect against future atrocities. Questions of forgiveness and reconciliation—secondary concerns, according to Kayigamba—must come much later.

Williams also contends that the international community should have done more to intervene in Rwanda and that, contrary to some analyses, international intervention could have significantly mitigated the violence. Williams claims that the genocide underlines serious weaknesses in international peacekeeping methods and questions whether these problems have been remedied. In particular, he highlights Britain's role, as a permanent member of the UN Security Council, in failing to advocate intervention in Rwanda—a failure that cannot be explained by Britain's lack of knowledge of what was unfolding in Rwanda, but only by a lack of political will on the part of John Major's government.

Chapters 4 to 9 navigate these complex issues of genocide memory and commemoration. The paths taken by the authors often diverge substantially.

Lemarchand employs Paul Ricoeur's categories of thwarted memory, manipulated memory and enforced memory to explore how the genocide has so far been remembered and in particular how elites have been *forced* to remember it, among whom the most prominent are—with very different motives—academic revisionists (including Helmut Strizek and Christian Davenport) and the current Rwandan government. Lemarchand sees danger in the government's 2002 law banning the use of the labels "Hutu" and "Tutsi" in public discourse and its emphasis on national identity based on the cultural unity of all Rwandans.

Helen Hintjens disagrees with Lemarchand's analysis, claiming that a departure from the use of "Hutu" and "Tutsi" constitutes a welcome attempt to overcome divisive racial and ethnic stereotypes in Rwanda. What is needed instead, she argues, is to create spaces for more complex voices, including Rwandans of mixed Hutu-Tutsi descent, Tutsi who have returned to Rwanda since the genocide and Hutu who are neither genocide perpetrators nor survivors. While cautiously welcoming the government's refusal to allow public discussion using racial or ethnic categories, Hintjens is highly critical of other areas of official policy, especially what she argues is the government's tendency to "globalise" the genocide guilt of the Hutu population. She suggests that more complex categories of Rwandan identity need to be recognised, and that the present regime should not portray itself to the international community as the only bulwark against future violence in Rwanda.

Ndahiro, the second of three survivors writing in this volume, analyses the RDR's attempts to deny the genocide and, more recently, to claim that the RPF was responsible for committing genocide against Hutu in 1994. Ndahiro argues, on the basis of rare primary sources, including documents that he gathered from Hutu refugee camps in eastern Democratic Republic of Congo (DRC), that the RDR had intimate connections to the political and military leaders who orchestrated the genocide. He notes that, as the Hutu government did during the genocide, the RDR describes the genocide as a "civil war", and that the international media tend to misinterpret events in Rwanda and provide the RDR and other extremists with a platform for their propaganda.

Susanne Buckley-Zistel, Solomon Nsabiyera Gasana and John Steward wrestle with questions of how to connect historical interpretations of the genocide with the objectives of reconciliation, healing, forgiveness and economic development. All three authors claim that there is a danger in some Rwandans' (and especially some survivors') desire to forget the past and move on. Buckley-Zistel argues that many Rwandans practise what she calls "chosen amnesia", a coping mechanism that prefers silencing continuing antagonisms rather than directly confronting them. She argues that history and memory in Rwanda have always been a "top-down political project", whether through colonial or national elites' attempts to politically manipulate ethnic identities and divisions or—here she echoes Lemarchand's argument—through the current government's desire to eclipse memories that do not promote its rhetoric of "national unity". Buckley-Zistel argues that without confronting the causes of conflict in Rwanda, sustainable reconciliation is impossible.

Gasana and Steward highlight the importance of a concept that has only recently gained currency in discussions of responses to mass violence: healing. Gasana, a Munyamulenge (a Congolese Tutsi from South Kivu), in a powerful survivor's account of violence in the Great Lakes, draws on his personal experiences to explore hatred and the elite manipulation of ethnic antagonisms in the region. Gasana and his family experienced Hutu violence in Zaire/DRC and Rwanda first hand, but only when he understood that Hutu were also the victims of oppression did he begin to experience healing of his "inner woundedness". Healing has allowed him to contribute meaningfully to peace-building and development programmes in the Great Lakes region, and he argues that reconciliation is a prerequisite for peace and development. In contrast to his fellow survivor Kayigamba, Gasana argues that not only is reconciliation possible in Rwanda and the Great Lakes generally but peace and prosperity in the region depend on it.

Steward explores practical approaches to psycho-social healing after the genocide, which he argues is important for facilitating forgiveness and reconciliation. Healing strategies, he argues, must account for complex post-genocide identities, similar to those explored by Hintjens and Buckley-Zistel, and different experiences of the genocide. Healing often involves a crucial ritual element that Steward argues is deeply embedded in Rwandan society, providing cultural resources upon which the population can draw. Furthermore, notions of communal negotiation, which are found in practices such as *gacaca*, are important for building trust and solidarity among parties previously in conflict, reinforcing their sense of inter-connectedness, which Steward argues is necessary for individual healing.

Post-genocide legal and political developments

Most reports on the tenth anniversary commemorations of the genocide were bogged down in distractions or revisionism, and also ignored questions of where Rwanda should go from here and, in particular, issues regarding justice, reconciliation and the overall reconstruction of the post-genocide society. Where commentators did consider such questions, they often focused on issues of accountability for alleged RPF atrocities, ignoring the challenge of how to effectively respond to Hutu-initiated genocide crimes. Considering the limited means and time available to address the enormous and multifaceted challenges post-genocide Rwanda faces, difficult choices must be made. Political and legal pragmatism must shape moral responses to the crimes of 1994: in an impoverished country like Rwanda, whose national judiciary was decimated by the genocide, not every perpetrator can be prosecuted. Therefore, it is necessary to focus first on the most severe offences, while leaving open the possibility of dealing with lesser criminals later. Critics of Rwanda's *gacaca* system of community-based courts, for example, have often accused it of failing to address crimes against Hutu. These commentators have failed to show, however, how *gacaca*, established largely because of the practical limitations of the legal realm in responding to the genocide, can prosecute lesser perpetrators while adequately addressing genocide crimes. Finite resources dictate that *gacaca* cannot achieve both and therefore must focus on the most egregious cases at hand (which, the government claims, still number in the tens of thousands, after *gacaca* has recently identified many more suspects, apart from those originally identified in the direct aftermath of the genocide[14]).

Meanwhile, the ICTR has been criticised both for its stated intention to address alleged RPF crimes (diverting resources, some contend, from dealing with genocide cases, and destabilising already fragile relations with the Rwandan government) and for failing to address them. The former claim was instrumental in the dismissal of Carla Del Ponte as the ICTR Prosecutor, as her intention to prosecute RPF members who allegedly perpetrated atrocities soured relations with Kigali, which responded by blocking the travel of witnesses from Rwanda to the Tribunal's headquarters in Arusha. While the ICTR is right to claim that there is a need for careful investigations into alleged RPF atrocities, it is not even able to deal adequately with its existing caseload of genocide suspects. Consequently, in 2007 the ICTR stated that starting in 2008 it would consider transferring some of its backlog of cases to the Rwandan national courts. When the task of prosecuting *génocidaires* (through *gacaca*, the ICTR and the Rwandan national courts) is complete, and if there are sufficient resources—which is likely to require the assistance of the international community—there may be scope for addressing other crimes allegedly committed in 1994. While this strategy may be considered one-sided, the most serious crimes, namely genocide, must be addressed first. Ideally, all crimes would be confronted, but the reality of the situation requires the setting of priorities.

In focusing on issues *after genocide*, this volume contends with recent legal and political developments in Rwanda, which can be interpreted through the six key concepts described above. After coming to power following the genocide, the RPF faced the challenge of dealing with approximately 120,000 genocide suspects whom the government rounded up in the latter half of 1994 and trans-

---

14   P. Clark's interview, Domitilla Mukantaganzwa, Executive Secretary, *Gacaca* Commission, Kigali (6 June 2006).

ported to prisons around the country that have been overflowing ever since. The national judiciary had been destroyed. Between 1994 and 1996, two key developments shaped the post-genocide legal landscape. On 8 November 1994, the UN Security Council authorised the establishment of the ICTR to prosecute those most responsible for the genocide. Modelled on the UN International Criminal Tribunal for the Former Yugoslavia (ICTY), the ICTR was intended to help end impunity in Rwanda by prosecuting the leaders of the genocide, while leaving lower-level perpetrators to the Rwandan national courts.[15]

The ICTR has been heavily criticised for its immense cost (an estimated $1 billion by the end of 2007) and for limited results (35 cases completed in 14 years of operation).[16] Over the past several years, there have been allegations that *génocidaires* work at the ICTR. Over time, the suspected number of such individuals participating in cases has increased. At first, it was thought that six suspected *génocidaires*—including an individual operating under the name "Sammy Bahati Weza," who was in reality Simeon Nshamihigo, a former deputy prosecutor of the Cyangugu prefecture of Rwanda accused of ordering and participating in the killing of Tutsi—were employed by the UN in Arusha.[17] More recently, it was reported that as many as twice that number of suspects may be working there.[18]

That even one *génocidaire* has served at the ICTR is reason enough to be concerned, as this is literally a life-or-death matter. A perpetrator working at the ICTR could gain access to confidential information about witnesses or co-conspirators, or manipulate evidence. Even if no direct harm is caused, the possibility of their presence alone has caused great concern over the IC-TR's competence and security among survivors of the genocide, adding to the already strained relationship between the ICTR and the Rwandan government and survivors' organisations, as discussed by Rwanda's President Paul Kagame in the preface to this anthology and in the chapter by the Rwandan Prosecutor-General Martin Ngoga.

Such a situation must be addressed immediately, but it also offers lessons for the future of international criminal justice. Most importantly, UN-backed tribunals (such as the ICTR, the ICTY, the Special Court for Sierra Leone and

---

15   United Nations, UN Doc S/RES/955 (8 November 1994).

16   Hirondelle News Agency, "ICTR's Judges Mandate Extended by UN", Arusha (15 June 2006) http://www.hirondelle.org/arusha.nsf/LookupUrlEnglish/1c6a1ddee99fa5a443257 18e0028b543?OpenDocument&Click=; United Nations, "ICTR Detainees – Status on 2 March 2008", available at www.ictr.org.

17   V. Peskin, "Rwandan Ghosts," *Legal Affairs* (September-October 2002), 21-25, http:// www.legalaffairs.org/issues/September-October-2002/feature_peskin_sepoct2002.html.

18   United Nations Office for the Coordination of Humanitarian Affairs, "Rwanda: UN Tribunal Investigating 12 on its Payroll" (29 June 2006) http://www.irinnews.org/report. asp? ReportID =54296 &SelectRegion= Great_Lakes&SelectCountry=RWANDA.

the Extraordinary Chambers in the Courts of Cambodia), as well as non-UN war crimes courts and tribunals (such as the ICC and the Iraqi Special Tribunal), must conduct thorough background checks on all personnel, especially those working on sensitive matters. The UN must also eliminate corruption and nepotism in its hiring practices or risk weakening the entire enterprise of international criminal justice and, more important, endangering individual lives.

At the domestic level, in 1996, with the assistance of the UN, foreign governments and NGOs, the Rwandan government began an overhaul of the national judiciary, training new judges and lawyers and establishing new courts across the country. In the same year, the government passed the Organic Law, which divided genocide suspects into four categories depending on the severity of their crimes, and established a plea-bargaining scheme.[19] The national courts were initially slow in hearing the cases of genocide suspects. However, over time, the courts became more efficient and were praised, albeit with reservations, by some international monitors for their speed and improved legal standards.[20]

2001 marked a sea change in Rwandan law, with the passing of legislation creating the *gacaca* jurisdictions. The *Gacaca* Law, based on the Organic Law, was modified in 2004 and 2006 and is set for further revision in 2001, 2004, 2006, 2007 and 2008 to help streamline the process. Three years of pilot phases led to the inauguration in June 2004 of *gacaca* courts in approximately 9,000 jurisdictions across the country. In March 2005, many of these jurisdictions began judging and sentencing approximately 35,000 genocide suspects— less than a third of those imprisoned since 1994—who had been provisionally released, beginning in January 2003, in several waves, first into civic education camps known as *ingando* or "solidarity camps", and then into their home communities, where they awaited appearance before *gacaca*.

The post-genocide period in Rwanda has also been characterised by political upheaval. After gaining control of the country in July 1994, the RPF quickly set about solidifying power in Rwanda. As Filip Reyntjens observes, the RPF "introduced a strong executive presidency, imposed the dominance of the RPF in the government, and redrew the composition of parliament."[21] Between 1995 and 2000, several prominent Hutu leaders, including Prime Minister Faustin Twagiramungu and President Pasteur Bizimungu, resigned from

---

19   Republic of Rwanda, "Loi Organique No. 8196 du 30/8/96 sur l'Organisation des Poursuites des Infractions Constitutives du Crime de Genocide ou de Crimes contre l'Humanité, Commises à Partir de 1er Octobre 1990", *Official Gazette of the Republic of Rwanda* (1 September 1996), Articles 2-9.

20   See, for example, Amnesty International, "Rwanda: The Troubled Course of Justice", AI Index AFR 47/10/00 (April 2000), 3-6.

21   F. Reyntjens, "Rwanda, Ten Years On: From Genocide to Dictatorship", *African Affairs*, 103 (2004), 178.

the government, citing their inability to work with the RPF. Twagiramungu fled into exile in Belgium, returning to contest the 2003 presidential elections, which he claimed were rigged, after Kagame won 95 per cent of the vote to his 3.7 per cent. Bizimungu was arrested in 2001 for attempting to create a new political party, which the government claimed was intent on spreading genocidal ideology. In February 2006, Bizimungu lost an appeal—during what many observers criticised as a sham hearing[22]—to overturn his 15-year prison sentence, handed down in 2004. President Kagame eventually pardoned Bizimungu and ordered his release in April 2007.

At the end of the official post-genocide transitional period in 2003, the government held a constitutional referendum and prepared the country for the first presidential and parliamentary elections since the genocide. In the lead-up to the elections, the government banned the *Mouvement Démocratique Républicain* (MDR), the largest Hutu opposition party and effectively the only significant Hutu voice in the Rwandan parliament, on the grounds of "divisionism" or what the government claimed were attempts to spread genocidal ideology.[23] The same allegations were levelled against the *Ligue Rwandaise pour la Promotion de la Défense des Droits de l'Homme* (LIPRODHOR), Rwanda's largest human rights organisation, which the government dissolved in January 2005.[24]

Legal and political developments: outline of chapters. Chapters 10 to 16 in this volume focus on post-genocide justice and reconciliation. Following Clark's conceptual chapter mentioned above, Schabas provides a vital introduction to these themes. "Everybody talks about battling impunity," he writes, "but few societies have done this with greater determination or more stubborn resistance to compromise than Rwanda." Schabas argues that, by incorporating the ICTR, Rwandan national courts and *gacaca* to prosecute genocide suspects, the Rwandan case represents a multi-faceted approach to transitional justice that covers a range of options available to conflict and post-conflict societies around the world. He argues that all systematic responses to crimes must contend with a multitude of needs and interests among affected populations and that, for this reason, Rwanda still struggles to find the most appropriate mechanisms for dealing with genocide crimes. What is clear, however, according to Scha-

---

22   See, for example, Human Rights Watch, "Rwanda: Historic Ruling Expected for Former President and Seven Others", HRW Background Briefing, Kigali: HRW (16 January 2006) http://hrw.org/english/docs/2006/01/16/ rwanda12429.htm.

23   For a thorough discussion of the plans in 2003 to ban MDR, see Human Rights Watch, "Preparing for Elections: Tightening Control in the Name of Unity", HRW Briefing Paper, Kigali: HRW, May 2003.

24   Amnesty International, "Rwanda: Human Rights Organisation Forced to Close Down", AI Index AFR 47/001/2005 (10 January 2005).

bas, is that harsh, retributive justice is not the best way forward and that other approaches—especially those that promote reconciliation—display greater potential for sustainable rebuilding of Rwandan society.

Kaufman focuses on one of the institutions explored by Schabas, the ICTR, and draws on interviews and recently declassified documents to present a new and comprehensive narrative of the history of the establishment of the Tribunal. While Williams' case study focuses on one member of the UN Security Council, namely Britain, Kaufman concentrates on another, the United States. The chapter focuses on what Kaufman argues was the primary role of the US in driving the form and structure of the Tribunal, although the chapter also discusses the critical part played by other states, such as France, New Zealand, Russia, Spain, the UK and Rwanda itself. Kaufman concludes that, despite the objections of Rwanda, the US led the establishment of the ICTR after abandoning its initial preference for a different design. Kaufman highlights the power politics involved in this decision-making process before outlining a number of puzzles that future research on the etiology of this Tribunal should address.

Hassan Bubacar Jallow, Prosecutor of the ICTR, outlines the contribution of the ICTR to Rwandan society and to international criminal law. Contrary to many of the critical perspectives on the ICTR, such as Kagame's and Ngoga's in this volume, Jallow argues that the ICTR's punishment of the orchestrators of the genocide contributes to deterrence of crimes and reconciliation. The trial process at the ICTR, he argues, facilitates individual and collective "catharsis". Jallow highlights the major legal developments of the ICTR, including the definition of the crime of genocide, the recognition of sexual violence and media incitement as tools of genocide, and the rejection of automatic immunity for heads of state.

Maria Warren and Alison Cole explore a range of practical issues regarding the collection and management of evidence at the ICTR. They consider the role of the Information and Evidence Section of the ICTR (of which, until recently, Warren was chief) in creating a historical record of the genocide. There is an immense need, they argue, for information-sharing among the ICTR and other stakeholders, such as civil society groups. In describing lessons learnt at the ICTR, Warren and Cole argue that the ICTR establishes a basis from which other international justice institutions, including the ICC, can effectively collect, manage and deploy information.

Ngoga, the current Rwandan Prosecutor-General and formerly the Rwandan government's special envoy to the ICTR, analyses domestic and international judicial responses to the problem of impunity in Rwanda. Ngoga argues that successive Rwandan governments before the genocide used domestic law to protect those responsible for orchestrating and committing mass crimes, creating the legal and political environment in which the 1994 genocide was possible. The chapter analyses domestic judicial attempts to eradicate the culture of impunity by prosecuting genocide suspects through the Organic Law, which governs the operation of the Rwandan national courts and lays the foundation for the *Gacaca* Law, and through recent legislation addressing the problems of ethnic "divisionism" and genocide denial. Ngoga argues that, despite major challenges, these domestic legal approaches display the potential to help foster reconciliation. In contrast, he argues, the ICTR has generally failed to meet its stated objectives—especially addressing impunity and contributing to national reconciliation—because of problems with the Statute establishing the Tribunal and the ICTR's inadequate judicial performance.

Finally, Clark focuses on the *gacaca* jurisdictions and argues that most commentators so far, especially Western human rights critics, have mischaracterised *gacaca* as a form of mob justice that sacrifices individual rights, especially those of suspects, for the sake of cheap, rapid prosecutions. Basing his analysis on more than 300 interviews with key stakeholders in the *gacaca* process and first-hand observations of hearings, Clark argues that *gacaca*'s legal critics ignore its deliberate pursuit of more fundamental objectives, especially reconciliation, by promoting genuine engagement among previous antagonists within and outside of hearings. Clark argues that *gacaca* represents an innovative approach to transitional justice that—perhaps more clearly than any post-conflict institution in the world—shows how it is possible to punish perpetrators of serious crimes in ways that promote reconciliation.

Lessons from the genocide for Rwanda and beyond

The Rwandan genocide raised questions with global consequences. One of the most tragic elements of the genocide was the readiness of the international community to play a subordinate role in the story. The failure of international actors to intervene to halt the genocide continues to haunt politicians and diplomats, looming whenever questions arise over how the world should respond to atrocities, such as those subsequently perpetrated in the DRC, Sudan and northern Uganda.

The genocide in Rwanda presented an opportunity to undertake what would have been one of the most legitimate cases of humanitarian intervention in history. The slaughter was massive and rapid. The victims were outnumbered and defenceless. Intervention would likely have been successful in mitigating the scope of the genocide, and that success would have made later humanitarian interventions politically more palatable. Instead, the world balked, still smarting from the failed intervention just months earlier in Somalia and unwilling to commit even minimal resources. The ignorance about the genocide was mostly wilful, as governments and other institutions ignored reports by the media, UN peacekeepers on the ground and Tutsi who escaped, all of which detailed the scale and nature of the unfolding atrocities.

Since the genocide, as Jennifer Welsh argues in this volume, the international community has attempted to redefine notions of sovereignty and establish criteria for humanitarian intervention. Maybe these steps will eventually help mitigate atrocities. For now, though, there appears little reason for optimism, especially considering the current situation in Darfur, about which there is still disagreement (among UN Security Council member states and experts) over whether to call the atrocities genocide. The international community is again reluctant to commit troops with a robust mandate. Darfur illustrates that those with the power to help rarely agree on the nature of atrocities and how best to respond to them.

Power politics fundamentally shapes decision-making. China blocks consensus on Darfur because of its investment in oil in Sudan. Powerful states will want to avoid establishing precedents that could legitimate external intervention in conflicts within their own territories, as in Russia's concerns over Chechnya and China's over Taiwan and Tibet. Powerful states also want to avoid committing the necessary resources if their militaries are already engaged in other conflicts. This is perhaps one of the worst and underreported consequences of the US occupation of Iraq: its vast deployment there means that the US military may be too stretched to commit to alleviating humanitarian disasters elsewhere. No matter what consensus about international principles such as the "responsibility to protect" may be reached in theory, in practice, when atrocities occur, whether the international community intervenes is determined on a case-by-case basis. Far from raising hopes, the Rwandan genocide, and subsequent conflicts in Darfur, the DRC and northern Uganda, underline the political reality that states intervene too late to halt mass crimes, if they intervene at all.

Rwanda and beyond: outline of chapters. Chapters 17 to 19 explore the political and legal significance of the genocide beyond Rwanda. Welsh explores normative developments in international relations and the evolution of the principle of the "responsibility to protect". International shame over the failure to intervene in Rwanda in 1994 and a desire to see "no more Rwandas" have driven a move away from an emphasis on blanket non-intervention in other states' affairs to the responsibility of those states to protect their citizens from aggression, such that a derogation of this responsibility may constitute sufficient grounds for external intervention. As the international community's slow and inadequate response to atrocities in Darfur shows, however, it is not clear that memories of Rwanda have resulted in clear, coherent and decisive policies that employ the "responsibility to protect" principle.

Morten Bergsmo and Philippa Webb argue that the pursuit of justice and peace after the genocide, particularly through the ICTR, has shaped international criminal justice, as seen in the creation and operation of the ICC. They claim that this development may seem paradoxical or ironic, given the international community's "confused and inadequate" responses during and after the genocide. Crucially, Bergsmo and Webb contend that the ICC builds upon conceptions of justice expressed in the ICTR's Statute, particularly that punishing perpetrators of mass crimes deters future criminals. The ICTR has also provided institutional and legal lessons for the ICC and inspired the creation of the ICC's *Legal Tools Project*. The first two cases before the ICC concern northern Uganda and the DRC, both neighbours of Rwanda. A third case before the ICC concerns Darfur, for which Rwanda, with its leaders motivated to help end atrocities, has provided African Union peacekeepers. Two Rwandan peacekeepers were killed in Darfur in August 2006 and four more in 2008 trying to protect civilians from the same fate that befell the Tutsi in 1994. The aftermath of the Rwandan genocide not only helped create the ICC but also decisively affects its early work.

Zaum considers a specific example of the impact of the genocide beyond Africa by exploring emerging norms of transitional justice and post-conflict reconstruction in Kosovo. He argues that the relationship between transitional justice and domestic order is more complex than has often been suggested. He questions, for example, the claims made by authors such as Kayigamba, Jallow, Ngoga, Bergsmo and Webb that punishing perpetrators can effectively facilitate broader social goals, such as ending impunity. Highlighting the lack of lessons learnt from the Rwandan example, Zaum argues that the Kosovo case illustrates that justice mechanisms only contribute partially to state-building after mass conflict and must be embedded within a carefully-designed system of legal, political and social institutions. He thus returns us to some of the fundamental questions of this volume: What is the role of law in rebuilding societies fractured by violence? And how can we respond holistically to the multitude of needs of conflict and post-conflict situations?

Finally, in Chapter 20, Clark, Kaufman and Nicolaïdis tease out tensions among the six key transitional justice themes—reconciliation, peace, justice, healing, forgiveness and truth—explored in the chapters of this volume. We argue that societies must often pursue several of these objectives simultaneously but that this endeavour can prove highly problematic, as the aims are not automatically or necessarily complementary. Greater recognition of the tensions among these themes, we argue, will not only bring about clearer theoretical discussions of transitional justice, post-conflict reconstruction and reconciliation, but also encourage more appropriate, practical responses to post-conflict societies.

This book is intended to help scholars and practitioners working on conflict and post-conflict issues to formulate clearer, more nuanced responses to the questions they confront and to aid a more general audience in understanding some of the subtleties of the Rwandan genocide and its personal, communal, national and international impact. The comprehensiveness of the debates in this volume constitutes an attempt to respond holistically to the complex challenges of rebuilding lives after genocide. In doing so, this book commemorates the lives lost during those three horrific months in 1994.

1

THE PAST IS PROLOGUE:
PLANNING THE 1994 RWANDAN GENOCIDE

Linda Melvern

In the course of those three terrible months in 1994, up to one million people were killed in Rwanda. The slaughter was not, as some media sources reported,[1] the result of spontaneous chaos. Rather, it was premeditated and systematic, the result of a deliberate government policy to kill citizens. The extermination was carried out according to a carefully prearranged strategy, involving youth groups, death squads and political parties. This chapter will describe in detail the conspiracy to plan and then perpetrate the genocide. My account of the Rwandan genocide conspiracy draws on personal interviews that I have conducted with key actors and confidential government papers that I have accessed.

The motive of those responsible for the genocide was to continue to monopolise power and to seek a final solution to their political opposition. Their primary means of killing was the mobilisation of Rwanda's unemployed youth into trained militias. A supplementary strategy employed propaganda to help local officials prepare the people of Rwanda to kill their neighbours. The killing methods were centrally controlled, and there was co-ordination among politicians, Rwandan army and *gendarmerie* units, and local militia. The methods used to quickly kill large numbers of people had been tried and tested. In the three years prior to the genocide, an estimated 2,000 citizens were murdered, using techniques well documented in human rights reports.[2] According to these reports, people were killed in organised massacres, involving the use of hate propaganda to persuade neighbour to kill neighbour and roadblocks to prevent escape. Local administrative leaders, including the communal police, par-

---

1   L. Hilsum, "Rwandan PM killed as Troops Wreak Carnage", *Guardian Unlimited* (8 April, 1994).

2   International Federation of Human Rights (FIDH), Africa Watch, InterAfrican Union of Human Rights, and International Centre for Rights of the Person and of Democratic Development, *Report of the International Commission of Investigation of Human Rights Violations in Rwanda since October 1, 1990* (7-21 January 1993).

ticipated in the killings. As Kayigamba describes in his first-hand account in the following chapter, these methods mirrored those used to kill Tutsi in 1959 and 1963, when there had also been roadblocks erected, targeted use of militia and propaganda, and massacres under the guise of "civilian self-defence".

A convergence of circumstances in 1994 provided the opportunity for genocide, allowing the extremists to distract the United Nations Security Council long enough to enable them to extend the genocide throughout the entire country. To prevent escape, and then to begin to identify and kill Tutsi, members of the Rwandan military, working alongside local militia known as *Interahamwe*,[3] established and operated a network of roadblocks in and around Rwanda's capital city, Kigali. On 6 April 1994, in the immediate confusion following the assassination of President Juvénal Habyarimana, Hutu extremists launched a coup designed to eliminate all political opposition. By that night, in northern Rwanda, the genocide plan was already under way. In Kigali, at first light the following day, soldiers and militia were on the streets with orders from the Hutu extremist leadership to kill anyone with a national identity card that showed that the bearer belonged to the minority Tutsi group. There were no sealed trains or secluded concentration camps in Rwanda. The genocide was carried out in plain view—in schools, hospitals, clinics and churches, the places where terrified citizens sought shelter.

There was little international condemnation, and yet the names of those orchestrating the massacres were well known.[4] By the end of the first week, as the International Committee of the Red Cross estimated a death rate of 10,000 people per day, a modest show of force mandated by the United Nations Security Council could have prevented the terror from spreading country-wide. Instead, those who were perpetrating the crime realised that a lack of outside interference gave them no reason to pause.

The genocide in Rwanda is the first attempted extermination since the Second World War to be genuinely comparable to the Holocaust. Both genocides were underpinned by similar ideologies: Hutu Power and Nazism were both based on racism. What Hutu Power adherents hoped to achieve was a "pure Hutu" state cleansed of the minority Tutsi. Hutu extremists infiltrated all walks of Rwandan life, including the military, local administration and government ministries. These extremists drove a massive wedge between Hutu

---

3   In Kinyarwanda, *Interahamwe* means "those who work closely together and who are united".

4   The names of the extremist Hutu Power adherents were widely known by the ambassadors in Kigali representing the US, France and Belgium. They were also known to human rights groups in those three countries. They included the members of the "Interim Government", hardline Prefects, the local leaders of the *Interahamwe*, and the journalists and technicians broadcasting the hate radio, RTLM.

and Tutsi living and working side by side. Through active recruitment, they expanded the ranks of people involved in state repression. Yet little attention is paid to the growth of Hutu Power.

The Hutu Power movement originated in northern Rwanda, among people conquered in the 19th century by Rwanda's Tutsi monarchy, which was later supported by the German colonialists. Chief among these German imperialist forces was the *Schutztruppe*, whose brutal invasions of northern Rwanda between 1910 and 1912 to subdue the kinglets, lineage heads and landowners, had terrible consequences eighty years later. In spite of their incorporation into the Rwandan state, the northerners maintained their distinct culture, determined to continue an independent tradition. The northerners harboured considerable bitterness toward the Tutsi and the southern Hutu, who had also helped to conquer them. The south of the country was traditionally more tolerant, and intermarriage between Hutu and Tutsi was common. Some experts believe that, had the Rwandan civil war of 1990 not been fought on ethnic grounds pitting Hutu against Tutsi, the fatal division in Rwanda might well have been north versus south.[5]

Precursors to the 1994 genocide

In genocide, racist ideology legitimises any act, no matter how horrendous. To commit genocide, it is necessary to spread an ideology that defines the victim as being outside human existence—vermin, subhuman. And so it was in Rwanda. An organised anti-Tutsi campaign began at the end of 1990, after Rwanda was invaded by an army from Uganda, the Rwandan Patriotic Front (RPF), whose leadership purported to represent up to one million Tutsi refugees. These refugees had been expelled from Rwanda during anti-Tutsi terror campaigns starting in 1959, after the Tutsi monarchy was ousted by politicians in the name of the downtrodden Hutu majority. The propaganda campaign against Tutsi soon became relentless in its incitement of ethnic hatred and violence. It was waged through newspapers, magazines and a radio station that incited genocide, *Radio Télévision Libre des Mille Collines* (RTLM). It was no coincidence that RTLM, with its catchy nationalistic theme tunes and racist jingles, began to broadcast in August 1993, within days of a peace agreement between the RPF and the Hutu government. This agreement sought to bridge the ethnic divide and provide a timetable for a power-sharing democracy, bringing an end to Rwanda's dictatorship by the northern oligarchs who had controlled the country for twenty years.

---

5   G. Prunier, *The Rwandan Crisis: History of a Genocide* (New York: Columbia University Press, 1995); A. Guichaoua, *Les crises politiques au Burundi et au Rwanda, 1993-1994* (Lille: Université des Sciences et Technologies de Lille, 1995), 185-210.

Towards the end of 1990, just after the RPF invasion, extremist elements of the Hutu government began planning mass murder of Tutsi, as outlined in a series of secret meetings held in the northern prefecture of Gisenyi.[6] The initial idea to eliminate the country's Tutsi minority involved death squads employed by the regime to secretly eliminate opponents. It was clear to the conspirators that to eliminate all Tutsi would require more than just the cooperation of the *gendarmerie* and the army.

The concept of genocide was not new to Rwanda. As Ngoga reminds us in his contribution to this volume, genocide occurred in 1959 and 1963 when the Hutu government mobilised the population to commit mass murder. In 1963, in response to an attempted invasion of Rwanda by Tutsi refugees, a campaign was instigated to kill Tutsi. The killing programme, supervised by a government minister in each prefecture, began with the elimination of the political opposition. At the local level, officials and skilled propagandists collaborated in encouraging Hutu to kill their Tutsi neighbours, using agricultural tools such as machetes. Roadblocks prevented escape. The genocide in 1963 was never officially acknowledged and no one was punished, but a pattern and method were established for future violence against Tutsi.

The 1994 genocide

Thirty years later, in response to the October 1990 invasion by the RPF, the Hutu government considered a proposal for the whole of Rwandan society to be militarised under the guise of "civilian self-defence" (*auto défense-civile*), whereby peasants in each *cellule*, the smallest of the country's administrative divisions, would be given weapons. The idea for such a peasant infantry can be traced to a 1989 confidential report to the Ministry of Foreign Affairs. The report was written by Rwandan diplomats in Rwanda's embassy in Zaire (now the Democratic Republic of Congo), and it predicted that Rwanda was in danger of being attacked again by Tutsi exiles. After an "analysis" of Rwandans living in Zaire, the Republic of Congo, Chad, the Central African Republic, Gabon and Cameroon, the report concluded that Rwanda's enemies were to be found in communities with a Tutsi majority. Some of these Tutsi, the report claimed, had received military training in Uganda. The report also noted that because of the weakness of the Rwandan army, it was necessary to create a civilian defence force to defend the country. The report recommended that the Hutu youth of Rwanda be trained in armed combat.[7] When, in October 1990, the RPF invaded from Uganda, one of the first government actions was to dis-

---

6   ICTR Prosecution Testimony, Military One case, Witness ZF.

7   ICTR Transcript, Jean Kambanda interrogation by ICTR investigators (1997), author's archive.

tribute weapons via communal officers to the army reservists living in each *commune*.[8] This was described as the "first line of defence." Each communal officer was told to write reports to the *bourgmestre* (mayor) about local civil defence planning, with copies sent to the Rwandan army command.

The following year, a more detailed plan for national civil defence was prepared by Col. Augustin Ndindiliyimana, then Minister for Defence and Security, and responsible directly to President Habyarimana. Ndindiliyimana proposed the training of militia in every *commune*.[9] He advised Habyarimana that Rwanda could not afford compulsory military service, and the means were not available to provide weapons to every person in the country. He noted, though, that the current financial situation in Rwanda would permit the creation of a civilian militia that could operate in tandem with the country's professional army.[10]

Later that year, at a meeting of all prefects from around the country, Ndindiliyimana said that henceforth army reservists would receive state salaries.[11] Each prefect was told to compile lists of the names of all young men who left to join the RPF. A more detailed plan for civilian defence was discussed the following month, in which all levels of public servants in the *prefecture* and *commune* were to be involved in civilian defence.[12]

That same year, each of the ten regional prefectures created a Council for Security, to examine the "*auto-défense*" of the population.[13] The government drafted a law setting out a plan to "protect" the population, "defend" against RPF attacks, "protect" the infrastructure and obtain information on the presence and the actions of "the enemy" in the *communes* and *cellules* and to

---

8   Until the administrative restructure of Rwanda, the country had ten *Préfectures*, each governed by a *Préfet*. The *Préfectures* are further subdivided into *communes*, which are placed under the authority of *bourgmestres*. The *bourgmestre* of each *commune* was appointed by the President of the Republic, Juvénal Habyarimana. A *bourgmestre* was responsible for public order. Each *commune* was further subdivided into *secteurs* and *cellules*.

9   Rwandan Republic, "Note to His Excellency The President, Subject: Study of the means necessary of defence and to allow the population to counter any attack from inside or outside the country." Undated, Col. Augustin Ndindiliyimana, author's archive.

10 Rwandan Republic, "To the Presidential Minister in charge of Defence and Security. Subject: Minutes of Meeting", Rapporteur: Lt. Grégoire Rutakamize (9 July, 1991), author's archive.

11 Rwandan Republic, "Account of a Seminar of Prefects" (11-12 September, 1991), author's archive.

12 Confidential, "Note to H. E. President of the Republic. Subject: A law for Civil defence. Kigali" (22 October, 1991), author's archive.

13 Prefecture of Kibuye, "Letter to the Minister of the Interior. Kigali. Subject: Recommendations of council for security," Prefect of Kibuye, Signed Gaspar Ruhumliza (26 November, 1991), author's archive.

"denounce" infiltrators. The Ministers of Defence and of the Interior were responsible for preparing the lists of soldiers and *gendarmes* living in each *commune*. The law also created a national committee of civil defence to bypass the parliament and to receive orders from a National Security Council, headed by the President.[14]

While the law was being drafted, the government was fighting a civil war against the RPF. The militarisation of society could therefore legitimately be described as country-wide protection. After October 1990, the Rwandan army grew rapidly, from 9,335 troops at the time of the RPF invasion to 27,913 by 1991. The vast majority of new recruits were uneducated peasants.

When some years later investigators from the UN International Criminal Tribunal for Rwanda (ICTR) considered the genocide conspiracy, they set great store in a military report that showed how the northern clique in the army had managed to legitimise its racist beliefs. This report revealed that extremists officially defined the enemy of the country as the Tutsi population within its borders. These extremists also organised the compilation of lists of Tutsi "infiltrators" to demonstrate that these individuals posed a danger to society, by which they meant Hutu society. Consequently, the extremists succeeded in popularising their beliefs within the military ranks.

Much of the planning of the genocide, investigators concluded, was carried out in military offices, although not all of the Rwandan army was extremist. In an extraordinary meeting on 4 December 1991, President Habyarimana summoned all of Rwanda's army and *gendarmerie* officers to a conference room of the *Ecole Supérieure Militaire* in Kigali. More than 100 uniformed officers assembled, depositing their weapons in a side room and awaiting the arrival of their commander-in-chief. It had been more than a year since the RPF invasion and the start of the civil war. What the meeting demonstrated was how bitterly the ranks were divided: while some officers wanted to continue to fight, others believed that negotiation with the RPF was the only chance for peace.

President Habyarimana was unable to reconcile the two groups and thus a dangerous power vacuum developed. "You could see his power eroding," one of the officers who attended the meeting told me.[15] In an attempt to save face, the President proposed a military commission to investigate how to defeat the enemy "in the military, media and political domains".[16] Ten officers were chosen for the commission and comprised both hardliners and moderates. The chair was a northerner named Col. Théoneste Bagosora, the

---

14   Law proposal, "Organisation of National Defence", (1991), author's archive.

15   Interview, Kigali (December 2001).

16   A. Des Forges, *Leave None to Tell the Story: Genocide in Rwanda* (New York: Human Rights Watch, 1999), 62.

man whom the international press portrays today as the mastermind of the genocide. Bagosora is currently on trial at the ICTR, accused of genocide in what is known as the "Military One" case. Another member of the commission, Col. Marcel Gatsinzi, is now Rwanda's Minister of Defence.[17] The commission's eventual report was not widely circulated, and not all members of the commission even saw it. Gatsinzi claims that he did not attend all of the military commission's meetings because he was not invited. But one key passage from the report was widely circulated and later constituted key evidence in the genocide prosecutions. The passage, crucial and chilling, states: "The principal enemy is the Tutsi inside or outside the country, extremist and nostalgic for power and who have never recognised and will never recognise the realities of the social revolution of 1959 and who want to take back their power by any means, including weapons. The accomplice of the enemy is anyone who supports the enemy."[18]

The passage was circulated among senior army officers, including Bagosora, who, according to one ICTR prosecution witness, played an important role in spreading the idea of genocide among the rank and file of the military. Bagosora claimed to possess secret evidence showing that the RPF was planning "to kill the Hutu". To foil this plan, Bagosora explained, the Tutsi needed to be exterminated.[19] "They were calmly speaking about the extermination of Tutsi," the ICTR prosecution witness claimed. "The main subject was that you had to unwind – or undo the enemy action and stop the extermination of Hutu by Tutsi, and in order to do that, the Tutsi had to be exterminated."[20]

Another ICTR prosecution witness testified how Bagosora instructed the general staffs of the army and the *gendarmerie* to establish lists of people identified as "the enemy and its accomplices." The army's military intelligence department, known as "G2", prepared lists of "accomplices" of the RPF.[21] The military provided weapons for the "civil defence" network[22] and trained a youth militia. In some places in the north, the military distributed weapons to civilians, aiming to arm one person per *cellule* in every community.

---

17   Interview with Maj. Gen. Marcel Gatsinzi, Kigali (December 2001).

18   Vénuste Nshimiyimana, *Prélude du Genocide Rwandais: Enquête sur les Circonstances Politiques et Militaires du Meutre du Président Habyarimana* (Paris: Quorum, 1995), 39.

19   ICTR Prosecution Testimony. Military One, Witness ZF.

20   Ibid.

21   ICTR Prosecution Witness statement, Witness AK.

22   Assemblée Nationale, Mission d'Information Commune, *Enquête sur la Tragédie Rwandaise (1990-1994)* (Paris: Assemblée Nationale), 209.

Militia groups and the genocide

Each time Rwanda made tentative steps towards power-sharing, there was violence. Youth gangs, who violently coerced support, were a component of each political party, and serious fighting broke out among rival groups that tried to steal members from each other. Most of the violence went unpunished. In 1991 President Habyarimana's party, the *Mouvement Républicain National pour la Démocratie et le Développement* (MRND), formed its own youth group, the *Interahamwe*, led by the MRND's president, Matthieu Ngirumpatse, a former ambassador and Minister of Justice.[23] This group was well organised with six committees covering social and legal affairs, research and development, propaganda, evaluation and documentation. It was intended to operate nationwide, organised by sector, with its members required to contribute monthly dues.[24] The Rwandan military trained *Interahamwe* members: witnesses from Camp Kigali, an army base in the heart of the capital, saw government buses arriving at the barracks in 1992 and transporting soldiers to secret training facilities.[25] *Interahamwe* recruits were initially taught to handle weapons and use explosives, and then later taught to kill with speed. To murder people swiftly and efficiently, recruits were told to immobilise their victims by cutting their Achilles tendons. Two men known to have been part of this training were Col. Léonard Nkundiye, a Belgian-trained Presidential Guard, and Col. Innocent Nzabanita, known as Gisinda, meaning "wild animal" in Kinyarwanda.[26] One witness later claimed that French military officers trained youth militia as early as January 1991, which, if true, supports Kagame's and Ngoga's claims in this volume that France played an active role in the genocide.[27] There were several training sites for youth militia: one near the international airport in Kigali, and another in Gisenyi, at the Bigogwe camp, where Maj. François Uwimana, a member of the Para-Commandos, was responsible for training exercises.[28]

---

23   ICTR Testimony, Jean Kambanda confession.

24   ICTR Prosecution Testimony, Media Trial, Witness X (February 2002).

25   ICTR Prosecution Testimony, Witness KL.

26   Both men have since died.

27   Janvier Africa, *Courrier International* (30 June-6 July 1994). The role of France in the Rwandan genocide is the subject of much research and controversy. For the present purposes, it is sufficient to state that France had been an ally from the very beginning of the twenty-year dictatorship of Juvénal Habyarimana. Although a former Belgian colony, Rwanda was considered by the French to be part of Francophone Africa. When the RPF invaded Rwanda in 1990, the decision was taken in the Elysée Palace, where the Africa Office was run by François Mitterrand's son, Jean-Christophe, to immediately send troops to shore up the regime. The French military later took charge of Rwanda's counter-insurgency campaign and provided substantial arms and expertise to both the Rwandan army and *gendarmerie*.

28   ICTR Prosecution Testimony, Military One case, Omar Serushago, (June 2003).

Exactly when the *Interahamwe* first took part in organised killing may never be known, but there are reports that as early as November 1991, some four months after Ndindiliyimana suggested the creation of a civilian militia, it was involved in the killing of Tutsi in the *commune* of Murambi, east of Kigali.[29] In March 1992, there were more killings by the *Interahamwe*, this time in Bugesera, a region in the south-east of the country with a higher percentage of Tutsi than anywhere else in Rwanda. The *Interahamwe* travelled to Bugesera from three sectors in Kigali—Remera, Cyahafi and Bilyogo—and arrived in two minibuses and a lorry. Presidential Guards wearing civilian clothes were also present during the killing. At the local Gako military camp, one witness described how the commander there received an order to put a company of men at the disposal of the operation intended to "neutralise the enemy".[30] This phrase increasingly became a euphemism in the military for killing Tutsi.

The official response from the government to the killings in Bugesera was to describe what happened as "self-defence". The US and Canadian ambassadors in Kigali went to see President Habyarimana to express concern at the violence, but the French ambassador, Georges Martres, refused to join them.[31] The Belgian ambassador, Johan Swinnen, cabled Brussels that the *Interahamwe* had taken part in the killings in Bugesera and that what happened had been carefully planned. In a desperate plea on 4 June 1992, the director of Amnesty International in France, Michel Forte, said on Radio France International:

Those responsible for these massacres are soldiers with help from the civil authorities. No one at all has been punished. Not to punish these people will lead to a repetition of these horrors. An independent commission must be created to judge those civilians and soldiers responsible....[32]

The truth of what happened in Bugesera later emerged when a group of Rwandan human rights activists held a press conference in Kigali to explain the role of propaganda and how the killings were directly linked to it.[33] Much of the propaganda, which convinced the Hutu population that the Tutsi "devils" were coming to massacre them to restore their monarchy, was masterminded by a Hutu intellectual, Ferdinand Nahimana, a professor and historian who was a member of the President's inner circle. In 1991 Nahimana, along with Hassan Ngeze, the editor of the racist, pro-Hutu newspaper *Kangura*, dis-

---

29   A. Guichaoua, *Les crises politiques au Burundi and au Rwanda 1993-1994*, 2nd edn. (Paris: Université des Sciences et Technolgies de Lille, Karthala, 1995), 265.

30   Belgian Senate, *Commission d'enquête parlementaire concernant les évènements du Rwanda*, Report (December 1997), 495.

31   Martres served until March 1993 when he retired. He was replaced by Jean-Michel Marlaud.

32   Guichaoua, 72.

33   Belgian Senate, 495.

tributed leaflets calling for violence against Tutsi. During massacres in March 1992, Ngeze was witnessed, together with a military escort, distributing petrol to burn houses.[34]

In October 1992, the existence of "a death squad" in Rwanda was announced in Brussels, during a press conference held at the Senate and organised by Prof. Filip Reyntjens and Senator Willy Kuypers. The death squad was described as similar to those in Latin America. Using information from an informer, Reyntjens and Kuypers claimed that the death squad was called *Reseau Zéro* (Zero Network), and that it comprised both civilians and soldiers. Some people speculated that the name indicated the number of Tutsi that the extremists intended to leave in Rwanda. A reputable source claimed that the death squad took part in the Bugesera massacres in March and helped to plan other politically-motivated killings.[35]

Later, it became clear just how very organised the extremists were: to co-ordinate their murderous activities, they created their own secret radio network. An ICTR prosecution witness, who is a communications expert, explained the rationale of those who used the system: "They did not want their communications or their conversations or activities to be heard... they did not want the other members of government or officers or members of the army to be aware of their activities and communications."[36] Zero Network was intended to be kept secret. According to another ICTR prosecution witness, it was divided into small groups of well-trained operatives, in charge of executing decisions made by people called "dragons", the codename for those who issued the identities of those to be killed. "The dragons were supposed to be the names of the masterminds – I do not know whether this word is the appropriate word – the groups that were behind those activities, that is, anti-enemy activities, activities directed against the accomplices."[37]

According to the same witness, another secret group called the *Amasasu* association was created within the military: "That was a group of persons who was made up of soldiers and who worked with the commanders of the dragons... The *Abakuzi*, a Rwandan word which means 'the workers,' was also used to describe death squads, but it was mainly used for those higher in rank, and who were considered as good 'workers.'" The witness further explained, "To work meant to rid oneself of the *Inyenzi* [cockroaches], of the enemy and

---

34   Guichaoua, 59.

35   Belgian Senate, 495.

36   ICTR Prosecution Testimony, Military One case, Witness ZF.

37   Ibid.

its accomplices who were, based on what I knew, who were considered to be Tutsi and their accomplices."[38]

Conclusion

By April 1994, many Hutu in Rwanda had come to believe that the elimination of the Tutsi was a civic duty and necessary to end their own poverty. The genocide plot was developed and perpetrated according to a conspiracy involving the Rwandan military, the *Interahamwe* and propagandists who helped spread the genocidal ideology throughout the population. Far from being a spontaneous atrocity, the 1994 Rwandan genocide was premeditated, meticulously planned and systematically perpetrated.

At the opening of the trial of the twenty Nazi criminals in the dock at Nuremberg in 1945, the prosecutor of the International Military Tribunal, US Supreme Court Associate Justice Robert Jackson, said of the defendants: "We will show them to be living symbols of racial hatreds, of terrorism and violence, and of the arrogance and cruelty of power. They are symbols of fierce nationalism and of militarisation, of intrigue and war-making.... [The Nazi defendants] represented sinister influences that would lurk in the world long after their bodies had returned to dust."[39] There are similarities between the defendants at Nuremberg and those in the dock at the ICTR, not least their failure to express guilt or regret of any kind about their deeds.

We have yet to fully establish the extent of the planning of the 1994 genocide. Today most of the Hutu Power conspirators are still at large: the planners, financiers, instigators, propagandists and many perpetrators, who currently benefit from foreign protection and looted funds from one of the poorest countries on earth, further ravaged by genocide.[40]

---

38 Ibid.

39 Summation for the Prosecution by Justice Robert Jackson (26 July 1945) http:// www.law. umkc.edu.

40 The ICTR has convicted or is in the process of judging the cases of 60 individuals. Initial lists of suspects in the author's archive indicate that some 240 Rwandans comprised the core group of *génocidaires*. Many of these people have not been investigated by the ICTR, and no attempts have been made to extradite them from the countries in the West where many of them reside.

2

WITHOUT JUSTICE, NO RECONCILIATION: A SURVIVOR'S EXPERIENCE OF GENOCIDE

Jean Baptiste Kayigamba[1]

Not all people understand in the same way the suffering of Rwandan Tutsi between the massacres of 1959 and the genocide in 1994. Observers of the violence and those who experienced it first-hand, like me, will often have different accounts of what took place. As a Tutsi and a genocide survivor, my account here is not neutral, but deeply personal. This is a narrative of how I survived the attempt to annihilate all Tutsi in Rwanda, and of the events that I witnessed, in the lead-up to, and during, the genocide. On several occasions during the genocide I came within inches of Hutu machetes. This is also a narrative of how I have since tried, day to day, to come to terms with the devastating personal legacies of these experiences.

Nearly all of my relatives, including my parents, two sisters and five brothers, were killed in 1994, perishing at the hands of the genocidal government, its army, its militias and Hutu mobs; only two of my sisters, one niece and I survived. Before the 1994 tragedy, most members of my family had survived repeated attempts to exterminate the Tutsi in Rwanda. In common wih all Tutsi, my whole life has been a chain of suffering, because of violent discrimination and extreme fear for my life and those of my loved ones.

It is not easy for me to recount what happened in Rwanda in 1994. Whenever I ponder the genocide, I revisit the agonising death of my family and friends, and the physical and emotional trauma I also suffered. It sickens me to think that they knew that one day they would be killed but never attempted to flee the country to find safety. I also relive the terrible days of the genocide, when all Tutsi in the capital, Kigali, were counting the hours until they would be killed. Each day was but one more day of horror. As Hutu militias prowled the streets looking for Tutsi, we experienced haunted mornings, and our fears continued

---

1   While commissioned for this edited collection, a short version of this chapter appeared in
     New Internationality, June 2006.

throughout the days and sleepless nights. Thinking of those days brings back horrible memories and makes me wish that I could forget what happened to me and the rest of the Tutsi population.

Despite these feelings, I cannot forget what happened during the genocide—it would be wrong to forget. It is crucial for survivors of the genocide to tell what they experienced, to describe the events they witnessed first-hand, so that the world understands the nature and magnitude of the violence that engulfed Rwanda, not only in 1994, but also throughout the entire second half of the twentieth century. When others learn and acknowledge what we survivors lived through, this helps restore some of the humanity that we lost during the genocide. If the world is willing to listen, this may also help prevent similar tragedies from occurring in other countries.

Impunity breeds impunity

I was born in Gikongoro province of Rwanda in 1963, the year after Rwanda gained independence from Belgium. This area in southwest Rwanda is known, even today, as a hotbed of Hutu extremism. Around the time of my birth, the hunt for Tutsi reached a climax. My parents narrowly escaped being butchered. Others were not so fortunate. Before being dumped into the Mwogo, the Rukarara or the Mbirurume, the three rivers that originate in Gikongoro and constitute major tributaries of the Nile, the Tutsi victims were beaten, so that they could not swim to safety. As a child, I grew up hearing my parents' harrowing stories of the sadism and cruelty that characterised the massacres of that time. My father once told me that the rocks on the banks of the Rukarara River had remained crimson for years after the 1963 massacres because the blood of thousands of Tutsi had flowed so freely there.

White people or other foreigners did not kill us, although some Western countries were accomplices in the killings which shattered Rwanda at different times for over three decades. Often drawing on racist ideologies propagated by colonial powers, successive post-colonial Hutu regimes in Rwanda considered Tutsi to be second-class citizens. Such a view often motivated violence against Tutsi, perpetrated by our own neighbours. The belief in inherent differences between Hutu and Tutsi was violently manifested in the so-called 1959 Hutu Revolution. The Hutu takeover of all social and political institutions in Rwanda succeeded, thanks to the unconditional support of the Belgian colonial masters, who themselves had earlier propagated the racist ideology that the Hutu in Rwanda represented the majority and rightful inhabitants of Rwanda, while the Tutsi were alien invaders from Abyssinia (Ethiopia) who had colonised and subjugated the Hutu for 400 years.

In implanting such views in the population, the colonial rulers sowed the seeds of hatred that led to later massacres of Tutsi. For over 30 years, many Hutu were trained to kill Tutsi, and did so with impunity. Few Hutu killers were ever brought to account, while many government figures who excelled in inciting the killings were rewarded with promotion. What we witnessed in 1994 was the culmination of a series of pogroms against Tutsi carried out regularly since our national independence.

At the grassroots, my family's experience reveals the culture of violence and impunity that characterised rural Rwanda. During several outbreaks of ethnic violence in the late 1950s and early 1960s, many Hutu not only killed Tutsi but also damaged or looted property, especially stealing and slaughtering cattle. During one killing spree in Gikongoro in 1959, my mother's wedding shoes were stolen. Several years later, my mother noticed one of her Hutu neighbours wearing the shoes. My mother knew that she could not claim them back from this woman because to do so would have triggered reprisal attacks against her or members of our family. Because the authorities were unwilling to bring perpetrators to account, and because the local population was too fearful to demand this, it was impossible to confront suspected criminals, regardless of the severity of their alleged offences, or to regain property that had been stolen or damaged during periods of violence. My mother's abject reluctance to claim back what was rightfully hers showed how severely a culture of impunity and fear had come to dominate Rwandan society.

Shortly before the 1994 genocide, I returned to my home village. My mother said to me, "Son, when you next come home, you will find that the Hutu have finished us off." My brothers told me how Hutu children from their neighbourhood taunted them, saying they would kill them and then move into our beautiful house. I have photographs showing how the house looked before the 1994 genocide and how it was then completely demolished during the genocide, by the Hutu who also looted all the furniture, doors and window frames. Had the guilty been punished for crimes in the years before the genocide, perhaps people would have hesitated before responding to the call to massacre their neighbours, with whom they had lived for generations. In 1994, it was not unusual to see the same people who had been involved in the massacres of the Tutsi in past decades participating in the pogroms that were aimed at decimating the Tutsi once and for all.

How I survived the genocide

In the years immediately preceding the 1994 genocide, I managed to gain a good education and subsequently worked as an international reporter. When the genocide broke out in April 1994, I had just begun to work as a stringer

for the Inter Press News Agency, covering Rwanda, Burundi and eastern Zaire (now the Democratic Republic of Congo). Late on the night of 6 April
1994, the extremist Hutu station *Radio Télévision Libre des Milles Collines*
(RTLM) reported that a missile had hit a plane that then burst into flames near
Kanombe airport. The announcer did not elaborate, promising to provide more
information later. Gunfire echoed around Kigali and my whole body shook
with fear. At 1 am, I heard on the BBC World Service on my shortwave radio
that the Hutu President Juvénal Habyarimana and his Burundian counterpart
and several colleagues had been killed in the plane crash and that their bodies
were charred beyond recognition.

That night neither my housemate, Ange Albert Rwiyegura, a long-time
friend, nor I could sleep. We spent the whole night pondering what might happen now that Habyarimana had been killed. We were both delighted at the
death of a man we considered a Hutu dictator but also scared and confused,
especially as we anticipated the anger and mayhem that was likely to follow.
"There's no doubt his death will give us the power-sharing arrangements in the
Arusha Accords," I told Ange. "But the *Interahamwe* will not let this happen
easily." Ange agreed with me; he had worked at Radio Rwanda for over fifteen
years and knew the sort of Hutu animosity towards Tutsi that Habyarimana's
death could unleash. Though Ange was a Tutsi and well educated, he worked
as a driver for many radio executive officials, all of them Hutu, who never hid
their anti-Tutsi feelings.

That fateful evening, killing began in many parts of Kigali, especially in the
Kimihurura neighbourhood where many Tutsi opposition leaders lived. Both
Tutsi and moderate Hutu leaders of the opposition were massacred with their
entire families. RTLM broadcast government communiqués ordering people
not to leave their homes and urging everyone to be on the lookout for alleged
"enemy infiltrators" in the area. I had no doubt that this was a clear invitation
to kill Tutsi; Ange and I knew that, if it was true that the *Umubyeyi*, or the
"father," as the late Hutu President was called, had been assassinated, reprisals
against Tutsi were inevitable. Further into the night, the rate of killings around
the city skyrocketed. There were roadblocks all around Kigali, as members of
the Presidential Guard and militia barricaded all streets and alleyways.

At dawn on 7 April, a national state of emergency was declared. Col. Théoneste Bagosora and the Presidential Guard took control of the state while an interim government was being established. Later that morning, a group of armed
Presidential Guard officers stormed the compound of the *Jeunesse Ouvrière
Catholique* (JOC) in Nyarugenge, where my family lived. Ange, several other
friends and I dashed through a nearby fence and sought refuge in the compound of the Centre for the Learning of African Languages (CELA), run by
the Catholic White Fathers. Later that afternoon, our camp swelled to 400

frightened Tutsi refugees and a few Hutu, including women and children. More continued to arrive that evening and over the following days. A surprisingly large number of people had managed to pass through roadblocks manned by the *Interahamwe* militias in the neighbourhoods of Gikondo, Nyamirambo, Biryogo and Muhima. Most of these people were survivors of the killings in the city, who saved themselves by paying hefty sums to influential militiamen to escort them from danger.

The fresh arrivals told terrible stories of entire families being butchered, which confirmed the updates we had already heard from the White Fathers, who seemed to enjoy keeping us abreast of the magnitude of the bloodbath ensuing around us. The White Fathers briefed us every day with communiqués, telling us the names of those who had been killed. These stories compounded our fears because we realised that, as the situation stood, we were unlikely to survive. The Fathers were soon evacuated by French and Belgian soldiers and left us with the keys to the camp. This evacuation of expatriates, embassy staff, and in some cases their pets, is commonly the first action by Western governments during mass violence. In the case of Rwanda, the evacuees were taken to Nairobi, where we heard they started drinking champagne to celebrate their survival.

Those of us hiding in the CELA camp started counting the days, convinced that the militias would attack. Some youths in the camp who were members of minor Hutu political parties began receiving messages from the outside telling them that they had nothing to fear because of their ethnicity. Many of these youths, all of them Hutu, were told that the killings targeted only the Tutsi. They were ordered to go back to their respective neighbourhoods and to join other Hutu in the massacres. Some eventually came back to CELA to warn us that the militiamen were planning to raid our camp.

Those of us left behind started to organise the camp, focusing on the need to maintain hygiene. We sent most of the women and children to the Sainte Famille parish, a large church down the road, where we believed they would be safe. To ensure that we had enough food to hold out for a long period, we contacted the Red Cross, which sent us a dozen sacks of beans.

Our camp was raided two weeks later, around 10 am on 22 April. We were attacked by a combination of soldiers, members of the gendarmerie, the local population and the *Interahamwe* (some armed with guns and grenades, others with traditional weapons, such as pangas, machetes and spears). Col. Thar-cisse Renzaho, the Mayor of Kigali City, and Maj. Gen. Laurent Munyakazi, Head of Muhima Police Station, led the attackers. Both men have now been arrested and charged with genocide and crimes against humanity—Renzaho by the United Nations International Criminal Tribunal for Rwanda (ICTR), where he is currently on trial at the ICTR's headquarters in Arusha, and Munyakazi by the Rwandan authorities after evidence of his crimes emerged through the *gacaca* courts (he has been sentenced by a military tribunal to life imprisonment).

Further back in the group was Father Wenceslas Munyeshyaka, nicknamed *"Umujeune"* (the young one). He used to move around in a flak jacket, armed with a pistol and grenades. He was notorious for protecting women and girls who had satisfied his raging libido. During the attack he stood where he could see us, and asked the killers not to harm the women and children. Despite Munyeshyaka's role in the genocide, he lived freely and peacefully in France for many years, seemingly untouchable by the law. The French authorities finally arrested him in August 2007 and opened discussions with the ICTR regarding his possible transfer to Arusha. Munyeshyaka is not the only killer to have found at least temporary safe harbour overseas. It is widely believed, especially among genocide survivors, that many masterminds of the genocide are hiding in Europe and the US, and that because of the apathy of Western governments they may never be brought to justice.

During the attack on the CELA, the killers rounded up and led away around 30 men accused of being accomplices of the Rwandan Patriotic Front (RPF), the predominantly Tutsi force that had invaded Rwanda from the north and was attempting to halt the genocidal campaign of the Hutu government. The killers had a list of people they wanted to murder. Being a Tutsi, a journalist and a graduate from the local university should have made me a prime target. Luckily, however, my name was not on the killers' list.

Before the young men accused of aiding the RPF were taken away, we were told that they would be interrogated before eventually being released. About an hour later, we heard gunshots nearby. Only two of the men accused of being RPF accomplices survived; one of those two told me that he was spared because one of the killers wanted his beautiful watch and took it in exchange for letting him live. The rest of the accused RPF accomplices were brutally executed, their bodies buried in a mass grave near the administrative office of Rugenge *secteur*.

We were traumatised, shaking uncontrollably and talking incoherently, and expected the killers to come back and finish us off. The following morning, a friend (who would later become my wife) sent someone to look for me. After the attack on CELA she had moved to the Sainte Famille parish. She convinced me that I should leave the hostel and join her at the parish. That morning, a friend and I left the hostel and began walking in the ditch along the main road heading towards Sainte Famille. Trucks of *Interahamwe* drove past on the main Rugenge highway. Upon seeing us, they reversed their truck. We mustered the last burst of energy we had and ran the final 200 metres to Sainte Famille and disappeared behind its gates. Had the militiamen caught us, they would have killed us. The next afternoon, my friend and I heard that we had escaped death for a second time: that morning, on 24 April, militiamen had arrived at the hostel where we had been hiding and killed all of the people sheltering there.

The Sainte Famille premises were immense: in addition to the church itself, there was a large compound containing a school and several accommodation units. The complex became overcrowded with both Tutsi and Hutu refugees, the latter fleeing the RPF advances in the southern and south-eastern neighbourhoods of Kigali, the former fleeing the killings by genocidal mobs. Some of us slept on the altar and did not have enough to eat. Father Munyeshyaka was not interested in helping us, instead continually insulting the refugees and blaming Tutsi for assassinating President Habyarimana.

The dominant feelings among the refugees were of fear and mutual distrust. The Tutsi were afraid that the Hutu refugees were spying on them. We noticed strange faces visiting the parish—we suspected they were there to gather information on who was sheltering inside. I changed my name from Jean Baptiste to Thacisse, to thwart plans by any newly arrived Hutu who may have wanted to reveal my whereabouts to the *Interahamwe*.

Meanwhile, one of my sisters who had reached the refuge of the famous *Hôtel des Mille Collines* in the centre of Kigali was informed that I was still alive, and hiding at Sainte Famille. With the help of some *gendarmes* stationed at the hotel, whom she knew personally, she managed to get me out of the church and escorted to the Mille Collines. I felt immense relief at having reached the hotel, which was considered the safest haven in the whole city. The Mille Collines was a privileged place, where many businessmen and intellectuals, among hundreds of ordinary Tutsi, hid from marauding Hutu mobs. The hotel was never raided, and not a single Tutsi or moderate Hutu was taken away to be killed. There was a rumour circulating in Kigali that the UN mission guarding the Mille Collines would soon evacuate everyone in the hotel to Nairobi.

At the hotel we had TV in our rooms, so we could follow the news and see what was happening around the country. The hotel manager, Paul Rusesabagina—recently depicted in the Academy Award-nominated film *Hotel Rwanda*—worked tirelessly to keep us alive. We survived by sending out some of the Hutu living in the hotel to the market in the city centre to buy commodities, such as rice and sugar, which had become scarce during the fighting. Our only drinking water came from the swimming pool and we stored it in the bathtubs of some of the rooms, most of which were being shared by three or four people.

Although the UN force had been reduced to a minimum, the few "Blue Helmets" that remained in Rwanda managed to encourage the RPF rebels and the genocidal government to strike a deal that allowed refugees caught behind enemy lines to travel to safe areas around Kigali. Along with other Tutsi hiding in the Mille Collines, my sister and I were evacuated in the middle of May to an area of town under RPF control, and so survived the rest of the genocide. If it were not for the actions of Lt.-Gen. Roméo Dallaire, the Canadian head of the UN peacekeeping mission, who protected the Tutsi sheltering inside the Mille Collines, we would never have survived.

The remainder of my family, however, was not so fortunate. They were massacred in late April in Musange, my home *commune*, in an office building where they had sought refuge at the start of the killings. One of my nieces, who was five years old at the time, was the only member of my family to survive the massacre at Musange. She later told me that she had received a machete blow and had fallen to the ground. She managed to hide under the corpses in the office and later crawled out and hid in the latrine of a Hutu's home nearby. A policeman who found her spared her life because he knew that, although my niece had been living with my parents, her father was Hutu. When one of my father's friends learned that I had survived the genocide and was still in Kigali, she brought my niece to me. My niece is now a student at the Kigali Institute of Science and Technology.

Fourteen years later, I resent bitterly that the world betrayed my people in their hour of most desperate need by refusing to intervene to halt the genocide. I am also surprised to see now that some powerful countries on the UN Security Council, most of which spent their days discussing the best terminology to give to the bloodletting in Rwanda, later formed a giant coalition to "liberate" Iraq. What was needed to stop the killings in Rwanda was not a huge force, but rather a few thousand troops to support the UN "Blue Helmets". Alas, Rwanda did not have any oil or other minerals that would have been of interest to the superpowers.

Continuing impunity and the problems of reconciliation

Today my fear is that, just as a failure to bring past perpetrators of violence to justice made the genocide of 1994 possible, so another culture of impunity is being cultivated in post-genocide Rwanda that may again sow the seeds of ethnic hatred and violence. The difference today is that this new culture of impunity comes under the guise of calls for reconciliation. Today, survivors are encouraged to forgive and forget the crimes committed against them. They are asked to live with some of the neighbours they know participated in the genocide. Many survivors feel that the present Rwandan government, and the world at large, are making the same grave mistakes as past Hutu regimes, by not administering full justice to those found guilty of genocide crimes. Without justice for genocide perpetrators, any attempt to reconcile the nation will prove futile. As long as survivors assume that justice has not been done, prospects for healing the nation's wounds remain bleak.

Unlike what is suggested in Rwanda, I have never heard survivors of the Holocaust being asked to reconcile with the Nazis. There is of course an urge to move forward in Rwanda, and to rebuild the country. However, my fear, and that of many survivors, is that any failure to deliver full justice after the genocide, either by the Rwandan national courts, *gacaca* or the ICTR—for example, by offering suspects plea-bargaining arrangements in the name of reintegration and reconciliation—could be seen as an absolution of the guilt of unrepentant killers and the leaders who during the genocide urged Hutu to participate en masse in the killings. As one Hutu leader announced over the infamous RTLM, "Once the job is done, nobody will be able to bring you to book!" After all, many individuals who killed in the 1960s repeated these crimes at different times during the next three decades, including during the genocide in 1994.

If this culture of impunity is not destroyed, Rwandans will never come to terms with their terrible past. My fears are compounded by an alarming surge of recent attacks against, and murders of, genocide survivors in parts of Rwanda. The intention of some of these killers, many of whom were among genocide suspects released from prison following the presidential communiqué in January 2003, is to intimidate potential witnesses who may testify against them during *gacaca* hearings in their home communities or at the ICTR. While the current regime in Rwanda, controlled by the RPF, urges every Rwandan to work for national reconciliation, the recent massive releases of thousands of genocide suspects from Rwandan prisons are seen by many survivors as a blanket amnesty. Is the RPF falling into the same trap as its predecessors, by abdicating its responsibility to provide justice to victims of mass violence? Only history will tell whether the current *gacaca* process will help achieve this goal. However, there are undoubtedly many problems ahead, with thousands of killers now roaming freely in the community.

Problems of distorted memory

Another problem that survivors face, in our attempt to deal with the legacies of the genocide, is a pervasive misunderstanding of the nature of ethnic divisions that have often led to violence in the country. Rwanda is possibly the only country in the world whose major ethnic groups speak the same language, have the same religion and share many of the same customs and traditions. However, what is painful for me today is that Rwanda's history has been trivialised and reduced by many commentators to a simple tale of ancient, visceral, tribal conflict between Hutu and Tutsi. This is yet another reason why survivors' testimonies of what they experienced during the genocide are so crucial. We have too often been denied the right to narrate the true and verifiable facts of the genocide and previous periods of violence that we survivors know better than the best historians and so-called political experts, many of whom could not even locate Rwanda on a map during the genocide. Perceived divisions between Hutu and Tutsi that have been manipulated by successive governments in Rwanda, rather than actual, unchangeable ethnic differences between these groups, are responsible for inciting the genocide. This would be made clear if survivors were permitted to describe in our own words the ordeals and tribulations that we have suffered and the causes behind them. We could then undermine clichéd, inaccurate views of the causes of violence in Rwanda that belittle and confuse understandings of the genocide by equating it with tribal war or primitive violence, as some media reports did during the genocide, and continue to do even today. Is it really possible to blame the genocide on inherent ethnic differences between groups of Rwandans, even though this sort of violence was never observed in Rwanda before colonialism?

I am angered and dismayed at what appears to be a growing tide of revisionism concerning the Rwandan genocide in some international quarters, fostered by people who seem intent on obliterating the truth of this tragedy. Some commentators have dared to suggest that, in fact, there was no genocide in Rwanda, but rather a civil war between two relatively equally powerful sides, while others, such as Prof. Christian Davenport at the University of Notre Dame, have argued that as many Hutu as Tutsi were killed in the "politicide" of 1994.[2] Such arguments are an insult to all genocide survivors, and encourage the form of impunity that permitted mass violence against Tutsi in the first place. 	.

Conclusion

The plight of genocide survivors is ongoing. We live with the legacies of the genocide every day, fighting the deepest emotional and psychological battles imaginable. Sometimes it is difficult to go on living. Nothing in this world will bring back those whom we loved and who loved us. However, those who failed to act to stop the genocide must reassess their betrayal and move beyond the mere expression of "*mea culpa*" to take concrete measures to help the survivors—including the orphans and genocide widows who were infected with HIV during the genocide—to overcome the aftermath of this horrific tragedy. Let us all hope that the world will learn from the mistakes of the Rwandan genocide, help rebuild a vibrant Rwanda where justice reigns, and prevent such tragedies from happening elsewhere.

---

2   See C. Davenport, "Genodynamics: Understanding Genocide through Time and Space", http://www.genodynamics.com.

3

THE PEACEKEEPING SYSTEM, BRITAIN AND THE 1994 RWANDAN GENOCIDE [1]

Paul D. Williams

This chapter reflects upon two questions: what do the international responses to the 1994 Rwandan genocide tell us about United Nations (UN) peacekeeping in general, and what does the genocide tell us about Britain's commitment to maintaining international peace and security in particular? I focus upon the British government's role for two reasons. First, as a permanent member of the UN Security Council, the British government has a greater responsibility than most states for maintaining international peace and security and was an important participant in the debates about how the UN should respond to Rwanda's civil war and then genocide. Second, despite its privileged position within the Security Council, with few exceptions, the literature discussing international responses to the genocide has failed to analyse Britain's role, concentrating instead upon the actions of the UN Secretariat and the US, French and Belgian governments. My focus on Britain is thus intended to help fill a gap in the literature on the genocide.

As one of the British officials I interviewed about this subject told me, one makes history facing forwards, but one writes about history looking backwards. This raises complicated methodological issues about the false clarity of hindsight, the difficulties of getting inside the minds of those who participated in this series of events, and, in this particular case, the challenges of gaining access to the relevant information. What follows are the reflections of a curious outsider without access to all of the relevant information, except what has been gleaned through the usual academic channels. There are at least two obstacles regarding the use of primary sources in this investigation. First, it is difficult for the public to obtain the documentary records of the most relevant discussions,

---

1   It would have been impossible to write this chapter without Linda Melvern, a fellow contributor to this book. We have worked together researching the British government's response to the genocide, and I am proud to acknowledge my debt to her here.

particularly private Security Council meetings, the UN Assistance Mission for Rwanda's (UNAMIR) cables, faxes and telephone calls from the field, and the British government's records of its policy-making process towards Rwanda and UN peacekeeping.[2] Second, important players in the British system have refused to provide full and frank accounts of what happened, sometimes citing legal constraints, sometimes other reasons. With that intellectual health warning in mind, what can we say in response to the two questions posed?

The peacekeeping system and the genocide

Throughout its history, international society has developed a variety of crude systems for pursuing what the UN Charter refers to as "international peace and security". Consequently, UN peace operations do not take place in a political vacuum but are part of an institutional system. For the purposes of this chapter, I will refer to this as the peacekeeping system; that is, those actors and institutions relevant to understanding the UN's attempts to promote peace and development in Rwanda. In Rwanda's case, the most important actors and institutions comprising the peacekeeping system were:

- The UN Secretariat, especially the Departments of Peacekeeping Operations (DPKO) and Political Affairs (DPA) and the Secretary-General's office;

- States represented on the UN Security Council;

- The United Nations Observer Mission to Uganda-Rwanda (UNOMUR) and then UNAMIR;

- States contributing troops to UNOMUR and UNAMIR;

- The UN's programmes, including the World Food Programme (WFP), the UN Development Programme (UNDP), and the UN High Commissioner for Refugees (UNHCR); and

- The UN's specialised agencies engaged in the reform of Rwanda's economy, particularly the World Bank and International Monetary Fund (IMF).

---

2   On the lack of transparency in the UN decision-making process, see H. Adelman and A. Suhrke, "Rwanda" in David M. Malone (ed.), *The UN Security Council* (Boulder, CO: Lynne Rienner, 2004), 495-6. In Britain's case, one unnamed source has suggested that the Foreign and Commonwealth Office's files on the subject show evidence of "weeding". See Linda Melvern, *Conspiracy to Murder: The Rwandan Genocide* (London: Verso, 2004), 261. Information about the private Security Council debates was subsequently leaked to the journalist L. Melvern. Her first account appeared in "Death by Diplomacy", *The Scotsman* (4 January 1995).

Theoretically, the peacekeeping system was coordinated through the UN Secretariat and Security Council. In practice, however, the system showed little evidence of coordination.[3] To take just one example, World Bank officials, who had been heavily engaged in the reform of Rwanda's economy since the mid-1980s, failed to inform the UN Security Council of the dramatic evidence they had of the rapid militarisation of Rwandan society.[4] At the time of the genocide, the peacekeeping system displayed several important features that made it unsuitable for the type of peace enforcement that was ultimately required in Rwanda. Analysing these characteristics can help us understand the system's reaction to the genocide and shed some light on our first question.

An emaciated system. Since its inception, the current peacekeeping system has been kept in a consistently emaciated condition. In 1994, UN peacekeeping cost US$3.5bn (although the regular peacekeeping budget had been allocated only US$1.3bn), while the world's states spent approximately US$770bn preparing for war.[5] This did not stop the Security Council from authorising 20 new peacekeeping operations between 1988 and 1993, many of which went well beyond the boundaries of traditional peacekeeping.[6] As a result, the system's resources were stretched thinly across numerous concurrent operations, and inevitably some missions were accorded greater priority than others. The deciding factor in the allocation of resources was the geopolitical considerations of the Security Council's permanent members.[7] Not surprisingly, therefore, by the time the genocide began in April 1994, Rwanda was not among the system's priorities. The top priority in doctrinal terms was to avoid crossing what became known as "the Mogadishu line" after the deaths of eighteen US soldiers in a botched operation in Somalia in October 1993. In Washington, this episode sparked an

---

3   For a discussion of this continuing problem, particularly in the context of the present-day "responsibility to protect", see chapter 17 by Jennifer Welsh.

4   L. Melvern, *A People Betrayed: The Role of the West in Rwanda's Genocide* (London: Zed, 2000), 5. See also, P. Williams, "Peace Operations and the International Financial Institutions: Insights from Rwanda and Sierra Leone," *International Peacekeeping,* 11, 1 (2004), 108-12.

5   A. J. Bellamy, P. Williams and S. Griffin, *Understanding Peacekeeping* (Cambridge: Polity, 2004), 53.

6   Traditional peacekeeping operations are intended to help ensure liberal and peaceful relations between states. In practice, this means that they work towards constructing the political space necessary for warring states to reach an agreement. Traditional peacekeeping takes place in the space between a ceasefire agreement between states and the conclusion of a political settlement. Traditional peacekeepers do not propose or enforce particular political solutions. Rather, they try to build confidence between the belligerents in an attempt to facilitate political dialogue. See ibid., 95-110.

7   Alternatively, M. Goulding suggested that "the peace efforts undertaken by the United Nations tend to reflect Western priorities." Cited in *Peacemonger* (London: John Murray, 2002), 26.

inter-agency debate about peacekeeping that resulted in the publication of US Presidential Decision Directive 25 in early May 1994. This set out strict criteria to judge whether or not to authorise UN peacekeeping operations.[8] By this stage, talk of not crossing "the Mogadishu line" had become shorthand for the argument that states should avoid being drawn into dangerous humanitarian peace enforcement operations in areas of the world they considered strategically insignificant. In practical terms, the system's priorities reflected the concerns of the great powers, which, at that stage, were with the so-called "safe areas" in Bosnia, particularly Gorazde, and the restoration of Aristide's government in Haiti, which the Clinton administration viewed as the best way to prevent more Haitian refugees from flooding into the US.

So, although overburdened and under-resourced, the system concentrated its resources on certain parts of the globe. Rwanda was not one of those places, and UNOMUR and UNAMIR were forced to operate on a financial shoestring. UNAMIR was chronically under-resourced in virtually all areas, from military to office equipment.[9] Yet even with UNAMIR's relatively small budget, the UN's member states failed to meet their financial obligations to it.[10] In many ways, the situation that developed represented the worst of all possible worlds: by helping to put the Arusha peace process together, supporting the exclusion of the extremists from the process, and then publicly signalling its commitment to the subsequent Accords, the peacekeeping system raised local expectations about the role that outsiders would play in Rwanda. Yet, at the same time, by failing to provide the resources necessary to assemble the Neutral International Force (NIF) envisaged at Arusha, the peacekeeping system denied the peace process any realistic chance of success. That UNAMIR was meant to represent a shadow of the envisaged NIF highlighted the fact that the international society was not serious about acting as a guarantor of the peace process, or as a guard against the resurgence of the extremists who organised the genocide.[11]

---

8   Specifically, PDD 25 determined that peacekeeping operations should only be authorised when:
-    there was a genuine threat to peace and security;
-    regional or sub-regional organisations could assist in resolving the situation;
-    a ceasefire existed and the parties had committed themselves to a peace process;
-    a clear political goal existed and was present in the mandate;
-    a precise mandate had been formulated; and
-    the safety of UN personnel could be reasonably assured.

    "Statement on the conditions for the deployment and renewal of peacekeeping operations", S/PRST/1994/22 (3 May 1994).

9   See Bellamy, Williams and Griffin, *Understanding Peacekeeping*, 131.

10   On 31 January 1994, the UN's member states owed UNAMIR US$50.7m in arrears. W. A. Knight, "Towards a Subsidiarity Model for Peacemaking and Preventive Diplomacy", *Third World Quarterly*, 17, 1 (1996), 40.

11   See B. D. Jones, *Peacemaking in Rwanda: The Dynamics of Failure* (Boulder, CO: Lynne

Deciding where responsibility for the peacekeeping system's emaciated condition lies is a complex issue that is usually reduced to asking only the UN Secretariat and the great powers to account for their behaviour. But the Rwandan case reveals that many of the UN's member states, including Rwanda's neighbours, watched from the sidelines and were guilty of not empowering the peacekeeping system with the resources that could have enabled it to respond "more confidently, more quickly and more effectively" to genocide.[12]

Information and communication problems. The peacekeeping system also lacked reliable and accurate information about Rwanda. This was partly because the UN failed to employ staff familiar with the intricacies of Rwandan history, who could accurately interpret the warning signs that were available. In addition, the staff assigned to work on UNOMUR and UNAMIR in New York were expected to cover the country as just one part of larger portfolios. As one British official put it, Rwanda always seemed to be "a little add-on to somebody's main mission".[13] Finally, there were also problems with the dissemination of information throughout the system. These three factors contributed to a situation in which the information that was collected was not interpreted in such a way as to make the strongest case for intervention in the face of genocide.

Three issues are particularly relevant here. First, during late 1993 and early 1994, the peacekeeping system was very poor at collecting, let alone acting upon, the series of reports and press releases highlighting the likelihood of imminent violence and the organised nature of what had already occurred.[14] Im-

---

Rienner, 2001). The NIF's mandate included:
- Help provide security throughout the country, for humanitarian assistance, and for the expatriate community;
- Monitor the ceasefire agreement, including the establishment and maintenance of a demilitarised zone around Kigali;
- Investigate all reported infractions of the ceasefire agreement;
- Help maintain public security by monitoring the activities of the *gendarmerie* and police; and
- Assist with the demobilisation and integration of the armed forces (expected to take seven to nine months and involve 50,000 government and RPF personnel).

Cited in M. Barnett, *Eyewitness to a Genocide: The United Nations and Rwanda*, (Ithaca: Cornell University Press, 2002), 62.

12   T. Erskine, "Blood on the UN's Hands? Assigning Duties and Apportioning Blame to an International Organisation", *Global Society*, 18, 1 (2004), 42.

13   Dr Lillian Wong, speech at The Rwanda Forum, Imperial War Museum, London, 27 March 2004.

14   For details of the early warnings available to the peacekeeping system see H. Adelman and A. Suhrke, "Early Warning and Conflict Management", Study II of *The International Response to Conflict and Genocide: Lessons from the Rwanda Experience*, (Copenhagen: DANIDA, 1996); Melvern, *A People Betrayed*, 56-57; and Melvern, *Conspiracy to Murder*, esp. chs 2 and 3.

portantly, these reports suggested that the violence apparent in Rwanda was not just a continuation of the civil war. They also contained documented evidence that organised massacres of approximately 2,000 Tutsi civilians had occurred since 1991, separate from fighting between the Rwandan Patriotic Front (RPF) and government soldiers. The peacekeeping system's failure to detect and act upon such warnings suggests it was primarily geared to managing and containing violent conflict, rather than preventing it in the first place.

Second, the flow of information within UN channels depicted what was happening in Rwanda in ways that downplayed the urgency of the situation, and initially framed events as solely an extension of the civil war.[15] For instance, after the shooting down of President Habyarimana's plane on 6 April 1994—an episode whose immediate sequel is described chillingly by Kayigamba in the previous chapter—one insider described the (formal and informal) information delivered by the Secretariat to the Council as "brief, vague, and indecisive".[16] As a result, Michael Barnett went on to argue, "an extraordinary chasm" developed between what Lt.-Gen. Roméo Dallaire, UNAMIR's force commander, told the Secretariat via his cables, faxes and telephone calls and what the Secretariat passed on to the Council.[17] This had important practical repercussions, because the information that the Secretariat passes to the Council plays a significant role in setting the parameters of the Council's discussions. The gap was evident in two main respects.[18] First, by 8 April, Dallaire's communications unmistakably characterised the violence as a civil war, and what he referred to variously as "ethnic killings", "ethnic cleansing", "massacres", and later "crimes against humanity" and even a "holocaust".[19] Second, Dallaire offered a prescription to end the massacres by calling for reinforcements to engage in coercive diplomacy against the *Interahamwe* and the Presidential Guard, in the hope that, when confronted with a show of international force, they would halt the massacres.

The final issue relating to the system's information gathering is that although UNAMIR became a crucial witness to the events in and around Kigali after most foreign diplomats, journalists and NGO workers had fled, it was not

---

15   C. Keating, "An Insider's Account" in Malone (ed.), *The UN Security Council*, 503-4.

16   Barnett, *Eyewitness to a Genocide*, 107.

17   Ibid., 110 and Melvern, *A People Betrayed,* esp. Ch. 14. Colin Keating is also heavily critical of Boutros Boutros-Ghali's role in not keeping the Security Council informed about events in Rwanda: see Keating, "An Insider's Account", 503. The Council received summarised briefings from Secretariat officials rather than verbatim copies of Dallaire's reports.

18   Barnett, *Eyewitness to a Genocide*, 109.

19   Dallaire used the latter two terms to characterise what was happening in and around Kigali in a letter to Col. Nazrul Islam, commanding officer of the Bangladeshi contingent, on 17 April 1994. It is not clear whether the Secretariat received a copy of this letter.

always in the best position to assess the situation in the rest of Rwanda. For example, eleven days after the plane crash, Dallaire informed the Secretariat that in all likelihood they were better placed than UNAMIR to understand what was happening in Rwanda. Dallaire's problem was that his assessments of the military situation on the ground were limited to events in Kigali and its environs. As he put it, "UNAMIR has lost its eyes and ears outside of Kigali ...[W]hereas in the first few days of the conflict we had a clear picture of the situation throughout Rwanda, we now are limited to knowledge of the Kigali area and the RPF zone. We are rapidly entering a phase where UN New York may well know more about what is going on than UNAMIR with intelligence information (satellite, EW [eyewitness] etc.) from its members of the situation outside Kigali."[20]

Early stages. These information problems were compounded by the fact that when UN peacekeepers were sent to Rwanda, the peacekeeping system was at an early and experimental stage in its development. Key elements of the system had only just been assembled. Crucially, the DPKO had only been established in February 1992, and it was still finding its feet, in terms of both its contribution to making peacekeeping doctrine and its relationship with other parts of the system. DPKO personnel were so overburdened and under-resourced that Dallaire referred to them as workers in "a thirty-sixth floor sweatshop". He also later recalled the rather strained relations that existed between the DPKO and the DPA during the early months of his mission.[21] In retrospect, the DPKO's establishment was a necessary and constructive reform of the peacekeeping system; for instance, until DPKO's creation the issue of where ultimate responsibility for peacekeeping lay within the UN was a frequent source of confusion. But it did not help the victims of Rwanda's 1994 genocide that the UN's peacekeeping teething problems came when they did.

In October 1993, when UNAMIR was established, the peacekeeping system's attention was fixed upon Somalia and the former Yugoslavia, and most of the incoming news was not positive. Consequently, in several important respects UNAMIR reflected an organisation whose institutional goal was increasingly becoming to avoid further peacekeeping failures. This, in turn, was interpreted by the Security Council as authorising only "scaled down" operations and "learning to say no" to difficult missions.[22] The fact that UNAMIR was initially seen as an easy mission highlights the lack of relevant expertise that plagued the peacekeeping system. What made UNAMIR seem an "easy"

---

20 Code Cable, "The military assessment of the situation as of 17 April 1994", Dallaire (UNAMIR) to Baril (New York, UN), 17 April 1994, para 12.

21 Lt.-Gen. R. Dallaire, *Shake Hands With The Devil: The Failure of Humanity in Rwanda* (Toronto: Random House, 2003), 48-51.

22 Barnett, *Eyewitness to a Genocide*, 72.

operation compared to the travails of the United Nations Operations in Somalia (UNOSOM), or the difficulties of the United Nations Protection Force (UNPROFOR) in Bosnia, was the fact that the RPF and the Rwandan Government had already agreed on terms for peace at Arusha in August 1993. This meant that UNAMIR's mandate could be authorised under Chapter VI of the UN Charter. In practice, however, while UNAMIR's tasks fell short of full peace enforcement, they went considerably beyond those of traditional peacekeeping. UNAMIR thus found itself in the all too common position of engaging in "wider peacekeeping" activities in a situation of ongoing conflict.[23] Given the problems experienced between June and October 1993 by UNOSOM II and American soldiers in Somalia, the UN Secretariat and Security Council were loath to grant UNAMIR a Chapter VII mandate authorising the use of "all necessary means" to accomplish its mission.

Apart from signalling the seriousness of the situation to the outside world, there were two main reasons why a more robust mandate might have been useful for UNAMIR. First, is that it would have made it easier to justify considerable numbers of additional personnel that would make it easier for UNAMIR to protect itself. As Dallaire made clear, the main danger to UNAMIR personnel did not come from RPF or Rwandan Government Forces (RGF) soldiers, although at various times throughout the genocide both of these forces fired upon UNAMIR buildings and personnel. The "most dangerous threat to UNAMIR" came from what Dallaire called a "third force" of "aggressive/brazen/militia" who displayed "no particular respect for anybody and essentially work to their own unruly/drunk/drugged tune. They are a very large and dangerous and totally irrational group of people."[24] A more robust mandate would have increased the likelihood of UNAMIR's expansion, and enabled it to more effectively engage in proactive self-defence and coercive diplomacy against this third force.

A second reason for granting UNAMIR a more robust mandate is that this would have allowed it to protect more civilians at risk of massacre than it was able to do under its Chapter VI mandate. This would have been a major decision for New York, and would have required the peacekeeping system to provide UNAMIR with resources (human and material) that it appeared unwilling

---

23   Wider peacekeeping operations are intended to fulfil the aims of traditional peacekeeping as well as certain additional tasks within an environment of ongoing conflict. They usually develop as an *ad hoc* response to the breakdown of ceasefires or political agreements that facilitated the original deployment of a peace operation, combined with a belief on the part of peacekeepers that they should continue to have some sort of role (often humanitarian) in the conflict area. For details on the concept of wider peacekeeping, see Bellamy, Williams and Griffin, *Understanding Peacekeeping*, Ch. 7.

24   Code Cable, "The military assessment of the situation as of 17 April 1994", Dallaire (UNAMIR) to Baril (New York, UN), 17 April 1994, para. 19.

to give. Consequently, as the genocide unfolded, Dallaire became increasingly blunt in presenting his superiors with the options as he saw them. On 17 April he told New York that UNAMIR

...cannot continue to sit on the fence of all these morally legitimate demands for assistance/protection, nor can it simply launch into a Chapter 7 type of operations without the proper authority, personnel and equipment. ... Maintaining the status quo on manpower under these severe and adverse conditions is wasteful, dangerously casualty-causing and demoralizing to the troops. Either UNAMIR gets changes in its parameters of works in order to get into the thick of things (with more resources), or it starts to thin out in order to avoid unnecessary losses and reduce the overhead and administrative burden to the negotiation process for a ceasefire and peace.[25]

However, in an internal UNAMIR letter to the commanding officer of the Bangladeshi contingent, also written on 17 April, Dallaire suggested that his force's current mandate allowed it to try to protect civilians in danger of massacre. As he told Col. Nazrul Islam,

Our orders from New York are quite explicit; we are to conduct the evacuation of the expatriate community and to offer protection when feasible of Rwandese citizens. Within our peacekeeping rules of engagement we can use force to defend persons under UN protection and to prevent crimes against humanity. We must however balance the use of force with the requirement to protect our men.[26]

The broader, more relevant point is that UNAMIR found itself in a difficult position that was not uncommon for UN peacekeepers at the time (or since), namely, that they were mandated to conduct activities that went beyond traditional notions of peacekeeping, but had neither the resources necessary for the job nor a peaceful environment in which to work. It was not until the publication of the *Report of the Panel on United Nations Peace Operations* (the so-called Brahimi Report) in 2000 that the UN took a clearer position (at least on paper) on the need to avoid such wider peacekeeping.[27]

---

25   Ibid., paras. 24-25.

26   Letter from Dallaire to Col. Nazrul Islam, 17 April 1994, p. 1. It should be noted that after the plane crash UNAMIR received numerous requests to rescue specific individuals and their families, usually foreign nationals or those with powerful friends outside Rwanda who felt they could pull strings within the UN peacekeeping system. By June 1994, UNAMIR had received 971 such requests. Cited in Melvern, *Conspiracy to Murder*, 237.

27   *Report of the Panel on United Nations Peace Operations*, UN Doc. A/55/305-S/2000/809 (21 August 2000). Among the most relevant of the Report's recommendations were:
- The military component of a peace operation should be robust enough to defend itself effectively and protect civilians under its care;
- The Security Council should not authorise a mission until it has the means to accomplish its goals; and
- "Impartiality for United Nations Operations must ... mean adherence to the principles of the Charter: where one party to a peace agreement clearly and incontrovertibly is violating its terms, continued equal treatment of all parties by the United

Internal rules and their consequences. A fourth issue that emerges from the Rwandan case is the extent to which the UN system exerts a powerful organisational logic upon its individual employees. It is inevitable that an organisation charged with, among other things, maintaining international peace and security will develop a bureaucratic logic of some sort. Since the UN cannot alleviate all of the world's suffering, it has to establish criteria for deciding where and when it should act. However, there was no *a priori* reason why this logic should come to resemble what the head of the DPKO in 1994 (and later UN Secretary-General), Kofi Annan, later described as an "institutional ideology of impartiality even when confronted with attempted genocide."[28] The important issue here is the need to understand how the parts of the UN system responsible for peacekeeping came to believe that abandoning the victims of genocide would actually bolster the UN's institutional reputation and image. Or as Michael Barnett put it, how was it that "with knowledge about the crimes against humanity, many in the Security Council and in the Secretariat concluded that withdrawal was ethical and proper"?[29] This disturbing observation raises issues not only about the power of individuals to alter the bureaucratic logic of their organisation, but also how the UN's internal rules should be balanced with its members' other international legal obligations.

To date, Barnett's work has revealed most about how the power exerted by the UN's internal rules helps explain the organisation's policy of non-intervention in response to genocide. Barnett has argued persuasively that the UN's bureaucracy was not simply a home for established and static ethical standards but was an active "incubator of ethical claims" that came to define watching from the sidelines as the most sensible response.[30] The short explanation for the UN's ineffectual response to Rwanda's 1994 genocide is that the individual employees who called the shots within the peacekeeping system[31] believed, quite correctly, that they had responsibilities to multiple constituencies—not only to Rwandans, but also to other populations in danger, to their own personnel at risk in the field, and to the UN as an institution. The problem was that those same individuals decided that their other responsibilities took priority over rescuing the victims of genocide. In short, the key decision-makers within the peacekeeping system acted as if the deaths of—as it turned out—approximately

---

Nations can in the best case result in ineffectiveness and in the worst may amount to complicity with evil".

28   Cited in Barnett, *Eyewitness to a Genocide*, 158.

29   Ibid., 4.

30   Ibid., 7.

31   In this case, the key players were in the Secretariat—especially the Secretary-General, Boutros Boutros-Ghali; Marrack Goulding, head of the DPA; and Kofi Annan, head of the DPKO—and the representatives of the most influential governments within the Security Council, especially the US, France, the UK and Rwanda itself.

800,000 Rwandans was a price worth paying to ensure the continuation of UN peacekeeping.

Barnett pushes this bureaucratic argument, going as far as to claim that "those who opposed intervention had the rules on their side."[32] But it is important to remember that the rules to which Barnett is referring are those constructed and enforced by the small clique of bureaucrats and the UN's most powerful members, who, after the bungled US operations in Somalia, had adopted a very restricted idea of what peacekeeping should entail. In contrast, one might reasonably argue, as, for example, the International Committee of the Red Cross (ICRC) and Oxfam did at the time, that those who supported intervention had more important rules on their side, especially the rules set down in the Convention on the Prevention and Punishment of the Crime of Genocide. It is also clear in retrospect that the bureaucratic logic of the peacekeeping system was incoherent even on its own terms, because withdrawal in the face of genocide did not ensure the future of peacekeeping nor bolster the UN's image. On the contrary, that logic heralded a (temporary) retreat from peacekeeping[33] and left the UN and its member states open to the most damning criticisms in the organisation's history.

Word games. Rwanda provides another example of the misleading way in which language is used to describe the peacekeeping system's activities. The episode also shows how important words can be. As genocide unfolded in Rwanda, the UN was becoming infamous for its misnomers, not least the designation of so-called "safe areas" in Bosnia. To the careful observer, these were supposed to indicate something qualitatively different from the "safe havens" established by the allied coalition in northern Iraq in the aftermath of Operation Desert Storm. Similarly the so-called UN Protection Force in Bosnia provided very little real protection to the victims of Serb and Croat ethnic cleansing. The word games of the peacekeeping system were also apparent in Rwanda. From at least January 1994, for instance, UNAMIR knew that the so-called "weapons secure area" in Kigali was patently awash with weapons that, in contravention of the Arusha Accords, were being moved without UNAMIR's permission.

But while words can obscure reality, they can also constrain and influence action. In this case, using the word "genocide" to describe the situation on the ground would have put significant pressure on the UN's member states, especially those states that had signed the Genocide Convention, to live up to a variety of moral, political and legal obligations. This may explain why Britain's ambassador to the UN urged his fellow diplomats on the Security Council not

---

32   Barnett, *Eyewitness to a Genocide*, 127.

33   On the subsequent retreat from peacekeeping, see Bellamy, Williams and Griffin, *Understanding Peacekeeping*, 81-85.

to use the word in public, or why the US State Department insisted that its spokespersons use the phrase "acts of genocide"—which, incidentally, is also included in Article VIII of the Genocide Convention. Of course, it is possible that these actors genuinely believed genocide was not occurring, or that it was premature to characterise the violence as genocide, or even that they were appropriately using a phrase that appears in the Genocide Convention. However, the fact that these actors never publicly articulated the third justification suggests it is not a plausible explanation for their behaviour. The first two justifications, while plausible explanations during the initial days of the genocide, became increasingly untenable as the genocide progressed. The point is that the UN's language, the peacekeeping system's use of terms, and the wider vocabulary of international law fuel high expectations about the degree of protection to which victims of mass crimes, and especially genocide, are entitled. In Rwanda's case, such expectations proved to be misplaced.

Institutional racism? On the basis of what happened in Rwanda, peacekeepers and commentators alike have asked whether the peacekeeping system is institutionally racist, inasmuch as the deaths of black people are considered less important than those of white people.[34] Whether the explanation for the lack of urgency that the peacekeeping system gave to Rwanda lies within geopolitical or racial factors is difficult to determine. Some recent work on the global distribution of peace operations suggests that although the UN has shown greater willingness to send missions to Europe, Latin America and the Caribbean than to Africa, it is civil wars in Asia, not Africa, that are least likely to receive UN help.[35]

It is also important to remember that in mid-1994 both the Secretary-General and the head of DPKO were Africans, and the UN was running eighteen missions, involving over 70,000 personnel, over half of which were in Africa. What does seem apparent, however, is that peace operations in Africa have often been downsized in the planning stages and under-resourced once authorised. For example, not only was UNAMIR significantly weaker than the NIF envisaged at Arusha, but Dallaire's initial assessments suggested a force of approximately 4,500 troops was required to carry out the mandate. The Security Council, however, authorised just over 2,500 personnel. This reflects the shallow commitment of international efforts (both African and non-African) to resolve wars on the continent. In short, Africa, more than other continents, can

---

34 Dallaire is convinced the system is racist. See Dallaire, *Shake Hands With The Devil*, 5. Others have posed the question but imply the answer is "yes", e.g. Tony Worthington (MP), *Hansard* (Commons), 24 May 1994, col. 308. Others have been more cryptic on the issue, e.g. "Wretched Rwanda", *The Economist*, 7 May 1994, 15.

35 M. Gilligan and S. J. Stedman, "Where do the Peacekeepers Go?", *International Studies Review*, 5, 4 (2003), 49.

legitimately claim to have experienced peace operations designed to salve the consciences of outsiders, rather than solve the problems facing insiders.

Imperfect but important. Finally, in spite of all the weaknesses exhibited by the peacekeeping system, its very existence, and particularly the presence of UNAMIR, affected the situation in Rwanda in significant ways. First, the UN's peacekeepers were witnesses to the unfolding genocide, although their testimony was often based on limited information. Second, UNAMIR personnel continued to affect some outcomes on the ground. This highlights how even a small number of the "right" sort of peacekeepers can have significant positive effects. Similarly, the "wrong" sort of peacekeepers can make a precarious situation more dangerous.

Despite their limited resources, within a fortnight of the plane crash, UNAMIR personnel—sometimes aided by soldiers from France, Belgium and Italy—had evacuated over 4,000 people and protected approximately 14,000 others at their outposts. It should not be forgotten that these were people who had been almost entirely abandoned by international society and international relief organisations (with the notable exception of the ICRC).[36] Indeed, during the 100 days of genocide, it has been estimated that UNAMIR at one time protected approximately 30,000 people.[37] These were people who could have been saved, had UNAMIR not been reduced to a skeleton presence.[38]

On the other hand, some of the behaviour by UNAMIR personnel undermined the mission's mandate. For example, local civilians have reported abuses suffered at the hands of UNAMIR personnel, primarily individuals from the Bangladeshi and Belgian contingents. Similarly, Dallaire was clearly annoyed and frustrated by the lack of professionalism and commitment of some of his troops. While the Bangladeshi contingent lacked equipment, was averse to taking risks and consistently refused to follow Dallaire's orders, many Belgian soldiers suffered from hubris and could not adapt to the needs of a Chapter VI operation, and some soldiers engaged in unprofessional, sometimes violent acts

---

36 Code Cable, "Sitrep on Rescue Missions", Dallaire (UNAMIR) to Annan (New York, UN), 20 April 1994, para 4. Some of those persons evacuated by UNAMIR to Kenya were subsequently forced back to Rwanda while the genocide was still raging because Kenyan authorities claimed they did not possess the correct visas.

37 A. des Forges, *Leave None To Tell The Story: Genocide in Rwanda* (New York: Human Rights Watch, 1999), 689. The difficulty with this figure is that many of these people were located within the RPF zone. Consequently, the extent to which UNAMIR was responsible for saving them is not entirely clear.

38 This was apparently the case with a contingent of 116 Ghanaian peacekeepers forced to endure daily and semi-daily changes to their orders stipulating whether they were to withdraw from or dig into their positions. Code Cable, "Urgent requirement to reduce UNAMIR to a residual force by last light Friday 22 April 1994", Booh-Booh (Kigali, UNAMIR) to Annan (New York, UN), 21 April 1994, para. 9.

towards civilians.[39] The following extract from one of Dallaire's code cables to New York displays his frustrations:

> The [Bangladeshi] contingent commander has consistently stated he is under national orders not to endanger his soldiers by evacuating Rwandese. They will evacuate expatriates but not local people. His junior officers have clearly stated that if they are stopped at a roadblock with local people in the convoy they will hand over these local people for inevitable killing rather than use their weapons in an attempt to save local people. This reticence to engage in dangerous operations and their stated reluctance to use their weapons in self-defence or in defence of crimes against humanity has led to widespread mistrust of this contingent among its peers in other units and amongst staff officers/UNMOs [UN Military Observers] at the headquarters when they are tasked to go with these men on dangerous missions.[40]

In contrast to the exemplary professionalism displayed by their Ghanaian, Senegalese and Tunisian colleagues,[41] the Bangladeshi and Belgian contingents were, for different reasons, ill-suited to achieving UNAMIR's mandate. Consequently, the withdrawal of these two contingents did not generate great surprise within UNAMIR.

Britain and the genocide

What was the British government's contribution to the peacekeeping system, and how did it respond to the civil war and genocide in Rwanda? Dallaire, for one, is clear about Britain's role, accusing it, along with others, of adopting indifferent, selfish and racist policies towards Rwanda, of "aiding and abetting" the genocide, and of sabotaging UNAMIR's efforts to fulfil its mandate.[42] These are serious accusations and warrant a far more detailed analysis of Britain's Rwanda policy than can be offered here.

Throughout its period in office, John Major's government consistently claimed that Britain was a good international citizen when it came to peacekeeping. In relative terms, Britain did indeed contribute resources to the peacekeeping system, concomitant with its position in the world economy: in June 1994 it was the fourth largest troop contributor and the sixth largest financial

39 See the anecdotes in Dallaire, *Shake Hands With The Devil*, especially pages 113, 182-5, 204-5, 243-4, 273, 323-4. The fact that Belgium was a former colonial power in Rwanda did not help the situation. Indeed Belgian's participation contradicted one of the central norms of UN peacekeeping developed during the Cold War: that states should not serve in missions in their former colonies. This norm had developed out of the recognition that former colonial powers were likely to have vested interests within their former colonies and their soldiers could easily become scapegoats for local propagandists hostile to the UN's presence.

40 Code Cable, "The military assessment of the situation as of 17 April 1994", para. 17.

41 See Dallaire, *Shake Hands With The Devil*.

42 Ibid., 5, 323, 375.

contributor.[43] In absolute terms, however, it was one of the many parties content to starve the peacekeeping system of resources. Indeed, despite the assertions of government officials to the contrary, Britain often failed to pay its peacekeeping contributions on time, including contributions to UNAMIR.[44]

In mid-1994, Britain had almost 3,800 troops engaged in UN peace operations in Cyprus (425), Kuwait (15) and the former Yugoslavia (3,350).[45] These figures highlight two issues: Britain clearly had spare military capacity during the period of the genocide, and Major's government was preoccupied with the war in Bosnia.[46] But even before the genocide, Britain had been reluctant to contribute significant numbers of troops to peace operations outside its areas of immediate interest. For example, Britain did not contribute any soldiers to the UNAVEM II, ONUMOZ, UNOSOM I or UNOSOM II operations in Angola, Mozambique and Somalia, and sent only 122 troops to participate in UNTAC in Cambodia.[47] On the other hand, Britain was interested in helping the DPKO operate more efficiently, and sent eight British military officers to help the DPKO in its work. Apparently, these British soldiers remained in the DPKO throughout the period of the genocide.[48]

Regarding the genocide, British policy towards Rwanda and the wider Great Lakes region must be understood within the context of the government's post-Cold War African policy more generally. After the Cold War, successive Conservative governments reduced the resources devoted to policies toward Africa and cut Britain's diplomatic presence on the continent. By 1994, the continent had become largely the remit of the Overseas Development Administration (ODA) under Baroness Lynda Chalker. Geographically, British policy focused on South Africa and the other large Anglophone states, particularly Nigeria, Kenya, Tanzania, Ghana and Uganda. In economic terms, the objective was to protect Britain's traditional sources of trade and investment on the continent, the majority of which were concentrated in southern and eastern Africa, especially South Africa. Politically, Britain continued its traditional policy of dam-

---

43   D. Hurd, "Why the UN is more important to the world than ever", *Evening Standard*, 20 June 1994. In 1994, the UK was the sixth largest economy in the world ranked in terms of GDP.

44   On 31 January 1994, Britain owed UNAMIR $3.2m in arrears. Knight, "Towards a subsidiarity model for peacemaking and preventive diplomacy", 40.

45   *Britain and UN Peacekeeping*, (London: FCO Background Brief, June 1994).

46   For details of the UK's relevant military capacity see House of Commons Defence Committee, *United Kingdom Peacekeeping and Intervention Forces*, Session 1992–93, 4th Report (London: House of Commons paper 369, 1993).

47   Mr Goodlad, *Hansard* (Commons), Written Answers, 22 April 1993, col. 148.

48   Mark Lennox-Boyd, *Hansard* (Commons), Written Answers, 20 July 1994, col. 233.

age limitation, with London keen to avoid becoming entangled in African crises unless it was absolutely necessary.[49]

Within this context, Britain's engagement with Rwanda was minimal and indirect. Although Major's government is reported to have been part of an international network that supplied the Rwandan government with military equipment,[50] Britain's main priorities in the region lay in Uganda and, to a lesser extent, Zaire, both of which, unlike Rwanda and Burundi, hosted British permanent diplomatic missions. At the time of the genocide, the British High Commissioner to Uganda, Edward Clay, was also non-resident ambassador for Rwanda and Burundi. What interests Britain did have in Rwanda revolved primarily around the relationship of Ugandan President Yoweri Museveni with the RPF, and the potential impact this might have on Anglo-French relations.

This is not to suggest that Britain had no policy towards Rwanda from 1993 to 1994, only that it was of minimal importance to Westminster and Whitehall. Before elaborating on the content of that policy, though, it is important to highlight what appears to be its fundamental contradiction. On the one hand, until very recently, British officials consistently claimed ignorance of what was happening in Rwanda, until early May 1994, when they claim that they adopted a more robust response to the slaughter. Claiming complete ignorance, however, did not mean that British officials sat silently and let other states with better information take the lead in policy-making within the peacekeeping system. Instead, Britain's ambassador to the UN, David Hannay, played a leading role in shaping the Security Council's response to the genocide.[51] Furthermore, throughout the genocide, other British officials and politicians consistently claimed with a remarkable degree of certainty that anything short of massive military intervention would not be able to stop the killings.

The argument that British authorities could genuinely claim ignorance of events in Rwanda has also appeared in the media and academic journals. The Executive Director of the Royal African Society, Richard Dowden, has suggested for example that the British government's "main source of information" about the genocide was CNN.[52] What exactly the British government knew

---

49 For more details see P. Williams, "Britain and Africa after the Cold War: Beyond damage limitation?" in Ian Taylor and Paul Williams (eds), *Africa in International Politics* (London: Routledge, 2004), 41-60.

50 OAU, *Rwanda: The Preventable Genocide* (Report of the International Panel of Eminent Personalities to Investigate the 1994 Genocide in Rwanda appointed by the OAU, July 2000), section 12.27.

51 The first detailed account of Britain's position was Melvern, "Death by Diplomacy". Colin Keating has recently confirmed that Britain's "interventions were clearly in a negative direction". Cited in Keating, "An Insider's Account", 508.

52 Dowden quoted a British diplomat making this argument in "Delay and they die", *The Observer*, 10 November 1996: "As one diplomat said later: 'We were taking our informa-

about events in Rwanda between mid-1993 and mid-1994 is currently unclear, but the idea that the government's "main source of information" was CNN is nonsense. The British government had access to a variety of information sources about what was going on in Rwanda before and during the genocide. First, there were the reports of its own non-resident ambassador to Rwanda, the first of which appeared in late February 1994, with subsequent communications following in the days after the plane crash. Second, between 21 and 23 April, Britain, along with Tanzania, the US and France, was also engaged in an initiative headed by Museveni, to arrange a ceasefire between the belligerents.[53] Third, Rwanda had been the subject of discussion at the Security Council even before the establishment of UNOMUR and UNAMIR, including the likelihood of massacres of civilians.[54] Fourth, the British government may have been receiving some information about Rwanda from their eight military officers on secondment to DPKO, and from their representatives at the World Bank, which sent five missions to Rwanda between June 1991 and October 1993.[55] Fifth, by 4 May 1994, David Clark, the shadow Defence Secretary, had called on the Conservative government to play a more robust role in stopping the "appalling slaughter of innocent people".[56] Sixth, Oxfam issued numerous press releases in Britain, both well before and during the genocide, about what was happening in the country and neighbouring Burundi. Oxfam also took the rare step of naming the violence "genocide" and calling for military intervention to help the victims.[57] In addition, the ODA was aware of the information being distributed by the ICRC's mission in Rwanda as early as 9 April.[58] Seventh, the British

---

tion off CNN. It was humiliating for us, a permanent member of the Security Council, to admit that we had no other source of information'." Dowden subsequently endorsed this diplomat's claim himself in "Comment: The Rwandan Genocide: How the Press Missed the Story. A Memoir", *African Affairs*, 103 (2004), 286.

53   A negotiation conference was arranged to take place in Arusha on 23 April. Interview with British official, December 2003 and Code Cable "Urgent requirement to reduce UNAMIR", para. 1.

54   S/PV.3244, 22 June 1993, 4.

55   On 19 April, the British government claimed, "Ministry of Defence staff have not been involved in United Nations contingency planning sanctioned operations in Rwanda. [Nor has ...] the Secretary of State for Defence ... had any discussions with either his NATO or UN counterparts relating to the situation in Rwanda". Cited in *Hansard* (Commons), 19 April 1994, Written Answers, col. 509. On the World Bank see Melvern, *A People Betrayed*, 66-68.

56   Dr David Clark, MP, Shadow Secretary of State for Defence, "Labour calls for military assistance for Rwanda", news release, 4 May 1994.

57   For more details see B. M. Rahman, "Constructing Humanitarianism: An investigation into Oxfam's changing humanitarian culture, 1942-1994" (Unpublished PhD thesis, University of Wales, Aberystwyth, 1999), Ch. 7.

58   Interview with British official, November 2003.

journalist Mark Doyle was in Kigali, and was writing a stream of reports for the BBC—with Dallaire's full cooperation and support.[59] And eighth, the RPF's representatives in New York, especially Claude Dusaidi, delivered detailed information to the members of the Security Council, including the British government, about militia training, arms caches, political murders, hate propaganda, and death lists in the weeks before the genocide, and daily updates of how events were unfolding after the plane crash.[60] The extent to which the British government chose to listen to these information sources and shape its policy accordingly remains unclear.

Before the genocide, British policy was to support the Arusha peace process and the resulting Accord. However, Britain was not keen on supporting a well-resourced and sizeable UN peace operation to help guarantee the Accord's implementation. In late February 1994 Britain, along with the US, opposed Belgium's proposal to the Secretariat and the Security Council to increase the size of UNAMIR and the strength of its mandate. This decision was apparently taken "for financial reasons".[61] The British government's main priority at this stage was the war in Bosnia, especially events around the "safe area" in Gorazde. As the Foreign Secretary Douglas Hurd reflected at the time, "I could not honestly list Rwanda among the major preoccupations at the Foreign Office."[62] Claiming that it was overstretched, Britain never publicly contemplated contributing troops to UNAMIR.[63]

Once the genocide erupted, the British government's immediate priority was to evacuate its nationals, including the honorary consul, David Wood, who left on 12 April. In the immediate aftermath of the plane crash and the deaths of the ten Belgian peacekeepers on 7 April, Britain and Belgium led the calls for UNAMIR to withdraw.[64] It was true, as Hannay suggested, that the Security Council was confronted with a rapidly haemorrhaging UNAMIR after a considerable portion of its troops (notably the Belgian and Bangladeshi con-

---

59   Dallaire, *Shake Hands With The Devil*, 332, 364. It should be noted, however, that Doyle's reports did not concentrate upon the slaughter of civilians.

60   Melvern, *Conspiracy to Murder*, 218, 259.

61   Belgian Senate, *Commission d'enquête parlementaire concernant les événements du Rwanda*. Report, 6 Dec. 1997, cited in Melvern, *A People Betrayed*, 104 and OAU, *Rwanda: The Preventable Genocide*, section 9.13. In spite of the financial constraints, Major's government contributed emergency aid to Rwanda and Burundi totalling £12m between February 1993 and June 1994: Cited in Douglas Hurd, *Hansard* (Commons), 25 April 1994, Oral Answers, col. 16.

62   Douglas Hurd, *Memoirs* (London: Little, Brown, 2003), 488.

63   Hurd recently made the extraordinary claim that "It never occurred to us, the Americans or anyone to send combatant troops to Rwanda to stop the killing. I record this as a bleak fact": Cited in ibid., 488-9.

64   OAU, *The Preventable Genocide*, section 15.11 and 15.49.

tingents) were withdrawn by their national governments.[65] Nevertheless, the resulting compromise codified in Resolution 912 (21 April), authorising UN-AMIR's reduction to a skeleton force of 270 personnel,[66] was not the only possible course of action the Security Council could have taken.[67] But this course of action fitted with the British government's depiction of events as an ethnic civil war between morally equivalent factions. It also reflected Britain's preferred solution for stopping the violence: a ceasefire between the RPF and government forces that would create a space for humanitarian assistance.[68] Finally, this course of action supported the British government's understanding of the internal rules of the peacekeeping system. After all, if there was no peace to keep, with both sides to the civil war rejecting a ceasefire, then UNAMIR—a Chapter VI peacekeeping force—had no business being there at all. In the crucial month of April, the British government's representatives emphasised the importance of the peacekeeping system's rules, and studiously avoided any public mention of the word "genocide", or discussion of Britain's obligations under the Genocide Convention. The latter subject did not come up for discussion until June, and only then because President Clinton had mentioned it in a meeting with John Major at Chequers.[69] The subsequent discussion was apparently not serious enough to warrant the participation of Sir Franklin Berman, the Foreign and Commonwealth Office's Legal Advisor.[70]

By mid-May, British policy altered to supporting the expansion of UNAMIR II under Resolution 918 of 17 May 1994. Until September 1994, the British government still refused to officially recognise that genocide was taking place.[71] But it now claimed to see the need for a reinforced UNAMIR, primarily as a means to provide greater humanitarian assistance. However, Britain, along with many other states, offered no troops for UNAMIR II.[72] Instead, the government offered 50 Bedford trucks—initially on condition of payment upfront, although this demand was later withdrawn. Dallaire recalled that when a British official informed him of this "most generous" offer, he "satirically asked,

---

65   Interview, Birmingham, 12 March 2003.

66   In reality, 456 peacekeepers remained.

67   In the weeks before Resolution 912, Dallaire provided the UN with a variety of operational scenarios and concomitant force structures. See, for example, Code Cable, "Concept and plan for options of retention of UNAMIR", Dallaire (Kigali) to Annan (New York), 14 April 1994.

68   See the statements to that effect by Mark Lennox-Boyd in *Hansard* (Commons), 20 April 1994, Written Answers, col. 538 and 21 April 1994, Written Answers, col. 613.

69   Anthony Seldon, *Major: A Political Life* (London: Weidenfeld & Nicolson, 1997), 467.

70   Interview, British official, November 2003.

71   Wong, op. cit.

72   The first troops of UNAMIR II took over three months to arrive.

'They do work, don't they?'" to which Dallaire said he was "answered first with silence, and then: 'I'll check and get back to you'." Some trucks did eventually arrive in Rwanda, but each broke down until all of them were unusable.[73] One week after Resolution 918, the Conservative MP Mark Lennox-Boyd told Parliament, "the United Kingdom was at the forefront of those insisting that the United Nations should remain engaged to the maximum extent feasible."[74]

After the RPF defeated the government forces and stopped the genocide, the British government increased its humanitarian assistance and emergency aid to the region. Most of these supplies were not channelled to the survivors of the genocide within Rwanda, but to the refugees and *génocidaires* in the numerous camps outside of Rwanda, especially in Zaire and Tanzania. Between August and November 1994, while the war in Bosnia continued unabated, the British government managed to further stretch its armed forces and deployed over 600 soldiers to Rwanda to provide medical assistance, vehicle maintenance, and bridge and road reconstruction.[75] In addition, Britain established an embassy in Rwanda, which, by all accounts, was successful largely because of the efforts of one British official.

When asked to reflect upon Britain's Rwanda policy in 1993 and 1994—and it is important to remember that most of the politicians making the decisions at the time have failed to publicly reflect upon this issue[76]—British officials have shifted their position slightly, and now claim that confusion combined with a lack of vision, rather than genuine ignorance, accounts for the government's failures.[77] As one decision-maker put it, "We weren't indifferent—it's just that we didn't know what to do."[78]

Conclusion

After the Cold War, the international society raised expectations about its willingness and ability to maintain peace and security, not just between states, but

---

73   Dallaire, *Shake Hands With The Devil*, 376.

74   *Hansard* (Commons), 24 May 1994, col. 313.

75   Unfortunately, the first units in what was known as Operation Gabriel arrived without adequate vehicle support and its substantial medical team arrived without medicines suitable for treating the local population and had to use supplies provided by a French NGO. See "Humanitarian Aid and Effects", Study 3, *The International Response to Conflict and Genocide: Lessons from the Rwanda Experience* (Copenhagen: DANIDA, 1996), Ch. 3.6.

76   For the ways in which the British establishment has collectively forgotten the genocide and Britain's response to it, see L. Melvern and P. Williams, "Britannia Waived the Rules: The Major Government and the 1994 Rwandan Genocide", *African Affairs*, 103 (2004), 11-20.

77   Wong, op. cit.

78   Cited in Melvern, *Conspiracy to Murder*, 261.

also within them. Yet it refused to provide anything more than token resources for a peacekeeping system that proved completely inadequate for the tasks demanded of it. By 1994, the international society had constructed a peacekeeping system that might have salved the consciences of the great powers, enough to make them believe their own "Never again!" rhetoric, but proved inadequate for rescuing victims of genocide. Britain was among the many states responsible for this situation. But, as a permanent member of the Security Council, Britain bears a heavier burden of responsibility than most states. Without access to all of the necessary information, it is impossible to deliver a final verdict on Dallaire's accusations that the British government pursued indifferent, selfish and racist policies towards Rwanda, aided and abetted the genocide, and sabotaged UNAMIR's efforts to fulfil its mandate. Nevertheless, it is clear that John Major's government failed to even countenance sending soldiers to save the victims of genocide. It is our collective responsibility to ensure that the British government lives up to the "Never again!" rhetoric that it espouses.

PART II
POLITICS OF MEMORY, IDENTITY AND HEALING

4

THE POLITICS OF MEMORY IN POST-GENOCIDE RWANDA

René Lemarchand[1]

"Never again! *Plus jamais!*" The message—so often heard, so seldom heeded—was delivered loud and clear to those present in the *Amahoro* stadium in Kigali, on 7 April 2004, on the tenth anniversary of one of the most monstrous bloodbaths of the last century. Relayed through public speeches, survivors' reminiscences, multiple banners, even the name of the venue—"Peace"—gave symbolic significance to that defining moment.

This was a time to remember the enormity of the crimes committed a decade before, while the international community looked the other way. This was a time for all Rwandans to commune in remembrance of their common suffering; a time for recognition. Unlike a similar occasion in 1995 when posthumous homage was paid to Hutu and Tutsi victims, this time, as in previous years, Kagame's discourse, in turn mournful and accusatory, made no mention of ethnic identities. To do so would have been superfluous and, in any case, contrary to the public ban on all references to ethnicity. There are no Hutu or Tutsi in today's Rwanda, only Banyarwanda.

To justify this drastic reconfiguration of collective identities, Rwandan officials are prompt to point out that the aim of the state at this critical juncture is to build a nation, and the first step towards this daunting task is to do away with ethnic labels once and for all. The logic of the argument is straightforward: "If awareness of ethnic differences can be learned, so too can the idea that ethnicity does not exist."[2] The rationale is equally clear: "divisionism"—ethnic,

---

1   A version of this chapter appears in R. Lemarchand, *The Dynamics of Violence in Central Africa*, Philadelphia: University of Pennsylvania Press, 2008.

2   M. Lacey, "Rwanda: There is no ethnicity there", *International Herald Tribune* (10 April

regional and political—has been the bane of Rwanda, and indeed the root cause of the genocide; the time has come to lay the foundation for a national community free of the stigma of ethnicity. This is why the crime of "division-ism" has been added to the penal code: besides providing the government with a convenient weapon to ban almost any type of organised opposition, it offers the new nation-builders a unique opportunity to legislate ethnic identities out of existence.

Although there are obvious and compelling reasons to remember the atroci-ties of 1994, the question is whether the exclusion of ethnic memories for the sake of a spuriously unifying official memory can bring the people of Rwan-da—Hutu, Tutsi and Twa—any closer to building the mutual trust necessary for a peaceful coexistence. Reconciliation, assuming it can ever be achieved, requires that the past be confronted, not obliterated. Recognition that guilt and victimisation transcend ethnic boundaries is not enough. No less crucial is how ethnic and individual memories alter perceptions of the past, and by implication the writing of history. What follows is an attempt to explore the politics of memory in post-genocide Rwanda in the light of the categories proposed by Paul Ricoeur—thwarted memory, manipulated memory and en-forced memory.[3]

The ambivalence of ethnic memory

Memory—official or ethnic, collective or individual—is a pre-eminently sub-jective phenomenon. It blurs the boundaries between fact and fiction, between factual truth and interpretive truth. Blind spots, ethnic amnesia, denials of his-torical evidence operate to mask unpalatable truths and magnify others out of proportion. "Memory," writes Stanley Cohen, "is a social product, reflecting the agenda and social location of those who invoke it."[4] This is true not only of the official memory invoked by the Kagame government, but of the ethnic and individual memories summoned by perpetrators and victims alike. In these conditions the distinction between good faith and bad faith is not always easy to pin down. The reason for this is nowhere more convincingly articulated than by Primo Levi, in his penetrating commentary on "the memory of the offense"[5]:

There are those who lie consciously, coldly falsifying reality itself, but more numerous are those who weigh anchor, move off, momentarily or forever, from genuine memories, and fabricate for themselves a convenient reality. The past is a burden to them; they feel repugnance for things done or suffered and tend to replace them with others. The substi-

---

2004), 2.

3   P. Ricoeur, *La Mémoire, l'Histoire, l'Oubli* (Paris: Le Seuil, 2002).

4   S. Cohen, *States of Denial* (Cambridge: Polity, 2001), 241.

5   P. Levi, *The Drowned and the Saved,* trans. Raymond Rosenthal (New York: Vintage Books , 1989), 27.

tution may begin in full awareness, with an invented scenario, mendacious, restored, but less painful than the real one; they repeat the description to others but also to themselves, and the distinction between true and false progressively loses its contours, and man ends by fully believing the story he has told so many times and continues to tell, polishing and retouching here and there the details which are least credible or incongruous or incompatible with the acquired picture of historically accepted events: initial bad faith has become good faith.

Anyone familiar with the discourse of the more radically inclined members of the Hutu and Tutsi communities on the roots of the genocide cannot fail to note the pertinence of Levi's comments: the "memory of the offence," whether falsified or fabricated, is always selective, and thus acts as a key mechanism in the construction of a "convenient reality."

The clash of ethnic memories is an essential component of the process by which the legacy of genocide—the "memory of the offence"—is being perceived or fabricated by one community or the other. Once filtered through the prism of ethnicity, entirely different constructions are imposed on the same ghastly reality, from which emerge strikingly divergent interpretations of why genocide occurred.

Not only is the past seen through a different ethnic lens, but there are also major differences *among* Hutu and Tutsi in the way in which it is remembered, or forgotten. There are those fortunate ones, overwhelmingly Tutsi, who survived the carnage and witnessed at close range the horrors of genocide, who saw friends and neighbours and members of their own families shot, speared, clubbed to death, or hacked to pieces by mobs of enraged Hutu youth. And there are the *Inkotanyi*, Kagame's refugee warriors, who killed tens of thousands of Hutu civilians in "liberated" zones and, according to credible testimonies from Rwandan Patriotic Army (RPA) defectors, did not shrink from inflicting horrendous tortures on their suspected enemies.[6]

There are the blood-soaked Hutu *génocidaires*, and there are the heroes who risked or lost their lives in order to save their Tutsi neighbours. And there are those countless, anonymous Hutu who were witnesses to the cold-blooded killings perpetrated by Kagame's troops in Rwanda and eastern Zaire (now the Democratic Republic of Congo, DRC).[7] All, to some extent, experience the same dysfunctions of memory and emotional traumas, so tellingly explored by Liisa Malkki among survivors of the 1972 genocide of Hutu in Burundi.[8]

---

6   See in particular Abdul Ruzibiza's devastating testimony, *Témoignage destiné a démontrer les erreurs commises par le gouvernement rwandais et le FPR qui ont permis la possibilité d'un génocide*, Brennasen, Norway (2004),18-19.

7   See Refugees International, *The Lost Refugees: Herded and Hunted in Eastern Zaire* (Washington, September 1997).

8   L. Malkki, *Purity and Exile: Violence, Memory and National Cosmogony and Hutu Refugees in Tanzania* (Chicago, IL, University of Chicago Press, 1995).

Finally, there are the ideologues who manipulate the historical record for political purposes. They are found on both sides of the ethnic divide, and beyond. Even in the absence of ulterior political motives, deliberate travesty of the facts is not uncommon among foreign observers. A case in point is Helmut Strizek, who, in a conference at the Sorbonne, on 6 April 2004, denied that the killings were planned, thereby implicitly denying the existence of a genocide. Christian Davenport, professor of political science at the University of Notre Dame, also contests the appropriateness of the term "genocide", arguing that what occurred was a "totalitarian purge, a politicide rather than ethnic cleansing or genocide." Moreover, the majority of the victims, according to Davenport, were Hutu, not Tutsi:

Our research strongly suggests that a majority of the victims were Hutu – there weren't enough Tutsi in Rwanda at the time to account for all reported deaths... Either the scale of the killing was much less than is widely believed, or, more likely, a huge number of Hutu were caught up in the violence as inadvertent victims. The evidence suggests the killers didn't try to figure to out who everybody was. They erred on the side of comprehensiveness.[9]

Such assertions are enthusiastically received by some Hutu deniers, all too eager to bolster their claims by quoting from European "authorities." One example among others of Hutu *négationisme* can be found in the statement released on 21 March 2004 by the *Association des Rescapés du Génocide des Réfugiés Rwandais en République Démocratique du Congo*, which states: "Since there is no proof that the genocide was planned... how can one say that a genocide has been directed against the Tutsi of Rwanda in 1994?" Leaks to the press of the report by the French investigating magistrate, Jean-Louis Bruguière[10]—in which strong circumstantial evidence implicates Kagame in the shooting down of Habyarimana's plane, on 6 April 1994—have given a new slant to the argument advanced by Hutu deniers: the mass murder of Tutsi was the direct outcome of the dastardly plot concocted by the RPF, and thus has nothing to do with the planning imputed to extremist Hutu elements. If one can speak of genocide, the argument goes, the responsibility lies squarely with Kagame. A closer look at the evidence reveals a more complex reality. Nonetheless, critical questions remain about the role of Kagame in paving the ground for the carnage, including those raised by Bruguière in his, as yet unpublished, report.[11]

---

9   See M. Green, "Rwanda Killings Weren't 'Genocide' – US Study," Kigali: Reuters, 3 April 2004, http://www.inshuti.org/davenpo.htm. See also www.genodynamics.com.

10   See S. Smith, "Révélations sur l'attentat qui a déclenché le génocide rwandais", *Le Monde* (10 March 2004), 1-3. For an English-language summary version, see S. Smith, "Rwandan president implicated in death of predecessor by French magistrate", *Guardian Weekly* (25-31 March 2004), 31.

11   At the time of writing, only excerpts of the report have been published.

Thwarted memory

There are many ways in which memory departs from reality. In his magisterial work on *Memory, History and Oblivion*, Paul Ricoeur refers to "thwarted memory, manipulated memory and enforced memory" (*"mémoire empêchée, mémoire manipulée, mémoire abusivement commandée"*). Our fixation on *"le devoir de mémoire"*, the "duty to remember", he argues, makes us lose sight of a more urgent task, which he calls *"le travail de mémoire"*, the "labour of memory", which involves a more sustained effort to probe the relationship between history and memory, and between memory and recognition. This is also Eva Hoffman's point when she writes, "the injunctions to remember, if reiterated too often, can become formulaic—an injunction precisely not to think or grapple with the past."[12] Thinking or grappling with the past is what is conspicuously missing from Rwanda's official memory—in other words, a sustained effort to recognise the profound ambivalence of the notion of guilt. What persists to this day, in Cohen's words, is "collective memory pressed into shape by being repressed."[13]

Ricoeur's notion of thwarted memory gives a clue to an understanding of the many blind spots in Rwanda's official memory. What is being thwarted through the ban on ethnic identities is the memory of atrocities endured by Hutu and Tutsi, where ethnicity, though singularly unhelpful for discriminating between victims and perpetrators, is crucial for addressing the roots of the injuries suffered by each community.

What is being thwarted is the memory of those generally referred to as "Hutu moderates", a "ubiquitous, undefined phrase", as Nigel Eltringham correctly shows, which "fails to communicate the pro-active resistance these actors demonstrated."[14] Among them were Prime Minister Agathe Uwilingiyimana, three government ministers, the president of the Constitutional Court, the entire leadership of the *Parti Social Démocrate* (PSD), 49 journalists killed because they aired criticisms of the genocidal crusade, and scores of human rights activists, along with tens of thousands of Hutu killed by other Hutu for no other reason than they happened to belong to an opposition party, or because they happened to look Tutsi, or because their spouses were Tutsi. What is being thwarted is the memory of those Hutu who steadfastly refused to surrender their Tutsi friends and neighbours to the militias, who gave them shelter and protection at considerable risk to themselves and their families.

---

12   E. Hoffman, "The Balm of Recognition", in Nicholas Owen (ed.), *Human Rights, Human Wrongs* (Oxford, UK: Oxford University Press, 1999), 296.

13   Cohen, *States of Denial,* 138.

14   N. Eltringham, *Accounting for Horror: Post-Genocide Debates in Rwanda* (London: Pluto Press, 2004), 97.

Exemplary is the story of Damas Mutezintare, a Hutu who saved nearly 400 Tutsi lives—300 children and 80 adults—in his orphanage at Nyamirambo. "I haven't done anything special," he told the correspondent of *La Libre Belgique*, Marie-France Cros. "I just said to myself I've got to do something, but I wasn't sure what the results would be... I've been lucky."[15] Not all such heroes were lucky enough to live to tell their story.

Summoning a de-ethnicised, victim-centred memory is not enough; what has yet to be given proper recognition is that Hutu and Tutsi were victims of a calamity, for which responsibility is shared by elements of both communities. This sharing of responsibility is what Rwanda's official ideologues refuse to acknowledge. Instead, every effort is made to manipulate memory, so as to exonerate the ruling elites of all responsibility in the circumstances that led to the abyss. Complex though they are, a key element in the chain of events leading to the butchery is the outbreak of the bitter civil war instigated by the RPF.

Manipulated memory

"*Tous les autres sont coupables, sauf moi*" ("All others are guilty except me"): Céline's phrase[16] provides a subtext to Kagame's commemorative discourse on 7 April 2004. There are excellent reasons for lambasting the ignominious attitude of the French government throughout the crisis, as Kagame does, as well as the culpable indifference of the international community and the disastrous consequences of Belgian colonial policies. Predictably, however, nothing was said of the responsibility borne by Kagame himself in unleashing the civil war that led to the genocide. This is not to deny the very obvious culpability of the Hutu *génocidaires* and their leaders in planning, organising and carrying out the murder of approximately 800,000 people, only to underscore that the climate of fear and paranoia created by the civil war did at least as much as *Radio Télévision Libre des Mille Collines* to heighten the receptivity of Hutu extremists to a "final solution". Again, it is not insignificant that among the one million Hutu internally displaced persons (IDPs) forced out of their homelands by incoming RPF troops[17]—most of them living in utterly inhuman conditions in makeshift refugee camps—many enthusiastically joined the killing spree. The key point here is that there would have been no genocide had Kagame not decided to unleash his refugee warriors on 1 October 1990, in

---

15   M.-F. Cros, "Portrait d'un juste", *La Libre Belgique* (5 April 2004), 12.

16   Quoted by P. Bruckner, *La Tentation de l'Innocence* (Paris: Grasset, 2001).

17   For a graphic description of the devastating attacks mounted by RPF troops on IDP camps, see "Rwanda: SOS pour une guerre oubliée", *La Croix* (25 February 1992), 3, which quotes extensively from the report written by a group of missionaries ("*Les prêtres du doyenné du Mutara crient la détresse des victimes de la guerre*" [10 February 1992]).

violation of the most elementary principle of international law. If he deserves full credit for stopping the killings, it can just as convincingly be argued that he bears much of the responsibility for provoking them.

Tempting as it is to see in President Kagame's government the embodiment of moral virtue for bringing the genocide to an end, the mourning of Tutsi lives must not be allowed to obscure the crimes against humanity committed by Kagame's army. If, as claimed by the UN-commissioned Gersony Report, between 25,000 and 45,000 Hutu were massacred by the RPA in only three *communes* of Rwanda between the months of April and August 1994,[18] how many were similarly killed in the whole of Rwanda during the same period?

Again, the systematic extermination by Rwandan troops in the eastern DRC of tens of thousands of Hutu refugees—conveniently lumped together as "*génocidaires*"—has been virtually "airbrushed out of history", to use Milan Kundera's phrase. Stephen Smith, in his absorbing sketches of Congolese history, estimates at 200,000 the number of Hutu killed in the course of search-and-destroy operations conducted by the RPA in 1996 and 1997, of whom "800 were machine-gunned in broad daylight in the port city of Mbandaka on May 16, 1997, the day Laurent-Désiré Kabila captured the capital."[19] Are we to assume that these victims of Kagame's "security imperative" are to be left out of the macabre accounting of 1994?

Admittedly, whether the killings in the eastern DRC can be seen as genocide is open to debate. The terms "war crimes" and "crimes against humanity", rather than "genocide", are generally used to describe the systematic elimination of refugee populations after the destruction of their camps in 1996. Nonetheless, the June 1998 UN report on violations of human rights in the DRC does not shrink from evoking the "G-word", but adds a cautionary note: "the killings perpetrated by the *Alliance des Forces Démocratiques* (AFDL) constitute crimes against humanity, as did the denial of humanitarian assistance to Hutu refugees. The members of the team feel that certain types of murder could constitute acts of genocide, depending on the intention of the perpetrators, and request that such crimes and their motives become the object of further investigation."[20] Arguably, even in the absence of wholesale massacres comparable to those perpetrated against Tutsi in 1994, the thoroughly inhuman treatment visited upon Hutu refugees would fit Helen Fein's definition of "genocide by attrition", which occurs "after a group is

---

18   See A. Des Forges, *Leave None to Tell the Story*, (New York: Human Rights Watch and Federation Internationale des Droits de l'Homme, 1999), 726-s9.

19   S. Smith, *Le Fleuve Congo*, (Paris: Actes Sud, 2003), 95.

20   "UN Report of the investigative team charged with investigating serious violations of human rights and international humanitarian law in the DRC", quoted in *Dialogue*, 206 (1998), 79.

singled out for political and civil discrimination. It is separated from the larger society, and its right to life is threatened through concentration and forced displacement, together with systematic deprivation of food, water, and sanitary and medical facilities."[21]

Enforced memory

If there is ample evidence that the regime is manipulating the historical record for the sake of an official memory, in what sense can one speak of an enforced memory? To start with, in a legal sense the decree regarding discourse on ethnicity rules out public expressions of ethnic memory. Suggestions that Tutsi killed Hutu or that Hutu killed Tutsi are subject to the same legal sanctions, regardless of the commonly accepted truth that Tutsi is synonymous with victim and Hutu with perpetrator. The writing of history, like the summoning of memories, thus takes on the quality of a fairy tale, where ethnic identifications rarely come to the surface.

No less important examples of enforced memory are the rituals of the annual genocide commemoration, which again unfold as a tribute to victims whose ethnic identity hardly needs to be mentioned. As Claudine Vidal points out, "at every commemoration, those in power have instrumentalised the representation of the genocide in the context of the political conflict at the time." Vidal continues, "The commemorations explicitly deny the status of victim to those Hutu who, even though they did not kill, were massacred so as to create a climate of terror. How can one speak of reconciliation when the exposure of skeletons has as its only purpose to remind the Tutsi that their own people were killed by Hutu? This is tantamount to keeping the latter in a permanent position of culpability."[22] This is a telling commentary on how the selectivity of public memory helps nurture ethnic enmities. As Vidal explicitly suggests, in essence, the official history inscribed in the commemoration ceremonies is meant to give ideological legitimacy to the consolidation of Tutsi power. The elimination of public references to ethnic identity conveniently erases from the record the memory of Hutu victims, or those "righteous" Hutu who died protecting Tutsi friends and neighbours. The only category left are the *génocidaires*.

The instrumentalisation of genocide—of which the commemoration rituals are but one example—has been the subject of scathing criticisms by three well-known experts, Vidal, Rony Brauman, and Smith. They convincingly argue that public sympathy for the victims of the genocide and, more importantly,

---

21   H. Fein, "Genocide by Attrition in the Sudan and Elsewhere", *The Institute for the Study of Genocide Newsletter*, 29 (Fall 2002), 7.

22   C. Vidal, "Les commémorations du génocide au Rwanda", *Les Temps Modernes* (2001), 613.

for the successor government that stopped the genocide has been instrumentalised in ways that allow the Kagame government to commit further crimes with impunity. "The global criminalisation of the Hutu community," they write, "poses a major threat to civil peace... Every Hutu is suspect since his community bears the onus of guilt for the genocide... The official history of genocide makes no reference to Hutu victims or Hutu survivors, or those Hutu who saved Tutsi lives at their own peril."[23] What Filip Reyntjens calls "the genocide credit"[24] enjoyed by Kagame has helped deflect attention from the crimes committed by the RPF, and to win the current Rwandan government the sympathies of an international community all too eager to atone for its shameful behaviour during the genocide. To a considerable extent, the skill with which the Rwandan authorities have capitalised on this "genocide credit" goes far in explaining the reluctance of most outside observers to criticise Kagame's human rights record, including his suppression of ethnic identities by decree (as if one could change society by decree!). Enforced ethnic amnesia is the most formidable obstacle to reconciliation, because it rules out the process of reckoning by which each community must confront its past and come to terms with its share of responsibility for the horrors of 1994.

The work of memory: recognition and reconciliation

What, then, is the relationship between the politics of memory and the prospects for national reconciliation in Rwanda? The short answer is that this relationship is highly problematic. To speak of national reconciliation as a realistic short-term goal is to make exceedingly short shrift of the gaping wounds each community has inflicted on the other. They will take generations to heal. The scars will remain forever etched into the collective consciousness of Hutu and Tutsi. But if forgiveness is not to be expected any time soon, can one find a redemptive element in what Eva Hoffman calls "recognition", that is, a "reckoning with the past", where "recognition of what actually happened – of the victims' experience and the perpetrators' responsibility, and ultimately the broader structures of cause and effect – can allow some healing to take place"?[25]

What makes the "duty to remember" so problematic as a path to reconciliation is that the phrase leaves out the crucial questions: What is to be remembered? How? By whom? And for what purpose?

---

23   R. Brauman, S. Smith and C. Vidal, "Rwanda: Politique de terreur, privilège d'impunité", *Esprit* (August-September 2000), 155.

24   F. Reyntjens, "Rwanda, Ten Years On: From Genocide to Dictatorship", *African Affairs*, 103 (2004), 199.

25   Hoffman, "The Balm of Recognition", 280.

No one was more dutifully conscious of the obligation to remember than President Kagame on 7 April 2004. But what was being remembered, in effect, was the collective agony of the Tutsi, not also the sufferings and losses of the Hutu. The exclusion of Hutu victims from Rwanda's official memory can only strengthen the conviction of the majority of the population, that the genocide has been shamefully instrumentalised for the benefit of the regime. "Memory is blind to all but the group it binds," writes Pierre Nora, "which is to say... that there are as many memories as there are groups, that memory is by nature multiple and yet specific, collective, plural and yet individual."[26] There is Kagame's official memory, "blind to all but the group it binds," and there is Hutu memory. There is Tutsi memory (which is not necessarily synonymous with official memory) and a plurality of memories among Hutu and Tutsi. Each must find its place in the annual mourning ceremonies of 7 April; oblivion is not an option if the promise of "never again!" is to be fulfilled.

What could be seen as the obvious alternative—giving free rein to ethnic memories—is no less problematic. These can be just as selective in their choice of victims, just as biased in their apportioning of blame, just as blind to the larger historical picture as official memories. This is made cruelly clear in some of the statements and *prises de position* issued by the more militant Hutu refugee organisations in exile.

A more fruitful approach is the one explored by Hoffman, in her wonderfully sensitive essay on "The Balm of Recognition". Commenting on "the current rhetoric," she writes,

Memory always stands for victimological memory, embraced by particular groups, and foregrounding the darkest episodes of various pasts... And yet there is something that troubles me about the current discourse of memory...[T]he uses of collective memory to bolster a group's identity, or a fixed identification with parental victimhood, seem sometimes to verge on a kind of appropriation or bad faith... What we see is the marshalling of victimological, defensive memory for the purposes of aggression.[27]

Instead, she invites us "to look beyond the fixed moment of trauma to those longer historical patterns, to supplement partisan memory with a more complex and encompassing view of history—a view that might examine the common history of the antagonistic groups and that might, among other things, enable us to question and criticise dubious and propagandistic uses of collective memory."[28]

Recognition in this sense means more than mere remembrance; it means coming to terms with the unspeakable atrocities inflicted on Hutu and Tutsi,

---

26   P. Nora, "Between Memory and History: Les Lieux de Mémoire", *Representations*, 26 (Spring 1989), 8.

27   Hoffman, 296-7.

28   Ibid., 302.

by Hutu and Tutsi; it means "to name wrongs as wrongs and to bring some of those responsible to account"[29] irrespective of ethnic identities; it means addressing the traumas experienced by the tens of thousands of survivors (and indeed many of the perpetrators); it means placing the horrors of genocide in the perspective of the broader historical forces that have led to violence. All of this and more are included in what Ricoeur has in mind when he urges upon us the exigencies of a *"travail de mémoire"*.

The phrase, Ricoeur tells us, harks back to Freud's concept of *Durcharbeiten* (which he translates as *"translaboration"*), which he used to call attention to the obstacles to the psychoanalytic cure, raised by the obsessive, repetitive memory of traumatising moments.[30] In Ricoeur's discourse it brings into focus the need for a "critical use of memory." Rather than a one-sided compulsive urge to rehash the sufferings endured by one group at the hands of the other, or allowing them to slip into oblivion, working through memory is first and foremost an exercise in narrative history. It aims at "narrating differently the stories of the past, telling them from the point of view of the other—the other, my friend or my enemy." As alternative perceptions are brought into view, past events take on a different meaning:

Past events cannot be erased: one cannot undo what has been done, nor prevent what has happened. On the other hand, the meaning of what happened, whether inflicted by us unto others, or by them upon us, is not fixed once and for all... Thus what is changed about the past is its moral freight (*sa charge morale*), the weight of the debt it carries... This is how the working of memory opens the way to forgiveness to the extent that it settles a debt by changing the very meaning of the past.

Both Ricoeur and Hoffman are sceptical of injunctions to remember; both reject the notion of oblivion as a vector of forgiveness; and both are aware of the need to give a central place to the claims of a "critical memory", immune to appropriation and manipulation.

Under any circumstances, the search for a critical memory in post-genocide Rwanda would be difficult enough, given the radically different narratives through which the past is interpreted. With the ban on ethnicity decreed by Kagame, the prospects are even bleaker. Enforced memory in today's Rwanda does more than suppress ethnic identities; it rules out "recognition" and makes the search for a "critical memory" an exercise likely to be denounced as a source of "divisionism" and therefore liable to legal sanctions. Ironically, while aimed at eliminating the "divisions of the past," the decree on ethnicity makes them all the more pregnant with mutual enmities. The imposition of an official memory, purged of ethnic references, is not just a convenient ploy to mask the

---

29   Ibid., 281.

30   P. Ricoeur, "Le pardon peut-il guérir?" *Esprit* (March-April 1995), 78.

brutal realities of ethnic discrimination; it institutionalises a mode of thought control profoundly antithetical to any kind of inter-ethnic dialogue aimed at a rethinking of the atrocities of mass murder. This is hardly the way to bring Hutu and Tutsi closer together in a common understanding of their tragic past.

5

RECONSTRUCTING POLITICAL IDENTITIES IN RWANDA

Helen Hintjens[1]

"race" has indeed become a fratricidal word [2]

...the caricature of manichean, collective categories still permeates representations of Rwanda. It cannot be overstated that giving contemporary credence to this simplistic image grants a posthumous victory to those who planned, propagated and perpetrated the 1994 genocide.[3]

Introduction

This chapter considers whether the transitional Government of National Unity has been able to reconstruct Rwandan political identities along non-racial lines a decade and a half after the genocide. During the genocide itself, the "local peasants in the hills, manipulated by the state to kill their erstwhile neighbours" were split irreconcilably along race lines.[4] In the aftermath of genocide, the question is how new forms of political identity can be forged that will enable Rwandans to live together in relative security.

---

1   An earlier version of this chapter was presented as a paper at the conference, "Why Neighbours Kill: Explaining the Breakdown of Ethnic Relations", University of Western Ontario, 4-5 June 2004. Thanks to David Kiwuwa (Department of Politics, University of Nottingham) for his help and encouragement with this chapter.

2   A. Montagu, *Man's Most Dangerous Myth: The Fallacy of Race*, 3rd edn. (New York: Harper & Brothers, 1953), 85.

3   N. Eltringham, *Accounting for Horror: Post-Genocide Debates in Rwanda* (London: Pluto Press, 2004), 100.

4   R. Karegyesa, Keynote speech delivered by Senior Trial Attorney Office of the Prosecutor of the ICTR on behalf of the Chief Prosecutor of the ICTR, Justice Hassan Bubacar Jallow, at the Conference: "The Rwandan Genocide and Transitional Justice: Commemorating the 10th Anniversary of the Genocide", organised by Phil Clark and Zachary D. Kaufman, St Antony's College, University of Oxford, 15 May 2004.

For ten years prior to the new constitution and the democratic elections of 2003, the past had been "looking over the shoulders" of ordinary Rwandans. The genocide haunts them, and the regime in power does not always represent what the current leaders and inhabitants claim they want to achieve: peace, good governance, order and security. Some critics warn that successive electoral majorities gained by President Paul Kagame and his party have created an illusion of national unity that is highly deceptive. When Kagame obtained around 95 per cent of the presidential vote in the August 2003, some viewed this as the result of relatively fair elections.[5] One newspaper report lauded Kagame for "generosity on an unimaginable scale" for releasing 40,000 genocide suspects from Rwandan prisons just months before the election.[6] However, the vote was viewed with suspicion by Kagame's critics, who complained that he had a complete stranglehold on state power, and alleged intimidation at the polls.[7] According to his critics, Kagame routinely uses the intelligence services to repress and discredit his political opponents.[8] Of his two main political opponents in the 2003 election, one was persecuted politically even during the election period and accused of wanting to divide Rwandans. According to the regime's supporters, the vote reflected the success of the Rwandan Patriotic Front (RPF) government in bringing peace and security to ordinary Rwandans: "I would simply say that a miracle has happened in Rwanda," said Foreign Minister Charles Murigande in 2004.[9]

There have been several kinds of criticism levelled at the government in post-genocide Rwanda. Some researchers concentrate on the question of selective remembering and highlight the selective amnesia of official accounts of the genocide and the immediate post-genocide period. Selectivity about remembering past events can be useful, to the extent that it allows neighbours to coexist on a daily basis. But such selective remembering also reinforces the dominance of political leaders over the majority of Rwandans.[10] Nigel Eltringham and Johan

5   Human Rights Watch, *World Report 2003: Rwanda* http://www.hrw.org/wr2k3/africa9.html.

6   J. Carlin, "New Dawn in Rwanda as a Nation Forgives," *The Observer*, 24 August 2003, 24.

7   J. Astill, "Intimidation Alleged in Rwanda Poll," *The Guardian*, 26 and 27 August 2003, 12.

8   F. Reyntjens, "Rwanda: Ten Years on: from Genocide to Dictatorship", *African Affairs*, 103, 411. (2004) 177-210; M. Dorsey, "Violence and power-building in post-genocide Rwanda", in R. Doom and J. Gorus (eds), *Politics of Identity and Economies of Conflict in the Great Lakes Region* (Brussels: VUB University Press, 2000), 311-48.

9   R. Walker, "Rwandans still Divided 10 years on," *BBC News*, 7 April 2004, http://news.bbc.co.uk/1/hi/world/africa/3557565.stm.

10   F. Reyntjens, "Rwanda: Ten Years on"; S. Buckley-Zistel, "Between Past and Future: An Assessment of the transition from Conflict to Peace in post-Genocide Rwanda," Confer-

Pottier, along with René Lemarchand in this volume, show that in Rwanda historical events are constantly being reinterpreted in light of current political priorities.[11] This is common in all political systems and regimes, but in Rwanda it is a process that potentially has important, even lethal consequences.

Critics say that the present government is not only failing to overcome social divisions in Rwandan society but is providing only a tiny and inter-connected minority with access to economic and political power.[12] Post-genocide efforts to renew the social contract between citizens and the state are seen as at best half-hearted, at worst public relations attempts to gain international acceptance. These arguments, however, give the government no credit for its sincere efforts to heal the rifts in Rwandan society. The government has consistently stressed the point that Rwandans should not be divided along racial lines. Attempting to reinvent Rwandan national identity by removing race labels from public political discourse is the government's way of trying to ensure genocide can never happen again.

Nonetheless, some commentators argue that genocide could happen again in Rwanda. As one recent review put it, in a few years' time Rwanda may again have "descended into hell."[13] Such a despondent view no doubt comes from decades of previous experience in the politics of the region. However, if such opinions have any basis in reality, then economic and military security must remain overwhelming priorities for the government. Ongoing Rwandan intervention in the Democratic Republic of Congo (DRC) has benefited the regime but cost many ordinary Rwandans dearly. Despite economic growth, few inroads are being made into tackling deteriorating and chronic rural poverty, and there are signs of rising social insecurity in urban areas.[14] Arguably, the human rights climate in Rwanda has also worsened in the past few years, with a disturbing purge of judges, mayors and other officials.[15] The role of the military, and especially the intelligence services, often overshadows civilian political leadership.[16]

---

ence, "The Rwanda Genocide and Transitional Justice: Commemorating th 10th Anniversary of the Genocide," St Antony's College, University of Oxford, 15 May 2004.

11   N. Eltringham, *Accounting for Horror*; J. Pottier, *Reimagining Rwanda: Conflict, Survival and Disinformation in the Late Twentieth Century* (Cambridge, UK: Cambridge University Press, 2002).

12   F. Reyntjens, "Rwanda: Ten Years On"; Pottier, *Reimagining Rwanda*.

13   F. Reyntjens, "Rwanda: Ten Years On," 210.

14   R. Walker, "Rwandans Still divided 10 years on."

15   See, for example, Human Rights Watch: Rwanda, World Report 2005 http://hrw.org/english/docs/2005/01/12/rwanda9860_txt.htm.

16   M. Dorsey, "Violence and power-building in post-genocide Rwanda". For the point about intelligence services and the military, Michael Dorsey, who was an aid worker in Rwanda for two years, has written a chapter that is problematic in many ways – being almost entirely unsourced, and replete with details that make no sense unless one is already ex-

Political opponents or those regarded as hostile to the regime, even if they are not politically active, are told to keep a low profile or face persecution.

Because of the advent of the *gacaca* community courts, which Gasana, Steward, Schabas, Ngoga and Clark explore in detail in this book, the prospects for achieving justice and reconciliation may have improved in the thousand hills and valleys beyond Kigali. However, can fostering a sense of national unity converge with demanding total obedience to the government, something rarely compatible with the search for peace and social justice? In the Rwandan context, civil obedience may be needed for peace and security, but suspicion of obedience is also well-founded, given the heavily orchestrated way in which the genocide was prepared and perpetrated. Unity may not always mean consensus, as *The Guardian* reported at the tenth anniversary commemorations: "The government says we are all Rwandan and we must not have Hutu and Tutsi in our heads. ..."[17] At the same time, Murigande pointed out that most Rwandans were living together peacefully and preparing for justice through *gacaca*.[18] Even so, there is the constant danger that in the new Rwanda, as in the old, "instruments of power and enrichment are concentrated in small networks based on a shared past."[19] The intelligence services, for example, are now almost 100 per cent Tutsi,[20] which represents a complete reversal of the situation under the previous Hutu-dominated regime.

The question is whether Rwandans are now freer to choose their political identities than they were before the 1994 genocide. Three profiles of Rwandans of mixed heritage presented in this chapter suggest that they may not be. Rwandans' political identity options may be restricted by the narrow set of political identities derived from the genocide. As the new national foundation myth, there is a latent danger that the official story of the 1994 genocide will become another source of stereotyping and prejudice. People's political identities will always be too complex to be expressed by simple fairytales of "goodies" and "baddies". While the terms "survivor", "new caseload refugees", "old caseload refugees" and "suspected *génocidaires*" are primarily descriptive, and can be useful, they can also be a misleading way to label entire groups of people. Most ordinary Rwandans live with economic, social and political insecurity on a daily basis. For them, the choice about their political identity is limited strictly to

---

tremely familiar with the who's-who of Rwanda. This chapter is nonetheless one of the few detailed (though as I say, largely unsubstantiated) accounts of the extent of military and political repression in post-genocide Rwanda. Dorsey particularly emphasises the role of the intelligence services and the youth wing of the RPA.

17   C. McGreal, "It's so difficult to live with what we know" *Guardian* (7 April 2004) 2.

18   R. Walker, "Rwandans still divided 10 years on."

19   F. Reyntjens, "Rwanda: Ten Years On", 188.

20   Ibid.

what is practicable. In this chapter, the central argument is that post-genocide Rwandan governments, having formally proscribed "race" labels, have instead reconstructed Rwandans' political identities according to their own interpretations of the events of the genocide itself.

I will first consider what has been learnt from the genocide. The three profiles of Rwandans of mixed heritage will be presented and reflected upon; at the end of the chapter, some possible alternative "future scenarios" are briefly explored, and other ways of conceiving political identity outside the confines of race categories, explicit or not, are tentatively proposed.

Counting the cost of genocide

Debates around numbers—the number of people killed, the number of killers, and the number of revenge killings, as well as the respective political identities of the perpetrators and victims—have tended to become more polarised during the first decade and a half after the genocide. Whenever such figures are disputed, what is also questioned is the contemporary meaning of the genocide itself, whether it benefited anyone and who were its victims. Exploring debates around numbers is potentially more interesting and revealing than it initially appears.

This chapter suggests that the ideology of those in power in Rwanda since 1994 is a peculiarly Rwandan variant of what Robin Cohen terms "victim diasporic" nationalism.[21] The assumption—implicit or explicit—is that a social group based on some common origin has been victimised for a long time, and that members of the group forced into exile have to return, in this case to Rwanda, to reclaim their "promised land." By implication, those in Rwanda who have victim status are allied by a common persecution, whether they were in exile or in Rwanda itself. Their victimisers, as a whole, are to blame for their exile and persecution. This is the founding myth upon which Rwandan nationalism is now in danger of being based. The emotional register centres on the twin themes of collective guilt on the one hand and collective victimhood on the other. It is not difficult to see how such an ideology might further polarise Rwandans, rather than bringing them together, as the post-genocide regime claims, in a shared national political identity as Rwandans. Victim diasporic nationalism in Rwanda is implicitly exclusive. The real complexity that is characteristic of the lives of everyday Rwandans of any background tends to disappear into a Manichean world of winners, losers and a tale of redemption. Those who fled Rwanda *en masse* after the genocide, and were reluctant to return after the RPF came to power, were seen to be in denial concerning their collective guilt, "unwilling to face the reality of genocide."[22]

---

21   R. Cohen, *Global Diasporas: An Introduction* (London: UCL Press, 1997).

22   J. Pottier, *Reimagining Rwanda,* 133; N. Eltringham, *Accounting for Horror,* 109.

Between 1994 and 1996, 2 million Rwandan refugees in the former Zaire (now the DRC), Tanzania and Burundi were effectively held hostage by militia members, soldiers and officials of the old regime, and were then attacked by the Rwandan Patriotic Army (RPA) in refugee camps and as they fled. Hundreds of thousands died and lost family members. Since 1994, as Steward discusses in chapter 9, "new caseload" returnees have returned to Rwanda to face collective suspicion, treated as if they were guilty *ab initio* of denial or active involvement in crimes of genocide. The story told is reflected in the debates about numbers. As Mahmood Mamdani observes:

> Every time I visited post-genocide Rwanda, I would ask responsible state officials... how many ordinary civilians they thought had participated in the genocide. Every time the answer was in the millions. Even more troubling, the estimate grew with each visit.[23]

The highest academic estimate calculates that ten per cent of Rwandan Hutu took an active part in the genocide in 1994, representing around 350,000 to 600,000 people.[24] In mid-2003, *The East African* reported that 571,934 suspected *génocidaires* were held on the computer database of Rwanda's then Prosecutor General, Gerald Gahima.[25] This appears to cohere with Human Rights Watch's report that, according to Gahima, 500,000 people would eventually be tried in *gacaca* courts.[26] There are even higher estimates: Kagame reportedly claimed that around one million Rwandans were genocide suspects; the Rwandan ambassador to Belgium later cited two million, equivalent to almost the entire adult Hutu male population.[27] Finally, at an Oxford conference in May 2004, the then Deputy Prosecutor General Martin Ngoga, who expands on his views in chapter 16, speculated: "Even if we find three quarters of the population guilty of genocide, it is not a problem."[28] In contrast to these rising estimates of the guilty, among those accused of crimes of genocide, acquittals actually increased from 9 per cent in 1997 to almost 25 per cent by 2002.[29] Ngoga's comments referred to the rising number of genocide suspects being identified during *gacaca* court hearings, and he stressed that all suspected *génocidaires* would be tried, whatever the cost, and however great their number. One possible cause of the rising number of named suspects is *gacaca*'s system

---

23   M. Mamdani, *When Victims Become Killers: Colonialism, Nativism and the Genocide in Rwanda* (Princeton, NJ: Princeton University Press, 2001), 266.

24   N. Eltringham, *Accounting for Horror,* 69.

25   *The East African,* 21-27 July 2003.

26   Human Rights Watch: , *World Report 2005: Rwanda.*

27   N. Eltringham, *Accounting for Horror,* 70.

28   M. Ngoga, Presentation on post-genocide justice systems in Rwanda, at "The Rwanda Genocide and Transitional Justice" Conference, St Antony's, 15 May 2004.

29   LIPRODHOR in Amnesty International, *Gacaca: a Question of Justice,* AI Index: AFR 47/007/2002 (2002), http://www.amnestyusa.org/countries/rwanda/document.do.

of plea-bargaining, which involves confessing to acts of genocide, as well as naming other suspects, as a means of reducing one's sentence or commuting it to community service.[30]

Immediately after the genocide, there were real fears that *Forces Armées Rwandaises* (FAR) and Hutu militias planned to return and "finish off the job" of the genocide of the Tutsi population. Estimates for Hutu Rwandan civilian casualties of the genocide and civil war, killed by the RPF inside Rwanda in 1994, vary between 25,000 to 100,000.[31] In 1996, the United Nations High Commissioner for Refugees (UNHCR) acknowledged that "many refugees did have genuine concerns about safety and justice in Rwanda" but declared that it was safe for them to return.[32] Following the Kibeho massacre in 1996, during which an estimated 2,000 to 4,000 refugees were murdered, an estimated further 200,000 Rwandan Hutu were killed or disappeared following armed attacks by RPA soldiers on camps in Zaire in 1997.[33] Remaining concerns about returning to Rwanda were not taken seriously after that, except by a few NGOs such as *Médécins Sans Frontières*.

The debate about numbers also raises the question of who exactly died during the war and during the genocide of 1994, and who was buried. As corpses continued to be unearthed in Rwanda, many Hutu claimed that their relatives were buried alongside Tutsi victims of the genocide.[34] Hutu victims of the civil war and genocide remain largely unacknowledged in official terms.[35] For instance, the RPF-dominated government has on occasion refused International Criminal Tribunal for Rwanda (ICTR) investigators access to documents needed to bring RPA soldiers to trial for alleged killings of civilians in 1994. This has potentially negative consequences, since "leaving these allegations unresolved allows those who would deny the genocide of Tutsi the freedom to inflate the size and nature of RPA abuses in order to argue for parity between the genocide and alleged crimes committed by the RPA."[36]

30   P. Clark, "When the Killers Go Home: Local Justice in Rwanda", *Dissent*, Summer (2005), 14-15.

31   N. Eltringham, *Accounting for Horror,* 103-6; F. Reyntjens, "Rwanda: Ten Years On".

32   J. Pottier, *Reimagining Rwanda,* 133.

33   J. Pottier, "Reporting on the 'New' Rwanda: the Rise and Cost of Political Correctness, with Reference to Kibeho", in R. Doom and J. Gorus (eds), *Politics of Identity and Economics of Conflict in the Great Lakes Region* (Brussels: VUB University Press, 2000), 121-47.

34   J. Pottier, *Reimagining Rwanda,* 160-4.

35   D. Walsh, "From Hell to Hollywood: The Tale of a Hotel in Kigali," *The Independent* (7 April 2004) 26.

36   N. Eltringham, *Accounting for Horror,* 110.

There are those who seek to deny or minimise the significance of the genocide of 1994, and the Rwandan government is right to be concerned by denialist propaganda. Around the tenth anniversary of the start of the Rwandan genocide, Professor Christian Davenport, then of the University of Maryland, claimed that the 1994 killings in Rwanda were not only genocide but also included "a totalitarian purge, a politicide",[37] a term that he failed to differentiate from genocide. According to Davenport, the majority of the victims in 1994 were in fact Hutu.[38] How Davenport comes to this conclusion is not clear, since neither forensic nor archival evidence has been conclusive in this respect and, as he himself admits, his own data analysis regarding the number of deaths in 1994 is currently incomplete.[39] When Davenport's research was published in the international press, President Kagame called the findings "malicious." There is, however, another part to this otherwise erroneous research: Davenport argues persuasively that Hutu victims of the genocide deserve more serious attention. He argues that "a huge number of Hutu were caught up in the violence as inadvertent victims", estimating their number at half a million.[40]

While this seems a huge overestimate, the RPF estimate of just 60,000 or so "moderate Hutu" being killed during the genocide seems a drastic underestimate. In effect, the RPF claims that only six per cent of the one million people who died in the war and genocide were Hutu.[41] Davenport claims that Hutu deaths constitute more than half of the total number of victims. There is no doubt that the genocide in Rwanda ended up "eating its own children", the Hutu, in large numbers.[42] Hutu as well as Tutsi, not to mention Batwa, suffered greatly through the genocide. But the main targets were Tutsi. It is useful to avoid using a purely racial definition of genocide; genocide can include all those who were killed, including those who were killed for political reasons (rendering superfluous Davenport's term "politicide"), because they opposed the genocide or were targeted for some other reason. After all, the term "holocaust", which is now associated only with the killing of Jews, was originally used to include all killings by Nazis, whether of Jewish people, Roma, Slavs

---

37   Reuters, "Rwanda 1994 killings weren't genocide", 3 April 2004.

38   Ibid.

39   C. Davenport, "Clarification of Exactly What we Did and Did not Say: wanda 1994: Genocide and Politicide", www.genodynamics.com.

40   Ibid.

41   F. Reyntjens, "Rwanda: Ten Years On", 178.

42   J. Kakwenzire and D. Kamukama "The Development and Consolidation of Extremist Forces in Rwanda 1990-94", in H. Adelman and A. Suhrke (eds), *The Path to a Genocide: the Rwanda Crisis from Uganda to Zaire*, (London: Transaction Publishers, 1999) 64; N. Eltringham, *Accounting for Horror*, ch. 3.

or the "unfit". Only later did "holocaust" refer solely to "racial" killings of a particular people.[43]

The true figure of Hutu victims is likely to fall somewhere between the lower estimate of 60,000 and the upper estimate of half a million. As a rough guess, it has been suggested that, since around one million Tutsi lived in Rwanda before 1994, and only around 200,000 survived, it follows that 800,000 of the victims were Tutsi. Almost all of the remaining 200,000 victims, of the estimated million dead, might be Hutu.[44] With around 800,000 victims of "race" killings, this leaves up to 200,000 victims of the war and genocide who were not racially defined. Refusing to acknowledge Hutu casualties during the genocide is just another form of denial and needs to be exposed as such. As one researcher stated: "We need to know what happened for the victims' sake",[45] so that the principle of the right to justice is applied to all, regardless of their origin or status.[46]

The Rwandan government rejected Davenport's research as "denialist" and "an insult to survivors and Rwandans in general."[47] The government is justified

---

43   P. Novick, *The Holocaust and Collective Memory* (London: Bloomsbury, 2001), 20-2. Interestingly, the parallel between Rwanda's genocide and the Holocaust is clearly understood by the Israeli government, which has had good relations with Kagame's transitional government (N. Eltringham and van Hoyweghen, "Power and Identity in Post-Genocide Rwanda," in R. Doom and J. Gorus (eds), *Politics of Identity and Economics of Conflict in the Great Lakes Region* (Brussels: Vub Brussels University Press, 2001), 215-42, 240. The two countries have friendly diplomatic relations, and in 2003 Kagame met with Shimon Peres for official talks where, "Mr Peres expressed full understanding and support for Rwanda as it works towards ensuring that Genocide does not occur again in that country" (Government of Rwanda website, http://www.gov.rw/government/240103_html, last accessed 19 August 2008). Israel has also provided Rwanda with some bilateral development aid since 1995, and for both regimes the defining basis for national identity is genocide and the return of a victim diaspora. For a fuller treatment of the Holocaust parallel see Eltringham (2004, Ch. 3); and Hintjens, "Explaining the 1994 Genocide in Rwanda," Jounral of Modern African Studies, 27, 2, (1999), 241-86.

44   F. Reyntjens, "Rwanda: Ten Years On," 178.

45   University of Maryland Newsdesk, "Rwandan Genocide 10th Anniversary: Correcting the Record", on Davenport's research, 30 March 2004, available at http://www.newsdesk.umd.edu.

46   A. Des Forges, Presentation on post-genocide justice and history of the genocide, at "The Rwanda Genocide and Transitional Justice" Conference, St Antony's 15 May 2004. There is substantial evidence to indicate that appearance, rumour, accusations and even bribery, rather than just one's official race status on an identity card, could determine whether a person actually lived or died during the genocide (See C. Taylor, *Sacrifice as Terror: The Rwanda Genocide of 1994* (New York: Berg, 1999); Eltringham, (2004), 26. Frantically seeking clarity amid a complex and messy reality meant that genocidal killers swept many people into their nets, including those "suspected" of being Tutsi or collaborators. Some Tutsi survived because their appearance was typically "Hutu" or because they were otherwise able to avoid detection (Eltringham, 2004: 26; Taylor, 1999: 72). Tutsi were rescued and protected by Hutu, some of whom were in command of militias or killing teams and themselves killed other Tutsi.

47   Reuters, "Rwanda 1994 killings weren't genocide".

in this regard. However, critics deplore the way in which the Rwandan government labels the Hutu as collectively guilty.[48] In official government discourse, there is a growing tendency to collapse the events of 1994 into those of 1959, as if the earlier period of mass violence were a practice run for genocide.[49] For the new caste of leaders in Rwanda, it is axiomatic that Hutu were/are collectively guilty of genocide, and anti-Tutsi genocide is dated back to the 1959 revolution. Although the exile of many who are now senior figures in Rwanda, including Kagame's own family, began in 1963, it is more often to 1959 that the genocide is traced.[50] In official accounts, Rwanda's past is reinterpreted as demonstrating a continuous genocidal threat against the Tutsi. "I am just sickened," said Jean Baptiste Kayigamba, a genocide survivor and an author who relates his harrowing story in chapter 2, at a conference in May 2004, "by the fact that we knew that one day we could be killed."[51] The problem with this statement is its implicit reference to a racially-defined "we", thus falling into the logic of the genocidal ideology of race hatred. For those whose families left Rwanda in 1959, 1963 or 1973, the continuities and connections between the past and the events of 1994 seem all too horribly obvious. Yet for many Rwandans, it is clear from other accounts that, while there were murder and hatred "in the air", the genocide caught them unawares when it started in earnest.[52] This is in the nature of something as premeditated, coldly planned, and widespread as genocide—murder on a national scale against a particular group.

The exhumation of bodies will not resolve questions of numbers; victims will never be identified by "race", since the notion is misleading in the first place.[53] A revealing report in *The Independent* at the time of the tenth anniversary of the genocide showed that, whatever the evidence, many Rwandan Hutu did in fact believe that Hutu remains were buried, unidentified, next to Tutsi genocide victims. The journalist complained about a "lack of open debate about Rwanda's painful past."[54] The ICTR has proven unable to exercise its mandate that could include trying RPA soldiers for alleged atrocities committed against Rwandan civilians in 1994. Facilitating this, following the lead of the former ICTR Prosecutor Carla Del Ponte, would have enhanced the Rwandan government's legitimacy, not only internationally, but also within Rwanda. Following

---

48   Pottier, *Reimagining Rwanda,* 205-6.

49   Eltringham, *Accounting for Horror,* 44-50.

50   Ibid., 36.

51   J.B. Kayigamba, Presentation on persecution and survival of a Tutsi family, "The Rwanda Genocide and Transitional Justice" Conference, St Antony's 15 May 2004.

52   C. Taylor, *Sacrifice as Terror: the Rwandan Genocide of 1994* (Oxford-New York: Berg, 1999).

53   A. Montagu, *Man's Most Dangerous Myth.*

54   D. Walsh, "From Hell to Hollywood," *The Independent* 7 April 2004.

this lost opportunity, the impunity of the military and political leadership of Rwanda remains a serious obstacle to national reconciliation.[55]

The official version

The RPF-dominated government's version of the genocide is that almost all Hutu benefited, or in some sense stood to benefit, from the event. Even if their own Tutsi relatives were killed, Hutu are not counted by the current government among the "survivors" of the genocide. Even among Hutu who remained inside Rwanda awaiting the arrival of the RPA, those with Hutu relatives active in the genocide can themselves be labelled "*génocidaires*."[56] Survivors' stories are almost always Tutsi stories. From scapegoats, Tutsi have been elevated to victims, not always a flattering image nor an easy one with which to live. Projected images of saints and sinners are unlikely to promote national reconciliation and instead are likely to promote a spirit of blaming one side for the sufferings of the other. The genocide memorials and remains found all over Rwanda do not always help to promote reconciliation. Most Rwandans say that, much as they try to put the events of the genocide behind them, they cannot: "How can you forget when there are genocide sites everywhere around us?"[57]

When the ICTR was established, its purpose was to promote prosecutions of war criminals and perpetrators of genocide and crimes against humanity, based on the recognised legal principles of individual responsibility, a fair hearing, and natural justice (the right to defend oneself against accusations). These principles are swept away by the story that the 1994 genocide was the spontaneous outcome of dangerous collective forces, a kind of "volcanic eruption" of collective feelings.[58] If relations of public trust are to be rebuilt between the rulers and the ruled, and private bonds between neighbours are to be re-established, then the history of the genocide needs to be thoroughly understood, not simplified or caricatured. Trauma affects all aspects of people's lives, including their relations with neighbours, and even their ability to maintain their farms.[59] Some recent testimonies collected by the filmmaker Anne Aghion and used in her films about *gacaca* indicate the high degree of complexity involved in any efforts towards bringing together post-genocide justice and reconciliation be-

55   A. Des Forges, *Leave None to Tell the Story: Genocide in Rwanda* (New York: Human Rights Watch, 1999); J. Pottier, *Reimagining Rwanda*, 157-9; D. Kiwuwa, "Slouching towards a Democracy: Rwanda and the Ethnic Hurdle", PhD thesis (2006) Department of Politics, University of Nottingham; F. Reyntjens, "Rwanda: Ten Years On", 204.

56   M. Mamdani, *When Victims Become Killers*, 267; Cases 2 and 3 below.

57   Nyemirango quoted in *The East African*, Nairobi, 21-27 April 2003.

58   Eltringham, *Accounting for Horror*, 66, 100; R. Karegyesa, Keynote speech at "The Rwanda Genocide and Transitional Justice" Conference, St Antony's, 15 May 2004.

59   Clark, "When the Killers Go Home", 17.

tween former perpetrators and survivors.[60] As Clark also notes, what Rwandans hope to obtain from *gacaca* is not only justice but "a chance to talk about their emotional experiences and for the community to acknowledge their pain and suffering."[61] The problem is that the pain and suffering of all parts of the community are not equally acknowledged; some people's pain is deemed more openly expressible than that of others.

Irrespective of whether Rwandan political identities may be becoming more inclusive at the level of communities, the government approach is to harden its repression of dissenting voices or political opponents. In the apparent belief that repression is the best antidote to "race" conflict, a new Organic Law was introduced in 2003, which allowed political parties to be registered only under certain strict conditions. This new law imposed tight restrictions on all political parties, stipulating that they must "reflect the unity of the Rwandan people"[62] and would be "prohibited from disseminating information [of] a denigrating or divisive nature." This included "words and acts that intend to denigrate or disparage a person in order to unlawfully remove him or her from leadership positions."[63] "Negationism or trivialisation of genocide" is prohibited under the law,[64] as is "betraying other politicians and the country."[65] It is not hard to see such sweeping clauses as giving incumbents a means of holding on to power, by harassing and intimidating their political opponents and perceived enemies.

Such fears were confirmed in 2004 when a wholesale purge of senior officials took place, mainly on charges of corruption, in both the judiciary and local government. Rwanda's major human rights organisation, Ligue Rwandaise pour la Promotion et la Défense des Droits de l'Homme (LIPRODHOR), was threatened with dissolution, and various other civil society organisations were accused of "divisionism" or even "genocidal ideology."[66]

The post-genocide governments of Rwanda have assiduously used the international and local media to cultivate their own "good guy" image. In this, the political leaders of Rwanda have partly succeeded. As Human Rights Watch argues, "Burdened by guilt over their inaction during the genocide, many foreign

---

60   A. Aghion, *In Rwanda we say...The family that does not speak dies* (2005), film details at http://www.anneaghionfilms.com/2004/index.html; A. Aghion, *Gacaca: Living Together Again in Rwanda* (2002), film details as above.

61   Clark, "When the Killers Go Home", 20.

62   Republic of Rwanda, Organic Law No 16/2003 of 27/06/2003 on Governing Political Organisations and Politicians, Article 5.

63   Ibid., 40.10.

64   Ibid., 40.14.

65   Ibid., 41.4.

66   Human Rights Watch, *Rwanda, World Report 2005: Rwanda.*

donors generously support the Rwandan government – credited with having ended the genocide – while ordinarily overlooking its human rights abuses."[67] Simple stories of "good guys" and "bad guys" are deeply problematic, since "seeking and imposing clarity is both the cause of *and* a response to genocide."[68] Dividing the world into categories of victims and perpetrators is unhelpful— to say the least—to individuals' own efforts to reconstruct their own political identities in the family and wider community along non-racial lines.

Repression of academic and human rights critics is also part of the Rwandan government's strategy. Those who have asked for RPA soldiers to be brought to trial for killings of Hutu civilians after the genocide, such as Del Ponte, have been accused of ill-will by the Rwandan government, and complaints about the Rwandan government's systematic obstruction of the ICTR have been largely ignored.[69] Western governments, including that of the United Kingdom, ignore the human rights abuses perpetrated in both Rwanda and neighbouring DRC by the current regime. By extension, they mostly refuse refugee status to Rwandan asylum seekers and do not acknowledge Kagame's political stranglehold as an impediment to democratic reform. Anyone inside Rwanda who asks for justice for Hutu victims of the genocide and of RPA atrocities in the DRC and in Rwanda has reason to fear retaliation. They can be accused of being members of the now banned Hutu opposition party, the *Mouvement Démocratique Républicain* (MDR), of trivialising the genocide, or of genocidal ideology.[70]

The official RPF state ideology thus tends to "globalise guilt according to ethnic identity."[71] Security may appear to be miraculously improved in the country, but this is due to considerable repression of dissent. Unable to voice their concerns, Rwandan Hutu, including those who find themselves losing their security of livelihood, could consider violence an option. If "race" tensions continue to bubble not far from the surface of Rwandan society, this is for material as well as political reasons.[72] On the other hand, such tensions would be difficult for any government to reconcile. The race markers so fatally employed in the past mean that the fault lines within Rwandan society will remain deeply marked by the experience of genocide.

"Race" terms are banned in public discourse in Rwanda, including in the media. Use of the words "Hutu", "Tutsi" and "Twa" is now illegal in public political discourse. In the past, these terms were often used to avoid analysing

---

67   Ibid.

68   Eltringham, *Accounting for Horror,* xiv.

69   Eltringham, *Accounting for Horror,* 110; Human Rights Watch, *Rwanda*, World Report 2005.

70   Ibid.

71   Eltringham, *Accounting for Horror,* 69.

72   Ibid.

Rwanda's social and political problems in depth; conflict was simply attributed to competition between "races" or "ethnic groups". While their replacement with other terms is certainly to be welcomed, the use of simplistic "race" markers should not simply be replaced with the government's way of labelling entire socio-political groups.

As Mamdani argues, "the immediate challenge in Rwanda is to undercut Hutu and Tutsi as political identities." However, as he also argues, "this will not happen so long as the minority monopolizes power."[73] In order to discern the nature of identity boundaries being constructed in any social setting, it can be helpful to look at people who are located on the borders, and whose identities span the main categories of politically constructed identities that cut across that society. In the following section, we consider three such individuals, each with a different profile, but all of mixed background, with elements of victim and perpetrator, Hutu and Tutsi in their personal makeup; in other words, three Rwandans.

Profiles of Rwandan exiles

These profiles are of three exiled Rwandans, whose political identities have been framed by stereotypes that seek to reduce all individuals to either victims or victimisers during the genocide and its aftermath. If political identity in post-genocide Rwanda is being reconstructed, then identity politics for these individuals remains a remarkably painful process. Their choices are almost entirely determined by others, and they find themselves unable to discard the "race" identity markers they inherited from the pre-genocide era. Their political identity labels have been changed since 1994; for Tutsi read "old caseload" or "survivor"; for "Hutu" read "new caseload" or "suspected *génocidaire.*" But in each case, the individual profiled has a background that exposes them to violence from the state, militias and even their own families and neighbours. As Rwandans of mixed heritage, they fall between all the old, but also the new, post-genocide forms of political identity available in Rwanda.[74] These profiles, all of which use changed names in order to preserve confidentiality, are presented in some detail, because they raise disturbing questions about how political identity is being reconstructed (or not) in the new Rwanda. The cases also suggest that polarised "race" identities of the past are not about to disappear under the consensual carpet of Rwandans' shared citizenship.

Case 1: Noelle Angelicas. Noelle's father was a prominent official under the Habyarimana regime, and this automatically makes Noelle a suspected *géno-*

---

73   Mamdani, *When Victims Become Killers*, 281.

74   Ibid., 45.

cidaire in present-day rural Rwanda. She is the only known survivor of a family of ten and the offspring of a mixed Hutu-Tutsi marriage. Her mother was Tutsi and was killed at the start of the genocide of 1994. Noelle inherited her mother's looks and is taken for a Tutsi. Her father and seven siblings are all presumed dead and either fled or were killed following attacks by RPA soldiers in their camp in the former Zaire in 1996. Noelle survived for years hidden in the house of a priest in Kivu. After being raped by an RPA soldier in 2001, she gave birth to a son the following year. When she was heavily pregnant, Noelle moved to Rwanda and lived with a relative. He too was involved in an opposition party, banned the same year for being "divisive" and "ethnicist." Shortly afterwards, he was arrested by RPA soldiers and disappeared. Noelle was warned that the soldiers were looking for her too. Fearing for her life, she fled Rwanda. Noelle has been trapped between her father's reputation as a prominent (though not active) former political official and her status as a victim of rape by an RPA soldier. She fears she could be silenced as a witness to RPA war crimes. She has not inherited her mother's political identity as a genocide victim, in spite of her "Tutsi" appearance. Noelle was refused asylum in the UK on the grounds that the government did not believe she had anything to fear from RPA soldiers who had threatened to silence her "for good."

This woman's Tutsi appearance and the Tutsi identity of her mother did not protect her from persecution after the genocide in the former Zaire, nor did she feel safe upon return to Rwanda. Instead, the political identity affixed to her was that of a "new caseload" refugee—and one active in the political opposition. Rather than disappear like her relative, Noelle went into exile, a journey ironically paid for by an RPA soldier who warned her that she was targeted and, taking pity on her, decided to help her escape to the UK.

Case 2: Julius Gasana. Julius is the son of a mixed marriage, and like Noelle, had a Hutu father and a Tutsi mother. His mother was killed at the start of the genocide, on 9 April 1994. Julius's father was killed for trying to defend his Tutsi wife. Julius is a survivor of the genocide. He remained inside Rwanda until the RPF took over, confirming his political identity as a survivor. However, one of his paternal uncles is on the official list of Category 1 genocide suspects, and was an active killer. As the oldest surviving male relative of this uncle, Julius became a target of Tutsi survivors in his home town. His neighbours spat on him and then attacked and badly injured him. He complained to the police but they did nothing to protect him. Julius's uncle was a genocide perpetrator, and even though Julius himself lost both his parents and remained inside Rwanda waiting for the RPA, he is not allowed to identify himself politically as a genocide survivor. He fits Tutsi ethnic descriptions and considers himself loyal to the RPF, which saved him when it took over the country. He is a survivor in every sense of the term except the official one, but he cannot escape

91

being labelled in the community as a suspected *génocidaire* by association with his uncle. Fleeing to the UK, Julius was refused asylum on the grounds that the Home Office did not believe that Rwandan survivors would persecute someone like Julius simply for being born the relative of a Category 1 genocide suspect.

Julius's story shows how misleading "Hutu" and "Tutsi" are when taken as synonyms for guilt and innocence. Terms like "survivor" or "suspected *génocidaire*", while they respond to the need to understand how the genocide cut across Rwandan society, have the potential to divide Rwandan people in other ways, some of them "racial."

Case 3: Modus Nzishura. Modus's father, a pastor, was Rwandan and his mother a Congolese Munyamulenge. In terms of his own identity, he describes himself as a Munyamulenge and claims to be of "Tutsi" appearance. Prior to 1999, Banyamulenge were encouraged to return to Rwanda as part of the RPF's diasporic form of nationalism. However, after 2000, this policy was reversed, and Modus's father was advised to divorce his mother because she was Congolese. He refused, and as a result, Modus was unable to obtain Rwandan citizenship. Under Congolese law he was not entitled to Congolese citizenship either. Modus's father campaigned against Rwanda's war in the eastern DRC and was shot in Kigali by the Rwandan army in 2003 for demanding Rwanda's withdrawal. His body was dumped in the road outside the family home. Modus's mother and sister were later arrested and have both disappeared. Modus is of Tutsi appearance and has lived for many years in Rwanda. He had a Rwandan father but cannot call himself a Rwandan. He is therefore stateless. In terms of his own political identity, Modus is trapped between a diasporic reality and the increasingly narrow definition of citizenship being employed by the Rwandan government. Claiming asylum on arrival in the UK, Modus was initially refused, as the story he recounted of his father's killing was not believed. However, on appeal, he was granted exceptional leave to remain for a limited period.

Modus's statelessness reflects the hardening boundaries of political identity in Rwanda today, as a group like the Banyamulenge is redefined as outside the bounds of Rwandan citizenship. Modus's complete loss of his personal identity obliged him, whether he considered himself Rwandan or Congolese, to subsist on the margins between the two countries. At home in neither place, he was branded as an opponent because his father spoke out openly against Rwandan involvement in the eastern DRC. His choices became very limited, and after members of his family were killed, he chose to flee into exile.

The political identities of all three of these individuals have been profoundly altered by the genocide, but also by the official account of the genocide. Their stories highlight the complexity and ambiguity of real events and the ways in which they translate to an individual's life circumstances. These complexities are largely lost among the post-genocide categories of guilt and innocence. The three narratives also illustrate how individuals are blamed for the sins of their relatives. All three find themselves trapped between polarised political identities, and this is mainly because of their parents' mixed heritage. Whereas in 1994 the terms "Hutu" and "Tutsi" were virtually compulsory, such terms are now proscribed, and the people who fall between the old "race" labels have almost as much difficulty establishing their mixed political identity as they did in the old Rwanda prior to the genocide.

If political identities are becoming more complex in Rwanda, then Rwandans should be brought together across "race" boundaries, and citizenship and Rwandan national identity should be creating new cross-cutting forms of political identification and allegiance. The opposite is suggested by these case studies of three mixed-race people; the influx and return of new kinds of Rwandans since the genocide has meant instead the appearance of new schisms in Rwandan society. Language has become an additional vector of identity formation, and while in theory this should prove useful in promoting new forms of national unity, in practice English is associated with the new political elite of returnees from Uganda, who in their higher ranks consist mainly of Kagame's inner circle of trusted allies. The danger is that official accounts of the genocide tend to "freeze" political identity formation at a certain point in time (around July 1994). It is as if genocide has become the foundation myth of the new Rwanda. The problem is that Rwandans are increasingly identified politically regarding their *presumed* role, rather than their *actual* role, in the genocide, as it is now officially remembered.

The category of "survivor" often excludes those with Tutsi mothers and Hutu fathers, even if they "look Tutsi" as in the above profiles. This may be, in part, because of a widespread presumption in Rwandan society that individuals are responsible for their relatives' actions. Even those who refused to flee to the camps, and made it alive into RPF-controlled Rwanda, could not always openly claim "survivor" status within their local communities. At the tenth anniversary commemorations, one journalist noted that, unlike the first genocide commemorations in 1995, which were a genuine exercise in mourning for all Rwandans, by 2004 the events reflected the regime's own particular take on the events of genocide and the identity of the victims.[75] The government now tends to label Hutu as *génocidaires* or accomplices to genocide, even if they were children at the time (as was the case with Case 3). It is certain that neither someone like Noelle nor someone like Julius feels able to claim the status of a "survivor" in Rwanda today.

---

75   J. P. Remy, "Hante par le genocide: Rwanda organise une difficile commemoration," *Le Monde*, 7 April 2004.

Permissible forms of political identification are almost as tightly restricted in today's Rwanda as they were in the past, but the actual terms of political identification are quite different, and more complex. Both completely ignore the real complexity of Rwandan people's daily lives during and since the genocide. This means that Rwandans with a mixed Hutu-Tutsi background, or those who have suffered at the hands of the RPF, cannot form independent political identities outside the confines of official categories.[76] In terms of political identities, the legacy of genocide has exacerbated rather than minimised "race" divisions.

There is anecdotal evidence emerging from Rwanda to suggest that inter-"race" marriages have become less, rather than more common since 1994.[77] The race markers of the First and Second Republics lurk behind the terms *"génocidaires"*, "new caseload refugees" or "old caseload refugees", "Ugandans" and "survivors." According to one seasoned observer, driving the terms "Hutu", "Tutsi" and "Twa" underground in Rwanda is a dangerous strategy which could simply reinforce the appeal of such terms as ways of mobilising opposition to the government in power today.[78]

During the genocide, any Hutu who expressed resistance, or tried to save Tutsi or half-Tutsi neighbours and relatives, were *ipso facto* targeted for killing. A few survived, like Paul Rusesabagina, manager of the Hotel des Mille Collines, profiled on UK radio[79] and in the recent Hollywood movie *Hotel Rwanda*. Some people consider him a hero, while others question the way he kept the senior military commander, Gen. Augustin Bizimungu, plied with free drinks from the hotel bar. Rusesabagina says that because of his mixed Hutu-Tutsi background, he saw himself as Rwandan first and foremost. The multiple affiliations, trials and tribulations of the profiles detailed here show the difficulty of erasing "race" markers from Rwandan political culture. People of mixed Hutu-Tutsi background may be as uneasy in the new, supposedly non-racial, Rwanda as they were in the old; they still do not fit into the neat, official categories of political identity.

Like other studies, this section has tried to "ease a number of complex voices back into the debate... the voices of people that have nuanced stories

---

76 Rwandans are not all equally at home in the new Rwanda; some are forced into exile and many more feel unwanted (Reyntjens, 2004: 194). Rwandans of mixed Hutu-Tutsi background, and relatives of *génocidaires* may be particularly vulnerable to persecution for their relatives' misdeeds rather than their own.

77 Kiwuwa, *Slouching towards a Democracy.*

78 T. Zack-Williams, Discussion at Review of African Political Economy Conference, University of Birmingham, September 2003.

79 BBC Radio 4, "Defying Rwanda's Killers", 20 January 2002.

to tell."[80] As Clark has observed, post-genocide strivings for justice through community participation in the *gacaca* courts depend on goodwill and trust among Rwandans; something that the actions of the present government do not always promote.[81] The overwhelming focus on "never again" has produced a rather simplistic folktale of good and evil within Rwandan society, a story of two opposites that cannot handle the increasingly complex processes of justice and injustice, and of political identity formation in Rwanda today. As always, real life in Rwanda is far more complex than the tidy logic of political ideology can recognise. Not everyone is either a victim or a perpetrator; in reality many people are neither, and some are both, and as the highlighted profiles show, this makes it impossible to talk of the situation in Rwanda today in terms of either the categories of colonial and post-colonial "race" ideology, or the categories of the official understanding of the genocide itself.

Prognoses for Rwanda

Conclusions by prominent scholars concerning Rwanda's future vary from the gloomy predictions of further rounds of civil war, and even genocide, to images of a future where democracy can flourish and militarisation can come to an end. This short selection of conclusions from recent works by scholars in the field provides an idea of the range of thoughts about the future. We start with the most pessimistic and end on a more positive note:

For someone like the present author, who warned against massive violence during the years leading up to 1994, it is frustrating to wonder whether, in two, five or ten years from now, the international community, again after the facts, will have to explain why Rwanda has descended into hell once more.[82]

The war [between the RPF and former Rwandan government] ...crystallised two volatile regional diasporas – one Hutu, the other Tutsi – each determined to set the region on fire if the demands it considered legitimate were not met.[83]

Without a vision of the past which acknowledges that different interpretations of history will exist, Rwanda...and the Great Lakes region generally, will remain entrapped in an official discourse which legitimates the use of violence and makes some, leaders and led, *génocidaires*.[84]

---

80   Pottier, *Reimagining Rwanda*, 202.
81   Clark, "When the Killers Go Home", 21.
82   Reyntjens, "Rwanda: Ten Years On", 210.
83   Mamdani, *When Victims Become Killers*, 263.
84   Pottier, *Reimagining Rwanda*, 207.

...a critique of colonialism and its effects on people's categories of perception was never allowed to develop and mature in Rwanda. Although this critique is not the only measure needed in order to bring about reconciliation in Rwanda, Rwandans must start here. They must acknowledge, then question, then criticize the enduring effects that colonialism has had on their own minds.[85]

For the Congo, as for Rwanda, Burundi and Uganda [a political solution]... implies the resolution of the crises of democratic transition by putting an end to governments established by the force of arms, and embarking on a path of genuine national reconciliation, justice and inclusiveness...[86]

Meanwhile, Eltringham has some advice for those who look to the past to solve the problems of the present and the future: "While Rwanda has a single past, a single, definitive history is unattainable. Given the role played by history in Rwanda's past, a recognition of the limits of historiography should be encouraged."[87] This brief sample of perspectives on the future shows an increasing readiness to be critical of the RPF and of military solutions to the problems of security and coexistence in the Great Lakes region. Today there is a danger that the international community will swing from giving the RPF the benefit of the doubt in all cases to extreme scepticism regarding the motives of those in power in Rwanda. This would be a mistake. Observers must view events in Rwanda in their longer historical and wider regional framework. Conflicts over history are not just academic. Outspoken critics of President Kagame have found themselves declared *persona non grata*,[88] including some who were previously close to the RPF, such as Gérard Prunier. With their excellent English and a sophisticated understanding of Western diplomacy and media, Rwanda's political leaders literally got away with murder in the DRC for two years without any loss of status or foreign aid. The regime needs to recognise that most criticism of its policies now arise as much out of the disappointed expectations of former admirers, as out of ill-will or genocide denial.[89]

---

85   Taylor, *Sacrifice as Terror*, 177.

86   G. Nzongola-Ntalaja, *The Congo: From Leopold to Kabila: A People's History* (London: Zed Press, 2003), 264.

87   Eltringham, *Accounting for Horror*, 182.

88   R. Doom and J. Gorus (eds), *Politics of Identity and Economics of Conflict in the Great Lakes Region*, 83.

89   On forms of denial by governments, see the exceptionally accessible and thought-provoking study by Stanley Cohen. His classification detailed below has been used in another paper by the author, "Silence and Distance: Genocide and Denial in Rwanda", originally presented at the conference organised by the Wiener Library in London, "Generations of Genocide", held at the School of Oriental and African Studies, London, 26-27 January 2002. Cohen's article provides a particularly helpful classification of the range of denial strategies used by governments in particular:
      (a) Silence. By ignoring accusations completely, the government chooses to remain silent and indifferent in the face of criticism. This was particularly the case prior to the

The varied conflicts between "old" and "new" caseload refugees, a growing urban middle class uprooted from rural life and a growing class of landless rural poor, with no secure claims to land and few livelihood choices, have all complicated Rwandan developmental possibilities over the past ten years. In place of two recognised languages, there are now three (English, Kinyarwanda and French),[90] with French much less widely spoken in official circles than before 1994. In part, the new regime's legal suppression of race identity labels has worked; references to Hutu, Tutsi and Twa are already less acceptable even in unmonitored internet and media outlets.

To reduce everything to a supposedly age-old conflict between two "races", Hutu and Tutsi, is no longer acceptable, and this development is to be welcomed. This has allowed other, more complex, perspectives on political identity to emerge. The realities that underpin Hutu, Tutsi and Twa political identities may remain, but many of the tensions surrounding these terms themselves seem to have been defused, and this surely constitutes a change for the better. Within Rwanda, and in the wider Rwandan diaspora, social divisions that cannot be reduced to the Hutu-Tutsi divide have been able to come to the fore, including divisions of class, region, politics and religion. The official categories of identity, survivors and *génocidaires*, "old" and "new" caseload refugees, rural and urban Rwandans, Anglophone and Francophone, have all taken on great significance in post-genocide Rwanda.

At the very least, it can be concluded that researchers, journalists and the Rwandan public have been challenged by the RPF regime to rethink the catego-

---

genocide itself.

(b) Righteousness. By invoking a higher moral or religious order, and claiming the right to act in promoting that order, whether that be "the revolutionary struggle, ethnic purity, Western civilization" (ibid.: 110).

(c) Necessity means arguing that what was done was done in self-defence to avoid greater problems in the future. This was the case prior to 1994 as well.

(d) Denial or blaming of victims. "The atrocities of the last few decades show there is no end to the historical spirals of conflicting claims about which group is the original, 'real' or ultimate victim" (ibid.: 111). In 1990-94, viewing Tutsi as eternal outsiders was presented as justification for eliminating them.

(e) Uniqueness. The government claims outsiders cannot understand the situation, or their judgement of the exceptional measures taken would be less harsh. This works more for the post-genocide government and its denial of political repression, human rights abuses, and war crimes than for the pre-genocide forms of genocide denial.

(f) Advantageous comparisons; in other words claiming that under similar circumstances your enemies, or others, would have done much worse, and that by comparison you have shown considerable restraint (S. Cohen, *States of Denial: Knowing About Atrocities and Suffering* (Cambridge, UK: Polity Press, 2002) 109-12)

These categories permit an interpretation of policies of denial, both prior to and during, as well as after the 1994 genocide in Rwanda.

90 Government of Rwanda website, http://www.rwanda1.com/gov.rw.

ries through which they explained Rwandan history and contemporary politics. Clichés and gross generalisations about "Hutu" and "Tutsi", which tended to inform most popular and scholarly understandings of Rwanda prior to 1994, have had to be complicated to fit with the law. On the other hand, perhaps they have not been complicated enough.

Conclusion

The new Rwanda is still divided, but not just as it was before the genocide. For instance, there are now Rwandans who speak better English than Kinyarwanda, and yet who feel fully Rwandan. The President recently learned to speak French fluently himself. He was reported to have been very proud to be able to make his first speech in "good French" not long ago.[91] Signs of "Kagamemania" in post-genocide Rwanda do not mean that his popularity will continue indefinitely. As well as standing against the genocide, the recently elected democratic government must now stand for a more positive alternative. This needs to involve greater material security for the majority of poor, rural Rwandans, and some shared achievements in concrete terms. It also has to involve less, rather than more, conformity and obedience. Unfortunately the link between genocide and obedience has not led to disobedience becoming acceptable politically in post-genocide Rwanda.[92]

Since it is not the researcher's role to sit, Cassandra-like, predicting disaster, I end this chapter with a story of how political identities can be reinvented through disobedience to authority. This story has been reported by African Rights, but it is worth repeating here, in order to comment briefly. In March 1997, *Interahamwe* broke into a girls' high school in northwest Rwanda and ordered the girls to divide themselves into groups of Hutu and Tutsi. Eyewitnesses interviewed by African Rights reported that the young women refused. In their frustration, the infiltrators shot into the classroom, killing several girls at random.[93] The girls' collective disobedience consisted in refusing to divide themselves. The story shows the extent to which the genocide project depended on the obedience of both the victimisers and the victims, but is simultaneously emblematic of the hope that a new Rwandan political identity is being formed among the post-genocide younger generation.[94]

If such a political identity is not allowed to find root among the population, then Rwandans will continue to be sacrificed on the altar of a version of the

---

91   Kiwuwa, *Slouching towards a Democracy.*

92   Eltringham and van Hoyweghen, "Power and Identity in Post-Genocide Rwanda," 234.

93   African Rights, *Rwanda: The Insurgency in the Northwest*, London: African Rights, 1998, 371-4.

94   Kiwuwa, *Slouching towards a Democracy.*

nation that only has room for two mutually antagonistic stories: that of the victors and that of the vanquished.

6

GENOCIDE-LAUNDERING: HISTORICAL REVISIONISM, GENOCIDE DENIAL AND THE ROLE OF THE *RASSEMBLEMENT RÉPUBLICAIN POUR LA DÉMOCRATIE AU RWANDA*

Tom Ndahiro

Introduction

Between April and July 1994, the world tried to ignore the annihilation of Tutsi in Rwanda. Today, it is impossible for anyone to forget the genocide. In particular, for survivors – those I call "living victims" – the genocide is a daily reality: it stole their friends and relatives, their plans and aspirations, and continues to haunt them. Raphael Lemkin argued that genocide is a coordinated plan to destroy the essential foundations of the life of a group so that it withers and dies like a plant that has suffered blight.[1] Genocide is a crime against all of humankind; against all notions of human civilisation. But it is also a deeply personal crime committed against individuals who re-live the memories of the genocide like a vicious, recurring nightmare.

As argued by my fellow survivors writing in this volume, Jean Baptiste Kayigamba and Solomon Nsabiyera Gasana, survivors remain victims of the perpetrators, many of whose ongoing preoccupation is to alter or erase the world's memory of the genocide. The perpetrators and orchestrators of the genocide may realise the weight of their crimes, but this has not stopped many of them publicly denying the nature and hideous significance of their actions. Perpetrators, international bystanders and their numerous supporters cannot feel safe and happy if both the living victims and other members of the international community keep the memory of genocide alive. It is always in the interest of the culpable to suppress or kill this memory, deploying all means possible. Such suppression or denial of the past is the last stage of genocide: as the killing spree

---

1   R. Lemkin, "Genocide – A Modern Crime," *Free World* (April 1945) 39.

sought to erase all Tutsi from the earth, so denial of the genocide seeks to erase all memory of the Tutsi who were slaughtered. Consequently, there should be justice and accountability for those who deny genocide, as well as for those who perpetrate it.

Many people have heard of money laundering, the objective of which is to generate a profit for certain individuals or groups by dispersing criminal proceeds through seemingly legitimate enterprises to disguise their illegal origins. This enables criminals to benefit without endangering the sources of their profits. Studies have shown that money launderers operate comfortably in countries and financial systems with weak or ineffective counter-measures. Many *génocidaires* and their allies have succeeded in doing the same regarding the most abominable crime: in propagating a revisionist view of the genocide that has gained great currency around the world, they have successfully distanced themselves from their involvement in the genocide. Their profit is not money, but impunity. For more than ten years, genocide-laundering movements have been extremely active, constructing influential and ultimately divisive reinterpretations of the past and allowing many *génocidaires* to distance themselves from their crimes. Efforts to counter genocide denial, highlighting how individuals and organisations around the world have been duped by the launderers, require determination and international solidarity, including efforts to prosecute the deniers.

The list of those who have laundered the 1994 genocide of Tutsi is long. Many of these individuals and organisations have gained great credence in the international community. As early as April 1994, various state governments and the United Nations were comfortable sitting with the orchestrators of the genocide, for example, members of the genocidal government who, by a quirk of history, at that time held a place on the UN Security Council (UNSC) and many of whom, as I contend below, have become prominent genocide launderers. The UNSC listened to their interpretations of the violence occurring in Rwanda and invited them to negotiate peace agreements. The international media, particularly French news agencies, aided the denial of the genocide as it was unfolding, by characterising the violence as simply the spontaneous flaring of ancient, tribal hatred.

The *génocidaires* gained greater assistance when, in July 1994, the world that had turned away when innocent people were being butchered came to the rescue of the killers. The UN endorsed the French government's humanitarian mission, *Opération Turquoise*, though its impact was decidedly inhuman, creating a security cordon through which tens of thousands of Hutu, including many orchestrators of the genocide, fled to Zaire (now the Democratic Republic of Congo [DRC]). Similarly, Kenyan and Zairean authorities afforded the *génocidaires* free movement and permitted the publication and circulation of hate literature, including the extremist newsletters *Kangura* and *Amizero*, which had originally been used to incite the genocide.

The responsibility for countering the spread of hate propaganda and new waves of genocidal ideology fell to the living victims and the Rwandan Patriotic Front (RPF), which had defeated the genocidal armed forces and halted the murder of Tutsi and their sympathisers. As the world focused on the plight of Hutu refugees in the camps in Zaire and Tanzania, and unwittingly helped feed, clothe and re-arm them through humanitarian aid, the RPF and genocide survivors were left to rebuild Rwanda and to safeguard it against the re-emergence of genocidal ideology. As this chapter will show, many prominent *génocidaires* fled to countries like Belgium, the Netherlands, France and Switzerland, where they established bases for genocide denial and plotted the exiled criminals' return to power. In these countries, the best-organised and most influential group involved in genocide laundering, the *Rassemblement Républicain pour la Démocratie au Rwanda* (RDR), or the Republican Rally for Democracy in Rwanda, was born and has grown with alarming speed. This chapter analyses the RDR's propagandist strategy for spreading genocide revisionism and denial, and the role of the international media in affording the RDR and other revisionist groups a global platform for their campaigns. In particular, this chapter focuses on official RDR propaganda as drawn from its public statements and from rare documents, including confidential *Forces Armées Rwandaises* (FAR) and RDR memoranda, which I have gathered from refugee camps in eastern DRC.

History of the RDR

It is necessary to understand what the RDR is, how it was created and what it intends to hide or protect. The RDR is the first Rwandan criminal organisation to acquire international recognition through genocide laundering. It was officially launched on 3 April 1995, with headquarters in France and later also in Belgium, the Netherlands and Canada, where it has operated since. On 4 April 1995, the FAR declared its support for the RDR[2], the Hutu genocidal army overrun by the RPF in July 1994. On 29 April 1995, the High Command of the FAR issued a statement in Bukavu, Zaire, divorcing itself from the Hutu "government in exile," the group of Hutu extremists that had been its partner in the genocide. The FAR believed that the exiled government had become ineffective in serving the interests of refugees in Zaire and Hutu everywhere and instead declared its unswerving support for the RDR. The FAR statement read:

---

2   FAR, "Declaration of Support to the 'RDR' by the Rwandan Armed Forces," 4 April 1995 (author's archive).

Since its creation on April 9, 1994, with the assistance of the Rwandan Armed Forces, the Government has been subjected to media and diplomatic embargo, and the Government reshuffle of November 1994 did not improve the situation. The absence of Government action for the refugees in the camps due to lack of adequate and efficient structures is remarkable....In the search of intermediate solutions to get out of the impasse, with the refugees' initiative, the "RDR" was recently created to address the concerns of the refugees and of the oppressed Rwandans inside the country. After examining the goal and the objectives of "RDR," the Rwandan Armed Forces saluted this good initiative setting up an organisation that can ensure efficient supervision of the population in exile, guarantee maximum cohesion and having a media and diplomatic influence, which are preliminary conditions to the refugees' return to their country. This is the reason why the Rwandan Armed Forces signed a declaration of support to the "RDR" on April 4, 1995....Conscious of their responsibilities and ...their strong willingness to work directly with and for the people... [t]he FAR believe that the Government must be aware of its responsibilities before History, the Rwandan people in general and the refugees in particular, by supporting the refugees' good initiative, and by resigning to let the "RDR" represent and defend their interests. Therefore, the Government must hand in all documents it has been keeping on behalf of the people in exile. The relations between the FAR and the Government are stopped as of April 29, 1995.[3]

This statement reveals the true intentions behind the creation of the RDR. The leadership of the FAR and the "government in exile" had taken refuge in neighbouring countries; many of them fugitives from justice. The RDR admitted in 1998 that it was established to bypass or circumvent the embargo imposed on the government in exile in Zaire. An RDR document published on 17 November 1998 and signed by the organisation's president, Charles Ndereyehe, revealed that it took the "refugees two months of serious thinking about setting up an organisation, which would be capable of breaking the media and diplomatic embargo affecting them." The document reads:

The idea of a large organisation was born during the meeting held in Bukavu in October 1994. To circumvent the embargo which had struck the government in exile during the 2-3 months while the refugees lived in exile, several series of refugee initiatives were launched in different places, particularly in the former Zaire and Tanzania, where more than 2 million Rwandans who fled en masse in July and August 1994 were living. But these initiatives lacked coordination. Mr. Nzabahimana François was among the organisers of this meeting, at which the refugees from Europe and the Americas were unfortunately under-represented. After two days of debates, the refugees were given 2 months for reflection before establishing an organisation which was able to break the media and diplomatic embargo under which the refugees were struggling. At the end of the first gathering of the organisation, the refugees published a charter for the rapid and peaceful return of refugees who fulfilled its requirements.[4]

---

3   Cited in "Declaration of the High Command of the Rwandan Armed Forces after its Meeting of 28 to 29 April 1995," Bukavu, document in author's archives.

4   Charles Ndereyehe, President RDR, "Sur les Traces du Rassemblement pour le retour des réfugiés et la Démocratie au Rwanda," on www.rdrwanda.org/english/historical_background/.

104

With the assistance of priests from the "Missionaries of Africa," a Belgian branch of the *Internationale Démocrate-Chrétienne* (IDC) and Belgian senator Rika De Backer, working with exiled Hutu, including known Hutu demagogues and *génocidaires*, the RDR was born. From 1995 until it changed its name in 2003, the RDR was the *Rassemblement pour le Retour et la Démocratie au Rwanda* or "Rally for the Return [of Refugees] and Democracy in Rwanda." Its members, particularly the hierarchy, were drawn from among the *génocidaires*. Some of them were former ministers[5], influential diplomats and senior civil servants. All of them were genocide ideologues[6] and many were highly active in the refugee camps in the ex-Zaire. The world was aware of this. In a public statement in June 1996, Richard McCall, Chief of Staff of the United States Agency for International Development (USAID) said, "Just as the international community failed to act to prevent the Rwandan genocide, the international community stands silent as the genocidal forces continue to work their will both inside Rwanda and in neighbouring Zaire. ...The seeds for this genocide were planted decades ago. The roots remain firmly embedded in an ideology that continues to be the principle guiding the ex-government and the RDR."[7]

McCall's claims are corroborated by the testimony given by Jean Kambanda, former Prime Minister of Rwanda, to the UN International Criminal Tribunal for Rwanda (ICTR). Kambanda told ICTR investigators that the RDR was formed by individuals close to the *Mouvement Républicain National pour la Démocratie et le Développement* (MRND), the ruling party that planned, and incited the population to carry out, the genocide, with full support by the FAR. In the camps, refugees were coerced to join this organisation. Kambanda explained:

It was impossible to belong to any other organization except the RDR. They were saying it openly, so it wasn't something that was said in hiding or in a concealed manner. You had to be in the RDR and nowhere else ... People were attacked since they didn't want to join or if they said they were not joining the RDR. They were physically attacked. ... I saw people who were beaten or insulted because they didn't want to join the RDR or because they said they were not going to join the RDR.[8]

---

5   The first president of the RDR was Francois Nzabahimana, Minister of Commerce in Habyarimana's government from 1991 to 1992.

6   Ndereyehe Charles Ntahontuye, who was the founding member of the RDR, and at one time its President, was the head of an extremist think-tank, *Cercle des Républicains Progressistes* (CRP). From CRP minutes in the author's possession, it is clear that the CRP was instrumental in the creation of the *Coalition for the Defence of the Republic* (CDR).

7   Statement of Richard McCall, Chief of Staff USAID, Rwanda Roundtable Conference, Geneva, 20-21 June 1996 (author's archive).

8   Ibid.; Testimony of Jean Kambanda, recorded on 22 May 1998, ICTR, Arusha, Tanzania (author's archive).

Kambanda was asked by the investigators to identify the individuals who exercised these physical and moral constraints. Kambanda answered, "It was mostly by the soldiers but also by the RDR officials in the region," adding that there were soldiers who did not remain in the camp but stayed with the civilians to convince them "to join the party."[9]

One conversation between Kambanda and the ICTR investigators regarding the RDR went as follows:

Q: When did you notice that the soldiers came to exert pressure? Was it when there was a negative report, or what?

A: From the very beginning, the entire RDR service was overseen by the army. From the very beginning. Be it at the higher levels of the party or at the levels of the camps.

Q: Okay. So it was an association to which a refugee had to belong as a matter of obligation?

A: He was obliged to join.

Q: They advocated to return to Rwanda using force, by launching attacks against Rwanda?

A: Yes.

Q: And the refugees were required to pay contributions?

A: Yes, each housing unit had to pay a dollar monthly.[10]

During the interview, Kambanda admitted, "My own family had to pay contributions. They sought my opinion and I told them that for their security it was in their interest to pay. I even gave my own money to pay." Kambanda described military incursions into Rwanda by ex-*génocidaires* from the camps, which targeted genocide survivors and witnesses.[11]

FAR military leaders, including Col. Théoneste Bagosora, orchestrated the creation of the RDR and, from the outset, sought to control it. Kambanda testified to ICTR investigators at length about how military officials held several meetings in preparation for launching the RDR and how officers such as Bagosora and Maj. Gen. Augustin Bizimungu announced the formation of the RDR even before it was officially established. Bagosora, according to Kambanda, "went to the camp to organize meetings and announce the good news that 'a new political organization' was going to be created, and that the military were henceforth taking charge." Kambanda claimed that the meetings to form

---

9   Ibid.
10   Ibid.
11   Ibid.

the RDR were convened by the FAR, and RDR leaders were appointed by the army.[12]

RDR and Genocide Denial

On the surface, the concepts and language used in the RDR's press releases may seem relatively innocuous. A careful analysis of the use of specific words, and their connotations in the Rwandan cultural context, however, exposes their nefarious intentions and insinuations. What follows here is an analysis of RDR press releases and other key documents, to display the organisation's attempts to describe Tutsi in racist or ethnically divisive ways and to deny that Hutu perpetrated the genocide in 1994 or that a genocide even took place. In the RDR's discourse, one easily uncovers claims and depictions of the genocide as a "civil war," "tragedy" or "crisis." It is also common to find claims that the RPF rather than the genocidal government was responsible for crimes in 1994. Such claims revolve around two forms of responsibility: the RPF as responsible for inciting the government's "response"; and the RPF as guilty of attacks on, even genocide of, innocent Hutu civilians.

As demonstrated above, the FAR played a crucial role in the establishment, growth, ideology and propaganda strategy of the RDR. In early April and May 1995, the FAR's department of military intelligence and two lawyers afforded the task of writing an account of Rwandan history, Charles Nkurunziza and Alberto Basomingera, published their first materials. In doing so, Nkurunziza and Basomingera attempted to provide a legal backing to the denial of Tutsi genocide, particularly by legally justifying the crime. Initially, both men acted as legal advisors to Dr. Theodore Sindikubwabo, the leader of the government that orchestrated the genocide. Their documents later greatly influenced the RDR's press releases and public statements, especially in their attempts to deny the genocide.

A text published in Bukavu in May 1995 by the *"Charles Nkurunziza Group"* includes the following statement which has become central to RDR ideology and propaganda: "It is not the Hutu who were the authors of the genocide; rather, it is the Tutsi who wanted to exterminate the Hutu, so that they will never have to share power. This is the truth that any person of good will and who loves justice should know to contribute to the restoration of the Rwandan people's rights...."[13]

---

12   Ibid.

13   Charles Nkuruziza Group, "Les aspects essentiels du problème rwandais" (Essential Aspects of the Rwandan Problem), May 1995 (author's archive). The report was prepared by a group led by "Charles Nkuruziza [for] the Ministry of Justice in Exile." I refer to this institution as "so-called" since, in my view, it could not exercise its duties as a "government ministry" in another country. The "Minister of Justice in Exile" was Stanislas

In a report published in April 1995, Albert Basomingera, formerly the Dean of the Faculty of Law at the National University of Rwanda in Butare and a consultant to the World Bank, argues that there was no plan to commit genocide in Rwanda. He contends that "it was the discovery of the RPF's brigades and arms caches that partly explains the violence and the intensity of the reaction of the populace and not the premeditation of genocide...[S]uch reaction is rather that of self-defence."[14] Linking the death of Hutu President Juvénal Habyarimana to the genocide, Basomingera argues that "it should be recalled that even some large-scale attacks by the RPF had already provoked popular 'punitive' reaction against true or suspected RPF's accomplices in the regions where the President enjoyed popularity...What was then expected in the event of the assassination of that same Head of State?"[15]

Basomingera furthermore defends Dr. Leon Mugesera who, in a famous speech in November 1992 when he was MRND vice-chairman for Gisenyi prefecture, incited people to exterminate Tutsi. Basomingera supports the incendiary discourse of *Radio Télévision Libre des Milles Collines* (RTLM), arguing, "It is tendentious to claim that the incriminated radio only called to the extermination of the Tutsi."[16] Reinforcing racist stereotypes used to de-humanise Tutsi, Basomingera defends RTLM depictions: "With regard to the term 'serpents', it was used to designate the Tutsi even before independence, referring partly to their *cunning, malicious and spiteful nature* and partly the dishonesty they are said to have been imbued with."[17]

Basomingera and Nkurunziza continue to propagate the views expressed in these original documents, which have served as a touchstone for RDR ideology. In May 2002, as a defence witness at the ICTR for Andre Ntagerura, former Transport Minister before and during the genocide, Nkurunziza told the Tribunal that he did not observe any massacres between April and July 1994 but alleged that mass killings by RPF soldiers led to "revenge by the government."[18] Nkurunziza, who was Rwanda's Justice Minister from 1977 to 1984 and Deputy Minister of Transport during the genocide, argued that the government set up roadblocks simply to bring calm and security because the justice system in

---

Mbonampeka.

14   Groupe Albert Basomingera, "A propos du rapport final de la commission des experts du conseil de sécurité des Nations Unies pour le Rwanda: Conclusions au génocide au prix d'une mise à l'écart de certains faits, d'altération d'autres et d'interprétation tendancieuse," also for the so-called Ministry of Justice of the Rwandan Government in Exile, Bukavu-Zaire, April 1995.

15   Ibid.

16   Ibid.

17   Ibid. (emphasis added).

18   See Shunah Kaliisa, "Cyangugu Trial: Prosecutor Challenges Former Minister's Credibility," *Internews*, 29 May 2002.

the country had broken down.[19] Underlying the importance of genocide denial for his discourse, Nkurunziza argued, "The massacres that bloodied the countryside were done by the RPF,"[20] claiming that he had never heard of the FAR nor the *interahamwe* militias killing Tutsi.[21]

RDR's Relativisation of the Genocide

The RDR's first four press releases, signed by its executive secretary, Dr. Innocent Butare, do not employ the word "genocide." In *Press Release No. 6*, the RDR refers to the genocide as the time "when, last year, misguided elements of the National Army were implicated in inter-ethnic massacres."[22] In the RDR political platform, the start of the genocide is referred to as "the resumption of hostilities on 6 April 1994."[23] Thereafter, the RDR argues, "the territory controlled by the government fell into the hands of renegade adventurers, looters and killers who launched a campaign of ruthless slaughter against defenceless civilians."[24] In an attempt to minimise the scale and terrible nature of the genocide, the RDR uses numerous dismissive phrases and metaphors to characterise the violence, such as "the unfortunate April 1994 massacres,"[25] "crimes committed in the ethnic conflict"[26] and "inter-ethnic massacres."[27]

The RDR also accuses the RPF and Tutsi generally of "sensationalising" the genocide and using their version of the facts as political capital, in an attempt to win international sympathy and donor aid, "using, for political benefits, the tragedy which has plunged into mourning the Rwandan people."[28] Elsewhere, the RDR argues, "Diplomacy under the RPF regime, like all its policies, rests upon a shameful exploitation of the 1994 genocide used as a business asset... The RPF believes that it is entitled to anything...and plays thoroughly on the chords of commiseration and culpability" and that "victims of these massacres are found in all ethnic groups, just like their perpetrators. It is therefore

---

19   Ibid.

20   See "Cyangugu Trial Adjourned to July" (Fondation Hirondelle, News Agency 29 May, 2002), http://www.hirondelle.org/hirondelle.nsf/0/444cd3eba80a2225c1256722007fc11 1?OpenDocument.

21   Ibid.

22   RDR *Press Release No. 6*.

23   RDR Political Platform, 23 August 1998, http://www,rdrwanda.org/english/basic_principles.RDR_Political_Platform.html.

24   Ibid.

25   Ibid.

26   Ibid.

27   Ibid.

28   RDR Political Platform.

sadistic, shameful and immoral for the Kigali regime to use these massacres as a political alibi...."[29] Such views buttress the RDR's claim that the genocide is in fact a useful invention exploited by an unpopular, Tutsi-led government. In this view, while "the tragedy" covers the whole period from 1990—when the RPF invaded Rwanda from Uganda, sparking the civil war that preceded the genocide—the attempted annihilation of Tutsi itself is little more than a product of RPF political spin-doctoring.

Not only are such descriptions obscenely dismissive of the genocide, they also deny any notion of the massacres as a deliberate policy of the government in power in 1994, as authors such as Linda Melvern have analysed in detail, including in chapter 1 in this volume. According to the denial accounts, nothing about the genocide was premeditated: it was unforeseeable and therefore unpreventable. The killings were not supported by government policy and the government was not in any way involved in the genocide. This historical account removes from the authorities of the day all blame for the massacres and denies that they had ever propagated a genocidal ideology and systematically planned the extermination of Tutsi. It also illustrates the RDR's approach to history, contrasting its descriptions of the genocide as "misguided," "unfortunate" or acts of "banditry" with its portrayal of the RPF's actions during and after the genocide ("the RPF decided to attack and systematically massacre Hutu refugees"[30]; "the Kigali dictatorial regime is still going on with its deliberate extermination plans of large segments of the population"[31]) as part of a carefully orchestrated strategy of Tutsi domination.

The RDR describes the genocide as "the aggression, assassination, tortures and massacres perpetrated against the Rwandese population since 1 October 1990" or "the war launched by the Tutsi-led RPF in 1 October 1990 and its ensuing extreme violence that enkindled and exacerbated the Hutu-Tutsi rivalry, accusing the RPF of inciting and perpetrating crimes.[32] The RDR refuses to identify the genocide as a distinct and heavily orchestrated event, describing instead the entire period from late 1990 to the present day as a time of general "violence" and "tragedy."[33] This historical account interprets the RPF inva-

29 RDR, "Memorandum to the Heads of State, Heads of Delegations and Mediators Participating in a Regional Conference on the Great Lakes Region," 21 November 1995 (author's archive).

30 Ibid.; RDR Political Platform.

31 RDR Basic Principles (17 August 1997,) http://www.rdrwanda.org/english/basic-principles/Basic-principles.html..

32 RDR, "Rwandese Crisis: The Other Side of the Story" (July 1996,) http://www.rdrwanda.org/english/documents/RDR/RWACRISIS071996/html.

33 See for example, RDR, Memorandum to Burkina Faso President and OAU Chairman Blaise Compaoré and copied to Heads of State and Government of OAU member states, 21 May 1998 (author's archive). In a section entitled "Appeal to the OAU to restore peace

sion of Rwanda as the cause of all "violence" in Rwanda, deflecting blame for the genocide from the Habyarimana regime and its extremist ideologues. Instead, the RPF—and the entire Tutsi community—become the perpetrators of all violence in Rwanda since 1990, including the genocide of Hutu. "The RDR strongly condemns the Tutsi genocide," one statement reads. "The RDR renews its vigorous condemnation of the genocide... perpetrated against Hutu."[34] To not only deny that the genocide of Tutsi occurred but to accuse the RPF and all Tutsi of committing genocide against Hutu is the ultimate insult to living victims of the genocide of Tutsi and to their loved ones butchered in 1994.

The RDR's use of statistics and historical details to support such claims is particularly misleading. *Press Release No. 32* of 25 October 1995 argues that one million Hutu were massacred by the RPF[35] during what the RDR argues were acts of genocide[36], and elsewhere implies that this figure may be even higher.[37] According to the RDR political platform, "hundreds of thousands of Hutu" were "thrown into prison," after being accused of genocide crimes[38], when most commentators estimate that approximately 120,000 suspects were rounded up and imprisoned after the genocide. Meanwhile, the RDR refuses throughout its public statements to cite a concrete number of Tutsi victims before or during the genocide.

The RDR's discussion of "national reconciliation" also belies the RDR's denial and revisionist agenda. The following passage is particularly illustrative of this:

A lasting solution to the Rwandan crisis requires a frank and sincere dialogue between authentic representatives of political opposition and the Kigali regime. It also requires reconciliation between the different components of the Rwandan people. To make this happen, all truth about all aspects of the war must be told so that all political and social main actors, whether nationals or foreigners, acknowledge their failures and responsibilities in creating the atmosphere and the conditions that led to the disintegration of Rwandan society, to the promotion of violence, to confrontation, and to the tragedy.

While on first reading this may appear to be a reasonable statement, calling for different parties in Rwanda to come to the negotiating table to formulate

---

and security in Rwanda" the word "tragedy" is used several times in place of "genocide." (published in Brussels May 21, 1998)

34   RDR Basic Principles.

35   RDR *Press Release No. 32*, "What is president Bizimungu Pasteur Afraid of?" (25 October 1995), http://www.rdrwanda.org/english/press-releases/RDR/25_OCTOBER_1995. htm..

36   Ibid.

37   Ibid.

38   RDR Political Platform.

strategies for rebuilding the country, the intentions behind it are highly divisive. Not only does the RDR employ dismissive and morally neutral terms like "crisis" and "tragedy" that undermine the severity of the genocide, it also seeks to apportion all blame for past violence to the RPF, while abdicating the responsibility of the RDR membership—characterised as "authentic representatives of the political opposition"—for the genocide.

Ethnic Stereotypes in RDR's Discourse

The RDR regularly paints a one-sided view of Rwandan history and uses divisive stereotypes of Tutsi. From the outset, in its *Political Platform*, it claims that historically "political power [in Rwanda] was characterized by absolutism and exclusion" and "the current territory of Rwanda grew out of bloody wars waged by Tutsi kings against Hutu kingdoms." Consequently, "a repressive regime against the Hutu was initiated" and "this ethnic evil has left an indelible mark on the socio-political evolution of Rwanda from the feudal-monarchic regime through the colonial and republican regimes up to the current RPF regime."[39] Absolutism, exclusion and bloody wars are all attributed to Tutsi since the beginning of Rwandan history. "Tutsi kings against Hutu kingdoms" implies that there were always distinct and opposed ethnic groups and that Tutsi have always been expansionist and imperialist.

The only repression mentioned in this instance is that of Tutsi against Hutu, with no suggestion that Tutsi have ever suffered from oppression or discrimination. The "ethnic evil" that marks Rwanda is attributed to the Tutsi. This false and divisive account makes no attempt to convey any of the complexity and problems of Rwandan history. In the *Political Platform*, the RDR states, "furthermore, upon [the RPF's] victory in July 1994, more than 2.5 million people chose to flee the country rather than be subjected to a regime imposed on them by military force."[40] There is no mention of the genocide—particularly many individuals' desire to flee accountability for their actions—as the main factor in the exodus of refugees, with the RPF presented as the sole aggressor in 1994.

According to the RDR's negative stereotyping, Tutsi are characterised by their cunning, manipulation, lying and underhandedness. Several RDR documents contain explicit references to Tutsis' lying, for instance when *Press Release No. 97* of 22 October 1996 accuses the RPF of "alleging fictitious infiltrations of *interahamwe* [into its own ranks]."[41] Elsewhere, the RDR asserts, "The RPF has so much benefited from its policy of lying that it has institu-

---

39   Ibid.

40   Ibid.

41   RDR *Press Release No. 97*, "Tutsi Internationalism Throwing the Great Lakes Region into an Unprecedented Chaos" (22 October 1996)

tionalised it...The RPF has developed in a refined manner the art of lying."[42] As the RDR attempts to reinforce the claim that the RPF is dominated by liars, it argues that the international community has come "to consider the aggressed as aggressor and the aggressor as the aggressed; the main killers who in fact launched the war in October 1990 are today considered as victims of a genocide."[43] Other references are more opaque but continually reinforce the image of Tutsi as cunning, deceitful and manipulative. Mention is made of an RPF "trap," whereby refugees in the Zaire camps were forced over the border into Rwanda and massacred by the army, acts characterised as typically "underhanded" Tutsi behaviour.[44] "During [the Habyarimana] regime," the *Political Platform* states, "recruitment of Tutsi into the army, security services and the local administration was very limited. To circumvent their political exclusion, Tutsi invested their energies in business, industries and the church with great success thanks to connections they created with some high-ranking dignitaries within the regime and, as a result, they wield real influence in Rwandan society, economics and politics."[45] This account makes no mention of the systematic repression and exclusion of Tutsi after Hutu came to power in Rwanda in 1959. Rather, it suggests that Tutsi "infiltrated" Rwandan society, enjoyed secretive power and influence, favoured ethnic over national identity and harboured expansionist intentions. Such an implication adds to the stereotype of Tutsi being conspiratorial and naturally subversive, the same characterisation employed by the architects of the genocide to incite the Hutu population to murder Tutsi in 1994.

The RDR consistently portrays the RPF and, by extension, all Tutsi as outsiders and usurpers. Such distortion and reversal of historical reality, which belittles the significance of the genocide, is common throughout the RDR's documents. The RDR refers regularly to Hutu refugees as "Rwandan and Burundian"[46] refugees, while Tutsi refugees are referred to simply as Tutsi. The implication here is that Tutsi belong to their ethnic group, rather than to their nation, and that Hutu are the rightful heirs to power in Rwanda and Burundi. The governments in Rwanda and Burundi are described as "Tutsi-led"[47] or "minority"[48] regimes, implying a lack of popular credibility or an inherent injustice in anything but majority—that is, Hutu—rule.

---

42   RDR *Press Release No. 6*, Untitled (24 May 1995) See also *Rwandese Crisis: The Other Side of the Story.*

43   Ibid.

44   Ibid.

45   RDR Political Platform

46   RDR *Press Release No. 6*, (24 May 1995)

47   Ibid.

48   Ibid.

Maintaining the argument that the RPF and all Tutsi are outsiders, *Press Release No. 11* of 1 July 1995 states that the RPF's high command "is exclusively made up of former members of a foreign army" and refers to "the so-called national assembly,"[49] while another statement refers to "the so–called national parliament"[50] in Rwanda, reinforcing the notion of the illegitimacy of RPF rule in Rwanda. Generally speaking, in the RDR's press releases, the terms "RPF" and "Tutsi" are used interchangeably and contrasted with descriptions of Hutu as "true Rwandans," "the Rwandan people" and "the population."[51] The RDR continually attempts to distance the RPF from the "Rwandan people," implying that the RPF is not truly Rwandan and instead a self-imposed and discredited government; "a clique of individuals, who are desperately trying to cling to power against the verdict of the people."[52] Such statements echo the claim in the RDR's *Political Platform* that the RPF government "has no political or social base; it is not representative of the population. It is a government that took power through military force by an ethnocentric oligarchy, which so far has not been able to win the hearts of the people over which it rules."[53] The RPF is portrayed as an occupying force; an administration of non-Rwandans subjecting true Rwandans— Hutu—to repressive, minority rule.

The myth of Tutsi being "foreigners" or "outsiders" is not new in Rwanda. After 1959, successive governments maintained that the Tutsi were foreigners who needed to be eradicated. Killing Tutsi by throwing them in the Nyabarongo River was considered part of sending them back to their purported origin—Ethiopia, via the River Nile. In a more modern version of this argument, the RDR's *Press Release No. 67* of 17 April 1996 describes economic migrants and foreigners who have been given legal rights to property in which they had been "squatting" since the genocide, allegedly as part of an attempt by the RPF to "enhance its political constituency."[54] Such a policy, the RDR argues, is "rewarding those aliens for their contribution towards the RPF war."[55] This implies that the RPF is not a party for Rwandans; that to maintain power it must buy support from outside of the country and can only govern with the help of foreigners. An RDR statement on 4 June 1996 accuses the RPF of needing to "pay a moral debt to Tutsi in Zaire who financed the RPF war," alleging

---

49   RDR *Press Release No. 11*, Untitled (1 July 1995)

50   Ibid.

51   Ibid.

52   Ibid.

53   RDR Political Platform.

54   RDR *Press Release No. 67*, Untitled (17 April 1996)

55   Ibid.

that the RPF relies on foreigners, especially members of the Tutsi diaspora, to stay in power.[56]

The RDR often claims that it desires to create a Rwanda free of ethnocentric politics, but its language frequently belies this. In its *Press Release No. 6*, the RDR argues that the ICTR was established to "judge Hutu suspected of having committed the crime of genocide."[57] Such a statement is unnecessarily divisive: why not speak of "suspected *génocidaires*" rather than "Hutu"? The RDR's implication here is that Hutu are unfairly singled out and subjected to ethnic discrimination by their accusers. Despite purporting to want to banish divisive ethnic considerations from politics and from the national conscience, the RDR makes explicit comparisons between ethnic groups. For instance, in the aforementioned communiqué, the RDR asks, "what would the commission [tasked with investigating deaths in the Kibeho refugee camp] have said if, during the regime of the late President Habyarimana, Tutsi who had taken refuge in Kiziguro parish... had been forced out by firearms?"[58] In April 1994, thousands were killed in the Church of Kiziguro. The reference to Kiziguro is intended to show that a commission by, or for the government, must be considered for the Tutsi only. Such language reinforces the idea of different treatment for Hutu and Tutsi, and is intended to create resentment among the former. In the RDR's discourse, the concept of irreconcilable differences among Rwandans is predominant.

Further allusions to ethnic victimisation appear in a statement published on 4 June 1996, wherein the RDR describes the government's attempts to "demonise Hutu refugees with a view to exacerbating animosity against them," reduce international humanitarian assistance to the refugees, and create insecurity in eastern DRC so as to cut food and other supplies to Hutu refugees.[59] This statement, claiming that the RPF, being "Tutsi-led," must therefore want revenge on all Hutu, propagates the idea that Rwandan politics must be ethnocentric and that members of an ethnic group with power must automatically want to wield it against the other group.

RDR and False Depictions of the RPF

The RDR takes great care to sound reasonable and even-handed in all of its public pronouncements. However, beneath this veneer lies a litany of threats and warnings of future violence to restore Hutu rule in Rwanda. In *Press Release No. 97*, the RDR warns the international community about its policies toward

---

56   Ibid.
57   RDR *Press Release No. 6*.
58   Ibid.
59   Ibid.

the Rwandan and Burundian governments, cautioning, "It should be recalled that such an appeasement policy towards Hitler's expansionism led to the Second World War."[60] Comparisons between the RPF and Hitler were common in the openly anti-Tutsi *Kangura* newspaper before the genocide and spread beyond Rwanda's borders in an attempt to mobilise its neighbours to support the *génocidaires*. The "RDR Basic Principles" contains the passage: "the Kigali dictatorial regime is still...going on with its deliberate extermination plans of large segments of the population. Therefore, it is quite legitimate to think of another way of stopping those crimes and of protecting the population."[61] The reference to "another way of stopping those crimes and of protecting the population"—meaning protecting Hutu—frighteningly implies the possibility of using what the RDR, in later documents, euphemistically refers to as "non-political" action or violence to return Rwanda to Hutu rule, overcoming "the expansionist policies of the Tutsi-led governments in Rwanda and Burundi," which the RDR compares to "Hitler's expansionist policy."[62]

In the Zairean refugee camps, the RDR and the FAR planned to attack Rwanda, including to eliminate genocide survivors. Some of the minutes of FAR and RDR meetings, which I have gathered, show their macabre plans. For example, in one military operations meeting, chaired by Brig. Gen. Gratien Kabiligi (currently on trial at the ICTR) and attended by some FAR commanders and officers, it was concluded that:

The adopted method is to cleanse the countryside to be able to live. That consists of the physical elimination of any supporters of the RPF cause (acolytes, sponsors, supporters...)—those who escape will find refuge in urban centres or in parishes. Ops will lay landmines and traps; destroy roads and public buildings. The war must be mobile: attack in urban centres and hide in the countryside. The principle of cleansing the countryside by eliminating RPF sympathizers and especially the best-known survivors has been approved. That will allow our men to settle easily into rural areas and to take action in small urban centres and against other specific positions.[63] RDR misrepresentations are meant to dupe people who may otherwise be unaware of who is

---

60   RDR *Press Release No. 97.*

61   RDR Basic Principles

62   RDR *Press Release No. 97.*

63   "The Minutes of Military Operations Meeting," Bukavu-Zaire, 25 April 1996, (author's translation and archive); Participants: Gen Bde Kabiligi Gratien Comd 2nd FAR; Lt Col Ruhorahoza J. Bosco (G3 1 Div); Capt. Ntirugiribambe J. C. (Offr G2 1 Div); Maj. Majyambere Léopold (Offr G3 1 Div); Lt. Malizamunda Juvénal (Offr G3 1 Div & Sec. to the meeting); Maj. Rwabukwisi Alexis (Comd 13 Bde); Capt. Nsanzabera Elie (Comd 136 Bn); Lt. Baziruwiha Frédéric (Comd 134 Bn); Lt. Turatsinze Victor (Comd Bn Kagoma); Lt. Maniraguha Damien (Comd Bn Vautour); Capt. Harelimana Gérase (Comd 132 Bn); Lt. Habyarimana Joseph (Comd 133 Bn); Lt. Ndangamira (S3 13 Bde) (In the author's archive). [author's translation]

responsible for the genocide, to legitimise the genocide planners' evil actions, and to obscure the RDR's dark past and current membership.

The conspiracy theory of Tutsi expansionism was one of the first hate discourses employed by the genocidal ideologues. As early as November 1990, *Kangura* published an editorial alleging the existence of a "plan" by the Tutsi to conquer all of central Africa in what it titled, "The Tutsi plan to colonise Kivu and the African Central region."[64] Léon Mugesera asserted the myth of a Tutsi empire in early 1991, when he co-authored a pamphlet with the *Association des Femmes Parlementaires pour la Défense des Droits de la Mère et de l'Enfant* (AFAPADEM), in which he claimed that Tutsi intended to "[e]-stablish in the Bantu region of the Great Lakes (Rwanda, Burundi, Zaire, Tanzania, Uganda) a vast kingdom of the Hima-Tutsi, an ethnic group that considers itself superior, on the model of the Aryan race, and which uses Hitler's Swastika as its emblem."[65]

In February 1993, the *génocidaires* again spoke of the Tutsi empire. A press release of the CDR warned that the RPF was planning genocide of Hutu throughout the country in its pursuit of a Hima–Tutsi empire. The CDR demanded that the government provide the people with the necessary means to defend themselves.[66] This coincided with the government's training and arming the *interahamwe* and *impuzamugambi* militias.[67]

To paint a negative picture of the RPF and to deflect attention from crimes committed under pre-1994 Hutu regimes, the RDR often accuses the RPF of carrying out offences known to have been committed against Tutsi. In *Press Release No. 3* of 27 April 1995, the RDR alleges that "in order to finish off Hutus, the RPF has decided to collectively label all of them '*interahamwe*'."[68] This is an exact inversion of the ideology that preceded the genocide, when all Tutsi were seen as legitimate targets because they were all "accomplices" of the "*inkotanyi*" or "*inyenzi*," the Tutsi "enemy" whose only dream was to exterminate Hutu. The statement by the RDR goes on to allege that "all Hutu or any other person who do not subscribe to the ideology of the RPF must therefore be eliminated at any cost"—again, an exact description, in reverse, of the thinking that drove the genocide. During the preparations of the geno-

---

64   Editorial, *Kangura* No. 4, 2, Kigali (November 1990)

65   L. Mugesera, "*Toute la vérité sur la guerre d'Octobre 1990 au Rwanda*" (March 1991)

66   CDR's Party Release (25 February 1993) (author's archive).

67   *Interahamwe* belonged to MRND, while *Impuzamugambi* belonged to CDR. Both groups had the same ideological goal of committing genocide against Tutsi.

68   RDR *Press Release No. 3*, "RPF Unveils its True Colour," (27 April 1995)

cide, the message sent by the planners was to brand as a "traitor" any Hutu who did not subscribe to their heinous plan.[69]

International Media's Response to Genocide: Neutrality or Complicity?

The RDR has received significant assistance from the international media in propagating its agenda of genocide denial and revisionism. Foreign journalists have often played a destructive role in the Rwandan genocide and its aftermath. Their failure to adequately identify and report the crimes in 1994 as genocide was a critical factor in the international community's failure to intervene to halt the violence. The global media were also a major factor in generating world-wide humanitarian relief for the refugees who fled Rwanda after the genocide, including thousands of *génocidaires*.

In 1996 the Steering Committee for Joint Evaluation of Emergency Assistance to Rwanda published a report which included an important observation on the failure of the international media during the genocide:

By and large, the international media chose not to report (nor to publish if news reports were filed) evidence of plans and organising for large-scale massacres. This contributed to the failure by the international community to perceive the genocide for what it was and to insist on an adequate response. This failure occurred in spite of local media, which became dominated in the early 1990s by a radio station and newspaper whose vitriolic propaganda incited hatred and violence. Inadequate and inaccurate reporting by the media on the genocide itself contributed to international indifference and inaction.[70]

During the genocide, the international media was at first obsessed with the violence as drama. Most journalists showed little interest in the details of the ensuing events, focusing instead on the headline-grabbing news that "tribes" were killing "tribes," neighbours killing neighbours. The emphasis on the closeness of the people killing and being killed was meant to show the abnormality of the "combatants." For many news consumers around the world, the inhabitants of Rwanda, and Africa generally, were not humans but ferocious, two-legged beasts. Much of the global audience will still remember one inter-

---

69   One good example is a threat issued in the extremist paper, *Kangura*, in the Ten Hutu Commandments. The tenth Commandment read in part, "...the Hutu Ideology must be taught to every Muhutu at every level. Every Hutu must spread this ideology widely. Any Muhutu who persecutes his brother Muhutu for having read, spread and taught this ideology is a traitor." See *Kangura* No 6 (8 December 1990).

70   Joint Evaluation of Emergency Assistance to Rwanda, *The International Response to Conflict and Genocide: Lessons from the Rwanda Experience* (March 1996) http://www.um.dk/Publications/Danida/English/Evaluations/RwandaExperience/index.asp.

national magazine's sub-heading: "There are no more devils in hell, they are all in Rwanda."

Throughout the genocide, the international media failed to investigate the political and organisational structures established to facilitate the extermination of all Tutsi. The genocide was consistently described as a spontaneous flaring of ancient tribal animosity, a violent flow of lava-like anger and hatred, unleashed by the sudden deaths of Rwandan President Habyarimana and Burundian President Cyprien Ntaryamina after their plane was shot down over Kigali on the night of 6 April 1994. A typical report claimed, "The president of Rwanda was assassinated and the Hutu who are on the side of the government turned against the Tutsi who are considered to be closer to the rebels of the Rwandan Patriotic Front."[71] Almost a month after the beginning of the genocide, *Agence France Presse* still reported that "mainly Tutsi rebel guerrillas were besieging Hutu-led government forces" and clashes spreading in the "corpse-littered and blood-splattered capital," much as it described "inter-ethnic bloodletting" a month earlier.[72] Such descriptions implied that what the world was observing was a civil war, between the Hutu government and the Tutsi rebel movement.

Prof. Richard Robbins argues, "If we examine cases of purported ethnic conflict we generally find that it involves more than ancient hatred; even the 'hatreds' we find are relatively recent, and constructed by those ethnic entrepreneurs taking advantage of situations rooted deep in colonial domination and fed by neo-colonial exploitation."[73] Robbins observes that "there is no better case than Rwanda of state killing in which colonial history and global economic integration combined to produce genocide. It is also a case where the causes of the killing were carefully obscured by Western governmental and journalistic sources, blamed instead on the victims and ancient tribal hatreds."[74]

The press can make a vital contribution to the strengthening of peace and international understanding and to countering racism and incitement to violence. The aforementioned examples of simplistic and irresponsible reporting include instances of racism, portraying Africans as savages. Journalists like Fergal Keane, who methodically explored the causes of events in Rwanda in

---

71   "UN spokesman reports fighting in Kigali and Ruhengeri." *AFP* News Agency, Paris (6 May 1994).

72   "French troops warned not to interfere in RPF advance on Kigali." *AFP* News Agency, Paris (9 April 1994).

73   Richard Robbins, *Global Problems and the Culture of Capitalism,* (Boston, MA: Allyn and Bacon, 1999, 2002), 269.

74   Ibid.

1994, spoke out against simplistic or racist reporting and misrepresentation of the genocide as a tribal mêlée:

We must not report on countries like Rwanda as if they were demented theme parks, peopled by savages doomed to slaughter each other in perpetuity... Too much of the reporting of Africa has been conditioned by a view of its people as an eternally miserable smudge of blackness stretching across the decades...In the aftermath of the Rwandan genocide, there was far too much reliance on tired clichés about ancient tribal hatreds. The fact that this was an act of systematically planned mass murder, a final solution of monstrous proportions, was too often lost in the rush to blame the catastrophe on the old bogey of tribalism.[75]

Neutrality and impartiality are necessary principles in the art of journalism. However, some forms of so-called neutrality and impartiality when reporting on crucial moral issues such as genocide are misplaced and highly damaging. The fundamental issue here is the journalist's furtherance of neutrality in the face of genocide. Is it possible for a reporter to maintain the idea of neutrality when confronting such a crime? Is it possible to be neutral between a Tutsi victim of genocide and an *interahamwe* militiaman committing genocide; between a Jew who was killed in an Auschwitz concentration camp and a Nazi who killed him or her; between a black Sudanese who is killed by the Janjaweed militia on their horsebacks? Such crimes must be identified and denounced. In the face of such atrocities, there is no place for the kind of "neutral" descriptions that appeared in many international media outlets during the Rwandan genocide, seeking to describe a "balanced" view of the role of "both sides" in the conflict.

To fail to describe genocide as genocide—to characterise it simply as a civil war or the result of spontaneous violence resulting from long-harboured tribal animosity—is anything but neutral. It insults the victims of such egregious crimes and paves the way for the kinds of genocide revisionism and denial we have seen in the analysis of RDR propaganda above.

International Media Aiding Spread of Genocide Revisionism and Denial

Many of the sins of omission and commission of the international press during the genocide have aided the cause of genocide deniers and revisionists such as the RDR. Furthermore, the international media must be vigilant that it does not inadvertently create an environment in which the RDR can propagate its views or actively help the RDR spread its racist and genocidal ideology.

In Jean Kambanda's testimony to the ICTR investigators, as quoted above, he also stated that the RDR had managed to bypass the media and diplomatic

---

75   F. Keane, "Spiritual Damage," *Guardian* (27 October 1995) T4.

embargo that all *génocidaires* deserve and blamed the international community for playing a crucial role in giving undue credibility to the RDR. "As soon as this organization was formed, everything was done for people to believe and hope that the return was imminent. And I think the international community played an important role by giving exaggerated attention to this organization. They received so much attention from the international radio stations that the population in the camps couldn't help having confidence in them although in reality it was just hot air."[76]

From available documents, the RDR and the FAR pursued what they called "*Redynamisation de la campagne médiatique*" or "reinvigoration of the media landscape." In a confidential communication, from Chris Nzabandora who was RDR's commissioner for information, based in Nairobi, to the FAR's commander, Gen. Bizimungu, whose code name at that time was "Kamanda Yves," it was recommended that they target the BBC Swahili service and the English and Kinyarwanda services of the BBC and Voice of America (VOA), suggesting direct contact with BBC and VOA producers of their choice.[77] The document, which was edited by the FAR's chief of intelligence, Lt. Col. Bahufite (code named Maneno Sother)[78], established the RDR's policy on media:

MEDIA POLICY
In light of the step already taken and our experience so far, the new components of the media policy should aim for the following objectives: To maintain the media offensive to prevent the extension of the embargo into the media sector; To change the image of the *génocidaire* who continues to move among the Hutu refugees; To train the refugees politically by disseminating the appropriate information; To make known the truth about the Rwandan drama; To make the population in the interior adhere to our cause; To counter RPF propaganda; To guide the international community toward supporting our cause.[79]

In light of Kambanda's comments and the unearthing of the RDR's media policy, international press agencies must be on high alert to avoid giving the RDR and other genocide deniers a platform from which to propagate their abhorrent views.

---

76   Kambanda's testimony.

77   Nzabandora and Bizimungu agree: "The Swahili service of the BBC, the English services of the BBC and VOA, as well as the Kinyarwanda service of VOA and the BBC must be exploited and direct contact with their producers is recommended." (author's translation and archive.)

78   For example, the military chief of intelligence in his memo of 3 October 1996, proposes on page 4, "Encourage the International Community to support our cause." On page 5, he lists the following points: "c) List potential sources; d) Intensive email contact; e) Maintain and improve relations with these agencies; f) Mount an aggressive offensive against the RPF and its supporters; g) Mount as a priority a media offensive against Tanzanian opinion-makers," (author's translation and archives).

79   Ibid. (author's translation).

Accountability for Genocide Launderers

If we are serious about preventing genocide recurring in Rwanda and elsewhere through universal solidarity, preserving the memory of the genocide and fighting genocide denial, we must confront some crucial issues. Paramount among post-genocide concerns is to bring to account organisations of genocide launderers like the RDR. Banning such organisations, and punishing their members who propagate heinous genocide ideology, is vital to making calls for "Never Again" a reality. Direct action to deal with organisations like the RDR requires the political will of host countries such as Belgium, France, the Netherlands, Switzerland and Canada. Without these countries' willingness to counter genocide denial and revisionism within their own territories, such crimes will continue to afflict all of humanity.

In 2004, four Dutch organisations, CORDAID, ICCO, KERKINACTIE and NOVIB, published a report, in which they advocate for an "inter-Rwandan dialogue" between the Government of Rwanda and what they call "a coalition of most important Rwandan political groups in exile."[80] An umbrella body of the majority of these groups is *Concertation Permanente de l'Opposition Democratique Rwandaise* (or the Permanent Consultation of Rwandan Democratic Opposition [CPODR]).[81] The report vehemently criticises the Rwandan government for refusing this dialogue and donor countries for not pressuring the government to speak to the exiled groups. In the report, the authors acknowledge that some of the so-called Rwandan "opposition groups" currently based in the DRC have "génocidaires in their midst with whom some political exile groups might have links."[82] The grand wish of these monitoring organisations is to produce from groups such as the RDR "born-again" *génocidaires*, whose eligibility for inclusion in the dialogue with the government is their co-operation with the ICTR and condemnation of the "genocide and its ideology."[83]

---

80   Rwanda Monitoring Project Report, The Hague (February 2003) 28-29.

81   The RDR is a member of this umbrella organisation (CPODR). The suggestion by these NGOs that these organisations were important members of opposition, was not their original idea, but from a network of deniers, based in Spain. See, for example, where RDR is referred to as "the world's foremost organisation of Rwandan exiles" in "The reasons for an acceptance" Juan Carrero Foundation S'Olivar Estellencs, Mallorca, 8 March 1999; also "Action for peace and human rights at the Africa of the Great Lakes" Palma, 1 July 1999, www.pangea.org/olivar; Messages and Letters of Support to the Candidature of Juan Carrero Saralegui for the Nobel Peace Prize of the Year 2000 by Committee for the Nobel Peace Prize 2000 for Juan Carrero Saralegui, Mallorca (Spain) July 2000. For more information see the website of the RDR or one of the links "Inshuti" of http://www2.minorisa.es/inshuti/.

82   Rwanda Monitoring Project Report.

83   Ibid.

Conclusion

Violent words can injure as much as, often more than, physical assault. Genocide scholar Israel Charny highlights this when he argues:

Denials of known events of genocide must be treated as acts of bitter and malevolent psychological aggression, certainly against the victims, but really against all of human society, for such denials literally celebrate genocidal violence and in the process suggestively call for renewed massacres—of the same people or of others. ...Such denials also madden, insult and humiliate the survivors, the relatives of the dead, and the entire people who are the surviving victims, and are, without doubt, continuing manifestations of the kinds of dehumanisation and disentitlement that we know are the basic psychological substrates that make genocide possible to begin with. The deniers also are attacking the fundamental foundations of civilization, namely the standards of evidence, fairness and justice, by flagrantly altering the historical record. Indeed, the deniers always engage in a totalitarian overpowering of the knowledge process, fully intending to subjugate the integrity of human history, memory, scholarships, and communication to their demagogy and tyranny.[84]

Much of Europe is acutely aware of the dangers of genocide denial and alert to the need to ensure that what happened to their continent during Hitler's Third Reich is never repeated. As a result, it is illegal to form a Nazi party in Germany. Denying the Holocaust is a punishable crime in both France and Germany. The same is not true in the case of Rwandan deniers of the Tutsi genocides such as members of the RDR, who are not punished but, instead, often treated in the international media and elsewhere as legitimate political voices.

As the current situation in Darfur shows, genocide in Africa is still occurring. The evil of Rwanda in 1994 is repeating because genocide, its nature and causes, are still not yet fully understood and are obscured by the continuing denial of past atrocities. Genocide denial is simply a continuation of the original crime. Roger Smith correctly observes that "denial of genocide is the universal strategy of perpetrators. Those who initiate or otherwise participate in genocide typically deny the events took place, that they bear any responsibility for the destruction, or that the term 'genocide' is applicable to what occurred. Denial, unchecked, turns politically imposed death into a 'non-event': in the place of words of recognition, indignation, and compassion, there is, with time, only silence."[85] We should expect, therefore, that *génocidaires* will find ever-creative ways to deny their crimes. We must formulate determined

---

84   I. Charny, "The Psychological Satisfaction of Denials of the Holocaust or Other Genocides by Non-Extremists or Bigots, and Even by Known Scholars", *Idea: A Journal of Social Issues*, 6, 1, 17 July 2001, http://www.ideajournal.com/articles.php?id=27.

85   R. Smith, "The Armenian Genocide: Memory, Politics and the Future," in *The Armenian Genocide: Memory, Politics, Ethics*, (Richard G. Hovanissian (ed.) (New York: St. Martin's Press, 1992), 8.

and systematic counters to this denial, lest it encourage future perpetrators to commit similar crimes.

On 3 December 2003, the ICTR sentenced three defendants, including Dr. Ferdinand Nahimana, a famous Rwandan historian, in what has become known as "the Media Trial," the first time anywhere in the world that journalists have been tried for genocide. In the early 1990s, Nahimana was the Director of Rwanda's National Office of Information (ORINFOR) and later the director of RTLM. In her judgement read in public, the South African judge, Navanethem Pillay, said:

Fully aware of the power of words, [Nahimana] used the radio — the medium of communication with the widest public reach — to disseminate hatred and violence.... motivated by his sense of patriotism and the need he perceived for equity for the Hutu population. But instead of following legitimate avenues of recourse, he chose a path of genocide. In doing so, he betrayed the trust placed in him as an intellectual and a leader. Without a firearm, machete or any physical weapon, he caused the deaths of thousands of innocent civilians.[86]

Words can heal but also kill. Mass media has an immeasurable ability to shape public opinion. Bolstering peace in the Great Lakes region means involving the media in countering genocide denial and revisionism. A more ethical use of the media can counterbalance the negative effects and help respond to the damage caused by hate messages, used initially by the orchestrators of the genocide and since by groups like the RDR. Genocide launderers—and those who support them—must be held accountable for their assault on historical truth, which perpetuates the heinous crimes committed in Rwanda in 1994. If we fail to counter genocide denial and damaging revisionism, such as those spread by the RDR, we stand by and watch while the seeds of future genocides are planted.

---

86   Read in the summary of Judgement and Sentence of "The Prosecutor v. Ferdinand Nahimana, Jean-Bosco Barayagwiza Hassan Ngeze" *Case No. ICTR-99-52-T.*

7

WE ARE PRETENDING PEACE: LOCAL MEMORY AND THE ABSENCE OF SOCIAL TRANSFORMATION AND RECONCILIATION IN RWANDA

Susanne Buckley-Zistel

How do we keep the past alive without becoming its prisoner?
How do we forget it without risking its repetition in the future?

—Ariel Dorfman, *Death and the Maiden* (1991)

After extreme violence, coming to terms with the past is a major challenge for any society. The experience of pain and suffering is deeply inscribed in individual and collective memory, and perpetuated through the stories people narrate about the event, often keeping the dichotomy of us/them or friend/enemy alive, and obstructing paths to reconciliation. A necessary social transformation, which renders future massacres impossible, therefore depends to a large extent on the way the past is remembered.

In Rwanda, people who lived through the 1994 genocide of Tutsi and their Hutu and Twa sympathisers, as well as the 1990-94 war between the Habyarimana government and the Rwandan Patriotic Front (RPF), have different recollections of the past, depending on their role at the time and their situation today. Yet Rwanda's memoryscape is not simply informed by recollection. Eclipsing the past, if only in parts, is also a feature of coming to terms with the atrocities. Remembering and forgetting are equally important in post-genocide Rwanda. At first sight, what is remembered and what is forgotten seem paradoxical: while the event of the genocide, its death and destruction, is constantly evoked in conversations among Rwandans, discussion of the causes of the genocide and the decades of tensions between Hutu and Tutsi, including pogroms against Tutsi in 1959, 1962 and 1973, is being silenced and the past portrayed as harmonious.

What becomes apparent upon closer examination is that the absence of memory about past cleavages is less the result of an inability to remember than a conscious strategy by my interviewees to cope with living in proximity to "killers" or "traitors."[1] At the local level today, many Rwandans are *pretending peace*. Consequently, the way of forgetting, as I shall explore it in this chapter, should not be confused with a mental failure to recall, but with the intentional silencing of some aspects of the past. To describe this phenomenon, I shall introduce the notion of *chosen amnesia*, the deliberate loss of memory.

The objective of this chapter is to understand local processes of social transition and reconciliation in Rwanda. After depicting how ethnic cleavages have been polarised, if not invented,[2] through history and memory since colonialism, I shall proceed by highlighting which memories of the genocide are presently evoked, and which ones are forgotten in local discourses. The focus on memory, reflected in narratives about the past, will help us understand how identities are constituted in discourse and language, and whether they allow for greater group cohesion or reinforce the ethnic cleavages between Hutu and Tutsi which gave rise to genocide and other massacres. This discussion will then lead to an examination of the dangers inherent in remembering some aspects of Rwanda's past while eclipsing others. I conclude the chapter with some thoughts on how outsiders can support processes of social transformation and reconciliation in Rwanda.

Reconciliation processes in Rwanda

Generally, since the end of the Cold War, there has been an increasing interest in reconciliation processes around the world.[3] The founding of academic research institutes such as International Conflict Research (INCORE, University of Ulster), the South Africa-based Centre for the Study of Violence and Reconciliation (University of the Witwatersrand) and the recently-established Centre for the Study of Forgiveness and Reconciliation (Coventry University) reflects the importance of this issue. Many responses to violent conflicts are centred around themes such as law (punishment, compensation, deterrence);

---

1   The argument is based on substantial field research in Nyamata district in Kigali Ngali province (in particular around Nyamata town and Ntarama) and in Gikongoro province (around the districts of Gikongoro Ville, Karaba and Nyaruguru) in 2003-4. The sites were selected for their proximity to mass graves and genocide memorial sites, including Murambi, Karaba, Kibeho, Nyamata and Ntarama. Although there are substantial differences between the two regions, these differences are not relevant to the argument of this chapter.

2   In this chapter, the notion of ethnicity is not understood as an essential, primordial concept, but as a form of belonging that has become significant over space and time.

3   For an overview see A. Rigby, *Justice and Reconciliation: After the Violence* (London: Lynne Rienner, 2001).

history (truth); theology (forgiveness); therapy (healing); art (commemorations and disturbance); and education (lesson learning).[4]

Regarding Rwanda, much of the literature on reconciliation processes focuses on justice.[5] This mirrors a wider tendency among observers to concentrate on serious crimes, and to make justice one of the preconditions for a reconciliation process.[6] A predominantly top-down, judicial view of war-torn societies, however, misses the serious social impact of violence at the community level, as critically remarked by Laurel E. Fletcher and Harry M. Weinstein, professors at the Human Rights Center, University of California at Berkeley:

To date, truth and justice have been the rallying cries for efforts to assist communities in (re)building in the aftermath of mass atrocities. These employ a paradigm that focuses on individuals who have been wronged (victims) and those who inflicted their wounds (perpetrators). Missing is an appreciation for the damage mass violence causes at the level of communities.[7]

This chapter adopts a different approach, seeking to draw attention to local experiences of the genocide and their impact on community-based reconciliation processes in Rwanda. The focus is therefore on local, intimate environments of mainly rural Rwandans and how they come to terms with the horrific experiences of the past. This seems even more significant since there appears to be a gap between assumptions about an advancing national reconciliation process and the reality on the hills.[8] On a more general note,

[a] crucial problem in the post-conflict agenda relates to the lack of reliable, quality knowledge. Ambassadors, aid coordinators, and programme managers often feel that they do not know what's 'really' going on, even in the areas of direct concern to them.

---

4   M. Minow, "Breaking the Cycles of Hatred", in M. Minow (ed.), *Breaking the Cycles of Hatred: Memory, Law, and Repair* (Princeton, NJ: Princeton University Press, 2002), 27.

5   See for instance C. Fisiy, "Of Journeys and Border Crossings: Return of Refugees, Identity, and Reconstruction in Rwanda", *African Studies Review*, 41, 1 (1998), 17-28; A. Corey and S.F. Joireman, "Retributive Justice: The *Gacaca* Courts in Rwanda", *African Affairs* 103, (2004), 73-89; E. Daly, "Between Punitive and Reconstructive Justice: the *Gacaca* Courts in Rwanda", *International Law and Politics* 34 (2002), 355-96; S. Gasibirege and S. Babalola, *Perceptions about the Gacaca Law in Rwanda: Evidence from a Multi-Method Study* (Baltimore: Johns Hopkins University School of Public Health, Centre for Communication Programs, 2001); J. Sarkin, "The Tension Between Justice and Reconciliation in Rwanda: Politics, Human Rights, Due Process and the Role of *Gacaca* Courts in Dealing with the Genocide", *Journal of African Law*, 45, 2 (2001), 143-72.

6   For instance, Jean Paul Lederach, professor of International Peace-building defines reconciliation as situated between justice, truth, mercy and peace. See J.P. Lederach, *Building Peace: Sustainable Reconciliation in Divided Societies*, (Washington DC: United States Institute of Peace, 1997), 30. His argument has been adopted by Rigby (2001).

7   L. Fletcher and H. Weinstein, "Violence and Social Repair: Rethinking the Contribution of Justice to Reconciliation", *Human Rights Quarterly* 24, 3 (2002), 637.

8   This perception is based on conversations with national and international actors in Kigali during the fieldwork period.

Why are certain policies adopted, and what are their likely consequences? What divisions exist within political elites and the military? ... What does the population think about these matters? In many post-conflict countries, especially those where insecurity still reigns and where authoritarian regimes are in power, donors are groping in the dark with these crucial questions.[9]

In order to increase the availability of knowledge, this chapter will illustrate how antagonisms based on ethnic identities of Hutu or Tutsi persist between the parties to the conflict, revealing the continuity of ethnic cleavages and the absence of social transformation. While this observation is of course not surprising, after little more than a decade as well as the scale and horror of the 1994 genocide, it nevertheless finds little recognition among many Rwandan and international researchers and policy-makers alike.

Ontological impact of memory and amnesia

According to the political scientist Sandra Hinchman and Lewis Hinchman, narratives can be defined as "discourses with a clear sequential order that connects events in a meaningful way for a definite audience, and thus offer insights about the world and people's experience of it."[10] A narrative approach thus recognises that stories "are not simple representations of a reality but that they involve selectivity, rearranging, redescription, and simplification. Narratives mediate between the self and the world."[11] In other words, the past is never portrayed as it actually happened, but rather it is always interpreted anew, involving the deliberate but also often unintentional inclusion and exclusion of information. The way people explain their past therefore serves a particular function which may change depending on their audience and circumstances. These narratives can serve the purpose of establishing a collective identity and bounded community of all who share the same interpretation of the past. There is therefore a

dialectic relationship between experience and narrative, between the narrating self and the narrated self. As humans, we draw on our experience to shape narratives about our lives, but equally, our identity and character are shaped by our narratives. People emerge from and as the products of their stories about themselves as much as their stories emerge from their lives.[12]

---

9   P. Uvin, "The Development/Peacebuilding Nexus: A Typology and History of Changing Paradigms", *Journal of Peacebuilding and Development* 1, 1 (2002), 10.

10   L. Hinchman and S. Hinchman, "Introduction" in L. Hinchman and S. Hinchman (eds), *Memory, Identity, Community* (Albany, NY: State of New York Press, 1997), xx.

11   Ibid., xvi.

12   P. Antze and M. Lambek, "Introduction: Forecasting Memory" in P. Antze and M. Lambek (eds), *Tense Past: Cultural Essays in Trauma and Memory* (New York/London: Routledge, 1996), xviii.

The narratives on which people draw to refer to their past thus have a strong ontological impact. In the case of Rwanda, for instance, people are not simply formed by their experience of, say, the genocide, but also by the ways in which they refer to it. This performative function of narratives is particularly important regarding collective identities, since a common interpretation of the past helps create group cohesion. Remembrance can have a coercive force, because it creates identity and a sense of belonging.[13] By defining the relationship to the past, memory shapes the future.

Chosen amnesia

It is not only what is articulated in collective memory, however, that has an ontological impact, but also what is not said.[14] In Rwanda, aspects of the past seem to be eclipsed from the discourse, creating a form of amnesia, albeit selective, or what I call *chosen amnesia*. The absence of memory and history is equally instructive in an ontological sense, regarding the constant harking back to a past in order to constitute an identity in the present and future.

Two aspects are central to my notion of *chosen amnesia* as a framework within which to discuss social reconciliation processes in Rwanda. First, the term *amnesia* is used as an analogy for eclipsing the past. This is different from its traditional, psychological form, which makes reference to the lack of memory about events that occurred during a particular period. Here the loss of memory may be caused by severe emotional trauma, and is often temporary in response to an event with which the mind struggles to cope. It is important to note, however, that my use of the term "amnesia" in this chapter does not derive from a psychological, medical condition of repressed memory, but should rather be understood as an analogy for eclipsing the past or for not wanting to remember. Significantly, amnesia is different from remembering differently. It does not refer to a fading of memory or a different interpretation of the past, but to not wanting to draw on a particular recollection that is nevertheless still stored in the mind.

Second, therefore, "chosen" suggests a degree of agency; that is, a conscious selection process by an individual or a community to eclipse sections of the past. As stated above, the issue is not the assessment of a mental condition, but of a societal strategy of dealing with its tormenting experiences. This strategy points to an immediate benefit of not remembering, and thus serves a particular

13   P. Nora, "General Introduction: Between Memory and History", in P. Nora (ed.), *Realms of Memory: Rethinking the French Past, Vol. 1: Conflict and Divisions* (New York: Columbia University Press, 1993), 11.

14   For similar argument, see S. Buckley-Zistel, "Remembering to Forget: Chosen Amnesia as a Strategy for Local Coexistence in Post-Genocide Rwanda", *Africa* 76, 2 (2006). See also: S. Cohen, *States of Denial: Knowing about Atrocities and Suffering* (Cambridge: Polity Press, 2002).

function, which I will illustrate later in this chapter. In sum, *chosen amnesia* signifies the deliberate choice to not remember some aspects of the past.

My coinage of the term *chosen amnesia* is inspired by Vamik Volkan's notion of *chosen trauma*, which occurs when a group, after the experience of a painful event, feels helpless and victimised by another group. In Volkan's words,

the group draws the mental representations or emotional meanings of the traumatic event into its very identity, and then it passes on the emotional and symbolic meaning from generation to generation. For each generation the description of the actual event is modified; what remains is its role in... the group identity.[15]

In this sense, *chosen trauma* is produced by, and at the same time produces, a collective identity. The repetition of narratives about the traumatic event constructs the group's identity in opposition to the identity of the opponent who caused the trauma, and as such it becomes a social reality for those who participate in this discourse. A common identity, a "we-feeling", is shared between the people who recall the same past, rendering their social interaction meaningful.

While one of the functions of *chosen trauma* is to encourage group cohesion and a collective identity, *chosen amnesia* has the opposite effect. Through eclipsing of memory, the collective experience of an event is neglected, preventing the interpretation of a shared, group-specific past and the production of a "we-feeling." *Chosen amnesia* does not introduce a sense of closure, nor does it produce a bounded identity, but rather it allows for more flexible inclusion in, and exclusion from, collective identities. As I will show, this might be necessary when survivors and perpetrators live together in one community.

Whether an event is remembered or eclipsed is highly dependent on circumstances, environments and audiences. In one example cited by anthropologist Liisa Malkki, people with the same background—in her case Burundian Hutu refugees in Tanzania—could either draw their memory into their very identity, as was the case with refugees living in isolation in refugee camps, or try to escape their history, as did the urban refugees who preferred to assimilate into the Tanzanian society in order to survive.[16] Importantly, however, in the Rwandan context, not only do people have many different stories to tell or eclipse, but these different stories are also told at different societal levels. There are, among other divisions, strong local/national and public/private divides. It is crucial therefore to note that my concept of *chosen amnesia*, and its reference to reconciliation, is applied exclusively to local public memory, where "local" signifies the societal level of bounded communities and neighbourhoods. This is

---

15   V. Volkan, "On Chosen Trauma", *Mind and Human Interaction*, 3, 13 (1991).

16   L. Malkki, *Purity and Exile: Violence, Memory and National Cosmology among Hutu Refugees in Tanzania* (Chicago, IL: Chicago University Press, 1995).

opposed to the national level, where memory work is a highly politicised, top-down governmental project.[17] In turn, "public" refers to the discourse at broad communal levels, including often mutually distrustful neighbours or strangers, such as researchers (both foreign and national). This can be juxtaposed with the private, intimate realm of the family, in the safety of which specifically Hutu or Tutsi views of past, present and future can be shared.

The question arises, why do people in Rwanda opt for eclipsing key aspects of the past, particularly when the past is as disturbing as Rwanda's experience in the twentieth century? What is the benefit of avoiding the production of rigidly bounded communities and firmly fixed boundaries demarcating friend and foe? After a brief account of how the interpretation of Rwanda's history has led to ethnic cleavages, the following section will illustrate what is remembered in Rwanda today, in order to then show what is deliberately forgotten.

Divided through history: the origins of ethnic antagonisms

History and memory have been the source of conflict in Rwanda for decades.[18] Since the beginning of historical writing, first by German and subsequently by Belgian colonial anthropologists, Rwanda's historical discourse has essentially been a top-down political project either to establish group cohesion or separation.[19] The colonial administration introduced the since-discredited "Hamitic hypothesis", which argued that the Tutsi originated from northern and eastern Africa, while Hutu belonged to the Bantu people and constituted the indigenous population of the country. This account was subsequently adopted by Rwandan scholars such as Alexis Kagame, and in turn by large segments of the population.[20] Moreover, Tutsi, who constituted the monarchy and who allegedly bore a physical resemblance to Europeans, were inculcated by the colonialists with notions of superiority, while Hutu were identified as common farmers. With the advent of independence, the feeling of inferiority grew among Hutu,

---

17   Nevertheless, the national policy of remembrance and history-writing also includes a selective recollection of the past, but to discuss the national nation-building discourse would extend the scope of this chapter.

18   See for instance C. Newbury, "Ethnicity and the Politics of History in Rwanda" in D.E. Lorey and W.H. Beezley (eds), *Genocide, Collective Violence, and Popular Memory: The Politics of Remembrance in the Twentieth Century* (Wilmington: Scholarly Resources, 2002), 67-84; S. Ngesi and C. Villa-Vincencio, "Rwanda: Balancing the Weight of History" in E. Doxtader and C. Villa-Vincenio (eds), *Through Fire with Water: The Roots of Division and the Potential for Reconciliation in Africa* (Claremont: David Philip Publishers, 2003), 1-63.

19   For a more detailed account, see S. Buckley-Zistel, "Dividing and Uniting: The Use of 'Citizenship' in Conflict and Reconciliation in Rwanda" *Global Society*, 20, 1 (2006).

20   A. Kagame, *Un Abrégé de l'ethno-histoire du Rwanda* (Butare: Editions Universitaires du Rwanda, 1972).

leading to the so-called "Social Revolution" of 1959, which marked the end of royal Tutsi supremacy and the first pogroms against Tutsi.

Regardless of whether ethnic cleavages in Rwanda predate colonialism or were invented by European anthropologists, they prevail in present-day Rwanda. Since independence, ethnic differences have been successfully manipulated for political ends by various heads of state, most notably under the presidency of Grégoire Kayibanda (1962-73), as well as in the lead-up to the genocide in 1994. This manipulation manifested itself, for instance, in the successful oppression of Tutsi by authorities through manipulation of ethnicity and the achievements of the "Social Revolution" under Kayibanda. This was followed by his successor Juvénal Habyarimana (1973-94), who promoted a national development discourse that emphasised the existence of a Hutu peasant class while turning the Tutsi into feudal "enemies of the agricultural revolution";[21] and inciting ethnic hatred as a political strategy to maintain power between 1990 and 1994.[22] Until 1994, Tutsi were portrayed as foreigners, authors of injustice and enemies of the Republic, while Hutu identity was defined as the indigenous majority and former victims of injustice who emancipated themselves from the Tutsi monarchy in 1959.[23] In the 1980s this racism was less visible, and therefore was neither questioned nor abandoned. Racist prejudice between Hutu and Tutsi, but also Batwa, "was a structural feature of Rwandan society, fulfilling simultaneously important political functions for the elites and socio-psychological function for the peasant masses."[24] Nevertheless, in Rwanda and elsewhere, ethnicities should not be considered primordial features, and as necessarily in conflict, but rather

[r]egardless of the historical components of different segments of the population, what matters is the political significance of ethnic identities. In other words, the political relevance of ethnic identities is shaped by political context. It is politics that makes ethnicity important (or, indeed, unimportant), not ethnicity which invariably defines politics.[25]

In this sense, in the lead-up to the genocide, Rwandan historians such as Ferdinand Nahimana, professor of history at the National University of Rwanda

---

21   P. Verwimp, "Development Ideology, the Peasantry and Genocide: Rwanda Represented in Habyarimana's Speeches", *Journal of Genocide Research* 2, 3 (2000), 327.

22   A. Des Forges, *Leave None to Tell the Story: Genocide in Rwanda* (New York: Human Rights Watch, 1999).

23   F. Rutembesa, "Le discours sur le peuplement comme instrument de manipulation identitaire", *Cahiers du Centre de Gestion de Conflits*, 5 (2002), 83.

24   P. Uvin, "Prejudices, Crisis, and Genocide in Rwanda", *African Studies Review* 40, 2, (1997), 91.

25   C. Newbury and D. Newbury, *Identity, Genocide, and Reconstruction in Rwanda* (1995), Paper presented at the European Parliament, Brussels.

and director of the infamous radio station *Radio Télévision Libre des Mille Collines* (RTLM), one of the key vehicles of hate speech before and during the genocide, successfully exploited these politically-manipulated ethnic divisions to incite violence against Tutsi.

An awareness of the damaging impact of history on Rwanda's past has generated fierce debates among Rwandan scholars and political leaders about how national history should be portrayed. To illustrate the struggle over different interpretations, in 1998 a conference was held at the National University of Rwanda in Butare, provocatively entitled, *"Changements politiques survenues en 1959. Oui ou non, y avait-il une révolution?"* ("The Political changes of 1959. Was there a revolution or not?"). The scholars and intellectuals present were unable to find an answer to the question, and Rwandan history has not officially been taught in Rwandan schools since 1994.[26]

Remembering and forgetting today

In societies with poor formal education and knowledge transmission, such as Rwanda, collective memory, expressed in day-to-day encounters and oral history, is of greater significance than official history.[27] At the local level, in particular, the social environment shapes what is collectively recalled and what is forgotten.[28] Not surprisingly, after the genocide, remembering in Rwanda is not uncontested: different groups in Rwanda have different views on the past.

Many survivors, for example, have lost not only their loved ones during the genocide but also all of their property, and many therefore struggle to make ends meet. In addition, many women are infected with HIV/AIDS, since rape was used as a strategic weapon during the genocide, and are today, together with their children, dying slowly from the consequences of the genocide.[29] A large proportion of impoverished, rural survivors feels neglected by the gov-

---

26   According to the Director of Curriculum Development, Rwanda is still in the early stages of developing a national history curriculum, even though history is taught at some schools at the discretion of the individual teachers: Interview with the Director of the National Curriculum Development Centre, Ministry of Education, Science, Technology and Scientific Research, Government of Rwanda, Kigali (4 December 2003).

27   J.-P. Schreiber, *"Le génocide, la mémoire et l'histoire"*, in R. Verdier, E. Decaux and J.-P. Chretien (eds), *Rwanda: Un Genocide du XXe Siecle* (Paris: Harmattan, 1995), 169. An important point is that memory and history are not identical concepts. For a discussion see P. Nora, "General Introduction: Between Memory and History" (1993).

28   M. Halbwachs, *On Collective Memory* (Chicago IL: University of Chicago Press, 1992).

29   During the genocide, many rapists were aware that they were HIV/AIDS positive, and used their infection as a way of killing. For further discussion, see African Rights, *Broken Bodies, Torn Spirits: Living with Genocide, Rape and HIV/AIDS*, Kigali: African Rights (2004); and AVEGA, *Survey on Violence Against Women in Rwanda*, Kigali: AVEGA (1999).

ernment; their call for compensation has so far been ignored, for financial and political reasons.[30] Since the experience of the violence is central to their existence, remembering the genocide is of major importance and each year groups of survivors gather at the numerous memorial sites for commemoration events. The significance of memory is reflected in the following quotes:

We have to remember people who died in 1994. It is important to remember someone that you love, a relative, a friend. We have to commemorate it in order to put a mechanism of prevention in place, and to ask God to help us. For me, we cannot forget what happened.

(Elderly female survivor, whose son has confessed to participating in genocide killings, Gikongoro)

Yes, of course we have to remember in order to fight the ideology and to avoid this happening again. And a lesson for Rwandan youth is to be aware of what happened. So, for instance, when you touch a fire it hurts, and teaches you to avoid touching it again.

(Young male, born in exile in Burundi, who returned after the genocide, Nyamata)

A different attitude to remembering is expressed by the accused and their families. While the genocide is a prime example of mass participation in violence,[31] it is mostly Hutu who have been accused and imprisoned, although some have recently been released provisionally after confessing to their crimes.[32] Since the Rwandan justice system is completely overstretched, and the *gacaca* tribunals only reached the judgement phase of the process in 2005 and only in a few jurisdictions, most detainees sense that they have little hope of a fair trial in the near future.[33] At home, having a family member in prison is an immense burden on an impoverished Rwandan household, and many Hutu wives struggle, and often fail, to simultaneously cultivate the land and care for their children. Moreover, some Rwandans also support their prisoner spouses by providing food and clothing, placing a further burden on the family. Consequently, as the quotes below illustrate, many accused and their dependants feel that they are the true victims of the genocide. Furthermore, many Hutu perished after the genocide in refugee camps in the Democratic Republic of Congo (DRC), in overcrowded prisons or at the hands of the post-genocide Rwandan Patriotic

---

30   The national Compensation Fund, which designates 10 per cent of the annual budget to survivors, remains a contested issue in Rwanda. Not only is the country's budget far too small to pay compensation, it is also not sufficiently transparent, and to many rural survivors it is unclear whether the Fund actually exists and who benefits from it.

31   R. Lemarchand, "Coming to Terms with the Past: The Politics of Memory in Post-Genocide Rwanda", *Observatoire de l'Afrique centrale* (23 July 2000), 1.

32   African Rights, "Prisoner Releases a Risk for the *Gacaca* System" (Kigali: *African Rights* 16 January 2003).

33   Personal fieldnotes.

Army (RPA). Having lost spouses, parents, siblings or other relatives, many Hutu do not understand why they are not allowed to mourn their dead publicly and why they are not included in the national commemoration ceremonies, as illustrated below:

To remember is good, but it should be inclusive. For instance, my parents were killed during the genocide. But when they [the public] remember they remember only Tutsi, so I am frustrated because they don't remember my family.

(Young rural woman, Nyamata)

It is important not to forget the past so that we can prevent the future. But the bad was not only the genocide but also the Hutu who died in the DRC from diseases, and also those who were killed in revenge when they came back. Nobody has won this war; everybody has lost at least one family member.

(Elderly rural man, Nyamata)

What becomes apparent from the above quotes is that even though memory of the genocide is significant in Rwanda, there is a conflict over how it should be remembered. While some, in particular the survivors and their families, insist that only the agony of the Tutsi should be recalled, others argue that all suffering needs recognition. A closer look reveals that this split goes along Tutsi/ Hutu lines, illustrating, yet also perpetuating, ethnic divisions.

Paradoxically, in contrast to my interviewees' memories of the genocide as illustrated above, their memories about the ethnic cleavages that led to the genocide have today disappeared, and the past is described as having been harmonious. This is apparent in the following statements in which my interviewees portray the killings as a sudden rupture:

The war was created by the state and the authorities. We as peasants did not know what was happening. Before we were living together, sharing everything. Only when the genocide started did divisions start.

(Young man, Nyamata)

According to me, I cannot determine who is responsible for the genocide. We heard that people were being killed without knowing who planned it.

(Young rural woman with husband in prison, Nyamata)

You know, we did not know how it came. We were friends, the same people, sharing everything. We are innocent in this situation.

(Elderly male farmer, Nyamata)

Against the backdrop of the pogroms against Tutsi in 1959, 1962 and 1973, the insistence on past harmony is surprising since, as I argued above and as has also been stated by political scientist Peter Uvin, the Rwandan genocide was situated in a context of deeply entrenched images of ethnic divisions and dynamics of social exclusion.[34] Today, these divisions still find expression in day-to-day attitudes. A rich person, for instance, is occasionally referred to as "a Tutsi" regardless of her or his ethnic identity, while "I am not your Hutu" is used to fend off exploitation.[35]

Pretending peace

The public forgetting of past cleavages and antagonisms, however, does not mean that these divisions are of no importance today. Rather, this *chosen amnesia* constitutes a deliberate social coping mechanism to deal with the disruptive experiences of the past. The code of silence that constrains much of the post-genocide discourse of these issues is expressed in the following quotation:

Just after the war there were many problems. People returned from exile; there were also revenge killings. People could not talk to each other. Everybody was afraid of everybody. Today, it is as if we have forgotten everything. At the moment it does not exist any more. People never talk about the past because it brings back bad memories and problems. We pretend it does not exist.

(*Elderly man who had just been released from prison, Nyamata*)

This coping mechanism is necessary since, against the backdrop of rural life, many Rwandans often feel that they do not have the choice to articulate their grievances publicly because it would upset the social balance. They are concerned instead with going about daily life in the community. According to the Rwandan historian Charles Ntampaka, it may be two or three generations before the situation permits individuals to speak out about their experiences of the genocide.[36]

In many cases, motivations for local coexistence oscillate between pragmatism and fear. As for pragmatism, on the one hand, Rwandans have an interest in living together, simply because they have no choice. In an environment in which all depend on all, as is the case on the Rwandan hills, survival and prosperity require collaboration. When people fall ill, for instance, neighbours help each other to carry the sick to hospital. Cultivation of the fields is also more efficient when carried out collectively. Moreover, some survivors even find themselves dependent on the murderers of their family to bring water to their sickbed. The dependency of survivors, in particular, is expressed in the following statement:

---

34   P. Uvin, "Reading the Rwandan Genocide", *International Studies Review*, 3, 3 (2001), 97.

35   Personal fieldnotes.

36   C. Ntampaka, "Memoire et Reconciliation au Rwanda: Ecart Entre les Pratiques Populaire et les Actions de l'Authorité", *Dialogue*, 226 (2002), 17.

We have to be courageous. Living in the community, we cannot live alone. A survivor cannot live alone. For example, we live with a family who killed our relatives. We have to relax and remain confident, and pretend that there is peace. *Kwishyra mu Mutuzo.*

(*Woman of mixed parentage who was married to a Tutsi and had lost all of her and most of her husband's family, Gikongoro*)

The Kinyarwanda phrases *Kwishyra mu Mutuzo* or *Kwihao Amahoro* mean "pretending peace" and signify a coping mechanism by which all antagonism is silenced to maintain the social equilibrium. According to my interviewees, this concept reflects many people's *modus operandi* and often constitutes the only possible way of living in the midst of mutual distrust. This coping mechanism is what I have described as *chosen amnesia.*

Fear of the other group, on the other hand, is often linked to the prospect of testifying at *gacaca* courts, regardless of whether this is as a victim, witness or perpetrator. According to my interviewees, this sense of fear was heightened by the murder of several survivors in Kaduha in Gikongoro province, in 2003.[37] However, while survivors are more concerned with being eliminated as witnesses, Hutu fear being accused and imprisoned unjustly for social or economic reasons: denouncing, rightly or wrongly, a genocide perpetrator has become a convenient way of getting rid of personal enemies and competitors.[38]

It is not surprising, however, that, generally speaking, insecurity is a greater issue for survivors than for suspects and the wider population. In particular, survivors who have chosen to stay on their family's land in rural Rwanda, and who are thus in many cases surrounded by the families of those who killed their kin, are often subjected to intimidation, which has increased with the first waves of releases of genocide perpetrators since 2003.[39] Nevertheless, a frequent, almost paradoxical response of my interviewees to questions about security was "cohabitation is peaceful since we don't dare to attack each other"[40]—or, as stated by a representative of AVEGA, the widows' survivor organisation:

---

37   The number of survivors killed in Kaduha is variously estimated between two and four. See for instance IRIN, "Rwanda: Genocide Survivor Group Denounces Killings, Harassment", Nairobi, 16 December 2003, www.irinnews.org; IRIN, "Rwanda: Kagame Dismisses District Leaders over Genocide-related Deaths", Nairobi, 14 May 2004, www.irinnews.org; IRIN, "Rwanda: Five Sentenced to Death over Killings of Genocide Survivors", IRIN: Nairobi, 1 March 2004, www.irinnews.org. The increasing fear of witnesses since the murders was also the theme of a Coexistence Network meeting on "*La protection des témoignages du génocide: une des conditionnalités de la réussite du processus gacaca*", Kigali, 25 February 2004.

38   Interview with human rights activist, Kigali (26 April 2004).

39   Personal fieldnotes from Gikongoro and Nyamata, 2003-4.

40   Personal fieldnotes.

We don't have any problems living together. But we also don't have a choice. If we don't live together the genocide will start again.

(*AVEGA representative, Nyamata*)

Absence of social transformation and reconciliation

As illustrated above, memory and forgetting in Rwanda are selective, and serve the purpose of maintaining some form of social harmony in an environment where victims and perpetrators live side-by-side. Arguably, therefore, *chosen amnesia* is a necessity for local communities emerging from atrocities. From an ontological perspective, to deliberately eclipse some stories about the past prevents a sense of closure and fixed boundary-drawing between one identity group and another. It constitutes a deferral and deliberate leaving open of bounded, in this case Hutu or Tutsi, communities, which is essential for day-to-day survival and allows for "pretending peace".

This phenomenon resonates in professor of Peace Studies Andrew Rigby's argument that too much memory obstructs healing wounds of war, since the past continues to dominate the present.[41] Rigby argues,

the desire to cover up the past can also be the wish of people at the grass-roots. This is particularly so if many of them share a past that they would rather forget because of their active involvement in, or complicity with, the evil that was perpetrated in their name. For people who have been involved in phenomena such as mass violence that can happen in a civil war, it can certainly seem as if the past is best left behind. To introduce it into the present might lead to further bloodshed, conflict and pain.[42]

In contrast, but with similar implications, anthropologist Murray Last suggests that after violence, communities need time to come to terms with the experience of the past. "As 'wounded'," he argues, "metaphorically people turn in on themselves, curl up, lie still—at least until they get their strength back and the pain goes."[43] Last's comment recalls the German experience, where addressing the Holocaust and dealing with disturbing memories and feelings of guilt and responsibility have taken many decades and continue today. What was peculiar to the German experience, though, was that only a small number of Jewish survivors remained in the country, thus avoiding much direct confrontation between victims and perpetrators, which would have required an immediate resolution.

---

41   Rigby, *Justice and Reconciliation: After the Violence*, 2.

42   Ibid.

43   M. Last, "Healing the Wounds of War", Lecture at University College London, London, 2000 (M. Last's personal notes).

Rwanda, however, does not have this luxury of time and distance. Given the harsh living conditions and the intimacy of life on the hills, as well as the mutual dependency of many Rwandans, ethnic cleavages simply cannot remain unattended. A "memory wall"[44] against the recent past would bear serious dangers, since an unresolved past inevitably returns to haunt a society in transition.[45] As argued in this chapter and elsewhere in this book by Melvern, Kayigamba and Gasana, the 1994 genocide was, among other things, the result of pre-existing ethnic cleavages and subsequent feelings of resentment which people harboured, enabling the authorities to manipulate these emotions and to incite large parts of the population to kill. These circumstances persist: today, the prevailing social structures could again be exploited through hate speech and propaganda, potentially leading to new outbreaks of violence.[46] Crucially, only a transformation of the ethnic cleavages that run through Rwandan society can prevent future massacres. To date, such a transformation has not taken place. Despite the unity discourse of the Rwandan government, which promotes an all-Rwandan identity based on citizenship and not on ethnic identity[47]—as also explored in this volume by Kayigamba, Lemarchand and Hintjens—the dichotomy of Hutu/Tutsi remains effectively unchallenged, and is perpetuated in the current form of memory and amnesia as illustrated in this chapter. What is absent, yet required to overcome this problem, is a transformation of the way in which different groups relate to one another. For Rwanda, such a transformation process would entail challenging and changing the prevailing social structures of ethnic identity, so that people would not identify themselves as exclusively Hutu or Tutsi, or at least would not view these identity labels as conflicting. As a result of such a transformation process, peace in Rwanda would no longer be defined in negative terms, as the absence of violence, but in

---

44   P. Connerton, *How Societies Remember* (Cambridge UK: Cambridge University Press, 1989).

45   J. Sarkin, "The Tension Between Justice and Reconciliation in Rwanda: Politics, Human Rights, Due Process and the Role of *Gacaca* Courts in Dealing with the Genocide", *Journal of African Law*, 45, 2 (2001), 147.

46   My conclusions resonate in the concerns raised in the report on the findings of the Ad-hoc Parliament Commission on Genocide Ideology, which states that "[t]hose who revive the genocide ideology spread words and acts that stir up ethnic hatred and conflicts amongst Rwandans". (Ad-hoc Parliament Commission on Genocide Ideology, *Final Report: English Summary*, Kigali: Parliament of Rwanda, June/July 2004).

47   To discuss the national unity and reconciliation strategy of the Rwandan government would exceed the scope of this chapter. Arguably, however, the promotion of an all-Rwandan identity takes place without addressing the cleavages and problems at the root of the conflict, and thus constructs a top-down unity without reconciliation. The introduction of closure through enforced unity bears the danger of new antagonism and resentment, since differences are being eradicated and legitimate grievances silenced. For a detailed discussion see S. Buckley-Zistel, "Dividing and Uniting", op. cit.

positive terms as being, ultimately, "about restoring sociality, about establishing the trust necessary not just to tolerate but to cooperate in partnership that can survive even the threat of failure."[48]

Supporting transition and reconciliation

From a more practical perspective, the question remains, how can such a local transformation process be encouraged by those outside these communities, such as national or international organisations? How can the mediation of different forms of memory and amnesia, as illustrated in this chapter, be assisted so that they support reconciliation processes?

Crucially, given the impact of the experience of violence at the local level, external organisations must find means of supporting transformative processes that originate within communities.[49] What is discernible, in conversations with individuals and groups of survivors, suspects and their families, and more impartial community members, is a request for mediation or facilitation between victims and offenders, in order to move out of their stalemate situation of *chosen amnesia*. In Rwanda, the necessary local change-agents, who seek to contribute to reconciliation processes in their immediate environment through mediating between Hutu and Tutsi communities, are few but nevertheless do exist. Their efforts are often hampered, however, by a lack of support and interest by larger national or international peace-building organisations. Asked about their requirements, these actors often reply that they would appreciate receiving support at their immediate, local level where their work can have the greatest impact, rather than being subsumed into national projects. Many change-agents state that national NGOs are often too involved in advocacy and politics in the capital, resulting in a poor local presence and the ignorance of needs at the community level.[50] They lack an understanding of the deep fissures that continue to run through local communities.

---

48 M. Last, "Reconciliation and Memory in Postwar Nigeria" in D. Veena, A. Kleinman, M. Ramphele and P. Reynolds (eds), *Violence and Subjectivity* (Berkeley, CA: University of California Press, 2000), 379.

49 D. Pankhurst, "Issues of Justice and Reconciliation in Complex Political Emergencies: Conceptualising Reconciliation, Justice and Peace", *Third World Quarterly*, 20, 1 (1999), 255.

50 This absence was very apparent during my interviews in rural areas of Gikongoro and Nyamata. With the exception of some individuals—mainly survivors in towns or recently established villages (*Umudugudu*) who were members of the survivors' organisations IBUKA or AVEGA—almost none of my interviewees had ever been consulted about their experience of the genocide and the reconciliation process. Although some had heard about national NGOs or the National Unity and Reconciliation Commission (NURC) they knew neither their mandate nor their programmes. Consequently, the majority of interviewees welcomed my interest in their circumstances, and the opportunity to articulate their views.

Consequently, my survey of non-governmental reconciliation projects revealed that—instead of seeking to mediate antagonisms between Hutu and Tutsi communities—most projects focus almost exclusively on justice-related issues such as *gacaca* or human rights[51] or on the needs of only one party, such as survivors (though all of these are of course important in their own right).[52] My survey exposed a shocking absence of projects dedicated to bringing the former parties to the conflict together—be they self-contained or in relation to *gacaca* or other projects—preventing them from addressing the underlying prevailing social structures of ethnic identity.[53]

This omission can be explained through current preferences in peace-building strategies.[54] In Rwanda and elsewhere, peace-building projects conducted or funded by international organisations, in particular, often give salience to visible demands and interests. These include the reintegration of demobilised soldiers, restoration of the justice sector, development assistance to deprived regions, and support for decentralisation and democratisation. While all of these

---

51 To what extent the *gacaca* tribunals can contribute to reconciliation processes in Rwanda remains to be seen. On the basis of the present trials to date, some tensions between *gacaca* justice and reconciliation are already discernible, although with varying degrees in different districts. In brief, the causes for setbacks include corruption of *gacaca* judges and witnesses, intimidation and harassment of witnesses prior to testifying, verbal abuse of survivors giving testimony, the opening of wounds, limited trust in truth being spoken during trials (according to a 2003 survey 60 per cent of the general population expects "a large amount of false accusations" to be made during *gacaca*: see NURC, *Sondage d'Opinion sur la Participation à la gacaca et la Réconciliation Nationale*, Kigali: NURC (2003) 13), debates over *de facto* limitation of *gacaca* jurisdiction to genocide crimes to the exclusion of war crimes, manipulation of outcomes through social and political power holders, partial or false confessions and enforced attendance of population at *gacaca* sessions. While NGOs such as African Rights and Penal Reform International (PRI) have drawn attention to the pitfalls of *gacaca* for some time, even the Rwandan parliament and government have recently acknowledged its flaws. (Ad-hoc Parliament Commission on Genocide Ideology, 2004, 10-12 and République du Rwanda/Service National des Juridictions *gacaca*, *Le Fonctionnement des Juridictions gacaca qui ont terminé leur 7ème Réunion*, Kigali: République du Rwanda/Service National des Juridictions *gacaca* (21 January 2004). See also African Rights, *gacaca Jurisdiction: A Shared Responsibility*, Kigali: African Rights (January 2003); LDGL, *Enquête sur l'Etat des Lieux des Juridictions gacaca au Rwanda: Rapport Provisionaire*, Kigali: LDGL (December 2003).

52 Survey conducted in the course of the fieldwork in Rwanda in 2003-4.

53 In recognition of this deficit, at a recent Coexistence Network meeting it was proposed to extend the *gacaca* tribunals with victim-offender mediation, and first steps have been taken to develop such a programme. (Coexistence Network meeting on *"La protection des témoignages du génocide: une des conditionnalités de la réussite du processus gacaca"*, Kigali, 25 February 2004).

54 For a discussion of the art of peace-building after civil conflicts, see, for instance, R. Paris, *At War's End: Building Peace after Civil Conflict* (Cambridge University Press, 2004); and for a critical appraisal of current donor projects in Rwanda, see S. Buckley-Zistel, "Between Past and Future: An Assessment of the Transition from Conflict to Peace in Post-Genocide Rwanda", DSF paper 15 (2008), www.bundesstiftung-friedensforschung.de

components are important, they are nevertheless based on an understanding of conflicts as deriving from incompatible goals, such as the distribution of resources, facilitating access to power, or overcoming injustice and inequality.[55] In short, they all revolve around "interests" that can be negotiated among the parties to the conflict. What is being left untouched, though, is the "identity" aspect of conflicts, such as between Hutu and Tutsi in Rwanda. According to Norbert Ropers, director of the Berghof Foundation for Peace Support,

> Disputes ... typically operate at two levels: the more or less openly negotiated level of political demands and interests, and the deeper level of collective experience, stances and attitudes integral to the formation of identity. An important role in constituting and shaping these two levels is played by events in which large numbers of the members of a group have been the victims of despotic rule, expulsion, military conquest, or some other form of violence. ... If, in such instances, conflict management is confined solely to the negotiation level and to an apparently "reasonable" balance of interests, there will be a danger that the neglected "deep dimension" of collective experiences, traumas, and attitudes will manifest itself as an inexplicable "irrational" derangement.[56]

In order to highlight the necessity to also address tensions at the identity level, this chapter has sought to illustrate these neglected "deep dimensions" of lingering antagonisms between Hutu and Tutsi, through referring to what is remembered and what is forgotten. Significantly, at the local, public level ethnic cleavages are subjected to *chosen amnesia,* silencing prevailing tensions and leading many external observers to conclude that there has been significant improvement regarding local reconciliation processes. However, to acknowledge these fissures—and the subsequent risk of future violence along ethnic lines—requires a shift of peacebuilding efforts, away from so far almost predominantly interest-centred approaches to one that also seeks to address the transformation of the prevailing ethnic cleavages between Hutu and Tutsi. Instead of being nationally driven, such an approach demands a locally situated, bottom-up strategy emanating from those whose lives have been most affected.

The progress of reconciliation at the community level, as portrayed in this chapter, might appear pessimistic and in contrast with many other accounts.[57] Given the enormity of the crime of genocide and the particularities of Rwanda's

---

55   For further discussion, see S. Buckley-Zistel, "Development Assistance and Conflict Assessment Methodology", *Conflict, Security and Development*, 3, 1 (2003), 119-29.

56   N. Ropers, "Roles and Functions of Third Parties in the Constructive Management of Ethnipolitical Conflicts" (Berlin: Berghof Research Center for Constructive Conflict Management, 1997), 8-9.

57   See, for instance, the media coverage of the reconciliation process in the Rwandan Anglophone national newspaper. e.g. "Rwanda is Moving Forward to a Unified, Peaceful, Just and Democratic Country – Kagame", *New Times* (17-19 March 2003), 3; "Interahamwe Courier, Survivor Reconcile", *New Times* (16-19 Oct. 2003) or the collection of speeches by Paul Kagame reprinted in Uma Shankar Jha/Surya Narayan Yadav, *Rwanda: Towards Reconciliation, Good Governance and Development* (New Delhi: AIA, 2004).

living conditions, this is not surprising. And yet, after fourteen years, it is time to face the past and to challenge the prevailing, antagonistic ethnic cleavages. Caught in the deadlock of past, present and future, it is time to ask how people can escape the prison of memory without choosing a form of amnesia that risks repeating the same crimes. How can Rwandans overcome the prevailing cleavages to establish a lasting peace?

8

CONFRONTING CONFLICT AND POVERTY THROUGH TRAUMA HEALING: INTEGRATING PEACE-BUILDING AND DEVELOPMENT PROCESSES IN RWANDA

Solomon Nsabiyera Gasana

Introduction

Emotional healing is vital in the process of achieving peace and human security, individually and collectively. In this chapter, I describe a healing process that allows individuals and groups to engage meaningfully in peacebuilding and poverty alleviation. This wider healing journey draws heavily from my personal experiences as a survivor of conflict in the Great Lakes region. As a witness to and victim of violence, I personally struggled for years with my inner woundedness. This blocked my ability to find meaning in my past and to understand the purpose of my future, until I discovered a journey towards healing that released my inner strength for resilience and growth. The experience of healing of my inner trauma has greatly shaped my peacebuilding efforts. In my work with the community development organisation World Vision in Rwanda, I have sought to help both genocide survivors and perpetrators regain a sense of inner freedom and recover functional capacities and the creativity necessary for social and economic productivity. Therefore, I draw on my dual experiences as a survivor and peacebuilding practitioner to offer insights into the importance of healing for responding to conflict and poverty.

That it is necessary to connect development and peacebuilding processes in post-conflict societies is no longer controversial among scholars and practitioners. The United Nations' Brahimi Report defines "peacebuilding" as "activities undertaken on the far side of conflict to reassemble the foundations of peace and provide the tools for building on those foundations something that is more than just the absence of war," including "promoting conflict resolution and

145

reconciliation techniques."[1] Meanwhile, the UN Development Programme (UNDP) defines "human development" as the ability of people to

> develop their full potential and lead productive, creative lives in accord with their needs and interests... expanding the choices people have to lead lives that they value... Fundamental to enlarging these choices is building human capabilities — the range of things that people can do or be in life. The most basic capabilities for human development are to lead long and healthy lives, to be knowledgeable, to have access to the resources needed for a decent standard of living and to be able to participate in the life of the community.[2]

Most sources accept that development and peacebuilding processes function symbiotically, and from this basis many have tried to integrate the two sets of processes in a variety of settings. These attempts at integration, however, have rarely achieved satisfactory results.

In my career in the field of peace-building and development, I have repeatedly confronted the issue of why the coordination of these two realms has so far had only a limited impact in terms of constructing a stable and strong Rwandan society. As Rwanda's reconstruction policies began to shift from emergency to development work in the late 1990s, I began to consult other NGOs to learn which frameworks they were using to integrate initiatives of development and peace-building. I quickly discovered that many organisations considered the integration of these processes as simply the concurrence of the two fields. In most instances, these organisations' processes of transforming conflict and eradicating poverty were kept separate in terms of their objectives and approaches. In many projects, the evaluation of objectives could not show whether development work had contributed to peace or vice versa. No framework of indicators existed to evaluate the common purposes and effects of the two fields. As well-intentioned as many activities of peace-building and development in Rwanda may be, they have rarely managed to coordinate their transformative processes and objectives.

My aim in this chapter is to explore strategies that can help poor communities in a conflict setting initiate their own processes of sustainable peace and economic growth. While my findings focus primarily on peace-building and development in Rwanda, I draw also on lessons from the Democratic Republic of Congo (DRC), where I have been involved in similar work.

In this chapter, I address three main sets of questions. The first is a logical issue. Regarding the domains of peace-building and development, should one constitute the foundation of the other? Should we begin to reconstruct

---

1   United Nations, "Report of the Panel on United Nations Peace Operations", UN Doc. A/55/305-S/2000/809, 21 August 2000, 3.

2   United Nations Development Programme, "What is Human Development?", UNDP, http://hdr.undp.org/hd/default.cfm.

post-conflict communities through peace-building or development initiatives? Is it necessary to begin both simultaneously? Are there common approaches or strategies that pursue the objectives of the two fields? In asking these questions, my intention is neither to suggest the supremacy of one field over the other, nor to imply that one field alone provides sufficient answers to the issues facing impoverished and conflict-ridden communities. Rather, my aim is to understand strategies to design efficient integrated peace-building and development interventions to rebuild post-conflict societies. In answering this question, I will argue that in post-conflict societies, peace-building is a necessary foundation for development.

Second, how do peace-building and development intersect? Conflict and poverty are, respectively, the main issues underlying peace-building processes and development work. Do conflict and poverty have interactive causes and effects? The means of coordination of the two fields can be found by analysing, first, the common causes of poverty and conflict and, second, how an increase in poverty affects the propensity to conflict and how violence causes and deepens poverty. In short, what are the common denominators in these fields that can be integrated in the same transformative processes?

To understand these common denominators, we must first define the causes and effects of both poverty and conflict and their intersection within a given social structure. On the one hand, an analysis of causes and effects should clarify why and how economic development often creates inequalities; on the other, we need to understand how divisions between different groups, along with the animosity and trauma that they generate—especially in communities affected by competing identity claims—influence productivity capacity and economic competition. In post-conflict societies, battles for economic, political and social power can produce fractured social structures, a culture of exclusion, human right abuses, bad governance, corruption and unhealthy competition for resources and violence.

Finally, what are the principles that underlie the structures or dimensions of conflict and poverty transformation in which we operate? Within which structures do we expect change to take place? What are the dimensions that provide and sustain this transformation? Uniting the various strands of my argument in this chapter is the contention that achieving peace and development after mass conflict involves healing through transforming human relations and social structures, which have been severely damaged during conflict. To achieve long-lasting peace and development means healing individual wounds, rebuilding solidarity among individuals and groups and revitalising fractured communities. In this sense, peace-building and development require systematic processes that address personal, emotional and psychological dimensions of conflict, as well as broader, structural questions of power and inequality.

147

Building transformative development processes on a peacebuilding foundation

If a practitioner decides to integrate processes to overcome conflict and poverty, where does she start? I argue here that transforming conflict and poverty must start from a foundation of peace-building initiatives. The reason why we should view peace-building as a necessary foundation for development is that conflict not only damages physical structures but also tears the communal fabric, leaving feelings of suspicion and mutual rejection among members of the community. After conflict, community members often experience a loss of shared interest and sense of belonging, which severely damages the community's ability to achieve economic development after conflict.

The Rwandan genocide was a cataclysm almost unparalleled in human history. It destroyed Rwandan society, greatly damaging local and traditional capacities for resilience. When people feel emotionally and physically unable to cope with daily life as a result of trauma, this hampers their ability to participate in development work. Furthermore, when the social structures that connect people and provide healing by building empathetic relationships are damaged, this weakens the community's capacity to fight poverty.

The damage wrought by conflict on local capacities for change is well highlighted in a recent survey conducted by the Rwandan National Unity and Reconciliation Commission (NURC). The survey aimed to assess the impact of efforts of post-genocide decentralisation, democratisation and development on national unity and reconciliation. The survey of 6,146 respondents concluded that the "the level of trust among community members is weak and constitutes an obstacle to community development because it is harder to undertake community development without a minimum of mutual trust."[3] Mutual suspicion and cleavages between groups based on ethnic divisions do not necessarily imply that community members from different groups would refuse to work together on community projects. In fact, many development workers throughout Rwanda have witnessed immense growth in the number of local micro-business associations that include members from both ethnic groups. However, the existence of such associations does not necessarily imply a restoration of healthy relationships or solidarity within the community. As the same NURC report argues, "people tend to rally in the face of adversity without there necessarily being a mutual trust among them," a claim supported by the fact that "41% of the interviewed said that nothing is done in the community unless the authorities force people to act."[4]

---

3   National Unity and Reconciliation Commission, "An Opinion Survey Report on the Process of Democratization in Rwanda" (Kigali: NURC, 2004), 27.

4   Ibid.

In such fragmented communities, many development efforts will achieve few tangible results because solidarity among community members is so severely lacking. It is clear from the findings of the NURC survey that the belief, held by many scholars and practitioners, that development work alone can restore relationships and build peace, does not apply in the case of Rwanda. That Rwandans from all ethnic groups can cooperate to pursue development objectives does not necessarily mean that they have rebuilt their relationships. Therefore, peace-building initiatives in a society as fractured as Rwanda's must constitute the foundation of sustainable development work. Without restored relationships, there can be no long-term development. While individuals can build solidarity around development activities, their energy often stems from extrinsic motivations based on personal gain, rather than on feelings of communal belonging. In such instances, solidarity and harmony are not in themselves community goals, but palliative means to attain certain objectives.

The fragility of post-conflict societies such as Rwanda's also calls into question the strength of solidarity built around work. How long can work-based solidarity withstand the trials of internal conflicts that can also result from intense work-related interactions? In many circumstances, development itself exacerbates conflicts of interest and identity. These conflicts can become more pronounced, as competing interests increase along with heightened productivity and demand for goods and services. For example, during my peace-building and development work in Rwanda, when I visited local sub-district offices, I was often struck by the multiplicity of legal cases of business and farmers associations in the local *gacaca* jurisdictions (which are explored in more detail elsewhere in this volume by Steward, Schabas, Ngoga and Clark).[5] Some of these cases lasted for years, deeply damaging the efficiency of the associations themselves, as well as relations between their members. Most of these conflicts have brought to the surface long-standing ethnic animosities between different individuals and groups.

Finally, cycles of violence always challenge the reconstruction of post-conflict communities. People who have been previously excluded from mainstream economic and social activities related to their livelihoods tend to treat others as they were treated. The process of estrangement recycles through future generations. Consequently, those who feel marginalised within certain economic and social structures often express their grievances by venting frustration and

---

5   I refer here to traditional *gacaca* jurisdictions facilitated by the local sub-district officers known as "executive officers of *secteurs*" to settle and mediate disputes among community members. These jurisdictions, which deal with low-level disputes, differ from the official *gacaca* hearings that prosecute genocide suspects. To differentiate the two jurisdictions, the Rwandan government recently renamed the former *abunzi*, a Kinyarwanda word meaning "mediators".

anger towards themselves, their families and even towards public economic and development programmes. They often develop risky and destructive behaviour such as having unprotected sex with multiple partners, alcoholism or drug abuse, and sometimes even commit suicide as means of expressing their need for recognition after conflict.[6]

To break this cycle of violence and poverty, economic and development work must build on social justice principles, good governance and social structures that respond to people's basic human needs, values and motivations, such as identity, security, recognition, participation, dignity and justice.[7] However, the first steps towards breaking the cycle of violence and poverty must incorporate a personal and community journey of psychological healing. Without healing, there can be no lasting peace and therefore no genuine development after conflict.

A personal journey of healing. My conviction that healing is central to any attempts to meaningfully connect peacebuilding to poverty alleviation stems from my personal experiences of healing, as a survivor of conflict in the Great Lakes. As a survivor who also engages in peacebuilding processes, I have often found myself in a difficult, but ultimately useful and rewarding, position of engaging—and helping others to engage—in rebuilding our personal and collective lives after the genocide in Rwanda. Many of my personal experiences of healing have inspired my efforts to help others seek healing, reconciliation and economic development in their communities.

I was born into a family of Banyamulenge (Congolese Tutsi) on the Mitumba plateau, currently known as Minembwe territory in South Kivu in eastern DRC, amid the period of turmoil and wars that characterised the aftermath of post-colonial independence in the Great Lakes in the 1960s. Three of my first eight years were spent in temporary shelters, as civil unrest and ethnic conflict forced my family and community to flee our homes. We lived in total poverty after losing all of our cattle during fighting, and the bitterness of my parents taught me to hate those who drove us to such destitution. Predictably, the repeated ethnic violence of the colonial and post-colonial periods has been passed on to subsequent generations of Rwandans and Congolese. I was not spared this education in ethnic cleavages, which was reinforced by the formal education system. The history and civic education we received as students emphasised supposed ethnic differences between Tutsi (Hamites), Hutu (Bantus) and Twa (Pygmies). In nearly every interaction with teachers and fellow stu-

---

6   L. Schirch, *The Little Book of Strategic Peacebuilding* (Intercourse, Pennsylvania: Good Books, 2004), 24.

7   J. Burton, *Resolving Deep-rooted Conflict: A Handbook* (Lanham: University Press of America, 1987), 54-8.

150

dents, I was reminded that I was a Tutsi, an alien, who originated in Ethiopia. Among my teachers were Rwandan Tutsi who had taken refuge in the east of Zaire (now the DRC). They told us of their experiences of ethnic violence; how Hutu massacred their relatives, looted their property and drove them out of their country, just as we had experienced violence in Zaire. Such stories produced constant fear within me, and I concluded that my entire ethnic group was threatened. My fears were reinforced by the ethnic hatred and practices in the political system that excluded all Tutsi from power. There was some respite in the 1970s, when my cousin Frederic Gisaro was a member of the Zairean parliament. After his death, all Banyamulenge were denied Zairean citizenship and the right to vote. We were also denied the right to join student unions and our parents were barred from any local administrative structures.

Such divisions created regional, ethnic coalitions among communities and institutions. The solidarity between Zairean Bantu/Hutu, originally from Rwanda and Burundi, against Tutsi in Zaire was the most threatening. I was a victim of such destructive solidarity. Once a group of Zairean Bantu and Burundian Hutu refugees caught and beat me badly, simply because I was a Tutsi. I was left unconscious with a broken arm. This was not an isolated incident. Many acts of violence and murder against Tutsi occurred in the 1980s on university campuses and in communities, perpetrated by a coalition of Hutu and other Zairean Bantu groups. The violence became more pronounced in eastern Zaire in the early 1990s, after a coalition of Tutsi from Uganda, called the Rwandan Patriotic Front, attacked Rwanda in 1990, and more so after the assassination of Melchior Ndadaye, the Hutu president of Burundi, in 1993. These events led partly to the genocide of Tutsi in Rwanda and Zaire, while the spiral of violence in Burundi continued to cause deep divisions between Hutu/Bantu and Tutsi/Hima.

The leadership in the region used these historical discriminations to promote national inequalities, based on ethnic identities. Major social and cultural institutions, such as churches, provided little opposition to the atmosphere of ethnic divisions and violence. As a young man, I was intrigued and confused by how the widespread conflict around me devalued the Christian faith, which was embraced by 90 per cent of the population but seemed to exert so little influence over people's views and actions. Individuals and groups who had different ethnic identities, but nonetheless claimed to share a Christian faith, lived in a state of perpetual animosity.

These community divisions and conflicts had an immensely negative effect on me. I held grudges and secretly nurtured a desire for revenge against those who subjugated my community, the Tutsi. These emotions were collectively shared by all members of my ethnic group, my clan and my family. The narrative of hatred and fear dominated the daily conversations and news throughout the entire community, increasing people's trauma.

I rationalised, and even actively defended, the violent retaliation of my ethnic group against other groups. Consequently, I lost emotional and psychological energy, which was consumed by a sense of personal unrest as I struggled to control my inner pain and anger.

As a young adult, however, I began to question the values I had acquired. In a state of internal revolt, I resolved to search for solutions to my sense of inner conflict that reflected the wider conflicts around me. One solution was to study human behavioural sciences to better understand the underlying issues in a conflict society such as Rwanda's or Zaire's, and thus to explain my personal pain and the deep divisions evident in my community. Shortly after my university studies, though conscious of my limited experience and the cultural prejudices related to my young age, I engaged in efforts to help my church community settle some of its internal conflicts related to questions of ethnicity. My efforts began to bear fruit, in terms of facilitating new forms of dialogue between different individuals and groups. This encouraged me greatly and started a period of personal growth as well as a commitment to peace-building processes in my society more broadly.

I soon discovered that working on peace-building and reconciliation processes aided my personal healing. Since 1997, my engagement in post-genocide peace-building and reconciliation has not only benefited others but has also allowed me to deepen my personal sense of healing and has increased my commitment to, and understanding of, issues related to conflict.[8] As I reflected on my personal transformation, I recognised that I had experienced a profound journey of healing and that this had involved seven stages. These stages simply reflect my efforts to explain the complex, undulating journey of healing. It is not as linear a reality as is described here, but rather a highly dynamic process involving many complicated intermediary experiences.

First, my whole journey of healing began with a desire to engage in peace-building work and to help those affected by the genocide. To begin healing, I

---

8   The main workshops that transformed my life are the following. First there was the "Personal and Community Development workshop (PDWs) designed by Prof. Simon Gasibirege of the National University of Rwanda (see Steward's chapter in this volume for further discussion of the PDWs). Later I participated in other similar processes such as "Healing the Wounds of Ethnic Conflict" (HWEC) designed by Dr Rhiannon Lloyd, and the "Healing of Memories" workshop designed by Father Michael Lapsley, a white South African priest who fought apartheid for many years before losing his two hands, an eye and an ear as a result of a letter bomb. Later I attended another workshop called "Strategies for Trauma Awareness and Resilience" (STAR) at the Center of Justice and Peacebuilding at the Eastern Mennonite University, Virginia, designed as a response to the psychosocial effects of the 9/11 attacks in the US.

first needed to look outward; to consider the needs of others. As I listened to other survivors' stories of incredible pain, I felt my own memories resurfacing intensely. They triggered anger, hatred and bitterness towards members of the ethnic group that oppressed mine. These emotions raised serious contradictions between my sincere commitment to peace-building work and my capacity to embody the peace and reconciliation message I was conveying.

Second, I chose to explore my past and how it fitted within a shared history of the conflict between Tutsi and Hutu. To explore history would help me answer some critical questions as an attempt to give meaning to my pain: How had the hatred between Hutu and Tutsi developed to the extent of causing genocide? What specific factors fuelled ethnic hatred? Are the effects of ethnic conflict reversible? What can we do to help ourselves and subsequent generations end cycles of victimisation and violence? I decided that I needed to find a group of Hutu and Tutsi willing to wrestle with these questions and to struggle honestly and openly together to find meaning in what happened to our nations.

Third, I discovered that the best way to engage truthfully with others in answering key questions about the past was to openly share and tend to others' emotional and psychological wounds. There is immense power in being able to express the personal meaning of past experiences to a sympathetic audience. I resolved to share my thoughts and emotions verbally and through many tears. Initially, during this process, I found myself condemning those whom I considered offenders: myself (my feelings of personal guilt from hating others and my inability to change the situations around me), God (for His failure to assist His children who were targeted during the massacres and genocide), and those who had perpetrated crimes. I was consumed by sorrow, anger and fear as I remembered my personal losses, especially those of family and friends who were killed in 1994 and in 1996 in Zaire/DRC, by Congolese and Hutu *interahamwe* militias from Rwanda.

Fourth, I chose to accept my past and sought to release myself from its grip. This proved to be the most difficult stage of my healing journey. To seek liberation from my pain generated an inner dilemma: I preferred to consider myself a victim because it attracted others' pity and gave me a sense of belonging as a member of the victim group. Being a victim allowed me to claim the right to revenge or at least to threaten my offender with revenge. However, I also wished to be free from the pain that consumed my emotional, psychological and physical energy and caused me to be constantly ill, haunting me with memories that connected me daily with the past and blocked my hopes and dreams for the future. Therefore, I had to decide consciously to pursue liberation from the past. Through sharing my experiences with others and continuing to help them with their own feelings of sorrow and loss, I gradually felt liberated from my own bondage of self-pity, sorrow, anger and hatred. My negative feelings were slowly transformed into virtues. I moved from fear to confidence, from sorrow to joy, from guilt and shame to an acceptance of myself and others, from hatred to love, from a desire for revenge to a commitment to help bring peace to my community.

Fifth, my healing journey required a stage of forgiveness. In most of the languages and dialects spoken in the Great Lakes, the word for forgiveness is *kubabarira*. The radical word *kubabara* means "feeling the pain." The deep meaning conferred on forgiveness in our culture is therefore to feel—to actively share in—someone's pain and suffering. Before my healing journey, I demanded an apology from those who had wronged me and my family, as a precondition of forgiveness. I asked myself, "How can I forgive the Hutu who vowed to exterminate us and who have never expressed a sign of guilt or shame to me or my ethnic group?" But as my inner pain decreased, I began to understand that the benefits of freedom gained through forgiveness are foremost my own. I needed to recover my lost humanity, my love of others and of myself. As I shared my pain with others and expressed my struggle to forgive, I regained a sense of inner peace and compassion. I felt more willing to understand the causes of the offenders' hatred of me and of Tutsi generally. I began to ask questions such as: What made them lose their humanity? How do they feel today about their actions? I began to understand how anger and hatred consumed their energies, how they struggled to master their guilt and continued to suffer the consequences of their actions. I felt pity and compassion towards them. My personal journey made me realise that I could not deepen my healing experience without first being willing to forgive those who had committed crimes against my loved ones and me. Healing required that I share in the pain of the perpetrators of genocide, for example, their pain and that of their families as they were detained for their crimes, often in terrible conditions. Forgiveness deepened my healing process, as it liberated me from the hatred of my offenders that I carried everywhere.

Sixth, after finding it possible to forgive genocide perpetrators, I moved towards a place of reconciliation, where I believed it was possible to live and interact with the people whom I previously hated. Although I could never identify the exact individuals who killed my relatives, I hated the perpetrators' entire ethnic group, all Hutu, and considered them my enemies. Over time, however, as some of them shared their pain with me and expressed shame and apology on behalf of their ethnic group, I felt willing to extend my forgiveness and my apology for the oppression of Hutu during the reign of the Tutsi monarchy in Rwanda and during Tutsi collaboration with the Belgian colonial regime. I began to build friendships with Hutu, particularly those who shared my vision and commitment to the work of reconciliation.

I found that connecting with Hutu in my work and visiting them in prison, to hear stories of their personal experiences, were acts of reconciliation. Connecting with perpetrators of the genocide of Tutsi in Rwanda was a most transforming experience. As I listened to their stories, I discovered that some of the Hutu in Rwanda succumbed to mass manipulation by the government of the day. One genocide suspect detained in Butare attended a World Vision group therapy workshop. During group sharing, he was overwhelmed by shame and guilt for what he did in 1994. He sobbed as he described his pain: "I will never understand why I took part in the genocide. Why did I decide to join the mob that went to kill my neighbours, simply because they were Tutsi, when at the very same time I was protecting eight other Tutsi in my home? I even rescued two Tutsi from the pit latrines where they were thrown after being mutilated by their captors. I also cannot understand why no one among my parents, elders, my spiritual leaders and friends tried to stop me committing crimes." The man expressed a sincere apology to all Tutsi. Later, I witnessed other Hutu sincerely confessing their crimes. These confessions made me rehumanise Hutu, people whom I previously viewed as beasts.

Finally, the efforts of my engagement in peace-building and reconciliation efforts began to bring rewards. As my work began to flourish, my commitment to it increased. My work with World Vision involved helping others along their own healing journeys. I heard amazing testimonies from people who experienced profound healing, forgiveness and reconciliation: Alexis, who forgave the killer of his relatives and offered financial assistance to his family; Elie, who confessed his genocide crimes and made reparations to his victims' families; Delphine, who forgave the killer of her father who had confessed his crime to her; Deborah, who forgave and adopted as her own child her son's killer, whose own parents were killed during the genocide. Observing others' experiences like these renewed and confirmed my life commitment to peace-building and reconciliation.

Healing: source of energy restoration for development initiatives. One of the most fundamental initiatives in development work in post-conflict societies is helping people to develop mechanisms of resilience and trauma healing. As illustrated in my personal narrative above, healing is central to peace-building work because all acts of violence leave emotional scars. People affected by conflict constantly relive painful memories of fear, sorrow, anger, hatred and hopelessness. Such pain must be healed to enable new or renewed social connections, through subsequent peace-building processes such as negotiation, mediation, restorative justice, governance and leadership development. Unless pain is healed, it is difficult to regain hope and to rebuild peaceful relationships.

Furthermore, until hope is restored and relationships healed in a given community, its members cannot focus on development work. People struggling with inner pain from atrocities often became dysfunctional and unproductive. In the aftermath of the genocide in Rwanda, survivors have often struggled to rebuild their lives, more than those who have returned to Rwanda from long exile in neighbouring countries, such as Uganda, Burundi and the DRC, because the former continue to wrestle daily with their inner turmoil. When I began working in survivor communities with World Vision in 1999, I was struck by how many survivors lacked energy and displayed immense apathy toward most aspects of their lives. Some of them came to my office to ask for assistance. I would reply with a single question: How can I help you most effectively? Their answers were almost always the same: give me food and build me a house. If World Vision provided construction materials, however, genocide survivors often sold them for personal gain. Most survivors wanted handouts and had little interest in productive activities. World Vision's first attempts to organise genocide survivors into micro-credit associations failed, because few survivors wanted to work together. Many survivors failed to generate income from the loans given to them and simply consumed the funds within a few weeks.

Initially, I judged the survivors as lazy. During counselling sessions with them, however, I came to understand their condition more deeply. I realised that many survivors simply lacked energy because of trauma after the genocide. Those who were able to begin a process of recovery and healing began to demonstrate a capacity for, and an interest in, productive work. I concluded that unless survivors experienced healing of their trauma, they would not be able to overcome their poverty.

I witnessed the same dynamic among the national staff at World Vision Rwanda. When I began working there, I observed that there was little acknowledgement of trauma within the organisation, until we began recognising signs of dysfunctional behaviour, a general lack of energy and even conflicts among workers. In a paper published in 2000, two colleagues and I noted that "national staff will be variously victims, agents and witnesses of all the violence that has gone before or may still be going on. Individuals may be shocked and traumatized, bitter and vengeful, fatalistic and apathetic, paralyzed by unexpressed grief."[9] Unless our Rwandan workers could deal with their own trauma, they could not be agents of change in their communities.

Trauma can be an individual and collective experience. In Rwanda, trauma is often collective because the traumatic events of the genocide—the attempt to exterminate the entire Tutsi population—were lived collectively. Through my

---

9   W. Nyamugasira, L. Ndogoni and S. Nsabiyera, "Telling a Different Story", in M. Janz and J. Slead (eds), *Complex Humanitarian Emergencies: Lessons from Practitioners* (MARC, CA: World Vision, 2000), 193.

practical experience, I began to reflect on how psychosocial healing processes help an individual or a whole community to sustain a process of resilience and productivity. I concluded that healing trauma occurs most effectively when people focus on emotional and physical sensations related to traumatic events and increased awareness of these sensations.[10] Such healing is vital to individuals' and communities' abilities to build peace and eradicate poverty.

The trauma healing journey: avoiding the traps of conflict and poverty. In Rwanda there are many testimonies, case studies and lessons documented by field practitioners that demonstrate how people can address their pain and begin a journey of healing, and how healing processes can in turn help transform individual and community peace and development capacities.[11] Inferring my conclusion from my own personal healing journey and learning principles from practice, I argue that healing in fact contributes to peace-building and development work, by encouraging individuals to embark on three separate "journeys."

First, healing provides a "Journey of Energy Recovery" that is crucial for development. People suffering from psychological and emotional pain survive through coping mechanisms that require immense supplies of energy. Emotional and psychological energy is lost during inner struggles to suppress regular explosions of anger, vengefulness and guilt that many survivors experience after conflict. Energy is also consumed through nightmares, insomnia and daily strategies to avoid contact with those considered to be the "enemy", such as those who killed or injured loved ones during the genocide. Rhiannon Lloyd, a Welsh psychiatrist who has been working in Rwanda since 1994, illustrates the concept of "restless energy consumption" with the metaphor of a string that binds the offender and the offended, even when one of them has died or lives far away. The string signifies the ways in which painful memories constantly haunt the victim. "Unforgiveness binds us forever to those who have sinned against us," Lloyd argues. "They will continue to devastate our lives until we release them in forgiveness."[12]

The journey of energy recovery often produces two main outcomes. First, individuals often experience a sense of liberation from inner emotional and

---

10   P. Levine, *Waking the Tiger: Healing Trauma* (California: North Atlantic Books, 1997), 173-220.

11   For example, people who attended the PDWs developed by Gasibirege and the HWEC designed by Lloyd (Nyamugasira, op. cit.) testify that these workshops allowed them to discover the painful emotions they harboured such as fear, anger, grief, hopelessness, hatred and suspicion. They chose to face them, to feel, name and process them, using verbal, physical and symbolic expressions in a space where mutual respect and empathy make participants more attuned to each other's vulnerability (Ibid).

12   M. Janz and J. Slead (eds), *Complex Humanitarian Emergencies: Lessons from Practitioners* (Monrovia, California: World Vision, 2000), 194-201.

psychological struggle. This increases their capacity to renew energy and direct it towards more productive initiatives, such as rebuilding previous relationships and fostering new interactions with others and their environment. Second, many individuals testify that once they have experienced healing, they can consider the possibility of forgiveness, repentance, reparation, justice and rebuilding relationships, even with their offenders or the person offended, or simply with people across the ethnic divide.

A second crucial healing process is a "Journey of Hope Renewal." Conflict kills not only people but also the survivors' sense of hope. Genocide survivors in Rwanda often demonstrate signs of incredible hopelessness and an inability to envision the future. I have heard stories of people who refused to send their children to school because, in many communities during the genocide, educated people were the first targets of violence. Other survivors sell construction materials because they cannot see far enough ahead to envisage ever living in new homes, or simply lack the willpower to build them. Some survivors claim to have lost the faith in the divine that they had before the genocide. They believe that God, or other supernatural powers that should have protected them and their families, have become powerless. Many survivors feel abandoned by God or protective spirits. Therefore, they believe that nothing remains beyond their own ability to build a better life in the future. As mentioned earlier, many survivors display signs of lethargy and withdrawal from society and many become dependent for their material survival on NGOs and their neighbours' charity.

Third, the healing process of a "Journey towards Togetherness and Connectedness" is crucial to peace-building and development. Many survivors suffer frequent flashbacks and sorrowful memories, which attach them to their deceased loved ones. I once heard of a man who lost his wife and three children during the genocide but remarried one year later. Although the new marriage gave him three more children, he confessed during a World Vision healing workshop that he never felt love and compassion toward his new family: "My true wife and children were those who died," he said. "These new ones were only like a band-aid on my wound." He confessed that he had never expressed love toward them nor hugged them until after his healing process began.

Survivors such as this man often struggle to reconnect with their wider communities after conflict because harmful memories prevent them from engaging meaningfully with others. As a result, many survivors become trapped in a state of miserable loneliness, thinking that they are the only ones who have suffered immense personal loss. On rare occasions when they dare to connect with others to release some of their pain, meetings with fellow survivors often lead only to more complaints, and to survivors' compounded sense of misery and victimhood.

Individuals who have gone through healing processes, however, claim that they have been able to create bonds of companionship and friendship with others, regardless of their ethnicity and whether they had previously considered them enemies. Such bonds of togetherness result from the sharing of past pains that individuals have experienced or caused. Many participants in healing processes discover a common past of suffering and a present state of inner woundedness. Having established these feelings of commonality, they often feel ready to offer mutual help and support to help nurse each other's pain and to pursue renewed relationships, which is the "journey of togetherness".

Healing is a key starting point for peacebuilding initiatives, as well as a firm foundation for any sustainable development. As Daniel Taylor-Ide and Carl E. Taylor argue, "a crisis weakens the community's vital resources. The wounds must be healed and strength rebuilt for forward progress. Otherwise, fracture lines may open up again, with crisis breeding further crisis."[13]

Conflict and poverty transformation processes

Having established the centrality of healing for peacebuilding and development processes after conflict, I turn now to the issue of how exactly we should integrate peace-building and development. This section describes a general process created to allow practitioners to design and implement integrated programmes to reduce poverty and conflict.

Two main implications emerge from this section. First, peace-building and development involve similar processes and use the same terminologies to describe the progression of the transformation envisaged. Conflict and poverty issues are interrelated in their causes and effects within a society. For example, both problems result from power inequalities, religious or identity-based ideologies or prejudices sustained within social, cultural and economic structures. Their effects include powerlessness and alienation. The ultimate common goal of peace-building and development interventions is therefore to transform broken or imbalanced relationships through healing, justice, education, empowerment, and social, economic and cultural integration processes.

Second, after identifying the shared domain of peace-building and development, it is possible to design an intervention that integrates processes that transform both conflict and poverty. There is a gap of knowledge in the intersection of the two fields, that is, in designing indicators that help practitioners to plan, monitor and evaluate evidence regarding how their interventions transform pov-

---

13   D. Taylor-Ide and C. E. Taylor, *Just and Lasting Change: When Communities Own Their Futures* (Baltimore, MD: Johns Hopkins University Press, 2002), 89.

erty and conflict. This knowledge gap explains why few practitioners have successfully designed programmes that integrate peace-building and development.

The following section does not attempt to design new indicators of peace-building and development or to critically review existing indicators. The task of designing a framework of indicators requires further research. The following section instead focuses on the second question outlined in the introduction to this chapter—exploring the intersection of, and particularly common denominators between, peace-building and development—by describing the overlapping causes, effects, objectives and strategies of processes of conflict and poverty transformation.

Analysis of causes and effects underlying structures of poverty and conflict.
Considering first the structures of violence and poverty, it should be noted that these things are often located in a cycle, in which poverty causes conflict and violence causes underdevelopment and poverty. These interconnected and complementary causes sustain structures of poverty and conflict. For example, social and economic injustice resulting from rejection, mistreatment and exclusion based on identity is likely to trigger conflict. When conflict escalates to violence, it causes loss, grief and trauma. Traumatised people lose creative and productive energy. Unproductive, impoverished communities sink progressively into poverty, while losing social, economic and political power. The poor often struggle to regain power through expressions of grievances without triggering further cycles of violence.

This cycle of violence and poverty is defined by James Gilligan and Lisa Schirch in the theory of "structural violence." Gilligan defines structural violence as "the death and disabilities that are caused by the economic structure of our society, its division into rich and poor."[14] Gilligan argues that "structural violence is not only the main form of violence, in the sense that poverty kills far more people (almost all of them very poor) than all the behavioural violence put together; it is also the main cause of violent behaviour." Gilligan suggests that "eliminating structural violence means eliminating relative poverty."[15] Discussing the strategic analysis of violent conflict, Schirch argues that "societies that permit or encourage economic and social disparity[...] exclude some groups' full participation in decision making and public life, or direct harm toward some people suffer more from all forms of violence."[16] Therefore, structural poverty can generate structural violence at all levels of society.

The importance of structural violence for understanding links between poverty and conflict is underlined by the finding of the Human Security Report

14   J. Gilligan, *Preventing Violence* (New York: Thames & Hudson, 2001), 101.
15   Ibid., 102.
16   L. Schirch, *The Little Book of Strategic Peacebuilding*, 23.

that "most of the world's armed conflicts now take place in sub-Saharan Africa. At the turn of the 21st century more people were being killed in wars in this region than in the rest of the world combined."[17] According to the report, the reason that sub-Saharan Africa suffers such disproportionate levels of violence compared to the rest of the world is that the region "remain[s] trapped in a volatile mix of poverty, crime, unstable and inequitable political institutions, ethnic discrimination, low state capacity and the 'neighborhoods' of other crisis ridden states—all these factors associated with the increased risk of armed conflict page."[18]

There is no inevitable link between poverty and conflict; clearly not all poor countries descend into violence. However, poverty constitutes one crucial cause of conflict. Addison identifies "a low per capita income and low (declining) growth rate as factors that significantly increase the risk of a country falling into conflict."[19]

Second, there are the power relations within poverty and conflict structures. For why do poor communities or entire nations like Rwanda remain trapped for generations in cycles of poverty and conflict? There are complex causes of this phenomenon, related to history, climate, political systems, land policies, culture, beliefs and prejudices, and stereotypes that dominate relationships between ethnic identity groups. Regardless of specific economic disparities between North and South, the structures of poverty and violent conflict are generated and sustained in the dynamic of power relationships between the rich and poor.

Capitalist economic systems that regulate resources and market competition create imbalanced power relationships between the poor and wealthy. Capital exchanges in Rwandan society create crucial class distinctions. In pre- and post-colonial Rwanda, the cattle economy dominated by the Tutsi minority enabled it to create hegemonic political and cultural structures that excluded the Hutu majority. The Hutu reaction to historical economic inequalities after independence was to construct new political and economic policies that ensured Hutu domination. One of these policies was to introduce ethnic quota systems in employment and education, to counteract perceived Tutsi power.

In capitalist systems, the best performing and/or those with more opportunities succeed in increasing their revenues, whereas the less skilled or the disadvantaged decrease their income and savings. The wealthy subjugate the poor

17   Human Security Report: *War and Peace in the 21st Century* (Canada: Human Security Centre, The University of British Columbia, June 2005), 4.

18   Ibid.

19   T. Addison, *The Global Economy, Conflict Prevention, and Post Conflict Recovery*, Helsinki: WIDER, UN University, 2004), 4, http://www.un.org/esa/peacebuilding/Action/DesaTask Force/papers.

socially, politically and economically and manipulate them to increase their power. For example, the majority of youth in the government forces and the RPF that fought each other in the war that preceded the 1994 genocide were recruited from uneducated, impoverished families. The majority of militiamen trained to carry out the genocide were also recruited from the poorest sections of the Rwandan population. Because of their powerlessness, it is easy to intimidate and alienate poor communities and use them to fuel and perpetrate identity-based conflicts.

Domination and manipulation have long characterised relationships between different groups in Rwanda. The rich class has dominated poor communities, drained their resources through taxation systems, the expropriation of land and low salaries, and manipulated them to stir up violence and kill each other. Such relationships, if they are not transformed, breed and perpetuate structures of violence and conflict. Poverty-based ethnic extremism often fuels identity-based violence and terror. Power imbalances between rich and poor create a dilemma for development policy-makers because they constitute a damaging result of normal market forces that often stimulate productivity in a society. A capitalist system reigns supreme globally after the collapse of feudal systems and the failure of communist economies. However, as we have already seen, capitalism also fuels poverty and therefore often contributes to violence in many communities.

Objectives and impact. Setting goals and objectives follows analysis. If analysis of conflict and poverty has shown the similarity of their causes and effects, the objectives to transform them are necessarily similar. The moment of establishing goals and objectives is the convergence point of conflict and poverty transformation processes. Many authors agree that the transformation processes of conflict and poverty aim at restructured relationships in which human needs of both the poor/weak and the oppressor/powerful are met. Schirch, for example, argues that "a core task of peacebuilding is to transform relationships so that those who harm and destroy move towards meeting the needs and ensuring rights."[20] Peace-building therefore aims at transforming relationships. Lederach argues that "relationship is perhaps the basis of both the conflict and its long term solution."[21] The question remains, then, how can relationships be effectively reconstructed? There are so many frameworks suggested by different experts in peace-building. One of them is the necessity and the process of healing. As Lederach maintains, "[p]eople need opportunity and space to express to and with one another the trauma of loss and their grief at that loss, the

---

20   Schirch, *The Little Book of Strategic Peacebuilding*, 25.

21   J.P. Lederach, *Building Peace: Sustainable Reconciliation in Divided Societies* (Washington DC: United State Institutes of Peace Press, 1997), 27.

anger that accompanies the pain and the memories of injustices experienced."[22] Healing can be an individual or a collective process, as described in the section of my personal journey of healing above. The remainder of this chapter takes up the question of how fractured relationships can be rebuilt to contribute to long-term peacebuilding and economic development.

Strategy to transform conflict and poverty. After setting goals and targets, it is critical to design a strategy to address conflict and poverty via the transformation of social relationships. By relationships I mean "the visible and invisible, immediate and long term"[23] dimensions of connections between individuals and between groups. At this point, the need to integrate conflict and poverty transformation processes is vital. Several strategies are used in different contexts by different practitioners. However, two strategies are particularly important for addressing both conflict and poverty.

First, education is necessary to build capacity and to empower people to transform their structures of conflict and poverty. Paulo Freire's model of "education for transformation"[24] is commonly used in developing countries. I have personally used its principles in Rwanda to integrate peace-building and development initiatives. Freire's model offers toolkits used by practitioners to build the capacity of communities trapped in poverty and fragmented by conflict, to liberate them from oppression. Freire argues that the oppressed possess the knowledge and power to confront injustice. This premise substantially changes strategies of peace-building and development, if we understand that the poor are aware of the injustices against them and possess capacities to break the cycle of conflict and poverty discussed above. Capacity building implies that there is within the oppressed the power to transform their livelihoods. The best education strategy does not aim at "erasing ignorance" but rather at consolidating and reaffirming people's knowledge of their needs and rights and helping them to discover their power to confront forces that alienate, manipulate or oppress them.

Second, advocacy is necessary to build the capacity of the powerless to confront the powers that keep them in a state of poverty and conflict. Effective advocacy to correct inequalities requires people's active participation. It addresses power structures, systems and institutions, as well as policies, values and behaviour that sustain them.[25] Some methodologies and strategies of

---

22   Ibid, 26.

23   J.P. Lederach, *The Little Book of Conflict Transformation* (Intercourse Pennsylvania: Good Books, 2003), 17.

24   A. Hope and S. Timmel, *Training for Transformation: A Handbook for Community Workers*, Book 3 (Harare: Mambo Press, 1988), 18.

25   L. VeneKlasen and V. Miller, *A New Wave of Power, People and Politics* (San Francisco: The Asia Foundation and World Neighbors, 2002), 17-24.

advocacy campaigns involve aggressive confrontation that threatens human emotional security or simply raises unhealthy tensions that risk escalating into further conflict. Some human rights advocates argue that risky confrontations are inevitable in advocacy campaigns. However, adherents of Gandhian non-violence argue that human needs of safety and growth of both the oppressed and the oppressor should be taken into consideration during advocacy.[26] In Rwanda, non-aggressive advocacy, founded on principles and values of relationship transformation within the structures of power and powerlessness, can contribute to peacebuilding and development.

Conflict and poverty transformational spaces

The structures of transformed relationships. Finally, I respond to the third question identified in the introduction: Within which structures should we pursue peacebuilding and development in a post-conflict society such as Rwanda? In practice, transformation of both conflict and poverty is a transformation of social structures. Conflict and poverty can be resolved in the process of mutual transformation of human beings and the structures in which they operate. As Peter Berge argues, "society is a dialectic phenomenon in that it is a human product, and nothing but a human product, that yet continuously acts back upon its producer."[27] Berge argues that human beings are a product of a "social process" that shapes individual identity to fit a given social structure. Therefore, human beings produce understandings of themselves within their given practices and institutions.

Tom Burns' discussion of two conceptions of human agency helps clarify how change takes place within social structures. Burns' version of rational choice theory holds that "each individual human being pursues his or her personal values and self interest, typically in the context of – and against others."[28] This conception of agency, however, begins to change when individuals realise that they cannot attain certain objectives in life, because some individual interests are not permitted by community values or law or simply cannot be attained without collaboration. Thus, individuals collaborate to create the "rules of the game" that regulate communal relationships.

In figure 1, transformed relationships emerge at the intersection of social structures of solidarity, communication and conciliation. I derive the notion of

---

26   Ibid., 279.

27   Cited in R.D. Worth, *Interdisciplinary Approaches to Human Communication*, 2nd edn. (New Brunswick, NJ: Transaction Publishers, 2003), 155.

28   T. Burns, "Two Conceptions of Human Agency: Rational Choice and Social Theory of Action" in P. Sztompka (ed.), *Agency and Structure: Reorienting Social Theory* (Langhorne, PA: Gordon and Breach Science Publishers, 1994), 197-249.

these structures from the work of Simon Gasibirege, professor of psychology at the National University of Rwanda in Butare. Gasibirege argues that the aim of conflict and poverty reduction is to rebuild these structures or spaces in such a way as to permit community members to reconnect and restore their relationships across ethnic and political divides.

Fig. 1. Structures of good governance, social justice and development. © Solomon N. Gasana, April 2005. Adapted from trauma healing modules, called "Personal Development Workshops" (PDWs), constructed by Prof. Simon Gasibirege.

The three structures of solidarity, communication and conciliation constitute spaces within which relationships are transformed. Interactions within these spaces engender other sub-spaces. Each space and sub-space is transformed with appropriate conflict and poverty transformation initiatives. The spaces of transformation operate as follows:

First, the "space of communication" constitutes a structure in which people living in post-conflict communities restore trust through open channels of information flow. Within this space, individuals communicate common interests, needs and strategies to share common resources. They express feelings, exchange ideas and share painful experiences. A common example of interaction within a space of communication is the habit of stopping by a neighbour's home to ask how he or she is doing. In these instances, people share news, family issues and community problems, and as a result, they foster common views about community life.

Second, the "space of solidarity-building" represents the forum in which community members demonstrate to each other through concrete actions that they are committed to values of mutual accountability. Attitudes and actions express commonly-held values and beliefs. Thus, individuals may feel connected to each other through interactions and relationships, mutual support, protection and companionship. For such actions to be truly meaningful, they

165

must be motivated by unconditional commitment to community values that foster connectedness.

Third, the "space of conciliation" represents the place where community members meet to settle their differences through cultural values and practices that combine healing, justice, reconciliation and reintegration. Community members feel a responsibility to abide by shared values, beliefs that serve to rebuild broken relations or sustain existing connections. Offences committed or received are dealt with in order to uphold the integrity of the community and the relationships of the people directly or indirectly affected.

Although cultural globalisation currently influences values, even in traditional societies, some cultures have preserved local modes of justice and governance. One example is the conflict conciliation mechanism known as "urubanza", employed by the Banyamulenge community in eastern DRC. Until 1998, when the second Congolese war broke out, there were no functioning classical courts, detention centres, nor prisoners in this community of about 400,000 inhabitants. In post-colonial Zaire/DRC, the Banyamulenge did not adopt the modern criminal justice system as many other groups did, because they rejected the lawless and corrupt state created by President Mobutu Sese Seko's dictatorship, characterised by arbitrary trials and violent punishment. Thus, the Banyamulenge rejected modern practices of governance and justice and maintained their own traditional systems. Through urubanza, every individual's misconduct or violence was dealt with according to restorative justice principles that upheld the victim's rights to have the crimes recognised and accounted for, and reintegrated the perpetrator into community life. These conciliation mechanisms are similar to the current gacaca jurisdictions in Rwanda designed to deal with genocide suspects. From my personal observations from living in Banyamulenge communities, these mechanisms have contributed to reducing the rate of community homicide, crime, theft, prostitution, and alcohol and drug abuse.

Restorative justice mechanisms such as gacaca or urubanza help rebuild fractured relationships in the community in three main ways. First, hearings during these processes are designed to be non-hierarchical and more participative. Law enforcement institutions are replaced by the dynamic of relationships between community members. For instance, the communities involved have no prisons, because every offender is reintegrated into the social structures during and after the justice process. Police institutions are not necessary because every community member is responsible for the security of people and property. The few criminals in the community are watched over by every member of the community under the supervision of elders. Criminal records are kept in the memories of the community, and can be transmitted orally or in written form from one clan's court to another.

Second, a communal mode of governance has constructed a culture of non-violence through unique community justice and security systems practised and transmitted throughout several generations. The communal governance that fosters restorative justice is participatory and democratic, built on values of freedom, solidarity and respect of people's rights. The aim of each trial of offenders within this system is to save the life and harmony of the community.

Third, the communities often integrate into restorative justice processes the Christian and traditional values that emphasise the need for peaceful and just relationships. Healthy relationships founded on love, care for one other, protection of the vulnerable, integrity and other community principles were considered as central to all social and economic structures.

According to Gasibirege, the three primary spaces above—of communication, solidarity building and conciliation—are the foundations of community life. Furthermore, as indicated in figure 2, the intersections of these spaces form four new spaces of social interaction. First, the "space of transformed relationships" is the central dimension where all three original spaces converge. This is the ideal space, the attainment of the goal of sustainable community capacity of peace and development. In this sphere, the community gains the necessary power to generate energy for economic growth and transformation from one step to another and the power to resist divisive influences. An example of effective community power occurs when advocacy processes grow from within the community and allow members to speak out against injustice and to protect the community from outside threats of violence and insecurity through non-violent means. Community members thus increase their energy to generate internal resources for sustainable peace and development.

Second, in the "space of healing and wholeness", grieving and healing occur when individuals can open wounds and tend to their grief and painful memories, in a space where values of listening, receptivity and empathy are genuinely practised, to soothe each other's pain and renew fractured relationships. Memories of individual and collective pain, as well as healing experiences, are shared and transmitted through informal networks of communication, as individuals provide mutual assistance and comfort.

Third, the "space of truth telling" constitutes the realm of restorative justice or *gacaca*, the Rwandan philosophy and practice that views all humans as inextricably connected to one other, in the process of doing justice. According to *gacaca*, truth is communicated to facilitate justice and reconciliation. Many truths are told, including expressions of hatred, desire for revenge and forgiveness, guilt, shame, confession and repentance. The truth is heard, processed and dealt with through the wisdom and integrity of the elders mandated to restore people's rights. In *gacaca*, for example, the truth is sensitive and can often involve explosive and violent emotional expressions. Nonetheless, *gacaca* insists

167

that truth must be told and dealt with publicly, to avoid the misconstruction of truth that may later fuel feelings of revenge. Truth-telling also helps the offender deal with feelings of shame with the support of the whole community.

Finally, the "space of unity-building processes" allows solidarity-building around justice and conciliation. Solidarity space is the space of the African *Ubuntu* philosophy and practice which Nomonde Masina defines as "the collective personhood" or "the art or virtue of being human", with fundamental characteristics such as "caring, compassion, unity, tolerance, respect, closeness, generosity genuineness, empathy, consultation, compromise and hospitality."[29]

In this space of solidarity, community members are committed to values of impartiality, integrity, cooperation and group support from everyone. The threat to an individual is a threat to every member of the community because it endangers the existence of the whole community. The process of unity-building requires that every community member, including those related to the offender and victims, participates in telling the truth, condemning and punishing the offence, forgiveness, reintegration and mending damaged relationships. This participation by all parties cements community solidarity.

All of the structures explored here—the original three spaces on Gasibirege's chart and the four spaces of intersection, which I have identified—are damaged by conflict and poverty. The process of transformation aims at reconstructing the society, the community and the individual by restoring the values that strengthen relationships within all of these spaces.

Conclusion

In "*Populorum Progressio*", Pope Paul VI wrote an encyclical centred on the issues of imbalances within the social structures of economic development. He linked violence with the absence of social justice, claiming, "development is the new name for peace."[30] This phrase encapsulates perfectly the interdependence between structural conflict and structural poverty. Conflict is largely linked with social and economic inequalities that recycle violence and poverty. Too often, efforts to address these issues of conflict and poverty have been carried out separately and even competitively. This lack of integrated initiatives in the field of peace-building and development limits the efficiency and impact of programmes in transforming the conflict and poverty structures. However, it

---

29   N. Masina, "Xhosa Practices of Ubuntu for South Africa" in I. William Zartman (ed.), *Traditional Cures for Modern Conflicts: African Conflict "Medicine"* (Boulder, Colorado: Lynne Rienner, 2000), 170.

30   N. O'Brien, *Island of Tears, Island of Hope: Living the Gospel in a Revolutionary Situation* (Eugene, OR: Orbis Books, 1993), 39.

is possible to design, implement, monitor and evaluate strategies that address these issues. Such processes may use the same framework to identify key problems, analyse the causes and effects on people's lives and design objectives that effectively transform conflict and poverty.

Moreover, in many conflict societies, an abundance of resources and energy has been expended on projects that have achieved little change in communities, because processes of reconstruction and development were not thoughtfully built on the foundation of peace and reconciliation. Only limited change will occur in a traumatised society unless people are encouraged to heal their pain and recover the energy for rebuilding solidarity and facilitating development. Because the causes of conflict and poverty are closely connected to power relations in social structures, any change must involve reconstructing community spaces to address the effects of fragmentation, estrangement and powerlessness. Restructuring community spaces of solidarity, communication and conciliation is the best way to empower people to take control of their destiny and to address the root causes of conflict and poverty.

9

ONLY HEALING HEALS: CONCEPTS AND METHODS OF PSYCHO-SOCIAL HEALING IN POST-GENOCIDE RWANDA

John Steward

Introduction

The purpose of this chapter is to discuss the role of psycho-social healing in Rwanda, in the context of my experience as a World Vision practitioner working for the recovery of individuals and the reconstruction of the social and communal fabric after the 1994 genocide. After explaining the complexity of needs in Rwanda after the genocide, and the additional effects of the mass return of Hutu from the refugee camps in Zaire, now the Democratic Republic of Congo, (DRC), this chapter introduces a strategy for healing that my World Vision colleagues (including Solomon Nsabiyera Gasana, also writing in this volume) and I developed and have used in Rwanda since 1997. This strategy involves the re-creation of trust through sharing in small groups of mixed ethnicity. The strategy encourages participants to become aware of the value of healing rituals and telling personal stories, speaking the truth and understanding and expressing emotions for personal and social well-being, while examining common misperceptions about forgiveness.

Our approach was supported by insights from the pastoral counsellor David Augsburger's framework of the four normal human responses of people affected by conflict and fractured human relationships. These responses of denial, revenge, forgiveness and reconciliation provide practical insights into the challenge of psycho-social healing after the genocide. This chapter examines healing in the wider context of restored relationships by outlining several post-genocide healing processes, encapsulated in two separate healing workshops that my colleagues and I have implemented, and by discussing further long-term needs for healing in Rwanda.

171

The complicated challenge

The challenge for Rwandans recovering from the genocide and its aftermath is not one of merely reuniting Hutu and Tutsi who before the genocide lived together as neighbours while suppressing their differences. Many Rwandans currently living side by side have never before lived in such close proximity. Since late 1994 up to one million Rwandans returned to their highly destabilised motherland, after living in exile in nearby countries for up to 40 years. By occupying the houses vacated by the fleeing Hutu, these "old caseload" refugees, who were predominantly Tutsi, heightened tensions after the Rwandan Patriotic Front (RPF) dispersed Hutu refugee camps in Zaire towards the end of 1996. This led to the mass repatriation of "new caseload" refugees, mostly Hutu. By early March 1997, people who had lived far apart, and had often never met before, faced each other for the first time, sparking renewed competition for houses and land, and triggering memories of decades of bitter rivalries.

Many Hutu were accused of involvement in the acts of 1994, and by the end of 1997 over 120,000 prisoners were crammed into nineteen jails throughout Rwanda. Meanwhile, Tutsi survivors pressed their case for retribution and recompense through bringing the accused to justice and receiving compensation for stolen or damaged property. In early 1998, the first trials of *génocidaires* saw 22 people convicted and publicly executed in local stadia, evoking the proclamation in the national media, "This day marks the end of the law of impunity and the beginning of justice in Rwanda."[1]

It was a bewildering time in Rwanda, with people struggling to re-establish some form of normality from a base of severe poverty, while enduring painful memories, unresolved questions of justice and forgiveness, and a government intent on stabilising, rehabilitating and advancing the country. Every day, I heard people saying, "We can't trust others any more, but we need to share our burden with someone." People were full of grief, fear, mistrust and blame. A Rwandan NGO worker observed in 1996, "Everyone in Rwanda is traumatised." A survey in 2000, in which three quarters of 1,676 adult respondents had experienced some form of loss or separation as a result of the genocide, concluded, "These findings point to the high level of trauma in Rwandan society."[2] Children were likewise affected, and highly vulnerable in cases where their parents had died. Almost everyone currently living in Rwanda has suffered some form of trauma and loss.

---

1   Cited to me by a Rwandan colleague in late April 1998.

2   S. Gasibirege and S. Babalola, *Perceptions about the gacaca Law in Rwanda: Evidence from a Multi-method Study*, Special publication no. 19 (Baltimore, MD: Johns Hopkins University School of Public Health, 2001), 6-7.

GROUP	ESTIMATED SIZE AND BACKGROUND	NEEDS OR DESIRES EXPRESSED BY THE GROUP	CHALLENGES CONSIDERED ESSENTIAL FOR RECOVERY
SURVIVORS	Up to 200,000 Tutsi who escaped death during the genocide	Justice; Social and legal protection; Housing, return of stolen goods or compensation for lost or destroyed possessions; Adequate income; Trauma healing; Better nutrition; Protection against injury or murder intended to prevent testimony about what they witnessed during the genocide.	Many raped widows (often with AIDS); 60,000 child-headed (under 18 years) households; Orphans, including in foster homes; The need to form associations of widows, HIV sufferers and participants in microcredit schemes; Individuals still being targeted by extremists.
INTERNALLY DISPLACED PERSONS	4+ million Hutu, many internally displaced during and after the genocide	To be cleared of suspicion of complicity in the genocide; To be healed from guilt, trauma and fear of reprisals; To overcome anger at the RPF's perceived failure to protect them from reprisals; To protect against reprisals aimed at preventing them testifying about militia activities during the genocide.	To separate the innocent from the guilty; Reparations for those unjustly imprisoned; Protection against false accusations or threats; To face responsibility for their actions and apologise to victims; To return stolen goods.
OLD CASELOAD	1+ million Tutsi, RPF members or sympathisers; long-term refugees from the 1960s and 1970s in neighbouring countries who have returned to Rwanda since late 1994	To adjust to a new country and circumstances; Housing; Acceptance back into the society; Dealing with fear, entrenched hatred, long-term pain and betrayal stemming from as far back as 1959; To see those who are guilty of genocidal acts punished.	Strong desire to get settled and recommence life; A source of major economic outflow to Uganda and Kenya; As often highly educated people, they desire rapid and high-level employment; Some want revenge, while also a desire to end the culture of impunity.
NEW CASELOAD	2+ million Hutu (and some Tutsi) who fled into refugee camps in the DRC and Tanzania and returned to Rwanda between December 1996 and May 1997	Justice for the planners of, and participants in, the genocide. If innocent, to be cleared of suspicion, given protection from revenge or arbitrary punishment and reintegrated into society.	Families are fragmented and separated; An initial backlog of 120,000 suspects in prison, mostly men; Dealing with guilt – and the indifference some express toward what has happened to others ; Fear of military reprisals (many were in hiding after the genocide); Some are trained to fight, and are armed; Often cannot be recognised as killers because they were active in a *commune* or *secteur* other than the one where they have been accused of genocide crimes.
RADICAL HUTU	300,000+ Hutu infiltrators, returnees, former *interahamwe*, former members of FAR (Armed Forces of Rwanda)	Power sharing and integration for the intellectuals; Victory over the RPF or to regain power in the north-west of Rwanda; To continue ethnic cleansing and genocide.	To offer a better alternative than a society dominated by one or other ethnic group; To become productive citizens and lay down their arms.
RADICAL TUTSI	Unknown number of Tutsi including army, sympathisers, survivors, returnees from Burundi	Revenge and ethnic cleansing.	To construct a just society; Healing for their pain and anger.
RWANDANS CHOOSING TO PERMANENTLY RESETTLE ELSEWHERE	50,000 + Hutu and Tutsi dispersed in other African countries, Europe, North America, etc	This grouping includes *génocidaires* (both real and falsely accused), as well as the Tutsi diaspora – their different needs were not documented since my colleagues and I were not involved	In general, many among this group have given up on Rwanda and resettled permanently elsewhere, either to evade justice, to avoid the politics and social complexities of Rwandan society, or for other

Table 1. Broad groupings of Rwanda's population in 1997 and their needs

When planning healing strategies at this time, my colleagues and I felt that it was necessary to recognise that the Rwandan community consisted of various groups with different needs. We assessed the needs of different groups and what they required to reclaim their place in society. The table above outlines the complexity of different groups' needs, as my colleagues and I discerned them in November 1997. We assessed different groups' needs on the basis of statements at that time in the Rwandan media and in discussions with Rwandan NGOs. The groupings are highly generalised but sufficiently distinct to enable an appreciation of the segmented and complex nature of people's post-genocide needs, and to facilitate appropriate responses to them. The column in the table marked, "Challenges to Consider for Recovery," represents diverse responses in healing workshops, which necessitate strategies that are neither partisan nor slanted towards the needs of one group at the expense of others.[3] Owing to the paucity of information at the time, we did not include the minority Batwa in our table.

Developing a healing strategy

As my colleagues and I set out to answer the question of how Rwandans may unite to rebuild as a nation, despite deep divisions, we found our strategy focusing on the potential of using psycho-social processes to catalyse change. Initially we noticed among many Rwandans a form of entrenched "group think"; that is, a popularly-held low expectation of the possibility of changes in attitude of one ethnic group toward the other. A common response to questions about attitude change in churches and community groups was, "This is Rwanda, that doesn't happen here." People told stories of misery, loss, victimisation, shame and blame, but invariably the conclusion tended towards the sentiment, "The other group caused the problem; why don't you work with them?"

Apart from blaming others, personal survival seemed to be the key motivator in people's daily lives. We concluded that trauma and/or hurt emotions, the consequent inner confusion, and multiple unresolved questions and problems of guilt, grief and shame resulted in an inward focus. Many Rwandans' psychological "energy" was diverted to protecting personal boundaries, rather than to relating to others and putting energy into rebuilding broken relationships. With time and reflection, we developed a healing strategy, based on observations of the attitudes of people with whom we interacted over a six-month period.

This healing strategy begins by inviting reflection on the past: to acknowledge key events and the attitudes and actions they elicited. In our interactions

---

3   This table was first published in W. Nyamugasira, L. Ndogoni and S. Nsabiyera, "Rwanda: Telling A Different Story", in Janz and Slead (eds), *Complex Humanitarian Emergencies*, (Seattle, WA: World Vision, 2000), 189.

with participants, it became clear that many of them had been deeply affected by the genocide; in response, many wanted to hurt others. These feelings fuelled tensions throughout the country, long after 1994. Individuals remembered what had been done to their family and group, desired revenge and sought to apportion blame to the "other." This perpetuated people's wish that the other might be made to suffer in some way.

However, by 1997, a process began to emerge from several initiatives, outlined below, that gave hope of change to some members of Rwandan society. Whereas most Rwandan churches preached a doctrine of forgiveness as *the* solution to Rwanda's ills, and the government stressed justice as the main priority, both invocations proved to be premature, because of many Rwandans' complex, unresolved psychological needs. Through our observations and interactions, my colleagues and I realised that some people began to gain new perspectives and rediscover aspects of their humanity when they mustered the courage to tell their story in a small, confidential and accepting group of mixed ethnicity. It seemed that reopening psychological "wounds" by speaking of people's losses and the painful experiences of their life enabled healing to begin.

As a sense of personal boundaries began to be restored, personal, psychological energy became available for the outer world of relationships and communal roles. This process of listening, reflecting and speaking required time and confidentiality, but many of those who chose to participate began to build inner confidence and stability. This led them to consider how they related to other individuals and groups: a choice whether to change their views of themselves (in some cases, to repent of their own mistakes in the past), and seek a new kind of relationship with the "other", or to maintain the status quo. This choice between two possible directions resulted in either a hardening of attitudes towards the other group or a desire to heal rifts. Those who chose the former remained locked in a divisive mentality. In the healing strategy, we defined such individuals as "peace-breakers", while the few individuals who decided to focus their energy on rebuilding broken relationships were termed "peace-makers." The latter, we believe, is Rwanda's most promising hope for the future: a strategy that invites those who are willing to participate in the healing process to decide to make a personal contribution to fostering peace in Rwanda. By their commitment, they may become the facilitators of peace in their community, and thereby invite others to experience the healing process. The context in which this strategy was used is outlined in the next section.

The human response framework

The shaping of the healing strategy was deepened by a practical insight gained during healing workshops (outlined below): that the concept of healing has

175

multiple levels. My colleagues and I began to relate these levels to what Augsburger describes as the four normal human responses to a painful experience between two parties: denial, revenge, forgiveness and reconciliation.[4]

First, *denial* is—as Susanne Buckley-Zistel explores through the concept of "chosen amnesia" in this volume—a useful way of surviving, which leads to statements such as, "Let's just get on with life and rebuild the country." While denial can be healthy up to a point, by stabilising people who would otherwise flounder in difficult circumstances,[5] it creates a false sense of peace within the person, and tends to foment suppressed anger. At some time, this "fire within" will express itself inappropriately. In Rwanda, many individuals have expressed denial of their experiences of the genocide, claiming to have no need to deal with their inner issues.

Second, *revenge* occurs when anger in the victim overflows into aggression against the perpetrator or a scapegoat. Revenge is a response of power and retribution and an attempt to impose a penalty on the "other." With revenge attacks now largely suppressed in Rwanda by government and military efforts to maintain law and order, the expression of revenge in Rwanda has become subtler, as suggested in reports of deaths through poisoning, or through favouritism in appointments to political and social positions. However, painful memories do not disappear but rather continue to nurture a thirst for revenge, a desire that persists until the person chooses a different course of action.

Third, *forgiveness* is a deeply complex human response to painful experience. Humans generally find it hard to forgive themselves for their failures to act in the past. This is common in Rwanda, where many people claim, "I failed to protect my family", or "I did not warn my friend about the coming danger." People who talk about their awareness of this failure and choose to forgive themselves experience inner release from their guilt. They begin to see how they blamed others for their predicament and, believing the other to be guilty, wished evil on them in return.

After forgiveness of self, it becomes possible to consider the hurtful acts of the "other." Those who reach this point of forgiving others for their deeds find that forgiveness removes a source of tension within themselves; that is, the absolute determination to hold the other personally accountable. Many victims may find that forgiveness benefits them, the injured person, and may not, on its own, directly benefit the perpetrator.

Finally, *reconciliation* is a two-way interaction, in which one party responds with forgiveness to the other's offer of an apology and some form of

---

4   D. Augsburger, *Helping People Forgive* (Kentucky: John Knox Press, 1996), 92.

5   L. Ndogoni, personal communication, November 1999.

restitution. This may lead to a degree of acceptance of each other and a *rapprochement* between the two parties.

Healing is an individual matter. Groups that undertake healing processes include people at several of the four points of response, but as one person finds healing in him- or herself, this offers hope to others. It was important for my colleagues and me to recognise that the Rwandan psycho-social healing process must respect this range of possible responses and provide room for appropriate options to emerge—for example, acknowledging the courage shown in speaking the truth, being free to state one's desire for revenge or unreadiness to forgive, or finding sufficient incentive to go against one's clan's opinion and pursue ideas that may resolve conflicts with traditional family enemies.

Processes of psycho-social healing

Traditional culture. Under normal circumstances, aspects of Rwanda's culture may have contributed to healing and unity after mass conflict. However, post-1994 circumstances in Rwanda have been far from normal. The inability of key traditional practices to respond to the post-genocide needs of the population necessitates the kind of healing processes explored in this chapter.

First, conflict resolution through the traditional form of *gacaca* was impossible immediately after 1994, both because of the loss of customary leadership and the radical breakdown in trust among Rwandans, especially towards community leaders. *Gacaca*, in its pre-genocide form, provided a forum where people could bring their disputes, air grievances and discuss them communally. It offered a negotiating "climate" which often helped parties come to agreement or accept each other's differences and foster the opportunity for reconciliation. A similar tradition was the airing of issues and open discussion between aggrieved parties, to find a resolution by consensus and to celebrate it by sharing banana wine.[6] There now exists in Rwanda a justifiable fear of drinks being poisoned as a form of retaliation for genocide crimes. Rumours abound of people believed to have died from poisoned drinks since 1994. Furthermore, in traditional Rwanda, according to the research of the anthropologist Christopher Taylor,[7] the giving of a poisoned drink was used on occasion as a way of testing the truthfulness of one party's testimony: in a form of trial by ordeal, the party whose word was in doubt was "accused" and subjected to a test in which they were given poisoned drink and exonerated if they survived. Nowa-

---

6   "Rwandans construct social relationships through the fluids they exchange in celebration, hospitality, and ordinary social interaction": C. Taylor, *Milk, Honey and Money* (Washington, DC: Smithsonian Institute Press, 1992), 105.

7   Ibid., 208.

days, this "therapy" would be considered an offence, leading to imprisonment for the person who applied such a test.

Third, the Rwandan cultural practice of blood pacts was derived from the "flow/blockage" symbolism on which pre-colonial Rwandan culture was based. According to Taylor, the image of flow in Rwanda conveyed ideas of fertility and order, whereas blockage spoke of loss.[8] Because of this liquids had a central place in society, and sharing a drink became, and remains, a metaphor for openness and exchange. Many Rwandans practised a ritual of exchanging and imbibing each other's blood, which bound them in a pact by which "men became 'brothers'."[9] According to some Rwandans, the blood-tie was stronger than ties of family or ethnicity. Taylor suggests that this act of bonding by exchanging blood is no longer a relational model, having been replaced in the 1970s and 1980s as a pact-creating practice by profit-making and accumulation.[10] In addition, the current awareness of the threat of AIDS has encouraged abandonment of the practice of blood pacts. For both of these reasons, the blood pact is no longer a viable or desirable practice.

I next introduce the two healing workshops in which my colleagues and I applied the key principles of the healing strategy discussed above,[11] while also reflecting the relevance of Augsburger's four human responses for the psycho-social healing process.

The Personal Development Workshop (PDW). The PDW was developed by Prof. Simon Gasibirege of the National University of Rwanda in Butare.[12] The PDW is based on the central concept of truth-telling;[13] that is, the notion that people should speak about their painful experiences to benefit from articulating personal truths to an empathetic audience, while hearing others tell their stories. Outcomes of this confidential sharing of experiences in a small group setting include a re-humanising of attitude—that is, a renewed openness to accept the "other" —and work towards the rebuilding of trust. Hundreds of Rwandans have participated in the PDW process, with over 100 graduates of the workshops now trained as trainers, many of whom currently volunteer as facilitators of the workshop in their local communities.

---

8   Ibid., 206.

9   Ibid., 206.

10   Ibid., 208 fn.

11   Other groups offer psycho-social healing programmes, but their documentation was not available to the authors for this study.

12   Initially the materials used consisted of loose-leaf handouts in French. One of the more experienced facilitators has translated the material into Kinyarwanda.

13   "Telling the truth is healing in itself"—from the *gacaca* educational video *Ukuri Kurakiza,* produced by a collaboration between the Ministry of Justice and Johns Hopkins University (2001).

The PDW is a skilfully crafted series of workshops with questions for personal reflection, small group assignments, plenary discussions and time for integration of insights before proceeding to the next topic. The table below outlines the five sessions of each PDW, as it was used by World Vision.

DURATION	TITLE	CONTENT OF MODULE	AIM
1. 1 day	Introduction day; video *Rwanda a country that went mad*	Agreeing on group norms (called "Rules of protection"); commitment to the process; Discussion of Rwanda's recent history	Work with the willing. Create understanding of the workshop. Rebuild trust and willingness to share.
2. 3 days (one month after the first work-shop)	Bereavement and loss (dealing with grief)	Denial, disorganisation, reorganisation, guilt, responsibility, and bereavement pathology. Small group process.	Provide a climate and safe environment where people can express their pain, grieve their losses and begin to open their wounds.
3. 3 days (one month after the second work-shop)	Emotions	Feelings and emotions of anger, sadness, joy and fear, explored through the eyes of the adult, parent and child within.	To understand and value the role of emotions; to get in touch with one's emotions and begin to express them; to relate them to levels of maturity within.
4. 3 days (one month after the third work-shop)	Forgiveness	What does forgiveness mean for the self and relationships with others? The concept of social violence, no forgiveness without justice, conditions of forgiveness	A journey towards forgiveness including "I must learn to forgive myself" ([see the "Twelve-step process of forgiveness" in Appendix 1)].
5. 1 day (one month after the fourth work-shop)	Evaluation and Celebration	What was important to me in the workshop? What effect have we found in our person? What impact does this have on my relationships?	Reflection and discussion on the impact of the workshop, with written feedback and recommendations, looking forward, celebrating hope and new life.

Table 2. The Personal Development Workshop.

PDW programme

One aim of the PDW is to provide time for each individual to participate in a process in which he or she applies concepts and internalises insights, while also becoming aware of the pain and struggle of others in the group, as they emerge through discussion. This was different from the many "reconciliation workshops" offered around the country in 1996 and 1997, in which people were often passive recipients of messages about the history of Rwanda and the necessity of accepting one another, without processing the thoughts and feelings that reinforced division. Workshop facilitators provide exercises for each step and stress the importance of trust and confidentiality. Participants respond at the level of openness that suits them. One strength of the workshop is the time-gap between modules, which allows participants to adjust their life according to the insights gained during the sessions.

As a general rule, participants reluctantly come to the forgiveness module, anticipating that they will be asked to forgive people who have harmed them or stolen or damaged their possessions. It therefore comes as a large surprise when the group works through the material in the Appendix to this chapter. This outstanding contribution profoundly personalises the matter of forgiveness and offers a healthy view of what forgiveness can and cannot achieve. Confidentiality is an important part of the workshop. On some occasions, however, participants agree to share comments with others. The following is the sense of celebration conveyed by one participant:

> *Oh! Let me tell you why I am very at ease within myself:*
> *I have just known what I did not know*
> *I have understood what I did not understand*
> *I have felt what I have never felt in me*
> *I feel good, I am well!*
> *For this reason my burden has fallen down*
> *Viva, these workshops!*[14]

Some participants echo one man who said, "We wish that every person in Rwanda could do this workshop."[15] One graduate said to me, "Intellectually, I know I must be at peace with others, but I cannot have reconciliation if I am still wounded inside."[16] In one town, the spouse of a participant approached the facilitators and said, "I want to know what is the medicine that you gave my husband. I would like to drink it too."[17]

After three years of running the PDW, two staff from the Trauma Clinic of the Centre for the Study of Violence and Reconciliation in South Africa evaluated the programme. They reported the strengths of the PDW as achieving:

- A sense of safety and trust in the small groups;

- Self-understanding and resolution of internal conflicts;

- Awareness of the importance of expressing emotions and suspending judgemental attitudes;

- Improved relationships between colleagues and family members, with reduced conflict in the home;

- Sufficient internal psychological resolution to result in participants' being more able to help others;

- Equipping individuals with knowledge and skills in assisting traumatised children to express their pain and anger.[18]

---

14   A participant in the Personal Development Workshop, from author's notes, as part of feedback during the evaluation day (August 1997).

15   Ibid.

16   J.-B. Ntakirutimana, personal communication, October 1997.

17   Author's notes, August 1997.

18   M. Robertson and H. Hajiyiannis, *Evaluation of the Psycho-social Support Program* (Kigali: World Vision Rwanda, 1999), 26.

Their study concluded that the PDW had not only helped participants deal with trauma and mental health issues but also helped facilitate the process of reconciliation. The study reinforced a key message of the PDW, that unless people have resolved their anger and hurt, it is not possible to talk about justice, forgiveness or reparation. The evaluators identified the main weaknesses of the PDW as the absence of mechanisms for follow-up, the emotional exhaustion of the facilitators, and the inability to run sufficient workshops in order to meet perceived needs. "Everybody [in Rwanda] has a story to tell, a wound to heal, a pain to share":[19] there may never be a truer word spoken about the people of Rwanda.

Relevance of PDW for the gacaca courts

My colleagues and I discovered over time that the PDW was not only important in itself, as a facilitator of post-genocide healing, but would also crucially support the *gacaca* courts, which are explored in greater detail elsewhere in this volume by Gasana, Schabas, Ngoga and Clark. In 2002, Gasibirege, the creator of the PDW, stated that "three things are needed to make *gacaca* work, all of which the PDW addresses: first, management of fear and sadness; second, telling the truth without fear; third, reconciliation based on tolerance and love."[20] As a result, each local PDW now includes at least one judge from the nearest *gacaca* tribunal, with the intention that after training, this person will more easily recognise people during *gacaca* hearings who show signs of urgent psycho-social needs. The judges can refer these people to their local PDW facilitators for follow-up.

Gacaca is a complex process that is proving intimidating for many community members who did not expect to hear detailed, often graphic, confessions of genocide crimes. As a result, by early 2005, I heard many Rwandans asking, "Is *gacaca* really worth it? Are we going backwards?" *Gacaca* affects many people, often inducing shock and re-traumatisation, making skilled psycho-social healing essential for victims and suspects alike.

Gacaca has great potential to contribute to peace and justice in Rwanda, but its success relies heavily on overcoming severe psycho-social challenges. The leaders of *gacaca*—judges and government overseers of the process—must pay close attention to crucial psycho-social issues raised by *gacaca*, particularly the peaceful management of anger and dealing with painful memories, feelings of shame, disappointment and injustice, and the general challenge of rebuilding trust and restoring relationships—national, local and personal. The genocide shredded the fabric of Rwandan society, which has since then been further

---

19   Nyamugasira, Ndogoni and Nsabiyera, "Rwanda: Telling A Different Story."
20   Ibid.

frayed by the detailed revelations by participants in *gacaca* of the fate of their loved ones during the genocide.

On the basis of my colleagues' and my own observations, and as a result of our interactions with participants of these workshops in Rwanda, I list here some of the psycho-social needs that must be met if survivors and suspects are to benefit from *gacaca* and to experience healing and justice that is lasting and restorative.

Victims/survivors may need some or all of the following:

- To hear the truth confessed in a sensitive but transparent way;
- To express their trauma and pain and be understood and believed by the accused;
- To know what happened to their loved ones and where to find their remains;
- To hear perpetrators' apologies;
- To see gestures of reconciliation by hearing a request for forgiveness, and to believe the request to be sincere and to find courage to accept it (that is, to forgive);
- To be compensated in some appropriate way for material losses;
- To see justice done to the accused who accepts guilt (or is proven to be guilty) according to law;
- To be supported while dealing with health effects suffered as a result of abuse;
- To be embraced as a worthy member of the community.

Suspects may need some or all of the following:

- To gain a fair hearing;
- To have the courage to speak the truth;
- To receive the appropriate sentence (with the right to appeal);
- To have courage to express regrets, show contrition, repent for actions;
- To have their offer of sincere apology accepted (that is, to be believed, even if not forgiven by their accusers);
- To make meaningful and fair material restitution;
- To be embraced as a worthy member of the community.

Currently, only a few genocide suspects have participated in the PDW. Detainees who have shared in the intimate personal context of this workshop describe it as creating within them a sense of feeling human again. This re-humanisation needs to extend to prisoners' families as a prerequisite for prisoner reintegration. The need for this is confirmed by the difficulties being by the tens of thousands of suspects released since 2003, many of whom are currently involved in, or awaiting, *gacaca* trials. Many returned detainees have been rejected by their families and ostracised or ignored by their communities.

According to Rwandan community workers, the return of prisoners from jail to the community has greatly increased the level of angst in the entire community, not just among survivors.

Whenever individuals have participated in the PDW, they have pleaded for all Rwandans to have the opportunity to attend. I have observed that, while the workshop enables participants to process their own thoughts, feelings and concerns, it is also a forum to meet those who perceive things differently. The PDW allows people to hear each other. This re-connection is crucial for the creation of civil communities in Rwanda. Testimonies given during the *gacaca* process also involve recalling detailed memories of the terrible events of 1994, making it all the more important to have a place to address these. PDW constitutes one such forum.

Workshop for religious and lay leaders

The workshop for religious and lay leaders, which integrates Christian teaching with psychological theory, was created by Dr Rhiannon Lloyd, a Welsh psychiatrist, who has mentored several Rwandans from the NGO African Enterprise (AE). The workshop employs two facilitators, one Hutu and one Tutsi. The three-day event was initially offered for clergy, priests and lay leaders. Christian theology is the starting point of this workshop, because the sessions focus on church leaders, who continue to wield strong influence over Rwandan society, despite the failure of the Church to oppose the slide towards genocide in 1994 or to provide an effective sanctuary for those who fled the Hutu militias. In this workshop, psychological concepts are deliberately included, to help relate Biblical teachings to the immediate need of rebuilding lives and restoring relationships in Rwanda.

The workshop for religious and lay leaders incorporates an important ritual element, to appeal to a perceived Rwandan affinity with the symbolic. In particular, the workshop employs the cross as a symbol of suffering and encourages participants to write their painful experiences on paper as a way of externalising what has previously been unexpressed. The nailing of the paper to the cross then symbolises an act of sharing one's struggles and hurt with the crucified deity, while burning the paper ensures confidentiality and symbolises that the knowledge of the hurt has ascended to heaven. These processes, when taken as a whole, constitute a solemn and profound experience.

The table below outlines the structure of the three-day workshop, using the symbol of building a house (foundations, walls, ceiling, roof), which in itself is a powerful symbol of justice for many victims of the genocide. A house is a tangible and central need for the survivors of the genocide, representing protection and a stable life. On several occasions during the workshops, widows who were HIV-positive as a result of being raped during 1994 said to me, "When I die, my children will at least have this house to live in."

DAY/FOCUS	WORKSHOP CONTENT	INTENDED EFFECTS
1. Laying a foundation: Understanding unconditional love	Images of the divine heart of grace and love for all people, emphasising the acceptance of the nature of human waywardness	Awareness of sacredness of all people and of divine love for humanity; human failure to love the other
2. Building the walls: Healing the wounds from past pain	Jesus, the exemplary pain-bearer; opening of our wounds by reflecting on and writing experiences that caused our personal pain; small group sharing; symbolic nailing to a cross, then removing and burning each person's papers	Understanding and identifying personal wounds, expressing painful memories appropriately, letting go of grudges and hurts that have been held within for years
3. The ceiling and roof: Forgiveness and repentance, acceptance of the other	Forgiveness, described as meaning "to let go, to release"; introducing the concept of "identification repentance" (defined in detail below); moving towards embracing the "other", i.e. accepting them as human, by forgiving individuals and representatives of the other group, celebrating hope of being able to live in relationship	Freedom and release, hope for change, offering forgiveness, commitment to encourage others to desire this freedom

Table 3. Healing and forgiveness workshop.

The teaching of Day 1 surprises many participants because it focuses on the love of God for all humanity, whereas many expect to hear a message of shame and condemnation. This approach helps participants feel open to the process that follows, in which each person identifies the personal negative effects of the genocide, including loss of family, friends, position, health, possessions and hope. Once these painful experiences are written down, it is easier for participants to share them in confidential groups of two or three people. Those who want to speak in the plenary that follows are encouraged to do so. In many cases, several people will muster the courage to publicly describe their experiences, having heard others do likewise.

The evening of Day 2 is significant, as participants who, having mourned their losses and recalled their pains, symbolically nail their wounds to a cross in a solemn religious ceremony. This action emphasises letting go of past experiences that have gripped them with fear and shame. As a result of this ritual, many participants claim to have experienced a profound sense of inner peace and find they can embrace the "other" as a fellow human being. During many workshops, participants literally embrace each other and dance in celebration. Their new feelings are described in the qualitative evaluation/feedback at the end of this section.

I next introduce the process of "identification repentance", which comprises a key element of Day 3. Identification repentance constitutes a response to structural abuse, in which some participants apologise for the past failures of their group. This practice of apology derives from three books of the Hebrew sacred texts: Ezra, Nehemiah and Daniel. In these books, the nation's leaders were divinely commanded to confess to God and to repent, not only of their own sins but also of the sins of their ancestors. Thus, they identified with the failures of their ancestors and apologised for their lasting effects, hence the description "identification repentance." When the healing workshops were being developed and tested in Rwanda in 1996-97, Rhiannon Lloyd invoked this Hebrew practice, when she identified herself as a European and apologised for the failure of Europe in 1994 to actively stop the genocide. Lloyd's American assistant/co-facilitator then apologised for the failure of her own government to act. For some Rwandans, these apologies constituted a statement of solidarity and concern that, albeit belated, affected them deeply, and provided a sense of comfort that, in retrospect, some Westerners did care about what had happened in Rwanda.

In the workshops run by Rwandans after Lloyd's introduction, Tutsi co-facilitators often reflected on the history of Rwanda and apologised for the ways in which their ancestors abused their power over Hutu for many years. This apology profoundly touched many Hutu participants. Such statements and apologies are extremely rare in Rwanda. Afterwards, Hutu co-facilitators often apologised to Tutsi for "what my brothers did to your families, and some of them are now trying to continue."[21] These apologies meant a great deal to many Tutsi survivors. The impact of the dual apologies was often deep, moving participants from blaming one another to facing the truth of what members of their own group had done, or desired to do, to the other group. According to many participants, stating these truths brought a feeling of relief and release. During many workshops, there were many tears, dancing and celebration. Many participants returned home stating that they believed that Hutu-Tutsi relations could change in their communities.[22]

Follow-up workshops occur two months later, with discussions of earlier lessons and new material. Once religious and lay leaders have completed the workshops, they take them back to their parishes and communities, focusing, for example, on child-headed households, survivors and participants in local *gacaca* tribunals. In particular, these leaders offer insights into questions regarding forgiveness, repentance and justice which arise readily in their communities.

Many participants provide qualitative feedback, such as the following, which offer insights into the effects of the workshops upon individuals:[23]

---

21   J. Nyamutera, personal communication, August 1999.

22   From an internal report, "The Role of the Church in Healing and Reconciliation in Rwanda", African Enterprise (1997), 20.

23   These quotations were extracted, with permission, from internal African Enterprise documents, comprising a collection of translations of feedback reported in the documentation of various AE workshops in Rwanda during 1997-99.

I hated and feared soldiers. Now I understand that they are also wounded by the genocide, which exterminated their relatives. I feel that I have to forgive them; they hate us because we have hurt them.

(A woman, whose four children were killed in crossfire between the army and rebels)

We are sorry for the genocide. We hated you, we mistreated you, we killed your families, we wounded you. We are sorry.

(A pastor apologising on behalf of his fellow Hutu)

I was overwhelmed after a Tutsi repented on behalf of his ethnic group. I went to the front and there I found myself repenting of the sins that the Hutu have committed in killing many Tutsi. Eventually I found peace.

(A Hutu man)

Three of my children died. One after another we buried them in a forest near the church. I was afraid to visit that burial site—even to look there…. [After] the seminar everybody offered to go with me to the grave site.

(A Tutsi woman)

I am a Hutu. But I hated Hutu. They killed my father in 1959. In 1994, they killed my two educated brothers who were working in Kigali. I became more resentful and angry against my fellow Hutu. Before we fled to Tanzania, I hid nearly 1000 Tutsi in my church. My fellow Hutu were mocking me… I only came back in December 1996. I was welcomed by the people I hid. After the workshop, I got delivered from my resentment and anger.

(A Hutu pastor)

Since my childhood I was taught to consider all Hutu as enemies. I hated them with all my energy… My grandfather nourished my hatred with many stories of awful things Hutu did in 1959, causing our exile. I only regretted that I was a weak little girl who could do nothing to take revenge.

(A Tutsi woman)

When we came back to Rwanda in 1994, I was at the height of my hatred … But when one of the workshop facilitators repented on behalf of the Hutu, I felt my heart was broken. I felt love flowing in me. I humbled myself before God and my brother, the facilitator. I offered him this rug [one of her skirts], to prove to him [a Hutu] that I love him. I said, "Whenever you wipe your feet on it, remember that I forgave Hutu."

(A Tutsi woman)

Insights from the two healing workshops

These workshops—the PDW and the workshop for religious and lay leaders—both contain elements that contribute to the healing of individuals, and of human relationships in Rwanda, leading to changes in attitudes from hopelessness to optimism. First, the workshops take a small-group approach that establishes a degree of trust, while alleviating the fear of invasion of personal boundaries. This is essential for people to feel confident talking about their feelings without being shamed or ridiculed. The events of 1994 affected the sensibility of many Rwandans. Many people became withdrawn after 1997, because of the chaos of the mass return from the camps in the DRC, and the conflicts that ensued as the returning people met former exiles living in their homes and neighbourhood, invading their personal space. At the same time, others were coerced into supporting the militia incursions and the ensuing violence. Every person either had lost loved ones or knew others who were implicated in some way. Thus, it was difficult for many Rwandans to accept the offer to meet and trust others with their personal thoughts and experiences.

Second, creating an environment of sufficient confidentiality to tell personal stories without fear of exposure or exploitation allowed participants to move beyond trust, to share what had been kept in their minds for several years. Bringing secrets into the open occurred by choice, not through the invasion of privacy, and required delicate and sensitive framing of discussion topics, as well as careful handling of the group sharing process. Group norms are important in this process, but the skill and experience of the facilitator are paramount. Both workshops were led by mature people who were experienced in their field. It took many months to develop and train the second and third level of leadership, and constant vigilance is needed to supervise these facilitators and guard against burnout.

Third, these workshops have demonstrated that it takes time to "open the wounds"; that is, to speak of deep feelings of pain, and to remember and recount its causes. Relatively few participants have been able to do this, and to speak of such hurts once is rarely enough. The wounds heal slowly.

Fourth, the time to grieve for losses and to let go of the memories of the painful death of loved ones cannot be underestimated. Large-scale losses have deep impact, and the grieving process takes a long time.

Fifth, the workshops allow participants to face personal experiences rather than denying them, confronting personal fears while also teaching participants to value their emotions and to reflect on their meaning. This is a slow process of education and awareness-raising. This, in part, provides some of the inspiration to envisage a better future, imagining a peaceful Rwanda in which citizens speak the truth and communicate openly and respectfully.

Sixth, the dialogue stimulated by the workshops promotes recognition that people from the "other" group have also suffered and are also becoming aware of the causes of their pain. I have been amazed, both as a participant and as an onlooker, to hear participants who have suffered and can recount great losses in 1994 admit that their traditional enemy also suffered, sometimes even more than themselves. I have heard these comments made by Tutsi survivors to Hutu, and vice versa.

Finally, in both workshops, participants often go away resolving to be just and to seek justice for others—for example, by setting a goal to participate in rebuilding broken relationships in their community, to challenge stereotypes in the group about the "other", or to apologise for what their ancestors did to the other.

Conclusion

When compared to the scale of need in Rwanda, the experiences of PDW and the AE Healing and Forgiveness Workshops in psycho-social healing are modest. Yet they contain methods and principles and suggest insights that may guide the expansion and deepening of long-term psycho-social recovery in Rwanda after the genocide. They show that opening inner wounds is where healing starts. Participants accompany others on their journey, but individuals are affected only insofar as they are willing to share openly with others. The telling of a story to an attentive audience both authenticates it and diminishes its power over the teller. In this sense, the experience of these workshops refutes the well known saying attributed to the Roman poet Terence, "Time heals all wounds." In the light of Rwandan history and current experience, I believe that while time does bring perspective, it does not heal the deepest wounds; *only proactive, conscious healing heals.*

Rwandans have taken years since the genocide to begin their healing journey. Reconciliation rarely happens, because it requires sustained involvement from both the offender and the offended. The journey from denial winds its way through revenge to face the questions of forgiveness, repentance, apology and acceptance. This journey takes time.

Forgiveness is a surprising process, often benefiting the forgiver before the transgressor. In Rwanda, I am convinced that forgiveness is difficult, but possible. Forgiveness is an act of healing the self, which releases the forgiver from the chain that binds him or her to hurt and nurtures the desire for revenge. Generally, people do not forgive others because they do not first forgive themselves for their own failures, both real and perceived. The willingness to look at personal shortcomings, and to let go of anger and disappointment in one's self, has been crucial in the ability of many Rwandans to move on to consider the question of forgiving another. In the Appendix, the steps that lead to forgiveness of oneself frequently allow an appreciation of this point. In my reflections with Rwandan colleagues, we have concluded that personal psychological energy is focused inwards until inner struggles over guilt, failure, grief and anger can be satisfactorily processed. Subsequently, some of the personal energy and focus can be directed outwards. That is why forgiving oneself is such a priority.

I have also observed in Rwanda that "I am sorry" are the most powerful words in the healing of broken relationships. As long as individuals blame others, they will avoid the truth about themselves, while claiming a position of superiority and power. By projecting their faults onto others, they make themselves feel safe. But when individuals come to see things from the perspective of the "other", which only happens by listening to their stories, they may discover why others suffered hurt in the past and they may begin to share in their humanity. Saying "sorry" is crucial to healing the "other": it is an act of support and empathy. Apology is difficult because it requires accountability and confession.

My colleagues and I have learned from our experiences of psycho-social healing in Rwanda that people must face the truth about the past, including their own actions, pay attention to their own emotions, take responsibility for their failures, identify and confront negative forces in their own lives and community, honour the dead and grieve their loss, practise forgiveness towards others, and find ways to bring justice that seeks to restore what has been lost.

APPENDIX
A TWELVE STEP PROCESS OF FORGIVENESS [24]

This is an abbreviated translation of a document used in the session on forgiveness in the PDW, to explain some of the steps by which one may reach forgiveness. It is not meant to be prescriptive, but a basis for discussion.

1. Forgiveness is not a unique (single/simple) act, but a form of inner pilgrimage, as encapsulated in the following statements:

2. *Not to take revenge, and to cease offensive actions.* The walk towards forgiveness begins with two decisions: to decide not to take revenge, and to stop the offensive situation. There is no point in wanting to forgive if the offensive situation continues.

3. *Recognise our inner wounds.* If we deny our woundedness, we block the possibility of healing. This person has hurt/is hurting me, s/he has offended me, and I suffer because of this. Denial, truth-minimisation and truth-avoidance are defence mechanisms that prevent us from reaching real forgiveness. They hold the energy inside us.

4. *Share our inner wounds with someone.* Rather than bear the wounds alone, tell the story to someone who will listen and not judge, moralise or offer

---

24 Adapted and translated from: R. Poletti and B. Dobbs, in J. Monbourquette, *Comment pardonner?: pardonner pour guérir et guérir pour pardonner* (Ottawa, Canada: Novalis, 1992).

advice. This allows us to see the situation in a larger perspective. Every telling shares our pain and the story loses a little of its power over us.

5. *Identify the loss and grieve it.* List all of the losses caused by the offence and grieve for what we have lost. Weep, wail, mourn, reminisce.

6. *Accept the anger and the desire for revenge.* It is natural, but it does not have to push us to destructive actions. Anger is necessary to express the need for justice; we need to fully imagine vengeance in images and then slowly the images will disappear.

7. *Forgive myself.* We feel guilt, shame, blame, desire for revenge, which affect our inner harmony and need for forgiveness, as do our mistakes. To forgive ourselves is the first condition of allowing us to forgive others.

8. *Understand our offender.* Put aside blame and place ourselves in the other's position, imagining her suffering, realising that what she did is irreversible. Recognise her value as a human being; accept her mystery.

9. *Find some meaning for the offence in our life.* With time we might see some positive value or meaning in what happened. But this cannot be felt straight after the event.

10. *Know that we are worthy of forgiveness and already forgiven.* Each of us has been forgiven many times; forgiveness gives us dignity and a sense of value. For those of us who accept the idea of a God who forgives, there is the possibility of feeling accepted unconditionally.

11. *Stop pursuing forgiveness.* Forgiveness is not a moral obligation. We cannot demand if from others. Not all people are ready to forgive and, furthermore, they will not respond to pressure. The process takes time and everyone has their own process. Pressure adds guilt and builds the wall of resistance and resentment.

12. *Open ourselves to the grace to forgive.* It is not natural, it is beyond comprehension—we do not understand in advance how we will forgive. We often need to call on divine help.

13. *Decide to end the relationship/friendship or renew it.* If forgiveness leads to reconciliation, it is impossible to meet each other in the way it was before the offence. The relationship will begin on a new basis. Forgiveness may be given and the relationship ends, for different reasons. It is still beneficial for the offended and the offender.

PART III
POST-GENOCIDE TRANSITIONAL JUSTICE, RECONSTRUCTION AND RECONCILIATION

10

ESTABLISHING A CONCEPTUAL FRAMEWORK: SIX KEY TRANSITIONAL JUSTICE THEMES

Phil Clark

Introduction

"Transitional justice" is an often ill-defined realm that encompasses a multitude of discrete, though overlapping, and often conflicting themes. At the heart of discussions of transitional justice are questions of what reconstructive objectives post-conflict societies should pursue and how they should pursue them. Given the complexity of issues surrounding rebuilding societies after mass violence, the immense confusion about what "transitional justice" entails is perhaps inevitable. Different transitional societies choose different objectives, and often pursue them in very different ways, usually because of political, social, economic and legal constraints after conflict. The truth commissions of Central and South America in the 1980s and 1990s, for example, sought to establish the truth about crimes committed by political and social elites and, in most instances, offered these individuals amnesty in exchange for the truth.[1] The South African Truth and Reconciliation Commission (TRC) similarly offered amnesty to apartheid leaders in exchange for disclosure about their crimes against the black majority. However, the TRC differed from previous truth commissions by enshrining reconciliation as a key objective. This policy represented a turning-point in the ideas and practices of post-conflict institutions globally. The TRC in South Africa has since served as a touchstone for other

---

1   P. Hayner, "Fifteen Truth Commissions—1974-1994: A Comparative Study", *Human Rights Quarterly*, 16, 4 (November 1994), 613-14, 621-3, 628-9, 653-5.

post-conflict institutions, inspiring in many cases (usually implicitly) the expressed pursuit of reconciliation, for example in Kenya, Nigeria, Sierra Leone and East Timor. Even the Statute of the United Nations International Criminal Tribunal for Rwanda (ICTR)—an institution designed primarily to prosecute and punish the main orchestrators of the Rwandan genocide—states that "prosecution... would... contribute to the process of national reconciliation and to the restoration and maintenance of peace."[2]

Out of the central question of transitional justice—what reconstructive objectives should post-conflict societies pursue? —two specific questions emerge: First, is it necessary and feasible to punish the perpetrators of mass crimes? Second, if it is necessary and feasible to punish these perpetrators, what is punishment designed to achieve: to fulfil a moral obligation to bring the guilty to account, to deter future perpetrators, or to contribute to wider objectives, such as reconciliation?

No post-conflict society can avoid addressing these questions. The creators of the Central and South American truth commissions argued that it was not feasible to punish perpetrators if they were to persuade perpetrators to tell the truth about their crimes.[3] The South African TRC held that punishing apartheid leaders was likely to foment civil conflict, and that therefore a political compromise—trading amnesty for the truth about crimes and for national reconciliation—was more appropriate.[4] The ICTR holds that it is necessary to punish perpetrators, in order to fulfil a moral obligation to bring them to account, but also contribute to national peace and reconciliation. In the South African case, punishment and reconciliation were deemed to be contradictory objectives. The ICTR, however, holds that punishment is a prerequisite of peace and reconciliation. What these examples show is that not only do different post-conflict institutions explicitly aim for different political, social, or legal outcomes, but even in cases where they claim to pursue the same objectives—as in the South African TRC's and the ICTR's claimed pursuit of reconciliation—they often define the same objectives, or the methods for achieving them, in very different ways. In the case of the ICTR, the reference to "national reconciliation" cited above is the sole occurrence of this term in the Tribunal's Statute, with no attempt to define it more clearly, nor to describe how punishing *génocidaires* may contribute to it. Serious

---

2 United Nations, "Statute of the International Criminal Tribunal for Rwanda", http:// www.un.org/ictr/ statute.html.

3 Hayner, "Fifteen Truth Commissions", 613-14, 621-3, 628-9, 653-5.

4 For a useful discussion of the political and social compromises behind the South African TRC, and their often problematic outcomes, see J. Sarkin, "The Trials and Tribulations of South Africa's Truth and Reconciliation Commission", *South African Journal on Human Rights*, 12, 4 (1996), 617-40.

questions therefore remain over whether the ICTR genuinely views reconciliation as a key objective and whether, and how, it actively pursues it.

This chapter investigates a range of potential post-conflict objectives that transitional societies may pursue; aims that are sometimes mutually reinforcing and sometimes in tension. The purpose of this chapter is to define and delineate some key terms of transitional justice, thus laying a foundation for the remaining chapters of this volume, which focus theoretically or practically on these concepts. This theoretical framework is not intended to be comprehensive but simply to clarify the transitional justice concepts most pertinent to the debates in the remainder of this volume. On the basis of the discussions in the following chapters, the final chapter of this volume explores the tensions between the terms that I introduce here, investigating in more detail the clashes between many of the key concepts associated with transitional justice.

This current chapter defines and distinguishes six key transitional justice terms—reconciliation, peace, justice, healing, forgiveness and truth—which constitute important post-conflict objectives, from which transitional societies must decide which aims to pursue. Other potential aims—for example the objective of establishing order and security in a society after conflict or providing victim compensation or reparation—can generally be considered components of one of these six objectives; for example, order and security, as I argue below, constitute important components of peace, while compensation and reparation represent outcomes of justice. The task of delineating these six objectives is vital because the field of transitional justice is afflicted by a severe theoretical poverty, which, in turn, affects the way that post-conflict objectives are pursued in practical terms. Many authors who discuss transitional justice themes, and many practitioners who actively pursue them, conflate these terms—for example by equating peace or healing with reconciliation—or, in the case of objectives such as healing and forgiveness, ignore them altogether. Defining and distinguishing these concepts therefore provides a better understanding of the nuances and prerequisites of each transitional justice objective, so that they may be more consistently and effectively realised. The aim of this chapter is not to provide an exhaustive investigation of each transitional justice theme, but rather to define and delineate each term sufficiently to outline the contours of what transitional justice entails, and to provide the basis for more detailed explorations of the aims that post-conflict societies should pursue (for example, the more detailed analyses of transitional justice themes in the following chapters of this volume).

Reconciliation

Where truth and justice have traditionally been the more common objectives of post-conflict institutions, reconciliation has recently become a focal theme. More regular considerations of reconciliation in transitional justice discourse, however, have rarely cultivated a clear understanding of what reconciliation is and how it may be achieved. It is important, therefore, to define what "reconciliation" means. In the broadest sense possible, reconciliation involves the rebuilding of fractured individual and communal relationships after conflict, with a view to encouraging meaningful interaction and cooperation between former antagonists. Reconciliation entails much more than peaceful coexistence, which requires only that parties no longer act violently towards one another. Non-violence may mean that the parties concerned simply avoid each other, seeking separation rather than mended relationships. Reconciliation, however, requires the reshaping of parties' relationships, to lay the foundation for future engagement between them. John Paul Lederach contends that a "relationship-centric"[5] interpretation of reconciliation holds that responses to conflict must penetrate to the level of individual relationships. "To enter reconciliation processes," Lederach argues, "is to enter the domain of the internal world, the inner understandings, fears and hopes, perceptions and interpretations of the relationship itself."[6] This internal dimension greatly affects reconciliation at the communal or national level, because these structures necessarily comprise individuals who have experienced violence. In this sense reconciliation, when defined in terms of rebuilding individual relations, lays the foundation for rebuilding wider social relations after conflict.

Reconciliation is both a process and an endpoint, requiring individuals and groups to interact and cooperate in often difficult circumstances, to discover solutions to their problems and thus to build stronger future relationships. Reconciliation is both backward- and forward-looking, seeking to address the causes of past conflict in order to produce a more positive dynamic in the future. Reconciliation must honestly and directly address the root causes of conflict, and the overwhelming feelings of grievance and anger that may have compounded over generations and led to violence, if the parties concerned are to overcome serious divisions in the future.

In defining reconciliation, it is also necessary to differentiate it from two terms with which is it often confused: peace and healing (I discuss these terms separately below). First, reconciliation differs from peace or any of its related processes such as peace-keeping or peace-building. The Report of the Panel on United Nations Peace Operations (commonly known as the "Brahimi Report"

---

5   J. Lederach, "Five Qualities of Practice in Support of Reconciliation Processes" in R. Helmick and R. Petersen (eds), *Forgiveness and Reconciliation: Religion, Public Policy, and Conflict Transformation* (Philadelphia: Templeton Foundation Press, 2001), 185.

6   Ibid.

after its chief author Lakhdar Brahimi) defines peace-building as "activities undertaken on the far side of conflict to reassemble the foundations of peace and provide the tools for building on those foundations something that is more than just the absence of war", including "promoting conflict resolution and reconciliation techniques."[7] Peace should be viewed as a prerequisite of reconciliation. If violence continues, it is nearly impossible for individuals and groups to consider rebuilding their relationships. The broader, systemic, society-wide peace-building aims of ending violence and safeguarding against future conflict therefore pave the way for reconciliation's deeper, inter-personal, relationship-focused processes.

Second, reconciliation differs from healing, which refers primarily to the ability of individuals and groups to overcome trauma experienced during or after conflict. Authors such as Johan Galtung often conflate reconciliation and healing: for Galtung, reconciliation entails "the process of healing the traumas of both victims and perpetrators after violence, providing a closure of the bad relation."[8] Reconciliation, however, with its focus on rebuilding broken relationships, constitutes much more than overcoming trauma, although this—like peace-building—is often an important prerequisite of reconciliation. Many individuals and groups may not feel that they have suffered extreme trauma after conflict. Nonetheless, their relationships may be severely damaged, for a host of reasons other than trauma, and they may therefore seek some form of reconciliation. In other cases, traumatised individuals may need to overcome feelings of anguish, loss, or hatred toward others before they can feel ready to reconcile with them.

Peace

Post-conflict institutions, particularly those like *gacaca* in Rwanda or the ICTR, that pursue justice in some form are usually connected to the objective of peace through the idea of deterrence. If we punish the orchestrators and perpetrators of mass violence, the argument goes, then we will send a clear message that future criminals will also be punished, thus dissuading them from committing atrocities. As explored elsewhere in this volume, one of the root causes of the genocide in Rwanda was a culture of impunity, as political leaders were rarely held accountable for their crimes, and this encouraged them to continue orchestrating violence and creating the conditions whereby

---

7   United Nations, "Report of the Panel on United Nations Peace Operations", *UN Doc. A/55/305-S/2000/809* (21 August 2000), 3.

8   J. Galtung, "After Violence, Reconstruction, Reconciliation, and Resolution: Coping with Visible and Invisible Effects of War and Violence" in M. Abu-Nimer (ed.), *Reconciliation, Justice and Coexistence: Theory and Practice* (Lanham, MD: Lexington Books, 2001), 3.

mass crimes such as genocide were possible. Eradicating the culture of impunity, by punishing those responsible for genocide and crimes against humanity, is therefore seen as vital for restoring stability in post-conflict societies and for replacing a culture of violence with a culture of peace.

Often on the basis of notions of deterrence, post-conflict institutions are regularly viewed as tools of peace-building, which the UN—in addition to the aforementioned definition in the Brahimi Report—defines as "in the aftermath of conflict... identifying and supporting measures and structures which will solidify peace and build trust and interaction among former enemies, in order to avoid a relapse into conflict."[9] This definition of peace-building contains two aspects of "peace": a negative component, in which peace (usually defined as the absence of conflict) has already been achieved, but must now be solidified in the immediate aftermath of violence; and a positive component, in which peace is a long-term condition that must be facilitated for the future, through building trust and encouraging greater interaction between previously antagonistic parties.

Each of these components comprises an interpretation of the timeframe and the necessary measures to bring about peace. In the negative version, peace involves short-term maintenance that shores up a recently-achieved situation of non-violence. In the positive component, peace constitutes a long-term process that requires building deeper mechanisms in a community to ensure that combatants do not return to conflict. Positive peace seeks to overcome what David Crocker describes as the "temptation in post-conflict or post-authoritarian societies... to permit euphoria (which comes from the cessation of hostilities...) to pre-empt the hard work needed to remove the fundamental causes of injustice and guard against their repetition."[10] Negative peace requires simply that the parties involved maintain security and stability, and no longer act violently towards one another. Such processes constitute forms of peace-keeping or peace enforcement, which are the stated purview of armed bodies such as UNAMIR. Positive peace, meanwhile, entails deeper engagement between previous protagonists, requiring new conflict resolution methods to safeguard against violence in the long-term. Negative peace is generally interpreted as a prerequisite of positive peace, as security and stability are necessary for the parties involved to begin constructing safeguards against future conflict. Both components of peace should be viewed as prerequisites for reconciliation, as negative peace helps

---

9   United Nations, "Glossary of UN Peacekeeping Terms", http://www.un.org/Depts/dpko/glossary/p. htm.

10   D. Crocker, "Truth Commissions, Transitional Justice and Civil Society" in R. Rotberg and D. Thompson (eds), *Truth v. Justice: The Morality of Truth Commissions* (Princeton, NJ: Princeton University Press, 2000), 107.

facilitate positive peace, which, in turn, may help parties to resolve their conflicts more effectively in the future and therefore build stronger, longer-lasting relationships.

Justice

The fundamental questions of post-conflict institutions—whether, and why, it is necessary to punish perpetrators of mass crimes (and the connected question, whether amnesty rather than punishment may ultimately better facilitate peace, reconciliation, truth or some other goal)—suggest the centrality of questions of justice in this context. As with reconciliation, however, the regular considera-tion of justice in post-conflict situations has rarely led to clear or comprehensive concepts or methods of justice. In particular, it is not always clear *why* certain institutions pursue justice after mass violence. This uncertainty may stem from what Ruti Teitel describes as the paradox of legal responses to mass crimes.

Law is between the past and the future....between retrospective and prospective. Transi-tions imply paradigm shifts in the conception of justice; thus, law's function is inher-ently paradoxical. In its ordinary social function, law provides order and stability, but in extraordinary periods of political upheaval, law maintains order, even as it enables transformation.[11]

Post-conflict legal institutions, such as the ICTR, are trapped uncomfort-ably between backward- and forward-looking pursuits, punishing perpetrators of past crimes while claiming—though usually failing to articulate precisely how—punishment will contribute to reconstruction or reconciliation. In order to more clearly explore justice as it manifests in the ICTR, *gacaca* and other post-conflict justice institutions, I outline the contours of justice here.

First, models of justice as responses to crime can be divided into three broad categories: retributive, deterrent and restorative. Retributive justice holds that perpetrators must be punished, to bring them to account and to give them what they supposedly "deserve." Some authors argue that retributive justice is also necessary for states to adhere to international legal conventions.[12] The deterrent view of justice meanwhile holds that punishment is necessary, but not simply because perpetrators deserve it. Rather, punishment should help discourage a convicted perpetrator from committing another crime, for fear of receiving punishment as he or she has in the past, and also to discourage current or potential criminals from continuing or initiating offences, lest they also receive punishment. Finally, a restorative conception of justice differs from

---

11   R. Teitel, "Transitional Jurisprudence: The Role of Law in Political Transformation", *Yale Law Journal*, 106, 7 (May 1997), 2014.

12   See, for example, D. Orentlicher, "Settling Accounts: The Duty to Prosecute Human Rights Violations of a Prior Regime", *New York Law Journal*, 100, 8 (June 1991), 2562-8.

the retributive or deterrent models, by holding that punishment alone is insufficient; punishment of criminals is necessary but should be facilitated in ways that allow perpetrators and victims to rebuild relationships, for example by requiring perpetrators to compensate victims or provide reparations, which may contribute to restoring fractured relations. In the case of mass crimes such as genocide, restorative justice often views the reconciliation of entire communities as the ultimate objective. Restorative justice therefore attempts to further explain the sorts of conceptual relationships suggested in the clichéd refrain of many commentators on post-conflict societies, that "no reconciliation is possible... without justice."[13]

Gerry Johnstone describes restorative justice as a new approach to criminality that

revolves around the idea that crime is, in essence, a violation of a person by another person (rather than a violation of legal rules); that in responding to a crime our primary concerns should be to make offenders aware of the harm they have caused, to get them to understand and meet their liability to repair such harm, and to ensure that further offences are prevented; that the form and amount of reparation from the offender to the victim and the measures to be taken to prevent re-offending should be decided collectively by offenders, victims and members of their communities through constructive dialogue in an informal and consensual process; and that efforts should be made to improve the relationship between the offender and victim and to reintegrate the offender into the law-abiding community.[14]

Second, methods of justice can be divided into two broad categories: formal and negotiated. In the formal interpretation, post-conflict institutions arrive at justice via pre-determined (usually legal) statutes and procedures. Due process during criminal hearings constitutes a key component of most formal models. In the negotiated interpretation, institutions achieve justice predominantly through communal discussions of evidence related to mass crimes. Negotiated justice, meanwhile, emphasises the role of the community in discussing and debating different versions of the truth about the past, and what responses that truth requires: for example, whether perpetrators should be punished and how. These two broad methods of justice—formal and negotiated—are not mutually exclusive. An institution could, theoretically, rely on very broad legal statutes that permit a large degree of communal negotiation within those formal boundaries.

At the theoretical level, formal and negotiated methods may lead to some combination of retributive, deterrent or restorative outcomes. For example,

---

13   J. de Gruchy *et al.*, "The Kairos Document: Challenge to the Church" (1985) http://www.
      bethel.edu/~letnie/AfricanChristianity/SAKairos.html.

14   G. Johnstone, *Restorative Justice: Ideas, Values, Debates* (Cullompton, Devon, UK:
      Willan Publishing, 2002) ix.

retributive or deterrent justice may be achieved via both formal or negotiated means: in the first instance, independent judges operating in the controlled environment of a conventional courtroom, adhering strictly to pre-determined legal statutes governing the running and the range of judicial outcomes of hearings, may punish perpetrators in a fashion consistent with the requirements of retributive or deterrent justice. These requirements could also be fulfilled via a negotiated process that affords the community a central role in debating and judging cases, but still punishes perpetrators. Similarly, restorative justice could theoretically be achieved by either formal or negotiated means. For example, the formal requirements of a judicial process could dictate that punishment must be systematically directed towards rebuilding relationships between parties, or in the case of negotiated processes, the very nature of the participatory methods employed could be viewed as a means towards restorative ends.

On this basis, we should view Johnstone's account of restorative justice above—with its emphasis on restorative punishment as necessarily "decided collectively... through constructive dialogue in an informal and consensual process"—as normative, rather than strictly definitional. In a theoretical sense, we can conceive ways to achieve restorative justice other than through collective deliberation, although Johnstone may be right to argue that, in practice, communal negotiation is the most justifiable and effective means to restoration. No *prima facie* reason exists to assume that one particular method of justice will lead automatically to one particular justice outcome, or that post-conflict institutions should be limited to employing either a formal or a negotiated method, rather than a hybrid of these approaches.

Healing

It is impossible to overstate the extent to which severe physical, emotional and psychological trauma characterises many post-conflict communities. In the case of Rwanda, nearly every citizen has been affected individually by violence, whether from direct involvement in perpetrating crimes, from personal injury, or from the injury or death of loved ones.[15] Trauma manifests itself in numerous ways in post-conflict societies, from individuals' feelings of helplessness and an inability to engage with others, to expressions of mistrust, paranoia, anger and vengefulness, and even to suicide.[16] In the face of such immense and various

---

15   L.A. Pearlman, "Psychological Trauma", lecture for "Healing, Forgiving, and Reconciliation" project, John Templeton Foundation, West Conshohocken, Pennsylvania, 13 March 2000, copy on file with author; N. Munyandamutsa, *Question du Sens et des Repères dans le Traumatisme Psychique: Réflexions autour de l'Observation Clinique d'Enfants et d'Adolescents Survivants du Génocide Rwandais de 1994* (Geneva: Editions Médecine et Hygiène, 2001).

16   Pearlman, "Psychological Trauma".

needs, concepts and processes of healing centre on helping individuals regain a sense of psychological or emotional wholeness that conflict has shattered. Individuals' trauma is not, however, necessarily the result only of physically, psychologically, or emotionally damaging experiences, such as mass violence. Trauma may also stem from material deprivation, resulting either from conflict or from later disasters, including famine, which may be natural or a consequence of conflict. For this reason, healing must take a holistic approach. In the context of post-conflict healing, holism refers to the need to rebuild the whole or complete person. If we identify the causes of trauma as a combination of psychological, emotional, material and other factors, then healing must incorporate holistic methods that seek effective responses to this range of causes. Because these causes often compound one another—for example when a lack of food and adequate shelter exacerbates a victim's sense of loss after the murder of a loved one—then methods of healing must respond simultaneously, and in an integrated manner, to all the identifiable causes of trauma.

The concept of healing has only recently become associated with the field of transitional justice. In recent years, greater attention has been paid to issues of psychosocial healing after conflict, largely as a result of the South African TRC, where Archbishop Desmond Tutu in particular emphasised the importance of truth, forgiveness and communal healing in the daily running of the TRC.[17] Where post-conflict reconstruction was once solely the domain of politicians and legal experts, trauma counsellors and other psychological experts now play a greater role in helping individuals come to terms with their personal experiences of conflict. Underlying this shift towards a greater consideration of psychosocial issues is a recognition that conflict not only damages entire nations or cultural groups, as emphasised in the use of the term "genocide", but crucially also the individuals within those groups. Post-conflict healing holds that societies require rebuilding from the level of the individual upwards, in concert with nationwide pursuits. Rebuilding from the level of the individual is a complicated undertaking, because individuals' needs are both highly varied and difficult to assess without evaluating the specific case of every person in the post-conflict society. However, as Mahmood Mamdani argues, overcoming individuals' feelings of trauma, resentment, and victimhood after conflict is vital because these perceptions have long-lasting effects, producing subsequent feelings of victimhood in future generations that plant the seeds of further violence. Mamdani argues that in the Rwandan case, a Hutu self-view of victimhood, particularly in the twentieth century, provided an emotional and psychological foundation for Hutu violence against Tutsi, as Hutu attempted to overcome

---

17   D. Tutu, *No Future without Forgiveness* (New York: Doubleday, 1999), chs. 6, 7, 10 and 11.

their victim status and to gain a greater sense of empowerment.[18] The inter-generational effects of trauma remind us of the need to facilitate healing not only to help individuals rebuild their lives, but also to protect entire societies from descending into further conflict. Healing therefore is integral to achieving positive peace and ultimately reconciliation.

Healing relates to crucial questions of individual identity. Processes of healing comprise important internal and external elements, as healing entails what Malvern Lumsden describes as "rebuilding a coherent sense of self and sense of community."[19] Post-conflict healing relates to individuals' regaining of a sense of inner wholeness—that is, healing of their own identity, as captured in the phrase "to find oneself again." Re-establishing individuals' sense of inner coherence often requires rebuilding a sense of how they as individuals relate to their communities, from which they gain much of their sense of self-worth and the meaning of their lives as a whole. Lisa Schirch argues that it is often necessary to "rehumani[s]e" survivors and perpetrators after violence.[20] These individuals have forfeited much of their personal sense of humanity through either perpetrating, or being the victims of, mass crimes. Perpetrators often dehumanise their victims in order to justify their violent actions, and in turn may suffer forms of dehumanisation themselves by committing crimes, when they forfeit feelings of common humanity and empathy toward their victims. Thus, healing requires rehumanising survivors and perpetrators to overcome the negative identities that they assumed during conflict.

Forgiveness

Like the questions related to healing, the consideration of the need for, and possibility of, forgiveness is a recent development in the study of post-conflict societies. Forgiveness is an even more controversial and more rarely discussed issue in this context because it is so readily connected with religious perspectives to which many people do not subscribe. Some critics argue that any discussion of forgiveness will inevitably require forfeiting retributive or deterrent justice; that is, perpetrators will not receive the punishment they deserve or that may be necessary to discourage future criminality. Some critics also argue that forgiveness will entail the enforced forgetting of crimes and an unjust demand

---

18   M. Mamdani, *When Victims Become Killers: Colonialism, Nativism, and Genocide in Rwanda* (Princeton, NJ: Princeton University Press, 2001) chs. 4, 5 and 7.

19   M. Lumsden, "Breaking the Cycle of Violence", *Journal of Peace Research*, 34, 4 (November 1997), 381.

20   L. Schirch, "Ritual Reconciliation: Transforming Identity/Reframing Conflict" in Abu-Nimer (ed.), *Reconciliation, Justice, and Coexistence*, op. cit., 152.

for survivors to "move on" from their pain and loss.[21] For all these reasons, it is often considered too emotionally costly or coercive to advocate forgiveness after mass violence.

Most political thought on post-conflict forgiveness has occurred within the last decade. However, Hannah Arendt explored the appropriateness of forgiveness in the aftermath of the Second World War and provided an important analysis of the relevance of this term after mass conflict. Arendt argues that "forgiveness is the exact opposite of vengeance, which acts in the form of re-acting against an original trespassing, whereby far from putting an end to the consequences of the first misdeed, everybody remains bound to the process."[22] Direct retribution, Arendt argues, fuels the cycle of violence. Therefore forgiveness, which entails foregoing feelings of resentment and a desire for personal, direct retribution, is necessary to start afresh and to allow people to deal with memories of the past in a more constructive manner. "Forgiveness does not imply forgetting... 'giving up', 'turning the other cheek' or 'letting the other off the hook',"[23] argues Wendy Lambourne. Rather, forgiveness should be seen as a "complex act of consciousness" that overcomes injury in order to restore lost relationships.[24] Forgiveness therefore requires active, sometimes public acknowledgement of crimes committed, and leaves open the possibility that victims will seek redress from perpetrators and perhaps insist on punishing them.

On this basis, forgiveness is not inherently opposed to all forms of punishment, provided punishment for perpetrators does not involve personal, direct retribution, or ongoing calls for retribution even after perpetrators have been punished. Because forgiveness suggests some form of renewed relationship between perpetrator and victim, it is often confused with reconciliation. The two concepts, however, are distinct. While forgiveness may, in practice, lead to parties resolving their differences to the extent that a renewed form of relationship is possible, nothing in the concept of forgiveness requires parties to reconcile. A victim may justifiably forgive his or her transgressor and still refuse to engage with him or her again, perhaps for fear of repeat offences. Forgiveness requires only that a victim should forego feelings of resentment and a desire for direct revenge against the perpetrator.

Truth

---

21   See, for example, these two main criticisms of notions of forgiveness after the Rwandan genocide by genocide survivor Jean Baptiste Kayigamba in Chapter 2 of this volume.

22   H. Arendt, *The Human Condition* (Chicago, IL: University of Chicago Press, 1958), 241.

23   Lambourne, "The Pursuit of Justice and Reconciliation", 4.

24   Ibid.

The theme of truth, its discovery, propagation, and the extent to which it should be pursued along with other objectives in the post-conflict environment, is a perennial consideration in transitional societies. Victims of violence often seek the truth about who organised, perpetrated and covered up crimes, and how they were able to do so. From the perspective of policymakers, a key reason why questions over truth arise so regularly is that the debate in most post-conflict societies is often framed as a stark choice between pursuing justice or truth.[25] Specifically, policymakers are often faced with deciding between establishing some sort of judicial structure, whether domestic, international, or some combination, which may try an individual without establishing a full account of the past, or creating some type of truth commission, which often incorporates a promise of amnesty in exchange for full disclosure of the truth.

What does "truth" entail in the context of post-conflict societies? Generally speaking, truth after conflict relates to people's understandings of what occurred during periods of mass violence. As Robert Rotberg argues, "If societies are to prevent recurrence of past atrocities and to cleanse themselves of the corrosive enduring effects of massive injuries to individuals and whole groups, societies must understand—at the deepest possible levels—what occurred and why."[26] Truth can be achieved through various processes, such as a legal procedure, if it involves the provision and weighing of evidence related to crimes, or an emotional process, when it concerns testimony related to personal experiences of conflict. A controversial feature of the truth commissions established in South and Central America was their attempts to construct an "official" version of the truth by producing reports that synthesised evidence gathered from thousands of citizens who had experienced, or witnessed, alleged atrocities.[27] Individuals' and groups' recollections of the past often clash, and may be expressed for a variety of well-intentioned or cynically instrumentalist reasons. Therefore, attempts to produce an account of the past that will adequately represent, and be acceptable to, all individuals and groups who engage in the post-conflict truth process are inherently limited and likely to prove acrimonious.

Despite these caveats, three processes related to uncovering truth after conflict can be distinguished: what I term "truth-telling", "truth-hearing" and "truth-shaping." First, truth-telling relates to parties' public articulation of the

---

25   For further discussion of the tensions between truth and justice, see A. Gutmann and D. Thompson, "The Moral Foundations of Truth Commissions" in Rotberg and Thompson (eds), *Truth v. Justice*, op. cit., 22-44.

26   R. Rotberg, "Truth Commissions and the Provision of Truth, Justice and Reconciliation" in Rotberg and Thompson (eds), *Truth v. Justice*, op. cit., 3.

27   See, for example, D. Bronkhorst, *Truth and Reconciliation: Obstacles and Opportunities for Human Rights* (Amsterdam: Amnesty International Dutch Section, 1995), 15-28, 74-6.

truth, for example with the aim of providing legal evidence at a war crimes tribunal, or in pursuit of some form of catharsis through emotional expression in front of a truth commission. In these instances, legal evidence that leads to the conviction and sentencing of perpetrators exemplifies how truth can constitute a means towards certain forms of justice; in the case of emotional discourse, truth may help facilitate healing.

Second, truth-hearing entails the reception of truth-telling, focusing on the ways in which different audiences respond to evidence or emotional expressions. Truth-telling and truth-hearing constitute the halves of a post-conflict dialogue; in the case of legal settings, this dialogue is less pronounced, as truth-hearers are usually judges who engage in dialogue only insofar as they ask questions of those providing evidence. In more negotiated settings, such as truth and reconciliation commissions or *gacaca* in Rwanda, there is a greater sense of dialogue, as perpetrators and victims are encouraged to speak face-to-face.

Third, truth-shaping relates to the ways in which parties external to the initial truth-telling and truth-hearing receive and re-mould evidence to serve purposes for which the original participants may not have intended their discourse. For example, historians and political leaders engage in truth-shaping when they use evidence gleaned from post-conflict institutions to serve wider social or political purposes, such as reinterpreting historical events or teaching the population moral lessons. This phenomenon can be abused, for example when elites manipulate evidence to serve self-interested, even corrupt purposes, such as purging history of their own crimes.

One source of complexity and controversy in the TRC in South Africa was that all three truth processes—truth-telling, truth-hearing and truth-shaping—occurred within the same institution: individual perpetrators and victims engaged in face-to-face dialogue, and their discourse was recorded, debated, and interpreted by a range of external parties, not least by the commissioners of the TRC tasked with producing the Commission's Final Report, which was supposed to provide a basis for post-apartheid nation-building.[28] That the truth related to past crimes emanates from many different sources and is expressed, and subsequently deployed, for many different reasons ensures that the three processes of truth often intersect and overlap and are invariably controversial.

Conclusion

---

28   For a detailed discussion of the role of the Final Report of the TRC in South African nation-building, see J. Cronin, "A Luta Dis-Continue: The TRC Final Report and the Nation Building Project", paper delivered at the University of the Witwatersrand, Johannesburg (June 1999), http://www.trcresearch.org.za/papers99/cronin.pdf.

This chapter has traced the conceptual contours of six key transitional justice themes—reconciliation, peace, justice, healing, forgiveness, and truth—which shape how post-conflict societies choose which reconstructive objectives to pursue. More clearly defining the realm of transitional justice is necessary not only for us to discuss more lucidly and consistently questions of how to rebuild societies after mass violence, but also for us to engage practically in that rebuilding process. Before processes of transitional justice, there are often lofty, deeply moral ideas about what rebuilding after conflict requires. These ideas, however, can nonetheless become conflated and confused, leaving societies vulnerable to inconsistent and detrimental practical decision-making. The remainder of this volume explores in depth the ramifications of ideas and practices of transitional justice for societies trying to reconstruct after mass conflict. In particular, the following chapters investigate the ramifications of Rwanda's and other transitional societies' attempts to simultaneously pursue several of the six objectives outlined in this chapter—for example, trying to balance the demands of truth, justice and reconciliation—often with unpredictable, volatile and long-lasting consequences for their citizens.

11

POST-GENOCIDE JUSTICE IN RWANDA: A SPECTRUM OF OPTIONS

William A. Schabas

Impunity has been a feature of Rwandan life since at least the time of independence in 1962, and no doubt since before then.[1] Successive waves of ethnic cleansing, beginning in the dying days of the Belgian regime, went unpunished and were officially condoned. The silence of the national courts only aggravated the campaigns of persecution based on ethnicity that were a feature of the country's history until the catastrophic genocide of 1994. In the aftermath of genocide, there was general recognition that the so-called "culture of impunity" had played its own role in contributing to the context in which genocidal ideologies could thrive.

Everybody talks about battling impunity, but few societies have done this with greater determination or more stubborn resistance to compromise than Rwanda. It is beyond the scope of this chapter to attempt to understand why Rwanda took, and continues to take, such an intransigent course. It certainly stands as an obstacle to those who theorise that, unlike Europeans and Americans, Africans are conciliatory and forgiving, and prefer rapid reconciliation to prolonged criminal justice. But no discussion can proceed on this topic without first observing that Rwanda's approach to transitional justice is one of the most principled manifestations of the commitment of international human rights law and policy. While many other post-conflict societies have delayed, postponed and even prevaricated, resisting the admonitions of various international organisations, personalities and NGOs,[2] Rwanda has insisted upon holding perpetrators accountable.

---

1   "Report of the International Commission of Inquiry into Human Rights Violations in Rwanda" (Paris/Brussels/Montréal, 1993); Odette-Luce Bouvier, "Magistrature: Sous le diktat de l'exécutif", *Dialogue*, 162 (January 1993), 4-24.

2   For example, "The Rule of Law and Transitional Justice in Conflict and Post-conflict Societies, Report of the Secretary-General" (2004), UN Doc. S/2004/616.

The post-conflict justice debate sometimes posits mechanisms for address-ing accountability as mutually exclusive alternatives.[3] It is perhaps better to approach the problem as one requiring a multi-faceted approach, drawing upon various models, ranging from international tribunals to national courts, as well as non-judicial or quasi-judicial institutions, such as truth and recon-ciliation commissions. The Rwandan experience is of great interest because it has combined several approaches, covering many of the range of options. In some respects, it is also quite innovative. The discussion would not be com-plete without at least a passing reference to attempts in other countries to as-sist Rwanda, by bringing alleged perpetrators to justice under the principle of universal jurisdiction.[4]

International criminal prosecution

The International Criminal Tribunal for Rwanda (ICTR) was established pur-suant to United Nations Security Council (UNSC) Resolution 955, adopted on 8 November 1994, only a few months after the retreat of the *génocidaires* across Rwanda's borders. As Kaufman discusses in detail in the following chap-ter, the ICTR was largely modelled on the International Criminal Tribunal for the Former Yugoslavia (ICTY), which had been established in May 1993.[5] The only other important precedents for such international prosecution were the post-Second World War trials held in Nuremberg and Tokyo. The establish-ment of the ICTY focused international attention on the repression of atroci-ties committed during conflict through judicial mechanisms. There is evidence that an international tribunal for Rwanda was being contemplated from the earliest days of the conflict.[6]

---

3   On the debate in Sierra Leone, where an international court and a truth commission oper-ated contemporaneously, see William A. Schabas, "A Synergistic Relationship: The Sierra Leone Truth and Reconciliation Commission and the Special Court for Sierra Leone", in William A. Schabas and Shane Darcy (eds), *Truth Commissions and Courts, The Tension Between Criminal Justice and the Search for Truth* (Dordrecht: Kluwer Academic Publish-ing, 2004), 3-54.

4   William A. Schabas, "National Courts Finally Begin to Prosecute Genocide, the 'Crime of Crimes'", *Journal of International Criminal Justice*, 1 (2003), 89.

5   UN Doc. S/RES/827 (1993).

6   On the reaction within the United Nations to the first reports of genocide, see Linda Melvern, "Genocide Behind the Thin Blue Line", *Security Dialogue*, 28 (1997), 341. See also Alison Des Forges, *Leave None to Tell the Story, Genocide in Rwanda* (New York: Human Rights Watch, Paris: International Federation of Human Rights, 1999), 638-40; Boutros Boutros-Ghali, *Unvanquished, A U.S.-U.N. Saga* (New York: Random House, 1999), 129-40. Pope John Paul II was apparently the first major international personality to use the term "genocide" to describe the situation in Rwanda, to a general audience on 27 April 1994, reported by *Osservatore Romano* on 3 May 1994. The report of the inquiry commissioned by the Secretary-General concluded: "*The delay in identifying the*

A UNSC resolution of 17 May 1994 requested the UN Secretary-General "to present a report as soon as possible on the investigation of serious violations of international humanitarian law committed during the conflict."[7] The Czech diplomat Karol Kovanda spoke in the UNSC of the importance of the report, adding that once it was delivered, "we will want to know how those responsible will be brought to justice."[8] On 8 June 1994, a UNSC resolution confirmed that "genocide constitutes a crime punishable under international law."[9] Referring to the preambular reference to genocide, Ambassador Kovanda said he was looking "beyond the horizon" of the resolution to such measures as a fact-finding mission to be established by the UNSC, and the determination that certain organisations participating in the carnage might be deemed "criminal organisations". The Argentine representative said that genocide "must be investigated and those responsible cannot go unpunished".[10] A mission of the United Nations Commission on Human Rights, led by the Ivoirian law professor René Degni-Segui, said that the United Nations should either establish an international *ad hoc* tribunal or enlarge the jurisdiction of the existing tribunal for the former Yugoslavia in order to bring those responsible for genocide to justice.[11]

The United States was also promoting the idea. At the end of June 1994, the US Secretary of State, Warren Christopher, indicated his government's support for an international war crimes tribunal for Rwanda.[12] In early August, a senior US Department of State official, John Shattuck, visited Kigali and convinced Rwanda's new regime to go along with the idea.[13] On 28 September 1994, Rwanda formally requested the UN to establish a tribunal.[14] Moreover,

---

events in Rwanda as a genocide was a failure by the Security Council. The reluctance by some States to use the term genocide was motivated by a lack of will to act, which is deplorable." See "Report of the Independent Inquiry into the Actions of the United Nations During the 1994 Genocide in Rwanda", issued 15 December 1999 by the United Nations (italics in the original).

7   UN Doc. S/RES/918 (1994), para. 18.

8   UN Doc. S/PV.3377 (16 May 1994).

9   UN Doc. S/RES/925 (1994), Preamble.

10   UN Doc. S/PV.3388 and Corr.l (8 June 1994).

11   "The Situation of Human Rights in Rwanda", A/49/508, S/1994/1157 (1994).

12   S. Greenhouse, "U.S., having won changes, is set to sign Law of the Sea", *New York Times* (1 July 1994), 1.

13   P. Lewis, "Rwanda agrees to a U.N. war-crimes tribunal", *New York Times* (9 August 1994), 6. After losing power in mid-July, the remnants of the Rwandan regime that had presided over the genocide issued a call for the creation of an international tribunal, adding that its jurisdiction should cover human rights violations in Rwanda since October 1990, when the civil war had begun. Jerry Gray, "At Rwanda border, mass graves and the start of a journey home", *New York Times* (26 July 1994), 1.

14   "Letter Dated 28 September 1994 From the Permanent Representative of Rwanda to the United Nations Addressed to the President of the Security Council", UN Doc.

in his October 1994 address to the UN General Assembly, President Pasteur Bizimungu of Rwanda declared that "it is absolutely urgent that this international tribunal be established".[15] But Rwanda subsequently quarrelled with the UN about the form the tribunal was to take.[16] The realisation that an international tribunal would not be equipped to undertake the prosecution of thousands of detainees was, in the view of two UN insiders, probably one of the reasons why the Government of Rwanda eventually withdrew its support for the ICTR.[17]

The causes of Rwanda's disagreement included the prohibition of capital punishment, the limitation on temporal jurisdiction to the 1994 calendar year, the lack of an independent prosecutor and appeals chamber, a desire to exclude nationals of "certain countries" believed to be complicit in the genocide from nominating judges, the possibility that sentences might be served outside Rwanda, and the refusal to commit to locating the seat of the tribunal within Rwanda itself. Adoption of the UNSC resolution was delayed by a week as the UN legal adviser Hans Corell travelled to Kigali to try to win the support of Rwanda.[18] He was unsuccessful, and UNSC Resolution 955 was adopted on 8 November 1994 with one dissenting vote, that of Rwanda,[19] and an abstention, by China.[20]

The first ICTR trial judges were elected in early 1995 and formally sworn into office in June. The Tribunal issued its first indictments on 12 December 1995, accusing eight persons of genocide with respect to the mass killing of several thousand men, women and children in the Kibuye prefecture of

---

S/1994/1115.

15   UN Doc. S/PV.3453, (1994) 14.

16   P. Smerdon, "PM paints bleak view of Rwanda", *The Guardian* (9 August 1994), 11; Barbara Crossette, "Rwanda asks quick start of tribunal", *New York Times* (9 October 1994), 19; David Beresford, "Rwanda dead 'need justice'; general warns peace is impossible unless the killers are brought before the courts", *The Guardian* (24 September 1994), 17; Victoria Brittain, "Rwanda threatens to bypass UN and start genocide trials", *The Guardian* (14 September 1994), 10.

17   D. Shraga and R. Zacklin, "The International Criminal Tribunal for Rwanda," *European Journal of International Law*, 7 (1996), 504.

18   "U.N. delays vote on Rwanda panel", *New York Times* (1 November 1994) 17; Raymond Bonner, "Rwandans divided on war-crimes plan", *New York Times* (2 November 1994), Section a, 10; "Major obstacles remain over court", *Reuters World Service* (6 November 1994).

19   More moderate members of the Rwandan regime felt they should accept the Resolution, despite disagreement with some of the conditions, but apparently the hard line Vice-President and military supremo Paul Kagame prevailed. See Raymond Bonner, "Rwandans divided on war-crimes plan", *New York Times* (2 November 1994), 10.

20   The Chinese representative said it was "an incautious act to vote in a hurry on a draft resolution and statute that the Rwanda Government still finds difficult to accept." UN Doc. S/PV.3453, (1994) 11.

western Rwanda.[21] By March 1996, the interim military ruler of Rwanda during the genocide was taken into custody, a development that indicated the ICTR might actually do rather better than its European counterpart in prosecuting those most responsible for the atrocities, rather than their underlings and subordinates.

The ICTR was plagued with administrative difficulties and even corruption. At one point, in 1997, the UN had to intervene, firing two of the most senior officials of the Tribunal, the Registrar and the Deputy Prosecutor. As Ngoga notes in chapter 16, the UN also fired the ICTR's former chief prosecutor, Carla Del Ponte, paving the way for a chief prosecutor for the ICTR who was separate from the ICTY. There were also severe problems with unethical defence lawyers, who took legal aid fees from the ICTR but then split them with their clients. The Rwandan prisoners were fractious and uncooperative, sometimes going on hunger strike or refusing to attend trials. Relations with Rwanda itself, whose cooperation was essential for investigations, were often stormy. Trials were tediously slow, with some defendants held in detention for several years before having their day in court. Frustrated by irregularities in the arrest and detention of suspects, in late 1999 the Appeals Chamber granted the motion of an important defendant and permanently stayed all proceedings in the case. Enraged at the resulting impunity, Rwanda threatened to block all access by ICTR officials to its territory, a move that would effectively have shut down the institution's ability to operate. A differently-constituted Appeals Chamber ate humble pie and reversed the decision.[22]

Though constantly overshadowed by its older sister in The Hague, the ICTR has managed to try and convict many of the most prominent and important participants in the 1994 genocide. It has also clarified the historical truth of the attempted destruction of the Tutsi, putting this beyond the reach of deniers and negationists. As Judge Patricia Wald, formerly of the ICTY, has written,

Many historians as well as the relatives of victims maintain that only the adjudicated findings of an impartial international body of jurists following accepted rules of legal procedure will quell the doubts of future generations that the terrible things did in fact happen. To chronicle accurately for history some of the world's darkest deeds is the special responsibility of the Tribunal. Many would say it explains and even justifies the extraordinary length of the Tribunal's judgements and what sometimes appears to be the Tribunal's near-obsession with minute factual detail.[23]

---

21   N. Pillay, "The Rwanda Tribunal and its Relationship to National Trials in Rwanda", *American University International Law Review*, 13 (1998), 1469.

22   *Prosecutor v. Barayagwiza* (Case No: ICTR-97-19-AR72), Decision (Prosecutor's Request for Review or Reconsideration), 31 March 2000.

23   Ibid.

This is something no national tribunal can accomplish in the same credible and enduring manner. Certainly, in the Rwandan context, national courts will always be dismissed as being unrepresentative and, therefore, biased against the majority Hutu. No such claim can be made about the ICTR. By mid-2005, the ICTR had convicted more than 20 individuals, many of them national leaders, and several trials were ongoing. In other words, it has delivered on its pledge to bring those most responsible for the 1994 genocide to justice. The ICTR has committed itself to complete prosecutions by the end of 2008, and to close its operations shortly afterwards.[24]

Setting the stage for national prosecutions

In September 1994, Rwanda's then-Minister of Justice, Alphonse-Marie Nkubito, working from an office whose windows had been knocked out, and whose walls were decorated only by gunshots, appealed to the international community for assistance in rebuilding the country's devastated justice system. The Rwandan judicial system had never been more than a corrupt caricature of justice, and there was little to "rebuild". Prior to the 1994 genocide, it comprised about 700 judges and magistrates, of whom less than 50 had any formal legal training. Of these, the best had perished during the genocide, often at the hands of their erstwhile colleagues. There were only aroud 20 lawyers with genuine legal education in the country when I visited Rwanda in November 1994 as part of the international response to Minister Nkubito's appeal.[25] Documents furnished at the time by the Rwandan Ministry of Justice noted the utter devastation of both material and human resources, perpetrated by the defeated Rwandan government forces during their retreat to Zaire (now the Democratic Republic of Congo) in June and July 1994.[26] A succession of international mis-

---

24   "Report of the International Criminal Tribunal for the Prosecution of Persons Responsible for Genocide and Other Serious Violations of International Humanitarian Law Committed in the Territory of Rwanda and Rwandan Citizens Responsible for Genocide and Other Such Violations Committed in the Territory of Neighbouring States between 1 January and 31 December 1994", 27 July 2004, UN Doc. A/59/183-S/2004/601.

25   Several international studies were produced at the time: "Pour un système de justice au Rwanda, Rapport d'une mission exploratoire effectuée par l'Hon. Jacques Lachapelle, juge à la Cour du Québec (Chambre civile), et le Pr William A. Schabas, directeur du Département des sciences juridiques, Université du Québec à Montréal, du 27 novembre au 6 décembre 1994", International Centre for Human Rights and Democratic Development, Montreal; "Rapport de la mission Union Interafricaine des droits de l'homme/Synergie à Kigali du 15 au 22 octobre 1994"; "Mission francophone d'évaluation des besoins prioritaires dans le domaine de l'état de droit et des droits de l'homme au Rwanda du 17 au 21 novembre 1994", Agence de Coopération Culturelle et Technique, Paris; "Report, Joint Mission to Evaluate Needs of Justice System, UNDP/UNCHR/UNHCHR/USAID/ Swiss Cooperation/ACCT/ICJ/IPA/Lisbon Forum/ICHRDD", 2 December 1994.

26   "Projet d'appui à la reconstruction du système judiciaire rwandais du Ministère de la

sions proposed a series of major aid programmes,[27] and at one point the UN Office of the High Commissioner for Human Rights, which had barely begun operations, attempted to assemble *curricula vitae* of foreign lawyers willing to work within Rwanda as judges, lawyers or other judicial officers. But when Minister Nkubito was replaced by his chief of staff, Marthe Mukamureni, in September 1995, the Rwandan government made it clear that large numbers of foreign jurists were not required, and that justice in Rwanda would be done by Rwandans, with assistance from abroad playing only a secondary role.

Faced with the massive arrests that followed the 1994 genocide, and above all the devastation of an already feeble administrative and judicial infrastructure, Rwanda was simply incapable of respecting the provisions of its own criminal law, not to mention its obligations under international human rights law and international criminal law. In November and December 1994, the prosecutor for the Kigali region, François-Xavier Nsansuwera, informed me that barely 1,000 cases had been prepared, although many multiples of that number were being held in detention, and the prison population was growing each day.[28] From 31 October to 4 November 1995, the Government of Rwanda convened an international conference to explore the various dimensions of accountability for genocide. At the conference, South Africans argued strongly that a truth and reconciliation commission, coupled with some form of amnesty mechanism, was the appropriate "African" approach to accountability for the atrocities that had taken place in Rwanda. Rwanda's president at the time, Pasteur Bizimungu, called for innovative forms of justice but at the same time ruled out any possibility of amnesty. The 1995 Kigali Conference recommended that new mechanisms be created to deal with the genocide cases, including specialised chambers of the existing courts, a classification scheme to separate the main organisers of the genocide from criminals with lesser degrees of responsibility, and a unique approach aimed at encouraging offenders to confess, in exchange for substantially reduced sentences.[29] The ICTR had only a modest and quite low-key presence at the Conference; its prosecutor, Richard Goldstone, did not attend.

---

justice", UN Doc. TCB/BT2/8/Add.9, 7 November 1994.

27   "Aperçu de la situation", in *La lettre hebdomadaire de la Fédération internationale des droits de l'homme*, 206 (June 1995), 25-6.

28   Lachapelle and Schabas, *supra* note 25.

29   Republic of Rwanda, Office of the President, *Recommendations of the Conference Held in Kigali from November 1st to 5th, 1995, on 'Genocide, Impunity, and Accountability': Dialogue for a National and International Response*, Kigali, 1995; Colette Braeckman, *Terreur africaine* (Paris: Fayard, 1996), 323-37. The author participated in the Kigali Conference and was responsible for delivering its conclusions and final report on 5 November 1995.

The Rwandan Ministry of Justice proceeded to prepare legislation giving effect to the conference recommendations, and the Cabinet approved a draft law in April 1996. The legislation then advanced to the National Assembly for adoption. It was reworked in a parliamentary committee in July 1996, and was finally adopted on 30 August 1996.[30] In early September, the Constitutional Court approved the new statute. The legislation adopted in 1996 defined four categories of offender.[31] The first category consisted of the organisers and planners of the genocide, persons in positions of authority within the military or civil infrastructure who committed or encouraged genocide, and persons who committed "odious and systematic" murders. This category accounted for a relatively small percentage of those who had been detained and overlapped with those over whom the ICTR has attempted to establish jurisdiction. The second category covered those not in the first category who had committed murder or serious crimes against the person that led to death. The third category comprised other serious crimes against the person, and the fourth category was made up of crimes against property.

The heart of the legislation was what has been called the "Confession and Guilty Plea Procedure". In return for a full confession, offenders in the second, third and fourth categories were to benefit from a substantial reduction in penalties. Confessions were required to include a complete and detailed description of the offences that the accused admitted to, including information about accomplices and any other relevant facts. The prosecutor had three months in which to confirm the truth of the confession. Even if the prosecutor challenged the truth of the confession, the accused was entitled to submit the matter to the court, which could overrule the decision of the prosecutor not to accept the confession. If the confession remained unchallenged during this time, it became a guilty plea and the case proceeded to the sentencing phase. Though not comparable to the South African approach, which offered amnesty in return for a full confession, the guilty plea procedure displayed key similarities to that method and was, to a large extent, inspired by the same principles. Of course, under the Rwandan system, a guilty plea did not result in immediate release, although there were substantial benefits in terms of a reduced sentence. Judgements at the ICTY have recognised the social benefits of encouraging guilty pleas:

---

30   *Organic Law No. 08/96 of 30 August 1996 on the Organisation of Prosecutions for Offences Constituting the Crime of Genocide or Crimes against Humanity committed since 1 October 1990*, J.O., 1996, Year 35, No. 17, p. 14. In the Rwandan system, an Organic Law ranks hierarchically immediately beneath the Constitution. Organic Laws are adopted with a view to specifying or completing provisions of the Constitution, according to special procedures which must be rigorously respected.

31   See: *Prosecutor v. Kambanda* (Case no. ICTR-97-23-S), Judgement and Sentence, 4 September 1998, para. 18.

In confessing his guilt and admitting all factual details contained in the Third Amended Indictment in open court on 4 September 2003 Dragan Nikolić has helped further a process of reconciliation. He has guided the international community closer to the truth in an area not yet subject of any judgement rendered by this Tribunal, truth being one prerequisite for peace.[32]

The Organic Law has been referred to regularly in judgements of the ICTR, generally in the context of sentencing convicted persons.[33] The prosecutor has often cited the national legislation with reference to Article 23(1) of the *Statute* of the ICTR, which directs: "The penalty imposed by the Trial Chamber shall be limited to imprisonment. In determining the terms of imprisonment, the Trial Chambers shall have recourse to the general practice regarding prison sentences in the courts of Rwanda."[34] The prosecutor has argued that offenders at the ICTR fall, by and large, within Category 1 of the Rwandan legislation. Were they to be tried in Rwanda, they would be exposed to life imprisonment (although the death penalty was used until its abolition in 2007), and this is invoked to justify a harsh sentence at the ICTR. Actually, Article 23(1) of the ICTR Statute was intended to ensure respect of the *nulla poena sine lege* principle. In other words, its purpose is to protect the defendant, rather than to justify severe punishment.[35]

Genocide trials before national courts under the 1996 legislation

Trials under the Organic Law began before Specialised Chambers of the ordinary Rwandan courts in the final week of December 1996, several weeks before the ICTR launched its first trial.[36] International observers had been impatient to see the trials begin. The resolution on the situation in Rwanda adopted

---

32 *Prosecutor* v. *Dragan Nikoli* (Case No. IT-02-60/1-S), Sentencing Judgement, 18 December 2003, para. 3. Similarly, *Prosecutor* v. *Sikirica* et al. (Case No. IT-95-8-I), Judgement on Defence Motions to Acquit, 3 September 2001, para. 149.

33 For example, *Prosecutor* v. *Rutaganda* (Case No. ICTR-96-3-T), Judgement and Sentence, 6 December 1999, paras. 453-454; *Prosecutor* v. *Musema* (Case No. ICTR-96-13-T), Judgement, 27 January 2000, paras. 983e-984; *Prosecutor* v. *Serushago* (Case No. ICTR-98-39), Sentence, 5 February 1999, paras. 17-18; *Prosecutor* v. *Ruggiu* (Case No. ICTR-97-32-T), Judgement, 1 June 2000, paras. 28-31; *Prosecutor* v. *Ntakirutimana* et al. (Cases No. ICTR-96-10 & ICTR-96-17-T), Judgement, 21 February 2003, para. 885; *Prosecutor* v. *Semanza* (Case No. ICTR-97-20-T), Judgement and Sentence, 15 May 2003, para. 561; *Prosecutor* v. *Ntakirutimana* et al. (Cases Nos. ICTR-96-10-A and ICTR-96-17-A), Judgement, 13 December 2004, para. 552

34 UN Doc. S/RES/955 (1994), annex.

35 See, on this point, William A. Schabas, "Perverse Effects of the *Nulla Poena* Principle: National Practice and the Ad Hoc Tribunals", *European Journal of International Law*, 11 (2000), 521.

36 *Prosecutor* v. *Akayesu* (Case no. ICTR-96-4-T), Judgement, 2 September 1998, para. 17.

by the UN General Assembly at the end of 1996, "urge[d] in particular that the processing of the cases of those in detention be brought to a conclusion expeditiously."[37] Moreover, the General Assembly "[n]ote[d] with deep concern the reports of the Human Rights Field Operation in Rwanda which state that government officials without legal authority to arrest or imprison continue to do so in several parts of the country, that detainees are held for very long periods before trial and that acute overcrowding threatens the safety of those in detention."[38] But when the trials finally began, there was much criticism that the proceedings had begun with undue haste. In the eyes of the "international community" Rwandan justice was damned if it did, and damned if it didn't.

The Field Office of the UN High Commissioner for Human Rights delivered a devastating initial verdict on the trials.[39] Amnesty International was also highly critical of the first trials, noting that the new legislation was inconsistent with international standards because it failed to ensure state-funded counsel for indigent defendants in capital cases.[40] *Avocats sans Frontières*-Belgium took the lead in ensuring that defence lawyers would be supplied to persons accused before the Rwandan courts, and in practice most defendants were well represented by competent counsel, generally foreigners, from Europe or elsewhere in Africa. The late-1997 report to the General Assembly by the High Commissioner was rather more charitable:

64. The steps taken towards bringing the perpetrators of the genocide to justice and compensating civil claimants are to be welcomed. Progress has been made since the commencement of the genocide trials, including the increased number of witnesses testifying in court; the improvement in detainees' access to case files; and the increase in the granting of reasonable requests for adjournments.

65. However, several aspects of the proceedings remain cause for concern, in particular the lack of full respect for some fair trial guarantees as required by Rwandan law and article 14 of the International Covenant on Civil and Political Rights, and the lack of legal representation in many cases, as well as a general lack of opportunity for category-one defendants to cross-examine witnesses. These shortcomings can be particularly serious given the fact that if found guilty, under Rwandan law, the accused may face the death penalty...[41]

---

37   "Situation of Human Rights in Rwanda", GA Res. 51/114, para. 10.

38   Ibid., para. 11.

39   C. Tomlinson, "UN Report Blasts Rwanda Trials", *Associated Press* (11 January 1997).

40   Amnesty International, "Rwanda Unfair Trials: Justice Denied", April 1997 (AI Index AFR 47/008/1997).

41   "Report of the United Nations High Commissioner for Human Rights on the Human Rights Field Operation in Rwanda", UN Doc. A/52/486, annex. See also "Decision 5(53) of the Committee for the Elimination of Racial Discrimination, adopted 18 August 1998", para. 10.

Some of the harsh initial judgements about the shortcomings in the trials were made by lawyers trained in common law jurisdictions, who misunderstood certain aspects of the "civil law" approach that Rwanda had inherited from Belgium and France. They were shocked, for example, at the relative brevity of the trials, the reliance on written evidence, and the lack of cross-examination. By contrast, trial observers who came from "civil law" traditions were relatively sanguine and even rather impressed with the proceedings.

I attended the January 1997 trial of Froduald Karamira, as an observer for the International Secretariat of Amnesty International. From my standpoint, the proceedings had all the appearances of fairness, and the presiding judge gave the accused and his lawyer every chance to rebut the charges. Karamira's so-called "defence" convinced nobody. It consisted essentially of accusations that the prosecution witnesses were liars. One witness, who was missing an ear and an eye, told the court how Karamira had manned a barricade close to his home in a Kigali suburb and ordered armed thugs to execute a defenceless woman. Another described how she had called Karamira on behalf of her employer, a Tutsi, asking him for protection; the Tutsi was a prominent local businessman and neighbour of Karamira, but Karamira hung up the phone and minutes later militia members came to the house to kill the unfortunate man and his family. Karamira denied accusations that he had fomented ethnic hatred. However, he was credited with coining the slogan "Hutu Power". He mobilised racists in different political parties around a common programme of genocide. When Karamira challenged the court to furnish proof, the prosecutor played a damning tape recording of a racist speech Karamira had delivered in a Kigali football stadium in October 1993.[42]

The "guilty plea and confession" concept set out in the 1996 legislation soon proved that it could work effectively. Only 500 prisoners confessed in 1997, but by December 1998 the number had grown to 9,000. By the end of 1999 there were 15,000 confessions, and by early 2000 more than 20,000. According to the High Commissioner for Human Rights, over the first eight months of 1997, judgements were delivered with respect to 174 defendants.[43] In his report to the United Nations, prepared in early 2000, Special Representative Michel Moussalli said that some 2,406 persons had been tried by the special genocide courts, of whom 348 (14.4 per cent) were sentenced to death, 30.3 per cent to life imprisonment, 34 per cent to jail terms of between

---

42   The judgement in Karamira is reported: *Ministère Public* v. *Karamira*, 1 Receuil de jurisprudence contentieux du génocide et des massacres au Rwanda 75 (1ᵉ inst., Kigali, 14 February 1997).

43   "Report of the United Nations High Commissioner for Human Rights on the Human Rights Field Operation in Rwanda", UN Doc. A/52/486, annex, para. 63.

20 years and one year, and 19 per cent were acquitted.[44] He added, "There is much to applaud in this process."[45] Jacques Fierens has reported that 346 accused were tried in 1997, 928 in 1998, 1,318 in 1999, 2,458 in 2000, 1,416 in 2001 and 727 in 2002.[46] Assuming comparable numbers for 2003 and 2004, this gives a total of approximately 10,000 who have been tried for genocide-related offences in Rwanda.

In other words, the whole idea of the Organic Law's plea bargaining scheme was a good one, and the experience might well provide a useful model for other post-conflict societies where there are very large numbers of offenders. The Rwandan justice system had trouble exploiting the volume of confessions and was unable to process them promptly.[47] Had there been greater certainty that a guilty plea and confession would lead to prompt treatment of the case and eventually release, there might well have been many more confessions. Moreover, things were not helped by the inability of the Rwandan authorities to separate those who had confessed from those who had not. In order to encourage confession, it was surely necessary to separate those participating from the general prison population, so as to reassure them of safety and protection from reprisals. Once again, had this been better organised, the confession programme might have delivered more than it did.

Assessing the record is like determining whether the proverbial glass is half-empty or half-full. Considering the impoverishment of Rwanda's justice system prior to the genocide, and the resource-problems that continue to confront development in the country, 10,000 trials is an impressive figure by any standard.[48] It is better than the performance of many European countries following the Second World War. Arguably, Rwanda has done more in this respect, in the ten years following the end of the conflict, than did the national courts of Germany, Italy and Austria from 1945 to 1955. Rwanda's experience recalls Georges Clemenceau's comment at the Paris Peace Conference, when the crea-

---

44   "Report on the situation of human rights in Rwanda submitted by the Special Representative, Mr. Michel Moussalli, pursuant to Commission resolution 1999/20," UN Doc. E/CN.4/2000/41, para. 136.

45   Ibid., para. 137.

46   J. Fierens, "*Les juridictions gacaca entre rêve et réalité*", *Journal of International Criminal Justice*, 3 (2005), 896-919. According to Amnesty International, the decline in the number of trials in recent years is a consequence of reduced donor funding: Amnesty International "*Gacaca*, A question of justice", December 2004 (AI Index: AFR 47/007/2002), 16.

47   Ibid., (AI Index: AFR 47/007/2002), 18.

48   See, e.g., M. Morris, "The Trials of Concurrent Jurisdiction: The Case of Rwanda", *Duke Journal of Comparative and International Law*, 7 (1997), 349; C. Carroll, "An Assessment of the Role and Effectiveness of the International Criminal Tribunal for Rwanda and the Rwandan National Justice System in Dealing with the Mass Atrocities of 1994", *Boston University International Law Journal*, 18 (2000), 163.

tion of the first international criminal tribunal was being debated. Clemenceau said, "The first tribunal must have been summary and brutal; it was nevertheless the beginning of a great thing."[49]

Yet with approximately 60,000 accused still languishing in prisons by 2005, it could take another 80 years just to prosecute those who are detained. The message sent by the "international community" seems to have been directed at mildly discouraging Rwanda from its insistence on prosecuting all cases of genocide. In his 1999 report, Special Representative Moussalli "commend[ed] the Government of Rwanda for its creative efforts to hasten the reduction of the caseload" and he "encourage[d] the Government of Rwanda to persevere in these efforts and to ensure that all such measures are in conformity with established human rights standards."[50] The Special Representative proposed to the Rwandan authorities that "serious consideration should be given to releasing, on humanitarian grounds, the sick and the elderly, minors and children for whom alternatives to imprisonment can be found, and those identified as having case files belonging to the lower categories according to the Organic Law, where the length of their pre-trial detention exceeds that of the sentence they are likely to receive."[51] The General Assembly, in its 1998 resolution on Rwanda, similarly "[w]elcome[d] and encourage[d] the release of minors, elderly prisoners, prisoners suffering from terminal illnesses and suspects with incomplete files, who were detained for their alleged involvement in the genocide and other abuses of human rights...."[52]

The genocide trials held pursuant to the 1996 legislation have generated an impressive body of reported case law, published as an initiative of *Avocats sans Frontières*. Beginning in 2002, these have been published annually in volumes of several hundred pages. The judgements deal principally with the assessment of factual issues and are of undoubted interest in this respect as an insight into the dynamics of the genocide. They will be of great practical use to Rwandan judges and lawyers engaged in the ongoing prosecutions, and establish principles for interpretation of the national legislation dealing with genocide prosecutions. Moreover, they are surely of interest to historians of the genocide. Some of the more lengthy judgements present fascinating, detailed accounts of specific episodes during the months of April, May and June 1994.[53] Perhaps

---

49 A. Link (ed.), *The Papers of Woodrow Wilson*, 56 (Princeton, NJ: Princeton University Press, 1987), 534.

50 "Report on the situation of human rights in Rwanda submitted by the Special Representative, Mr. Michel Moussalli, pursuant to resolution 1998/69", UN Doc. E/CN.4/1999/33, para. 76.

51 Ibid., para. 77.

52 "Situation of Human Rights in Rwanda", U.N. Doc. A/RES/53/156, para. 14.

53 *Ministère Public* v. *Barayagwiza*, 3 *Receuil de jurisprudence contentieux du génocide et*

most importantly, the judgements provide a reassuring portrait of a judicial system hard at work, contending with the rights of the accused, conflicting evidence, legal questions and attempting to come to a fair result.

The judgements show that the "confession and guilty plea" scheme that underpinned the 1996 legislation works in practice. There are reported judgements in which an accused has confessed, pleaded guilty, apologised to the victims and denounced accomplices.[54] In some cases, the confession procedure was not invoked, or its strictures were not respected; nevertheless, the courts tended to view a confession, guilty plea and expression of remorse as mitigating circumstances with respect to sentencing.[55] Confessions were sometimes not accepted, because they were made too late, or because the courts judged them to be contradictory or insincere.[56] There are also examples of confessions being withdrawn at the hearing stage.[57] One court of first instance applied the confession procedure even though it had not been invoked, and for this reason the decision was overturned by the Court of Appeal.[58]

Several cases address the issue of *nexus*, that is, of a common crime determined to have no connection with the genocide, and therefore, one outside the jurisdiction of the special tribunals.[59] Several reported judgements conclude with acquittals, occasionally at the request of the prosecutor, a positive sign that some form of justice is being done.[60] Amnesty International has cited fig-

---

des massacres au Rwanda 309 (Conseil de Guerre, Kigali, 26 November 1998).

54   *Ministère Public v. Murindangwe*, 1 *Receuil de jurisprudence contentieux du génocide et des massacres au Rwanda* 63 (1st inst., Kibungo, 28 July 2000).

55   *Ministère Public v. Nzirasanaho & Munyakazi*, 1 *Receuil de jurisprudence contentieux du génocide et des massacres au Rwanda* 147 (1st inst., Nyamata, 9 September 1998); *Ministère Public v. Bizuru* et al., 3 *Receuil de jurisprudence contentieux du génocide et des massacres au Rwanda* 175 (1st inst., Kibungo, 22 September 2000; *Ministère Public v. Nsabimana*, 5 *Receuil de jurisprudence contentieux du génocide et des massacres au Rwanda* 139 (1st inst., Kibungo, 3 February 2000).

56   *Ministère Public v. Ndikubwimana*, 2 *Receuil de jurisprudence contentieux du génocide et des massacres au Rwanda* 9 (1st inst., Butare, 7 July 1997). Also: *Ministère Public v. Ndererehe & Rwakibibi*, 2 *Receuil de jurisprudence contentieux du génocide et des massacres au Rwanda* 181 (1st inst., Nyamata, 21 October 1999).

57   *Ministère Public v. Namahirwe*, 2 *Receuil de jurisprudence contentieux du génocide et des massacres au Rwanda* 23 (1st inst., Byumba, 19 November 1997); *Ministère Public v. Nduwumwami*, 2 *Receuil de jurisprudence contentieux du génocide et des massacres au Rwanda* 35 (1st inst., Cyangugu, 6 October 1997); *Ministère Public v. Munyawera* et al., 2 *Receuil de jurisprudence contentieux du génocide et des massacres au Rwanda* 45 (1st inst., Gikongoro, 28 March 1997).

58   *Ntimugura* et al. v. *Ministère Public*, 5 *Receuil de jurisprudence contentieux du génocide et des massacres au Rwanda* 261 (C.A., Cyangugu, 24 July 2002).

59   *Ministère Public v. Sebishyimbo* et al., 2 *Receuil de jurisprudence contentieux du génocide et des massacres au Rwanda* 263 (C.A. Ruhengeri, 30 December 1998).

60   *Ministère Public v. Mukansangwa*, 3 *Receuil de jurisprudence contentieux du génocide*

ures indicating that approximately 20 per cent of the more than 7,000 persons tried between 1996 and 2002 were acquitted.[61] In one case, a Court of Appeal reversed a conviction by a trial court, finding that it had refused to hear the evidence of relevant witnesses "*par crainte de la manifestation de la vérité*".[62]

The case law reports consist of decisions of the special chambers of the courts of first instance throughout the country, of the regional Courts of Appeal, and of the War Council (*Conseil de Guerre*). The first ones are from early in 1997, and the latest reported decisions are from 2003. Several decisions include participation by the *partie civile*, and result in awards of damages as well as convictions. In some cases, the Rwandan state is also condemned as being jointly and severally liable, because it was incapable of preventing the massacres.[63]

The gacaca system

In February 1997, Paul Kagame, then Vice-President, declared that alternative methods of transitional justice ought to be considered in Rwanda, giving as an example some form of community service. The following year, President Pasteur Bizimungu established a commission to examine possible mechanisms for increasing public participation in judicial proceedings. The 15-member commission was chaired by the Minister of Justice, and its conclusions, published on 8 June 1999, were to establish "*gacaca*" courts,[64] an idea that had been mooted as early as the 1995 conference in Kigali. *gacaca* is a word in Kinyarwanda, the national language of Rwanda, that literally means "grass" or "lawn". Jeremy Sarkin has explained that "[t]he name [*gacaca*] is derived from the word for 'lawn,' referring to the fact that members of the *gacaca* sit on the grass when listening to and considering matters before them."[65] It was an ancient

---

et des massacres au Rwanda 221 (1st inst., Nyamata, 31 July 2000); *Ministère Public v. Munyaneza*, 5 *Receuil de jurisprudence contentieux du génocide et des massacres au Rwanda* 117 (1st inst., Gitarama, 17 August 1998).

61 *Amnesty International*, "*Gacaca*, A Question of Justice", December 2004 (AI Index: AFR 47/007/2002), 17.

62 *Munyangabe v. Ministère Public*, 3 *Receuil de jurisprudence contentieux du génocide et des massacres au Rwanda* 255, at p. 261 (C.A. Cyangugu, 6 July 1999).

63 *Ministère Public v. Munyangabo et al.*, 4 *Receuil de jurisprudence contentieux du génocide et des massacres au Rwanda* 89 (1st inst., Gikongoro, 10 June 1998).

64 L. D. Tully, "Human Rights Compliance and the *gacaca* Jurisdictions in Rwanda", *Boston College International and Comparative Law Review*, 26 (2003), 385, citing an unpublished paper by Stef Vandeginste.

65 J. Sarkin, "The Tension Between Justice and Reconciliation in Rwanda: Politics, Human Rights, Due Process and the Role of the *Gacaca* Courts in Dealing with the Genocide", *Journal of African Law*, 45 (2001) 159. See also, Jeremy Sarkin, "Promoting Justice, Truth and Reconciliation in Transitional Societies: Evaluating Rwanda's Approach in the New Millennium of Using Community Based *Gacaca* Tribunals to Deal with the Past", *International Law Forum*, 2 (2000), 118; Idi T. Gaparayi, "Justice and Social Reconstruc-

dispute resolution method used at the local level, administered by respected local leaders or elders.[66] Historically, it dealt mainly with disputes concerning property matters, such as inheritance, and family law issues, although there is apparently some evidence of the system being used in a criminal law context as well. The system fell into some obscurity when European justice models were imported, following colonisation by the Germans in the 1890s and their subsequent replacement by the Belgians under a League of Nations mandate. *gacaca* had some resurgence following independence and continued to function as a mechanism to resolve disputes at the local level, subject to review by the formal courts. Following the genocide, in 1994, the Minister of Justice proposed that *gacaca* be revived in order to relieve the struggling judicial system of the burden of minor cases.[67]

The development of *gacaca* tribunals was greeted by many observers as a move away from the retributive justice approach trumpeted by the Rwandan authorities since 1994. In this logic, Rwanda seemed to be increasingly influenced by examples like that of the South African Truth and Reconciliation Commission.[68] Others viewed it as drawing inspiration from "alternative dispute resolution" mechanisms that had been fashionable among law reformers for many years.[69] Many warned that informal, indigenous tribunals might not fully respect international due process standards.[70] According to Carsten Stahn, "[s]uch a far-reaching transformation of a country's legal system, allowing legally untrained members of a local community to impose formal criminal sanctions on persons suspected of having committed medium-level or even severe crimes, raises serious concerns relating to the right to be tried

---

tion in the Aftermath of Genocide in Rwanda: An Evaluation of the Possible Role of the *gacaca* Tribunals", *African Human Rights Law Journal*, 1 (2001), 83.

66   The phenomenon has been studied by F.-X. Nzanzuwera, who was formerly a prosecutor in Kigali and is now a Belgium-based academic. See F.-X. Nzanzuwera, *Les juridictions 'gacaca', une réponse au génocide rwandais ou le difficile équilibre entre châtiment et pardon*, *La répression internationale du génocide rwandais* (Brussels: Bruylant, 2003).

67   L. Danielle Tully, "Human Rights Compliance and the *Gacaca* Jurisdictions in Rwanda", 396-7.

68   E. Daly, "Transformative Justice: Charting a Path to Reconciliation", *International Legal Perspectives*, 12 (2001-2002), 73; E. Daly, "Between Punitive and Reconstructive Justice: The *Gacaca* Courts in Rwanda", *New York University Journal of International Law & Policy*, 34 (2002), 355. Others remain doubtful about how much legal approaches can contribute to reconciliation: Mark A. Drumbl, "Punishment, Postgenocide: From Guilt to Shame to Civis in Rwanda", *New York University Law Review*, 75 (2000), 1121.

69   M. Day, "Alternative Dispute Resolution and Customary Law: Resolving Property Disputes in Post-Conflict Nations, a Case Study of Rwanda", *Georgetown Immigration Law Journal*, 16 (2001), 235.

70   For example, P. Wald, "The Omarska Trial - A War Crimes Tribunal Close-Up", *Southern Methodist University Law Review*, 57 (2004), 271.

by a competent, independent, and impartial tribunal by means of procedures established by law."[71]

The Transitional National Assembly of Rwanda adopted Organic Law No. 40/2000 of 16 January 2001, "on the Establishment of *'gacaca* Jurisdictions' and the Organisation of Prosecutions for Offences Constituting the Crime of Genocide or Crimes Against Humanity Committed between 1 October 1990 and 31 December 1994." The 2001 Organic Law began with a lengthy preamble that read, in part:

> The establishment of such a legal system is justified by the fact that offences that constitute the crime of genocide or crimes against humanity were committed publicly in full view of the population. This non-dissimulation resulted from the fact that the public authorities, whose role is to plot the course for the population to follow, themselves incited the population to commit crimes in order to generalize participation in them and thus be able to leave no survivors. This inspired the population, manipulated by the politicians, not even to attempt to conceal its criminal actions, since it was confident it was following the path indicated by the very persons who should have apprehended the population. For that reason it is essential that all Rwandans participate on the ground level in producing evidence, categorizing the perpetrators of the offences by taking into consideration the role they played, and establishing their punishments without applying the classic system of repression of offences, but instead, re-establishing peace and the return of citizens who were manipulated to commit crimes to the right path. As a result, the population who witnessed the atrocities committed shall achieve justice both for the victims and the persons suspected of being perpetrators of the offences, a justice based on evidence and not on passion. This justice shall be implemented within the framework of the *'gacaca* jurisdictions', meeting at the cell, sector, commune, and prefecture level and composed of honourable persons appointed by their neighbours.

The preamble continued with a list of objectives of the *gacaca* courts:

1. Find out the truth about what happened since residents shall be called upon as eyewitnesses to the acts committed in their cells, and they shall compile a list of victims and perpetrators;

2. Accelerate the prosecution of genocide since those who know what happened shall testify in the presence of their neighbours on their hills. In addition, the trials shall be resolved by almost 11,000 *'gacaca* jurisdictions', while 12 specialized chambers used to take on this task. Finally, it should be hoped that the defendants can no longer seek to deny the evidence as a delaying tactic since they will be in front of eyewitnesses to their actions;

3. Continue the eradication of the culture of impunity by using any method that makes it possible to identify a person who took part in the tragedy, since once the truth is known, none of those who were complicit shall escape punishment, and

---

71   C. Stahn, "Accommodating Individual Criminal Responsibility and National Reconciliation: The UN Truth Commission for East Timor", *American Journal of International Law*, 95 (2001), 964.

the people will understand that an offence results in the conviction of the criminal without any exception whatsoever;

4. Punish those who played a part in the tragedy, reconcile the Rwandans, and strengthen their unity since the '*gacaca* jurisdictions' system shall induce the residents of the same cell, sector, commune, and prefecture to collaborate in judging those who participated in the genocide, to discover the victims, and restore their rights to innocent people. The '*gacaca* jurisdictions' system shall thus be the basis for collaboration and unity, especially since, once the truth is known, there shall no longer be any suspicions of guilt. The perpetrator shall be punished, and justice shall be rendered both to the victim and to any innocent imprisoned person who will be reintegrated into Rwandan society;

5. Prove the capacity of the Rwandan society to settle its own problems through a legal system based on Rwandan custom, since, although the cases that the '*gacaca* jurisdictions' will have to hear, are different from these that are normally resolved within the *gacaca* framework, these jurisdictions fit well into the custom of settling differences by arbitration, even amicable arbitration.

In many respects, the legislation was built upon the 1996 Organic Law, which continued in force, as amended by the *gacaca* Law. Like the 1996 legislation, the 2001 statute was predicated upon encouraging perpetrators to admit guilt and express remorse. To this extent, it also resembled alternative approaches to accountability, like truth and reconciliation commissions. In addition to the temporal jurisdiction (which, incidentally, corresponds to Rwanda's unsuccessful proposal regarding the ICTR), the *gacaca* courts were also similar to the Specialised Chambers in that they applied the four-tier categorisation of crimes. Category 1 consisted of planners, organisers, and framers of genocide or crimes against humanity and was broadly similar to Category 1 in the 1996 legislation, where this designation had the consequence of exposing the offender to capital punishment. The 2001 law added the crime of rape to Category 1. As the most serious crimes, Category 1 offences were excluded from the jurisdiction of the *gacaca* courts and were to be judged by the ordinary courts, according to the system set out in the 1996 law. Category 2 consisted of homicide or attempted homicide, and Category 3 of "serious attacks without the intent to cause the death of the victims". Category 4 comprised crimes against property.

The Belgian colonisers had left behind a highly organised and centralised system of local government that has persisted to the present day. The lowest level is the cell or *cellule*, of which there are more than 9,000 in Rwanda. A *cellule* may consist of less than 100 people and averages perhaps 500. *Cellules* are grouped within the country's 1,500 sectors, and these are then organised into districts. The *gacaca* system is based upon this structure of local government, with a separate court or tribunal established for each *cellule* and each *secteur*. Each *gacaca* court consists of a General Assembly, a Bench, and a Coordinating

Committee. The General Assembly at the *cellule* level is made up of all inhabitants aged 18 years or older. The General Assembly of each *cellule* elects 24 people over the age of 21 of "high integrity", known as *inyangamugayo*. Five members of the elected group are to serve as delegates to the General Assembly at the *secteur* level, with the remaining 19 serving on the Bench at the *cellule* level. Five members of the Bench comprise the coordinating committee. On the basis of the 2001 legislation, approximately 250,000 elected officials are required for the system.

Elections for judges were held in October 2001, and hearings began in mid-2002. Some preliminary experiments, known as "pre-*gacaca*," presented encouraging results and appear to have convinced many sceptics to give the scheme a chance.[72] Special Representative Mousalli described the pre-*gacaca* proceedings:

The first stage of this process involved the identification, review, completion and establishment of files for the 3,434 prisoners from Kibuye. The 544 files which contained no or very little evidence of participation in the genocide, (17 per cent) were kept for the second phase: presentation of the detainees to the population. These detainees were then presented to the public one by one, over a period of six weeks, and members of the population were invited to give testimony in favour or against the person in question. Of the 544 detainees, the population decided that 256 (47 per cent) should be released.[73]

From 2002 to 2004, Rwanda conducted a "pilot phase" of the *gacaca* programme. Initially, in June 2002, *gacaca* tribunals were organised for only 80 *cellules*, but this was enlarged to 750 in November 2003. By this time, there were functioning *gacaca* tribunals in at least one *secteur* of each district in the country. A third phase, involving the entire country, was originally scheduled to begin in March 2004, but it was postponed, initially because of the genocide commemoration activities of April 2004, and subsequently because of the adoption of new legislation. The enabling legislation for the *gacaca* tribunals was amended in 2004, by Organic Law No. 16/2004, of 19 June 2004. The structure of the tribunals was simplified somewhat, eliminating two levels of superior jurisdiction, and reducing the number of judges required to about 170,000. The categories of offenders were redefined yet again. Category 1, which is excluded from the *gacaca* jurisdiction, has been slightly expanded to include crimes of torture, indignity to a dead body, and a somewhat broader range of crimes of sexual violence. Categories 2 and 3 are merged.

---

72   "Observations and Recommendations concerning recent human rights developments in Rwanda of the Special Representative of the Commission on Human Rights, Michel Moussalli, following his visits to Rwanda in October 2000 and February/March 2001", UN Doc. E/CN.4/2001/45/Add.1 (2001), para. 29.

73   Ibid., para. 25.

Yet the terrible and completely unexpected result of the *gacaca* pilot process was not to provide the fabled "closure", but rather to reveal that the numbers of those responsible for genocide may have exceeded 100,000 by a factor of ten. Rather than resolve the outstanding cases and end the blight of mass detentions under appalling conditions, the initial *gacaca* hearings appear to have opened a Pandora's box. The numbers of suspects continue to grow because the *gacaca* scheme encourages perpetrators to confess and to name their accomplices. On 14 January 2005, Domitilla Mukantaganzwa, executive secretary of the National Service of *gacaca* Jurisdictions, announced that over one million Rwandans were to be tried under the revised *gacaca* system. "Drawing from the experience and figures accruing from the pilot trials, we estimate a figure slightly above one million people that are supposed to be tried under the *gacaca* courts," Mukantaganzwa told Reuters in Kigali.[74]

The estimates are derived by extrapolating from the list of suspects developed by the 750 *gacaca* tribunals in the pilot phase. But confirmation of the enormity of the suspect pool comes from the ICTR, whose investigators have prepared a database listing 550,000 suspects. It is based on 87,000 genocide files assembled by prosecutors over the last six to seven years, as part of a project carried out by the German technical assistance company GTZ. The genocide-related database is to be provided to the *gacaca* tribunals by the ICTR,[75] whose judgements have made a few perfunctory references to the *gacaca* proceedings.[76]

The number of suspects constitutes a staggering percentage of the current population of Rwanda, which totals about 7 million. But many of those 7 million were not living in Rwanda in 1994, and perhaps half of them were either not yet born, or too young to engage criminal responsibility, even if they did participate in atrocities. Charging one million Rwandans with genocide amounts to an indictment of perhaps one-third of the country's adult population.

In January 2005, Mukantaganzwa said that suspects who have pleaded guilty and asked for forgiveness would be judged by the *gacaca* tribunals beginning in February 2005. "We will start with trials of people who have confessed," Mukantaganzwa said. "We should have completed all phase one hearings before the genocide anniversary [of the 1994 genocide] which is commemorated on April

---

74   A. Meldrum, "1 million Rwandans to face killing charges in village courts", *The Guardian* (15 January 2005).

75   "UN tribunal's database of genocide suspects ready for use", *Xinhua News Agency* (20 December 2004).

76   *Prosecutor v. Kamuhanda* (Case No. ICTR-95-54A-T), Judgement (22 January 2004), para. 395; *Prosecutor v. Gacumbitsi* (Case No. ICTR-2001-64-T), Judgement, (17 June 2004), paras. 73, 77-78.

7 each year," she added. At the beginning of the judgement phase of *gacaca*, approximately 60,000 case files were ready and in a position to proceed.[77]

Conclusion

Rwanda continues to struggle to find the appropriate approach to accountability. The history of prosecutions since 1994 reveals a number of conflicting values (or "tensions", as discussed in the final chapter by Clark, Kaufman, and Nicolaïdis), and these have influenced the evolution of the various approaches. There are contending interests within Rwanda. Survivors, including Kayigamba writing in this volume, are by and large unwavering in their determination to prosecute or otherwise seek retributive or punitive treatment of perpetrators. On the other hand, the vast majority of the population appears to fall into the perpetrator camp, where there is less enthusiasm for uncompromising justice. To some extent, the current plan to prosecute more than one million seems almost implausible. Can the majority of Rwandans really have voted for a government that plans to prosecute a large proportion of the electorate for genocide? It has always been expected that as some form of democracy, or majority rule, took over in Rwanda, there would be no heart for further prosecutions. But this is not what seems to be happening.

At the same time, there are odd messages of reconciliation. One of them is Rwanda's abandonment of the death penalty. In April 1998, following the first trials under the 1996 legislation, some 22 accused were executed publicly in football stadiums; there had been a debate in the cabinet about the wisdom of capital punishment, but the hard-liners prevailed. Yet since then, there have been no executions, despite death sentences on many hundreds. In 2007, the Rwandan government abolished capital punishment. This provision fulfils the requirement established by the ICTR for the transfer of certain genocide cases from the ICTR to the Rwandan national courts. Thus, since 1998, Rwanda has forsaken capital punishment in terms of its actual practice. This can only reflect an understanding, if only an implicit one, that harsh, retributive punishment is probably not the best way forward.

---

77   "60,000 genocide cases ready for Rwandan courts", *Xinhua News Agency*, 8 January 2005.

12

THE UNITED STATES ROLE IN THE ESTABLISHMENT OF THE UNITED NATIONS INTERNATIONAL CRIMINAL TRIBUNAL FOR RWANDA

Zachary D. Kaufman[1]

Introduction

Following Schabas's introduction to the United Nations International Criminal Tribunal for Rwanda (ICTR), this chapter discusses the history of the establishment of that tribunal, setting the stage for Jallow's and Ngoga's evaluation of its performance in later chapters. This chapter is the first publication to report on detailed "elite interviewing," especially of current and former United States Government (USG) officials, and recently declassified documents on this topic. The origin of the ICTR is complicated and controversial because of the number, attractiveness and precedence of alternative transitional justice mechanisms, and the pitfalls of establishing such a tribunal for investigating, prosecuting and punishing the suspected perpetrators of the 1994 Rwandan genocide. This chapter focuses on the role of the USG in the establishment of the ICTR for two reasons. First, the USG was one of the primary—if not the most important—actors in the establishment of the ICTR. Second, for better or worse, the USG's reaction to international crises often significantly shapes the

---

1   The author wishes to thank the following individuals for their comments on an earlier draft of this chapter: Fahim Ahmed, Adrienne Bernhard, Phil Clark, Howard Kaufman, Sarah Martin, Vipin Narang, and Katherine Southwick. All statements and any errors are, of course, the responsibility of the author. This chapter draws upon the author's thesis for the MPhil (Master's) degree in International Relations at the University of Oxford. For the full thesis, see: Zachary D. Kaufman, "Explaining the U.S. Policy to Prosecute Rwandan *Génocidaires*", Unpublished Master's Degree Thesis, University of Oxford, 2004: on file at the University of Oxford and with the author. The author wishes to thank his thesis supervisor and general academic adviser, Dr Jennifer M. Welsh, for her critical guidance and invaluable mentorship.

global response, owing to the US's preponderance of resources in the post-Cold War era. Because of space constraints, this chapter will not analyse the rationale for the USG's support for the ICTR, concentrating instead on the mechanics of creating the institution.

Much of this chapter includes a detailed historical account of the USG's involvement in establishing the ICTR. This narrative is important because, as Schabas discusses, the ICTR is critical to transitional justice in post-genocide Rwanda specifically, and, as Jallow notes, to the development of both international criminal law and war crimes tribunals more generally. The reader will learn several key facts from this chapter. First, the USG exercised leadership, perhaps more so than any other state, in the development of the ICTR. Second, two other permanent members of the United Nations Security Council (UNSC), Russia and France, played leading roles, especially in opposing the USG on its optimal preference for a transitional justice institution for post-genocide Rwanda. Finally, two non-permanent members of the UNSC at that time, Spain and New Zealand, also played critical roles in the establishment of the ICTR.

Background

During the Rwandan genocide, besides the United Nations Assistance Mission for Rwanda (UNAMIR) and the controversial French-initiated *Opération Turquoise*, neither the UN nor the world's sole superpower, the United States, intervened, despite evidence of mass atrocities and the likelihood that even minimal efforts would have mitigated the scope of the genocide.[2] After the genocide, however, the UN, acting through the UNSC, where the USG took a proactive role, and on which the Government of Rwanda (GoR) coincidentally held a non-permanent seat during 1994, actively engaged in the post-conflict transitional justice process in Rwanda. Some USG officials involved in deliberations claim that the idea to establish the ICTR originated in late July 1994 within the USG[3] and that "the primary initiative for the action was that of the United States and we were the ones who moved it through the [UN Security] Council."[4] Indeed, among all states, the USG played the most significant role in all phases of the establishment of the ICTR—from being the first

---

2   Organization of African Unity (7 July 2000), Rwanda: The Preventable Genocide, http://www.visiontv.ca/RememberRwanda/Report.pdf.

3   See: Interview with Michael Matheson, former Deputy Legal Advisor to the US Department of State (11 Nov. 2005); Interview with David Scheffer, former US Ambassador for War Crimes Issues (18 Nov. 2005); Interview with John Shattuck, former US Assistant Secretary of State for Democracy, Human Rights, and Labor (9 Oct. 2003); Interview with Gregory Stanton, former Political Officer, Office for United Nations Political Affairs, US Department of State (26 June 2003).

4   Interview with Matheson (11 Nov. 2005).

state to publicly declare its support for the idea, to lobbying the international community for its acceptance, to lobbying the UN Independent Commission of Experts on Rwanda to issue an interim report including a recommendation to that effect, to playing a leading role in drafting the UNSC resolution that would create the ICTR, and, finally, to contributing the most financial support for its establishment.[5]

Several other states also played important roles in the establishment of the ICTR. First, the Spanish government proposed the establishment of the UN Independent Commission of Experts on Rwanda. Second, the French and Russian governments objected to the USG's initial proposal to expand the jurisdiction of the UN International Criminal Tribunal for the Former Yugoslavia (ICTY) to include the Rwandan genocide (what I call the "ICTY-Expanded" option), favouring instead the creation of a separate *ad hoc* UN international criminal tribunal (ICT) for Rwanda (what I call the "ICT-Separate" option). Finally, the New Zealand government proposed the compromise design of the creation of an *ad hoc* UN ICT for Rwanda (established by the UNSC's Chapter VII powers) that would share some bureaucracy, such as an appeals chamber and/or chief prosecutor, with the ICTY (what I call the "ICT-Tied" option), which is the option that would become the ICTR. These three ICT options—ICTY-Expanded, ICT-Separate and ICT-Tied—were the three main options discussed for the establishment of an ICT for Rwanda and are therefore critical to the following history of the etiology of this institution.

Sources

My research draws upon three sets of sources. First, I researched primary sources, including published and unpublished USG documents, UNSC resolutions and reports, statements by USG and other state and inter-governmental officials reported in the press, and documents from the GoR. Most importantly, through submitting Freedom of Information Act requests to the USG, I successfully obtained—and, here, am the first to publicly report on—relevant documents regarding the USG role in the establishment of the ICTR. In total, the USG declassified and released to me several hundred pages of documents comprising 125 cables in whole or in part.[6] This is a gold mine of specific information about the USG decision-making process on the establishment of the ICTR. Such primary sources provide vital and unfiltered insight into the evolution of

---

5   The USG has also claimed to be the largest single government contributor of humanitarian assistance to the Rwanda crisis. See United States Department of State (3 August 1994), Cable Number 207687, "Press Guidance – August 3, 1994."

6   Where cables are cited in this chapter, they should be assumed to be declassified to and on file with the author.

the USG decision-making process, including the perspectives of key individuals. That said, one problem with such a declassification process is that, because the USG withholds some documents in whole or in part, it presents a self-selective portrait of USG internal discussions and decision-making.

Second, I conducted personal interviews with current and former USG officials involved in, or familiar with, US foreign policy regarding suspected *génocidaires*. I also interviewed other individuals who are knowledgeable about USG policy-making, including those from NGOs (human rights organisations, think tanks, etc.), academia, other state governments and the ICTR itself. Such elite interviewing provides additional information not available through existing primary or secondary sources, especially the views of those involved in making these decisions. However, like declassification, elite interviewing is not without its potential problems. For example, information derived from interviews may be biased because of accessibility only to certain individuals. Furthermore, intentionally or not, a decade or more after certain events, USG officials might not tell the whole truth or be completely thorough: first, being involved in a decision may inherently prevent impartiality; second, there may be incentives to exaggerate or lie, such as the desire to self-aggrandise, to make oneself appear more of a visionary, or to avoid criticism; third, these individuals may not remember or know (or both) why they supported a particular decision.[7] I obtained primary sources and conducted interviews in Oxford, Washington DC, New York City, The Hague, Arusha and Kigali. Furthermore, I attempted to correct potential problems with these sources by using, where possible, triangulation to corroborate events or explanations with more than one source, whether through interviews or by surveying the declassified documents or secondary literature on this topic. Finally, I consulted secondary sources to review the existing literature on the USG role in the establishment of the ICTR and other transitional justice institutions. Such documents provide crucial information on the background on and theoretical framework through which USG policy on transitional justice can be analysed.

Establishment and design of the ICTR

On 8 November 1994, acting under Chapter VII of the UN Charter, the UNSC adopted Resolution 955 to establish the ICTR.[8] The statute constituting the ICTR is annexed in this UNSC resolution. The *ratione materiae* (subject-matter jurisdiction) of the ICTR is limited to genocide, crimes against humanity and violations of Article 3 common to the Geneva Conventions of 12 August

---

7   For a discussion of elite interviewing, including its potential pitfalls, and further information on the author's research methodology on this topic, see Kaufman (2004), 8-14.

8   UNSC Res 955 (1994).

1949 for the Protection of War Victims and of the Additional Protocol II thereto of 8 June 1977. The *ratione tempore* (temporal jurisdiction) is limited to crimes committed between 1 January and 31 December 1994. The *ratione personae et ratione loci* (personal and territorial jurisdiction) are limited to crimes committed by Rwandans in the territory of Rwanda or of neighbouring states, as well as by non-Rwandan citizens for crimes committed in Rwanda. UNSC Resolution 977, adopted on 22 February 1995, located the seat of the ICTR at Arusha.[9]

When established, the ICTR shared an appeals chamber and chief prosecutor with the ICTY and was endowed with UNSC Chapter VII powers to compel state compliance with, *inter alia*, the arrest and extradition of suspected *génocidaires*. The ICTR marks a watershed in the development of international law and justice because, in contrast to the ICTY, which treated the Balkans crisis as an ongoing international armed conflict, it is "the first international court having competence to prosecute and punish individuals for egregious crimes committed during an *internal* conflict."[10]

In the case of Rwanda, the USG therefore chose to support a judicial process that would deal with only a few dozen *génocidaires*, be relatively expensive compared to other transitional justice options, be located outside the victimised country, create the precedent of establishing an ICT for a purely civil conflict, share some resources and bureaucracy with an existing transitional justice institution (the ICTY) and affirm the precedent (established by the ICTY) of the UNSC's use of its Chapter VII powers to investigate selectively and to prosecute alleged atrocity perpetrators.

The history of USG support for the establishment of the ICTR

The following narrative describes the development of USG support for the creation of the ICTR, from the date on which the Rwandan genocide began, 6 April 1994, to the date on which the UNSC voted to establish the ICTR, 8 November 1994.

During the genocide: April – July 1994. USG support for the creation of the ICTR began both publicly and privately before the genocide had even concluded. Publicly, immediately after the killing started on 6 April 1994, the USG began issuing general statements denouncing the atrocities and declaring a need for accountability for the genocide.[11] Indeed, the day after the genocide began, President Clinton declared that he was "shocked and deeply saddened...

---

9   UNSC Res 977 (1995).

10   R. S. Lee, "The Rwanda Tribunal", *Leiden Journal of International Law,* 9 (1996), 37-61, at 37 (italics added).

11   Interview with Scheffer (24 June 2003).

233

horrified that elements of the Rwandan security forces have sought out and murdered Rwandan officials... condemn[ed] these actions and... call[ed] on all parties to cease any such actions immediately...."[12] That same day, the UNSC president for April 1994, Colin Keating, New Zealand's permanent representative to the UN, issued a statement supported by the USG (as UNSC presidential statements are unanimous), condemning "these horrific attacks and their perpetrators, who must be held responsible."[13] A week and a half later, the US National Security Adviser Anthony Lake called on "the leadership of the Rwandan armed forces, including Army Commander-in-Chief Col. Augustin Bizimungu, Col. [Léonard] Nkundiye, Capt. Pascal Simbikangwa and Col. [Théoneste] Bagosora, to do everything in their power to end the violence immediately."[14] According to the historian and Human Rights Watch senior adviser Alison Des Forges, that statement "was the first by a major international actor to publicly assign responsibility for the ongoing killing to specific individuals, but it stopped short of calling the slaughter genocide."[15] Perhaps the most forceful early public statement by the USG concerning accountability for the Rwandan genocide came on 28 April. That day, the US Department of State spokesperson Christine Shelly read a prepared statement that the USG "strongly condemns the massacres" and said that the USG was in touch with all parties to the conflict and would be "working very strongly through the United Nations". During that press briefing, Shelly also indicated that there were four general transitional justice options for promoting justice and accountability: domestic prosecutions within Rwanda, the use of an ICT, referral to the UN, and the use of the International Court of Justice (ICJ).[16]

Private USG efforts to condemn and seek accountability for the genocide started at approximately the same time. On 26 April, the US Department of State decided that Prudence Bushnell, Principal Deputy Assistant Secretary of State for African Affairs, would make telephone calls to GoR officials leading the genocide and to rebel leaders. Bushnell spoke to Bagosora on 28 April, Bizimungu and Rwandan Patriotic Front (RPF) Major General Paul Kagame on 30 April, and Kagame again on 1 May. She tried unsuccessfully to call Bagosora again that week, but spoke to Bizimungu several more times in early

12 "100 Days of Slaughter: A Chronology of U.S./U.N. Actions." (1999). Frontline, http://www.pbs.org/wgbh/pages/frontline/shows/evil/etc/slaughter.html.

13 UN Doc. S/PRST/1994/16 (7 April 1994).

14 Press Release, Office of the Press Secretary, The White House, "Statement by the Press Secretary", 22 April 1994. Non-classified. Online. United States National Security Archive. Internet. Available: http://www.gwu.edu/~nsarchiv/NSAEBB/NSAEBB53/rw042294.pdf.

15 Des Forges (1999), 284.

16 United States Department of State (29 April 1994). Cable Number 112290. "Daily Press Briefing of Thursday, April 28, 1994."

May.[17] Bushnell told Bizimungu, "I am calling to tell you President Clinton is going to hold you accountable for the killings."[18] In her conversation with Bagosora on 28 April, Bushnell urged him to "end the killings," emphasising that "in the eyes of the world, the Rwanda military engaged in criminal acts" and stressing that "it would behoove [sic] the GoR military to show some responsible leadership and a willingness to compromise... we were looking to him personally to do the right thing."[19] The US Assistant Secretary of State for African Affairs, George Moose, also repeatedly spoke by telephone to representatives of various sides of the conflict.[20] The implication of these discussions was that the USG was watching the genocide and taking note of its perpetrators, with the intention of eventually holding them individually accountable for their crimes.

The USG was not alone in calling for perpetrators to be brought to justice. Some Rwandans also did so, though they were much more specific (and, as it would turn out, accurate) about the precise form the accountability mechanism should take. Rwandans opposed to the genocidal Hutu regime, though not in power, almost immediately began demanding that the UN apprehend and try *génocidaires*. One week after the genocide began, Claude Dusaidi, the RPF representative to the UN, wrote to the UNSC president that a "crime of genocide" had been committed in Rwanda and requested that the UNSC immediately establish a UN ICT and apprehend those responsible for the killings.[21] After the genocide, the five reasons cited by the RPF-led GoR for its request for an ICT were: "to involve the international community, which was also harmed by the genocide and by the grave and massive violations of international humanitarian law" and "to enhance the exemplary nature of a justice that would be seen to be completely neutral and fair"; "to avoid any suspicion of its [the GoR's] wanting to organize speedy, vengeful justice"; "to make it easier to get at those criminals who have found refuge in foreign countries"; to

---

17   Interview with Prudence Bushnell, former Principal US Deputy Assistant Secretary of State for African Affairs (2 January 2004).

18   S. Power, *"A Problem from Hell": America and the Age of Genocide* (New York: Basic Books, 2002), 370.

19   United States Department of State (29 April 1994), Cable Number 113672.

20   United States Department of State (20 July 1994), Cable Number 194391, "Press Guidance – Wednesday, July 20, 1994."

21   Independent Inquiry into the Actions of the United Nations during the 1994 Genocide in Rwanda. S/1999/1257, "Annex: Letter Dated 15 December 1999 from the Members of the Independent Inquiry into the Actions of the United Nations during the 1994 Genocide in Rwanda addressed to the Secretary-General." 16 December 1999; Independent Inquiry into the Actions of the United Nations during the 1994 Genocide in Rwanda. S/1999/1257. "Enclosure: Report of the Independent Inquiry into the Actions of the United Nations during the 1994 Genocide in Rwanda." 16 December 1999.

emphasise that "the genocide committed in Rwanda is a crime against human-kind and should be suppressed by the international community as a whole"; and "above all... to teach the Rwandese people a lesson, to fight against the impunity to which it had become accustomed since 1959 and to promote national reconciliation."[22]

Two weeks later, on 30 April, the UNSC suggested that responsibility for atrocities in Rwanda should take the form of prosecution, but did not endorse a specific forum. The UNSC president's statement called "on the leadership of both parties... to commit themselves to ensuring that persons who instigate or participate in such attacks are prosecuted and punished" and recalled that "persons who instigate or participate in such acts are individually responsible. In this context, the Security Council recalls that the killing of members of an ethnic group with the intention of destroying such a group in whole or in part constitutes a crime punishable under international law"; the Council president requested the UN Secretary-General "to make proposals for investigation of the reports of serious violations of international humanitarian law during the conflict."[23] Without employing the word "genocide," this statement alluded to its definition under international law.

RPF officials were not satisfied, however, with the progress being made in the UN and therefore lobbied publicly for an ICT using the tactic of alleged racism and regionalism. In May, the RPF prime minister designate Faustin Twagiramungu posed a rhetorical question at a press conference: "[i]s what is happening different from what happened in Nazi Germany? Was a war crimes court not set up in Germany? Is it because we're Africans that a court has not been set up?"[24]

The same month, the USG began daily inter-governmental agency briefings on Rwanda.[25] Many of these discussions occurred in the US Interagency War Crimes Working Group, which had been founded in response to the Balkans crisis. The US Department of State led this interagency working group, which included representatives from the US National Security Council and the US Departments of Justice and Defense. From the US Department of State, represented were the Bureau of Democracy, Human Rights and Labor; the Bureau of International Organization Affairs; the Office of the Legal Adviser; and the US Mission to the UN. The US Interagency War Crimes Working Group was chaired or co-chaired during the genocide and immediately afterwards

---

22   UN Doc. S/PV.3453 (1994), 14, 16.

23   UN Doc. S/PRST/1994/21 (30 April 1994).

24   E. Neuffer, *The Key to My Neighbor's House: Seeking Justice in Bosnia and Rwanda* (New York: Picador, 2001), 129.

25   "100 Days of Slaughter: A Chronology of U.S./U.N. Actions." (1999).

(leading up to the 8 November UNSC resolution 955) by John Shattuck,[26] David Scheffer,[27] and/or Michael Matheson.[28] Other members of this interagency working group included Conrad Harper,[29] Crystal Nix,[30] and Gregory Stanton.[31/32] The product of one meeting was a classified internal discussion paper, outlining goals, tactics and options for the daily USG taskforce on Rwanda. On the topic of "Genocide Investigation: Language that calls for an international investigation of human rights abuses and possible violations of the genocide convention," the paper cautions, "Be careful. Legal at State was worried about this yesterday – Genocide finding could commit USG to actually 'do something.'" On the topic of "Pressure to Punish Organizers of Killings," the paper also cautions, "NO. Hold till Ceasefire has been established—don't want to scare off the participants."[33] Political considerations about automatic USG involvement and the disruption of the potential ceasefire agreement prevented the USG at this point from calling for the investigation of, and punishment for, the massacres.

Two weeks later, on 16 May, Joan Donoghue, US Department of State Assistant Legal Adviser for African Affairs, prepared a legal analysis for Christopher finding that "[t]here can be little question that the specific listed acts [of genocide] have taken place in Rwanda."[34] Shortly thereafter, Toby Gati, Assistant Secretary of State for Intelligence and Research, sent a memorandum to Moose and Harper, concluding that "[t]here is substantial circumstantial evidence implicating senior Rwandan government and military officials in the widespread, systematic killing of ethnic Tutsis, and to a lesser extent, ethnic

---

26   Assistant Secretary of State, Bureau of Democracy, Human Rights, and Labor, US Department of State.

27   Senior Adviser and Counsel to Ambassador Albright, US Mission to the United Nations, US Department of State.

28   Deputy Legal Adviser, Office of the Legal Adviser, US Department of State.

29   Legal Adviser, US Department of State.

30   Counsellor, Bureau of Democracy, Human Rights, and Labor, US Department of State.

31   Political Officer, Office for UN Political Affairs, Bureau of International Organization Affairs, US Department of State.

32   Interview with Matheson (26 Aug. 2003). See also: Interview with Stanton (26 June 2003); Interview with Scheffer (24 June 2003).

33   Discussion Paper, Office of the Deputy Assistant Secretary of Defense for Middle East/Africa Region, Department of Defense, 1 May 1994, Secret, United States National Security Archive, http://www.gwu.edu/~nsarchiv/NSAEBB/NSAEBB53/rw050194.pdf.

34   Draft Legal Analysis, Office of the Legal Adviser, Department of State, drafted by Assistant Legal Adviser for African Affairs Joan Donoghue, 16 May 1994, Secret, United States National Security Archive, http://www.gwu.edu/~nsarchiv/NSAEBB/NSAEBB53/rw051694.pdf.

Hutus who supported power-sharing between the two groups."[35] On 21 May, several US Department of State officials, including Moose, Shattuck, Douglas Bennett[36] and Harper, sent a memorandum, "Has Genocide Occurred in Rwanda?" to Christopher, recommending that he authorise US Department of State officials to use the formulation "acts of genocide have occurred," noting that "[t]his is the same formulation that we use with respect to Bosnia." The memorandum, which had the file name of "nonamerwandakilllgs,"[37] also notes that such a statement

would not have any particular legal consequences. Under the [Genocide] Convention, the prosecution of persons charged with genocide is the responsibility of the competent courts in the state where the acts took place or an international penal tribunal (none has yet been established); the US has no criminal jurisdiction over acts of genocide occurring within Rwanda unless they are committed by US citizens or they fall under another criminal provision of US law (such as those relating to acts of terrorism for which there is a basis for US jurisdiction).[38]

Publicly and internally, the USG was careful not to describe the conflict as "genocide", in part for fear of what using that term might legally oblige the USG to do, such as apprehending and prosecuting the perpetrators.[39] While Rwandan men, women and children were being slaughtered by the hundreds of thousands, the US Department of State, which literally placed them in a category apart from American casualties, continued wrestling with what precisely to call the killings.[40]

During this same month (May), the USG began to urge the UN to take a more proactive role in responding to the genocide.[41] Human rights advocate Holly Burkhalter implies that Shattuck's pressure on UN officials resulted in

---

35   Memorandum from Assistant Secretary for Intelligence and Research Toby T. Gati to Assistant Secretary of State for African Affairs George Moose and Department of State Legal Adviser Conrad Harper, "Rwanda – Geneva Convention Violations", circa 18 May 1994. Secret/ORCON (originator controlled), United States National Security Archive, http://www.gwu.edu/~nsarchiv/NSAEBB/NSAEBB53/rw051894.pdf.

36   US Assistant Secretary of State, Bureau of International Organization Affairs.

37   See also: Power (2002), 362.

38   United States Department of State (21 May 1994). See also US DoS (20 and 21 May 1994). "Has Genocide Occurred in Rwanda?" Action Memorandum to the Secretary of State, through P – Mr. Tarnoff and G – Mr. Wirth, from AF – George E. Moose, DRL – John Shattuck, IO – Douglas J. Bennett, and L – Conrad K. Harper.

39   See e.g.: Jared A. Cohen and Zachary D. Kaufman (15 July 2005), "A Genocide by Any Other Name: Debating Genocide in Rwanda and Sudan," Opinion Editorial, Broward Times (South Florida newspaper), 6; "100 Days of Slaughter: A Chronology of U.S./U.N. Actions." (1999)

40   See e.g., US DoS (13 May 1994): "White House Press Guidance", US DoS (26 May 1994), Office of the Spokesman, "Taken Question."

41   Ibid.

the appointment of a special rapporteur on Rwanda.[42] The UN also responded to such pressure in other ways, such as by sending the UN High Commissioner for Human Rights, José Ayala Lasso, to Rwanda to investigate allegations of serious violations of international humanitarian law and to publish a report on his 11-12 May trip. Thus, even before the Rwandan genocide had ended, various agencies of the UN, such as the UN Office of the High Commissioner for Human Rights, the UN Commission on Human Rights, and the UNSC (including the USG), with the imprimatur of the RPF, had the launched investigation of crimes and made known that their perpetrators would be held individually responsible. [43]

Also in May, the USG held bilateral meetings with relevant non-state actors to explore issues concerning pursuing transitional justice for Rwanda. Among other efforts, the US Ambassador to Belgium, Alan Blinken, met the ICJ Judge, Raymond Ranjeva, to explore "the notion of an international inquiry into gross violations of human rights in Rwanda."[44] USG officials consulted NGOs, such as the International Committee of the Red Cross, on the possibility of creating an ICT for Rwanda and recruiting witnesses to testify.[45] The USG would later consult and lobby UN officials, including Lasso, on creating an ICT for Rwanda, specifically through the ICTY-Expanded structure.[46]

The following month, in June, momentum developed within the UN to establish a "commission of experts to gather evidence related to breaches of the genocide convention and other violations of international humanitarian law in Rwanda." This commission would eventually become the UN Independent Commission of Experts on Rwanda. On 10 June, Spain circulated a draft resolution calling for the establishment of such a commission.[47] Spain's initiative

---

42   H. J. Burkhalter, "The Question of Genocide: The Clinton Administration and Rwanda," *World Policy Journal,* Volume 11, Issue 4, (Winter 1994/95), 44-54, at 52.

43   UN/HCHR. E/CN.4/S-3/3. (19 May 1994). Annex; UNSC Res 918 (1994); UN/HCHR. E/CN.4/S-3/3. (19 May 1994). Paragraphs 10, 20, and 32.

44   United States Department of State (16 May 1994). Cable Number 05416. "International Jurist Comments on Human Rights Inquiry in Rwanda."

45   United States Department of State (24 May 1994). Cable Number 137577. "Under Secretary for Global Affairs Wirth's Meeting with Director of Operations for ICRC, Jean de Courten, May 17, 1994."

46   United States Department of State (5 August 1994). Cable Number 06844. "Meeting with High Commissioner for Human Rights: Rwanda, Cuba, China, and Other Issues."; United States Department of State (27 September 1994). Cable Number 08272. "Meeting with High Commissioner for Human Rights: Burma, Rwanda, Cuba."; United States Department of State (27 September 1994). Cable Number 08273. "Meeting with High Commissioner for Human Rights: Burma, Rwanda, Cuba."

47   United States Department of State (15 June 1994). Cable Number 02491. "Rwanda: Bringing the Guilty to Justice." See also: United States Department of State (9 July 1994). Cable Number 182529. "Africa Bureau Friday Report, 07/8/94."

prompted further internal USG discussion about whether and how to support the commission and whether to propose or at least support a transitional justice option. Specifically, at this time, the USG was considering at least three options: ICT-Separate, ICTY-Expanded, and the establishment of a permanent international criminal court.[48] Later that month, the USG decided to co-sponsor a UNSC resolution establishing a commission of experts for Rwanda.[49]

At approximately the same time, from 9 to 20 June, the UN conducted another investigation in Rwanda. René Degni-Ségui, who had been appointed the UN Commission on Human Rights Special Rapporteur on the human rights situation in Rwanda on 25 May, visited Rwanda and its neighbouring countries, Burundi, Zaire (now the Democratic Republic of Congo) and Kenya. He was accompanied by Bacre Waly Ndiaye, the UN Commission on Human Rights Special Rapporteur on extrajudicial, summary or arbitrary executions, and Nigel Rodley, the UN Commission on Human Rights Special Rapporteur on the question of torture. Their mission was to investigate allegations of violations of human rights, particularly crimes against humanity and genocide.[50] After their return, on 28 June, Degni-Ségui issued a report that "recommends, *inter alia*, the establishment of an ad hoc international criminal tribunal or, alternatively, the extension of the jurisdiction of the [ICTY]."[51] This report was the first time that specific transitional justice options for Rwanda were publicly proposed. Degni-Ségui mentioned ICTY-Expanded or a new ICT, which implicitly included ICT-Tied and ICT-Separate. During this same period, the USG continued to publicly characterise the atrocities in Rwanda as "acts of genocide," denied that it had any legal obligation to act, and stressed that it was supporting an active UN role to help stop the massacres.[52] Midway through the June investigation, the USG had still not determined whether it would support an ICT for Rwanda.[53] On 1 July, the UNSC took a further step in pursuing transitional justice for Rwanda: it adopted UNSCR 935, declaring that atrocity perpetrators would be held individually accountable, and requesting the UNSG to establish the UN Independent Commission of Experts

---

48   United States Department of State (15 June 1994). Cable Number 02491. "Rwanda: Bringing the Guilty to Justice."

49   United States Department of State (2 July 1994). Cable Number 177024. "Press Guidance – Friday, July 1, 1994."

50   UN/HCHR. S/1994/867 (25 July 1994). Introduction, Annex Paragraph 26.

51   UN/ICER. S/1994/1125 (4 October 1994). Article II, Section B, Paragraph 27. See also: United States Department of State (7 July 1994). Cable Number 05974. "Human Rights Commission: Special Rapporteur Concludes Genocide has Occurred in Rwanda."

52   United States Department of State (13 June 1994). "L Press Guidance."; United States Department of State (14 June 1994). "L Press Guidance."; United States Department of State (16 June 1994). "To Prudence Bushnell for Hill Briefing."

53   United States Department of State (14 June 1994). "L Press Guidance."

on Rwanda to collect evidence of those crimes, which would later serve as the basis for seeking the creation of an ICT for Rwanda.[54]

The USG supported or supplemented these UN efforts, including the UN Independent Commission of Experts on Rwanda. Responding both to pressure and to overwhelming evidence, on 10 June Secretary of State Christopher for the first time called the slaughter in Rwanda "genocide."[55] On 30 June, Christopher testified before the US Senate Committee on Foreign Relations that "it's clear that there is genocide, acts of genocide in Rwanda, and they ought to be pursued..." and also stated that, even though the USG had no unilateral responsibility, the international community had a collective obligation under the Genocide Convention to punish acts of genocide. Christopher also made an unsolicited comparison with Bosnia, stating, "I have no hesitation in saying that there was genocide in Rwanda and had been genocide, is genocide, in Bosnia as well." Christopher publicly stated for the first time during this testimony that the USG supported "the creation of an international war crimes tribunal" for Rwanda and that he had recently met with the ICTY's deputy prosecutor to discuss the matter.[56] At this point, the USG envisaged that the ICT could take one of two forms: an ICT specifically for Rwanda (although Christopher did not suggest whether this would occur outside or through the UN) or a permanent international criminal court.[57] In doing so, Christopher led the US to become "the first country to go on record in favor of the establishment of an international tribunal for Rwanda."[58]

Shortly after the vote to establish the UN Independent Commission of Experts on Rwanda, the US representative on the UNSC, Edward Gnehm, Jr., stated, "[o]ur goal must be individual accountability and responsibility for grave violations of international humanitarian law in Rwanda. We must fix responsibility on those who have directed these acts of violence. In so doing, we can transform revenge into justice, affirm the rule of law and, hopefully, bring this horrible cycle of violence to a merciful close."[59] Also around that

---

54   UNSC Res 935 (1994), Preamble, Paragraph 3; Interview with Scheffer (24 June 2003).

55   William Ferroggiaro, ed., "The US and the Genocide in Rwanda 1994: Evidence of Inaction," United States National Security Archive (20 August 2001), http://www.gwu. edu/~nsarchiv/NSAEBB/NSAEBB53/press.html.

56   "Christopher Urges Trial Over Genocide in Rwanda." *Washington Post* (1 July 1994), A29. See also: Julia Preston, "U.N. to probe genocide in Rwanda." *Washington Post* (2 July 1994), A15; US/SCFR (30 June 1994); United States Department of State (30 June 1994). "June 30, 1994 Appearance of Sec. Christopher before the Senate Foreign Relations Committee."

57   "Christopher Urges Trial Over Genocide in Rwanda." (1 July 1994).

58   V. Morris and M. P. Scharf, *The International Criminal Tribunal for Rwanda.* Vol. 1. (Irvington-on-Hudson, NY: Transnational Publishers, 1998, 2 Vols.), 64-5.

59   UN Doc. S/PV.3400 (1994), 4.

time, as Scheffer notes, the US Interagency War Crimes Working Group began collecting its own evidence of the genocide, in part to assist the UN Independent Commission of Experts on Rwanda.[60] On 15 July, the White House joined the US State Department in publicly supporting the establishment of an ICT for Rwanda, expressing the hope "that the United Nations would act swiftly... to create a War Crimes Tribunal."[61] At approximately that time, the USG was pressuring individual states, such as Tanzania and France, to begin detaining certain suspected *génocidaires*,[62] and the USG also began curtailing diplomatic relations with the GoR, refusing to recognise it, closing its embassy in Washington DC, and freezing its assets in the US.[63]

A parallel development was the selection of the ICTY Chief Prosecutor, who would ultimately also become the ICTR Chief Prosecutor, though this broadened mandate was not decided at the time. On 6 July, at a meeting in Moscow, Shattuck and Russia's deputy foreign minister Sergey Lavrov agreed to appoint Richard Goldstone, a prominent South African jurist, as the ICTY Chief Prosecutor.[64] On 8 July, UNSC Resolution 936 formalised that decision,[65] and Goldstone began serving as the ICTY Chief Prosecutor on 15 August.[66]

After the genocide: July – September 1994. The genocide stopped in mid-July 1994, when the RPF defeated the remaining GoR troops. The RPF then gave Dégni-Ségui a list of 55 people it considered to be the core group of *génocidaires*.[67] Meanwhile, Rwanda's new government was sworn in on 19 July, after which it lobbied for the establishment of an ICT for Rwanda, and France began withdrawing its forces (deployed under *Opération Turquoise*) later that month.[68] Also around this time, the Government of Tanzania declared its will-

---

60 Interview with Scheffer (24 June 2003).

61 The White House (15 July 1994). See also: United States Department of State (20 July 1994). Cable Number 194391. "Press Guidance – Wednesday, July 20, 1994."

62 United States Department of State (7 July 1994). Cable Number 180972. "Human Rights Violations: Detention of Gatete and Associates."; United States Department of State (9 July 1994). Cable Number 183627. "Gatete Departure from Benaco."; United States Department of State (11 July 1994). Cable Number 184429. "Gatete."

63 United States Department of State (15 July 1994). Cable Number 190358. "Non-Recognition of Interim Government of Rwanda."

64 J. Shattuck, *Freedom on Fire: Human Rights Wars & America's Response* (Cambridge, MA: Harvard University Press, 2003), 325.

65 UNSC Res. 936 (8 July 1994).

66 R. J. Goldstone, *For Humanity: Reflections of a War Crimes Investigator* (New Haven, CT: Yale University Press, 2000), 74, 81.

67 L. Melvern, *A People Betrayed: The Role of the West in Rwanda's Genocide*. (New York: Zed Books, 2000), 60 (footnote 20).

68 United States Department of State (20 July 1994). Cable Number 002972. "Rwanda: 19 July Security Council – Rwanda Absent; French Intent on Leaving by August 21."; United

ingness to cooperate "fully" with the international community in bringing *génocidaires* to justice,[69] a pledge that would later prove important both for apprehending suspected *génocidaires* and also for establishing the ICTR in that state.

Notwithstanding the White House's public and apparently unconditional support for an ICT for Rwanda, the US Department of State remained only conditionally supportive. In a response three and a half weeks after Tony Hall, a senior member of Congress, had sent a letter on 1 July to Christopher, advocating the immediate establishment of an ICT for Rwanda,[70] one of Christopher's deputies, Wendy Sherman, stated that "[w]e will support the creation of an international tribunal if the Commission of Experts confirms that violations of international humanitarian law have occurred."[71]

In the immediate aftermath of the genocide, the US Interagency War Crimes Working Group was actively considering two of the options outlined in Degni-Ségui's 28 June report to prosecute genocide leaders: ICT-Tied and ICTY-Expanded. At this point, according to Scheffer, and as made clear by internal US State Department documents, the USG favoured the latter option, which Matheson recommended, in part to facilitate the expansion of the ICTY into a permanent international criminal court.[72] The USG proposed that any ICT for Rwanda would not only share "common resources and registry staff with the ICTY, but would also share with the ICTY a common statute, trial and appellate chambers and chief prosecutor."[73] The USG also decided then to declare its preference and to commit itself to support domestic criminal justice efforts to prosecute other *génocidaires*.[74] Also at this time, as it could not assume that the ICTY and the ICTR would share a chief prosecutor, the USG was actively researching and considering candidates for the position of ICTR Chief Prosecutor, including Leopoldo Torres Boursault, a Spanish attorney.[75]

States Department of State (23 July 1994). Cable Number 197812. "Rwanda: 22 July Security Council Meeting."

69   United States Department of State (3 August 1994). Cable Number 004940. "Rwanda War Crimes – Tanzania's Position."

70   United States Department of State (1 July 1994). "Letter from Tony P. Hall, Member, House of Representatives, to Warren Christopher, Secretary of State."

71   United States Department of State (27 July 1994). Letter from Wendy R. Sherman, Assistant Secretary, Legislative Affairs, United States Department of State, to Tony P. Hall, Member, House of Representatives.

72   Interview with Scheffer (24 June 2003).

73   United States Department of State (28 July 1994). Cable Number 202027. "Rwanda War Crimes."

74   Interview with Matheson (26 Aug. 2003). See also: Interview with Stanton (26 June 2003).

75   United States Department of State (19 July 1994). Cable Number 07697. "Leopoldo Tor-

The USG made at least six attempts to lobby the international community to support the establishment of an ICT for Rwanda, especially as ICTY-Expanded. First, on 26 July, the USG informed its embassies around the world "to advise their host governments of the US support of an international tribunal to prosecute violations of the Genocide Convention and other grave violations of international humanitarian law in Rwanda and to seek their support as well," and also to advise them that the "present thinking" of the USG was in favour of ICTY-Expanded or ICT-Tied; that the USG requested them to begin detaining suspected *génocidaires*; and that the new ICTY Chief Prosecutor, Goldstone, "seems ready to supervise both the Yugoslav and Rwanda prosecutions" and had South African President "[Nelson] Mandela's personal endorsement for this position." The cable also requested its embassies to begin identifying African prosecutors and judges who could serve on an ICT for Rwanda.[76]

As part of the second lobbying effort, from mid-July to 8 November (the date the ICTR was established), USG officials conducted frequent and detailed bilateral meetings with various governments, including those of France, Spain, the UK, China, Ireland, Belgium, the Netherlands, Tanzania, South Africa, Kenya and Uganda, to lobby them to support the establishment of an ICT for Rwanda, and specifically through ICTY-Expanded.[77]

---

res Boursault for Rwanda War Crime Tribunal."; United States Department of State (19 July 1994). Cable Number 192051. "Rwanda War Crimes Tribunal."

76   United States Department of State (26 July 1994). Cable Number 198848. "Rwanda War Crimes."

77   See the following sources: United States Department of State (13 July 1994). Cable Number 19216. "Consultations with France on Rwanda War Crimes Issues."; United States Department of State (15 July 1994). Cable Number 188919. "Next Steps in Addressing War Crimes in Rwanda."; United States Department of State (18 July 1994). Cable Number 07165. "Rwanda: War Crimes, Non-Recognition, and APC's."; United States Department of State (19 July 1994). Cable Number 11339. "British Response Muted in Considering Next Steps in Addressing War Crimes in Rwanda."; United States Department of State (27 July 1994). Cable Number 08330. "Human Rights Tribunal - Rwanda."; United States Department of State (28 July 1994). Cable Number 04815. "Rwanda War Crimes Demarche: Minister of Home Affairs Reaction and Pitch for Financial Aid."; United States Department of State (29 July 1994). Cable Number 04148. "Irish Reaction to President Clinton's and AID Administrator Atwoods' Letters on Rwanda."; United States Department of State (29 July 1994). Cable Number 08418. "Human Rights Tribunal - Rwanda."; United States Department of State (29 July 1994). Cable Number 10774. "South Africa: Goldstone Involvement in Yugoslavia War Crimes Tribunal Should Insure South African Support for Concept."; United States Department of State (29 July 1994). Cable Number 202705. "Human Rights Tribunal - Rwanda."; United States Department of State (1 August 1994). Cable Number 205480. "Human Rights Tribunal – Rwanda."; United States Department of State (2 August 1994). Cable Number 08559. "Human Rights Tribunal – Rwanda."; United States Department of State (5 August 1994). Cable Number 210227. "Visit of A/S John Shattuck."; United States Department of State (6 August 1994). Cable Number 211528. "Talking Points for AF A/S Moose's Use with GOF and GOB Officials."; United States Department of State (8 August 1994). Cable Number

The USG's bilateral communication with the Russian, French, South African and Chinese governments is particularly noteworthy. The USG focused on lobbying the Russian and French governments because, as two of the five permanent members of the UNSC, their support was critical to establishing an ICT for Rwanda, and to varying degrees they both opposed the USG's preference for ICTY-Expanded, instead preferring to establish the ICTR as a legally separate ICT. Reaching agreement with France was of particular concern to the USG because of the French government's history and relationship with Rwanda, which was seen as, *inter alia*, logistically critical to establishing a successful transitional justice mechanism. As one internal US Department of State document states,

France is a key player on this issue, not only because of its current involvement in Rwanda, but because it may have the most complete information of any western government on war crimes in Rwanda and access to witnesses, evidence and even perpetrators. France's support for the work of the Commission [of Experts] may be critical to

---

21685. "A/S Moose Briefs Quai on his Rwanda Trip."; United States Department of State (8 August 1994). Cable Number 14073. "Visit to Kenya of A/S Shattuck."; United States Department of State (9 August 1994). Cable Number 06337. "Interim Trip Report – Kigali and Goma."; United States Department of State (11 August 1994). Cable Number 12721. Draft reporting cable of A/S Shattuck meeting with British officials for Shattuck's comment/approval; United States Department of State (12 August 1994). Cable Number 22245. "A/S Shattuck's Meeting with French on Rwanda War Crimes Tribunal and Burundi."; United States Department of State (13 August 1994). Cable Number 22398. "DRL/MLA Director Rosenblatt's Meeting with Belgian Official on Rwanda Tribunal and Monitors."; United States Department of State (15 August 1994). Cable Number 23223. "Demarche to Russian MFA on UN War Crimes Tribunal for Rwanda."; United States Department of State (15 August 1994). Cable Number 12901. "A/S Shattuck's Discussion on the Proposed Rwanda War Crimes Tribunal with HMG."; United States Department of State (20 August 1994). Cable Number 224856. "Establishment of UN War Crimes Tribunal for Rwanda."; United States Department of State (20 August 1994). Cable Number 224672. "Establishment of UN War Crimes Tribunal for Rwanda."; United States Department of State (25 August 1994). Cable Number 24407. "UN War Crimes Tribunal for Rwanda: Russian Position."; United States Department of State (25 August 1994). Cable Number 09371. "Assistant Secretary Moose's 8/23 Discussions with Belgian Foreign Minister on Rwanda, Burundi, Zaire."; United States Department of State (30 August 1994). Cable Number 234040. "Establishment of a War Crimes Tribunal for Rwanda: Dutch Views."; United States Department of State (31 August 1994). Cable Number 005510. "Rwanda War Crimes Tribunal Demarche to GOT."; United States Department of State (16 September 1994). Cable Number 251046. "UN War Crimes Prosecutions for Rwanda."; United States Department of State (19 September 1994). Cable Number 25531. "French Perspective on Rwanda War Crimes Tribunal."; United States Department of State (19 September 1994). Cable Number 26935. "UN War Crimes Prosecutions for Rwanda."; United States Department of State (15 October 1994). Cable Number 280506. "Resolution Establishing War Crimes Tribunal for Rwanda."; United States Department of State (21 October 1994). Cable Number 286662. "Rwanda War Crimes."; United States Department of State (24 October 1994). Cable Number 006900. "Tanzanian Views on War Crimes Tribunal."; United States Department of State (27 October 1994). Cable Number 008705. "Rwanda War Crimes Tribunal."

the success of its efforts, and France's views on next steps will be critically important in the [Security] Council.[78]

As a result, the USG focused much of its lobbying efforts on these two governments. By mid-September, when both continued to oppose ICTY-Expanded, the USG began employing new tactics, other than just appealing to the merits of its preferred option. To the Russian government, to which it privately referred as having "stubbornly defended" its opposition to ICTY-Expanded,[79] the USG offered to support a Russian candidate for one of the new judges of an expanded ICT. This tribunal would have jurisdiction over cases arising from the conflict in the former Yugoslavia, which was of cultural and emotional concern to Russians, as it involved their historic Orthodox Christian Slavic brethren, the Serbs. Specifically, the USG argued to the Russians,

One of the advantages of expanding the current tribunal to include Rwandan offences is that in doing so, additional judges would be added, giving the tribunal a broader geographic base. In particular, the USG would be prepared to support a qualified Russian candidate, who would, if elected, thereby be able to participate in the handling of both Yugoslav and Rwandan cases. On the other hand, if a separate tribunal is created for Rwanda, there would be no opportunity to bring a Russian judge into the handling of the Yugoslav cases.[80]

The USG simultaneously made a similar appeal to the French government: "the USG would welcome the appointment of a Deputy Prosecutor and staff prosecutors from other French-speaking countries to handle the Rwandan cases, as well as the election of an additional French-speaking judge to deal with both Rwandan and Yugoslav cases."[81]

The USG believed that having South Africa's support for an ICT for Rwanda and, in particular, that of its president, Mandela, and its foreign minister, Alfred Nzo, would "lend great credibility and momentum for this important effort."[82] In bilateral discussions with the South African Government, including directly with Mandela (in which the USG addressed him as "Africa's most

---

78   United States Department of State (12 July 1994). Cable Number 184612. "Consultations with France and Others on Rwanda War Crimes Issues." See also: United States Department of State (23 July 1994). Cable Number 197812. "Rwanda: 22 July Security Council Meeting."; United States Department of State (5 August 1994). Cable Number 210227. "Visit of A/S John Shattuck."

79   United States Department of State (19 September 1994). Cable Number 26935. "UN War Crimes Prosecutions for Rwanda."

80   United States Department of State (16 September 1994). Cable Number 251046. "UN War Crimes Prosecutions for Rwanda."

81   Ibid.

82   United States Department of State (3 August 1994). Cable Number 206761. "Rwanda War Crimes."; United States Department of State (6 August 1994). Cable Number 211529. "AF A/S Moose's Talking Points for His Meeting with President Mandela."

respected leader"), the USG further argued that lending its support was in South Africa's interest: "South Africa could and should play a prominent role in this effort, thereby promoting human rights and furthering its moral leadership in the international community. This will be particularly true if, as we hope, Justice Goldstone will oversee both Yugoslav and Rwanda war crimes."[83] Indeed, several African states, including South Africa, eventually provided support for an ICT for Rwanda, specifically through ICTY-Expanded. The USG suspected that staffing selection, not the merits of the proposal, provided part of the motivation: "We have received favorable preliminary reactions from key African governments for expanding the current tribunal to include Rwanda. This is probably due, at least in part, to the fact that the current head of one of the two trial chambers (Judge Karibi-Whyte) is from Nigeria, and the current chief prosecutor (Judge Goldstone) is from South Africa and has the personal support of President Mandela."[84]

The USG also specifically focused on lobbying China to support the establishment of an ICT for Rwanda, since by mid-August China was the only one of the five permanent members of the UNSC that still resisted the idea. China explained that it was hesitant because it did not want the international community to violate the GoR's sovereignty. In order to lobby China, the USG made direct bilateral appeals and also enlisted the support of other states, including Burundi, Congo, Uganda, Kenya, Tanzania, Djibouti, Ethiopia and Nigeria.[85] On 30 August, the Chinese government informed the USG that it would support the USG's proposal for ICTY-Expanded.[86]

A third lobbying effort by the USG occurred in early August, when USG officials secured support from Goldstone for the ICTY-Expanded option.[87] Then, in a fourth effort, the USG convened meetings (on 4 and 9 August) of the legal advisers of the five permanent members of the UNSC, to discuss establishing an ICT for Rwanda, and to lobby specifically for ICTY-Expanded. On 4 August, according to the USG, Russia "strongly supported" and France "generally supported" the USG proposal, whereas China and the UK remained non-commit-

---

83   Ibid.

84   United States Department of State (16 September 1994). Cable Number 251046. "UN War Crimes Prosecutions for Rwanda."

85   United States Department of State (20 August 1994). Cable Number 224856. "Establishment of UN War Crimes Tribunal for Rwanda."

86   United States Department of State (30 August 1994). Cable Number 03594. "War Crimes Tribunal for Rwanda."

87   Interview with Matheson (26 Aug. 2003). See also: Interview with Graham Blewitt, former Deputy Prosecutor, ICTY (11 June 2003).

tal.[88] By 9 August, only China remained non-committal.[89] Another meeting of the legal advisers of the five permanent members of the UNSC was convened later, on 18 August, by UN Legal Counsel Hans Correll. During that meeting, the USG continued lobbying for its preference for ICTY-Expanded, and Correll stated that transitional justice options for Rwanda included ICT-Separate established through either Chapter VI or Chapter VII of the UN Charter, the USG proposal (ICTY-Expanded), or an augmentation of the GoR's national courts with foreign judges.[90] At this meeting, France (seconded by the UK) restated its preference for legally separate ICTs for Rwanda and the former Yugoslavia, but, from the USG's perspective, was "not, however, adamantly opposed to US approach."[91] A few days later, UN Deputy Legal Adviser Ralph Zacklin told USG officials that he personally preferred two legally separate ICTs for Rwanda and the former Yugoslavia. He also said that while he believed they could share an appeals chamber, he preferred separate trial chambers and chief prosecutors, and he suggested that whatever part of an ICT for Rwanda was to be located in Africa should be in Nairobi, as a first choice, or alternatively in Addis Ababa.[92]

A fifth USG lobbying effort occurred from 4 to 10 August, when four USG officials (Shattuck, Nix, Josiah Rosenblatt,[93] and Frederick Barton[94]) travelled to Uganda, Rwanda, Burundi, Zaire and France for bilateral discussions about various USG objectives relating to post-genocide Rwanda.[95] In Rwanda, part of the delegation's objective was to convey that the USG strongly supported an ICT for Rwanda, without specifying whether it should be ICTY-Expanded or ICT-Tied, and also to persuade the GoR to support such a tribunal, in part by requesting that the UNSC establish it.[96] In Rwanda they met with Kagame, who

88 United States Department of State (5 August 1994). Cable Number 03237. "Rwanda War Crimes."

89 United States Department of State (10 August 1994). Cable Number 215074. August 10 Daily Rwanda/Burundi Sitrep Prepared by U.S. Department of State Bureau of African Affairs Office of Central African Affairs (AF/C).

90 United States Department of State (19 August 1994). Cable Number 03437. "Rwanda – Crimes Tribunal – Meeting with UN Legal Counsel."

91 Ibid.

92 United States Department of State (24 August 1994). Cable Number 03495. "Rwanda War Crimes Tribunal UN Sect. Views."

93 Director, Office of Multilateral Affairs, Bureau of Democracy, Human Rights, and Labor, US Department of State.

94 Director, Office of Transition Initiative, US Agency for International Development.

95 United States Department of State (4 August 1994). Cable Number 207893. "Travel of A/S Shattuck to Uganda, Rwanda, Burundi, Zaire and France."

96 United States Department of State (5 August 1994). Cable Number 209882. "A/S Shattuck Visit to Rwanda: Objectives."

had become Vice-President and Minister of Defence, Alphonse-Marie Nkubito,[97] Twagiramungu, and Jacques Bihozagara.[98/99] The USG delegation arrived in Kigali on 5 August, where they were joined by the US Ambassador to Rwanda, David Rawson, and General John Shalikashvili.[100/101] According to Shattuck, the purposes of the trip were to "seek Kagame's support for a Security Council resolution to establish an international criminal tribunal for Rwanda to investigate the genocide and bring its leaders to justice... [and to] urge Kagame to work with the United States to rebuild the country's shattered justice system...". Shattuck also delivered a letter (drafted by himself, Scheffer and Nix) to Nkubito and Kagame, endorsing the establishment of an ICT for Rwanda, which he asked the GoR to send to the UNSC.[102] On behalf of the GoR, Nkubito submitted the letter to the UN Secretary-General on 8 August,[103] and the UNSC issued a presidential statement on 10 August welcoming the letter.[104]

The USG then took a sixth step to lobby for an ICT for Rwanda (specifically as ICTY-Expanded). On 1 September, the USG began circulating a draft resolution and annex, including a statute to create an ICT for Rwanda through ICTY-Expanded.[105] The USG followed up by circulating another draft document to UNSC members on 20 September, arguing that prosecution of the Rwandan cases "can be most effectively done by adding this responsibility to the mandate of the [ICTY]."[106]

After Shattuck, Nix, Rosenblatt and Barton returned from their multi-state trip, the US State Department increased its focus on Rwandan criminal justice issues. On 12 August, the US Department of State established a separate US In-

---

97   Rwandan Minister of Justice.

98   Rwandan Minister of Rehabilitation and Social Integration.

99   United States Department of State (11 August 1994). Cable Number 06441. "A/S Shattuck Urges Support for War Crimes Tribunal."

100   Chairman of the Joint Chiefs of Staff.

101   United States Department of State (8 August 1994). Cable Number 212243. "Press Guidance – August 8, 1994."

102   Shattuck (2003), 59-66; United States Department of State (9 August 1994). Cable Number 06337. "Interim Trip Report – Kigali and Goma."

103   United States Department of State (9 August 1994). Cable Number 213680. "Press Guidance – August 9, 1994." NOTE: For the full text of the letter, see: United States Department of State (9 August 1994). Cable Number 02676. "International Tribunal for Rwanda – Further Thoughts."; United States Department of State (20 August 1994). Cable Number 224856. "Establishment of UN War Crimes Tribunal for Rwanda."

104   United States Department of State (11 August 1994). Cable Number 03310. "Rwanda: SC Statement Issued August 10."

105   United States Department of State (1 September 1994). Cable Number 237220. "Resolution Establishing War Crimes Tribunal for Rwanda."

106   "Try Rwandan War Cases in Hague, Says U.S." (21 September 1994). *The Record.* A17.

teragency War Crimes Working Group on Rwanda and indicated that it would press for a rapid completion of the UN Independent Commission of Experts on Rwanda's work.[107] Almost two weeks later, Shattuck published an editorial in *The Washington Post*, stating, "it is vital that the international community rapidly create a war crimes tribunal for Rwanda that will hold the perpetrators of genocide and other atrocities accountable to their victims and to the international community."[108] Also in mid-August, the USG, through Albright and in other ways, began pressuring the UN Independent Commission of Experts on Rwanda and the UN High Commissioner for Human Rights to support the establishment of an ICT for Rwanda, and especially for the UN Independent Commission of Experts to issue an interim report including a recommendation to that effect.[109] The idea of the UN Independent Commission of Experts on Rwanda issuing an interim report apparently arose from this USG pressure, after an 18 August meeting between Spiegel, Matheson and three members of the Commission, including its chairman, Atsu-Koffi Amega.[110] The USG made several offers of assistance to the Commission at this point, offering for example to provide legal staff and urging the UN to provide adequate office equipment.[111]

Soon thereafter, President Clinton sent a high-level mission, co-chaired by Congressman Donald Payne and C. Payne Lucas of Africare, to Central Africa, including Rwanda, to investigate post-genocide issues in the region. Upon their return, mission members briefed the White House, the US National Security Council and the US Department of State, and appeared on various news programmes and were quoted in the media. According to the US Department of State, their conclusions and recommendations "track closely with U.S.G. policy," including the recommendation for quick establishment of an ICT for Rwanda.[112] One mission member, Aspen Institute president S. Frederick Starr,

---

107　Interview with Matheson (26 Aug. 2003).

108　J. Shattuck, "War Crimes First," *Washington Post* (23 August 1994), A19.

109　United States Department of State (17 August 1994). Cable Number 221084. "Rwanda: Pending Meetings in Geneva with Ayala Lasso and the Commission of Experts."; United States Department of State (24 August 1994). Cable Number 228408. "Demarche for International Tribunal in Rwanda."; United States Department of State (12 September 1994). Cable Number 245815. Summary of [illegible]'s meeting with Assistant Secretary Moose.

110　United States Department of State (18 August 1994). Cable Number 07233. "Rwanda: Initial Meeting with Commission of Experts."

111　Ibid.

112　United States Department of State (9 September 1994). Cable Number 243592. "Presidential Mission Returns from Central Africa; Recommendations Track Closely with U.S.G. Policy."

published an op-ed in *The Washington Post* on 6 September recommending, *inter alia*, the establishment of such an ICT.[113]

That same month, the USG sent another team to Rwanda—an inter-agency evidence-gathering team to assist the efforts of the UN Independent Commission of Experts on Rwanda, which had completed its preliminary work in Rwanda on 5 September.[114] Nix, Assistant US Attorney Stephen Mansfield, Major General Patrick O'Hare and about three other officials travelled to Rwanda to conduct an assessment of the political and security climate, to collect evidence, and to interview witnesses, all data and findings of which they provided to the Commission.[115] The Commission acknowledged these contributions in its 1 October Interim Report, stating that the US Department of State "forwarded to the Commission documents... that prove the existence of a plan for genocide against Tutsis and the murder of moderate Hutus."[116] The USG sent yet a third mission to Rwanda later that month. In mid-September the Undersecretary of State for Global Affairs, Timothy Wirth, made a four-day visit to Rwanda to investigate developments on the ground and further lobby for the establishment of an ICT for Rwanda.[117]

The UN Independent Commission of Experts on Rwanda's interim report made recommendations on the form the prosecutions should take. The report recommended prosecution by an international rather than a municipal tribunal and, like Degni-Ségui's 28 June report, discussed only two options for dealing with suspected *génocidaires*: ICTY-Expanded and a new ICT, either ICT-Tied or ICT-Separate.[118] The Commission stated its preference for ICTY-Expanded, arguing that "[t]he alternative of creating an *ad hoc* tribunal alongside the al-

---

113 S. Frederick Starr, "It's up to us to Defuse the Rwandan Time Bomb," *Washington Post* (6 September 1994), A17.

114 United States Department of State (7 September 1994). Cable Number 01509. "Visit by UN Commission of Experts; Recommendation for U.S. Assistance."

115 Interview with Scheffer (24 June 2003); Interview with Scheffer (18 Nov. 2005); United States Department of State (12 September 1994). Cable Number 246554. "USG Interview Trip to Rwanda." Also see: Interview with Alison Des Forges, author of *Leave None To Tell the Story: Genocide in Rwanda* (24 May 2003); Interview with Shattuck (9 Oct. 2003); United States Department of State (17 September 1994). Cable Number 008006. "UN Human Rights Program: Getting it all Together."

116 UN/ICER. S/1994/1405 (9 December 1994), Article II, Section A, Paragraph 35.

117 United States Department of State (23 September 1994). Cable Number 259321. Updated Press Guidance – September 23, 1994; United States Department of State (24 September 1994). Cable Number 259570. "Press Guidance – September 23, 1994."; United States Department of State (26 September 1994). Cable Number 260743. "Press Guidance – September 26, 1994."; United States Department of State (27 September 1994). Cable Number 261704. "Press Guidance – September 27, 1994."

118 UNSG. S/1994/1125 (4 October 1994), Annex, paragraphs 133-45; 149-52. Also see: L. G. Sunga, *Human Rights Law Journal*, 121-4.

ready existing international criminal tribunal in The Hague would not only be less efficient from an administrative point of view of staffing and use of physical resources, but would be more likely to lead to less consistency in the legal interpretation and application of international criminal law."[119] According to Stanton, he was seconded to the Commission in August, wrote the first half of this interim report, and consulted on the second half.[120] A cable from the US Embassy in Kigali states, "IO/UNP Stanton was a most effective liaison to the Commission. He was instrumental in ensuring the Commission's commitment to an early interim report recommending an international tribunal."[121]

The GoR remained dissatisfied with the progress of the international community in bringing *génocidaires* to justice. On 28 September, the permanent representative of Rwanda to the UN sent a letter to the UNSC president, noting "evident reluctance by the international community to set up an international tribunal."[122] On 4 October, the GoR publicly declared its preferences: that proceedings take place in Rwanda and that convicted *génocidaires* receive the death penalty.[123] Two days later Rwanda's President, Pasteur Bizimungu, stated to the UN General Assembly,

it is absolutely urgent that this international tribunal be established. It will enable us to prosecute in a completely open setting those responsible for the genocide. Since most of the criminals have found refuge in various corners of the world, what we seek is a tool of justice that knows no borders. Moreover, the very nature of the events—considered to be crimes against humanity—warrants the international community's joining forces to prevent their reoccurrence.

Bizimungu also stated the GoR's preference for an ICT created by the UNSC's Chapter VII powers, so that the ICT could compel state compliance.[124] However, none of these GoR statements indicated its preference for either ICTY-Expanded, ICT-Tied, or ICT-Separate.

The narrowing option: ICT-Tied: September – November 1994. Between the 26 July cable indicating USG preference for ICTY-Expanded and 28 September, USG preferences shifted from ICTY-Expanded to ICT-Tied. Although the UN Independent Commission of Experts on Rwanda endorsed ICTY-Expanded in its interim report, several UNSC member states, most notably Russia and France, preferred ICT-Tied (China and the UK did not have a preference either

---

119   UNSG. S/1994/1125 (4 October 1994), Annex, paragraph 140.

120   Interview with Stanton (26 June 2003).

121   United States Department of State (7 September 1994). Cable Number 01509. "Visit by UN Commission of Experts; Recommendation for U.S. Assistance."

122   UN Doc. S/1994/1115 (29 September 1994). Also see: Shraga and Zacklin (1996), 504.

123   Haq, Farhan (4 October 1994). "Rwanda: Government Scorns U.N. Proposal for Outside Trials." *Inter Press Service.*

124   UN Doc. A/49/PV.21 (1994), 5.

way).[125] According to Matheson and internal US Department of State documents, one reason why Russia and France favoured ICT-Tied was to avoid creating the institutional framework for a permanent international criminal court, which these two governments did not support at that time.[126] According to Matheson and Scheffer, because the USG had only a *weak* preference for ICTY-Expanded over ICT-Tied, and given the value of French and Russian support, the USG revised its own position to reflect the shifting preferences of those states among the five permanent UNSC members that had voiced opinions.[127] The USG characterised its new position as "the latest USG proposal for the [Rwanda] war crimes tribunal, based on the New Zealand approach."[128] That decision occurred on 28 September, as reflected in an internal US Department of State cable that stated:

In light of continuing opposition from Russia and France to the expansion of the jurisdiction of the current tribunal for the former Yugoslavia, we have decided to pursue the New Zealand approach of creating a separate tribunal for Rwanda, but providing that the appeals judges and prosecutor for the former Yugoslavia would serve also as the appeals judges and prosecutor for Rwanda.... You should emphasize that we are making this compromise in the interest of quick Council action on Rwanda prosecutions, which is essential in light of the situation in Rwanda.[129]

The GoR advised the USG that it agreed with the "New Zealand approach" and wanted trials to take place in Kigali.[130] The French, British, and Belgian governments also advised the USG that their group "agrees to pursue the New Zealand approach of creating a separate tribunal for Rwanda, and additionally agrees that the appeals judges and prosecutor for the former Yugoslavia

---

125   United States Department of State (27 July 1994). Cable Number 03089. "Rwanda War Crimes Tribunal – Russian Demarche."; United States Department of State (28 July 1994). Cable Number 202027. "Rwanda War Crimes."; United States Department of State (14 August 1994). Cable Number 218325. "Establishment of UN War Crimes Tribunal for Rwanda."; United States Department of State (23 September 1994). Cable Number 004014. "Rwanda War Crimes."

126   Interview with Matheson (26 Aug. 2003); United States Department of State (30 August 1994). Cable Number 003604. "War Crines [*sic*] Tribunal for Rwanda."

127   See: Interview with Matheson (26 Aug. 2003) and Interview with Scheffer (24 June 2003).

128   United States Department of State (29 September 1994). Cable Number 04101. "A/S Shattuck Discussions with Secretariat, ICRC, and Missions Regarding Haiti, Rwanda, Burundi, China, Turkey, and Funding for UN Human Rights Activities."

129   United States Department of State (28 September 1994). Cable Number 262739. "Resolution Establishing War Crimes Tribunal for Rwanda." See also: Interview with Matheson (26 Aug. 2003).

130   United States Department of State (29 September 1994). Cable Number 04101. "A/S Shattuck Discussions with Secretariat, ICRC, and Missions Regarding Haiti, Rwanda, Burundi, China, Turkey, and Funding for UN Human Rights Activities."

would serve also as the appeals judges and prosecutor for Rwanda."[131] Scheffer reports that, in addition to offering the "New Zealand approach," which ultimately produced the ICTR, the New Zealand government was crucial to the establishment of the ICTR in other ways: "New Zealand... was a key negotiating partner in the establishment of the ICTR. New Zealand often hosted in its UN Mission in New York our negotiating sessions with various UNSC members, including Rwanda that year, concerning creation of the ICTR. They served as an honest broker and were critical to the ultimate success of the venture."[132] On 28 September, the USG and the New Zealand government circulated among Zacklin and the five permanent members of the UNSC a draft UNSC resolution for the establishment of the ICTR, which they then circulated to all UNSC members the following day.[133] A revised text was then introduced by the USG, the New Zealand government and the British government two weeks later, in mid-October.[134] Despite an initial USG preference for ICTY-Expanded, the USG shifted its support to ICT-Tied, because of its desire and perceived need to seek consensus among the five permanent members of the UNSC. Also at this time, the USG decided to establish a ministerial-level operational support group, entitled "The Friends of Rwanda," to coordinate further efforts to assist post-genocide Rwanda.[135]

Even after the decision to support ICT-Tied emerged among the five permanent members of the UNSC and some other critical states, such as New Zealand, Uganda and Tanzania (the last of which, in October, offered Arusha as a venue for any ICT for Rwanda[136]), some other states and other parties raised concerns. For example, the UN Secretary-General Boutros Boutros-Ghali objected to Goldstone as chief prosecutor, preferring instead a Francophone

---

131   United States Department of State (29 September 1994). Cable Number 26809. "French Confirm Concurrence on Rwanda War Crimes Tribunal." See also: United States Department of State (29 September 1994). Cable Number 04101. "A/S Shattuck Discussions with Secretariat, ICRC, and Missions Regarding Haiti, Rwanda, Burundi, China, Turkey, and Funding for UN Human Rights Activities."

132   Interview with Scheffer (18 Nov. 2005).

133   United States Department of State (30 September 1994). Cable Number 04112. "Resolution and Statute Establishing War Crimes Tribunal for Rwanda."

134   United States Department of State (15 October 1994). Cable Number 280506. "Resolution Establishing War Crimes Tribunal for Rwanda."

135   United States Department of State (29 September 1994). Cable Number 04101. "A/S Shattuck Discussions with Secretariat, ICRC, and Missions Regarding Haiti, Rwanda, Burundi, China, Turkey, and Funding for UN Human Rights Activities."; United States Department of State (19 October 1994). Cable Number 28295. Evening Notes 10/18/94 Eyes Only for A/S Douglas Bennett W/ Strobe Talbott Party from George F. Ward.

136   United States Department of State (24 October 1994). Cable Number 006900. "Tanzanian Views on War Crimes Tribunal."

African.[137] Furthermore, in mid-October, Japan's government expressed its concern that the UNSC was apparently engaged in the proliferation of *ad hoc* ICTs, a practice to which it objected.[138]

Most notably, though, the GoR continued lobbying for the establishment of an ICT for Rwanda (without stating a preference for a particular version) and some of its details. GoR representatives voiced objections to Matheson and other USG officials regarding the draft ICTR statute, concerning for example the temporal jurisdiction, the number of judges, the seat of the tribunal and the text of Articles 3 (on crimes against humanity), 4 (on war crimes), 26 (on sentencing) and 27 (on pardon or commutation of sentences). Specifically, the GoR stated, *inter alia*, that it wanted a voice in the selection of tribunal staff and a veto over all releases and pardons, and insisted all convicted *génocidaires* to be incarcerated only in Rwanda.[139] The GoR demanded more control over a process perceived as crucial to the development of its state and also that atrocities committed before 1994 should be included in the ICT's jurisdiction, as the GoR argued they were inextricably linked to the genocide and should also be punished. At this time, Twagiramungu again publicly demanded the establishment of an ICT for Rwanda: "[w]hy do we have to beg for the international court to be set up?"[140] USG officials continued meeting with their GoR counterparts in mid-October through early-November, including a phone meeting between Wirth and President Bizimungu on 19 October,[141]

137   United States Department of State (19 October 1994). Cable Number 28295. Evening Notes 10/18/94 Eyes Only for A/S Douglas Bennett W/ Strobe Talbott Party from George F. Ward; United States Department of State (19 October 1994). Cable Number 283000. "Rwanda War Crimes."

138   United States Department of State (21 October 1994). Cable Number 004514. "Rwanda War Crimes Tribunal – Japanese Views."

139   Interview with Matheson (26 Aug. 2003); United States Department of State (15 October 1994). Cable Number 280506. "Resolution Establishing War Crimes Tribunal for Rwanda."; United States Department of State (19 October 1994). Cable Number 283000. "Rwanda War Crimes."; United States Department of State (19 October 1994). Cable Number 01872. "Rwandan Position on Rwanda War Crimes Tribunal."; United States Department of State (4 November 1994). Cable Number 004749. "Rwanda War Crimes Tribunal – Meeting of Co-Sponsors."; United States Department of State (5 November 1994). Cable Number 004783. "Rwanda War Crimes Tribunal."; United States Department of State (19 October 1994). Cable Number 28295. Evening Notes 10/18/94 Eyes Only for A/S Douglas Bennett W/ Strobe Talbott Party from George F. Ward; United States Department of State (20 October 1994). Cable Number 04459. "Rwandan Views on War Crimes Tribunal."; United States Department of State (20 October 1994). Cable Number 01883. "Follow-up Demarches on Rwanda War Crimes Tribunal Resolution: Prime Minister and Justice Minister."; United States Department of State (22 October 1994). Cable Number 06331. "Rwanda War Crimes."

140   Morris and Scharf (1998), 67.

141   See e.g.: United States Department of State (19 October 1994). Cable Number 283000. "Rwanda War Crimes."; United States Department of State (19 October 1994). Cable

but according to Scheffer did not discover "until the last day or so prior to the vote in the Security Council that the Rwandan government would not budge on their objections to the ICTR statute."[142] Part of the problem may have been communication difficulties that the GoR delegation at the UN claimed to be having with its home government in Kigali, which prevented the former from receiving timely and thorough guidance.[143]

On 3 November, the USG convened a meeting of the co-sponsors (France, New Zealand, Russia, Spain, the US and the UK; Argentina would join later as a co-sponsor) of a resolution to establish an ICT for Rwanda. According to an internal US Department of State cable, the group decided at that meeting to confer with GoR officials the following day to try to persuade them "to vote in favor or not participate" in the resolution; to bring the resolution to a vote on 7 November, "irrespective of Rwandan position"; and "that no changes would be made in text of resolution or statute unless Rwanda indicated one or another minor cosmetic change would enable them to vote yes on the resolution." Members of the group varied in terms of their strict adherence to these positions: French and Russian representatives urged no further amendments to the resolution and insisted a vote should be taken on 7 November, US and Spanish officials supported the French/Russian position, and the government of New Zealand was willing to both negotiate further with the GoR and delay any vote on the resolution.[144]

As planned, on 4 November the co-sponsors of the resolution met with GoR officials, including the GoR's permanent representative to the UN, Manzi Bakuramutsa. They conveyed to the Rwandan delegates the decisions they had made the previous day, including their intention to vote on the proposed resolution on 7 November, and said they hoped the GoR would vote yes or abstain. GoR officials responded that they had not yet received instructions from more senior officials in their government back in Kigali, in part because, according to a US Department of State cable, "time was differently perceived

---

Number 01872. "Rwandan Position on Rwanda War Crimes Tribunal."; United States Department of State (20 October 1994). Cable Number 04459. "Rwandan Views on War Crimes Tribunal."; United States Department of State (20 October 1994). Cable Number 01883. "Follow-up Demarches on Rwanda War Crimes Tribunal Resolution: Prime Minister and Justice Minister."; United States Department of State (22 October 1994). Cable Number 06331. "Rwanda War Crimes."; United States Department of State (22 October 1994). Cable Number 286781. "Rwanda War Crimes Tribunal: Zero Hour."

142 Interview with Scheffer (24 June 2003).

143 United States Department of State (20 October 1994). Cable Number 01883. "Follow-up Demarches on Rwanda War Crimes Tribunal Resolution: Prime Minister and Justice Minister."

144 United States Department of State (4 November 1994). Cable Number 004749. "Rwanda War Crimes Tribunal – Meeting of Co-Sponsors."

in Rwanda... it simply took weeks for them fully to grasp" the proposal. Bakuramutsa also reiterated some of the GoR's objections to the draft resolution. The co-sponsors responded that they were amenable to increasing the number of judges but not to increasing the involvement of the GoR in their selection because the ICT "could not be seen as in any way prone to bias." The meeting concluded with an agreement to meet as a group as soon as the GoR delegates received instructions. Members of the co-sponsoring group continued to vary in terms of their resolve, with the French and Russians insistent on voting on the current version of the resolution on 7 November and New Zealand most willing to compromise with the GoR and delay the vote. USG officials present at the meeting added that, although no agreement with the GoR had been reached, the meeting had been productive in conveying the "message to Rwandans that time had come to make their decision and slight firming up of New Zealand and UK resolve to act on Monday."[145]

Scheffer reports that further meetings among GoR, USG and UN officials on this topic did occur between 5 and 7 November, but in Kigali, not New York City. Scheffer further recalls that, during this time, GoR officials in Kigali sent instructions to their representatives at the UN to vote against the proposed tribunal statute. Finally, Scheffer believes that the delay from 7 November to 8 November in ultimately voting on the UNSC resolution on the tribunal statute is not significant. Instead, he suggests that such delays are common and, in this case, probably reflected the last-minute meetings occurring in Kigali and the time it took to relay messages from there to New York.[146]

The decision to create the ICTR: 8 November 1994. On 8 November, the UNSC adopted Resolution 955, establishing the ICTR through the UN Charter's Chapter VII authority. The vote was 13 in favour, one abstention (China), and one—Rwanda—against. Along with the US, those voting in favour of the resolution were: Argentina, Brazil, the Czech Republic, Djibouti, France, New Zealand, Nigeria, Oman, Pakistan, Russia, Spain and the UK.[147] China abstained from the vote, as explained by its Permanent Representative to the UN Li Zhaoxing, both because it was opposed, in principle, to overreaching the UNSC's authority by invoking Chapter VII to establish an ICT through a UNSC resolution and because China believed that the UNSC should have consulted the GoR further.[148]

---

145   United States Department of State (5 November 1994). Cable Number 004783. "Rwanda War Crimes Tribunal."

146   Interview with Scheffer (18 Nov. 2005).

147   UN Doc. S/PV.3453 (8 November 1994).

148   Ibid., 11.

After issuing broad public statements condemning *génocidaires* and calling for their accountability, and privately and directly threatening the genocide's leaders, the USG decided to act only after the genocide. Specifically, the USG decided to support prosecutions through ICT-Tied after abandoning its initial position of favouring ICTY-Expanded.

Puzzles

The case of USG support for the ICTR presents a series of puzzles, which should be investigated in future research on this topic. First, why, given the USG decision not to intervene in the Rwandan genocide, did the USG not only decide to "do something" about the transitional justice process, but also choose to support and to lead a relatively expensive (compared to other transitional justice options), labour-intensive and resource-draining transitional justice option?

Second, the precise form of the transitional justice option is itself puzzling. There was, at least theoretically, a vast array of other non-prosecutorial and prosecutorial options outside or through the UN, including the only other option that the USG seriously considered, ICTY-Expanded. Why, then, did the USG initially favour expanding the ICTY to eventually become a permanent international criminal court if it subsequently opposed the ICC? In addition, why did the USG support ICT-Tied, given apparently contradictory developments, such as the division of the ICTY/ICTR chief prosecutor into two separate offices? Moreover, why did the USG ultimately favour ICT-Tied, considering that it and the UN Independent Commission of Experts on Rwanda initially preferred ICTY-Expanded? Furthermore, why did the USG support an option that could not employ the death penalty, a punishment implemented in the US and one which the GoR sought? Finally, why did the USG support any option that would be an expansion of, tied to, or based on the ICTY, given the valid reasons the USG had to be sceptical of that model?

Third, it is curious—given the GoR's vote against UNSC resolution 955— that the USG supported the ICTR but cited the GoR's preferences in making other decisions leading up to that vote. Fourth, why did the USG support the ICTR, given that in other post-conflict situations the USG employed alternative options, such as amnesty, exile, assassination, and prosecution in a court established by multilateral treaty outside the UN? Fifth, given the UN's failure to prevent, stop, or even mitigate the Rwandan genocide, why did the USG rely upon the UN to facilitate and then administer the transitional justice solution for Rwanda? Finally, considering the enormous number of suspected *génocidaires*, why did the USG pursue an option that would focus on a limited number of them, even if they were the genocide's suspected leaders?

These puzzles bear directly on evaluating the USG's motives in supporting the establishment of the ICTR, and therefore merit further investigation. Conclusions about these puzzles can be drawn by considering the logic, necessity and persuasiveness of arguments put forth in interviews with USG officials involved in, and others knowledgeable about, USG decision-making on transitional justice issues; by analysing events since the ICTR's establishment; and by consulting the international law, institution creation and transitional justice literatures.

Conclusion

The establishment of the ICTR, in which the USG played a leading role, was a momentous advance in international relations. The creation of the ICTR marked a significant development in international cooperation, especially among Great Powers. The creation of the ICTR (and the ICTY), including the bilateral cooperation between the US and Russia on the appointment of Goldstone as ICTY and then ICTY/ICTR chief prosecutor, serve as a barometer for how far international cooperation had developed by 1994. Previously, during the Cold War, the US-USSR superpower rivalry paralysed the UNSC and otherwise prevented effective collaboration on international issues, including transitional justice. On the other hand, it is ironic that, whereas in 1994 some states objected to the USG's plan to establish a permanent international criminal court, just four years later those same states objected to the USG's opposition to doing so.

The establishment of the ICTR also represents a significant development in transitional and international justice. The ICTR established the precedent of the international community's response to crimes limited to an internal conflict. It also affirmed the power and legitimacy of the UNSC to use its Chapter VII powers to create *ad hoc* tribunals to prosecute suspected offenders of atrocities. Most important, the establishment of the ICTR presented the opportunity to identify, try and punish *génocidaires*; to document the history of, and responsibility for, the Rwandan genocide; to deter future atrocities and to provide reconciliation for the people of Rwanda. As Jallow notes in the following chapter, the ICTR has already established significant international legal precedents: it was the first ICT to receive a guilty plea for genocide,[149] it handed down the first genocide conviction,[150] it indicted and subsequently convicted a head of government for genocide for the first time,[151] it defined

---

149   Prosecutor v. Kambanda, Case No. ICTR-97-23, Judgment (4 Sept. 1998).

150   Prosecutor v. Akayesu, Case No. ICTR-96-4, Judgment (2 Sept. 1998).

151   Prosecutor v. Kambanda, Case No. ICTR-97-23, Judgment (4 Sept. 1998).

rape in international law and held that it could constitute genocide,[152] and it passed the first genocide conviction of journalists.[153]

The hope is that "genocide"—what the ICTR has called the "crime of crimes"[154]—and other atrocities will cease to occur in the future. Sadly, we have little reason to believe that this will be the case. As long as such crimes persist, the international community will be forced to make difficult choices like the ones described in this chapter, regarding whether and how to deal with their perpetrators.[155]

---

152   Prosecutor v. Akayesu, Case No. ICTR-96-4, Judgment (2 Sept. 1998).

153   Prosecutor v. Barayagwiza, Case No. ICTR-97-19, Judgment (3 Dec. 2003); Prosecutor v. Nahimana, Case No. ICTR-96-11, Judgment (3 Dec. 2003); Prosecutor v. Ngeze, Case No. ICTR-97-27, Judgment (3 Dec. 2003).

154   Prosecutor v. Kambanda, Case No. ICTR-97-23-S, Judgment and Sentence (4 September 1998), Paragraph 16; Prosecutor v. Serashugo, Case No. ICTR-98-39-S, Sentence (2 February 1999), Paragraph 15.

155   For an analysis of some case studies (e.g. people's tribunal in Japan, exile in Nigeria, prosecution in Darfur) outside the scope of this chapter that reflect the breadth of problems and controversies involved in choosing among various transitional justice options, see: Zachary D. Kaufman, "Transitional Justice Delayed Is Not Transitional Justice Denied: Contemporary Confrontation of Japanese Human Experimentation During World War II." *Yale Law & Policy Review.* Volume 26, Issue 2 (Spring 2008), 645-59; Zachary D. Kaufman, "Sudan, the United States, and the International Criminal Court: A Tense Triumvirate in Transitional Justice for Darfur" in Ralph Henham and Paul Behrens (eds), *The Criminal Law of Genocide: International, Comparative and Contextual Aspects* (Ashgate, 2007), 49-60; Zachary D. Kaufman, "Justice in Jeopardy: Accountability for the Darfur Atrocities", *Criminal Law Forum.* Volume 16, Issue 4 (April 2006), 343-60; Zachary D. Kaufman, "The Future of Transitional Justice." *St. Antony's International Review* (University of Oxford Journal of International Relations). Volume 1, Number 1 (March 2005), 58-81.

13

THE CONTRIBUTION OF THE UNITED NATIONS INTERNATIONAL CRIMINAL TRIBUNAL FOR RWANDA TO THE DEVELOPMENT OF INTERNATIONAL CRIMINAL LAW

Hassan Bubacar Jallow

Introduction

The twentieth century distinguished itself not only for its great advances in science and human development, but also for being the bloodiest in recorded history. The trail from Armenia to Rwanda is littered with the shattered corpses of the victims of senseless conflict, owing in large measure to a culture of impunity. In its final decade, however, there was a watershed: the advent of the first truly international effort to deal with gross outrages to human life and dignity. Freed at last from the paralysis of the Cold War, the United Nations Security Council (UNSC) presided over the renaissance of international criminal justice in the establishment of two *ad hoc* tribunals: the United Nations International Criminal Tribunal for the Former Yugoslavia (ICTY) in 1993, and the United Nations International Criminal Tribunal for Rwanda (ICTR) in 1994.

The purpose of these Tribunals was to prosecute those responsible for genocide, crimes against humanity and war crimes in the former Yugoslavia and Rwanda. Their creation heralded a new era in supranational justice—for here, judicial sanction was to be applied not by victors, as in Nuremberg and Tokyo after the Second World War, but by the collective conscience of humanity, under the aegis of the United Nations. Rendering justice in conflict and post-conflict societies was now a legitimate international concern in the nascent but evolving global legal order and was subsequently institutionalised in the Rome Statute, which established the International Criminal Court (ICC), the world's first permanent tribunal mandated to address atrocities.

This chapter examines the contribution of the ICTR to the development of international criminal law, an achievement that even the ICTR's critics, such as Ngoga writing in chapter 16, acknowledge. The first part looks briefly at the establishment of the Tribunal, which Kaufman explores in greater detail in the previous chapter, and the ICTR's mission. The second examines the contribution of the ICTR to the evolving jurisprudence of international criminal law through its landmark decisions, and suggests that the ICTR has significantly broadened the scope for future international prosecutions of suspected atrocity perpetrators.

The establishment of the ICTR and its mission

Recognising that serious violations of international humanitarian law had been committed in Rwanda, the UNSC, acting pursuant to Chapter VII of the UN Charter, established the ICTR to prosecute persons responsible for genocide and other serious violations of international humanitarian law that occurred in Rwanda in 1994. In Resolution 955 of 8 November 1994, the UNSC expressed its determination to "put an end to such crimes", convinced that such prosecutions would serve the ends of justice and "contribute to the process of national reconciliation and to the restoration and maintenance of peace."[1]

The normative basis for UNSC involvement in establishing the ICTR, therefore, was Chapter VII of the UN Charter, and the four pillars of the global legal order—International Human Rights Law, International Humanitarian Law, International Criminal Law and International Refugee Law.[2] Furthermore, the UNSC's involvement was predicated on an understanding that justice, as a function of the restoration of the rule of law in a post-conflict society, was a *sine qua non* for the consolidation and maintenance of a peace that could not be achieved without judicially addressing the grievances arising from the genocide, through legitimate structures for dispute settlement with due process. Yet Rwanda had been devastated by genocide and was without the means or the institutional capacity to bring the perpetrators to justice without external intervention.

The ICTR was never expected to pursue these ends single-handedly; the UNSC resolution called for "international cooperation" to strengthen the Rwandan judicial system, so that it could process the large number of genocide cases with which it had to contend. As Schabas observes in chapter 11, the establishment of the ICTR must therefore be seen as just one of a broader range of mechanisms and processes associated with an agenda for post-conflict

---

1   UN Document S/RES/955, (8 November 1994).

2   UN Document S/2004/616, *The Rule of Law and Transitional Justice in Conflict and Post-conflict Societies*, Report of the Secretary General to the Security Council (3 August 2004).

transitional justice in Rwanda, which seeks to ensure accountability, to achieve reconciliation, and to secure a lasting peace.

In the Rwandan context, a peculiar hybrid exists to seek redress for crimes stemming from the genocide and comprises:

- international prosecutions at the ICTR;
- national prosecutions before Rwanda's domestic courts;
- prosecutions before community courts known as *gacaca*, derived in part from traditional Rwandan conflict resolution mechanisms;
- education and coordination of unity programmes through a National Unity and Reconciliation Commission.

It is beyond the remit of this chapter to discuss the last three components; it will instead focus on prosecutions at the ICTR.

A discussion of prosecutions at the ICTR requires a brief consideration of the dual objectives of its mission as highlighted by the wording of UNSC Resolution 955—first, accountability and deterrence and, second, reconciliation and peace. The mission of the Tribunal to render retributive justice through prosecutions is informed by an understanding that criminal trials can achieve several objectives in a transitional society. While the ICTR Statute does not provide for reparations, the trial process is, in itself, an important means of promoting peace and reconciliation in Rwanda, providing catharsis to survivors. Trials help to establish an official historical record, individualise criminal responsibility rather than ascribing group guilt, officially acknowledge the victims' suffering, and incapacitate extremist elements.[3]

The nature of a judicial forum in which victims and survivors testify adds gravitas to witness narratives: not only will the suffering of the victims be heard and acknowledged, but their testimony in a court of law assists in the compilation of an official record of who did what and why, thereby curbing denials and false revisionism, which denigrate the worth of the survivors and are inimical to a lasting peace in a fractured society. By affording victims this opportunity, the ICTR, according to François-Xavier Nsanzuwera, a legal officer in the ICTR's appeals section, former prosecutor in Rwanda and former Secretary General of the *Fédération Internationale des Ligues des Droits de l'Homme*, "rendered human dignity back to the survivors of the genocide."[4] No longer faceless nor nameless, survivors testifying as witnesses before the ICTR are reminded that they are not objects, but individual human beings whose hardships are deserving of formal and official recognition. The act of giving testimony offers solace

---

3   R. J. Goldstone, "Reconstructing Peace in Fragmented Societies", in *Facing Ethnic Conflicts,* (ZEF Bonn: Centre for Development Research, October 2000) and UN Document S/2004/616.

4   F.-X. Nsanzuwera, "The ICTR Contribution to National Reconciliation", *Journal of International Criminal Justice*, 3 (2005), 944-49.

and relief from a silence that only perpetuates fear and suspicion. Witness JJ,[5] a Tutsi rape victim who testified in the trial of the former Taba mayor, Jean-Paul Akayesu, articulated this sentiment when asked to describe her experience in court. "When I saw Akayesu with my eyes, I was afraid," she said. "But at the same time, I had something heavy on my heart. After I testified, it went away."[6] It is through the act of testifying that many victim witnesses attain a sense of inner peace.

The official acknowledgement of victims' plight and the public exposure of the criminality of the perpetrators not only lay a foundation for healing on the part of the victims but also avoids ascribing guilt to the community or group from which the perpetrators come, and thereby contributes to ending the cycle of violence between antagonistic groups.[7] Prosecutions, by relieving victims of the need to take justice into their own hands—which often becomes an imperative when there is a perception that nothing has been done to make perpetrators pay for their crimes—therefore lend gravity and strength to the reconciliation process.[8] In the words of Alexis Rusagara, former advocacy officer for the Rwandan National Unity and Reconciliation Commission: "In post-genocide Rwanda, justice is the key to reconciliation. We believe true reconciliation should be based on justice."[9]

Similarly, the public exposure of the criminality of military and civilian leaders through evidence adduced at trial not only brings to account those arrested and prosecuted but incapacitates those fleeing the law, thereby excluding extremist tendencies from the national transitional process. International criminal tribunals also serve as models of legal norms and standards and thereby lay the foundation for restoration of the rule of law in a post-conflict society. Promotion of the rule of law is an additional and necessary precondition for successful reconciliation in a society struggling with its genocidal past. By championing the rights of the accused to a public, fair and timely trial, the ICTR sets a positive example in Rwanda and elsewhere, regarding the realisation of basic and universal human rights. Similarly, by adhering to fair trial standards, international criminal tribunals restore the integrity of, and trust in, the law and its

---

5   ICTR witnesses are given pseudonyms to protect their identities.

6   D. Eviatar, "Judging the Tribunals", *The Nation*, (May 2002), http://www.thenation. com/doc/20020527/eviatar .

7   R. Goldstone, "Reconstructed Peace in Fragmented Societies".

8   Minow argues that although vengeful acts promise a degree of relief in theory, they often fail to meet expectations, and instead convert a victim into a guilty perpetrator. M. Minow, *Between Vengeance and Forgiveness: Facing History after Genocide and Mass Violence* (Boston: Beacon Press, 1998).

9   G. Mutagoma, "Truth and Reconciliation: The Way forward for Rwanda?" *Internews*, (8 April 2004), http://www.internews.org/regions/africa/justice_reports/justice_20040408b. htm.

enforcing authorities. In so doing, the UN tribunals may be regarded as transformative tools, paving the way for a conflict society to become one based on accountability and the rule of law, thereby fostering national reconciliation, peace, and order.[10]

Holding perpetrators accountable and punishing them for their criminal conduct inevitably has a deterrent effect, and, responding to the concerns of Rwandans like Kayigamba and Ngoga expressed in this book, contributes to replacing a culture of impunity with one of accountability.[11] One structural precondition that appears to have paved the way towards genocide in Rwanda was immunity from prosecution for those who had perpetrated violence against the Tutsi minority in the second half of the 20th century.[12] As a consequence, when orders to eliminate Tutsi were propagated down the rungs of the Rwandan hierarchy after the death of President Juvénal Habyarimana, those who joined in the carnage acted without fear that their crimes would result in punishment.[13]

Expectations of impunity were challenged, however, when my earliest predecessor submitted his first indictments in late 1995 and early 1996. Through the establishment of an international tribunal, whose primary purpose is to prosecute perpetrators of genocide and other serious violations of international

---

10 H. Shinoda, "Peace-building by the Rule of Law: An Examination of Intervention in the Form of International Tribunals", *International Journal of Peace Studies*, 7, 1 (2002), http://www.gmu.edu/academic/ijps/vol7_1/Shinoda.htm.

11 The first Prosecutor of the ICTR, Richard Goldstone, cites two cases within the context of the war in the former Yugoslavia that suggest that fear of prosecution before an International Tribunal has a deterrent effect. The first instance concerns the late Croatian President Franjo Tudjman, who specifically ordered his troops to avoid perpetration of war crimes. Goldstone claims that "these crimes would almost certainly have been worse and more plentiful had the Croat government not publicly taken a 'no war crimes' stance, and [that] the government would not have taken this stance had President Tudjman… not been mindful that a criminal tribunal was watching." In addition, Goldstone cites NATO's 1999 military campaign to halt ethnic cleansing in Kosovo as evidence of leadership evading criminal prosecution by limiting civilian casualties. "For the first time in over 100 years," Goldstone writes, "countries made sustained aerial bombing the centerpiece of their war strategy *without* specifically targeting civilians." R. Goldstone, *The Development of International Criminal Justice*, Rohaytyn Center for International Affairs, Middlebury College (2005), http://www.middlebury.edu/NR/rdonlyres/40DCB816-8656-4386-82B2-986AB6F94B6A/0/ GoldstonePaper.pdf.

12 In November 1959, Hutu targeting of Tutsi officials and their families resulted in the deaths and displacement of thousands. Widespread killings were also perpetrated against the Tutsi in December 1963, in 1967 and in 1972. The years 1991 and 1992 were additionally characterised by a series of Tutsi massacres bearing the hallmark of state inspired violence. See generally A. Des Forges, *Leave None to Tell the Story: Genocide in Rwanda* (New York: Human Rights Watch, 1999) G. Prunier, *The Rwanda Crisis: History of a Genocide* (New York: Columbia University Press, 1995).

13 P. J. Drew, *Dealing with Mass Atrocities and Ethnic Violence: Can Alternative Forms of Justice be Effective? A Case Study of Rwanda* (2005), http://www.cfcj-fcjc.org/full-text/rwanda.htm.

humanitarian law in Rwanda, the UNSC was sending an important message: the international community was not only aware of the violence committed in Rwanda and neighbouring states, but willing to take action and hold those responsible to account. Although it is impossible to quantify the anti-Tutsi violence that would have happened had impunity continued, there is evidence that the efforts of the ICTR contributed to ending the violence perpetrated directly after the genocide. According to Nsanzuwera, the violence in the refugee camps of eastern Zaire (now the Democratic Republic of Congo) subsided as a consequence of the indictment and arrest of principal *génocidaires* by the ICTR, thereby paralysing the genocidal movement.[14] To date, the ICTR has completed the trials of 35 high-level accused, securing 29 convictions for genocide, crimes against humanity and war crimes, while cases against 29 others are in progress. Seven accused are in custody awaiting trial, while 13 accused are on the run from the law.[15]

Notwithstanding the singularly punitive objective expressed in the mandate of the Tribunal, the ICTR acknowledges that retributive justice alone is no panacea for post genocide Rwanda, and can only complement and supplement further measures aimed at securing restorative or socio-economic justice as a basis for lasting peace and national healing.[16] It was from the Registry of the ICTR, for example, that the idea of a court-administered trust fund was born. Monies from such a fund were to be made available for financial support for the victims, as well as medical and psychological care and legal assistance.[17] To achieve similar ends, the ICTR Registry also issued the *Note on a Victim-Oriented Approach*, "urging [a] restorative approach to victims and specifically... that victims should receive the necessary material, medical, psychological and social assistance through governmental and voluntary means."[18]

---

14   F.-X. Nsanzuwera, "The ICTR Contribution to National Reconciliation," 944-49.

15   "Report on the completion strategy of the International Criminal Tribunal for Rwanda," Letter from the President of the International Criminal Tribunal for Rwanda to the President of the United Nations Security Council as of 1 May 2008, http://www.ictr.org/default.htm.

16   See generally W. Lambourne, "Post-Conflict Peacebuilding: Meeting Human Needs for Justice and Reconciliation", *Peace, Conflict and Development,* 4 (April 2004); R. Goldstone, "Reconstructing Peace in Fragmented Societies."

17   Following the precedent set by the ICTR, the ICC is to establish a Trust Fund—financed by individual perpetrators as well as through voluntary government contributions—for the compensatory benefit of victims and their families: Roger S. Clark and David Tolbert, "Toward an International Criminal Court", in Y. Danieli, E. Stamatopoulou and C. J. Dias (eds), *The Universal Declaration of Human Rights: Fifty Years and Beyond* (Amityville, NY: Baywood Publishing Company, 1999), 99-114.

18   I. Melup, "The United Nations Declaration of Basic Principles of Justice and Victims of Crime and Abuse of Power" in Y. Danieli, E. Stamatopoulou and C. J. Dias (eds), *The Universal Declaration of Human Rights: Fifty Years and Beyond* (Amityville, NY: Bay-

The former ICTR President Judge Navenathem Pillay expressed a similar sentiment in her speech to the UN General Assembly in November 2000, in which she addressed the issue of reparations for victims. Judge Pillay "reiterated her concern about compensation for victims and more specifically its indispensable contribution to the process of national reconciliation and the restoration and maintenance of peace."[19] That same year, the former ICTR Registrar Agwu Okali initiated an assistance programme for victim witnesses, under which the ICTR would award grant money to Rwandan NGOs to help legal and psychological assistance programming, as well as the administration of housing construction projects.[20]

Regrettably, the ICTR is limited both by resources and by mandate so that reparatory justice remains principally outside its jurisdiction and capabilities. A December 2001 statement from UN Headquarters in New York, written in response to the Registrar's initiatives, is instructive. The report reads, "The task of the ICTR is, in the first place, the pursuit and punishment of perpetrators of international crimes. The ICTR's mandate does not allow for social assistance programs."[21]

Prosecutorial discretion. The ICTR has been mindful of its mission in the indictment and prosecution of the principal perpetrators of the genocide, as reflected in its policy and practice of prosecuting those who bear the gravest responsibility for crimes. The exercise of prosecutorial discretion in the selection and prioritisation of targets for prosecution has taken into account, in addition to the traditional legal considerations, such factors as the dual objectives of its establishment (outlined above), the nature of the crimes and the prominence of perpetrators in the context of concurrent jurisdiction.[22]

The nature of crimes during the genocide, particularly the extent to which these crimes were heavily orchestrated by the state, shapes the ICTR's policy concerning which suspects to prosecute. The Rwandan genocide is unparalleled in recent human history, both in its intensity and its depravity. Over 100 days in the spring of 1994, close to one million people were ruthlessly butchered because of their birth or their political views. In a country of approximately eight million inhabitants at the time, that translates to over 10 per cent of the population, or about 10,000 murders a day. The methods used were rudimentary—there were no gas chambers, nor other scientific means of mass execution and

---

wood Publishing Company, 1999), 53-66.

19   H. Rombouts, *Victim Organisations and the Politics of Reparation: A Case Study on Rwanda* (Oxford: Intersentia, 2004).

20   Ibid.

21   Ibid.

22   For a more detailed discussion see H.B. Jallow, "Prosecutorial Discretion and International Criminal Justice", *Journal of International Criminal Justice*, 3, 1 (2005), 145-61.

disposal. Victims were brutally killed with gardening implements (such as hoes, axes and machetes) and traditional weapons (such as spears and clubs), and left to rot in open fields to the prey of dogs and vultures, or thrown into rivers and cesspits. Perpetrators used guns and grenades sparingly, as the civil war preceding the genocide, and then an arms embargo, drastically limited supply of this heavier materiel. Therefore, firearms were often only used to stun and disable victims, before marauding gangs of extremist militia hacked them to death. This pattern was consistent throughout the country.[23]

Today, it is tempting for a distant observer or revisionist to argue that this carnage was a "spontaneous combustion" triggered by the assassination of the Hutu President, Juvénal Habyarimana, on 6 April 1994. To the contrary, investigations by reputable NGOs, human rights activists, journalists, scholars and the UN during, and in the immediate aftermath of, the genocide point to a deliberate, well-conceived and meticulously executed criminal campaign to blot an entire ethnic group out of existence.[24] Subsequent investigations by the ICTR Office of the Prosecutor (OTP), assisted by expert opinion, confirmed that what had occurred in Rwanda in 1994 was indeed a genocide, contrived at the highest levels of state, and reliant for its efficient execution on the military, media, local government authorities, extremist party militia, businessmen and finally, the local peasantry, manipulated by hate ideologues to kill their erstwhile neighbours.[25]

---

23   See generally Des Forges, *Leave None to Tell the Story* (New York: Human Rights Watch, 1999).

24   See e.g. Des Forges, *Leave None to Tell the Story* (New York: Human Rights Watch, 1999); Prunier, *The Rwanda Crisis 1959-1994: History of a Genocide* (1995); L. Melvern, *Conspiracy to Murder: The Rwandan Genocide* (London: Verso, 2004); Samantha Power, *"A Problem from Hell:" America and the Age of Genocide* (New York: Basic Books, 2002); A. Destexhe, *Rwanda and Genocide in the Twentieth Century* (New York: New York University Press, 1995); A. J. Kuperman, *The Limits of Humanitarian Intervention: Genocide in Rwanda* (Washington DC: Brookings Institutution Press, 2001); R. Dallaire, *Shake Hands with the Devil: The Failure of Humanity in Rwanda* (Toronto: Random House Canada, 2004); P. Gourevitch, *We Wish to Inform You That Tomorrow We Will Be Killed With Our Families* (New York: Picador, 1999); International Panel of Eminent Personalities, *Special Report: Rwanda: The Preventable Genocide* (Organization of African Unity, July 2000); United Nations Security Council, *Report of the Independent Inquiry into the actions of the United Nations during the 1994 Genocide in Rwanda* (United Nations, December 1999); Report of the Special Representative of the Commission on Human Rights on the Situation of Human Rights in Rwanda. A/52/522; General Assembly Resolution on the Situation of Human Rights In Rwanda, A/RES/49/206; General Assembly Resolution on the Situation of Human Rights in Rwanda, A/RES/54/188.

25   See e.g. *Akayesu* Trial Judgement, para 126; *Kayishema & Ruzindana* Trial Judgement, para 291; *Musema* Trial Judgement, para 316; *Kayishema & Ruzindana* Appeal Judgement, para 143; *Semanza* Trial Judgement, para 424. Indeed, the ICTR Appeals Chamber recently took judicial notice of the Rwandan genocide stating, *inter alia*, that "There is no reasonable basis for anyone to dispute that, during 1994, there was a campaign of

In short, the crimes of the Rwandan genocide were neither isolated nor spontaneous but were committed in concert as part of a broader criminal enterprise, whose objective was the extermination of the Tutsi and any form of political opposition. Given the number of potential perpetrators, the ICTR focused on targeting the leadership without whose evil architecture and encouragement these egregious crimes would probably never have been committed. In many cases, these individuals had found safe haven abroad, and were comfortably beyond the reach of Rwandan judicial authorities.

Another justification for targeting the genocidal leadership was the fiduciary duty they owed to their victims and the international community, a breach of which warranted rigorous international condemnation. An analysis of the 90 indicted, 77 of whom have been arrested by the Tribunal, indicates a spread across various levels of leadership: the central government, military, local government, business, the clergy, the media, intelligentsia, corporate executives and political party operatives of established notoriety [26] In addition to adopting this thematic approach, the ICTR has sought to prosecute suspects according to the location of their alleged crimes, ensuring that key perpetrators in all regions were brought to account. This equitable geographic spread was particularly necessary because the crimes were committed throughout Rwanda, which rendered it imperative, in the interests of justice, to reach all the communities involved in equal measure. The conclusions reached, and the theory adopted by the OTP, about the conception and execution of the genocide were confirmed by the confession and guilty plea of Jean Kambanda, Prime Minister of the Interim Government during the genocide, who was convicted and sentenced to life for genocide, extermination and murder as crimes against humanity, as discussed in further detail below.[27]

---

mass killing intended to destroy, in whole or at least in very large part, Rwanda's Tutsi population... That campaign was, to a terrible degree, successful; although exact numbers may never be known, the great majority of Tutsi were murdered, and many others were raped or otherwise harmed. These basic facts were broadly known even at the time of the Tribunal's establishment; indeed, reports indicating that genocide occurred in Rwanda were a key impetus for its establishment, as reflected in the Security Council resolution establishing it and even the name of the Tribunal." *Prosecutor v Karemera et al, Decision on Prosecutor's Interlocutory Appeal of Decision on Judicial Notice*, 16 June 2006, para 35.

26   See Status of Detainees, ICTR website, http://www.ictr.org/default.htm.

27   *Prosecutor v Kambanda; Case No. ICTR 97-2-T.* See ICTR Judgement of 4 September 1998. Among the several acknowledgments made by Kambanda in his plea of guilt is that he, together with other members of his government and the military, actively supported, facilitated and instigated the killing of Tutsi through the use of the media, the distribution of weapons to the *Interahamwe* militia, the setting up of roadblocks for purposes of identifying the Tutsi and generally "making public engagements in the name of the government, he addressed public meetings, and the media, at various places in Rwanda directly and publicly inciting the population to commit acts of violence against Tutsi and

The contribution of the ICTR to international criminal law

Despite the limitations to its mandate, and the varied challenges of its execution, the ICTR has purposefully interpreted the law, thereby broadening the scope for future international prosecutions. By taking a contextual approach to the interpretation of historical treaties and adapting international humanitarian law to contemporary realities, the ICTR has, through its groundbreaking judgements, provided clarity and definition to the concept of genocide, acknowledged the importance of sexual violence as a form of destruction, prosecuted the media as a weapon of hatred, clarified the application of the Geneva Conventions to civilian perpetrators and shown that sovereign immunity has no place in the modern world.

Defining genocide. On 2 September 1998, the ICTR delivered the world's first ever judgement against an individual accused of genocide before an international court. The significance of this should not be underestimated. For while to a layperson the term "genocide" probably still means killing on a massive scale, the term had never been interpreted legally. With the term clearly defined, the international community is better armed to deal with future violations of the Genocide Convention more quickly and, it is hoped, with greater success than hitherto.

This ground-breaking judgement was delivered in the case of *Akayesu*. In reaching its conclusions, the ICTR Trial Chamber had to consider whether the massacres that took place in Rwanda between April and July 1994 could constitute "genocide" and whether Akayesu as an individual was guilty of this crime—a first in an international court. Although the Genocide Convention of 1948 "created" the crime, before 1997 no one had come before a trial chamber charged with such an offence, and there was much ambiguity as to what a prosecutor would be required to prove in such a case.

In reaching its judgement, the Tribunal had to reconcile the limited wording of the Genocide Convention with the realities on the ground. The Convention sought to protect "national, ethnic, racial or religious" groups from deliberate destruction, but the Tutsi victims of massacres in Rwanda in 1994 could not so easily be defined. For the Tutsi were not a *nation*, nor were they, by this time, an *ethnic* group, having no distinct cultural or social identity. They could not be defined as a *racial* group either, since generations of intermarriage had wiped out any physical distinction between them and the Hutu. Equally, the Tutsi in pre-1994 Rwanda were largely Christian, as were the Hutu, and could not therefore be defined as a distinct *religious* group either. While lawyer and layperson alike described the situation as one of genocide, if the Tutsi could not

---

moderate Hutu."

be fit into one of the types of groups defined by the Genocide Convention, the absurd conclusion might be drawn that, legally, no genocide had occurred in Rwanda, and therefore no one could be held accountable for such a crime.

The Trial Chamber had to question, therefore, whether "it would be impossible to punish the physical destruction of a group... if the said group, although stable, and membership is by birth, does not meet the definition of any one of the four groups expressly protected by the Genocide Convention."[28] The Chamber concluded that too narrow a reading of the Convention went against its purpose and intention, which was to ensure the protection of *any* "stable and permanent group."[29] Thus, the ICTR overcame this potentially shattering difficulty by taking an expansive approach to the definition of the victims of genocide, and thereby widened the possibility of future prosecutions. But what of the perpetrators, and the means of perpetration? Was it really necessary to destroy a "stable and permanent group" for genocide to have occurred? Again, the Trial Chamber looked at the reality of the situation in Rwanda, where it found that there was a determined intention to destroy the Tutsi, whether or not such destruction actually took place. It concluded that all that was necessary for conviction was the so-called "special intent" of the accused to destroy, in whole or in part, a particular group, and proof that at least one person had been killed or dealt serious bodily harm in pursuit of this. As a result of this decision, it is now theoretically possible for a successful prosecution of genocide to take place where there is only one victim.

The importance of this jurisprudence has already been shown by its use in the ICTY, where, before *Akayesu*, "genocide" had not been among the charges. As a result of the judgement of 2 September 1998, the ICTY looked afresh at what had occurred within its jurisdiction, and in 2001 convicted Radislav Krstic of genocide, concluding that the intent to kill all the Bosnian Muslim men of military age in Srebrenica constituted an intent to destroy in part the Bosnian Muslim group and therefore qualified as an act of genocide.[30] The ICTR has, in clearly defining genocide, opened the door to a greater number of prosecutions for this horrendous crime, and has, through its jurisprudence, signalled to the world that the intended destruction, whether it occurs or not, of a particular stable and permanent group, will not be tolerated.

Acknowledging that sexual violence is a form of genocide. The *Akayesu* judgement generated another hugely significant development in international humanitarian law: conviction for rape as a crime against humanity and as genocide. No individual had been convicted of rape specifically under the rubric of

---

28   *The Prosecutor v. Akayesu*, ICTR-96-4-T, 2 September 1998, para. 516.

29   Ibid.

30   *The Prosecutor v Radislav Krstic*, IT-98-33, para. 598.

crimes against humanity by an international court, and, as discussed, no one had been convicted of genocide at all in such a forum. Indeed, historically, although it was well established that rape or other acts of sexual violence were frequently part of a layperson's concept of "genocide", "crimes against humanity" or "war crimes", the perceived difficulty in proving sexual violence meant that, where it was mentioned, it was classified under the umbrella of inhumane treatment, complicating attempts by advocates of the human rights of women (in particular) to bring such cases before international tribunals.

The ICTR has shown that sexual violence is to be treated seriously as an international crime, finding that it can be an act of genocide in itself. The Trial Chamber in *Akayesu* gave the first-ever definition of rape in international criminal law. Interestingly, when the trial began, neither rape nor any act of sexual violence was alleged against the accused in the indictment. Yet following evidence that Akayesu, by his presence, demeanour, and utterances, had encouraged sexual violence and mutilation of Tutsi women, the Trial Chamber allowed the indictment to be amended, and subsequently found Akayesu criminally responsible for these acts, including rape—and found that rape and sexual violence were within the scope of causing "serious bodily or mental harm" as a means of committing genocide. In its judgement, the ICTR recognised that sexual crimes are used intentionally during conflicts to control and devastate the enemy, and that in Rwanda they were part of a deliberate strategy to destroy the Tutsi and their supporters. Such crimes were perpetrated as "an integral part of the process of destruction".[31]

Akayesu was additionally convicted of rape as a crime against humanity *in itself*, rather than under the umbrella of "cruel and inhumane acts"—making rape a substantive crime in its own right for the first time in international law. Prior to the judgement, rape had not even been defined in international law. The ICTR took a groundbreaking liberal approach to this task, finding that rape was an act of aggression which "cannot be captured in a mechanical description of objects and body parts".[32] The definition provided was: "a physical invasion of a sexual nature, committed on a person under circumstances which are coercive"[33]—which goes far beyond the definitions widely used in national jurisdictions that focus on the question of consent and penetration. The definition of sexual violence provided by this judgement is equally broad: it need not even involve physical contact. Indeed, sexual violence was held to have occurred when a student was forced to perform gymnastics in the nude.[34]

---

31   *The Prosecutor v Akayesu*, ICTR-96-4, 2 September 1998, para. 731.

32   Ibid., para. 687.

33   Ibid., para. 688.

34   Ibid., para. 688.

The significance of the convictions for sexual violence in *Akayesu* is monumental, for while women's rights campaigners have long argued for the inclusion of sexual crimes in international humanitarian prosecutions, this precedent has vastly improved the likelihood of investigation and prosecution of rape and other sexual violence as international crimes. One interesting demonstration of this improved climate for the prosecution of sexual crimes is the case of Pauline Nyiramasuhuko, the Minister of Women and Family Affairs of Rwanda in 1994; her indictment was amended in 1999 to include the charge of rape as a crime against humanity.[35] The trial is still in progress but whether or not she is convicted, it is yet another example of the pioneering work of the ICTR that a woman has been charged with rape.

Acknowledging the media's role in genocide. In this modern age of mass communication, where rapid technological advances make it ever easier to disseminate opinion, the convictions of the three accused in what is commonly known as the *Media* trial were hugely significant. Not since the celebrated case of Julius Streicher by the Nuremberg Tribunal had a journalist been convicted in an international court, and no one had ever been tried on the basis of their editorial policy for incitement to genocide.[36] The judgement not only established potentially far-reaching law, which clarifies the boundary between freedom of expression and freedom from discrimination, but it also provided some answers to the question of what causes a genocide, and will thereby hopefully contribute to the future prevention of such atrocities.

The *Media* judgement was delivered on 3 December 2003. It provided the first thorough analysis of "direct and public incitement to genocide," which was proscribed in the Genocide Convention. Over 50 years earlier, when the Convention was drafted, the inclusion of *incitement* to genocide had caused considerable debate, because of its perceived threat to freedom of speech. Today, the conflict between this democratic principle and the prevention of so-called "hate crimes" is increasingly at the forefront of national legislative debate. The importance of the ICTR judgement in the *Media* trial is that it has drawn afresh the line at which free speech must stop, thus removing any ambiguity regarding the role of the media in humanitarian crimes. In explicitly rejecting the American model for interpreting incitement,[37] the Tribunal acknowledged that the application of a democratic principle such as freedom of expression must vary from state to state—in other words, what works in a politically "free" country

---

35   *The Prosecutor v. Nyiramasuhuko*, Amended Indictment, ICTR-97-21-I, 10 August 1999, Count 7, 42.

36   Jean Paul Akayesu had been convicted of direct and public incitement to genocide on the basis of his speeches.

37   Within the American model of interpreting incitement, free expression, free speech, and maximum latitude are to be the norm.

like the United States cannot be said to work in countries where, for example, a government has vastly disproportionate power and means for disseminating information.

The main organs of incitement in the *Media* case were *Radio Télévision Libre des Mille Collines* (RTLM) and the *Kangura* newspaper. While acknowledging the importance of protecting political expression—particularly the expression of opposition views and criticism of government—the ICTR found that these media were not used simply to report or to freely express opinion. Rather, by consistently identifying the Tutsi as "the enemy", identifying particular Tutsi, and facilitating the logistical execution of the genocide by giving their exact location, and further combining stereotyping with denigration, public broadcasting by these two organs clearly amounted to incitement. As the Trial Chamber said of one of the accused, "without a firearm, machete or any physical weapon, he caused the deaths of thousands of innocent civilians."[38]

The principles followed in the *Media* case came from *Akayesu*, where the limit to freedom of expression was held to lie in the intention of the "orator". Incitement might take place through, *inter alia*, public speaking, shouting or threats, or through the public display or dissemination of written or printed material, but the significant element that renders it genocidal is that the accused must himself or herself intend to commit genocide. In determining whether or not this intent was held by the accused, the Tribunal considered not only the individual's actions and words, but the editorial policy of the media he or she controlled. The Tribunal concluded that, for example, the cover of one edition of *Kangura* was a "graphic impression of genocidal intent", showing as it did a machete alongside the question: "What weapons shall we use to conquer the *Inyenzi* once and for all?"[39] In the light of this kind of material, there was little difficulty in concluding that genocidal intent existed.

In reaching its judgement, the Tribunal had to resolve the question of what amounted to "direct" incitement. It rejected the argument that "direct" meant, as it does in the American legal system, provoking an immediate response, but went so far as to say that a newspaper published several years before the genocide could constitute direct incitement. This is particularly significant in view of the absence of a requirement to prove any resultant act of genocide—indeed, the Tribunal heard no evidence from any individual listener or reader that they had been provoked into killing another as a result of what they heard or read.

In delivering the *Akayesu* and *Media* judgements, the ICTR has narrowed the parameters of freedom of expression, and thereby broadened the scope for future prosecutions, highlighting the accountability of those who use mass

---

38   *The Prosecutor v. Nahimana, Barayagwiza & Ngeze,* ICTR-99-52-T, 3 December 2003, para. 1099.

39   Ibid., para. 962.

media as a tool for dangerous propaganda. The trial of Simon Bikindi, which began on 2 October 2006, and has been completed and is awaiting judgement, will no doubt provoke debate about the freedom of artists: Bikindi was the most famous pop singer in Rwanda at the time of the genocide, whose virulently anti-Tutsi music warranted the charges against him. The *Media* judgement has paved the way for his conviction because it is clear now how political speeches, articles, and songs can be distinguished from incitement to genocide. If Bikindi intended to incite others to commit genocide by his singing, then he committed a crime.

War crimes and civilian perpetrators. In convicting Georges Rutaganda[40] and Laurent Semanza[41] of war crimes, the ICTR has once again blazed a trail in international criminal law. Hitherto it had been generally assumed that the laws of war, as enunciated in the Geneva Conventions of 1949, applied to members of the armed forces and government agents alone,[42] since Article 3 Common to the Geneva Conventions binds only a "party to the conflict". But the situation in Rwanda was ambiguous. Many civilians in positions of authority had exercised quasi-military functions during the genocide, while many atrocities were committed under the aegis of war.

The question of whether a civilian could be liable for breaches of the Conventions was first raised in *Akayesu*. Akayesu was a mayor, not a soldier. The Trial Chamber, when considering the allegations of war crimes against him, held that for a civilian to be convicted, the Prosecutor must prove that he was in

---

40   Georges Rutaganda held the position of second vice-president of the *Movement Républicain National et Démocratique* (MRND) party's youth wing, the *Interahamwe*. Further, he was one of three shareholders in the radio station RTLM, established to articulate the extremist Hutu message. He was convicted by the Trial Chamber of genocide, crimes against humanity, extermination and crimes against humanity, and murder, and sentenced to life in prison.

41   Laurent Semanza served as *bourgmestre* of Bicumbi *commune* for 20 years until 1993 and was subsequently selected to represent the MRND in the National Assembly envisioned by the Arusha Accords. The Trial Chamber sentenced him to 25 years' imprisonment, finding him guilty of complicity in genocide, aiding and abetting the crime against humanity of extermination, and instigating the crimes against humanity of rape, torture, and murder for his participation in attacks committed in Bicumbi and Gikoro *communes* in April 1994, including massacres at Musha Church and Mwulire Hill.

42   There appears to have been an erroneous assumption that, in addition to members of the armed forces, only civilians legitimately mandated to support the war effort could be held liable for war crimes, a position taken by the Trial Chamber in *Akayesu*, but clarified on appeal: see *Akayesu* Trial Judgement paras. 630-34; 640-44 and *Akayesu* Appeal Judgement paras. 437-46. In the *Kayishema* Judgement the Trial Chamber, while acknowledging that civilian perpetrators could indeed be held liable for war crimes, nevertheless required them to have a link to the armed forces in the conduct of the hostilities. See *Kayishema* Judgement paras. 616-24.

some way legitimately, or directly, mandated to fulfil or support the war effort. Since this could not be proven, Akayesu was acquitted on this count.

The Prosecutor of the ICTR appealed for clarification on this point, even though any decision in its favour would not alter Akayesu's acquittal on war crimes charges. The Appeals Chamber examined, for the first time in an international forum, the provisions of Article 3 Common to the Geneva Conventions concerning the class of perpetrator. It noted that Article 3 did not clearly identify the persons covered by its provisions, nor did it require the identification of any specific link between the perpetrator and one of the "parties" to the conflict. The Appeals Chamber concluded that the protection of victims was the core notion of Article 3 and necessitated effective, non-discriminatory punishment of persons who violate it.[43] In stating that "international humanitarian law would be lessened and called into question if it were to be admitted that certain persons can be exonerated…under the pretext that they did not belong to a specific category,"[44] the Appeals Chamber of the ICTR has dramatically broadened the scope for the future prosecution of war crimes.

Following the *Akayesu* Appeals Chamber decision, the test for the applicability of Common Article 3 could be summarised as follows: (a) the offence must have been committed within the context of an armed conflict, (b) the victims must have been non-combatants, and (c) there must have been a nexus between the offence and the armed conflict. These elements had been set out in the jurisprudence of the ICTY,[45] but the nexus had never been clearly defined.

Once again, the ICTR led the way. Rutaganda, acquitted of war crimes at first instance, was later convicted by the Appeals Chamber following a detailed analysis of the "nexus" requirement, which resulted in the first clear definition of the term, and effectively lowered the threshold for liability once again, by broadening the range of situations in which such a "nexus" could be proven. The Appeals Chamber held that the "nexus" need not be a causal link between the armed conflict and the commission of the crime, but that the conflict must have played a substantial part in the perpetrator's ability to commit it, the manner in which it was committed, or the purpose for which it was committed. If a relevant crime is committed "under the guise of the armed conflict" the nexus has been shown.[46] The principles established in *Rutaganda* and the *Akayesu* Appeal judgement were followed in the *Semanza* Case, resulting in

---

43   *Akayesu v. The Prosecutor,* ICTR-96-4-A, 1 June 2001, paras. 442-43.

44   Ibid.

45   *The Prosecutor v. Kunarac et al.,* IT-23&23/1.

46   *Rutaganda v Prosecutor,* Judgement, ICTR-96-3-A, 9 February 2004, paras. 569-70.

a war crimes conviction of a civilian who held no public office at the time he committed the offences.[47]

Another important development regarding the prosecution of war crimes is found in the judgement in the *Imanishimwe* case. Samuel Imanishimwe, a Lieutenant and army camp commander in the government's armed forces, was convicted of war crimes even though the place where the crimes were committed was hundreds of miles from the "battlefield". Again, there was held to be a sufficient "nexus" between his crimes and the armed conflict. It is now clear that there is no requirement for proximity between the war crime and the arena of conflict, as long as a "nexus" is established. As with the conviction of a civilian for violations of the Conventions, this decision has broadened the scope for future prosecutions, and shown that in times of war—even civil war—crimes committed by soldier or civilian, if committed under the guise of the war, will not be tolerated.

Challenging sovereign immunity. While the Nuremberg trials following the Second World War appeared to herald a new era, in which heads of government could be held accountable for their actions under international law, there has always been a substantial body of opinion that the Nuremberg Tribunal represented only "victors' justice".[48] Subsequently, the question of whether a head of state can be held personally accountable for breaches of international law remained unanswered. The ICTR has now made it clear that sovereign immunity no longer applies: individuals, even heads of state, can be held responsible, as subjects bound by international legal obligations, for breaches of those obligations.

This significant development in international jurisprudence came about on 4 September 1998, when the former Prime Minister Jean Kambanda was sen-

---

47   *The Prosecutor v Semanza.* It may merit mention here that Fulgence Niyonteze, a civilian mayor in Rwanda at the time of the genocide, was tried and convicted for war crimes committed during the genocide by a Swiss Military Court sitting in Laussane in 1999.

48   V. Morris and M. P. Scharf, *An Insider's Guide To The International Criminal Tribunal For The Former Yugoslavia* (Irvington-on-Hudson, New York: Transnational Publishers Inc., 1994) 332: "A primary criticism of Nuremberg was that it amounted to victors' justice, since the tribunal was composed exclusively of prosecutors and judges from the victorious countries and the defendants were limited to Germans, even though the allied personnel also committed serious violations of humanitarian law during the war." See also A. Cassese, *International Criminal Law* (Oxford, UK: Oxford University Press, 2003) 332 discussing the one-sided nature of the Nuremberg and Tokyo Tribunals. "These sets of experiences were nevertheless one-sided, as everybody knows. They imposed 'victors' justice' over the defeated. The major drawback of the two 'international Tribunals' was that they were composed of judges (respectively, four and eleven) appointed by each of the victor powers; the prosecutors too were appointed by each of those Powers and acted under the instructions of each appointing State... Thus, the view must be shared that the two Tribunals were not independent international courts proper, but judicial bodies acting as organs common to the appointing States."

tenced to life imprisonment, following his guilty pleas to six counts of genocide and extermination and murder as crimes against humanity. Indeed, this was the first time ever that the head of a government has been convicted under an international treaty. The effect of this legal precedent was seen shortly afterwards, when the United Kingdom's House of Lords ruled that General Augusto Pinochet, the former president of Chile, was not immune from prosecution for international crimes.[49] The universal jurisdiction created by the 1949 Geneva Conventions has, since the establishment of the *ad hoc* tribunals, come to be increasingly accepted. It is now a realistic possibility that former dictators will be pursued and prosecuted for crimes committed within their own states. Whereas an ex-dictator could flee his national jurisdiction and be confident that he could escape punishment for his crimes—like Idi Amin of Uganda, who eventually died in exile in Saudi Arabia—others, like Chad's former president, Hissène Habré, now in Senegal, or Ethiopia's former leader, Mariam Mengistu, who currently resides in Zimbabwe, are not comfortable in exile, as there are international arrest warrants for them for violations of international criminal law. It remains to be seen whether the implications of this remarkable development in international law will result in many further prosecutions, but the subsequent indictment of Slobodan Milošević at the ICTY and Charles Taylor at the Special Court for Sierra Leone suggest that, in principle at least, no head of state can now escape accountability for crimes against humanity.

Conclusion

Established in the shadow of the ICTY, the ICTR has significantly contributed to the evolving international criminal justice regime in several key respects. First, through a clear definition of genocide, its scope as a crime was extended to cover the intended destruction of a particular stable and permanent group, and it was acknowledged that rape and sexual violence could constitute genocide. Second, by recognising the role of the print and electronic media in inciting genocide, the ICTR sounded a warning to the abuse of freedom of expression in the incitement of international crimes. Third, through clarification of the Geneva Conventions' applicability to civilian perpetrators in armed conflict, such civilians can no longer evade the long arm of the law. Fourth, by shattering the myth of sovereign immunity, the ICTR gave impetus to the assertion of universal jurisdiction by states seeking to prosecute former leaders for atrocities

---

49   See Regina v. Bartle and the Commissioner of Police (Appellants) Ex Parte Pinochet (Respondent); Evans and Another and the Commissioner of Police and Others (Appellants) Ex Parte Pinochet (Respondent), Decision of the House of Lords on appeal from a Divisional Court of the Queen's Bench Division (25 Nov. 1998), available at http://www.publications.parliament.uk/pa/ld199899/ldjudmnt /jd981125/pino01.htm.

committed while still in office. Finally, as ICC Prosecutor Luis Moreno Ocampo indicates in his Foreword and Bergsmo and Webb observe in chapter 18, the ICTR, alongside other *ad hoc* tribunals, provided the building blocks upon which the permanent ICC was founded, and will bequeath it a substantial corpus of law, both substantive and procedural, that will guide it in the execution of its challenging mandate.

14

PROSECUTING GENOCIDE IN THE DIGITAL AGE: AN INFORMATION MANAGEMENT PERSPECTIVE

Maria Warren and Alison Cole[1]

Introduction

The practical operation of transitional justice institutions is often overlooked but it is crucial to understanding the potential, limits, and expense of their functioning, as discussed in this volume by President Kagame, Schabas, Jallow and Ngoga. The techniques and technologies that the UN International Criminal Tribunal for Rwanda (ICTR) has developed are central to its efforts to manage the complexity of prosecuting genocide perpetrators. These advances in information management have been invaluable to transitional justice for Rwanda and internationally. Transitional justice is evolving in the digital age, and the experience of the ICTR has contributed substantially to this phenomenon.

This chapter provides insight into how the Information and Evidence Section in the Office of the Prosecutor (OTP) at the ICTR facilitates the work of UN prosecutors in the quest for justice for the victims of the Rwandan genocide. After analysing that Section's mandate, and discussing some of the key practical challenges it has faced in trying to manage evidence related to the genocide, this chapter outlines critical lessons learned for future information management, and the potential for evidence, when effectively gathered, managed, and shared among key stakeholders, to contribute to peace and reconciliation after mass conflict. This chapter argues that the establishment and imposition of information management standards in international war crimes trials and the appropriate use of information technology can lay a foundation

---

1   This chapter precedes developments in the case before the International Criminal Court against Thomas Lubanga.

281

for more effective international prosecutions and for establishing a clearer historical record of crimes committed around the world.

The mandate of the Information and Evidence Section

The mandate of the Information and Evidence Section arises out of Rule 41 of the ICTR's Rules of Procedure and Evidence.[2] At first reading, the rule appears simple and direct:

Rule 41: Preservation of Information

- A. The Prosecutor shall be responsible for the preservation, storage and security of information and physical evidence obtained in the course of his [sic] investigations.

- B. The Prosecutor shall draw up an inventory of all materials seized from the accused, including documents, books, papers, and other objects, and shall serve a copy thereof on the accused. Materials that are of no evidentiary value shall be returned without delay to the accused.

Rule 41 is operationalised by Rule 66 and Rule 68, which oblige the Prosecutor to disclose evidence and information to the Defence. Previous Prosecutors of the ICTR have identified how this disclosure obligation creates certain challenges in the logistics behind information management.[3] This critical obligation of the Prosecutor to disclose information is detailed in Rule 66:

Rule 66: Disclosure of Exculpatory and Other Relevant Material.
Subject to the provisions of Rules 53 and 69;

- A. The Prosecutor shall disclose to the Defence:

    1. Within 30 days of the initial appearance of the accused copies of the supporting material which accompanied the indictment when confirmation was sought as well as all prior statements obtained by the Prosecutor from the accused, and

    2. No later than 60 days before the date set for trial, copies of the statements of all witnesses whom the Prosecutor intends to call to testify at trial; upon good cause shown a Trial Chamber may order that copies of the statements of additional prosecution witnesses be made available to the Defence within a prescribed time.

---

2   See International Criminal Tribunal for Rwanda, "Rules of Procedure and Evidence", adopted on 29 June 1995, as amended on 7 June 2005, http://65.18.216.88/ENGLISH/rules/070605/070605.doc.

3   L. Arbour, "The Status of the International Criminal Tribunals for the Former Yugoslavia and Rwanda: Goals and Results," 3 *Hofstra Law and Policy Symposium* (1999), 37.

- B. At the request of the Defence, the Prosecutor shall, subject to Sub-Rule (C), permit the Defence to inspect any books, documents, photographs and tangible objects in his custody or control, which are material to the preparation of the defence, or are intended for use by the Prosecutor as evidence at trial or were obtained from or belonged to the accused.

Rule 66(A) is self-explanatory and relates to the pre-trial disclosure of information relating to witnesses, and the evidence upon which the Prosecutor has built his *prima facie* case in confirming the Indictment. The content of Rule 66(B), however, is not entirely clear. It is modelled on the US Federal Rules of Criminal Procedure, which state that the Defence can request disclosure of certain evidence it suspects the Prosecution to possess and which is material to the Defence case. The ICTR and the UN International Criminal Tribunal for the Former Yugoslavia (ICTY) share a common Appeals Chamber in order to, *inter alia*, ensure the consistent development of the law in the two *ad hoc* tribunals, including in this matter.

In addition to the foundational requirements of Rule 66, Rule 68 places further obligations on the Prosecutor:

Rule 68: Disclosure of Exculpatory and Other Relevant Material

- A. The Prosecutor shall, as soon as practicable, disclose to the Defence any material, which in the actual knowledge of the Prosecutor may suggest the innocence or mitigate the guilt of the accused or affect the credibility of Prosecution evidence.

- B. Where possible, and with the agreement of the Defence, and without prejudice to paragraph (A), the Prosecutor shall make available to the Defence, in electronic form, collections of relevant material held by the Prosecutor, together with appropriate computer software with which the Defence can search such collections electronically. [...]

- D. The Prosecutor shall apply to the Chamber [...] to be relieved from an obligation under the Rules to disclose information in the possession of the Prosecutor, if its disclosure may prejudice further or ongoing investigations, or for any other reason may be contrary to the public interest or affect the security interests of any State [...]

In interpreting Rule 68, the Appeals Chamber has held that the Prosecutor's obligation under the rule is of special significance.[4] Rule 68 imposes a continuing disclosure obligation, meaning that the Prosecutor must diligently monitor the collection of information by investigators and must inform the Defence, as soon as practicable, of the existence of such exculpatory material through the trial phase, and in the case of convictions, through the appeals stage if one

---

4   *Blaskic* Appeal Judgement, paras 270-303.

is mounted,[5] and also beyond the initial appeal into review proceedings. This is achieved primarily through motions permitted under Rule 115, in which parties can argue for the admission of additional evidence after the closure of trial hearings. These Rule 115 motions often concern evidence found to be in the possession of the Prosecution and alleged by the Defence to fall under Rule 68—that is, exculpatory information that is required to be disclosed prior to and during trial.[6]

For the Defence to avail itself of a remedy for breach of Rule 68, it must not only show that there has been a violation of Rule 68 obligations by the Prosecution, but also that the Defence has suffered material prejudice as a result of the alleged breach.[7] In addition, it has been held in the *Kajelijeli* case[8] of the ICTR that the Defence must first show that the evidence in question was known to the Prosecutor. "Known" in this case was interpreted to mean that the evidence was in the custody, control or possession of the Prosecution. The Defence must also establish a *prima facie* case that the material sought would be exculpatory. Once the above criteria are satisfied, and if it is shown that the Prosecution has failed to comply with its obligations under Rule 68, then the Chamber can apply the appropriate remedy, such as ordering disclosure.

The Appeals Chamber has demonstrated that it takes the Prosecutor's obligations under Rule 68 very seriously. In the *Krstic* case the Appeals Chamber found that delay in compliance with Rule 68 had occurred but that no prejudice was caused; however, it specifically noted that, while the Defence had not shown that the delay by the Prosecution was deliberate, the failure of the Chamber to sanction the Prosecution should not be "mistaken for the Appeals Chamber's acquiescence in questionable conduct by the Prosecution."[9] The Chamber further noted that it "will not tolerate anything short of strict compliance with the disclosure obligations, and considers its discussion of this issue to be sufficient to put the Office of the Prosecutor on notice for its conduct in future proceedings."[10]

The scope and category of material covered under Rule 68 includes "any material, which...may suggest the innocence or mitigate the guilt of the accused or affect the credibility of Prosecution evidence." Such a definition is intended to ensure fairness and equality between litigants, and a proper administration of international criminal justice. The Appeals Chamber has stated that "given

---

5   This is achieved primarily through Rule 115 motions, in which parties can argue for the admission of additional evidence after the closure of trial hearings.

6   See for example, Ibid.

7   *Krstic* Appeal Judgement, para. 153

8   *Kajelijeli* Appeal Judgement, para. 262. See also *Blaskic* Appeal Judgement, para. 268.

9   *Krstic* Appeal Judgement, para. 215

10   Ibid.

the fundamental importance of disclosing exculpatory evidence, however, it would be against the interests of a fair trial to limit the Rule's scope."[11]

The Prosecution is also obliged to disclose exculpatory material arising from other related cases. In the case of the ICTR, as with other war crimes tribunals, aspects of some cases are inter-related.[12] This reality obliges the Prosecutor to monitor the testimony of witnesses in all trials. The Prosecutor is required to disclose material relevant to the impeachment of witnesses, during or after testimony, particularly where the same witnesses testify in different cases. This requirement also applies to closed session testimony that would normally be unavailable to Defence teams from separate trials.

The timing of the disclosure envisaged under Rule 68 is also essential. The Rule envisages disclosure done "as soon as practicable." In the *Blaskic* case, the Appeals Chamber held that the "Prosecution cannot take an inordinate amount of time to disclose exculpatory material."[13] Timely disclosure was also held to be imperative in the determination of compliance in the case of *Krstic*.[14]

Despite the wide scope of the obligation imposed by Rule 68, it is not un-limited. The first constraint, as shown before, is that the alleging party must establish that the material in question is within the possession of the Prosecutor. The Appeals Chamber in *Niyitegeka* stated that "something which is not in the possession of or accessible to the prosecution cannot be subject to disclosure: *nemo tenetur ad impossibile* (no one is bound to impossibility)."[15] Where the Prosecutor is not in possession of any documents, it is not his or her duty, under the Rule, to obtain those documents.[16]

To operationalise Rule 68 more efficiently the Prosecutor has implemented an electronic disclosure suite (EDS). The EDS is a central electronic repository in which the OTP places its documentary evidence in a searchable database, from which the Defence can conduct its own searches. The EDS contains public or redacted versions of more than 34,000 documents. Whereas previously Rule 68 required disclosure of information "known" by the Prosecutor, the amendment requires disclosure of material "in the actual knowledge of the Prosecutor." This amendment may suggest the relaxation of the obligation of the Prosecutor by requiring actual and not imputed knowledge. Various Chambers have offered differing opinions on whether or not by availing itself of material in the EDS the Prosecutor satisfies the obligation under Rule 68

---

11   *Blaskic* Appeal Judgement, para. 265.

12   *Bagosora* Appeals Chamber Decision, 6 October 2005.

13   *Blaskic* Appeal Judgement, para. 275.

14   *Krstic* Appeal Judgement, para. 195.

15   *Niyitegeka* Appeal Judgement, para. 35.

16   *Kajelijeli* Appeal Judgement, paras. 262 and 263.

to disclose.[17] However, the Appeals Chamber has held that the mere deposit of information in a database accessible to the Defence does not relieve the Prosecutor of the obligation to identify exculpatory material under Rule 68. Instead, it was held that "[i]t might be helpful if the Prosecution either separates a special file for Rule 68 material or draws the attention of the Defence to such material in writing and permanently updates the special file or the written notice."[18] This demonstrates that advances in information management tools are still subject to judicial interpretations of the rights and obligations of the parties.

Implementing practical information management in the OTP

In the early days of the ICTR, when the first indictments were prepared, and the OTP dealt with no more than a few folders of documents, compliance with the disclosure obligation as set out in Rules 41, 66 and 68 posed relatively few managerial challenges. But as the ICTR progressed and the mass of information grew, the task became more complex and burdensome. To illustrate: the OTP currently has a collection of over half a million pages of documents, thousands of hours of audio and video tapes, and tens of thousands of transcripts of proceedings, and the numbers continue to expand significantly as additional cases go to trial.[19]

The ICTR is not alone in amassing mountains of information. The Commission of Experts that was the forerunner to the ICTY was the first entity connected with international criminal justice to encounter modern-day information-overload. Over the course of 35 missions to the former Yugoslavia, the Commission produced "65,000 pages of documents, a database cataloguing the information in these documents, over 300 hours of videotape, and 3300 pages of analysis."[20] The ICTY inherited these documents, and by June 2003 the ICTY's OTP held over 4.2 million pages of written material, and over 6,400 video and audiovisual tapes.[21] As trials are scheduled to continue beyond the end of this decade, one can imagine that these numbers will continue to grow significantly.

17   *Bizimungu et al.* Trial Decision, 1 December 2004; *Halilovic* Trial Decision, 27 July 2005 p. 5; *Limaj et al.* Trial Decision, 7 June 2005 para. 21.

18   *Karemera et al.* Appeals Chamber Decision on EDS, 30 June 2006, para. 15.

19   ICTR OTP Information Management Report, notes of file with Maria Warren.

20   M. Cherif Bassiouni, "Versailles to Rwanda in Seventy-Five Years: The Need to Establish a Permanent International Criminal Court," *Harvard Human Rights Journal* 10 (1997), 11, 40.

21   D. Pimmentel, "Technology in a War Crimes Tribunal: Recent Experience of the ICTY" (2004) 12 *William and Mary Bill of Rights Journal*, 715, 720.

The imperative of managing information was formally acknowledged as a distinct and specialised aspect of prosecutorial practice and procedure, when the ICTR's Information and Evidence Section was established in 1998 with the intention that all information produced or acquired by investigative and trial teams was to be centralised and shared among all the teams.[22] In practice, investigative and trial teams rely on the Information and Evidence Section to organise the massive store of information in a way that will make access and analysis more efficient. Usually, computerised tools help accomplish this goal. Six computer-based electronic repositories of information are used by the OTP on a daily basis: Zy Evidence Database,[23] Casemap,[24] GELOD,[25] TRIM Judicial Database,[26] Lotus Notes,[27] and EDS.[28] The OTP's JALAW intranet[29] and the LiveNote transcript management system[30] have also become part of this stable of electronic productivity tools.

The overall feedback from trial teams is that these information management tools are appreciated and do improve the ability to comply with disclosure obligations.[31] The fundamental caveat underlying these information tools is that the limits of their utility are set by their users. Obviously, a computer-based

---

[22]   ICTR OTP Information Management Report, notes of file with Maria Warren.

[23]   The OTP maintains an electronic repository of evidence, using the commercially available software product Zyfind. Documents are scanned as image files and their full text indexed to make them searchable and accessible to users on the OTP computer network.

[24]   Casemap is a knowledge management database that allows all the key information about a case to be registered in the database (such as witnesses, places, charges etc.) and linked to each other, to comments from trial team members, and to transcripts of the trial. It allows every member of the trial team to have access to the same information at any time and facilitates the preservation of institutional memory.

[25]   GELOD—Global Evidence for Legal Officers Database—is a witness management database devised by the OTP to keep a record of details of prosecution witnesses who testified in ICTR cases.

[26]   The ICTR maintains an official repository of all its official records, including all court documents (e.g. transcripts, motions), using a commercially available records management system called TRIM.

[27]   Lotus Notes by IBM Lotus is the main email communications platform of the ICTR.

[28]   The Electronic Disclosure System (EDS) is a central electronic repository of evidence that is made available to the Defence by the OTP via the local computer network on the internet, subject to security authorisation. Also see discussions on exculpatory evidence above.

[29]   The OTP has been named JALAW—Judicial and Legal Advisers' Workplace—and is coincidentally a play on the current Prosecutor's surname: Jallow. JALAW has been developed as a web-based information channel, available to all OTP staff members to accelerate the sharing of information among trial teams and other relevant sections of the OTP.

[30]   Livenote transcript management system is used by the OTP to search and retrieve information from the thousands of pages of transcripts of most of the past and current ICTR trials.

[31]   ICTR OTP Information Management Report, notes on file with Maria Warren.

program is of little use if it is not actually employed by trial teams, as has been the experience of the Special Court for Sierra Leone.[32]

Even for those lawyers who actively integrate computer technology into their case management, the benefits of these electronic information repositories are entirely dependent on reliable data. If data are not entered correctly and errors are allowed to go unchecked, the electronic repositories and the computer programs that run them will have little to no utility. Information management protocols are essential to set the standards and the benchmarks against which quality control can be imposed. It is critical to provide continuous training, and to give lawyers a choice of convenient times and settings: one on one, online or classroom style. The use of these computerised tools is greatly enhanced by the implementation of sound information policies that take into consideration the notion of fair access to information, the imperative of cost and time efficiencies, the protection of witnesses, and the physical and mental welfare of the members of the trial teams who spend long hours labouring over the thousands of pages of evidentiary materials.

Information management in other contexts— lessons worth learning

It is often noted that international law and international legal exchanges can benefit immensely from advances in technology and information management systems.[33] Indeed, concerns regarding information management are not unique to the ICTR. Many lessons learned at the ICTR relate to shared experiences from legal processes in other contexts, including those seemingly unrelated to international criminal prosecutions.

For example, some sectors normally foreign to international criminal prosecution, such as Alternative Dispute Resolution and other branches of private law, currently exploit the rapidly increasing opportunities offered by technological advancements. Various jurisdictions around the world have evolved their legal and judicial processes to integrate electronic courtrooms into litigation practices.[34] It is increasingly common for innovators in corporate law to seek the development of information-sharing devices such as

---

32   D. Crane, "Dancing with the Devil: Prosecuting West Africa's Warlords: Building Initial Prosecutorial Strategy for an International Tribunal after Third World Armed Conflicts" (2005), 37 *Case Western Reserve Journal of International Law* 1, p.6.

33   H. H. Perritt, Jr, "Cyberspace and State Sovereignty," *Journal of International Legal Studies*, 3 (1997), 181-94.

34   Australian Law Reform Commission, "Managing Justice: A review of the federal civil justice system, Report No 89," (31 December 1999), http://www.austlii.edu.au/au/other/alrc/publications/reports/89/

regional repositories of relevant contract law.[35] In some countries, online "virtual deal rooms" have enabled secure document exchange and inspection sites, often using software that summarises long documents.[36] Many entities in the private sector are also developing tools for using the internet to facilitate communication between parties through hearings and conferences by video link.[37] The ICTR has recently included similar audiovisual initiatives with the implementation of its video-conferencing facilities, which are proving extremely useful, especially in light of the need to reconcile the timeframe of the ICTR's completion strategy[38] with the fact that various participants in the trial process (prosecutors, defence counsel, witnesses) come from many nations. The postponement of cases can be reduced and trials are facilitated by, for example, using video-links to conduct examination of witnesses who are based in other countries and unable to travel to Arusha. There are cautions to keep in mind in this area, however, as the rights of the Accused require a public hearing and possibly a hearing where the Defence is able to see the witnesses give live testimony.

Professional fields unrelated to the practice of law also increasingly recognise the need to develop electronic information management solutions to manage vast amounts of information, and synthesise data from diverse sources such as the economy, politics and the environment.[39] This system is known as Geographic Information Systems (GIS). A good example of the utility of GIS occurs during a de-mining mission. Military units can supply a "layer" of data showing areas where mines or unexploded ordnances exist. A humanitarian agency then provides a second layer showing school or other civilian locations. Combining the two sets of data and creating buffer zones around the schools indicate initial areas for de-mining. A third layer of data, such as the footpaths used by children on their way to school, provides an intersection of areas of priority sites for de-mining.[40] At the ICTR, similar exercises occur when matching witnesses with documentary evidence, or

---

35   D. Kallweit, "Towards a European Contract Law: For a Prosperous Future of International Trade," *Victoria University of Wellington Law Review*, 35, 2 (2004), 295-96.

36   R. J. Howe, "The Impact of the Internet on the Practices of Law: Death Spiral or Never-Ending Work," *Virginia Journal of Law and Technology* (2003), 8.

37   F. A. Cona, "Focus on Cyberlaw: Application of Online Systems in Alternative Dispute Resolution," *Buffalo Law Review*, 45 (1997), 990-2.

38   United Nations, "Letter dated 5 December 2005 from the President of the ICTR to the President of the Security Council," Doc. S/2005/782, http://65.18.216.88/ENGLISH/completionstrat/s-2005-782e.pdf.

39   W. B. Wood, "Geography and the Boundaries of Confidence: A Lesson for Diplomats," *Fletcher Forum of World Affairs* 23, 5, (1999), 16-18.

40   P. Currion, "Learning from Kosovo: the Humanitarian Community Information Centre (HCIC), Year One," http://www.odihpn.org/report.asp?ID=2278..

indictment paragraphs with oral testimony, especially through the Casemap tool discussed above.

One example of a situation similar to the ICTR's regarding issues of storage and use of information concerns the Truth and Reconciliation Commission (TRC) in South Africa. The TRC faced a monumental task in managing information. Over 21,000 persons gave statements to the TRC, requiring intricate systems to record, verify and corroborate testimony.[41] These processes represented a crucial demonstration of how an independent domestic transitional justice body can interact with national criminal justice systems. During the life of the TRC, there was a need to reconcile its work with the concurrent national judicial process, as both addressed related criminal incidents. A "dual carriageway" of information was pioneered, in which it was the official policy of the South African Attorney General's offices to allow the TRC's staff to examine its files and take notes from its documents; in return, prosecution staff would attend some of the TRC's amnesty hearings to gather information useful to its cases.[42] This demonstrates the type of mutual judicial assistance and information-sharing discussed later in this chapter, regarding proposed international standards for information management.

In line with this development, it is notable that several commentators have emphasised that the electronic recording of information provides greater opportunities for knowledge-sharing and the ability for nations to learn alternative approaches to their own law.[43] This is of particular assistance to international war crimes tribunals, where judges will often review the legal practices of national jurisdictions when guidance outside of international jurisprudence is required.[44] A good example of these online databases is the work of the Supreme Court of the Philippines, which developed the Action Program for Judicial Reform through the launching of the Court Administration Management Information System, which is a publicly accessible

---

41   S. Garkawe, "The South African Truth and Reconciliation Commission: A Suitable Model to Enhance the Role and Rights of Victims of Gross Violations of Human Rights?" *Melbourne University Law Review,* 27 (2003), 367.

42   M. Mutua, "Republic of Kenya Report of the Task Force on the Establishment of a Truth, Justice and Reconciliation Commission," *Buffalo Human Rights Law Review* 10, 15, (2004) 202.

43   See for example, F. R. P. Romero, "Legal Challenges of Globalisation, Delivered as Part of the Indiana Supreme Court Lecture Series at Indiana University School of Law," *Indiana International and Comparative Law Review,* 15 (2005), 507.

44   See for example, the discussion of rape with reference to national laws in the ICTY case *Furundzija,* Case No. IT-95-17/1-T & A, as most recently discussed in the ICTR case *Muhimana* Trial Judgement, paras 95-102; and also *Gacumbitsi* Appeal Judgement, paras 147-157.

and comprehensive database of all cases under its jurisdiction.[45] The utility of sharing information on legal developments is apparent in the references made by national courts to the jurisprudence of international war crimes tribunals.[46] Other international tribunals, including the International Court of Justice, the European Court for Human Rights[47] and the Inter-American Commission on Human Rights,[48] refer to the jurisprudence of international war crimes tribunals. Furthermore, it has been stated that decisions from the international war crimes tribunals are absolute "gold mines of information", crucial, for example, to the drafting of the United States Joint Services Law of War Manual.[49] It is clear that the electronic sharing of information on international justice greatly enhances the legacy of the Tribunals.

Information networks: strategy for securing justice and promoting peace

Information-sharing and the innovative use of information networks have the potential to enable international prosecution to fully connect with the larger purpose behind international justice, namely the promotion of peace and reconciliation.[50] An example of using electronic means to promote reconciliation is the process known as "conflict mapping", which was pioneered to help address crimes committed in Kosovo. Several post-conflict societies have expressed an interest in benefiting from the insight of the Kosovo process. The Kosovo conflict mapping initiative pooled the information from civil society organisations on the one hand, and international agencies such

---

45   Supreme Court of the Philippines, "Court Management Information System", http://jrn21.supremecourt.gov.ph/files/documents/Day2/Information%20Communication%20Technology%20in%20the%20Judiciary/paper-Velasco%20(SC-OCA).pdf.

46   See: Stephanie K. Wood, "A Woman Scorned for the Least Condemned War Crime", *Columbia Journal of Gender and Law*, 13 (2004), 293.

47   See the comments of Patricia Viseur-Sellers in "Symposium, War Crime Tribunals: The Record and the Prospects: The Contribution of Ad Hoc Tribunals in International Humanitarian Law," *American University International Law Review*, 13, 1509 (1998), 1531.

48   See the comments of Robert K. Goldman in "Symposium, War Crime Tribunals: The Record and the Prospects: The Contribution of Ad Hoc Tribunals in International Humanitarian Law" *American University International Law Review*, 13, 1509 (1998), 1536.

49   See the comments of W. Hays Parks in "Symposium, War Crime Tribunals: The Record and the Prospects: The Contribution of Ad Hoc Tribunals in International Humanitarian Law" (1998), *American University International Law Review*, 13, 1509 (1998), 1532.

50   See for example, the preamble of Security Council Resolution 955 (1994) referring to the objective of contributing to national reconciliation in the creation of the ICTR, http://www.un.org/ictr/english/Resolutions/955e.htm.

as the ICTY and the Organisation of Security and Co-operation in Europe (OSCE) on the other. The information was analysed according to geography and time, and proved to be of immense evidential value to the ICTY's international prosecutions, including the Milošević trial. The data were equally important to providing the local population with a synthesis of the historical record of the atrocities, including extra-judicial information and evidence from the ICTY.[51] Furthermore, the Prosecutor of the International Criminal Court (ICC) cites the creation of an international network of information among judicial and extra-judicial organisations as key to galvanising international cooperation and maximising the impact of the Court.[52]

It is important to note that information-sharing during the humanitarian response to mass atrocities also contributes to real-time peace efforts. The United Nations Office for Coordination of Humanitarian Affairs (OCHA) established the Kosovo Humanitarian Community Information Centre (HCIC) to provide multiple methods of access to data resources, including a drop-in centre, printed fact sheets, emails, interactive CD-ROMs and a website. The success of the Balkans experience has now expanded to other regional centres around the globe.[53] Following the HCIC model, such information centres can pool information on humanitarian concerns, to identify areas of need and working strategies.

While applauding the benefits of information-sharing, it is also necessary to acknowledge the challenges, especially regarding sensitive information. This has long been a difficulty in sharing criminal investigation intelligence, where the relevant agencies within states are often reluctant to share data,[54] although steps being made in this field are particularly successful when there is development of regional structures, most obviously in the case of the European Union.[55]

---

51   Wendy S. Betts and Gregory Gisvold, *Human Rights Brief*, 10 (2003), 24.

52   Draft ICC Policy Paper, "Maximising Impact of the Court of International Relations," July 2006.

53   R. Schofield, "Information systems in humanitarian emergencies", http://www.odihpn.org/report.asp?ID=2277. For a critique on the development of information centres and their contribution to improved management of humanitarian situations, see Paul Currion, "A little learning is a dangerous thing: five years of information management for humanitarian operations", http://www.odihpn.org/report.asp?ID=2797. Draft ICC Policy Paper, "Maximising Impact of the Court of International Relations"; Evolution of OCHA's Use of IM in Humanitarian Response, http://www.humanitarianinfo.org/IMToolbox/web/07_info_centre.html.

54   Bryan F. MacPherson, "Building an International Criminal Court for the 21st Century," *Case Western Reserve Journal of International Law*, 13 (1998), 22-23.

55   For example, Europol, Eurojust and the European Convention for Mutual Assistance in Criminal Matters, http://conventions.coe.int/treaty/Commun/QueVoulezVous.asp?NT=030&CM=8&CL=ENG.

International standards of information management in international trials

The ICTY and the ICTR were the first international criminal tribunals since Nuremburg and Tokyo.[56] The trials conducted at these tribunals face unprecedented challenges in evidence and information management. Such challenges for international criminal justice will continue after the completion of the work of the ICTY and the ICTR, through fora such as the recently-established ICC and any future tribunals mandated to prosecute international crimes. In fact, commentators have identified information management as one of the most important foundations for the future work of the ICC.[57] The following five key points will help develop critically needed international standards of information management in international trials.

Reflection. First, it is important and indeed incumbent upon the ICTY and the ICTR to distill their lessons learned and best practices in the field of information management.[58] It is also essential to compile reflections from all potentially useful sources relating to information management.[59] As discussed above, a wide range of contexts encounter similar information management challenges to those faced in international criminal prosecution. Second, these institutions must organise these best practices and useful tools into a schema reflecting the stages of an international criminal prosecution. With continuing collaboration among international prosecutors, these best practices could evolve into accepted international standards that can be applied to all international criminal investigations and prosecutions.

Competent body. It is imperative that the international community establishes a competent body to oversee the collection of evidence in war-torn areas. Such a body would require the drafting of internationally approved protocols for the purpose of preserving evidence, until it is possible to hand over to a tribunal with rightful jurisdiction over the evidence.

Access. A primary consideration in setting international guidelines on information management is the issue of access. There should be an Information Ac-

---

56   M. C. Bassiouni, "The Role of Justice in Building Peace: Justice and Peace, the Importance of Choosing Accountability over Realpolitik," *Case Western Reserve Journal of International Law*, 35 (2003),195-201.

57   J. Schense, "Necessary Steps for the Creation of the International Criminal Court," *Fordham International Law Journal*, 25 (2002), 724-30.

58   See *Final Report of Proceedings at the Colloquium of Prosecutions of International Criminal Tribunals*, 25-27 November 2004, http://65.18.216.88/ENGLISH/colloquium04/reports/final_report.pdf..

59   See generally F. I. Lederer, "The Potential Use of Courtroom Technology in Major Terrorism Cases", *William and Mary Bill of Rights Journal*, 12 (2004) 887.

cess Protocol to cover those governments, organisations and individuals that acquire, use and store documents and objects in the course of their work in a conflict area. The Protocol would, among other issues, identify the parties that have the right of access to the information prior to, during, and after international judicial proceedings. It would also spell out the appropriate ways and means of handling information.

Institutions such as the ICTR and the ICTY are creations of the international community. As such, they are partnerships among nations to establish the truth and create a historical record.[60] It is imperative that a common understanding and commitment to information-sharing should be reached, so that officers of international judicial institutions can gain access to information in government archives and personal collections. In the experience of the *ad hoc* tribunals, access to information in the countries where the atrocities occurred, as well as in other states, continues to be crucial in the preparation and conduct of trials. When countries withhold evidence, as documents or through witnesses, the judicial process is obstructed, perpetrators are not held fully accountable, and victims continue to be denied justice.

Top among the legacy issues that the ICTY and the ICTR are currently considering are the safekeeping of, and access to, their archives when they close their doors. This is a potentially controversial issue because the question of "access" is closely allied to the question of "ownership." Who "owns" the archives? The party that "owns" has the right to grant "access." Are the archives owned by the UN which created and funded the *ad hoc* tribunals, or by the countries where the crimes occurred and whose citizens suffered, or by the international community at large? So far, representatives of all of these parties have expressed interest in rightful ownership. A high-level international panel with representatives drawn from all relevant sectors will be necessary to resolve these issues. They must, however, be resolved soon.

Technology. Undoubtedly, technology plays a crucial role in building opportunities for efficiency in the ICTR and other war crimes tribunals. One critical lesson we have learned is that technology is only an enabler of good practice. Appropriate application of technology is required, rather than technology *per se*.

The ways in which technology can assist during pretrial preparation, the trial itself, and post-trial procedures need to be assessed. In the pretrial stage, the initial challenge is to create the case through the collection and processing of information collected from the field and generated within the office. This exercise primarily requires a master-database to record and link information, ideally in a multi-media format; that is, in document form as well as audio-

---

60   See generally on the purpose of international justice: E. Stover and H. Weinstein (eds), *My Neighbour, My Enemy* (Cambridge UK: Cambridge University Press, 2004).

visual. Most important, technology should be used to facilitate the sharing of this information among the trial teams and investigators as well as all relevant external parties.

During the trial itself, creating tools to assist the input of information into the case-database is vital, as are tools to assist translations and recording of transcripts. It is also important to consider methods for facilitating public access to courtroom proceedings, for example through live-video feeds of trials. Furthermore, tribunals must investigate the applicability of video conferencing to enable remote witness testimony, while keeping in mind the question of whether the Defence is entitled to live witness testimony. This concept can possibly be extended to remote engagement between lawyers and judges. Another essential application of technology that must be considered is the preservation of institutional memory, so that the unexpected absence of a trial team member, for example, will not hamper the progress of the trial. In the post-trial stage, it is essential to consider tools for robust preservation of evidence and the efficient transfer of trial records to the appeals team. Once these initial tasks have been performed and the best tools and plans of action formulated, it is then necessary to take a long-term view and provide for future integrations of information management technologies facilitating international criminal trials.

Funding. Finally, institutions that fund the operation of international tribunals should better direct their efforts to eliminate redundancy. Recently, the European Commission funded an ICTR project to upgrade the information management capabilities of the OTP.[61] Projects of this kind have also been funded in the ICTY and the ICC. Efficiency dictates that funding organisations must consider, when assessing proposals, the possibility of overlap, and take steps to avoid inadvertent re-invention of the wheel. An example of addressing such concerns is the recent resolution of international prosecutors to formalise and share their best practices, in order to document lessons learnt and the initiatives of each tribunal and court. Funding institutions should be encouraged to add this to their checklist when assessing funding applications. In this way, development and operating standards can be promoted and costs leveraged across similar initiatives.

Conclusion

Managing information and evidence can be overwhelming. The volume of documents and materials, coupled with disclosure obligations, can give one the sense of playing a never-ending game of paper chase instead of seeking justice for victims of atrocious crimes. It is essential to keep sight of the ultimate pur-

---

61   Memorandum of Agreement between the European Commission and the ICTR, dated 2003, on file with Maria Warren.

pose of information management in international criminal prosecutions, which is best illustrated in the following anecdote.

In 1996, when asked by a journalist what he considered the mission of the *ad hoc* tribunals, the first joint ICTY/ICTR Prosecutor, Richard Goldstone, answered that it was to break the cycle of vengeance-inspired ethnic violence. He explained:

Such interethnic violence usually gets stoked by specific individuals intent on immediate political or material advantage, who then call forth the legacies of earlier and previously unaddressed grievances. But the guilt for the violence that results does not adhere to the entire group. Specific individuals bear the major share of the responsibility, and it is they, not the group as a whole, who need to be held to account, *through a fair and meticulously detailed presentation and evaluation of evidence,* precisely so that the next time around no one will be able to claim that all Serbs did this, or all Croats or all Hutus.[62]

Goldstone's view demonstrates the ultimate purpose of information management in international prosecutions: to facilitate the conduct of a fair and meticulously detailed presentation and evaluation of evidence in the quest for justice.

---

62   Lawrence Weschler, "International Humanitarian Law: An Overview", http://www. crimesofwar.org/thebook/ihl-overview.html. (emphasis added).

15

THE RULES (AND POLITICS) OF ENGAGEMENT: THE *GACACA* COURTS AND POST-GENOCIDE JUSTICE, HEALING AND RECONCILIATION IN RWANDA

Phil Clark

Introduction

In the direct aftermath of the genocide in Rwanda, around 120,000 genocide suspects, mostly Hutu, were rounded up and transported to jails around the country built to hold only 45,000 inmates.[1] Most detainees were never formally charged with any crime and were forced to live in hellish conditions: underfed, drinking dirty water and crammed into tiny rooms where they were often made to sleep in latticework formations for lack of space.[2] Outside the prisons, genocide survivors demanded justice and compensation for the crimes committed against them and to know the truth of who had killed or injured their loved ones in 1994. Meanwhile, the economic impact of imprisoning so many young Hutu men has been immense, both for the population that has had to cover for the loss of labour and for the government that has had to care for so many detainees.

In response to the social, political, economic and legal problems created by the overcrowded prisons, the Rwandan government in 2001 instituted the *gacaca* jurisdictions. *Gacaca* comprises around 9,000 community-based courts, each overseen by locally-elected judges, designed to hear and judge the cases of genocide suspects, most of whom have been imprisoned for more than a decade.

---

1   International Centre for Prison Studies (King's College), "Prison Brief for Rwanda" (London: ICPS, 2002), http://www.kcl.ac.uk/depsta/rel/icps/worldbrief/africa_records. php?code=39.

2   Prison Fieldnotes, Prison Centrale de Butare, Butare, 4 February 2003, notes on file with author.

Two judicial documents establish the legal basis and mechanics of *gacaca*, the Organic Law of 1996 and the *Gacaca* Law of 2001; the latter modified five times, to a minimal extent in June 2001 and June 2006 and more substantially in June 2004,[3] March 2007 and May 2008 to help streamline the institution to deal with the immense backlog of genocide cases. The Organic Law is organised to prosecute "the crime of genocide or crimes against humanity" or "offences... committed in connection with the events surrounding genocide and crimes against humanity" between 1 October 1990 and 31 December 1994.[4] The Organic Law defines "genocide" and "crimes against humanity" in accordance with three international conventions to which Rwanda is a signatory: the 1948 United Nations Convention on the Prevention and Punishment of the Crime of Genocide, the 1949 Geneva

---

3   Republic of Rwanda, "Loi Organique No. 8196 du 30/8/96 sur l'Organisation des Pour-suites des Infractions Constitutives du Crime de Genocide ou de Crimes contre l'Humanité, Commises à Partir de 1er Octobre 1990", *Official Gazette of the Republic of Rwanda*, 1 September 1996, Articles 2-9 (from here on, referred to as the "Organic Law"). Repub-lic of Rwanda, "Organic Law 40/2000 of 26/01/2001 Setting Up *Gacaca* Jurisdictions and Organising Prosecutions for Offences Constituting the Crime of Genocide or Crimes against Humanity Committed Between 1 October 1993 and 31 December 1994", *Of-ficial Gazette of the Republic of Rwanda*, October 2000, Articles 72-81 (from here on, referred to as the "*gacaca* Law"). The three documents that comprise the modifications are: Organic Law Modifying and Completing the Organic Law Setting Up *gacaca* Juris-dictions and Organizing Prosecutions for Offences Constituting the Crime of Genocide or Crimes against Humanity Committed Between 1 October 1993 and 31 December 1994, No. 22/2001 of June 22, 2001 (Rwanda), in *Official Gazette of the Republic of Rwanda*, June 2001 (hereinafter, Gacaca Law (Modified 2001)); Organic Law Establishing the Or-ganization, Competence and Functioning of *gacaca* Courts Charged with Prosecuting and Trying the Perpetrators of the Crime of Genocide and other Crimes against Humanity, Committed between 1 October 1990 and 31 December 1994, No. 16/2004 of June 19, 2004 (Rwanda), in *Official Gazette of the Republic of Rwanda*, June 19, 2004 (herein-after, Gacaca Law (Modified 2004)); Republic of Rwanda, "Organic Law No. 28/2006 of 27/06/2006 Modifying and Complementing Organic Law No. 16/2004 of 19/06/2004 Establishing the Organisation, Competence and Functioning of *Gacaca* Courts Charged with Prosecuting and Trying the Perpetrators of the Crime of Genocide and Other Crimes against Humanity, Committed between October 1, 1990 and December 31, 1994" in *Of-ficial Gazette of the Republic of Rwanda*, June 2006 (hereinafter, Gacaca Law (Modified 2006)); Republic of Rwanda, "Organic Law N° 10/2007 of 01/03/2007 Organic Law Modifying and Complementing Organic Law n°16/2004 of 19/6/2004 Establishing the Organisation, Competence and Functioning of *Gacaca* Courts Charged with Prosecut-ing and Trying the Perpetrators of the Crime of Genocide and Other Crimes against Humanity, Committed between October 1, 1990 and December 31, 1994 as Modified and Complemented to Date", Official Gazette of the Republic of Rwanda, March 2007 (hereinafter, Gacaca Law (Modified 2007)); and Republic of Rwanda, "Organic Law N° 13/2008 of 19/05/2007 Modifying and Complementing Organic Law n°16/2004 of 19/6/2004 Establishing the Organisation, Competence and Functioning of *gacaca* Courts Charged with Prosecuting and Trying the Perpetrators of the Crime of Genocide and Other Crimes against Humanity, Committed between October 1, 1990 and December 31, 1994 as Modified and Complemented to Date", *Official Gazette of the Republic of Rwanda*, May 2008 hereinafter, Gacaca Law (Modified 2008)).

4   Organic Law, Article 1.

Convention on the Protection of Civilian Persons in Time of War, and the 1968 Convention on the Non-Applicability of Statutory Limitations to War Crimes and Crimes against Humanity.[5]

Broadly speaking, the purpose of *gacaca* is two-fold, responding to pragmatic and more complex social needs respectively: first, to decrease the prison population by processing the massive backlog of genocide cases more rapidly than is possible in conventional courts such as the Rwandan national courts or the UN International Criminal Tribunal for Rwanda (ICTR); and second, to deal with a range of community-based problems arising from the genocide, such as those related to truth, reconciliation and the overall reconstruction of Rwandan society. *Gacaca* is the centrepiece of the government's justice and reconciliation programme. Whether hopes for rebuilding Rwandan society after the genocide are fulfilled or dashed will depend largely on the success of *gacaca*. In March 2005, *gacaca* entered its most crucial phase, as it began judging and sentencing the first wave of genocide suspects, many of whom, as a result of their *gacaca* convictions, have now been sentenced to new prison terms.

Two broad camps of opinion have developed among observers of *gacaca*. The first (made up mostly of non-Rwandan legal commentators and human rights critics[6]) claims that *gacaca* is destined to fail; that it will violate principles of legal due process or even lead to mob justice, greater insecurity and perhaps widespread violence. The second (consisting of some Rwandan government

---

5   Ibid., Article 1.
6   For examples of such human rights critiques, see African Rights, "Gacaca Justice: A Shared Responsibility," Kigali (2003) 65; Amnesty International, "Rwanda: Gacaca— Gambling with Justice" (19 June 2002); William Burke-White, "A Community of Courts: Toward a System of International Criminal Law Enforcement", 24 Michigan Journal of International Law, (2002) 54–61; Allison Corey and Sandra Joireman, "Retributive Justice: The Gacaca Courts in Rwanda", 103 *African Affairs* 73 (2004); Sandra Joireman, "Justice for a Genocide?", 2 *Global Review of Ethnopolitics* 65, 66 (2003); S'fiso Ngesi and Charles Villa-Vicencio, "Rwanda: Balancing the Weight of History", in Erik Doxtader and Charles Villa-Vicencio (eds), *Through Fire with Water: The Roots of Division and the Potential for Reconciliation in Africa* (2003) 21-23; Penal Reform International, "PRI Research Team on Gacaca, Report III" (2002); Jeremy Sarkin, "Gacaca Courts and Genocide", in Charles Villa-Vicencio and Tyrone Savage (eds), *Rwanda and South Africa Dialogue: Addressing the Legacies of Genocide and a Crime Against Humanity* (2001) 54. It should be noted that some non-Rwandan commentators offer more favourable analyses of gacaca's attempts to pursue, among other aims, justice and reconciliation after the genocide. See, for example, Helena Cobban, "The Legacies of Collective Violence: The Rwandan Genocide and the Limits of Law", *Boston Review*, http://www.bostonreview.net/BR27.2/cobban.html, (April/May 2002); Erin Daly, "Between Punitive Justice and Reconstructive Justice: the Gacaca Courts in Rwanda", 34 New York University Journal of International Law and Politics 355 (2002); Mark A. Drumbl, "Punishment, Postgenocide: From Guilt to Shame to Civis in Rwanda", 75 New York University Law Review (2000) 1221-1292; Drumbl, *Atrocity, Punishment, and International Law*, Cambridge: Cambridge University Press (2007) 85-99.

officials) argues that *gacaca* is the answer to all of Rwanda's post-genocide ills, a guaranteed vehicle for truth, justice, reconciliation and a vast array of other objectives.

In this chapter, I will respond to three questions: First, what is *gacaca*, and, perhaps more importantly, what is it not? Second, what are the main political, social, cultural and legal features that influence how *gacaca* operates? Finally, how effective is *gacaca* likely to be in responding to the legacies of the genocide? I will argue that most commentators on *gacaca*—particularly its legal critics—have misinterpreted its aims and methods and therefore have criticised it for failing to achieve goals for which it was never intended. In particular, these critics have ignored *gacaca*'s capacity to facilitate *restorative justice* via meaningful *engagement* between parties previously in conflict, in the form of communal dialogue and cooperation, which are crucial to fostering reconciliation after the genocide. As outlined in Chapter 10 of this volume, restorative justice holds that perpetrators should be punished for their crimes, but that the methods and outcomes of punishment should be facilitated to promote reconciliation between perpetrators and victims. Gerry Johnstone argues that restorative justice

revolves around the idea that crime is, in essence, a violation of a person by another person (rather than a violation of legal rules); that in responding to a crime our primary concerns should be to make offenders aware of the harm they have caused, to get them to understand and meet their liability to repair such harm, and to ensure that further offences are prevented; that the form and amount of reparation from the offender to the victim and the measures to be taken to prevent re-offending should be decided collectively by offenders, victims and members of their communities through constructive dialogue in an informal and consensual process; and that efforts should be made to improve the relationship between the offender and victim and to reintegrate the offender into the law-abiding community.[7]

I will argue that *gacaca*, as an institution of restorative justice, punishes those convicted of genocide and crimes against humanity explicitly in order to promote reconciliation, an objective that critics of *gacaca* have largely overlooked. Furthermore, most commentators have ignored the forms of engagement that *gacaca* facilitates between parties previously in conflict and the importance of this engagement for fostering reconciliation. A useful definition of engagement, which can be applied in the context of *gacaca*, comes from Norman Porter in his analysis of the potential for reconciliation in Northern Ireland. Porter emphasises the importance for reconciliation of creating spaces for public discourse and debate, in which a vital element is open and fair engagement between previously antagonistic parties. Speaking in terms applicable

---

7   G. Johnstone, *Restorative Justice: Ideas, Values, Debates* (Cullompton, Devon, UK: Willan Publishing, 2002), ix.

beyond Northern Ireland, Porter argues that meaningful engagement entails "practices involving honest, committed encounters with others, not least those with whom we disagree most."[8] In these settings, individuals make themselves vulnerable to others and the most important result is that "through [these practices] others are opened up to us and we to them, others are permitted to be heard in their terms and we in ours."[9] As we shall see, *gacaca*'s capacity to facilitate engagement, particularly between genocide suspects and survivors, is crucial to generating the sort of dialogue about the root causes of conflict in Rwanda that reconciliation requires.

Finally, I will argue that the two main camps of current opinion on *gacaca*— one extremely pessimistic and the other extremely optimistic—are equally mistaken. I will argue that something in between these two views—a sense of qualified optimism regarding *gacaca*'s contribution to justice, healing and reconciliation after the genocide—is a more appropriate analysis of its current and future success. Because *gacaca* only began judging suspects and handing down sentences to convicted perpetrators in March 2005, it is too early to gauge categorically how successful *gacaca* will be as a tool of post-genocide reconstruction. However, there are signs that, in some communities, *gacaca* is likely to achieve impressive results, while in others it faces serious problems.

My research is based on five months of fieldwork conducted in Rwanda in 2003 and a further six weeks each in 2006 and 2007, mainly in rural areas. During this time, I carried out around 100 interviews concerning issues of justice and reconciliation with confessed *génocidaires* in the *ingando* or "solidarity camps" (civic education centres where detainees spend several months between leaving prison and being provisionally released into the community, where they will eventually face *gacaca*) and a further 250 interviews with survivors, the general population, Rwandan government officials and NGO workers.[10] I also observed *gacaca* hearings in numerous communities around Rwanda. A key component of my research involved tracking a selected group of detainees through various stages of the release process, first in prison, then upon their release into the solidarity camps, afterwards inside the camps and finally in their home communities where they awaited their appearances before *gacaca*, including follow-up visits several years after their initial return. I was one of only a handful of non-Rwandans present on 5 May 2003, when more than 20,000 confessed perpetrators were provisionally released from prison and returned to their home towns and villages for the first time in more than a decade. In

---

8   N. Porter, *The Elusive Quest: Reconciliation in Northern Ireland* (Belfast: The Blackstaff Press, 2003), 108.

9   Ibid., 108.

10   Throughout this chapter, the names of all genocide suspects and survivors and members of the general population have been changed for legal and security reasons.

one instance, I rode on an old Mercedes Benz bus with 70 detainees (some as young as 19 years old, meaning they had allegedly committed genocide crimes when they were 9 or 10 years old) as they returned to their homes in southern Rwanda, near the Burundi border, where I interviewed them and genocide survivors regarding the prospects of perpetrators' and survivors' living side byside in the future.[11]

Defining gacaca

Before asking how successful *gacaca* is likely to be, we must first understand what it is and what it is designed to achieve. In a historical sense, post-genocide *gacaca*, as the Rwandan government has designed it, is founded on the broad principles of earlier practices of *gacaca* which have been employed at least since the 16th century. Modern *gacaca* however, diverges in crucial ways from the pre-genocide institution. Before the genocide, *gacaca* constituted a dispute resolution system whereby individuals brought before a group of male heads of households their conflicts over relatively uncontroversial matters concerning land use, livestock and damage to property. Hearings were conducted outdoors, either on a patch of grass or in the village courtyard. Women were barred from participating as judges or witnesses. The primary aim of *gacaca* was not punishment alone but also reconciliation, seeking to restore a sense of social cohesion by facilitating a face-to-face resolution between victims and perpetrators.[12] Any punishment handed down by the village elders incorporated a restorative element, often the sharing of food or beer between previously antagonistic parties, and never resulted in the imprisonment of those found guilty.[13]

In the post-genocide environment, *gacaca* maintains the outdoor setting of the pre-genocide hearings and the high value placed on the community's participation, which now manifests in its election of judges, themselves members of the community, who decide the guilt or innocence of genocide suspects on the basis of open communal deliberations of the evidence presented; it also maintains the emphasis on punishment leading to restoration. Modern *gacaca* differs from pre-genocide *gacaca* by relying on written law, by involving

---

11   For a more detailed account of my tracking of these detainees from prison to *gacaca*, see P. Clark, "When the Killers Go Home: Local Justice in Rwanda", *Dissent*, Summer (2005), 21-28.

12   A. Karekezi, "Juridictions *Gacaca*: Lutte contre l'Impunité et Promotion de la Réconciliation Nationale" in E. Ntaganda (ed.), *Les Juridictions Gacaca et les Processus de Réconciliation Nationale*, Cahiers de Centre de Gestion des Conflits, No. 3 (Butare: Université Nationale du Rwanda, May 2001), 32.

13   S. Vandeginste, "Justice, Reconciliation and Reparation after Genocide and Crimes against Humanity: The Proposed Establishment of Popular *Gacaca* Tribunals in Rwanda", paper delivered to the All-Africa Conference on African Principles of Conflict Resolution and Reconciliation, Addis Ababa (8-12 November 1999), 15.

women both as judges and as witnesses, and by including the possibility of sentencing suspects found guilty of particular genocide-related crimes to prison terms. These sentences are greatly reduced, though, and in some cases can be voluntarily commuted to community service if perpetrators confess before their crimes are exposed at *gacaca*.

The *Gacaca* Law of 2004, which modifies statutes contained in the Organic Law, classifies crimes against humanity and genocide crimes committed between 1 October 1990 and 31 December 1994 in three categories: Category 1 includes individuals who planned or orchestrated the genocide or who committed torture, rape or acts of sexual violence; Category 2 includes individuals who committed murder or caused injury; and Category 3 includes those who committed property crimes.[14] *Gacaca* prosecutes suspects in Categories 2 and 3 only, while the cases of suspects in Category 1 are transferred to either the Rwandan national courts or to the ICTR.[15] Under *gacaca*'s plea-bargaining scheme, which Schabas explores in more detail in his chapter in this volume, an individual found guilty of committing murder in connection with the genocide or crimes against humanity during the specified dates must be sentenced to 25-30 years' imprisonment, the most severe punishment possible at *gacaca*. However, if the individual confesses to murder before the beginning of his or her *gacaca* trial, he or she is eligible for a reduced sentence of 7-12 years' imprisonment, with the possibility of commuting half of this to community labour. All sentences handed down at *gacaca*, with the exception of those passed on individuals convicted of murder before they confess, can be half-commuted to community service.[16]

In terms of transitional justice institutions around the world, *gacaca* is unique. *Gacaca* incorporates elements of both war crimes tribunals and truth commissions by punishing convicted genocide perpetrators and by encouraging the community to engage in open, communal, often emotional and non-legal discourse about their experiences of conflict, with the aim of eventually achieving reconciliation. However, *gacaca* is more than a hybrid of processes employed in other countries.[17] What distinguishes *gacaca* from transitional justice institutions used elsewhere is the central role played by

---

14 *Gacaca* Law (Modified 2004), Article 51.

15 The 2008 modifications to the *gacaca* law, among other changes, moved the majority of category 1 cases, including concerning crimes of sexual violence, to the *gacaca* jurisdictions (*Gacaca* Law (Modified 2008)). This chapter analyses *gacaca* as it functioned to the end of 2007 and therfore does not account for 2008 reforms.

16 Ibid., Articles 72-81.

17 For a more detailed exploration of notions of "hybridity" in the history and operation of *gacaca*, see, P. Clark, "Hybridity, Holism and 'Traditional' Justice : The Case of the Gacaca Courts in Post-Genocide Rwanda", *George Washington International Law Review*, 40 (December 2007), 171.

the general population in all facets of its daily operation. The spirit of *gacaca*, which is enshrined in the *Gacaca* Law and—as I discovered in my interviews with participants in *gacaca* across Rwanda, discussed further below—resonates throughout the general population, is the notion that the population must feel a sense of ownership over *gacaca* and must be its primary actor.

For this reason, the *Gacaca* Law excludes certain groups of elites from being judges, including magistrates, elected officials and clergy. The *Gacaca* Law also excludes lawyers from all official involvement.[18] The government argues that the population's ownership over *gacaca* will ensure its popular legitimacy and help encourage communal participation. Part of the reason why *Gacaca* is difficult to define in terms of its intentions and methods is that, once the population takes control, it often shapes the institution to its own ends, in line with local norms and beliefs and in response to the needs of particular communities. *gacaca* is thus a moving target, taking on new meanings and forms as more and more communities engage in the process. As we will see later in this chapter, this explains why most commentators, as well as parts of the population, express great confusion over what *gacaca* is designed to achieve.

An example of a *gacaca* hearing that I attended in 2003 is particularly illustrative of these points. This hearing shows how the population often interprets *gacaca* as contributing to objectives that are not necessarily captured in its legal statutes, in particular notions of healing from trauma or from feelings of pain and loss. It also shows how the dynamism of *gacaca* can produce great confusion among participants concerning the aims of the institution.

The *gacaca* hearing took place in Ruhengenge district of Kigali Ville province on 6 April 2003.[19] Before the start of this hearing, the president of the judges' bench ordered a group of women to drag two large blue tarpaulins, containing the recently-exhumed remains of genocide victims in the community, beneath the thatched shelter where the hearing would take place. The week before, two detainees from the nearby prison had confessed in front of this *gacaca* to the murder of several children during the genocide and to dumping their bodies in a mass grave. On hearing this confession, the president ordered the exhumation of the site that the detainees had described.

The two tarpaulins were opened at the *gacaca* hearing of 6 April to display a pile of rotten clothes in one, and a heap of cracked and decayed bones, evidently those of children, in the other. On seeing the remains, the audience of community participants in the hearing (known as the General Assembly) showed signs of great distress. Women and children began crying. Several men expressed anger that the president had allowed such traumatising evidence

---

18   *Gacaca* Law, Articles 14-15.

19   *Gacaca* Observations, Kigali Ville, Ruhengenge, 6 April 2003, notes on file with author.

to be displayed at an already fraught *gacaca* hearing, in which the General Assembly was constructing a list of people who had died in the community during the genocide. This *gacaca* was also taking place in an especially emotional environment in early April, the day before 7 April which marks the official anniversary of the start of the genocide in 1994, and at the start of a month-long national remembrance of those who died during the genocide.

Through my interviews with survivors I discovered that over time many had developed a view of *gacaca* as an important means of discovering the truth of what happened to their loved ones in 1994. This discovery had, in turn, helped them deal with emotions of anger and loss by providing the necessary facts about the death of their friends and family. It allowed them to understand precisely what had happened, and to speak more clearly and assuredly about their experiences. For these survivors, the distress of the exhumation appeared to undermine many of the benefits associated with their previous experiences of *gacaca*. The president replied to the community's concerns by saying the exhumation of the children's remains served a dual purpose: it verified the testimony of the two detainees at the previous *gacaca* regarding the location of the mass grave and, with later forensic analysis, would help verify how many children were buried there, their identities and how they had been killed; and it was a way of shaming the detainees who had committed these crimes. A third outcome that the president did not mention was that survivors would now have a chance to bury their loved ones properly, which was crucial for their personal healing.[20]

At this particular hearing, conflicting understandings of the role of *gacaca* were expressed, and had the potential to alter the way in which the hearing was conducted. What is evident here is that *gacaca*'s *raison d'être* can be interpreted in a multitude of ways by different participants in the process: in this particular instance, as a forum for the broad search for the truth, a realm of truth-discovery within the limits of healing, or as a means for pursuing some form of justice through shaming. This confluence, and for many participants confusion, of objectives was characteristic of many of the *gacaca* jurisdictions that I observed.

Although *gacaca*'s legal statutes lay the foundation for how the institution should operate, it is also influenced by a wide range of political, social, cultural and legal phenomena, ranging from the population's views of how *gacaca* was practised before the genocide to the specific, local needs—for example, a need

---

20 This third interpretation of the events surrounding the exhumation at Ruhengenge was suggested to me by Martin Ngoga, then Deputy Prosecutor General, Republic of Rwanda, during a panel session at the conference, "The Rwandan Genocide and Transitional Justice: Commemorating the 10th Anniversary of the Genocide", St. Antony's College, University of Oxford, 15 May 2004, notes on file with author.

for healing, as expressed by participants at Ruhengenge—that the population expects *gacaca* to fulfil.

A major influence on *gacaca* that most observers have overlooked is religion. In a country where approximately 56 per cent of the population (both Hutu and Tutsi, though mostly Hutu) is nominally Catholic, and around 26 per cent is Protestant (predominantly among Anglophone Tutsi, a large percentage of whom identify themselves as Anglican, Pentecostal and Seventh Day Adventist), it is perhaps not surprising that many Rwandans subsume religious principles into *gacaca*.[21] In particular, in my interviews, many genocide suspects and survivors claim that forgiveness is one of *gacaca*'s main objectives. The *Gacaca* Law makes no mention of victims seeking or granting forgiveness, stating only that detainees who wish to benefit from *gacaca*'s plea-bargaining scheme must publicly confess to, and apologise for, their crimes. Nonetheless, many survivors claim that they have a Christian duty to forgive genocide perpetrators and that they will do so at *gacaca*. Many suspects, in turn, claim that they will actively seek forgiveness from the families of their victims during *gacaca* hearings. Jean-Baptiste, a survivor in Nyamata, argued after a *gacaca* hearing that "we must forgive because God forgives," adding, "it is our Christian duty and if we do not forgive then we ourselves become the sinners."[22] During a *gacaca* hearing I attended in Save district of Butare province, a local pastor gave a short talk at the beginning of the hearing, in which he exhorted the General Assembly to tell the truth and to be ready to forgive because "truth is the liberator and we must help detainees to confess their crimes." He continued: "We won't hurt them with lies and we will welcome them home, ready to forgive them, so they will tell the truth about what they have done."[23] Some detainees reverse this process and argue that, by telling the truth, they will encourage survivors to forgive them. "It is not easy to confess to crimes like mine," said Alexis, a detainee in the solidarity camp at Gashora, who confessed to participating in the group killing of a woman during the genocide when he was 11 years old. "But I want to help the community forgive me at *gacaca*...One day I hope the community will let me go back to my farm and start my life again."[24]

---

21   Rwandan government figures quoted by US Department of State, "Rwanda: International Religious Freedom Report 2007", 14 September 2007, http://www.state.gov/g/drl/rls/irf/2007/90115.htm.

22   *Gacaca* Interviews, Jean-Baptiste, Kigali Ngali, Nyamata, 19 May 2003, notes on file with author. [author's translation]

23   *Gacaca* Observations, Butare, Save, 15 May 2003, notes on file with author. [author's translation]

24   Solidarity Camp Interviews, Gashora (no. 18), 18 April 2003, tape on file with author. [author's translation]

In many parishes around Rwanda, a version of Christian *gacaca* called *"gacaca nkiristu"* has evolved, in which believers confess their everyday sins to one another and seek and grant forgiveness. Many church leaders intend Christian *gacaca* to be a precursor to official *gacaca*, which deals with genocide crimes, and expect many of the beliefs and principles from the former to flow naturally into the latter.[25] I do not intend here to explore the motivations and methods of these practices, or the wider effects in the community of linking *gacaca* with religious concepts, but only to draw attention to the fact that much of the population explicitly and consistently connects *gacaca* with religious objectives and practices, in ways that cannot be captured in *gacaca*'s legal documents alone.

The human rights critique of gacaca

How have most commentators interpreted *gacaca*? Is there a single, overriding view that drives most critiques of the institution in the existing literature? The study of *gacaca* is a new but growing field and already more detailed and varied accounts are beginning to emerge. A small number of Rwandan academics and observers has discussed the importance of *gacaca* for pursuing a variety of objectives, including healing and reconciliation.[26] I do not incorporate the views of these authors into what I describe as the dominant discourse on *gacaca* because, in terms of the existing literature on this topic, their work currently constitutes a minority (albeit crucial) view. Over time, it is likely that the local literature on *gacaca* will grow and some local authors will respond more directly to the critiques of *gacaca* by non-Rwandan legal authors.

The majority of published critiques comes from non-Rwandan observers and draws on a form of human rights analysis that views justice as the primary virtue by which *gacaca* should be evaluated.[27] That most non-Rwandan observers of *gacaca* come from a legal background means that they tend to interpret *gacaca* strictly as a judicial remedy to the legacies of the genocide. Discerning the success of *gacaca* in terms of social outcomes other than justice, such as healing or reconciliation, is thus sidelined, rendering these virtues secondary considerations to justice if in fact they are considered at all.

---

25 For a more detailed discussion of Christian *gacaca*, see Karekezi, "Juridictions *gacaca*", 34.

26 Most prominent among these Rwandan authors are Alice Karekezi and Simon Gasibirege, both formely of the National University of Rwanda in Butare. See, for example, Karekezi, "Juridictions *Gacaca*"; S. Gasibirege, "L'élection des juges Inyangamugayo: rupture ou continuité?" in E. Ntaganda (ed.), *De la Paix à la Justice: Les Enjeux de la Réconciliation Nationale*, Cahiers de Centre de Gestion des Conflits, No. 6 (Butare: Université Nationale du Rwanda, November 2002), 93-127.

27 See, supra note 7.

While most commentators consider justice and the protection of human rights as the primary lens through which to interpret and analyse *gacaca*, they define justice in a very particular fashion. The form of justice that most commentators employ when analysing *gacaca* is *formal* in method and *deterrent* in outcome. Regarding the formal nature of this version of justice, the dominant discourse on *gacaca* draws on a longstanding tradition in Western philosophy that holds that justice should be a neutrally-determined, universal virtue and free from all value-laden claims made by specific individuals or groups.[28] The only way to achieve such neutrally-determined justice, this view dictates, is to follow pre-determined principles and procedures. In the context of *gacaca*, formal justice requires that the processes of the institution adhere to commonly-accepted precepts of due process, such as those requiring defendants to have access to competent legal counsel of their choosing and hearing of cases by an unbiased judiciary.

According to the dominant interpretation, the most important outcome of the *gacaca* process—like that of the Rwandan national courts and the ICTR, with which *gacaca* operates concurrently—is the punishment of genocide perpetrators, which, in turn, will help deter future criminals and eradicate the culture of impunity that in the view of many commentators prevailed in Rwanda before and during the genocide. In this view, justice will be achieved and *gacaca* will be deemed successful only when genocide perpetrators have been found guilty and sentenced according to the severity of their crimes. Any failure to mete out punishment to those found guilty of genocide crimes, and to do so according to commonly accepted principles of due process, will render *gacaca* an unjust and illegitimate institution and will foster greater impunity.

Three examples of human rights critiques of *gacaca* illustrate the most common arguments against it. All three critiques assume that *gacaca* is an institution aimed primarily at formal, deterrent justice. On this basis, they conclude that *gacaca* is an unjust and illegitimate attempt to deal with the legacies of the genocide.

In a report published in December 2002, Amnesty International (AI) argues,

the legislation establishing the *Gacaca* Jurisdictions fails to guarantee minimum fair trial standards that are guaranteed in international treaties ratified by the Rwandese government....[*G*]*acaca* trials need to conform to international standards of fairness so that the government's efforts to end impunity...are effective. If justice is not seen to be done, public confidence in the judiciary will not be restored and the government will have lost an opportunity to show its determination to respect human rights.[29]

---

28 The paradigmatic example of this view comes from John Rawls in his model of distributive justice, as presented in J. Rawls, *A Theory of Justice* (Oxford: Clarendon Press, 1972).

29 Amnesty International, "*Gacaca*: A Question of Justice", AI Doc. AFR 47/007/2002

Elsewhere, AI argues that it is

principally concerned with the extrajudicial nature of the *gacaca* tribunals. The *gacaca* legislation does not incorporate international standards of fair trial. Defendants appearing before the tribunals are not afforded applicable judicial guarantees so as to ensure that the proceedings are fair, even though some could face maximum sentences of life imprisonment.[30]

In July 2002 Human Rights Watch (HRW) analysts Kenneth Roth and Alison Des Forges published an article critical of interpretations of *gacaca* expressed by Helena Cobban. According to Cobban, deterrent justice is not *gacaca*'s only function and, for example, "therapy" or the healing of emotional and psychological wounds after the genocide for both perpetrators and survivors is also among *gacaca*'s aims.[31] In response, Roth and Des Forges argue,

[I]t is precisely at a time of atrocities…that a policy of trial and punishment is essential. Justice reinforces social norms and deters some would-be perpetrators…[O]ne can only imagine the long line of perpetrators who would choose therapy instead of prison cells. Before we agree to counselling instead of punishment [through *gacaca*], we owe it to the victims of the Rwandan genocide – and to all future victims of genocide – to contemplate the [idea of therapy at *gacaca*] from their perspective.[32]

I do not question here the validity of Roth's and Des Forges' specific critique of Cobban's argument. What is important to note instead is the primacy that groups such as AI and HRW give to methods of "trial and punishment" in the context of *gacaca*, with the aim of deterring potential criminals, and the implication that these methods must comply with international standards of judicial procedure. Nowhere in the literature do human rights critics explicitly state that deterrent justice is the *only* objective of *gacaca*, although quotes such as the one above from Roth and Des Forges come close to making such a point. However, objectives that—so legal commentators imply—do not relate to methods of punishment and more specifically to ideas of deterrence, such as "therapy", "healing", "rehabilitation" or "reconciliation", are generally treated with scepticism,

---

(December 2002), 2.

30   Amnesty International, "Rwanda: *Gacaca* – Gambling with Justice", press release, AI Index: AFR 47/003/2002, 19 June 2002, 1. It should be noted that AI's final statement regarding *gacaca*'s ability to sentence individuals convicted of certain genocide crimes to life in imprisonment was correct when it was published in 2002 but, after modifications to the *Gacaca* Law, no longer pertains.

31   H. Cobban, "The Legacies of Collective Violence: the Rwandan Genocide and the Limits of Law", *Boston Review* (April/May 2002), http://www.bostonreview.net/BR27.2/cobban.html.

32   A. Des Forges and K. Roth, "Justice or Therapy? A Discussion on Helena Cobban's Essay on Crime and Punishment in Rwanda", *Boston Review* (Summer 2002), http://bostonreview.net/BR27.3/rothdesForges.html.

if in fact they are considered at all. Therefore, we can conclude that the prevailing discourse considers deterrent justice to be the primary objective of *gacaca*.

The current academic literature on *gacaca* is relatively small, but where such analyses have appeared, particularly from non-Rwandan authors, they have largely mirrored the human rights arguments cited above. For example, Allison Corey and Sandra Joireman argue that *gacaca* threatens security in Rwanda by failing to adequately punish *génocidaires* in two key respects.[33] First, they argue that *gacaca* fails to punish perpetrators in a formal sense, as embodied in principles of due process, such as participants' right to competent legal counsel and to have their cases heard by neutral third parties, rather than by members of the community who themselves may be involved in the cases under consideration. Second, these authors argue that *gacaca* fails to uphold principles of judicial fairness by focusing only on crimes committed by *génocidaires* and neglecting crimes against Hutu committed by members of the Tutsi minority and the RPF. Corey and Joireman contend that this selectivity of cases to be heard at *gacaca* leads to a form of "politicized justice"[34] which intensifies "a desire for vengeance among the Hutu majority... thereby contributing to, rather than curtailing, the risk of ethnic violence in the long run."[35] Many observers, including those from AI and HRW, have criticised *gacaca* on these same grounds of legal due process and judicial fairness.[36] Corey's and Joireman's argument, however, differs slightly from these critiques by claiming that the politicised justice will lead to insecurity rather than simply being a derogation of a moral duty to try all crimes equally or a failed attempt to eradicate the culture of impunity, which constitute the human rights organisations' main justifications for pursuing punishment through *gacaca*.

In the current literature on *gacaca*, there are several variations of these formal critiques as outlined above. However, the examples from these human rights organisations and academics are representative of the dominant discourse on *gacaca*. Some critics emphasise either the formal or the deterrence shortcomings of *gacaca* more than others, while some emphasise both of these aspects. Both components of this view of justice, however, predominate in the existing literature and constitute a largely coherent view among most commentators of what *gacaca* is and what it is designed to achieve (or more crucially, given the critical nature of most commentaries, what *gacaca* supposedly is not and what it supposedly fails to achieve).

---

33   Corey and Joireman, "Retributive Justice", op. cit.; Joireman, "Justice for a Genocide?", op. cit.

34   Corey and Joireman, "Retributive Justice", 86.

35   Ibid., 74.

36   Des Forges and Roth, "Justice or Therapy?" 1-2; AI, "*Gacaca*: A Question of Justice", 2-11.

Countering the human rights critique of gacaca

We have good reason to reject the dominant discourse on *gacaca*. Human rights critics' sole focus on formal, deterrent justice when analysing *gacaca* is unsatisfactory for two main reasons. Consequently we require, for a more appropriate assessment of *gacaca*, the more nuanced analysis of its aims and achievements that I provide later in this chapter. First, human rights critics analyse *gacaca* solely in terms of a set of legal statutes which, they argue, represent flawed procedures of justice.[37] However, *gacaca* is a dynamic social institution that functions very differently in practice from how it may appear on paper. In particular, legal documents cannot capture the complex array of local beliefs and expectations according to which the population interprets *gacaca*, or the often unpredictable results of community interactions during *gacaca* hearings, exemplified in the hearing at Ruhengenge described earlier. In neglecting the importance of popular interpretations of *gacaca*, human rights critics fail to judge it on its participants' own terms.

It is important to justify the contention that the population's interpretations of *gacaca* should warrant a central status when interpreting its objectives and judging its effectiveness. It may appear that such an approach gives undue consideration to what many observers may view as merely participants' misunderstandings or deliberate contraventions of the laws governing *gacaca*— in essence, a "warping" of the original intentions of the makers of *gacaca* that should carry no moral or practical weight in our interpretations. There are, however, very good reasons for closely analysing the ways in which ordinary Rwandans' interpretations of *gacaca*, as manifest in their verbal discussions of the institution and in their practices and interactions during *gacaca* hearings, contribute to the functioning of the institution. The fundamental reason why interpreting popular perceptions of, and participation in, *gacaca* is important for understanding the institution as a whole is that *gacaca*'s driving ethos is one of popular ownership and participation. The Rwandan government emphasises the importance of popular participation, and most Rwandans, at least in their verbal expressions, also view themselves and not the state as the driving force behind *gacaca*. The spirit of *gacaca* emphasises that the community should play a central role in all aspects of the process and that the objectives of *gacaca* should not be pursued through the agency of national or local elites but through communal engagement in a public setting.

The government stresses that *gacaca* judges must allow the General Assembly, with minimal interference from judges or other community leaders,

---

37 For a rare example of a legal scholar's analysis of *gacaca* based on first-hand observations of hearings over several years, see L. Waldorf, "Mass Justice for Mass Atrocity: Rethinking Local Justice as Transitional Justice", *Temple Law Review* 79 (Spring 2006), 1-87.

to openly discuss cases and wider (often emotional, non-legal) issues stemming from the genocide. Fatuma Ndangiza, Executive Secretary of the National Unity and Reconciliation Commission (NURC), describes *gacaca* as "a form of justice originating from and serving Rwandan culture" and a demonstration of "Rwandans' ability to manage their [own] conflicts."[38] As the *Gacaca Manual*, which the government produced with the assistance of the Belgian legal organisation Avocats Sans Frontières (ASF) to guide judges in their daily running of *gacaca*, exhorts: "Don't forget that the population is the main actor in the *Gacaca* Jurisdictions and that you represent the population."[39] Judges are on hand primarily to encourage what Hannington Tayebwa, former Head of Judicial Services at the Rwandan Ministry of Justice, calls "facilitated problem-solving."[40] This process holds that the General Assembly should engage in a largely open discussion at *gacaca* hearings, in which judges act as mediators to help the community achieve certain legal and social objectives. *Gacaca* judges, in this view, function as democratically-elected officials, pursuing the good of the populace by allowing the General Assembly to control much of the running of *gacaca*, except in instances when judges believe that communal discussions may lead to damaging levels of discord or violence, in which case judges should intervene to ensure participants' security and the productivity of hearings.

Much of the Rwandan public echoes the government's understanding of the importance of popular participation in *gacaca*. In my interviews, many Rwandans discuss at length the importance of public dialogue during *gacaca* hearings and the need for all members of the community to openly discuss their experiences and concerns. A *gacaca* judge in Buhoma district of Ruhengeri province argued, "*Gacaca* is important because it brings everyone together, to talk together. When we come together, we find unity... Sometimes there is even too much talking and I have to slow the people down."[41] Many Rwandans view *gacaca* as a forum in which all members of the community, suspects, survivors and the general population, can debate and discuss legal and non-legal issues related to the genocide.

---

38 F. Ndangiza, "Transitional Justice and Reconciliation", paper delivered to the Conference on Policy Research, Ottawa (21 November 2002), 7.

39 Republic of Rwanda, "Manuel Explicatif sur la Loi Organique portant Création des Juridictions *Gacaca*", Kigali: Supreme Court of Rwanda, 6th Chamber (*gacaca* Commission), 2001, 10. (From here on, referred to as the "*Gacaca* Manual.") [author's translation]

40 Government Interviews, Hannington Tayebwa, Head of Judicial Services, Ministry of Justice, Republic of Rwanda, Kigali, 30 January 2003, tape on file with author.

41 *Gacaca* Interviews, Alice, Ruhengeri, Buhoma, 4 May 2003, notes on file with author. [author's translation]

Gacaca's popular ethos necessitates an analysis of popular interpretations of its objectives, if we are to rigorously interpret its aims. This is a difficult undertaking because it is impossible to propose a single, paradigmatic interpretation of *gacaca* and its aims, as it is shaped largely by the needs, beliefs and methods of local communities. These local factors vary greatly among, and within, different communities, which leads inevitably to different and often-changing understandings of *gacaca*. This dynamism should make us wary of interpreting the aims of *gacaca* too rigidly. Nevertheless, to neglect the ramifications of popular ownership of *gacaca*, as most human rights critics do, is to neglect the important public spirit of the institution and thus to fail to judge it on its own terms.

Furthermore, the very legal documents governing how *gacaca* operates explicitly state that *it* should facilitate something more than formal, deterrent justice. Underlining the importance of *gacaca* for restorative justice and reconciliation, the *Gacaca* Law states that it is designed "not only with the aim of providing punishment, but also reconstituting the Rwandan Society that had been destroyed by bad leaders."[42] As quoted earlier, the *Gacaca* Manual emphasises that the population must be the central actor of *gacaca*, highlighting its discursive—rather than strictly formal—methods of *gacaca*. Therefore, even on the grounds of the legal documents upon which human rights critics base their analyses, they offer an unsatisfactory interpretation of *gacaca*'s methods and objectives.

Second, in a more substantive sense, human rights critics argue unjustifiably that simply punishing perpetrators is enough to rebuild individual and communal lives in Rwanda after the genocide. Punishing the guilty may contribute partially to fulfilling some of the population's needs but overall it is, on its own, an insufficient response. At best, punishment alone amounts to the imprisonment of the guilty and therefore the physical separation of perpetrators and victims. *Gacaca* recognises that punishment is necessary both to express moral outrage at genocide crimes and to satiate survivors' desire to see some form of retribution meted out to the guilty. However, *gacaca* also holds that something more than punishment is necessary to reconstruct Rwandan society. In particular, *gacaca* shows how a cliché of transitional societies can work in practice, namely, that there can be no reconciliation without justice.[43] The key to understanding how *gacaca* breathes life into this cliché is to understand how it deliberately shapes justice toward reconciliatory ends, in ways that human rights critics fail to recognise.

---

42   *Gacaca* Law, Introduction, p.2.

43   See for example, J. de Gruchy *et al.*, "The Kairos Document: Challenge to the Church", 1985, http://www.bethel.edu/~letnie/AfricanChristianity/SAKairos.html.

Gacaca aims at restorative justice—reconciliation through punishment—in two ways: through the process and the outcomes of justice. First, the *gacaca* justice process encourages active engagement between parties previously in conflict, which may lead to their rebuilding relationships fractured by violence. As the quote from Porter at the beginning of this chapter expresses, engagement involves committed encounters between individuals and groups, often those who have previously considered each other as enemies, in which each is open to listening, and responding honestly and wholeheartedly, to the other. Engagement is a critical component of *gacaca*, given the degree to which the entire community is encouraged to participate and to interact face-to-face at all levels of the institution. The ethos of *gacaca* holds that there can be no reconciliation without genuine engagement between parties previously in conflict.

Engagement occurs via different means in *gacaca*, from the public discussions surrounding the election of judges to the various phases of the hearings themselves, the focus of the latter being the often non-legal and largely undirected dialogue in the General Assembly, in which judges act as mediators rather than direct participants. In particular, engagement entails antagonistic parties' debating the root causes of their conflicts. It recognises that there will be deep-seated animosity between individuals and between groups after an event as destructive as genocide. Implicit in the notion of engagement through *gacaca* is the view that reconciliation after the genocide will require difficult dialogue, a genuine confrontation with the sources of conflict, and parties' mutual dedication to rebuilding fractured relationships. Such a confrontation may on occasion prove detrimental to chances of reconciliation if it only produces further acrimony. Engagement is not an inherently positive dynamic; when not managed effectively, it is equally capable of fomenting discord, as I discuss further below. For engagement to produce positive results, it requires the immense dedication of the parties involved, a genuine sense of trust between them and effective forms of mediation, to ensure that this sense of trust is maintained.

The forms of engagement that *gacaca* facilitates distinguish it from other transitional justice institutions, such as war crimes tribunals, which rarely allow open or meaningful interactions between victims and perpetrators and which limit discourse to legal matters, to the exclusion of more emotional concerns. Where conventional courtrooms separate suspects and accusers, *gacaca* brings them together to engage in mediated dialogue, a process which in itself—if mediated effectively—can help participants begin to deal with some of the conflicts between them. *Gacaca* also facilitates a form of engagement that few truth commissions around the world have attempted. The Truth and Reconciliation Commission (TRC) in South Africa, for example, gave survivors the opportunity to tell their stories in front of government-appointed commissioners, but it rarely generated the sort of face-to-face dialogue between perpetrators and victims that is central to *gacaca*. The discursive approach to justice in *gacaca*, with its emphasis on fostering meaningful engagement between participants—as opposed to the strictly formal variety advocated by human rights observers—is one means to reconciliation.

Second, the outcomes of *gacaca* justice have the potential to facilitate reconciliation more effectively than other judicial structures. *Gacaca* does this in two main ways. First, its plea-bargaining system, and in particular its use of community service as punishment for certain crimes, reintegrates perpetrators more rapidly into the community and involves them in labour programmes, for example, rebuilding genocide survivors' houses or maintaining communal gardens. Community service may therefore contribute to economic reconstruction and may in some instances involve perpetrators and survivors working side by side—another form of engagement that continues after *gacaca* and may help parties rebuild broken bonds.

The second form of reconciliatory punishment in *gacaca* focuses on compensation and reparation. Especially in the case of property crimes committed during the genocide, *gacaca* requires perpetrators to compensate victims for the damage caused and, where possible, to contribute to a nationwide Compensation Fund designed to assist survivors.[44] Concrete acts of reparation, supporting reconciliatory statements made during *gacaca* hearings, are important for convincing survivors of the sincerity of perpetrators' remorse and desire to rebuild relationships damaged by violence. *Gacaca*'s emphasis on compensation as punishment also addresses one of the key issues that critics of the South African TRC said was neglected by that Commission: the need to improve the living conditions of individual victims of mass crimes, alongside pursuing nationwide objectives such as reconciliation.[45]

Assessing gacaca's success

Having discussed how *gacaca* pursues objectives such as restorative justice and reconciliation, I conclude by asking how effectively *gacaca* can meet these ends. *Gacaca* constitutes an immense social, cultural, political and legal gamble after the genocide. Giving control of the country's central justice and reconciliation programme to a heavily divided, traumatised population entails a great risk, but a calculated one, as the government hopes that engagement between participants at *gacaca* will kick-start reconciliation via communal dialogue and collaboration during hearings and in other social processes started at *gacaca*, such as community service programmes. In some communities that I visited in

---

44   *Gacaca* Law (Modified 2004), Articles 94-96.

45   For an example of this critique of the South African TRC, see M. Mamdani, "Reconciliation without Justice," *South African Review of Books* (November/December 1996), 3-5.

2003, 2006 and 2007, *gacaca* was working effectively, generating important communal discussions, involving suspects and survivors, about the causes of the genocide and possible remedies to these. Many participants in hearings describe the importance of being able to engage in communal discussions at *gacaca* that few of them had previously experienced. As Boniface, a genocide survivor in Kigali Ville, argued,

> At *gacaca* the truth frees us from the weight we have carried around since the genocide. *Gacaca* is important because it allows us to be together and to hear the truth and to learn to live together again...I will go to *gacaca* and ask the prisoners who come from the jail to speak the truth about what they did...There are many lies at *gacaca*. But the community will refute them and the judges will get to the truth and make a record of the prisoners' crimes. Then I will feel as if all these things have finished and life will start again.[46]

Many Rwandans view *gacaca* as a forum in which all members of the community, suspects, survivors, and the general population, can debate and discuss legal and non-legal issues related to the genocide.

Many survivors claim to have experienced a sense of healing especially from discovering the precise details of what happened to their loved ones in 1994 and from discussing traumatic experiences with others. Many survivors claim to have never had this opportunity prior to participating in *gacaca*. For many women, who in all the hearings I observed participated much more readily than the men (who often had to be coaxed to speak), *gacaca* has been empowering, affording them a more central role in the community.

One example of the importance of healing through *gacaca* and the central role of women in the institution comes from a hearing in Nyarufonzo district of Kigali Ville province. Several women brought to this *gacaca* framed photographs of loved ones who died during the genocide. They clutched these photographs tightly throughout the hearing and pointed to them when they stood and gave evidence. When these women sat down again, many of them cried and hugged each other. Elderly women moved from the fringes of the gathering to comfort those in distress. The women holding the photographs appeared to gain solace and strength from those who showed them concern, sitting up more confidently and soon participating again in deliberations. The solidarity displayed by those around them affirmed them as members of the community and acknowledged their traumatic experiences. Bringing the photographs to *gacaca* also afforded a greater sense of humanity and dignity to the individuals whose deaths the General Assembly was discussing. Though they were reluctant afterwards to discuss why they had brought the pictures, the women's aim seemed to be to give a face to the otherwise disembodied names that the judges

---

46   Survivor Interviews, Boniface, Kigali Ville, Kacyiru, 22 May 2003, notes on file with author. [author's translation]

recorded in their notebooks, and to remember their deceased friends and family members more meaningfully. Thus, through their actions rather than their words, these women viewed *gacaca* as a memorial for their loved ones, a place where they could receive comfort from others in the community, and thus a possible source of healing as belonging.[47]

In other places, however, *gacaca* appears to have increased community tensions, leading to acrimony during hearings that has spilled over into daily life outside *gacaca*. At several hearings I attended, *gacaca* judges were powerless to intervene as long, heated arguments broke out, causing further animosity between participants and distracting them from the objectives at hand. Hearings are often volatile and dredge up traumatic details that, for many survivors, prove overwhelming. In one instance, on a patch of grass beside a football field in Kacyiru district of Kigali Ville province, a detainee wearing a bright red T-shirt, who had been released from a solidarity camp less than a week before, arrived halfway through a *gacaca* hearing. A woman sitting in the assembly spotted him and accused him of burning the roof of a house belonging to an elderly woman in the village, whose murder the community was discussing. After the woman described the alleged act of arson, the accused man stood at the back of the gathering and began shouting first at the woman who was giving evidence, then at the president of the judges' panel for allowing this testimony to continue. The president told him to stop talking and to let the woman speak. The accused man refused and kept shouting. Some friends of the man also began shouting at the president to stop the woman from talking. A group of other women in the gathering told the man to sit and wait for his turn to speak, which he did momentarily, but he soon he leapt to his feet again. The president could do nothing as the man screamed at the assembly, "I know many things that I will never tell. Everyone here today should be on that list of killers." Eventually he sat down and allowed the hearing to continue.[48] In many cases difficult, messy arguments at *gacaca* can prove beneficial to the community's attempts to resolve its conflicts. However, effective mediation is necessary to guide these arguments toward constructive ends.

Contrary to the analysis of most human rights commentators, the biggest problem facing *gacaca* is not the danger of mob justice, in which individual rights are violated to suit the needs and desires of the broader community. The biggest challenge to *gacaca* is instead the low turnout of the population in many jurisdictions around the country. In other words, the main challenge currently facing *gacaca* is not too much engagement (in the form of mob justice) as its legal critics contend, but rather too little engagement in the daily operation of

---

47   *Gacaca* Observations, Kigali Ville, Butamwa, 21 May 2003, notes on file with author.

48   *Gacaca* Observations, Kigali Ville, Kacyiru, 11 May 2003, notes on file with author. [author's translation]

hearings. One hearing I attended in Butare province was cancelled altogether because so few people turned up.[49] ASF has reported that many hearings, especially in rural areas, are delayed or called off altogether because people who attend refuse to engage in the communal dialogue.[50] Various factors, some more serious than others, contribute to many Rwandans' reluctance to participate in *gacaca*. At the community level, *gacaca* is extremely time-consuming, in many places taking up an entire day that would otherwise be spent working. In farming communities, this loss of labour hours has a huge effect on people's economic wellbeing, forcing many people to forego participating in or witnessing *gacaca* in order to put food on the table. Many survivors also claim that they are not yet ready to participate in *gacaca*: they are still too traumatised to publicly discuss the events of the genocide and to confront suspects. "I have already experienced so much pain," said Augustine, a survivor in Gisenyi whose parents were killed during the genocide. She claimed:

The government has given us no explanation for why the prisoners have been released. Why are they back here now? *Gacaca* will be dangerous for us survivors because we will have to see them face-to-face. This scares me.[51]

Furthermore, the majority of the population appears dazed by the flurry of events in Rwanda in the last few years. In the first five months of 2003 alone, while I was conducting fieldwork in Rwanda, the population faced the first of several mass releases of genocide suspects, first from prison into the solidarity camps and then into the community; the expansion of *gacaca* from 750 to nearly 9,000 jurisdictions nationwide; the government's banning of the *Mouvement Démocratique Républicain* (MDR), the largest Hutu opposition party, generally considered a moderate voice of the Hutu majority; a referendum on a new constitution; preparations for the first parliamentary and presidential elections since the genocide; Rwanda's increased involvement in conflict in the Democratic Republic of Congo; and an escalation of tensions with its neighbour and previous ally Uganda that many feared would lead to all-out war.

In the midst of these events, many Rwandans complained that they could not grasp what was happening in their country. One elderly man in Ruhengeri province claimed that the government failed to properly explain why so many genocide suspects were returning to the community. "We heard on the radio in

---

49 *Gacaca* Observations, Butare, Kibingo, 14 May 2003, notes on file with author.

50 *Avocats Sans Frontières*, "Les 'Juridictions *gacaca*' au Jour le Jour", ASF, 19 June 2002-27 July 2003, http://www.asf.be/FR/Frameset.htm. (Within these reports, see for example, ASF *Gacaca* Report, Kigali Ville, Kanombe, 28 May 2003; Kigali Ville, Kicukiro, 31 May 2003; Kigali Ngali, Rulindo, 29 November 2002.)

51 Survivor Interviews, Augustine, Gisenyi, Gisenyi Ville, 23 May 2003, notes on file with author. [author's translation]

January," he said, "that the *génocidaires* were coming back. At first, we were very scared. Since then, the government has told us nothing."[52] In the climate of confusion and uncertainty, many Rwandans feel that confronting the worst legacies of the genocide through *gacaca* is asking too much. This situation illustrates the importance of the wider political, social and cultural sphere for the success of a transitional justice institution such as *gacaca*. Because *gacaca* relies so heavily on the public's confidence and participation, the prevailing environment of tense uncertainty in Rwanda has an immense impact on how effectively it runs. How to motivate the population to consistently and wholeheartedly participate in *gacaca*—not how to ensure the pursuit of formal, deterrent justice, as human rights commentators suggest—is the biggest predicament that the government faces if *gacaca* is to succeed.

Conclusion

Fourteen years after the genocide, beneath the sometimes peaceful veneer of communities across Rwanda, old antagonisms still fester, and the release of detainees and the start of *gacaca* have only magnified many of these tensions. *Gacaca* represents a risky, but necessary, circuit-breaker to the fear, distrust and violence of the past. If *gacaca* fails, especially in encouraging popular participation in hearings, attempts to facilitate justice, healing and reconciliation in Rwanda will be severely undermined. *Gacaca* will probably succeed in many communities, where Hutu and Tutsi have begun engaging with one another in crucial ways. However, praise for these successes must be muted until communities across the country reap the same benefits. As *gacaca* continues judging and sentencing waves of genocide suspects, most human rights critics, operating on flawed interpretations of *gacaca*'s objectives and methods, have already dismissed it prematurely as an illegitimate or ineffective response to the legacies of the genocide. *Gacaca* entails much more than simply punishing perpetrators to destroy the culture of impunity. However, we must wait to see if the gamble of *gacaca* pays dividends in achieving, via communal engagement, the sorts of objectives with which the population identifies it, namely restorative justice, healing, reconciliation and the reconstruction of Rwandan society after the genocide.

---

52   Survivor Interviews, Stefan, Ruhengeri, Ruhengeri Ville, 5 May 2003, notes on file with author. [author's translation]

16

THE INSTITUTIONALISATION OF IMPUNITY: A JUDICIAL PERSPECTIVE ON THE RWANDAN GENOCIDE

Martin Ngoga

Introduction

The purpose of this chapter is twofold: to discuss the roots of the 1994 Rwandan genocide, particularly the culture of impunity fostered by successive Rwandan governments through inadequate legislative responses to mass killings since 1959;[1] and to analyse the practical attempts after the genocide to bring perpetrators of serious crimes to account. The failure of previous governments to bring such perpetrators to justice allowed the organisers and perpetrators of the 1994 genocide to commit crimes with no fear of punishment. This chapter highlights domestic and international judicial responses to the genocide, which seek to prosecute those responsible for the widest, most devastating period of violence in Rwandan history and thus to overcome the long-term problem of impunity in Rwanda. As this chapter shows, post-genocide domestic and international justice institutions have experienced significant successes and failures. It is important to explore current attempts to combat impunity in Rwanda, in order to ensure the effective delivery of justice in the future, as a means to building a peaceful, stable society.

Prelude to genocide and the institutionalisation of impunity

After the divisive era of colonialism, Rwanda suffered the first waves of mass murder in 1959, resulting not only in the loss of tens of thousands of lives but also in the widespread destruction of property and the mass exodus of refugees,

---

1   Although the mass murder of 1959 comprised all the necessary legal ingredients to be qualified as genocide, there has not been, at the international level, a decision, legal or political, to that effect.

many of whom remained in neighbouring countries for more than three decades. The violence of 1959 began a decades-long pattern of Rwandan governments passing what I call "legislations of impunity", in which leaders consistently used the law to protect themselves and their supporters from prosecution for serious violations of human rights. Over time, this pattern of legislative behaviour became so entrenched that we must call it the "institutionalisation of impunity". This impunity created the necessarily permissive legal environment for governments to carry out successive campaigns of mass violence, culminating in the 1994 genocide.

The institutionalisation of impunity in Rwanda began with the passing of legislation by the government of President Grégoire Kayibanda on 6 August 1962.[2] This legislation afforded amnesty to individuals responsible for atrocities between 1 April and 1 December 1961. The legislation stated, "On the occasion of the anniversary of the proclamation of the Republic of Rwanda, a general amnesty is accorded for all crimes committed in Rwanda, which, because of their form, motivation, objective, circumstances or the events that inspired them, constitute political crimes, even those constituting violations of common law, except for murders."[3]

The 1962 law also provided amnesty to those who had committed crimes before April 1961, as follows:

Article 2:

The same amnesty is accorded for the same violations if they were committed before 1 April 1961, with the following exceptions:

1. Assassinations;
2. Violations falling outside of the United Nations amnesty for reasons of their exceptional gravity;
3. All violations against persons necessitating special condemnation or demanding a prison sentence of more than 10 years.[4]

Because some cases which fell within the remit of Article 2 had already been heard, the 1962 law invalidated them, as follows:

---

2   *Loi du 06 Août 1962 portant amnistie général des infractions politiques.*

3   In the original: "*A l'occasion de l'anniversaire de la proclamation de la République Rwandaise, amnistie générale est accordée pour toutes les infractions commises au Rwanda de leur nature, de leur mobile, de leur but, de leurs circonstances ou des motifs qui les ont inspirées, revêtent un caractère politique, même si elles constituent des infractions de droit commun, à l'exception des assassinats.*"

4   In the original: "*La même amnistie est accordée pour les mêmes infractions si elles ont été commises avant le 1ᵉʳ avril 1961, à l'exception des infractions suivantes : 1° Les assassinats ; 2° Les infractions écartées du bénéfices de l'amnistie de l'O.N.U. en raison de leur exceptionnelle gravité ; 3° Toutes les infractions contre les personnes qui ont fait l'objet d'une condamnation unique ou cumulée à une peine supérieure à 10 ans de servitude pénale principale.*"

Article 4:

The amnesty supersedes all previous judgements and sentences, with the exception of civil judgements. However, the execution of civil judgements cannot involve civil imprisonment beyond the end of a period of 5 months from the entry into force of this law.[5]

The law of 20 May 1963 granted amnesty for all political crimes committed between 1 October 1959 and 1 July 1962.[6] This law provided amnesty to all persons implicated in atrocities that were considered part of fighting colonialism and feudalism, which the government equated with earlier regimes. The amnesty for politically motivated crimes was rendered thus:

Article 1:

A general and unconditional amnesty is granted for all violations during the Social Revolution, from 1 October 1959 to 1 July 1962, which, because of their nature, their motivations, the circumstances or the events which inspired them, constitute participation in the fight for national liberation and are therefore of a political nature, even if they constitute breaches of common law.[7]

The amnesty, however, was not extended to those who held different political views from the government of the day. Article 2 of the law stated that "amnesty will not be afforded by the first article of this law for violations committed during this period by persons who fought against the liberation of the masses oppressed by feudal-colonialist rule."[8] To create clear distinctions between those eligible and ineligible for the amnesty, Article 8 of the 1962 law created a "Commission for Political Amnesty" to screen and publicise all applicants for the amnesty.

These amnesties for perpetrators of mass crimes were largely responsible for continued massacres across Rwanda throughout the early 1960s. The institutionalisation of impunity did not end with the passing of the Kayibanda regime. Maj. Gen. Juvénal Habyarimana toppled Kayibanda's regime in a coup on 5

---

5   In the original: "*L'Amnistie anéantit les poursuites et les condamnations pénales à l'exclusion des condamnations civiles. Toutefois, l'exécution des condamnations civiles ne pourra être poursuivie par voie de contrainte par corps avant l'expiration d'un délai de 5 mois à dater de l'entrée en vigueur de la présente loi.*"

6   *Loi du 20 mai 1963 portant amnistie générale des infractions politiques commises entre le 1er octobre 1959 et le 1er juillet 1962.*

7   In the original: "*Amnistie générale et inconditionnelle est accordée pour toutes les infractions commises à l'occasion de la Révolution Sociale pendant la période du 1er octobre 1959 au 1er Juillet 1962 et qui, en raison de leur nature, de leur mobile, des circonstances ou des motifs qui les ont inspirées, rentrent dans le cadre de la participation à la lutte de libération nationale et revêtent ainsi un caractère politique même si elles constituent des infractions de droit commun.*"

8   In the original: "*Sont écortées du bénéfice de l'amnistie accordée par l'article premier de la présente loi les infractions commises durant cette période par des personnes qui ont lutté contre la libération des masses opprimées par la domination féodo-colonialiste.*"

July 1973, citing atrocities against minority groups and other social injustices as the main justifications for the overthrow. This political acknowledgement, however, did not translate into reformed judicial processes. The Habyarimana government soon repeated the pattern of its predecessor, committing atrocities against minorities and passing legislation that protected political leaders and their supporters from prosecution for these crimes.

The early days of Habyarimana's administration displayed positive signs that it would protect human rights throughout the country. On 12 February 1975, the government passed law N° 8/75, which ratified several international conventions on human rights, disarmament, prevention and punishment of acts causing insecurity and disturbing the peace. Included among the ratified statutes was the international Genocide Convention.

It soon became clear, though, that the Habyarimana government had little intention of adhering to the international conventions to which it was a party. For example, on 15 February 1979, the government signed Law N° 03/79, which afforded former President Kayibanda an amnesty, following case N° 0001/74/CM, conducted by the Special Military Court on 29 June 1974. Other former and current political officials received amnesties for the mass crimes they had planned or committed. Consequently, violations of human rights became the norm in Rwanda, as minorities were constantly persecuted and abused.

The impact of the institutionalisation of impunity under Habyarimana was clear during the advent of multi-party politics in the early 1990s. Opposition parties and their supporters were constantly attacked. With the stated intention of strengthening democracy and encouraging inclusive politics, the government passed law N° 54/91 on 15 November 1991, which granted amnesty for the perpetrators of those attacks.[9]

Post-genocide domestic justice

The 1994 genocide marked a major shift in Rwandan legislation, overcoming deficiencies in existing law and responding to the major legal and political challenges of the post-genocide environment. Foremost among the challenges for the Rwandan government was the lack of domestic legislation for punishing the crime of genocide. Even though Rwanda had long been a party to the Genocide Convention, it had not enacted laws to deal with such crimes committed within its territory. After domestic genocide legislation was passed, the government also had to deal with the issue of how to match newly enacted law with the need to punish perpetrators of crimes committed before the law was passed. An immense practical challenge for Rwanda's judiciary was processing the cases of genocide suspects, which the government estimated at 200,000 in 1996.

---

9   *Loi N° 54 BIS/91 DU 15 Novembre 1991 portant amnistie de certaines infractions.*

The first major legislation passed after the genocide was the Organic Law of 30 August 1996, which laid the foundation for bringing *génocidaires* to justice through the Rwandan national courts. The Organic Law signified the government's dedication to bringing perpetrators of mass crimes to justice. Article 1 of the Organic Law defined the purpose of this legislation as:

to organise the putting in trial of persons prosecuted for having, between October 1, 1990 and December 31, 1994, committed acts qualified and punished by the penal code and which constitute:

Either crimes of genocide or crimes against humanity as defined by the Convention of December 9, 1948 preventing and punishing the crime of genocide, by the Geneva Convention of August 12, 1949 relating to protecting civil persons in wartime and the additional protocols, as well as in the Convention of November 26, 1968 on impre-scriptibility of war crimes and crimes against humanity;

Or offences aimed at in the penal code which, according to the charges by the Public prosecution or the evidences for the prosecution or even what admits the defendant, were committed with the intention of perpetrating genocide or crimes against humanity.

Another key feature of the Organic Law was its division of genocide suspects into four categories, according to the severity of their alleged crimes, as outlined in Article 51:

Category 1:

The person whose criminal acts or criminal participation place him among the planners, organisers, incitators (*sic*) or supervisors of the crime of genocide or crimes against humanity;

The person who, acting in a position of authority at the national, provincial or district level, within political parties, army, religious denominations or militia, has committed these offences or encouraged others to commit them;

The well-known murderer who distinguished himself in the location where he lived or wherever he passed, because of zeal which has characterised him in killings or excessive wickedness with which they were carried out;

The person who has committed rape or acts of torture against a person's sexual parts.[10]

Category 2:

The person whose criminal acts or criminal participation place him among the authors, co-authors or accomplices of deliberate homicides or serious attacks against persons which caused death. The person who, with intention of giving death, has caused injuries or committed other serious violence, but from which the victims have not died.

---

10   During investigations, the Public Prosecutor of the Supreme Court updates a list of persons prosecuted or convicted of having committed acts placing them in Category 1. This list is published in the *Official Gazette of the Republic of Rwanda* twice a year, in June and December.

Category 3:

The person who has committed criminal acts or been an accomplice of serious attacks, without the intention of causing death to victims.

Category 4:

The person having committed offences against property.

The categorisation of suspects was necessary for two reasons. First, it acknowledged the fact that, although the population's participation in the genocide had been extremely high, a small number of leaders had planned and incited the genocide. The categorisation of suspects identified the level of their responsibility for crimes committed. Second, it helped the government manage the cases of hundreds of thousands of genocide suspects, identifying the most serious perpetrators whose cases constituted the priority for the Rwandan judiciary.

Finally, the Organic Law instituted a plea bargaining system for sentencing those found guilty of genocide crimes. Introducing a system which traded decreased sentences for suspects' confessions of their crimes was intended to help discover the truth of what happened between 1990 and 1994. Although the plea bargaining scheme central to the Organic Law was designed to deal with a situation specific to the post-genocide environment, it also mirrored plea bargaining systems employed in other jurisdictions around the world.

On the basis of the Organic Law, the Rwandan judicial system—which was dysfunctional before 1994 and decimated by the genocide—succeeded in hearing thousands of genocide cases. Despite the scepticism of many vocal international commentators, the Rwandan government displayed a dedication to prosecuting and punishing those found guilty of serious crimes. Nonetheless, it was immediately clear that the national courts—or any form of classical justice—were insufficient to deal with the massive backlog of genocide cases. The Rwandan government estimated that, at the rate at which the national courts could hear genocide cases, it would take at least 200 years to complete the task of bringing all genocide suspects to trial.

Gacaca courts

Faced with the sort of challenges after the genocide that have confronted few societies in human history, Rwanda needed creative judicial solutions. For this reason, the *gacaca* jurisdictions were established by the passing of law n° 40/2000 on 26 January 2001.[11] The *gacaca* Law has since been amended on

---

11 Organic Law N° 40/2000 of 26/01/2001 setting up "GACACA Jurisdictions" and organising prosecutions for offences constituting the crime of genocide or crimes against humanity committed between October 1/1990 and December 31/1994.

five occasions, helping to streamline the process and aiding the more efficient hearing of genocide cases.

The *gacaca* Law retained the categorisation of suspects and plea bargaining scheme enshrined in the Organic Law of 1996, assigning to *gacaca* jurisdictions—overseen by communally elected judges and involving the active participation of the population in all hearings—the responsibility for categorising suspects in their particular communities. Eventually, as discussed in greater detail below, because the Rwandan government intends to handle all remaining Category 1 cases (including those cases which the ICTR will not have heard before the end of its mandate), the *Gacaca* Law has been modified to account for this change in policy.

The *gacaca* jurisdictions have faced many challenges, many of which have been inevitable, given the immensity of the legal task confronting them. The *gacaca* process began more slowly than the government had initially hoped, taking nearly four years of community evidence-gathering before trials of genocide suspects commenced. *Gacaca*, however, has already succeeded in prosecuting and punishing thousands of *génocidaires*, in the process encouraging a community-based dialogue that may not have otherwise been possible and thus increasing the community's sense of ownership of the institution. This sense of ownership and the community's general participation are central to encouraging reconciliation after the genocide. There is currently no large-scale participatory justice institution like *gacaca* operating anywhere else in the world. The Rwandan government believes not only that *gacaca* is the key to delivering reconciliatory justice after the genocide, but also that it represents a model for other conflict and post-conflict societies of how the population may be mobilised to deliver justice and, in the process, help mend fractured relationships.

Confronting divisionism and genocide denial

Combating impunity in Rwanda requires more than simply punishing those responsible for serious crimes committed between 1990 and 1994. In recent years, what the Rwandan government calls "divisionism"—the deliberate propagation of genocide ideology—and forms of genocide revisionism and denial have become common. Intentional spreading of genocide ideology through the media and political discourse repeats many of the principles and tactics employed by genocidal ideologues in the lead-up to the mass murder of 1994. Furthermore, revisionism, including attempts by some Rwandan and international commentators to deny altogether that a genocide occurred in 1994, is an assault against truth and an insult to all genocide survivors. Genocide ideology and revisionism, if not confronted head-on, sow the seeds of future violence. Like the impunity fostered by the previous legal regimes, they seek to minimise

327

the seriousness of crimes committed and send a message that future criminals can commit atrocities without fear of sanction.

To deal with attempts at revisionism or denial of the genocide, the government passed law N° 33 bis/2003 on 6 September 2003. Article 4 states that the courts must sentence

to an imprisonment of ten (10) to twenty (20) years, any person who will have publicly shown, by his or her words, writings, images, or by any other means, that he or she has negated the genocide committed, rudely minimised it or attempted to justify or approve its grounds, or any person who will have hidden or destroyed its evidence.

Where the crimes mentioned in the preceding paragraph are committed by an association or a political party, its dissolution shall be pronounced.[12]

Legislation outlawing divisionism and denial of the genocide displays the dedication of the Rwandan government to combating impunity via a comprehensive approach to post-genocide justice. Confronting crimes against the truth of the genocide, by punishing ideologues who would deny the nature and moral bankruptcy of the crimes committed in 1994, supports the work of the national courts and *gacaca* in prosecuting genocide suspects. Such laws provide the justice that genocide survivors demand and lay the foundations of a fair and stable society.

The United Nations International Criminal Tribunal for Rwanda

Even before the genocide ended, Rwandans discussed with the leading international powers the necessity of bringing *génocidaires* to account. Rwandans expressed their preference for the UN to assist Rwanda in rebuilding its own judiciary as the primary means of delivering transitional justice, while remaining open to some form of international tribunal.

As Schabas and Kaufman note in chapters 11 and 12, respectively, the Rwandan government, coincidentally sitting on the UN Security Council in 1994, called for an international tribunal for Rwanda and then voted against the proposed form the International Criminal Tribunal for Rwanda (ICTR) would take. The government objected to locating the tribunal outside of Rwanda and the possible involvement of judges and other staff who were nationals of countries suspected of aiding the organisers and main perpetrators of the genocide. The Rwandan government criticised the ICTR's exclusion of the death penalty, the punishment many Rwandans considered most appropriate for the principal *génocidaires*. The government also objected to the fact that, because of the

---

12   The law N° 33 bis/2003 OF 06/09/2003 repressing the crime of genocide, crimes against humanity and war crimes.

ICTR's "primary jurisdiction", the international community could prosecute whichever genocide cases it wanted, when it was the international community that had abandoned the Rwandan population during the genocide. Many Rwandans were angry that the international community effectively ignored the government's objections when the Security Council passed Resolution 955 on 8 November 1994, creating the ICTR. Despite some achievements, which Jallow stresses in chapter 13, the government's initial concerns over the ICTR have ultimately been vindicated.

ICTR successes. From its inception, the ICTR has served an important purpose in sending a clear signal to genocide deniers about what really happened in Rwanda in 1994. For example, the ICTR recently issued a judicial opinion confirming that genocide occurred.[13] Thus has there been not only political recognition of the genocide, but also legal acknowledgement.

The ICTR has also removed major genocide suspects from political activity within Rwanda and deterred other suspects from attempting to become involved in Rwandan politics. Thus, the ICTR has assisted in promoting political stability within Rwanda.

The ICTR has been effective in trying some of the "big fish", or planners and inciters, of the genocide. The former Prime Minister of Rwanda, Jean Kambanda, and many members of his Cabinet are in the ICTR's custody. The ICTR has already tried, or received guilty pleas from, some of these individuals. The ICTR Office of the Prosecutor has also pursued a strategy of indicting individuals from various aspects of Rwandan society, including religious leaders, artists and media personalities, and military and political officials, to demonstrate the broad and diverse conspiracy behind the genocide.

The ICTR has contributed substantially to the development of international law. Among other significant rulings, the ICTR found that rape was used as a tool of genocide.[14] It has also extended the principle of "command responsibility" from its traditional use by the International Military Tribunal at Nuremberg, where it was restricted to the military, to cover other influential members of the community.[15] This change reflects the reality of modern, hierarchical political and social dynamics, especially in developing countries.

ICTR failures. Since voting against the ICTR, despite some of its successes and the enormous potential the ICTR had after being endowed with great human and material resources, the Rwandan government's concerns about the tribunal have only been reinforced. The ICTR's failures can be divided into those that are not its fault and those for which it is responsible.

---

13   Prosecutor v. Edouard KAREMERA.

14   Prosecutor v. Jean Paul AKAYESU.

15   Prosecutor v. Alfred MUSEMA.

First, the ICTR's statute is the basis for many of the tribunal's failures. The statute located the ICTR outside Rwanda, in Arusha, Tanzania. Such physical detachment from Rwanda has impeded the ICTR's efforts to promote unity and reconciliation in Rwanda. The ICTR's location in another country, even one adjacent to Rwanda, means that only academics, policymakers and other elites can follow its proceedings, leaving the bulk of the Rwandan population largely uninformed about its activities. At a performance level, the ICTR's lack of an effective outreach programme has further weakened its ability to make its work relevant for ordinary Rwandans.

Unlike, for example, the Special Court for Sierra Leone (SCSL), which is located within the country whose atrocities it investigates and which assists the development of the domestic judiciary, the ICTR, because of its location, is also limited in its role in judicial capacity-building within Rwanda. Because of its proximity to the Sierra Leonean population, the SCSL has been much more successful than the ICTR (or its twin *ad hoc* UN tribunal, the UN International Criminal Tribunal for the former Yugoslavia [ICTY]) in achieving its goals and conveying the international community's concerns for the post-conflict plight of the local population after conflict.

The ICTR's ill-defined mandate has caused significant problems and fostered antagonism between the Rwandan government and the ICTR. The precise relationship between the ICTR and Rwanda's domestic judiciary is unclear. It is some measure of that problem that the international community sought to clarify such relationships when it established the ICC. The Rome Statute provides for the principle of "complementarity", stating that the ICC will investigate and prosecute major suspects only when domestic judicial systems are unwilling or unable to do so.[16]

Finally, a further statutory weakness of the ICTR is that, until recently, it lacked its own chief prosecutor. The chief prosecutor of the ICTR originally also served as the chief prosecutor of the ICTY. Although there was no statutory obligation for the prosecutor of both tribunals to reside in The Hague, the first three prosecutors, Richard Goldstone, Louise Arbour and Carla Del Ponte, chose to do so. Consequently, the ICTR's Office of the Prosecutor was left without close supervision, which led to poor performance in the early years of the ICTR.

Second, there have been performance-based failures. Cases before the ICTR are tried very slowly and its budget has risen significantly since it was established in 1994. This situation raises the question of whether the Rwandan government could have used at least part of the ICTR's resources to process domestically the backlog of genocide cases. For example, the government

---

16   Rome Statute, article 17(1)(a), http://www.un.org/law/icc/statute/romefra.htm.

would have only needed a fraction of the ICTR's budget to rebuild its judicial infrastructure and to finance the *gacaca* jurisdictions.

The ICTR's previous chief prosecutor, Del Ponte, sought to bring charges against leaders of the Rwandan Patriotic Front (RPF). The Rwandan government opposed these efforts, insisting that the matter be left to Rwanda's domestic judiciary. Del Ponte's intentions were problematic for several reasons. First, it was the RPF that had to contend with the *génocidaires* as Rwanda was abandoned by the international community, and any crimes the RPF may have committed in doing so paled in comparison to the crimes committed by the *génocidaires*. Second, the Rwandan government is already equipped to deal with alleged RPF crimes, as it has shown by previously punishing rogue elements of the RPF for their crimes in 1994. Del Ponte's initiative represented a misguided ICTR prosecutorial strategy and a lack of clarity in its mandate, diverting the ICTR from its primary objective of trying the leaders of the genocide.

The ICTR's administrative weaknesses represent a second type of performance failure. The credibility and effectiveness of the ICTR have been seriously undermined by the nepotism and corruption rampant within the institution, which Schabas notes in chapter 11. On several occasions, the UN has investigated such practices, which include fee splitting between defendants and defence lawyers and recruitment and hiring of friends and relatives of current employees. Consequently, the UN has issued reports containing various recommendations for reforming the ICTR. One of the most serious administrative problems undermining the ICTR's work has been the revelation that the tribunal hired several genocide suspects as defence investigators. This gross negligence in hiring practices has endangered witnesses. The ICTR has also lacked a clear and realistic policy on witness protection. It has, in some situations, failed to protect vulnerable witnesses against harassment in courtrooms. Regarding witnesses residing in Rwanda, who are the majority of those testifying at the ICTR, the tendency has been to inflate the ICTR's role when in reality these witnesses are protected by the state.

All of the ICTR's weaknesses have resulted in its failure to complete its mandate within the time allotted to it by the UN, thus undermining Jallow's overly sunny portrayal of the Tribunal in chapter 13. Efforts by the Rwandan government are ongoing to transfer those cases to the Rwandan domestic judiciary. The Rwandan parliament voluntarily abolished the death penalty in Rwandan law, thus fulfilling the UN's key requirement for Category 1 genocide cases to be transferred from the ICTR to Rwandan domestic jurisdictions. After more than a decade of frustration with the ICTR, the Rwandan government is ready and willing to process these cases, to finally deliver justice for the victims of the genocide. Hearing the cases of these major suspects will make post-genocide justice accessible to Rwandan survivors and the population as a whole. It is vital that the UN and other international bodies support Rwanda's efforts to deal with its existing genocide caseload—being processed through the national courts and *gacaca*—and with the cases that are expected to soon be transferred from Arusha to Rwanda. Foreign governments must also aid the ICTR and the government in tracking down and transferring major *génocidaires* who continue to find safe haven overseas. While the fundamental challenges of doing justice after the genocide confront the Rwandan judiciary, they are also global issues and thus require global cooperation.

Conclusion

Rwanda's long-term peace and stability require a break from its past. Whereas impunity for atrocities has been an institutional element of Rwanda's history, since the end of the 1994 genocide Rwanda has sought new strategies to combat heinous crimes, blending international and domestic approaches to accountability.

Rwanda continues to confront the difficult task of rebuilding after genocide. That effort requires the support and participation of individuals and institutions at all levels—local, as well as global. Limited resources and the immense number of accused have also required creative judicial solutions, such as the implementation of *gacaca*. After the genocidal perpetrators are brought to account, Rwanda will face the regular criminal justice problems of other societies. With new institutions and values, we hope to permanently replace the culture of impunity that wrought such devastation upon our country.

PART IV
LEGAL AND INSTITUTIONAL LESSONS AFTER RWANDA

17

THE RWANDA EFFECT:
DEVELOPMENT AND ENDORSEMENT OF THE
'RESPONSIBILITY
TO PROTECT'

Jennifer M. Welsh

Today, roughly 1,000 miles north of Rwanda, tens of thousands of Africans are herded onto death marches, and Western leaders are again sitting in offices. How sad it is that it doesn't even seem strange.

—Samantha Power[1]

Introduction

This chapter addresses not the Rwandan genocide itself, but rather the impact of the failure of outside actors to intervene on subsequent normative developments in international relations. While the horrors committed by the *génocidaires* in Rwanda garnered international condemnation, so too did the action (or more accurately, the inaction) of individual members of the UN Security Council (UNSC) and the Secretariat of the UN in New York. From the many reports and scholarly works published since the genocide, two facts have become painfully clear: that genocide might have been prevented by timely action on the part of outside actors prior to 6 April 1994; and that after the brutality began, opportunities were missed to mitigate its destructiveness. The UNSC's continued depiction of the events on the ground as a civil war (as opposed to genocide),[2] combined with a breakdown

---

1 S. Power, "Remember Rwanda, but take action in Sudan," *New York Times* (6 April 2004).

2 For an account of how the members of the Council sought to portray the events tran-

in communication between UN forces in the field and officials in New York,[3] prevented swift and decisive action to buttress the United Nations Assistance Mission in Rwanda's (UNAMIR) capacity to protect Rwandans from slaughter. This has naturally led to much questioning about the current international legal order (particularly the rules on non-intervention), the capacity of international institutions, and the lack of political will on the part of developed countries to engage in areas perceived to be of limited strategic interest.

I argue that the Rwandan genocide, and the international community's inadequate response, played an important part in the origins and evolution of the principle of the "responsibility to protect" (RtoP).[4] Drawing upon the work of constructivist international relations scholars, such as Richard Price, Martha Finnemore and Kathryn Sikkink,[5] I suggest that the genocide in Rwanda acted as a catalysing event (akin to what they refer to as a "chance occurrence") that stimulated discussion and debate on the existing normative framework surrounding intervention. As Finnemore notes, the genocide and its aftermath differed from instances of mass human rights violations that occurred during the Cold War,[6] in that states were *not* arguing that outside intervention would have been illegitimate. Rather, Finnemore suggests, "[s]tates understood very well that legally and ethically this case required intervention, and because they did not want to intervene for other reasons, they had to work hard to suppress information and to avoid [using] the word 'genocide'."[7] The former US President Bill Clinton's subsequent

---

spiring in Rwanda, see C. Keating, "Rwanda: An Insider's Account", in D. Malone (ed.), *The UN Security Council: From the Cold War to the 21ˢᵗ Century* (London: Lynne Reiner, 2004), 505. The characterisation as genocide would have given the Council not only a clear legal right to act, but also a duty to do so: Article 1 of the Convention on the Prevention and Punishment of the Crime of Genocide obliges state parties to undertake to punish acts of genocide.

3   The most glaring illustration of this breakdown is the fact that UNAMIR General Roméo Dallaire's cabled reports, which contained strong warnings of ethnic slaughter, were not communicated fully to the UNSC. See Paul Williams' chapter 3 for more discussion on this point.

4   *The Responsibility to Protect*, The Report of the International Commission on Intervention and State Sovereignty (Ottawa: International Development Research Council, 2001).

5   R. Price, *The Chemical Weapons Taboo* (Ithaca: Cornell University Press, 1997); and Martha Finnemore and Kathryn Sikkink, "International Norm Dynamics and Political Change," *International Organization, 52* (1998), 887-917.

6   The most frequently cited examples are the Indian invasion of East Pakistan (1971), the Tanzanian invasion of Uganda (1979), and Vietnam's intervention in Pol Pot's Cambodia (1979). For more on these episodes, and the international community's opposition to intervention, see N.J. Wheeler, *Saving Strangers: Humanitarian Intervention in International Society* (Oxford UK: Oxford University Press, 2000), Chaps 2-4.

7   M. Finnemore, *The Purpose of Intervention: Changing Beliefs About the Use of Force* (Ithaca, NY: Cornell University Press, 2003), 79-80.

apology in 1998 for US inaction during the genocide confirms that states (during and after the genocide) were aware of their obligations.

Soon after Clinton's acknowledgement of unfulfilled responsibilities, the former UN Secretary General Kofi Annan suggested that blame could be spread even more widely. "Why did no one intervene?" he asked. "The question should not be addressed only to the United Nations, or even to its member states. Each of us as an individual has to take his or her share of responsibility."[8] In a September 1999 address to the UN General Assembly (UNGA), Annan challenged the international community to prevent "another Rwanda" and to develop a new consensus on how to respond more quickly and effectively to humanitarian tragedies within the sovereign jurisdiction of states.[9] A key plank in that emerging consensus has been an attempt to reframe the traditional understanding of sovereignty, and its corresponding right of non-intervention, through the principle of RtoP. As this chapter will show, the fall-out from the Rwandan genocide interacted with a more permissive context for intervention, to produce a new discourse about the protection of civilians in international society. It also influenced the endorsement of RtoP in two significant documents: the Constitutive Act of the African Union and the Outcome Document of the 2005 UN Summit of World Leaders.

Yet, at the same time, this chapter concludes that RtoP's evolution has not been a linear one—as suggested by Finnemore and Sikkink's "lifecycle" model[10]—but rather an uneven process that by no means ensures international action when ethnic cleansing or genocidal acts occur. While heads of state and government endorsed the principle of the "responsibility to protect" in the Outcome Document of 2005, the text circumscribes its application in important ways. Moreover, the ongoing crises in different parts of Africa, most notably in the Darfur region of Sudan, demonstrate that the endorsement of words is not sufficient to bring about a change in state behaviour, and that words themselves can be manipulated by actors to prevent that change from occurring.

The emergence of RtoP

While debates concerning the extent and limits of state sovereignty have long been a feature of international relations,[11] the development of universal human

---

8   Secretary General, 35th Annual Ditchley Foundation Lecture, UN Press Release, SG/SM/6613, 26 June 1998.

9   Secretary General's Annual Report to the UNGA, UN Press Release, SG/SM/7136, 20 September 2000.

10   M. Finnemore and K. Sikkink, "International Norm Dynamics and Political Change," 898. The three phases of the lifecycle are: norm emergence, norm cascade (broad norm consensus), and norm internalisation (when norms take on a "taken-for-granted" quality and are no longer a matter of heated debate).

11   See R.J. Vincent, *Nonintervention and International Order* (Princeton, NJ: Princeton Uni-

rights norms after the Second World War has given this controversy added potency in contemporary international society. Central to today's debates is the alleged incompatibility between the human rights provisions written into the UN Charter—particularly in the preamble and Article 1(3)—and the strong commitment elsewhere in the document to sovereign equality and non-intervention, most notably in Articles 2(1), 2(4) and 2(7).[12]

There are a number of developments in contemporary international relations that have shone a spotlight on this supposed tension between sovereignty and human rights, and given impetus to those calling for more interventionism: the phenomenon of so-called failed states, which create opportunities for criminal activity, arms proliferation and terrorism; the increased vulnerability of civilians in the context of civil conflict; the effect of global media, where instantaneous access to information heightens popular awareness of human suffering; the increased activism of human rights NGOs in raising concern about massive violations of human rights; and the search by many Western governments for a moral dimension to their foreign policies. In short, we are living in a climate of heightened expectations for the international community to "do something" when populations are experiencing natural disasters or man-made catastrophes.

Yet, the "when," "how" and "who" of such action remain subjects of intense controversy among nation-states. If the international community's failure to act to stop the genocide in Rwanda in 1994 provoked condemnation, so too did NATO's military campaign to address the ethnic cleansing of Kosovar Albanians in 1999. China, arguably the most powerful developing country in the contemporary international system, was only one of a number of states to register its staunch opposition to the NATO action within the chambers of the UN. Indeed, the failure to gain UNSC authorisation for the use of force against Serbia led many to conclude that, while the action could be considered legitimate (using moral criteria), it was antithetical to the ruling principles of international law.[13]

For Annan, whose previous role as UN Under Secretary General for Peacekeeping Operations during the Rwandan genocide made him acutely aware of the international community's failure,[14] this seeming deadlock over the legiti-

---

versity Press, 1974).

12   For more on the impact of human rights norms on sovereignty, see J.S. Barkin, "The Evolution of the Constitution of Sovereignty and the Emergence of Human Rights Norms", *Millennium: Journal of International Studies*, 27 (1998), 229-52.

13   This was the conclusion of the Independent International Commission on Kosovo. See *The Kosovo Report: Conflict, International Response, Lessons Learned* (Oxford UK: Oxford University Press, 2000), 4.

14   For an assessment of the role of the UN Department of Peacekeeping Operations (which Annan led during the genocide), see M. Barnett, *Eyewitness to a Genocide: The United Nations and Rwanda* (Ithaca: Cornell University Press, 2002), 155-66.

macy of intervention was untenable. Indeed, Annan claimed in 1999 that of all his objectives as Secretary General, he was *most* committed to ensuring that the UN never again failed to protect a civilian population from genocide.[15] "*If* humanitarian intervention is, indeed, an unacceptable assault on sovereignty," he asked, "how should we respond to a Rwanda, to a Srebrenica – to gross and systematic violations of human rights that affect every precept of our common humanity?"[16] Annan was searching for a way to make civilians inside sovereign states more secure ("no more Rwandas"), but in a way that would command the support of international society as a whole ("no more Kosovos").

The International Commission on Intervention and State Sovereignty (ICISS), established by the Canadian government in September 2000, became an organisational forum for taking up Annan's challenge. In fact, representatives of the Government of Canada, along with the Commission's co-chairs—Gareth Evans, former foreign minister of Australia, and Mohamed Sahnoun, a senior Algerian diplomat and former special adviser to the UN Secretary General[17]—can be characterised in the language of Finnemore and Sikkink as "norm entrepreneurs"[18] in the promotion of new guidelines for the use of force for humanitarian purposes. The Commission set out to answer a central question: when (if ever) is it appropriate for states to take coercive—and in particular military—action against another state for the purpose of protecting people at risk in the latter? Although the ICISS had much to say about the operational aspects of military action by the international community, its main contributions to the debate on humanitarian intervention were primarily conceptual: in changing the language from a "right of intervention" to a "responsibility to protect", and in setting out a spectrum of action for the international community, ranging from prevention to military action to post-conflict reconstruction.[19]

The ICISS report offers one solution to the dilemma expressed by the Secretary General: the international community should view the relationship be-

---

15   K. Annan, "Two Concepts of Sovereignty," *The Economist*, 352 (1999), 49-50.

16   K. Annan, "We the Peoples," *Millennium Report* (New York: United Nations, 2000), 48.

17   The other commissioners came from diverse regional and vocational backgrounds and perspectives: Gisele Côté-Harper (Canada), Lee Hamilton (United States), Michael Ignatieff (Canada), Vladimir Lukin (Russia), Klaus Naumann (Germany), Cyril Ramaphosa (South Africa), Fidel V. Ramos (Philippines), Cornelio Sommaruga (Switzerland), Eduardo Stein Barillas (Guatemala), and Ramesh Thakur (India).

18   M. Finnemore and K. Sikkink, "International Norm Dynamics and Political Change," 896-7.

19   The overview of the ICISS Report in the following section draws on J. Welsh, C. Thielking and S.N. MacFarlane, "The Responsibility to Protect: Assessing the Report of the International Commission on Intervention and State Sovereignty," in R. Thakur, A. F. Cooper and J. English, *International Commissions and the Power of Ideas* (Tokyo: United Nations University Press, 2005), 198-220.

tween sovereignty and intervention as complementary, rather than contradictory.[20] This solution is made possible by reshaping the very notion of sovereignty and linking it more closely to the responsibility of states to their citizens.[21] This move draws on deeper theoretical foundations, namely social theory, under which the rights of the state derive from the implicit consent of citizens, and can be forfeited if a state fails to further their interests and rights.[22] Under this formulation, sovereignty is no longer conceived as undisputed control over territory, but rather as a conditional right, dependent upon respect for a minimum standard of human rights. As the Commissioners put it:

> It is acknowledged that sovereignty implies a dual responsibility: externally—to respect the sovereignty of other states, and internally, to respect the dignity and basic rights of all the people within the state. In international human rights covenants, in UN practice, and in state practice itself, sovereignty is now understood as embracing this dual responsibility. Sovereignty as responsibility has become the minimum content of good international citizenship.[23]

For the Commission, it logically follows that intervention is permissible, and an integral part of sovereignty, if it is aimed at protecting civilians. Here, as the background meetings and preparatory papers for ICISS reveal, the effect of Rwanda was clearly at work. But the Commissioners also outline a "Just War"[24] framework of six principles to guide decision-makers contemplating such action. A military intervention to protect civilians from harm would be legitimate only if it met the criteria of just cause, right intention, last resort, proportionate means, reasonable prospects of success, and proper authority. Significantly, regarding the last criterion, the Commissioners state that while military action should be authorised by the UNSC,[25] authorisation can be found elsewhere if the UNSC fails to act.

---

20   *The Responsibility to Protect.*

21   One of the earliest attempts to reformulate sovereignty in this way can be found in the work of the Brookings Institution's project on Conflict Resolution in Africa. See *Sovereignty as Responsibility: Conflict Management in Africa* (Washington: Brookings Institution, 1996).

22   D. Rodin, "The Responsibility to Protect and the Logic of Rights," Programme for Strategic and International Security Studies, Geneva (5 May 2006).

23   *The Responsibility to Protect,* 8.

24   What has been referred to as the "Just War" tradition dates back to as early as St Augustine. A definitive modern treatment can be found in M. Walzer, *Just and Unjust Wars: A Moral Argument with Historical Illustrations,* 3rd edn (New York: Basic Books, 2000).

25   The Commissioners were cognisant of the objections to such a recommendation: the slowness of UNSC decision-making, the under-representation of key regions on the UNSC, and the political nature of vetoes of the five permanent members. There is also the more obvious point that by requiring UNSC authorisation, one ensures that RtoP will not be applied against a P5 member. Nonetheless, they believed that recourse to unregulated unilateralism was an even more unpalatable alternative. In the end, the Report warns that

In sum, the ICISS maintains that sovereign states still bear the greatest responsibility to protect their own citizens from avoidable catastrophe. Such responsibility, the Commission argues, is embedded in the very notion of sovereignty. However, when individual states are reluctant or powerless to fulfil those obligations, these responsibilities shift to the broader community of states: "Where a population is suffering serious harm, as a result of internal war, insurgency, repression or state failure, and the state in question is unwilling or unable to halt or avert it, the principle of non-intervention yields to the international responsibility to protect."[26]

Implementing RtoP

Kofi Annan believed the ICISS recommendations had brought the world closer to preventing another Rwanda, by taking "away the last excuses of the international community for doing nothing when doing something can save lives."[27] But a wide gulf remained between the enunciation of a principle and its effective implementation, so that civilians threatened by massive violations of their human rights could actually experience greater protection. As the Commissioners themselves stated in the final chapter of their report:

It remains the case that unless the political will can be mustered to act when action is called for, the debate about intervention for human protection purposes will largely be academic. The most compelling task now is to work to ensure that when the call goes out to the community of states for action, that call will be answered. There must never again be mass killing or ethnic cleansing. There must be no more Rwandas.[28]

As part of their strategy for implementing the ICISS report, the Commissioners and the Government of Canada envisaged a series of initiatives within the UN: a UNGA Resolution embodying the basic framework of RtoP (akin to the 1970 Declaration on Friendly Relations among States); UNSC guidelines for responding to military interventions with a humanitarian purpose and UNSC agreement to suspend use of the veto in situations where mass violations of human rights were occurring; and leadership by the Secretary General to advance the report's findings. These efforts, however, faced two obstacles: reluctance by the Permanent Five members of the UNSC (China, France, Russia, the UK, and the US) to agree to any principles in advance that would commit them to

---

if the UNSC "fails to discharge its responsibility to protect in conscience-shocking situations crying out for action, concerned states may not rule out other means to meet the gravity and urgency of that situation - and that the stature and credibility of the United Nations may suffer thereby", *The Responsibility to Protect*, xiii.

26   *The Responsibility to Protect*, xi.

27   K. Annan, Address to the International Peace Academy Seminar on "The Responsibility to Protect," Press Release SG/SM/8125, 15 February 2002.

28   *The Responsibility to Protect*, 70.

action or curtail their use of the veto; and objections from a vocal segment within the developing world, which feared that RtoP might be used as a licence for more intervention by the great powers. This latter worry had a particularly detrimental effect on RtoP's prospects in the wake of the invasion of Iraq in 2003, when a humanitarian rationale was twisted into a *post facto* justification for regime change.[29]

When former Canadian Prime Minister Jean Chrétien took up the cause of RtoP at the Progressive Governance Summit in London in the summer of 2003, he encountered strong resistance from developing countries, such as Brazil, which feared any moves on the part of the international community to bypass the UN system in authorising the use of force. For many developing countries, the legal architecture provided in the Charter (as laid out in Article 2) provides a mechanism to protect weak states from the ambitious agendas of the strong, by limiting the lawful use of force to situations of self-defence or collective action mandated by the UNSC. The degree to which factions within the international community were suspicious about the principle of the "responsibility to protect" was further demonstrated in late 2002, when the Non-Aligned Movement[30] (NAM) blocked Canada's procedural resolution on RtoP in the UNGA. The "Bush Doctrine,"[31] and its implications for intervention, had made many non-Western states suspicious—if not outright hostile—towards any moves that might broaden the list of legitimate exceptions to the prohibition on the use of force. At this point, the supporters of RtoP changed their tactics; rather than seeking to push RtoP within the UN, they attempted to gain traction for the principle within a regional context. The next section will analyse efforts and developments in Africa in particular.

The Constitutive Act of the African Union. Within Africa, the memories of Rwanda had already created an environment conducive to rethinking traditional rules concerning the use of force. The International Panel of Eminent Personalities (IPEP), created in 1998, marked the first time in the history of the Organisation of African Unity (OAU) that African governments created a commission

---

29   For more on how the war against Iraq affected efforts to build a new consensus around RtoP, see G. Evans, "When is it Right to Fight?," *Survival*, 46, 3 (2004), 63.

30   The Non-Aligned Movement was created in 1955, as a platform for Third World countries to resist the entangling alliances favoured by the US and the USSR during the Cold War. Today, it has over 100 members (mainly from the developing world) and is focused on struggles for independence, the eradication of poverty, economic development and opposition to neo-colonialism and imperialism.

31   This doctrine, first outlined by President George W. Bush in a speech at the US Military Academy at West Point, NY, and formalised in the 2002 National Security Strategy of the United States, refers to a set of foreign policy guidelines that places emphasis on the use of preemptive force, military superiority, unilateral action and a commitment on the part of the US to "extending democracy, liberty, and security to all regions."

that would be independent of its creators in its findings and recommendations. The effect of Rwanda had encouraged OAU member states to admit their individual and collective weaknesses, particularly in relation to peace and security for civilians in Africa.

In addition to tracing the origins of the genocide, and analysing how it was perpetrated, the IPEP assessed why, in this instance, the international community did not enforce the 1948 Genocide Convention. As Williams recounts in chapter 3, not only did outside powers fail to expand the mandate and strengthen the effectiveness of the existing UN peacekeeping mission in Rwanda—as requested by the acting head of that mission, Roméo Dallaire—but, two weeks after the genocide began, the UNSC decided to *reduce* the mission's size to 270 peacekeepers.[32] These actions were not only misguided but tragic, for according to the IPEP members, the "conspirators may have seemed formidable in local terms, but in fact they were small in numbers, modestly armed, and substantially dependent on the outside world."[33] The final report of the IPEP, *Rwanda: The Preventable Genocide*, attributes blame to a variety of actors and organisations. In particular, it chronicles the limitations of Africa's regional architecture.

The release of the damning report coincided with the efforts of African heads of state to create a new regional organisation, with its own Peace and Security Council, to manage conflict on the African continent. According to the international lawyer Jean Allain, Article 4(h) of the Constitutive Act[34] of the recently formed African Union (AU) represents one of the most serious challenges to the UNSC's management of international peace and security—far greater, in fact, than the wars in Kosovo and Iraq. The challenge is twofold. First, in drafting their new charter, African states suggest that they can act militarily within their region without prior authorisation from the UNSC. Second, the Constitutive Act widens the scope of permissible use of force set out in the UN Charter[35] to include "grave circumstances" such as war crimes, genocide and crimes against humanity.[36]

---

32   SC Res. 912 of 21 Apr. 1994. UNAMIR had been created by SC Res. 872 of 5 Oct. 1993 to monitor the ceasefire between the government and the Tutsi-dominated Rwandan Patriotic Front and to secure a weapons-free zone in Kigali.

33   *Rwanda: The Preventable Genocide*, Report of the International Panel of Eminent Personalities, (Addis Ababa: Organisation of African Unity, 2000), Chap. 10, paragraph 2.

34   Article 4(h) enshrines "the right of the Union to intervene in a Member State pursuant to a decision of the Assembly – in respect of grave circumstances, namely: war crimes, genocide, and crimes against humanity."

35   Under Article 2(4) of the Charter, the use of force is prohibited. The two exceptions to this blanket prohibition are self-defence (as outlined in Article 51) and collective security actions taken under a Chapter VII Security Council resolution.

36   J. Allain, "The True Challenge to the United Nations System on the Use of Force: The Failures of Kosovo and Iraq and the Emergence of the African Union," *Max Planck Year-*

Allain argues that, in moving away from the UN framework, African states were motivated not only by the relatively successful interventions by the Economic Community of West African States (ECOWAS) in Liberia and Sierra Leone during the early 1990s (which initially proceeded without UNSC authorisation),[37] but, more importantly, by the failure of the UNSC—and Western states in particular—to act to prevent the carnage in Rwanda. In Allain's words:

One cannot over emphasise the traumatic effects the 1994 Rwanda Genocide had, in moving African states to establish a mechanism to ensure that such mass killing would not happen again. The memory of African leaders and the Continent as a whole, remains scarred by the mass slaughter which transpired in its midst and the indifference manifest by the international community....[38]

For African leaders, the UNSC's image was eroded still further by its controversial authorisation of *Opération Turquoise,* a French mission which many observers believe allowed *génocidaires* to escape to the eastern part of Zaire (now the Democratic Republic of Congo) and did little to protect refugees fleeing the killing fields.[39] This experience led heads of state on the continent to believe that Africans had to take control of their own destiny.

The fall-out from Rwanda had an even more direct impact on the wording of the Constitutive Act. As one scholar has shown, while African leaders desired a new capacity for regional peace and security, and Libya acted as the catalyst for bringing it about, there was less consensus over the precise scope of that capacity.[40] The final wording of Article 4(h) gives the AU prerogatives to intervene that are more ambitious than anything originally envisioned by the Secretariat of the outgoing organisation, the OAU.[41] The original draft the Secretariat presented for negotiation permitted intervention in a member state of the AU *only* with the state's consent, and did not mention intervention in cases of war crimes, genocide, or crimes against humanity.

---

book of *International Law*, 8 (2004), 237-89.

37   The UNSC gave *post facto* authorisation in the case of Liberia.

38   J. Allain, "The True Challenge to the United Nations System", 263.

39   J. Mayall, "Humanitarian Intervention and International Society: Lessons from Africa", in J.M. Welsh, *Humanitarian Intervention and International Relations* (Oxford University Press, 2004), 137.

40   For an in-depth analysis of the drafting process, see C. Haggis, "The African Union and Intervention: The Origins and Implications of Article 4(h) of the Constitutive Act", unpublished Masters thesis, University of Oxford, April 2005, Chaps 2 and 3.

41   It should be noted that the ECOWAS Protocol Relating to the Mechanism for Conflict Prevention, Management, Resolution, Peacekeeping and Security (signed in December 1999) also endorses in Article 22(c) "humanitarian intervention in support of humanitarian disaster."

The release of the IPEP report in May 2000, just before an important ministerial conference of African states in Tripoli, had a notable impact on the shape of Article 4(h), by assisting the proponents of a so-called "right of humanitarian intervention" for the new AU. Their call to address the capacity of African states to protect "their own" now had a powerful endorsement in the form of the IPEP. Moreover, institutionalising a new right to use force for humanitarian purposes had appealing rhetorical value vis-à-vis the rest of the world: "Even if the 'so-called international community' could not be counted on to prevent another Rwanda, *Africans* could."[42]

RtoP in a reformed United Nations. The general question of new criteria to regulate the use of force, and the principle of RtoP in particular, were addressed by the High-level Panel of Experts chosen by Annan in September 2003 to address the growing problems in the UN's collective security system. Mindful of the crisis which the Iraq war had created within international society, the Panel set out five criteria (reminiscent of those identified by ICISS) to determine whether a military action—whether between or within states—would be considered legitimate: seriousness of the threat, proper purpose, last resort, proportional means, and the balance of consequences (meaning that force cannot be justified if it is likely to make matters worse). In addition, the Panel's final report, *A More Secure World,* included as part of "proper purpose" actions designed to save civilians from genocide, ethnic cleansing or other comparable human rights atrocities.[43] The assumption underpinning the Panel's recommendations was that simplifying and standardising criteria for the use of force would make the global collective security system more responsive and legitimate.[44] In other words, a UNSC guided by agreed principles would help to avoid both another Iraq *and* another Rwanda.

This view was echoed by Annan in his report to the UNGA in March 2005, *In Larger Freedom,* a document which was to serve as the basis for discussion at the 60th anniversary of the UN in New York later that year. More specifically, the Secretary General called upon the UNSC to adopt a Resolution setting out the five criteria listed above, and to express its intention to be guided by them when deciding to authorise or mandate the use of force. If states could not reach a consensus on such questions, Annan warned, then the UN risked becoming a stage on which to act out differences, rather than a forum for resolving them. Annan was also clear that he wished to see heads of state agree on the principle of RtoP. In 2004, on the occasion of the tenth anniversary of

---

42   Haggis, "The African Union and Intervention," 80.

43   High-level Panel, *A More Secure World: Our Shared Responsibility,* Report of the Secretary General's High-Level Panel on Threats, Challenges and Change, UN doc. A/59/565 of 2 Dec. 2004, 65-6.

44   Evans, "When is it Right to Fight?", 74.

the Rwandan genocide, the Secretary General had presented a five-point action plan for the prevention of future cases like Rwanda, which included early warning through a new Special Adviser on the Prevention of Genocide. *In Larger Freedom* built on these provisions, by calling for closure of the gap between the rhetoric of support for international humanitarian law, and the reality of state responses to infringement of that law:

It cannot be right, when the international community is faced with genocide or massive human rights abuses, for the United Nations to stand by and let them unfold to the end, with disastrous consequences for many thousands of innocent people ... I believe that we must embrace the responsibility to protect, and, when necessary, we must act on it.[45]

Annan's ambitious plans to overhaul the UN ran into the realities of international politics at the anniversary summit in September 2005. Many of the provisions of *In Larger Freedom,* including reform of UNSC membership and new criteria for the use of force, proved too divisive to gain acceptance by key member states. However, heads of state did agree to enshrine the "responsibility to protect" as a new principle of international conduct.[46] The key clause of the Summit Outcome Document, Article 139, states:

The international community, through the United Nations, also has the responsibility to use appropriate diplomatic, humanitarian and other peaceful means, in accordance with Chapters VI and VII of the Charter, to help protect populations from genocide, war crimes, ethnic cleansing and crimes against humanity. In this context, we are prepared to take collective action, in a timely and decisive manner, through the Security Council, in accordance with the UN Charter, including Chapter VII, on a case by case basis and in cooperation with relevant regional organizations as appropriate, should peaceful means be inadequate and national authorities manifestly failing to protect their populations ....[47]

While Annan and others have referred to this passage as a "historic breakthrough",[48] there are a number of ways in which RtoP has been weakened, and made subject to conflicting interpretations. Both the negotiation process and its outcome suggest that while RtoP has emerged as a potential norm, it has not yet clearly passed through the second stage of Finnemore and Sikkink's norm lifecycle, the "norm cascade". Thus, in the words of the Secretary General's own Special Adviser on the Responsibility to Protect, "in

---

45   K. Annan, *In Larger Freedom: Towards Development, Security, and Human Rights for All*, Report of the United Nations Secretary-General, UN doc. A/59/2005 of 21 Mar. 2005, 48-9.

46   This discussion of the Outcome Document draws on my earlier analysis in "The Responsibility to Protect: Securitizing the Individual in International Society", in Benjamin Goold and Liora Lazarus (eds), *Security and Human Rights* (Oxford: Hart, 2007), 363-83.

47   "2005 World Summit Outcome", UN doc. A/Res/60/1 of 16 Sep. 2005.

48   See UN doc. SG/SM/10161 (12 October 2005).

344

normative terms this historic step is better described as evolutionary than as revolutionary."[49]

To begin, it is worth noting *where* this principle appears in the Summit Outcome Document. Whereas the 2004 High-level Panel had endorsed the notion of a "collective international responsibility to protect" in its discussion of collective security and Chapter VII, the Outcome Document discusses it under the rubric of human rights and the rule of law. I would argue that this represents an aversion on the part of member states to considering intervention for human protection purposes as part of the UN's "standard" practice of collective security.

It is also important to delineate the parameters of the principles. First, the clause places the specific entity of the UN at the heart of this new responsibility. While the ICISS and the High-level Panel spoke of the "international community" or "collective responsibility", the Outcome Document makes clear that the existing inter-governmental processes of the UN will be employed to decide when intervention takes place. This notion of a "UN responsibility to protect" was likely designed to alleviate the fears of some developing countries that powerful states would intervene unilaterally. But by tying RtoP explicitly to the UN (and Chapter VII), the statement does not provide any new legal obligations on the part of individual states, or groupings of states, to prevent the slaughter of civilians. It also moves away from the boldness of the ICISS report, in terms of its willingness to entertain alternatives, should there be failure by the Permanent Five in the UNSC to agree on military action. In this respect, the Outcome Document is less path-breaking than the Constitutive Act of the AU. Second, the threshold for justifying action by the international community is carefully circumscribed. While the ICISS set as its trigger for intervention "large scale loss of life, actual or apprehended, with genocidal intent or not" and "large scale ethnic cleansing, actual or apprehended",[50] Article 139 delimits a more specific set of actions. Interestingly, with the exception of ethnic cleansing, it is identical to the acts mentioned in Article 4(h) of the Constitutive Act of the AU. In the negotiations leading up to the signing of this Act, the question of thresholds generated much debate. Egypt's Foreign Minister, Amr Moussa, was particularly concerned that too general a formulation, referring to gross violations of human rights, would create too wide a space for outside intervention. His preference, which was shared by many others, was to use the less controversial Rome Statute of the International Criminal Court (ICC) as a reference point for determining what would constitute legitimate grounds

49   E. C. Luck, "The Responsible Sovereign and the Responsibility to Protect", in J.W. Muller and K.P. Sauvant (eds), *Annual Review of United Nations Affairs* (Oxford UK: Oxford University Press, forthcoming 2008).

50   *The Responsibility to Protect*, paragraph 4.19.

for intervention.[51] It is plausible to suggest that the diplomats negotiating the Outcome Document took the same approach. And third, the Article leaves scope for differing interpretations on the thorny question of *when* peaceful means have been exhausted. As seen in countless crises—including Kosovo in 1999 and Iraq in 2003—it is extremely difficult to garner a consensus that force really is a last resort, and that no further opportunities for diplomatic negotiation remain.

Perhaps the most significant aspect of Article 139's articulation of the responsibility to protect is what precedes it. Article 138 of the Outcome Document firmly declares that individual sovereign states still bear the responsibility to protect their population from atrocities such as war crimes or ethnic cleansing. The international community's role remains a fall-back position. Subsequent to the World Summit, a number of states—including Algeria, Brazil, China, Egypt, Russia and the United States—have emphasised the hierarchy of responsibilities set out in the Outcome Document as a way of constraining international intervention.[52] As Alex Bellamy and Paul Williams have shown, this hierarchical relationship also enables states to argue about the appropriate trigger for moving from national responsibility to international intervention.[53] Thus, for example, those states that have consistently opposed the application of sanctions against Sudan over the humanitarian catastrophe in Darfur have insisted that sovereign states must be given sufficient time and space to live up to their responsibilities, and that Sudan has not yet definitely proved its "manifest failure" to protect its citizens from mass violations of human rights.

Despite these limitations, the Outcome Document's articulation of RtoP does represent a significant step forward in the protection of civilians. As with all Declarations and Resolutions emanating from the UN, it has questionable status in international law; yet, it stands as a significant statement of political commitment by member states to act in ways not explicitly provided for in the UN Charter: first, to protect their own populations from genocide, war crimes, ethnic cleansing and crimes against humanity; and second, to participate in international efforts (where warranted) to encourage and assist other

---

51   C. Haggis, "The African Union and Intervention," The Rome Statute lists genocide, crimes against humanity, war crimes and the crime of aggression as the most serious actions of concern to the international community as a whole.

52   See, for example, the interventions of these states during the December 2005 Security Council debate on "The Protection of Civilians in Armed Conflict." UN document S/PV.5319 and Resumption 1, 9 Dec. 2005.

53   A.J. Bellamy and P.D. Williams, "The Responsibility to Protect and the Crisis in Darfur," *Security Dialogue*, 36, 1 (2005), 27-47.

states in meeting these obligations.[54] Moreover, the negotiation process over RtoP saw a shake-up in traditional coalitions within the UN—particularly the tendency of "northern" developed countries to encounter resistance from "southern" developing countries, suspicious about unilateral interference in their sovereign jurisdiction. While certain developing countries, such as Pakistan, Algeria and Egypt, continued to vociferously oppose RtoP as weakening the cherished principle of territorial integrity and thereby giving a licence to powerful states to intervene, a series of African states—most notably Rwanda, Botswana and South Africa—stood up in the UNGA to speak in favour of it. This disagreement made it impossible for a developing country "bloc" to paint the responsibility to protect as an interventionist ploy on the part of the developed world. At the time of writing, these African states, along with Western countries such as Canada and the UK, have formed an active "Group of Friends" dedicated to promoting the operationalisation of RtoP.

Finally, the relevant articles of the Outcome Document (138 and 139) were reiterated by the UNSC in its Resolution on The Protection of Civilians in Armed Conflict (UNSC Res. 1674), passed on 28 April 2006. During the UNSC's subsequent open debate on the Resolution, the representative of Tanzania (a non-permanent member of the UNSC) made a strong plea to advance implementation of RtoP:

Appropriate measures in protecting civilians threatened by armed conflicts should go beyond statements of intent or expressions of concern... [W]e urge Member States and international organisations, armed groups, the private sector and other non-state actors, to live up to their responsibilities and continue to display their necessary commitment to ensure decisive and rapid actions to move the war-torn societies from vulnerability to security and from war to peace.[55]

Despite the initial lack of clarity over what the Outcome Document had actually committed states to do, and a degree of "buyers' remorse"[56] on the part of states wary about RtoP, the diplomatic activity surrounding its implementation has recently received a burst of energy. Annan's successor as UN Secretary General, Ban Ki Moon, has made RtoP a key priority for his office and has overseen efforts to limit the principle's scope to the four crimes specified in the outcome document. In addition, the Secretary General has appointed

---

54   Luck, "The Responsible Sovereign and the Responsibility to Protect". Luck argues that the primary task of the international community should be in preventing these four violations from occurring.

55   Representative of Tanzania, UN Security Council Open Debate on The Protection of Civilians in Armed Conflict, 28 June 2006, http://www.reformtheun.org.

56   This phrase was first used in this context by Ed Luck, Special Adviser on the Responsibility to Protect.

a Special Adviser of RtoP who is tasked with developing a programme to operationalise the principle within the various agencies of the UN system.[57]

Conclusion: never again?

Ultimately, successful implementation will determine whether RtoP evolves into a powerful norm within international society. In this regard, there is a hint of irony in Kofi Annan's speech to assembled delegates at the end of the 2005 Summit: "Excellencies, you will be pledged to act if another Rwanda looms."[58] Yet, a continent away, *real* civilians were facing constant threats to their security in Darfur. A year earlier, in July 2004, the UNSC had passed Resolution 1556, condemning the human rights atrocities being committed by *Janjaweed* militia against Sudanese civilians, and threatening the Government of Sudan (GoS) with economic sanctions, if it failed to disarm the militia and bring the perpetrators to justice.[59] Yet, as Bellamy and Williams point out, the Resolution's attempt to bridge the divide between those advocating international action and those resisting intervention on sovereignty grounds resulted in a contradiction. While "there was clear recognition on the part of Western journalists, human rights organisations, and some states of an international responsibility to protect the people of Darfur... [t]here were also significant doubts about how the... responsibility should be allocated in practice, particularly what roles the GoS, AU and UN should assume."[60] In the end, the UNSC was suggesting that the primary responsibility for protecting civilians remained with the GoS, with the AU assisting as a regional partner.

The slow action in Darfur therefore illustrates that, in spite of the "Rwanda effect," where the locus of responsibility for responding to the massacre of civilians within a state remains unclear. Even after the then US Secretary of State Colin Powell stated in September 2004 that his government believed genocide had been committed in Sudan, the response of the UNSC remained limited to monitoring the peace agreement, implementing an arms embargo against parties to the civil conflict and establishing a commission to investigate reports of violations of international humanitarian law.[61] While the UNSC did

---

57   UN doc. S/2001/721, 7 December 2007.

58   K. Annan, "Address to the 2005 World Summit" (New York: 14 September 2005).

59   SC Res. 1556, 30 July 2004. Interestingly, while Article 41 was referred to, the Resolution did not mention the word "sanctions"—a concession to those who still objected to the Council taking this forceful step. In the end, China and Pakistan abstained in the vote on the Resolution.

60   A.J. Bellamy and P.D. Williams, "The UN Security Council and the Question of Humanitarian Intervention in Darfur", *Journal of Military Ethics*, 5, 2 (2006), 150.

61   See the Report of the International Commission of Inquiry on Darfur to the UN Secretary-General (Geneva: 25 January 2005). While the Commission found evidence of attacks

eventually refer the Darfur case to the ICC, it took almost two years before Council members were ready to contemplate a UN force to support the under-resourced African Union.[62] The intransigence and obstructionism of the Khartoum government—particularly around the issue of non-African troops on Sudanese soil—are a large part of the explanation for the UNSC's half-hearted response. However, the unimpressive track record of external actors also reflects the fact that, despite efforts to change the debate from "humanitarian intervention" to "responsibility to protect", we still have not overcome the reluctance of many member states of the UN to act in the affairs of a sovereign state without that state's consent—even on the basis of universal human rights.[63] Above all, the Darfur case demonstrates the UN's inability to force member states to contribute troops to missions with a humanitarian purpose. Although the Council has mandated a joint AU/UN force to take all necessary action to protect civilians in this region, the mission remains critically short of personnel and heavy equipment and is therefore severely compromised in its capacity to fulfil its responsibilities.[64]

The ICISS and High-level Panel member Gareth Evans believes that what most inhibited international action in situations of massive human rights violations in the second half of the 20th century was the "perceived constraint imposed by the UN Charter."[65] While UNSC members had the freedom and authority to interpret threats to international peace and security in an expansive way, the force of Article 2(7) of the UN Charter meant that states, in practice, were not willing to allow the use of external force in response to a catastrophe occurring *within* a sovereign state. The effect of the Rwandan genocide, and the development of the principle of RtoP, appeared to offer a way out. A new discourse on intervention was launched at the start of the 21st century, one that focused more on the protection of civilians at risk, rather than the rights of potential interveners.

that were deliberately and indiscriminately directed against civilians, it concluded that the Government of Sudan was *not* pursuing a policy of genocide. Here, the issue was the absence of clear genocidal intent on the part of the government.

62   In May 2006, the Council passed a Resolution accelerating plans for a UN peacekeeping mission. See SC Res. 1679 of 16 May 2006. In July 2007, in deference to Sudan's demands, it established an AU/UN Hybrid Operation (UNAMID) which would continue to employ a large number of African troops. See SC Res. 1769 of 31 July 2007.

63   See A.J. Bellamy, "Responsibility to Protect or Trojan Horse? The Crisis in Darfur and Humanitarian Intervention after Iraq," *Ethics and International Affairs,* 19, 2 (2005), 31-53.

64   At the time of writing, only about half of the promised 20,000 personnel were on the ground in Darfur.

65   G. Evans, "The Responsibility to Protect: Unfinished Business," *G8 Summit 2006: Issues and Instruments* (15-17 July 2006), http://www.crisisgroup.org/home/index.cfm?id=4269.

But, while RtoP has been formally endorsed both regionally and internationally, it has yet to "cascade" as a norm, let alone become internalised by most states. This suggests that Evans' assessment of what is preventing international action in cases of humanitarian catastrophe may be missing the mark. Significant ambiguity remains, regarding both the moment at which the responsibility for civilians becomes internationalised and the appropriate agent for carrying out that international responsibility. These divisive issues, combined with the fatigue and military overstretch of those who have been strong advocates of RtoP, mean that we are not yet in a position to promise "no more Rwandas".

18

SOME LESSONS FOR THE INTERNATIONAL CRIMINAL COURT FROM THE INTERNATIONAL JUDICIAL RESPONSE TO THE RWANDAN GENOCIDE

Morten Bergsmo and Philippa Webb

Introduction

As Ocampo observes in his Foreword, the establishment of a permanent international criminal court is closely connected to the tragedy of the Rwandan genocide. It may be strange to think that the confused and inadequate international responses to the death of some 800,000 Rwandan Tutsi and moderate Hutu could one day contribute to the founding of the International Criminal Court (ICC), but this is what has occurred. As Kaufman details in chapter 12, the UN Security Council (UNSC)'s decision to establish the UN International Criminal Tribunal for Rwanda (ICTR) in November 1994 came only 18 months after the adoption of the resolution creating the UN International Criminal Tribunal for the former Yugoslavia (ICTY). From the post-World War II trials until the early 1990s, there were no international criminal tribunals. The founding of the ICTR therefore signalled the emergence of an international criminal justice system, rather than being an isolated jurisdictional experiment. The hybrid international criminal jurisdictions in Kosovo, East Timor and Sierra Leone quickly followed. The Iraqi High Tribunal and the Cambodian Extraordinary Chambers arrived a short time later.[1]

The ICTR has clearly had an impact on the way the international community thinks about achieving peace and justice in the wake of mass atrocities. As

---

1   See also R. P. Alford, "The Proliferation of International Courts and Tribunals: International Adjudication in Ascendance," *American Society of International Law Proceedings*, 94 (2000), 160 ("Depending on one's count, more than fifty international courts and tribunals are now in existence, with more than thirty of these established in the past twenty years").

Jallow and Ngoga note in chapters 13 and 16, respectively, the ICTR's establishment and operation have helped define the contemporary understanding of international criminal justice and reinforced the notion of individual criminal responsibility, even for leaders. This chapter will consider some of the ways in which the ICC has been influenced by the international judicial response to the Rwandan genocide—from the emphasis on the role of international justice in preventing crimes to the institutional and legal lessons learned and applied in this fledgling international organisation.

A renewed commitment to prevention and deterrence

The delayed and inadequate response of the international community to the systematic slaughter of approximately 800,000 Rwandans was inexcusable. As the UN Independent Inquiry on the Genocide in Rwanda found, "The international community did not prevent the genocide, nor did it stop the killing once the genocide had begun."[2] This catastrophic failure of political will still looms large more than fourteen years later. Its repercussions can be observed in numerous places, such as the appointment of a UN Special Adviser on the Prevention of Genocide; the World Summit's declaration, discussed further in the previous chapter by Welsh, that every state has the "responsibility to protect" its populations; and the readiness of some governments and organisations to describe events in the Darfur region of Sudan, as "genocide".

This renewed expressed commitment to prevention and deterrence can also be observed in the language of the Preamble of the Rome Statute, which was adopted in Rome on 17 July 1998 and entered into force on 1 July 2002. The Preamble enshrines the fundamental values that underpin the ICC, the world's first permanent international criminal tribunal, and guide all of its work. The Preamble commits States Parties to preventing, punishing, and ultimately deterring the most serious crimes of concern to the international community as a whole. Paragraph 1 of the Preamble establishes the context by acknowledging that there is a consciousness that the "delicate mosaic of our shared heritage" may be shattered at any time, as it was from April to July 1994. Paragraph 2 provides that the Court is established in the shadow of "unimaginable atrocities," such as the Rwandan genocide. Paragraph 3 recognises that such atrocities are not just "ordinary crimes", with which society has learned to live, but "such grave crimes" that they endanger the "peace, security and well-being of the world."[3] As Otto Triffterer, a leading authority on international criminal

---

2   "Report of the Independent Inquiry into the actions of the United Nations during the 1994 genocide in Rwanda" (1999) UN Doc S/1999/1257, 3.

3   O. Triffterer, "Preamble - Paragraph 3: Recognition of protected values" in O. Triffterer (ed.), *Commentary on the Rome Statute of the International Criminal Court* (Nomos

law, argues, this formula refers to both the basic, inherent values of the community of nations and those values "which belong to *national* legal orders, but need *supplementary* protection by the *international* legal order to counter the threat of abuse of State power."[4] This makes clear that attacks by states on their own populations cannot be considered merely internal affairs, but invoke the concern of the international community as a whole.

Paragraph 4 of the Preamble of the ICC Statute is central to understanding the strengthened commitment to achieving accountability for crimes such as the Rwandan genocide. It provides that "the most serious crimes of concern to the international community as a whole must not go unpunished, and that their effective prosecution must be ensured by taking measures at the national level and by enhancing international cooperation."[5] This paragraph affirms the objective of punishing the most serious crimes, acknowledging the necessity of indirect enforcement at the national level. The experience of the ICTR, with its current track record of 35 judgements, clearly shows that even among "the most serious crimes of concern to the international community as a whole" not all crimes committed can, in practice, be prosecuted by the ICC.[6] It is therefore necessary to engage national jurisdictions and to adopt a co-operative approach to ensure effective prosecution.

The apparent objective of punishment described in paragraph 4 of the Preamble is logically developed in paragraph 5, which addresses the real objective of prevention by enforcement: "Determined to put an end to impunity for the perpetrators of these crimes and thus to contribute to the prevention of such crimes."[7] The prosecution of international crimes fulfils the repressive function of criminal law. The ICC also aims to fulfil the more important second function: prevention. The sheer number of victims and perpetrators of the Rwandan genocide alone reminds us that crime prevention or deterrence is generally held to be the more effective method of protecting legal values in practice. Needless to say, it would have been better for the genocide never to have taken place than for its perpetrators to be effectively prosecuted after the event. The ICC aims to contribute to the prevention of such crimes by building awareness and showing potential criminals that the perpetrators of the "most serious crimes of concern to the international community as a whole" will no longer enjoy immunity from effective enforcement mechanisms.

Baden-Baden, 1999), 9.

4   Ibid., emphasis in original.

5   Preamble of the Rome Statute, paragraph 4.

6   O. Triffterer, "Preamble – Paragraph 4: Affirmation of aims to be achieved" in Triffterer (ed.), *Commentary on the Rome Statute*, 11.

7   Preamble of the Rome Statute, paragraph 5.

The irrelevance of suspects' official capacity in Article 27 is a clear manifestation of the determination to put an end to impunity.[8] The ICTR has led the way in this respect. The 35 persons who have received judgements to date at the ICTR include one prime minister, four government ministers, two *préfets* and five *bourgmestres*, as well as media and military leaders.[9] The guilty plea and subsequent conviction of Jean Kambanda, former Prime Minister of Rwanda, marked the first time that a head of government had been convicted for the crime of genocide.

The ICC is only one aspect of what appears to be a renewed commitment to prevention and deterrence, and it cannot put an end to atrocities such as the Rwandan genocide on its own. Many take the view that the ICC should be integrated with other mechanisms such as national investigations and prosecutions, fact-finding missions, public education, decisive UNSC action, and civil proceedings focused on redress for victims, to replace a culture of impunity with a culture of accountability.[10] This is a reasonable hope, although it remains to be seen how effective the ICC's contribution will be.

Some institutional lessons learned: organising for effectiveness, flexibility and speed

Important institutional lessons have been learned from the international judicial response to the Rwandan genocide, and the subsequent experiences of the ICTR.

A standing court. The problem of the slow international judicial response to Rwanda was an important rationale for creating a standing court. International inaction, conflict and confusion characterised the Rwandan genocide and its aftermath. Although the UNSC resolution establishing the ICTR was passed in November 1994, the Tribunal had no courtrooms, offices, prison, legal officers, or secretaries until September 1995. Judges were not regarded as having officially taken office until 19 June 1996, and it was not until September 1996 that they were able to take up residence in Arusha.[11] The first indictment was confirmed in a hotel room.[12] These delays were not unique to the ICTR. Mak-

---

8   O. Triffterer, "Preamble - Paragraph 5: Prevention by Enforcement" in Triffterer (ed.), *Commentary on the Rome Statute,* 12.

9   E. Møse, "Main Achievements of the ICTR", *Journal of International Criminal Justice,* 3 (2005), 932.

10   P. Kirsch, "Introduction" in Triffterer (ed.), *Commentary on the Rome Statute,* xxviii.

11   Møse, "Main Achievements of the ICTR", 922.

12   *Kayishema et al (Decision)* ICTR-95-I (28 November 1995), Review of indictment by Judge Navanethem Pillay. Referred to in E. Møse, "Main Achievements of the ICTR", 922.

ing the ICTY an operational UN criminal justice mandate in 1993 to 1996 was very difficult indeed, with particular challenges in areas such as recruitment, investigative missions, witness protection, and court management.[13] The accumulation of such experiences, with the difficult establishment and activation of internationalised criminal jurisdictions, gave significant weight to the arguments for a permanent Court that would be prepared at short notice to analyse, investigate, and prosecute international crimes.

Unlike the *ad hoc* Tribunals, the ICC was established as a permanent court with prospective jurisdiction running from 1 July 2002. It can potentially address crimes committed anywhere in the world. In contrast to the hybrid courts in places like Sierra Leone and East Timor, the ICC is an independent international organisation with international staff based in The Hague. It has a standing administrative and operational capacity to deal with new allegations of crimes within its jurisdiction.

Professional, highly qualified staff. During the establishment of the ICTR, the necessary professional group of international judges, lawyers, and administrators with expertise in international criminal law and justice barely existed. In addition, it was almost impossible to recruit Rwandan lawyers, because virtually all of them had been killed or had fled the country. By comparison, the ICC was in an enviable situation when it was being established, in that many professionals with experience from internationalised criminal jurisdictions after 1993 were prepared to join the ICC during the first few years of its existence. The ICC aspires to maintain a core staff of highly qualified professionals, equipped with innovative legal tools and effective training. This approach aims at keeping human resource costs low and encouraging better communication and swifter action.

External networks. Over time, the human and financial resources of the ICTR and the ICTY have dramatically increased. This has attracted some criticism, for example by Ngoga in chapter 16, and arguably precipitated the strict monitoring by the UNSC of the so-called completion strategy of the Tribunals. The ICC is trying to learn from this experience by maintaining a small, flexible office, and by relying on extensive external networks of support, rather than bringing that expertise in-house. The ICC tries to build bridges with states, civil society, multilateral institutions, academics, and the private sector. It is hoped that this approach may enable the Court to benefit from skills, ideas, and perspectives from around the world without significantly expanding its budget or staff. This is an objective over which both the Court and the public can easily monitor actual achievements.

---

13   The co-author, Morten Bergsmo, was the first lawyer in the staff of the ICTY Office of the Prosecutor, commencing service in May 1994.

The difference is clear when one compares figures from the ICTR and ICC. For 2008-9, the UN General Assembly decided to appropriate to the ICTR a total net budget of US$280,386,800, and authorised 1,032 posts.[14] In the case of the ICC, the Assembly of States Parties approved a budget of €90,382,000 (or around US$131 million) for 2008, and, as of October 2004, there were 679 posts.[15] As more cases go to trial, the ICC will inevitably need significantly increased resources. It remains to be seen how the policy of using external networks wherever possible will affect this increase. A comparison of the ratios in the ICC and the ICTR/ICTY of the overall number of staff and those working full time on cases could be indicative.

Contingency Fund. The delays in setting up the ICTR and the ICTY can be traced in part to the insufficient funds available in the first years of operation. It appears that the ICC States Parties have learned from this start-up difficulty. The ICC Assembly of States Parties has approved the establishment of a Contingency Fund in the amount of €10,000,000. With these resources, the Court can meet costs associated with unforeseen complications, following, for example, a decision by the Prosecutor in mid-budget to commence an investigation in response to fresh allegations of crimes in a new situation, or unavoidable expenses for developments in existing situations that could not be accurately estimated at the time of the adoption of the budget. The Fund could also be used for costs associated with an unforeseen meeting of the Assembly of States Parties itself.

Addressing the impunity gap. The challenge of achieving accountability for mass atrocities is epitomised in the situation in Rwanda. The death of some 800,000 people within 100 days involved thousands upon thousands of perpetrators. At the same time, Rwandans have insisted upon criminal prosecution for all alleged offenders. For nine years after 1994, more than 100,000 people were in detention in Rwanda. Despite the provisional release of 25,000 prisoners in 2003, the International Committee for the Red Cross (ICRC) estimated that 89,000 were still detained as of January 2005.[16] National trials began in 1996, and approximately 10,000 suspects have been tried.[17] For its part, the ICTR had rendered judgements in respect of 33 accused, with six acquittals

---

14   "General Information – Budget and Staff," ICTR official website, http://www.ictr.org.

15   Official Records of the Assembly of States Parties to the Rome Statute of the International Criminal Court, Sixth session, The Hague,30 November to 14 December 2007 (International Criminal Court publication), Part III, 74.

16   W. A. Schabas, "Genocide Trials and *Gacaca* Courts", *Journal of International Criminal Justice*, 3 (2005), 880.

17   Ibid., 888.

so far. Trials involving an additional 29 suspects are in progress, and seven people are awaiting trial.[18]

The combination of the potential global reach of the ICC, the expanded range of crimes that come under its Statute, and its resource constraints means that the ICC must be selective in taking on cases. To this end, the ICC Office of the Prosecutor (OTP) has taken a policy decision to focus its efforts:

The Court is an institution with limited resources. The Office will function with a two-tiered approach to combat impunity. On the one hand it will initiate prosecutions of the leaders who bear most responsibility for the crimes. On the other hand it will encourage national prosecutions, where possible, for the lower-ranking perpetrators, or work with the international community to ensure that the offenders are brought to justice by some other means.[19]

The risk is that focusing on those who bear the greatest responsibility may leave an "impunity gap" unless national authorities, the international community, and the Court work together to ensure that other perpetrators are brought to justice, in a way that corresponds to reasonable expectations. To this end, co-operation between the ICC and other actors will be crucial. There should be international assistance for strengthening or rebuilding the national criminal justice systems in states where serious crimes have been committed. As Warren and Cole argue in chapter 14, widespread sharing of knowledge, tools and methodologies for cost-effective and fair documentation, investigation, and prosecution of international crimes will be of great significance.

Legal lessons learned: empowerment through preparedness

When the ICTR and the ICTY began operating, they lacked the systems or tools to analyse, investigate, and prosecute the core international crimes committed in Rwanda and the former Yugoslavia. Nuremberg happened in another era, and there were no comparable or model programmes of national trials to copy. Work processes, models and tools had to be developed from scratch. Procedural and substantive commentaries on international criminal law did not exist. A visitor to the ICTR in 1998 found that the Tribunal's library "consisted of two small wheeled trolleys piled with a random assortment of donated international legal reference books."[20]

This lack of preparedness made the initial task of building the credibility of the ICTR and the ICTY very difficult. As Ngoga observes in chapter 16, while

---

18   See "Status of Detainees Cases" at http://www.ictr.org (updated 2 March 2008).

19   "Paper on some policy issues before the Office of the Prosecutor," September 2003, http://www.icc-cpi.int/library/organs/otp/030905_Policy_Paper.pdf, (4 November 2005), 3.

20   S. Power, "Rwanda: The Two Faces of Justice," *The New York Review of Books*, 50, 1 (16 January 2003).

staff and budgets grew, progress was at times described as sluggish, while ICTR and ICTY principals failed to adequately explain the dimensions of the challenge at hand. Understanding these challenges, however, the states that negotiated and set up the ICC provided in its first budget for the development and maintenance of networked legal tools and services, by the Legal Advisory Section (LAS) of the Office of the Prosecutor (OTP). The tools and services were meant to serve several purposes:

1. To empower staff to find for themselves, through a computer network, answers to most legal questions they encounter, in work on core international crimes. This increases the autonomy and efficiency of existing staff, thus reducing the need for growth in human resources, and avoiding strain on the Court's budget;

2. To avoid duplication of legal research and drafting exercises within the Court, and its Organs and participants. Legal issues tend to return or appear in multiple contexts, albeit with slight differences of nuance. Responding to them can consume much time and many resources. Ensuring efficient availability of the relevant legal information on earlier work is important;

3. To increase the quality of legal submissions and other legal drafting in relation to both procedural and substantive aspects of the practice of international criminal law. The quality of submissions and decisions is decisive for their weight and capacity to serve as precedents, which again has an essential impact on the efficiency of work processes in an international jurisdiction.

The Legal Tools Project. Since 2003, the LAS of the OTP has developed a range of electronic and web-based legal tools and services, collectively known as the *Legal Tools Project.* The Project provides more than ten collections and databases of legal information, three commentaries and two applications. It offers a complete collection of resources relevant to the theory and practice of international criminal law and justice, and brings modern technologies to the investigation and prosecution of core international crimes. By 2008, the Legal Tools Project amounted to some ten gigabytes of legal information. As a whole, it represents the most important single research resource in international criminal law.[21]

Among the key components of the Legal Tools Project are the following:

• The *Elements Commentary*: A doctrinal, electronic commentary on each element of the crimes and legal requirements of the modes of liability in the ICC Statute. It draws on all main sources of international criminal law, and gives users direct access to important sources on the substantive law of the ICC Statute. The Commentary incorporates and takes fully into account the influence of the ICTR jurisprudence regarding, for example, the interpretation of the crime of genocide, the

---

21 Information about the *Legal Tools* can be found at the website of the ICC (http://www.icc-cpi.int).

affirmation of rape as an international crime, and the prosecution of incitement to commit genocide.

- The *Means of Proof Document*: A service that provides a detailed compilation of commentary and international criminal jurisprudence, from sources including the ICTR, on the type or category of facts which can constitute potential evidence for the existence or satisfaction of the specific legal requirement of an international crime or mode of liability. By 2008, the *Document* amounted to more than 6,000 A4 pages of text.

- The *Proceedings Commentary*: A detailed commentary on criminal law proceedings as contained in the ICC Statute, the Rules of Procedure and Evidence, and the Regulations of the Court. It provides a far-reaching analysis of key legal issues of international criminal procedure and evidence.

- The *ICC "Preparatory Works" Database*: A database that contains more than 9,000 official and unofficial documents, related to the negotiation and drafting of the ICC Statute, the Rules of Procedure and Evidence, and the Elements of Crimes, issued by states, NGOs, academic institutions, the UN, and other international organisations between December 1989 and September 2002.

- Selected documents from international criminal jurisdictions: The collection includes the primary law, indictments, judgements and other selected decisions of international and allied military tribunals sitting in Nuremberg and Tokyo, the ICTY, the ICTR, UN Mission for Kosovo (UNMIK) courts and tribunals, the Special Court for Sierra Leone, the East Timor Panels for Serious Crimes, the Iraqi High Tribunal and the Cambodian Extraordinary Chambers.

- Selected documents from national criminal jurisdictions: The collection includes national instruments implementing the ICC Statute and the most relevant decisions issued by domestic courts and tribunals concerning genocide, crimes against humanity, and war crimes.

- The *Legal Tools Project* also includes selected international treaties, decisions of regional and international human rights bodies, internet websites with relevant legal information, and academic works relevant to the research and practice of international criminal law, as well as public international law, international human rights law, and international humanitarian law.

The Case Matrix. An important component of the *Legal Tools Project* is the *Case Matrix*, a unique, law-driven case management application representing a significant innovation in how to approach the analysis, investigation, and prosecution of international crimes. It is tailor-made for core international crimes cases. The *Case Matrix* incorporates some of the legal tools described above, such as the *Elements Commentary* and the *Means of Proof Document*. The *Matrix* provides a database service to organise and present the potential evidence in a case, in a manner that can be customised to different users such as prosecutors, judges, defence counsel and victims' counsel. This gives a "snapshot" overview of the status of a case at any stage of the work processes. The emphasis on this feature is a direct result of the observation, which Warren and Cole also make in chapter 14, that it is difficult to develop and preserve proper overview of information and potential evidence in large core international crimes cases, which may lead to lengthy and costly proceedings, as can be seen in several internationalised criminal jurisdictions.

The *Case Matrix* application has been introduced both within and outside the ICC. It has been translated into Bahasa Indonesia and Arabic to facilitate the work of the Indonesian Prosecutor General's directorate for international crimes cases and the Iraqi High Tribunal. It has also been translated into Khmer for the Cambodian Extraordinary Chambers. A French version also exists. There are other national expressions of interest in the *Matrix*, notably from Canada, Denmark, Germany, Italy, Norway, Serbia and Montenegro.

The intention of the ICC is to make the *Legal Tools Project*, including the *Case Matrix*, common property or public goods. In early 2006, the legal tools were gradually made available to the public on the website of the ICC, making the ICC the host of the most comprehensive virtual international criminal law library. The website should become the focal point for practitioners and scholars of international criminal law around the globe.

The public release of the *Legal Tools* serves several purposes. First, it is hoped that the *Legal Tools* will play a role in harmonising the development of substantive international criminal law. Second, the *Tools* have the potential to help rationalise the work processes linked to the analysis, investigation, prosecution, and adjudication of core international crimes cases by domestic and other internationalised user-institutions. Finally, by sharing tools and methodologies developed within the Court with national criminal justice systems, the ICC contributes to local competence building.

Conclusion

The ICC is preparing organisationally and legally to respond faster and more effectively to atrocities like the Rwandan genocide, and ultimately, to contribute to preventing such tragedies from occurring in the first place. By 2008, the Court had received three state referrals from Uganda, the Democratic Republic of Congo (DRC) and the Central African Republic. The ICC had also received one UNSC referral regarding Darfur, whose situation some states initially—and, given the ICC's aforementioned strengths over the ICTR, unwisely—suggested referring to the ICTR.[22]

---

22   Z. D. Kaufman, "Justice in Jeopardy: Accountability for the Darfur Atrocities" *Criminal Law Forum*, 16, 4 (April 2006), 343-60.

The Rwandan genocide has influenced the establishment and management of the ICC in conceptual and practical terms. From the drafting of the ICC Statute to the investigative approach to events in Uganda and the DRC—particularly the ICC's focus on investigating the most serious crimes committed by high-ranking military leaders in these countries, as the ICTR has sought to do in the Rwandan context—the ICC has been trying to apply lessons learned since those hundred catastrophic days in 1994. The *ICC Legal Tools*, in particular, are a significant illustration of this learning process. The *Tools* provide practitioners of international criminal law with a unique combination of collections, databases, commentaries and applications to work rationally and in a cost-effective manner. They constitute an important contribution to the activities of users such as national criminal justice systems, and NGOs concerned with documenting and reporting gross human rights violations which may amount to core international crimes. Thus, the ICC seeks to hasten the evolution of international criminal law, a process that reached a critical phase in the operation of the ICTR in the aftermath of the Rwandan genocide.

19

BALANCING JUSTICE AND ORDER: STATE-BUILDING AND THE PROSECUTION OF WAR CRIMES IN RWANDA AND KOSOVO

Dominik Zaum

Issues of transitional justice have been central to many conflicts in the post-Cold War period, as societies, governments and international organisations try to come to terms with major human rights violations, to encourage reconciliation, and to devise structures and institutions to hold the perpetrators accountable. Different countries have chosen different paths to attain transitional justice, weighing concerns about domestic order, justice and reconciliation when establishing institutions of transitional justice.[1] However, the international debates that followed the Rwandan genocide—about military intervention to prevent genocide, the responsibility to protect, and the establishment of international judicial institutions to deter major human rights violations—have resonated in the demands and discussions during later conflicts.[2] This chapter aims to provide a comparison to the Rwanda case, looking at the ways in which transitional justice issues have been addressed in the context of the international intervention and state-building efforts in Kosovo, and how these efforts have been influenced by the experience of Rwanda.

The case of Kosovo differs from Rwanda in particular because of the major role that international actors have played in the governance and reconstruction of post-conflict Kosovo. Transitional justice in Kosovo, in addition to addressing past atrocities, was also thought to contribute to the building and strengthening of governance institutions. In addition to peace-building, it was part of the state-building effort. Furthermore, the deep involvement of the US and European states, and of international organisations like the United Nations (UN), the European Union (EU) and the Organisation of Security and Coopera-

---

1   J. Snyder and L. Vinjamuri, "Trials and Errors: Principle and Pragmatism in Strategies of International Justice", *International Security*, 28/3 (Winter 2003/04), 5-44.

2   See, e.g., Jennifer Welsh's chapter 17.

tion in Europe (OSCE) in post-conflict peace- and state-building processes led to an emphasis on formal justice mechanisms to hold accountable perpetrators of war crimes, crimes against humanity, and other atrocities. These states and organisations often sought to ensure the application of stringent international procedural standards for the administration of justice when dealing with war crimes, and pursued the internationalisation of the institutions responsible for guaranteeing these standards, either through the UN International Criminal Tribunal for the Former Yugoslavia (ICTY) or by including international legal personnel in domestic courts. As a consequence, the UN Interim Administration Mission in Kosovo (UNMIK) prioritised the use of formal justice mechanisms in Kosovo over alternative, indigenous procedures, such as the Comissão de Acolhimento, Verdade e Reconciliação, Commission for Reception, Truth, and Reconciliation, known by its Portuguese abbreviation, CAVR, in East Timor[3] or the *gacaca* process in Rwanda, both of which were established on local initiative.

Traditionally, the relationship between order and justice has been described as characterised by tensions, with justice seen to be realisable only within the context of order.[4] In recent years, however, this relationship has often been reversed, and international organisations and liberal Western states have increasingly viewed justice issues as a condition for order, peace and stability, as reflected in John Rawls's dictum, "Justice is the first virtue of social institutions".[5] In the words of Hansjörg Strohmeyer, legal adviser to the Special Representative of the Secretary General (SRSG) both in Kosovo and in East Timor,

a functioning judicial system can positively affect reconciliation and confidence-building efforts within often highly traumatized post-crisis societies, *not least because it can bring to justice those responsible for grave violations of international humanitarian and human rights law*.[6]

Pursuing transitional justice is viewed as helping to instil confidence and trust in public life, and to enhance the credibility of newly established democratic and human rights institutions, as it shows that perpetrators of war crimes

---

3   P. Pigou, *Crying Without Tears - In Pursuit of Justice and Reconciliation in Timor-Leste: Community Perspectives and Expectations*, International Centre for Transitional Justice (ICTJ) Occasional Papers (New York: ICTJ, 2003).

4   Snyder and Vinjamuri, "Trials and Errors", 6.

5   J. Rawls, *A Theory of Justice*, revised edition (Oxford, UK: Oxford University Press, 1999), 3.

6   H.-J. Strohmeyer, "Collapse and Reconstruction of a Judicial System: The United Nations Missions in Kosovo and East Timor", *American Journal of International Law*, 95, (2001), 60 (emphasis added).

cannot commit them with impunity.[7] So, it is claimed, transitional justice is a condition not only for peace and security, but also for the establishment of functioning political institutions; it contributes not only to peace-building but also to state-building.

The example of Kosovo provides a useful case study to explore the influence of emerging international norms of transitional justice which have been significantly shaped by the Rwandan experience,[8] emphasising accountability through the formal judicial system, and to assess to what extent this contributes to post-conflict peace- and state-building. In Kosovo, international involvement has been extensive. Unlike Rwanda, where the national government runs the domestic judicial system, Kosovo has been under UN administration since 1999, with UNMIK maintaining full responsibility for the administration of justice, including the prosecution of war crimes and crimes against humanity, together with the ICTY.[9] In addition, Kosovo's location in Europe has meant that European institutions, like the OSCE, the EU and the Council of Europe, all of which have strongly favoured formal judicial mechanisms for the prosecution of such crimes, have been deeply involved in the transitional justice process. The lack of trust that ethnic minorities in particular have in the judicial institutions, and the lenient response by the courts to the violence against ethnic minorities in March 2004, suggest that the contribution of transitional justice efforts to state-building and peace-building have been limited—an issue to which I will return at the end of the chapter.[10] This chapter will show that, while Rwanda's experience of bringing genocide suspects to account has influenced approaches to transitional justice in Kosovo in key respects, justice institutions in the Kosovo case have faced similar problems to those concerning Rwanda and often repeated their mistakes. This suggests a failure to learn important lessons from the past but also highlights some intrinsic limitations of transitional justice after mass atrocity, particularly as a result of unavoidable political challenges to delivering justice.

This chapter is divided into three parts. The first provides the background for the main discussion: it will briefly look at the nature of the conflict in Kos-

---

7   E. Newman, "'Transitional Justice': The Impact of Transnational Norms and the UN", in Albrecht Schnabel (ed.), *Recovering from Civil Conflict: Reconciliation, Peace and Development* (London: Frank Cass, 2002).

8   See, e.g., chapter 13 by Hassan Bubacar Jallow.

9   UNMIK, UNMIK/Regulation/1999/1, "On the Authority of the Interim Administration in Kosovo", 25 July 1999.

10   According to two surveys conducted in November 2006 and February 2007, only 5 per cent of Kosovo Serbs trusted the Kosovo judicial institutions "fully" or "very much." See Saferworld, *Human Security in Kosovo: a Survey of Perceptions*, London, May 2007, 33. On the judiciary's response to the March 2004 riots, see OSCE, *The Response of the Justice System to the March 2004 Riots* (Pristina, December 2005).

ovo and the crimes committed during and afterwards. The second will look at the different methods chosen to address war crimes in Kosovo, examining both the role of the ICTY and the use of domestic and "hybrid" courts, highlighting crucial similarities to, and differences from, transitional justice approaches in the Rwandan case. The final part will outline some tentative "lessons learned" from the Kosovo experience of accountability for major perpetrators and assess the effect of these mechanisms on peace-and state-building and their relevance for transitional justice more broadly.

The war and human rights in Kosovo

Throughout the 1990s, Kosovo remained relatively calm despite the revocation of its autonomy in 1989 by Slobodan Milošević and the conflicts that engulfed several of its neighbours, in particular Bosnia and Herzegovina and Croatia. From the early 1990s onwards, ethnic Albanians were effectively excluded from public life and lost their jobs in the public sector and socially owned enterprises. Increasingly, Kosovo's majority population was subjected to arbitrary police violence.[11] Until 1998, the Kosovo Albanians responded with peaceful resistance and the establishment of a parallel, shadow state, providing healthcare and education.[12] However, growing disillusionment with the policy of peaceful resistance after the 1995 Dayton Agreement, which failed to address the Kosovo issue, led to emerging armed resistance, in particular from the Ushtria Çlirimtare e Kosovës (UÇK or Kosovo Liberation Army). In 1998, this development triggered a violent response from Serb security forces, leading to the displacement of more than 200,000 Kosovo Albanians. Violence escalated despite the presence of international observers from October 1998 onwards, and the failure to forge a political settlement led to NATO's military action against Yugoslavia, starting on 24 March 1999.

War crimes and crimes against humanity committed by Serb police, security forces and paramilitaries, before and during the war, have been extensively documented in the harrowing report, *Human Rights in Kosovo: As Seen as Told*,[13] compiled by the OSCE after the war. As a result of the Serb ethnic cleansing campaign, at least 860,000 Albanians fled Kosovo, often at gunpoint, and a further 250,000 were internally displaced. More than 70 per cent

---

11   T. Judah, *Kosovo: War and Revenge* (2nd edition) (New Haven: Yale University Press, 2002), 61-98; Noel Malcolm, *Kosovo: A Short History* (Basingstoke: Macmillan, 1998), 344-6.

12   See H. Clark, *Civil Resistance in Kosovo* (London: Pluto Press, 2000).

13   OSCE, *Human Rights in Kosovo: As Seen, As Told (Volume I: October 1998-June 1999)* (Pristina: OSCE, 1999).

of the Albanian population was forced out of their homes by Serb forces.[14] In most municipalities, mass killings of civilians were carried out. Among the most prominent and most hideous incidents were the Racak massacre of January 1999, in which 45 Albanians, mostly civilians, were killed, some of them decapitated;[15] and the killing of 22 civilians by the Yugoslav army in Podujevo, on 24 March 1999.[16] Since the end of the war, the ICTY has exhumed approximately 4,300 bodies from mass graves.[17]

However, not only Serb forces but also the UÇK committed war crimes and major human rights violations. Both during and, in particular, after the conflict in Kosovo, UÇK fighters not only abducted and killed Serb civilians and people of the Roma and other minorities, but also Albanians they considered to be "collaborating" with the Serbs.[18] After the withdrawal of Serb police and military forces in June 1999, and the arrival of the NATO-led Kosovo Force (KFOR) troops and UNMIK, violence against Serb and Roma civilians started almost immediately: houses and churches were torched, and members of minority groups were rounded up, beaten, and tortured.[19] Much of the violence was aimed at encouraging Serbs and Roma to leave Kosovo, and of the estimated 250,000 to 300,000 Serbs and Roma who lived in Kosovo before the war, only around 100,000 have remained.[20] Four years after the war, the ICRC still listed 3,525 persons as missing from Kosovo,[21] among them 1,200 non-Albanians, mostly Serbs and Roma.[22]

Transitional justice in Kosovo

At the outset of UNMIK, supported by UN Security Council (UNSC) Resolution 1244, the UN asserted that all executive and legislative power, including the ad-

---

14 Conflict Security and Development Group (CSDG), *A Review of Peace Operations: A Case for Change - Kosovo Study* (London: King's College, 2003), para. 12.

15 OSCE, *As Seen, As Told (Vol.I)*, 602-28.

16 Ibid., 71-2.

17 Human Rights Watch, *Under Orders: War Crimes in Kosovo* (New York: Human Rights Watch, 2001), 122.

18 Ibid., 70-1.

19 W. G. O'Neill, *Kosovo: Unfinished Peace* (Boulder: Lynne Rienner, 2002); OSCE, *Human Rights in Kosovo: As Seen, As Told (Volume II: July 1999 - October 1999)* (Pristina: OSCE, 1999).

20 Figures from Statistical Office of Kosovo.

21 Cited in OSCE, *War Crimes Before Domestic Courts: OSCE Monitoring and Empowering of the Domestic Courts to Deal with War Crimes* (Belgrade: OSCE, 2003), 15.

22 ICG, *Finding the Balance: The Scales of Justice in Kosovo*, ICG Balkans Report No. 134 (Pristina: ICG, 2002), 17.

ministration of justice, would be exercised by UNMIK.[23] While legislative and executive functions have been largely devolved to Kosovar institutions,[24] the development of the judiciary has experienced the opposite phenomenon, and international control over judicial institutions has strengthened since 1999.[25] The responsibility to prosecute war crimes has so far remained mostly under the authority of UNMIK and the ICTY. Unlike in Rwanda, the authority in Kosovo under which crimes are addressed is not shared between the Tribunal and a sovereign government, but between the Tribunal and the UN-led international administration. The international community has relied exclusively on the formal justice system to prosecute war crimes—through the ICTY and through local courts in Kosovo—and has tried to uphold international standards, particularly procedural standards, in the domestic court system in Kosovo.

If transitional justice is supposed to be a condition for successful peace- and state-building, how successful, and how important have the contributions by the ICTY and the domestic courts been? Although the Tribunal has been prominent among Kosovar Albanians, in particular because of the trial of the late Slobodan Milošević, in the context of the Kosovo war it has played only a very limited role in bringing war criminals to justice, as it has been under strong resource constraints and thus has decided to focus on the main decision-makers. Of the 99 cases and indictments listed on the ICTY website, only six relate to the Kosovo conflict. The following analysis will therefore only look briefly at the ICTY and will focus more on the role of the courts in Kosovo.

The ICTY. A unique aspect of transitional justice in Kosovo has been that one of the key justice mechanisms—the ICTY, which would later serve as the model for and be institutionally tied to the ICTR—had already been in place before the conflict had fully broken out. While the ICTY had been established in 1993 in response to the atrocities in the Bosnian conflict, its jurisdiction potentially covered all of the former Yugoslavia, including Kosovo. As Bergsmo and Webb point out in the previous chapter, the tragedy of the Rwandan genocide contributed to a renewed commitment to preventing and deterring such atrocities, and with a court with jurisdiction over Kosovo in place already, advocates hoped that its presence and the fear of prosecution could act as a deterrence, or

---

23   UNMIK Regulation 1999/1 of 25 July 1999.

24   Resolution 1244 mandated UNMIK to build democratic institutions of self-governance, and work towards the resolution of Kosovo's status. The resolution of Kosovo's status is still ongoing. On 31 October 2005, the UN Secretary-General appointed the former Finnish President Martti Ahtisaari as his special envoy for the status of Kosovo. Ahtisaari presented his proposal for the resolution of the status question on 15 March 2007 to the Security Council. Kosovo unilaterally declared independence in February 2008.

25   For a detailed account of the development of the judiciary in Kosovo, see Dominik Zaum, *The Sovereignty Paradox: The Norms and Politics of International Statebuilding* (Oxford: Oxford University Press, 2007), 144-53.

at least limit the amount of violence—a hope that remained unfulfilled, as the atrocities committed during the conflict suggest.[26] As early as March 1998—a year before NATO's air strikes—the ICTY emphasised its jurisdiction over crimes that were reported to have been committed in Kosovo at the time,[27] and the UNSC urged the ICTY Prosecutor to start gathering evidence for war crimes committed in Kosovo.[28] Almost immediately after the end of the war, the Tribunal opened an office in Pristina to start investigations, particularly to exhume the known and suspected sites of mass graves.

The ICTY, like the ICTR, has primacy over domestic courts for the prosecution of war crimes in Kosovo. It has been the strategy of both tribunals to focus on key decision-makers and individuals in command positions, and increasingly to hand over investigations to national courts.[29] Thus the most high-profile cases, in particular cases of members of the Serbian political and military leadership from the time of the Kosovo war, have been tried at the ICTY, and not in domestic courts. Consequently, there have only been six public indictments made by the ICTY for crimes committed in Kosovo: four against Serbian political and military leaders[30] and two against Albanian UÇK fighters, including an indictment against Ramush Haradinaj, a former UÇK commander and Prime Minister of Kosovo in 2004-5.[31] In total, the ICTY has charged only 20 individuals with war crimes and crimes against humanity in Kosovo. No one has yet been charged with genocide. By August 2008, proceedings in the Milošević trial had been terminated, and judgements in two cases led to four acquittals and one jail sentence of 13 years.

The most prominent defendant in front of the ICTY has undoubtedly been the now-deceased Slobodan Milošević. This case also highlighted one of the main problems of the ICTY, namely, the unwillingness of the Belgrade govern-

---

26   On deterrence in Kosovo, see Christopher Rudolph, "Constructing an Atrocities Regime: The Politics of War Crimes Tribunals", *International Organization*, 55/3 (2001), 672; Payam Akhavan, "Beyond Impunity: Can International Criminal Justice Prevent Future Atrocities?", *American Journal of International Law*, 95/1 (2001), 7-31. Akhavan, however, argues that the threat of prosecution by the ICTY marginally discouraged vengeance attacks by the UÇK: ibid., 9.

27   Human Rights Watch, *Under Orders*, ch.18.

28   UNSC, Resolution 1160 (1998), UN.Doc. No. S/RES/1180 (1998), 31 March 1998, art. 17.

29   C. Del Ponte, "Address to the United Nations Security Council by the Prosecutor of the International Criminal Tribunals for the former Yugoslavia and Rwanda, Mrs. Carla Del Ponte", 27 November 2001.

30   Milutinović *et al.* (IT-99-37), "Kosovo; Milošević (IT-02-54), Kosovo, Croatia and Bosnia"; and Pavkovic *et al.* (IT-03-70). On 6 July 2006, a joinder indictment to Milutinović *et al.* was issued by the court, Djorevic (IT – 05 – 87/1.I). All indictments are available at http://www.icty.org.

31   Limaj *et al.* (IT-03-66); Haradinaj *et al.* (IT – 04 – 84).

ment to co-operate with the Tribunal. Only under strong American economic and political pressure did Belgrade agree to hand over Milošević and other indictees, and to allow the Tribunal access to witnesses and archives in Serbia.[32] In this respect, the ICTY has mirrored the problems faced by the ICTR, which has regularly had difficult relations with the Rwandan government, particularly after the then chief prosecutor Carla Del Ponte announced in 2000 that the ICTR would begin investigating alleged crimes committed during the time of the genocide by the Rwandan Patriotic Front (RPF), today the ruling party in Rwanda. The government responded by blocking the travel of ICTR personnel and witnesses between Rwanda and the Tribunal, effectively stalling all Tribunal operations. Some commentators have argued that Del Ponte's failure to cultivate better working relations with the Rwandan government was one key reason why she was sacked as ICTR chief prosecutor in 2003.[33] Since 1999, Del Ponte had been chief prosecutor of both the ICTY and ICTR. Following her dismissal from the ICTR, she retained her role at the ICTY until 1 January 2008. Given Del Ponte's key role in both the ICTY and ICTR, perhaps it is not entirely surprising that the two institutions have faced similar problems regarding cooperation with sitting governments and the challenges of pursuing "even-handed" investigations and prosecutions for various "sides" to a conflict, including those who gain power after violence. More broadly, such issues reflect key challenges at the heart of the transitional justice enterprise.[34]

In the case of the ICTY, as most of the alleged Serb perpetrators left Kosovo after the withdrawal of the army and the police, and now live in Serbia, Belgrade's co-operation with the Tribunal is vital. However, as the Serb population generally views the ICTY as anti-Serb, such co-operation has been politically unpopular. Furthermore the trials, which have been televised in Serbia, gave Milošević and unapologetic extremists like Vojislav Šešelj, leader of the Radical Party, a public political platform on which to campaign for their ideas. In the parliamentary elections in 2003 and 2007, Šešelj's Party became the strongest party in Serbia.

The Serb authorities have also been highly reluctant to prosecute war crimes committed by Serbs in Kosovo through the domestic court system. Regarding investigations by the Serb government, the OSCE wryly noted that:

---

32   HRW, *Under Orders*, ch. 18.

33   See, for example, A. McFerran, "Violated and Isolated", *The Sunday Times*, 4 April 2004, http://www.timesonline.co.uk/tol/life_and_style/health/article1051767.ece?token=null&offset=0.

34   For further discussion of the impact of such political considerations on transitional justice, see P. Clark, "Law, Politics and Pragmatism: ICC Case Selection in the Democratic Republic of Congo and Uganda" in N. Waddell and P. Clark (eds), *Courting Conflict? Justice, Peace and the ICC in Africa*, London: Royal African Society, March 2008, 37-45.

[t]he Ministry of Interior has largely investigated crimes committed by KLA soldiers and only a few cases where potential perpetrators were Serbian police and security forces. The underlying reason for the latter investigations was that the public had learnt about them, and the police had no choice but to begin an investigation.[35]

Given that after increasing pressure from the Security Council, the ICTY is supposed to finish first-instance trials by the end of 2008 and appeals by 2010, this raises important questions about the extent to which war crimes and crimes against humanity committed in Kosovo by Serbs will be brought to justice in the domestic system.[36]

Attempts to prosecute Albanian atrocity perpetrators have been limited to two indictments. The first was the case of a UÇK prison camp commander, Fatmir Limaj, and two guards under his command, accused of arresting, torturing, and murdering Serb and Albanian civilians during the war.[37] On 30 November 2005 Limaj and one of his co-defendants were acquitted, and one co-defendant was found guilty of torture and cruel treatment and sentenced to thirteen years' imprisonment. The second indictment has been against Ramush Haradinaj, a former UÇK commander and Prime Minister of Kosovo. Haradinaj, who received strong support from the head of UNMIK and politicians in the US and Europe, was granted conditional release from the trial, and returned to The Hague in February 2007 for the trial, and was acquitted.

The ICTY has also failed to address the issue of war crimes and crimes against humanity committed after June 1999, when UNMIK and NATO moved into Kosovo, again raising the problem of "even-handed" justice discussed above in the context of both the ICTY and ICTR. Indeed, until 2001, it was debated whether the ICTY actually had jurisdiction over these crimes, the debate hinging on the question of whether there was still an "armed conflict" in Kosovo after NATO-led KFOR troops and UNMIK had assumed authority. To avoid this politically sensitive issue, Del Ponte asked the UNSC to amend the Tribunal's statute to omit the reference to "armed conflict."[38] Although the statute was not amended, she asserted in March 2001, in part echoing her controversial approach to alleged RPF crimes at the ICTR, that war crimes and crimes against humanity committed by Albanians after June 1999 would be investigated as well.[39] In light of the time and resource constraints faced by the Tribunal, it seems unlikely that there will be any prosecutions for these crimes by the ICTY.

---

35   OSCE, *War Crimes Before Domestic Courts*, 13.

36   See Security Council Report, *Update Report: International Criminal Tribunals*, New York, December 2006.

37   Limaj *et al.* (IT-03-66).

38   ICG, *The Scales of Justice in Kosovo*, 18; O'Neill, *Kosovo*, 53.

39   ICG, *The Scales of Justice in Kosovo*.

The role of Kosovo's courts. For transitional justice to contribute to the credibility and stability of newly established political institutions, it requires the
support and the ownership of the local population and political elites. For institutions to be sustainable, they require the trust of the local population and must
be considered legitimate; otherwise, the population may seek justice through
alternative, possibly violent, means. Local ownership contributes to the legitimacy of democratic institutions, and to some extent also of judicial institutions,
as it creates the perception that the law is interpreted in accordance with a society's preferences and understandings of the law. Furthermore, the local participation that ownership implies supports legal capacity-building and in this way
strengthens new judicial institutions in the long term. From this perspective,
it is not surprising that the international community heavily emphasised the
development of the local justice system, and relied on Kosovar courts for the
prosecution of the bulk of war crimes. As Kagame and Ngoga discuss in their
contributions to this book, this has not been the case in Rwanda, where the
population has generally seen international justice as an expensive irrelevance
and the international community has contributed little to the development of
the national judiciary.

At the outset of the mission, UNMIK decided to eschew the participation
of international judges and prosecutors in Kosovo's judiciary, for two reasons.
First, international judges and prosecutors would have to acquaint themselves
with domestic Yugoslav law, the applicable law of Kosovo.[40] Not only would
this have been more costly than relying on local judicial personnel, but the
necessary training would also have delayed the establishment of the judiciary.
Second, many Kosovars viewed the heavy reliance on international judges as
undermining their ownership of the judicial system. Although the OSCE had
argued in favour of using international judges to deal with transitional justice
issues in May 1999, it was overruled during the planning of UNMIK by those
who did not want to repeat the approach taken in Bosnia, which had been
criticised for its heavy international involvement.[41]

Nevertheless, the decision to rely exclusively on Kosovar judges soon proved
problematic. Kosovo's judicial system had all but dissolved with the departure
of the Serb authorities after the war: as in Rwanda after the decimation of
the judicial system during the genocide, there were no judges and prosecutors,
no defence lawyers, and no jailers left in the province, and the withdrawing
Serb forces had looted and destroyed the physical infrastructure of the justice
system.[42] UNMIK quickly moved to appoint judges and prosecutors to the

---

40   UNSG, *Report of the Secretary General Pursuant to Paragraph 10 of Security Council
      Resolution 1244 (1999)*, UN Doc. S/1999/672, 12 June 1999.

41   O'Neill, *Kosovo*, 97.

42   Ibid., 75.

emergency judicial system, to deal with the consequences of the ensuing general lawlessness. An estimated 500 murders and other serious crimes, mostly against minorities, were committed between June and December 1999.[43] As UNMIK's legal adviser observed at the time, the absence of a judiciary that could investigate and try those arrested by KFOR "led to a backlog of more than 200 detainees, many of them held for such serious criminal offences such as arson, violent assault and murder."[44]

The post-war judicial system was characterised by ethnic bias by Albanian judges against minorities, and intimidation of judges and witnesses by the UÇK.[45] Serb judges were furthermore subjected to pressure from Belgrade and Serb extremists in Kosovo. Within months, all remaining Serb judges and prosecutors had resigned, and most left Kosovo. The now almost exclusively Albanian judiciary frequently released Albanian suspects despite strong evidence of serious crimes including murder. In contrast, Serbs and Roma were often charged and detained for very minor crimes, and were held in detention even without an indictment.[46] By July 2002, out of seventeen indictments for war crimes and crimes against humanity committed between May 1998 and June 1999 that had been issued by local courts, only one was against an Albanian, all the others against Serbs. The indictments against the latter also included four charges of genocide.

After a court released a man who had shot at French KFOR soldiers in Mitrovica in February 2000, UNMIK quickly passed a regulation appointing international judges and prosecutors first to the district court in Mitrovica and later to all five of Kosovo's district courts, to counter the obvious ethnic bias of Kosovo Albanian judges.[47] The presence of the international judges and prosecutors, however, failed to fully redress the partiality of the courts. According to the applicable law, the Yugoslav Criminal Procedure Code, panels on district courts consist of two professional and three lay judges, with majority verdicts and equal votes for all judges. Consequently, international judges were in a minority on the panels, and were regularly outvoted by their Albanian colleagues. Furthermore, their presence on the bench created the perception of increased legitimacy of biased judgements. By the end of the year, to ensure the independence and impartiality of the judiciary, the SRSG promulgated Regulation 2000/64, granting prosecutors, defence counsel and the accused

---

43   CSDG, *A Review of Peace Operations*, para.198.

44   Strohmeyer, "Collapse and Reconstruction of a Judicial System", 49.

45   M. Hartmann, *International Judges and Prosecutors in Kosovo: A Model for Post-Conflict Peacekeeping*, USIP Special Report (Washington, DC: USIP, 2003), 6-7.

46   O'Neill, *Kosovo*, 75-88.

47   Ibid., 89-90; UNMIK, Regulation/2000/6, "On the Appointment and Removal from Office of International Judges and International Prosecutors", 15 February 2000.

the right to petition UNMIK's Department of Justice to assign international judges and prosecutors or to change the venue of the proceedings.[48] Cases are transferred to panels with a majority of international judges, according to four main criteria: the existence of threats and intimidation of the local judiciary; significant public demand for a judicial decision; ethnic or political diversity among defendants, victims, and witnesses; and the severity of the offence.[49] Consequently, all war crimes cases have since been held in front of majority international courts.

Before international judges were appointed to Kosovo's courts, UNMIK in September 1999 launched the idea of establishing a Kosovo War and Ethnic Crimes Court (KWECC), with local and international judges and prosecutors. All war crimes and serious crimes committed on the basis of race, ethnicity, religion, or nationality committed in Kosovo were to be tried in this court, and UNMIK prepared a draft regulation to establish it. The initiative encountered strong objections from Albanian politicians, who wanted to limit the jurisdiction of international judges to war crimes—predominantly committed by Serbs—and to keep ethnic crimes, predominantly committed by Albanians after June 1999, under the jurisdiction of the locally-run judicial system.[50] More important, though, was the UN's and donor countries' fear of the high costs of such a court, and the unwillingness of donors to establish a "Mini-ICTY" in light of the introduction of international staff in Kosovo's courts, which made the prospect of establishing a separate court less attractive.[51] Thus, the KWECC initiative was formally abandoned in August 2000.[52]

Has the pursuit of war crimes through the domestic courts in Kosovo contributed to the peace- and state-building efforts of the international community? The record is clearly mixed. The ethnic bias displayed by Albanian judges vis-à-vis Serbs and Roma discussed above, and the intimidation of judges and witnesses by the UÇK, have deepened divisions between ethnic groups and have undermined the trust of ethnic minorities in the judicial system.[53] With the transfer of all war crimes cases to courts with a majority of international judges, the ethnic bias has been redressed. All the cases that had been handled by purely local courts were reviewed, and in many cases the conviction was overturned. Thus, none of the four genocide indictments has been upheld.

48   UNMIK, UNMIK/REG/2000/64, "On Assignment of International Judges/Prosecutors and/or Change of Venue", 15 December 2000.

49   CSDG, *A Review of Peace Operations*, para. 207.

50   Ibid., para. 200.

51   M. Baskin, *Lessons Learned on UNMIK Judiciary*, Pearson Paper (Clemensport: Peacekeeping Press, 2002), 19.

52   CSDG, *A Review of Peace Operations*, para. 205.

53   Saferworld, *Human Security in Kosovo*, 33.

However, while the structural changes and the increased internationalisation of the judiciary might have increased the courts' impartiality and independence from the Kosovar government, judges—in particular foreign judges—are not independent from UNMIK. The Kosovo Judicial and Prosecutorial Council (KJPC), the body responsible for appointments and disciplinary measures, has a majority of international members appointed by the head of UNMIK.[54] Furthermore, all judges and prosecutors originally received only three-month contracts; only since January 2002 have all local legal personnel been appointed until the end of UNMIK's mission.[55] International judges are selected and hired by UNMIK, and as UNMIK civilian employees they have six-month contracts. In the absence of a disciplinary procedure for international judicial personnel (the KJPC only deals with local judges and prosecutors), not renewing their contract is the only sanctioning mechanism available. However, this sanction is not a mechanism that would meet the procedural standards UNMIK promotes for Kosovar institutions.

Furthermore, the SRSG has sometimes interfered in the administration of justice, most prominently in the case of Afrim Zeqiri, who was accused of killing a Serbian boy in the village of Cernica in 1999. A local prosecutor ordered his release in May 2000, a decision upheld by the international judge. The SRSG at the time, Bernard Kouchner, now the French foreign minister, overruled the judge's decision by executive order and extended Zeqiri's detention, without giving detailed reasons or a proper justification for his decision.[56] UNMIK's own actions on occasion have thus undermined the independence and credibility of the judiciary in Kosovo.

Similarly, some decisions by the SRSG have created the impression that prominent Kosovar politicians receive different treatment by comparison with the rest of the population. Thus, Hasim Thaci, former UÇK commander and leader of the PDK, one of the major Albanian parties in Kosovo, complained in 2000 about being harassed by UNMIK police. The police had, according to Thaci, "raided his party premises, targeted his family members for police inspections and created a general impression of personal prosecution."[57] Kouchner apologised to him for these actions, and instructed UNMIK police not to engage in intrusive investigations of public figures—creating the impression that certain political leaders received favourable treatment regarding investiga-

---

54   UNMIK Regulation 2001/8 of 6 Apr. 2001, sec.2.

55   Interview with OSCE official, Pristina, 30 April 2003.

56   O'Neill, *Kosovo,* 86.

57   Cited in M. Brand, *The Development of Kosovo Institutions and the Transition of Authority from UNMIK to Local Self-Government*, Centre for Applied Studies in International Negotiations (CASIN), (Geneva: CASIN, 2003), 16.

tive measures.[58] As a range of senior politicians had come from the ranks of the UÇK, this did little to strengthen the credibility of Kosovo's democratic and human rights institutions.

The response by members of Kosovo's political elite to the judgement in the so-called "Llapi Case," the first major indictment for war crimes committed by Kosovo Albanians, suggests that judicial independence from the Kosovo government remains an important concern. The four accused Albanians were charged in connection with the detention, torture, and murder of Serb and Albanian civilians in a UÇK detention centre. After their arrest by the police, the Kosovo government issued a press release, accusing UNMIK of taking "political prisoners".[59] They were sentenced to prison terms of between five and seventeen years. After the judgement was announced in the summer of 2003, the acting Prime Minister claimed that the judgement was fabricated by people who used to work for the Serb regime, and accused the court of being "detrimental for the future of Kosovo".[60] The distinct lack of respect for an independent, impartial judiciary in Kosovo suggested by comments like this is the main reason why UNMIK has insisted that international control over the judiciary is essential to maintain the rule of law; it reflects the continued divisiveness in Kosovo of the issue of prosecuting war crimes through the formal judicial system.

"Lessons learned" —implications for peace- and state-building

The analysis of the prosecution of war crimes through the formal justice system in Kosovo leaves one sceptical about the claim that transitional justice is a condition for successful peace- and state-building. The reluctance of the Serb authorities to cooperate with the ICTY, and to prosecute Serb war criminals through the domestic judicial system, suggests that the work of the ICTY has had only limited effect on Serb willingness to recognise responsibility for atrocities perpetrated, not only in Kosovo but also in Bosnia and Croatia. In this respect, the ICTY has encountered similar challenges of legitimacy and efficacy to those of the ICTR and it is not evident that there has been sufficient learning of lessons from the Rwanda case. In Kosovo, the trial of Fatmir Limaj at the ICTY led to demonstrative support by the political class for an "Albanian hero" and

---

58   Ibid.

59   CSDG, *A Review of Peace Operations,* para. 219. However, in contrast to the political elite, the wider population hardly reacted to the judgement. See Tom Periello and Marieke Wierda, *Lessons from the Deployment of International Judges and Prosecutors in Kosovo,* Prosecution Case Studies Series, International Centre for Transitional Justice, New York, March 2006, 30.

60   OSCE, *Case Report: The Public Prosecutor's Office vs Latif Gashi, Rrustem Mustafa, Naim Kadriu and Nazif Mehmeti - The "Llapi Case"* (Pristina: OSCE, 2003), 10.

"Fighter for Albanian freedom", but certainly not to public acknowledgement that the UÇK has also been involved in war crimes and ethnic crimes.

The role of the domestic courts in contributing to peace- and state-building in Kosovo has been more complex. The lesson from a range of peace-building missions in the 1990s, among them the one that took place in Kosovo, has been that a functioning legal system is essential to restore public order and is a precondition for any political process, such as the building of democratic institutions. Reflecting on the beginning of his term as the High Representative in Bosnia and Herzegovina, Paddy Ashdown emphasised that "we should have put the establishment of the rule of law first, for everything depends on it: a functioning economy, a free and fair political system, the development of civil society, public confidence in police and the courts."[61] Similarly, this sentiment is reflected in the UN's Brahimi Report on the future of UN peacekeeping missions, which, in its section on transitional administrations, predominantly addresses rule of law issues.[62]

Yet, as the analysis above has shown, the effects of pursuing transitional justice on order and stability are not always positive. While the emphasis on local ownership of the judicial system at the outset of UNMIK certainly had positive effects on institution building, it also exacerbated the tensions between the different ethnic groups, and failed to contribute to establishing peace in the province. The internationalisation of the judicial system in 2000 contributed to peace-building by redressing the existing ethnic bias, and the presence of international judges and prosecutors arguably increased domestic judicial capacity, as they worked together with less experienced Albanian legal professionals—even if this effect has been limited by language problems and by the fact that many international legal professionals have worked alone rather than with Kosovar counterparts.[63] On the other hand, the internationalisation of the judiciary undermined the local ownership and support for the judicial system, as suggested by the remarks following the Llapi trial discussed above.

Still, without the attempts to bring perpetrators of war crimes and crimes against humanity to justice, the situation would certainly be even worse today. The ICTY's indictments against Milošević and Šešelj removed them—though not completely—from the political stage in Serbia, making it more difficult for them to obstruct the ongoing process of political reform. Without the internationalisation of the judicial system in Kosovo, former UÇK members could

---

61   P. Ashdown, "What I learned in Bosnia", *New York Times*, 28 October 2002.

62   UN, *Report of the Panel on United Nations Peace Operations (The Brahimi Report)*, UN Doc. S/2000/809, 21 August 2000, paras. 76-83.

63   Periello and Wierda, *Lessons from the Deployment of International Judges and Prosecutors in Kosovo*.

have continued to kill Serbs and Roma, and to burn their houses with impunity, creating an atmosphere of fear and intimidation.

The Kosovar justice system's handling of the March 2004 riots underlined the weakness of the judicial institutions. By November 2005, 316 participants had been tried, with 209 convictions.[64] However, the trials were often characterised by the intimidation of witnesses and very lenient sentences against the perpetrators of violence.[65]

UNMIK and the main donor countries declared that the prosecution of the perpetrators is an immediate priority, and made this an implicit condition for addressing the future of Kosovo's political status.[66] However, even though the so-called "Eide Report" on the situation in Kosovo, examining its readiness for the resolution of the status, highlighted the weakness of the judiciary, status negotiations resumed.[67]

The analysis thus suggests three "lessons" to be learned for future state-building efforts that incorporate transitional justice. First, the relationship between transitional justice, domestic order and stable institutions is more complex than is made out by many who view justice as a simple condition for successful peace- and state-building. As the analysis above has shown, the international community cannot necessarily achieve both order and justice for past crimes. The policies necessary for one of these goals might well compromise the other, whether in Kosovo, Rwanda, or elsewhere.

Second, in the light of the uncertain relationship between justice and order, transitional justice might better be viewed as an end in itself, rather than a means to broader social goals. If it is seen as an end, the prosecution of war crimes would be justified accordingly, and not in terms of its contribution to a stable democratic society. Only if transitional justice is not supposed to serve potentially contradictory goals can effective judicial institutions be designed, providing justice for past crimes.

Finally, the analysis suggests modesty about what transitional justice can achieve in the context of state-building. If maintaining that transitional justice is instrumental to peace and security, it must be recognised that it is not a panacea for all problems of post-conflict societies, and that one needs to be modest and precise about what it can achieve. Only then can judicial institutions—whether domestic courts or international tribunals like the ICTY

---

64 For detailed figures, see OSCE, *The Response of the Justice System to the March 2004 Riots*, Annex 1.

65 Ibid. See also Iain King and Whit Mason, *Peace at Any Price: Hoe the World Failed Kosovo* (London: Hurst, 2006), 194-5.

66 UNMIK, *Kosovo Standards Implementation Plan, 31 March 2004* (Pristina: UNMIK, 2004), 3.

67 UN Doc. S/2005/635 of 7 Oct. 2005, paras. 33-43.

and ICTR—be designed accordingly and embedded within a broader set of institutions necessary for the transition from conflict to stable political development. Excessively strong demands on transitional justice and excessively high ambitions will lead only to frustration and the danger of de-legitimising transitional justice in the eyes of affected populations such as those in Kosovo and Rwanda.

20

TENSIONS IN TRANSITIONAL JUSTICE

Phil Clark, Zachary D. Kaufman and Kalypso Nicolaïdis

Introduction

Transitional justice resembles the minefields it is meant to transcend. Whether for analysts or practitioners, this field requires both extreme prudence and bold risk-taking. While this volume explores a range of themes, including the history and memory of the genocide, post-conflict reconstruction and reconciliation, this final chapter focuses on transitional justice because we view this as the volume's primary theme, into which the others are crucially drawn. As this book demonstrates, transitional justice is a nascent yet dynamic field in which key concepts and their bearing upon concrete conflict and post-conflict situations are constantly defined and redefined. Daily realities in war-torn societies demand nuanced and specific responses attuned to the peculiar stories that have plagued and haunted them. Yet, in all of these cases, the same key themes or goals always seem to recur: reconciliation, peace, justice, healing, forgiveness and truth. The complex contours of transitional justice research can be seen as reflecting the diversity of interpretations of these concepts and the multitude of practical approaches to conflict and post-conflict situations, often as a result of these different interpretations. In such a landscape, the Rwandan genocide and its aftermath may stand as a unique and momentous landmark in confronting atrocities, but they also exhibit the tensions that we find in transitional justice around the world and throughout history.

The purpose of this chapter is to tease out such key tensions from the rich material provided in this volume. A better awareness and understanding of these tensions, we believe, is a necessary prerequisite for more effective study and practice of transitional justice. Some of these tensions may be avoidable, if instances of theoretical or operational ambiguity can be navigated, often by prioritising one objective over another. Other tensions are inevitable because of the inherent complexity of the conflicts under examination and because post-conflict recovery may involve objectives of equal value. In all cases, the tensions must be identified and addressed.

This chapter proceeds in four stages. First, we analyse tensions *within* the six specific transitional justice themes explored by the authors in this book. Second, we examine tensions *among* those themes. Third, we turn to the tensions caused by the practical operation of transitional justice institutions. Finally, we discuss the appropriateness of the term "transitional justice" to describe the range of concepts and processes explored in this volume.

Tensions within transitional justice themes

Seldom is it clear to stakeholders and observers what particular concepts, such as "justice" or "reconciliation," mean and how (or even whether) they can be operationalised. One simple way to frame, if not resolve, these difficulties is to highlight the tensions inherent in each of the goals, ideals or "themes."

Tensions within every term: aspiration v. capability. The tension between ideal and practical means of achieving particular objectives is not unique to transitional justice. Yet it is particularly acute in this field, as the very problem that actors seek to address greatly inflates both sides of the equation. Aspirations literally bound up with "life after death" cannot but reach for ultimate redemption and atonement, at least in their initial incarnation. However, post-conflict countries often have limited capabilities to fulfil these aspirations, and these capabilities are further crippled by past or even ongoing conflict. Other factors, such as the traumatised condition of the population after mass violence—as Buckley-Zistel, Gasana and Steward discuss in their chapters regarding the psychosocial effects of the genocide on Rwandans—heavily influence what objectives can and should be pursued.

In the case of Rwanda, as Schabas, Ngoga, and Bergsmo and Webb note in this book, there were few qualified attorneys available after the genocide, as many of the country's lawyers were killed, disappeared or fled during the violence. The criminal justice infrastructure, including courtrooms and staff, which even before the genocide was modest, had been decimated. We could examine the gap between desirable and feasible outcomes within each of our broad themes, namely reconciliation, peace, justice, healing, forgiveness and truth. If we take, for instance, the issue of justice, many survivors and observers aspired to bring all suspected *génocidaires* to justice, but the sheer number of those who allegedly committed crimes against people or property, and the limited judicial staff and infrastructure, presented a formidable obstacle to doing so. As Bergsmo and Webb argue in chapter 18, the limited resources of transitional justice institutions such as the ICC mean that they must be highly selective in choosing which criminal cases to pursue. Kaufman shows in chapter 12 how, given the political context in Rwanda at the time, only suspected perpetrators of the most egregious crimes during the genocide were to be dealt with through an international criminal tribunal established by the Chapter VII powers of the UN Security Council. As a result, as described by President Kagame, Schabas, Clark and Ngoga, *gacaca*, the ancestral institution of local justice, was resurrected in a modified form to address, among other objectives, the need to prosecute the huge number of individuals suspected of participating in the genocide who were not being—and probably could never be—tried through the ICTR or Rwanda's national judicial system. Is it better to prosecute large numbers of (particularly low-level) suspects through a controversial judicial system such as *gacaca* than not to prosecute them at all? On the whole, we believe so, as it provides for more rapid justice which the victims themselves can own. However, we must also seriously consider the arguments of critics who stress the due process imperfections and pressure for forgiveness and reconciliation that may come with *gacaca*.

Reconciliation is another core theme in the transitional justice constellation that highlights acute tensions between aspirations and capabilities, or perhaps between different sources of aspirations. Reconciliation entails the renewal of fractured relationships and the capacity for sustained interactions between parties after conflict. As Kayigamba argues in chapter 2, many genocide survivors find it emotionally impossible to pursue renewed relationships with those who killed or injured their loved ones: this is simply asking too much. Reconciliation often implies imposing the aspirations of local or foreign elites on the population at large. Is it not enough, ask individuals or communities who have suffered mass violence, to pursue peaceful coexistence, the long-term cessation of hostilities? It may be less ambitious than reconciliation but is nonetheless a remarkable achievement after conflict. Should post-conflict societies aim for reconciliation, which requires sustained and often harrowing engagement between avowed enemies, as they come to terms with the root causes of their conflicts? As such forms of confrontation may in fact fuel tensions, should they not settle for peaceful coexistence?

We believe that while individuals and societies should strive for reconciliation, some are more prepared than others, for a host of social, cultural, religious, economic and political reasons. For instance, Gasana, Steward and Clark all highlight how the Christian beliefs of many Rwandans have inspired their pursuit of healing and reconciliation after the genocide, helping them overcome—or at least find ways to manage—their deep-rooted fears and animosity. In other societies, reconciliation may indeed be asking too much, especially of survivors, who must contend with their personal anguish before considering whether to seek to rebuild broken relations with those who have caused their pain. Undoubtedly, questions of reconciliation are riddled with the tension between what is desired and what is achievable. The key is to recognise that in some instances, reconciliation is both sought *and* practical. In such cases, to dismiss reconciliation as a fantasy is to quash the aspirations of those who, against incredible odds, seek to build a new and more engaged, cooperative future with their erstwhile enemies.

Tensions within specific terms: retributive v. deterrent v. restorative justice. Tensions can also be specific to an individual theme, as with the tension among retributive, deterrent and restorative justice. As stressed by Clark in chapter 10, while these variants all assume that punishment is a necessary response to crimes, they differ on the question of what justice is ultimately designed to achieve and, consequently, what form it should take. Retributive and deterrent justice hold only that perpetrators should be punished, usually by sentencing them to pay financial restitution to the state or victims, or to serve prison terms or suffer capital punishment. The primary intention of retributive justice is to voice the community's disapproval of perpetrators' actions, while deterrent justice tries to persuade potential criminals that it would be too costly to initiate or repeat such crimes. Retributive justice holds that perpetrators should be punished to a degree commensurate with the severity of their crimes. Deterrent justice, on the other hand, holds that perpetrators be punished to a degree that deters them or others from committing crimes in the future—a punishment that may be of a greater, lesser or commensurate degree compared with their crimes. In other words, the degree of punishment should not necessarily be related to the severity of the crime; it must simply be harsh enough to discourage individuals from offending in the future. In contrast to deterrent and retributive justice, restorative justice holds that in some instances it is necessary to alter the form or degree of punishment to help rebuild relations between perpetrators and victims and therefore to gradually restore the fabric of society as a whole. Proponents of restorative justice therefore do not necessarily oppose the need for punishment, but rather argue that in some cases there may be a compelling need to shape punitive measures towards more reconciliatory ends.

Depending on the context, these different conceptions of justice may be mutually supportive or mutually exclusive. In chapter 2, Kayigamba argues that reconciliation in Rwanda is impossible without retributive justice—giving convicted *génocidaires* the form and degree of punishment that Kayigamba and many others believe they deserve—because, otherwise, victims of the genocide will not feel that justice has been done and therefore will not be willing to reconcile with perpetrators, an attitude that may lead to further conflict. Schabas, on the other hand, argues in chapter 11 that retributive justice after the genocide "is probably not the best way forward" because of the practical and social costs, especially regarding reconciliation (a term Schabas also scrutinises), of attempting to prosecute the vast numbers of genocide suspects. It is difficult to decide what justice is supposed to achieve after conflict but, as these authors show, even if we can agree on the ultimate objective to which justice should contribute—for example, reconciliation—it is not immediately clear which form of justice is best equipped to achieve that end. Whatever the case, it seems that the ICTR privileges retributive and deterrent justice over restorative justice. As Bergsmo and Webb argue that the ICC has drawn much from the ICTR's design and experience, it appears that the aftermath of the Rwandan genocide has contributed to establishing an international system where restorative justice takes second place, which may be problematic given the emphasis placed on restorative justice in many post-conflict societies.

There are numerous other tensions that we cannot address here, for example between the sometimes competing methods of achieving retrospective and prospective or short-term and long-term objectives. Specifically, short-term and long-term peace in a post-conflict society may be in tension, as when amnesty and a secure exile are afforded a former perpetrator so that he or she will leave a conflict region, or when authorities delay, perhaps indefinitely, the issuance of indictments and arrest warrants so that peace negotiations can commence or continue. Such actions may contribute to short-term stability but, if punishment of suspects is forfeited in the long term, they may not achieve a lasting peace.

Tensions among transitional justice themes

Transitional justice initiatives often fail to take a holistic approach to post-conflict reconstruction, whereby rebuilding individual and communal lives, contributing to reconstruction in both the short and the long term, and holding offenders accountable are seen as interconnected goals. Holism refers to the need to rebuild entire societies, responding to the various needs of individuals and groups after conflict, which in turn correspond to the key goals identified at the outset of this chapter, namely reconciliation, peace, justice, healing, forgiveness and truth, as well as the more operational translations of these various goals. It is no surprise that the simultaneous pursuit of these goals often produces tensions among them. The hope is to find approaches that can effectively combine multiple objectives, reflecting the complexity of the practical situations to which they respond.

Tensions among terms generally: profound v. pragmatic objectives. Transitional justice may ultimately be about achieving sustainable peace through reconciliation between yesterday's intimate enemies and by healing the wounds of the many victims of fratricidal conflict, but these grand goals do not constitute the bulk of its day-to-day vocabulary. Indeed, Clark stresses in his work the fundamental tension between "profound" and "pragmatic" objectives.[1] Profound objectives relate to complex issues of rebuilding individual lives and relationships between parties previously in conflict. Pragmatic objectives consist in solving the various practical problems that arise after violence. In Rwanda, such pragmatic objectives include addressing the country's massively overcrowded prisons, dealing with children growing up without parents, and facilitating economic development in remote areas of the country. Limits to available resources (such as time, money, staff) unavoidably lead to setting priorities between profound and pragmatic objectives which may ultimately prove to be mutually exclusive. Where should a post-conflict society such as Rwanda begin: with the physical rebuilding of a shattered society, providing physical and psychological healthcare to survivors and reconstructing homes and roads, or with social reconstruction, pursuing the aims of justice and reconciliation? The needs of a population that has experienced mass violence range from profound to pragmatic concerns, so that governments and key actors must constantly juggle different categories of needs.

Tensions among specific terms: reconciliation v. truth v. justice. The aims of reconciliation, truth and justice ought to be viewed as one single whole. Yet, this is where we find some of the most intractable tensions. Truth commissions, which often employ amnesty as a way of discovering the "truth" and, in the case of the South African Truth and Reconciliation Commission, as a way of facilitating reconciliation, may produce results considered unjust at least by those who subscribe to the retributive view of justice. Critics of truth commissions often question whether it is morally justified to forfeit punishment for the sake of truth or reconciliation. In this volume, Lemarchand, Hintjens, Buckley-Zistel, Gasana, Steward and Clark all explore tensions between truth and reconciliation in the Rwandan context. Each in his or her own way considers the fraught politics of post-genocide memory, where discovering and debating difficult historical truths may often prove to be initially contentious and thus appear to threaten prospects of reconciliation. All of these authors argue, however, that genuinely confronting the truths about Rwanda's past is vital to fostering reconciliation after the genocide, though they highlight the immense challenges in pursuing truth and reconciliation concurrently.

On the other hand, as Jallow argues in chapter 13, the ICTR holds that it is necessary to punish perpetrators in order not only to fulfil a moral and legal obligation—bringing them to account—but also to contribute to national peace and reconciliation. Trials such as those at the ICTR, however, may not always reveal the truth of past atrocities, especially if, as is often the case, perpetra-

---

1   P. Clark, "Justice without Lawyers: The *Gacaca* Courts and Post-Genocide Justice and Reconciliation in Rwanda", unpublished PhD thesis, University of Oxford, 2005, 27-8.

tors are unwilling to offer incriminating testimony; if witnesses are murdered or otherwise die, or are unwilling to testify; if evidence is lost or destroyed; or if the legalistic nature of trials bars disclosure of crucial emotional "truths" related to past crimes. Furthermore, the investigation, prosecution and punishment of alleged perpetrators may not promote genuine reconciliation among antagonists, especially if the imprisonment of convicted perpetrators separates them physically from victims of violence and the rest of the population, thus minimising the capacity of offenders and victims to engage, and reconcile, with each other. If not conducted with sensitivity and the approval and cooperation of survivors, trials may cause additional trauma. Furthermore, if suspects seek to avoid arrest or feel they have been wrongly accused, efforts to bring them to justice may also foment further conflict.

At a more individual level, the search for some degree of healing may also in turn conflict with truth and justice gains. For the sake of their emotional or psychological wellbeing, some victims may prefer to ignore calls to pursue the punishment of those guilty of crimes, especially if they were committed by individuals who have subsequently died or fled the region. Similarly, perpetrators may want to avoid the stigma of accepting blame, if they must return to be neighbours of their former victims, who may remain vengeful. Some victims may prefer to avoid the potential retraumatisation associated with justice processes that involve addressing difficult truths about the past, including painful memories and feelings. To what extent should transitional processes address the past, and to what extent should they allow victims and perpetrators to simply "move on"? Who has the moral authority to make such difficult tradeoffs and how can they be translated into institutional frameworks? What if the response given to these questions varies geographically and across different local realities? None of these questions can simply be addressed through broad and vague concepts such as "justice" or "reconciliation."

Tensions caused by the practical operation of transitional justice institutions

In addition to the tensions manifest between various transitional justice themes, there are those regarding the actual design and operation of transitional justice institutions themselves: Where should they be based? How should they work?

Tensions in the location of transitional justice institutions. In designing transitional justice institutions, one of the first decisions that must be made is where to locate the institution. There is in fact a simple choice: whether or not to situate the institution close to the site of the atrocities concerned. For example, the ICTR is located in Arusha in Tanzania, which is adjacent to Rwanda; *ad hoc* war crimes tribunals for Cambodia, Iraq and Sierra Leone are all located within the states where crimes under their jurisdiction are alleged to have been committed; and the ICTY and the ICC are located in The Hague in the Netherlands, far from the sites of the atrocities they address. There may be compelling reasons for these decisions concerning the relative proximity of institutions to the conflict zones concerned, and certain decisions will appeal to particular stakeholders. For example, the decision to locate a transitional justice institution away from the site of the atrocity being addressed is often linked to security concerns. In the aftermath of an atrocity, as in Rwanda, and especially if an atrocity is ongoing, as in the case of the ICTY—which was created while the conflict in the Balkans still raged—those designing the transitional justice institution may only consider it safe for the institution's infrastructure, staff, witnesses and even suspects to locate the institution away from the conflict zone. Furthermore, having a transitional justice institution operate in or near the site of an atrocity may trigger further unrest if, for example, the supporters of a suspect who has been detained by the institution seek to disrupt the proceedings.

Conversely, there are often compelling reasons to establish a transitional justice institution in or at least close to the scene of the alleged crimes it is mandated to address. The practical operation of a transitional justice institution depends on access to witnesses, evidence, suspects and experts, all of which may be facilitated by having the institution situated close to the atrocity site. Furthermore, the presence of the transitional justice institution in or near the location of the crime is often critical to post-conflict reconciliation and reconstruction. A common criticism levelled by, among others, Ngoga (in chapter 16) at the ICTR—an institution located closer to the atrocity site concerned than, for example, the ICC (at least with respect to its first cases), but still considered by many to be too far (physically and in the minds of the national population) from Rwanda—is that, because of physical distance and its lack of an effective outreach programme, the ICTR has little relevance for everyday Rwandans, who are unable to attend hearings or gain regular and useful information concerning developments at the Tribunal. Given the ICTR's claimed objective of contributing to national reconciliation in Rwanda, its physical distance and apparent detachment from social realities in Rwanda make its location highly problematic.

Locating transitional justice institutions far from the atrocity sites concerned is also potentially damaging if we consider that a purpose—or at least a side effect—of some transitional justice institutions is to help jump-start the legal system of the state in question. Accordingly transitional institutions may employ survivors, not only to use their expertise but also to train them in the investigation, prosecution and adjudication of mass crimes. The institutions may also initiate campaigns, through publicising of investigations, convictions and sentences, and may themselves be the subject of local reports, which raise local public awareness about the utility and desirability of international justice. Such public education efforts are especially critical in societies with low literacy rates, poor education and/or a lack of access to mainstream media—all of which are common in areas where atrocities are perpetrated and may indeed have also been among the contributing factors to the outbreak of heinous crimes in the first place. Demonstrating the importance of accountability can facilitate, and be a critical component of, broader post-conflict reconstruction and nation-building, which may in turn enable post-atrocity communities themselves to better prevent heinous crimes.

Tensions among principles to which transitional justice authorities subscribe when administering various institutions. Besides the issue of location, transitional justice authorities must make decisions on the basis of principles that might also turn out to be contradictory. Thus, for instance, many Western legal scholars and human rights activists have argued that the Rwandan government, in apparently failing to include certain elements of due process in *gacaca*, violates international standards of judicial procedure, including those recognised in international treaties that the Rwandan government has signed, for example the International Covenant on Civil and Political Rights and the African Charter on Human and Peoples' Rights.[2] This may again be an instance of the aspiration-capacity gap discussed earlier, between what the Rwandan government is legally bound to provide, such as ensuring that genocide suspects are tried by an impartial judiciary in *gacaca*, and what it may have the resources to achieve. The Rwandan government may thus be faced with a choice of whether to (continue to) violate international agreements or to formally withdraw from them. Government officials may also believe themselves that leaving the *gacaca* process to follow a life of its own will facilitate the healing or reconciliation process. Such a conflict between principles to which a transitional justice authority (in this case, the Rwandan government) subscribes and practices in different contexts may cause that authority to incur costs in terms of its international reputation, but these costs in turn must be weighed against internally generated tradeoffs and decisions.

Other examples of tensions relating to the practical operation of transitional justice institutions include problems arising from the use of plea-bargaining in the investigation and prosecution of suspected atrocity perpetrators. Plea-bargaining can be used to expedite a backlog of cases, especially when, as in Rwanda, there are tens of thousands of genocide suspects, and to reintegrate these individuals more rapidly into society, in the cause of reconciliation, or to gather evidence from foot soldiers against more high-level targets of investiga-

---

2   See discussion in Clark's chapter 15; see also Amnesty International, "*Gacaca*: A Question of Justice", AI Index AFR 47/007/2002, 12 December 2002, 30.

tion. Plea-bargaining can also lead to false confessions when suspects believe—or are intimidated into believing—that the evidence against them is sufficient to convict them and that, consequently, they will receive much harsher sentences than if they cooperate before trial.

Clearly then, tensions can occur when a single actor administers a single transitional justice institution, or when multiple actors (for example community-level authorities, the Rwandan government, the United Nations) simultaneously or sequentially employ multiple transitional justice institutions, perhaps involving the same suspects, witnesses, evidence and even objectives. Such tensions can be welcome and beneficial, by forcing a society or various authorities, whether working together cooperatively or independently, to prioritise among them and to set clear and achievable goals. These tensions, though, can also frustrate and cause conflict among key actors, such as the international community, human rights organisations, government officials and survivors, who may disagree about which goals should be prioritised and therefore disagree further about which transitional justice institutions or processes should be promoted in order to achieve them. In the end, success will depend on the capacity of actors and society to peacefully negotiate compromises among their respective conceptions of life after conflict.

Conclusion: appropriateness of "transitional justice"

"Transitional justice" has recently become a popular term to describe the field of judicial and non-judicial mechanisms used to respond to atrocities, and the tensions raised in doing so. But is "transitional justice" really an appropriate term for such a wide and heterogeneous range of mechanisms? Should we not question some of the very assumptions that underpin this book and the field more broadly?

First, what do we actually mean by "transitional"? The mechanisms in question will help societies to move from one state of affairs to another, and will at the same time be made obsolete by such evolution. In the process, however, attempts to promote, for example, accountability and reconciliation may be merely aspirational and fail to encourage genuine transition. They may even create perverse effects by exacerbating or indirectly causing renewed conflict. Individuals may have preferred to suppress memories of atrocities, or may, through the work of transitional justice institutions, learn new information, either of which may prompt new unrest. In short, in a context that does not result in any sort of transition, the transitional aspect of "transitional justice" may be a misnomer.

Second, is it appropriate to prioritise *the idea of* "justice" over all other themes? For example, some actors or observers would argue that in cases where these two objectives are not complementary, the stability of a society must be prioritised over justice. As discussed above, there are many facets in the "justice agenda", and some approaches, especially in the realm of retributive or deterrent justice, may further inflame feelings of revenge in a society and thus prove detrimental to any genuine transition away from conflict. Even short of this worst case, "justice" cannot be made to capture all of the other goals pursued in the aftermath of a conflict.

In short, the phrase "transitional justice" will often be a poor description of the actual dynamics of post-conflict societies as it fails to capture the tensions among the many goals pursued by different actors or the various outcomes—intended or unintended—which may prevail. It may sometimes be more useful to use the phrase "post-conflict reconstruction", which does not purport to make predictions or to prioritise any single transitional justice theme. If the fundamental challenge for theorists and practitioners alike is to navigate the tensions that arise from dealing with an impossible but all too recent past, it may be desirable to stress that the prize will be long-lasting, sustained reconstruction: a new beginning.

INDEX